BEETHOVEN

BEETHOVEN

THE MAN REVEALED

JOHN SUCHET

Atlantic Monthly Press
New York

This edition is adapted from *Beethoven: The Man Revealed* published
in 2012 in England by Elliott & Thompson.

Book design by Charles Rue Woods and Fearn de Vicq

Printed in the United States of America
Published simultaneously in Canada

ISBN 978-0-8021-2206-3
eBook ISBN: 978-0-8021-9291-2

Atlantic Monthly Press
an imprint of Grove/Atlantic, Inc.
154 West 14th Street
New York, NY 10011
Distributed by Publishers Group West
www.groveatlantic.com

13 14 15 16   10 9 8 7 6 5 4 3 2 1

For my children, grandchildren, and their children,

safe in the knowledge that all will know Beethoven's music

CONTENTS

Contents

Contents

Contents

PREFACE

THIS IS AN ACCOUNT OF BEETHOVEN'S LIFE, in accordance with current scholarship and research. Given that new facts and information emerge constantly, there are some aspects of this book that will inevitably become outdated or even prove incorrect. This is true of all biographies of great figures. I have not let it deter me from setting down the life as we perceive it today.

I make no great claim to having unearthed previously undiscovered facts about Beethoven's life. Everything in this book has been published in source material or previous biographies. But I do believe that a substantial amount of the information I have included, particularly about his childhood, has not been published for many decades, in some cases for a century or more, and I am certain never in English.

Beethoven's childhood and teenage years, I believe, were the making of him as a man and musician. For that reason I have examined them closely, and some of his experiences I have recounted in forensic detail. His trip with the court orchestra up the Rhine, for instance, rarely merits a mention in biographies, or is accorded at most a line or two, yet it provided the youthful Beethoven with a bank of memories—and a physical artefact—that he treasured for life.

Of Beethoven it is perhaps more true than of any other composer that if you know what is going on in his life you listen to his music through different ears. Beethoven's life—its dramas, conflicts, loves, and losses, his deafness coupled with continuous health problems, his epic struggle with his sister-in-law for custody of her son, his nephew—is there in his music. Without such knowledge his music is still extraordinary, and I believe many people who today love it do so without any deep understanding of his life. But to know what is happening to him at the time of a particular composition puts that work on a different level for the listener. Beethoven's music is his autobiography.

My approach to the life of this great artist, as in my previous publications on him, is that of enthusiast and lover of his music, rather than musicologist. Consequently this book is aimed primarily at like-minded people, though I hope the academics will give it their approval. It is, for instance, of more interest to me that Beethoven initially dedicated the 'Eroica' Symphony to Napoleon Bonaparte than that he chose to write it in E flat. At all times I have striven to set the music into the context of his life, to explain where he was living at the time of a particular composition, why he chose to write it, the reasons behind the dedication, the state of his health, his nonmusical activities, rather than present an analysis of the movement structure, key signature, thematic links.

In a nutshell I have tried to portray a difficult and complex character, struggling to continue his profession as musician despite increasing deafness, alienating friends with unprovoked outbursts of anger one moment, overwhelming them with excessive kindness and generosity the next, living in a city in almost constant turmoil because of war with France, rather than the godlike immortal portrayed in statues and paintings in heroic pose garlanded with laurel leaves.

He might have been one of the greatest artists who ever lived, but he was a still a man who had to live among fellow mortals, eat and drink, buy clothes, pay his rent. That is the Beethoven of this book.

PROLOGUE

I N THE EARLY AFTERNOON OF 29 MARCH 1827, thousands of people flocked towards the Altes Schwarzspanierhaus, as word spread across Vienna that Beethoven had died. Their numbers grew, and soon they thronged the courtyard of the building to such an extent that the gates had to be closed. They crowded along the Alsergasse and spilled onto the green Glacis that sloped up to the Bastei, the city wall. Soon there was barely space between Beethoven's residence and the Votivkirche, where the funeral mass was to be held.

On the second floor of the Schwarzspanierhaus, inside Beethoven's apartment, a small group of men made final adjustments to the polished oak coffin and the corpse it contained. Beethoven's head, adorned with a wreath of white roses, lay on a white silk pillow. It was a grotesque sight, belying the identity of Europe's most revered composer. The temporal bones, along with the auditory nerves, had been removed at post-mortem for further investigation, leaving the joint of the lower jaw with no support. The famously leonine face, with strongly defined jawbone, was distorted almost beyond recognition.

Into the folded hands a wax cross and a large lily were placed. Two more large lilies lay on either side of the body. Eight candles burned alongside the coffin. On the table at the foot of the coffin stood a crucifix, holy water for sprinkling, and ears of corn. At 3 p.m. the coffin was closed, and the group prepared to move it down the staircase and out into the courtyard.

By this time the crowd had grown restless. Soldiers from the nearby barracks were drafted in to keep order. There was a fear that the horses could be frightened or, worse, that the coffin could be disturbed. The soldiers cleared the courtyard and the gates were again closed. As the coffin was brought out of the building, the crowd surged forward, but the gates, soldiers on the inner side, held firm. As nine priests offered blessings and the Italian court singers intoned a funeral song, a heavy pall was spread over the coffin and a large wreath laid on the embroidered cross.

When everything was ready, the gates were opened, but the crowd surged forward again, overwhelming the soldiers. They pushed against the bier, dislodging the pallbearers and chief mourners. It took several minutes to restore order. Eight *Kapellmeister*, four on each side, took hold of the pall with one hand, a candle wrapped in crepe in the other. On both sides of them stood around forty torchbearers. Behind the coffin were the chief mourners, close friends and family; in front of it musicians, civic dignitaries, and the clergy.

The order was given, the four horses took the strain, and amid a clatter of chains and a cacophony of hooves, the procession moved off. Vienna, for so many centuries capital of the Holy Roman Empire, seat of the Holy Roman Emperor, had never seen scenes like it, nor had so many thousands of people ever thronged its streets.[1]

It was an appropriate tribute to a man whose music had touched people in a way that no composer's had before, who had changed the course of music, and whose compositions would speak to people down the generations and for all time. But it was also somewhat unfitting, given that Beethoven's music was not unanimously applauded in his lifetime, that his circle of friends and supporters was really quite small, that no great effort had been made in his difficult and painful final years to make his living conditions more palatable, and that on the whole there was no great stir in Vienna when it became clear their most famous resident was terminally ill.

In fact, the extraordinary homage he was accorded in death was simply the final inexplicable act in a lifetime of paradox and contradiction.

CHAPTER ONE

THE SPANIARD

IN WHICH A MOMENTOUS
LIFE BEGINS

IT WAS AN INAUSPICIOUS START. WE CANNOT BE certain of the day on which Beethoven was born, since his birth certificate has not survived, and in the baptismal register his mother is given the wrong first name, Helena rather than Magdalena (possibly because both names share the diminutive Lenchen). The date given in the register for the baptism of the Beethoven infant Ludovicus is 17 December 1770, and the place St. Remigius's Church in Bonn. It was customary for baptism to be carried out within twenty-four hours of birth; therefore it is likely that Beethoven was born on 16 December, with the lesser possibilities of the 15th in the late evening or 17th in the early hours. Given that there is a strong likelihood that the birth certificate was wilfully destroyed (as I will recount later), it is probable that we shall never know for sure the date of his birth.

More auspiciously, there is a legend that Beethoven was born with a caul, that is with part of the amniotic sac covering the face. Traditionally this carries beneficial supernatural qualities, such as protecting the individual from drowning, giving healing powers, or endowing clairvoyance. He himself lent weight to the legend (or possibly created it) by writing to a publisher that he was born 'with an obbligato accompaniment'. The passage in the letter, which refers to his Septet, Op. 20, is clearly written in jest: 'I cannot compose anything that is not obbligato, seeing that, as a matter of fact, I came into the world with an obbligato accompaniment.' I have not found any other reference to it in any source.

Beethoven was the eldest, but not the firstborn, and to say that his arrival brought unbridled joy to his parents, or even to say that he was born into a normal and loving family, would be a considerable over-statement. For a start, both sides opposed the marriage of his parents, Johann van Beethoven and Maria Magdalena Leym née Keverich. It seems the reason was the same for both families: that both were thought to be marrying beneath themselves.

To take the Beethoven family first. Ludwig van Beethoven the elder, the future composer's grandfather, had established himself as the most senior, and therefore the most respected, musician in Bonn. He had left his hometown of Malines in Flanders (today Mechelen in Belgium) at the age of twenty-one and settled in Bonn, where he was given a position as bass soloist and singer in the court choir. At the age of forty-nine he was appointed *Kapellmeister*, which put him in charge of music at court—in the chapel, concert hall, theatre, and court ballroom. This earned him a substantial salary and enormous prestige. In addition he ran a wholesale wine business on the side. It was probably not on any grand scale, but his income from the court, together with proceeds from the sale of wine, allowed him to rent two apartments, as well as cellars for storage. He was also wealthy enough to lend money to a number of people.

Ludwig's son Johann gained a position as tenor in the court choir. This brought him in a modest salary, which he supplemented by giving clavier and singing lessons to sons and daughters of well-off English and French families attached to the embassies, as well as to members of the nobility.

Father and son lived together in a large and well-furnished apartment at Rheingasse 934 (where, later, Ludwig van Beethoven was to spend many childhood years). In a later memoir, the child of the owner of the house, who remembered the Beethoven family living there, described the *Kapellmeister*'s apartment as being *beautiful and proper and well arranged, with valuables, all six rooms provided with beautiful furniture, many paintings and cupboards, a cupboard of silver service, a cupboard with fine gilded porcelain and glass, an assortment of the most beautiful linen which could be drawn through a ring, and everything from the smallest article sparkled like silver.*

But there was a cloud hanging over the Beethoven family. The *Kapellmeister's* wife, Maria Josepha Poll, became an alcoholic and had to be moved out of the family apartment to be cared for in a special home. It is not known when this action was taken, but it was almost certainly before Johann's marriage, because at the wedding Ludwig senior was reported to have tears streaming from his eyes, and when asked about it he replied that he was thinking about his own wedding and marriage. It is known that Maria Josepha stayed in seclusion until her death in 1775.

There is no evidence that any member of the Beethoven family ever visited Maria Josepha in the home, and although Ludwig van Beethoven was nearly five when his grandmother died, he is not reported to have spoken about her a single time in his life, nor did he ever refer to her in correspondence. This is all the more remarkable since the elder Ludwig predeceased his wife by nearly two years and yet Beethoven spoke about his beloved grandfather and wrote about him time after time, and treasured his portrait (which stayed with him almost all his adult life and was in his apartment when he died).

Of course he took pride in his grandfather's accomplishments as a musician, and presumably felt shame at his grandmother's descent into alcoholism, but it seems as if he erased his grandmother's existence from his mind. This is more than likely due to the fact that he watched his own father descend into alcoholism, thus making the whole question of alcohol something that was not for discussion. But that did not stop Beethoven himself in later years consuming enormous quantities, as will become clear as the story progresses, to the extent that it brought about the cirrhosis of the liver that was the probable cause of his death.

Clearly the Beethoven family had a liking for alcohol— Beethoven's grandmother and father were both alcoholics, and he himself was probably a victim of it. It is tempting to suggest that ready quantities of wine in the household from the elder Ludwig's business sideline meant it was easily accessible for the family, and certainly early biographers attribute the family tendency to this. It is indeed likely that there was a generous supply of wine on the table, although the *Kapellmeister* kept his wine in storage in rented cellars, and there are no reports that he himself ever over-imbibed.

But alcohol and its effects aside, the Beethoven family was highly respected, thanks to the accomplishments of Ludwig senior, and lived in a certain amount of comfort. So when Johann announced to his father, as a fait accompli, that he intended marrying Maria Magdalena Leym, of Ehrenbreitstein, the *Kapellmeister* was appalled. He made enquiries and established not only that she was a widow, but had been a housemaid. The Fischers at Rheingasse 934 heard him explode to his son, 'I never believed or expected that you would so degrade yourself!'

In fact his misgivings were largely misplaced. Maria Magdalena's family included a number of wealthy merchants, as well as court councillors and senators. Her late father, Heinrich Keverich, had been chief overseer of the kitchen at the palace of the Elector of Trier at Ehrenbreitstein. True, he was 'in service,' but it was a senior position, and he was in the employ of the most powerful and prestigious local dignitary, the Prince-Elector.[1] Furthermore, there is no evidence that Maria Magdalena was ever a housemaid.

Where Ludwig senior was correct was that Maria Magdalena was already widowed. More than that, she had experienced more sadness than a teenage woman should have had to bear. At sixteen she married a certain Johann Leym, and bore him a son. The child died in infancy, and her husband died not long after. She was thus a widow who had lost a child before she was nineteen.

Ludwig senior might have been influenced by the fact that Maria Magdalena's father had died many years before, leaving her mother as the family breadwinner, working as a cook at the court. Her mother was clearly already in fragile mental health, because she suffered a psychological breakdown soon after the marriage. She had one other surviving child, a son (four other children having died in infancy), and there was patently no prospect of a substantial dowry coming with the intended bride.

It seems an accumulation of unfortunate circumstances, combined with his own prejudices, turned Ludwig senior against the marriage, to such an extent that he refused to attend the ceremony 'unless the thing were quickly over with'.

The Keverich family was apparently no more enthusiastic about the union; this, if nothing else, cemented the absence of any dowry. The evidence for this is that the wedding took place in Bonn, rather than the bride's hometown, which would have been normal, and there is no evidence that any member of Maria Magdalena's family attended. One can imagine that any pride they might have had that she was marrying into the family of the *Kapellmeister* was undone by Johann's documented lack of charm (admittedly more evident in later years), and his clear obsession with money.

This latter attribute is evidenced by the fact that four months after the marriage a petition was sent to the Elector of Trier on Johann's mother-in-law's behalf, reporting that 'through an ill-turned marriage of her only daughter up to 300 Thalers disappeared'. This is a barely concealed accusation that Johann relieved his mother-in-law of the bulk of her savings, although it is likely the petition was deliberately written in an exaggerated way to increase Frau Keverich's plight. It is quite possible that this transfer of money, however it took place, occurred before the marriage, or at least that the process started then, which would be another reason for the Keverich family to be against the union.[2]

Exactly what took Johann van Beethoven up the Rhine to the fortress town of Ehrenbreitstein in the first place is not known, but one can imagine his father's frustration at the frequent absences as he pursued a young woman with an unenviable history before she was out of her teens from another town a good thirty-five miles away. With both families set against the marriage, we can assume that the wedding of the couple who were to be the parents of Ludwig van Beethoven was a small and one-sided affair, attended reluctantly by Ludwig senior, whose tears at his own memories might have hardened his heart still further.

The marriage took place in Bonn on 12 November 1767, and it would not be long before more heartache ensued, first for Maria Magdalena and then for both her and her husband. After the marriage Johann moved out of the large well-appointed apartment he had shared with his father, and rented a small apartment at the back of a building in the Bonngasse for himself and his wife. At the same time his mother-in-law's already precarious mental health went into sharp decline. The same petition that cited the loss of her savings stated that she had begun to live a life of such penitence that she stopped eating and could not be expected to live long. Sometimes, it reported, she lay outside the church all night in the bitterest cold, wind, and rain. She died less than a year after her daughter's marriage, and it must be the case that Maria Magdalena felt considerable guilt that her choice of husband, not to mention her departure from her hometown, had caused her mother so much distress.

In the weeks before her mother's death, Maria Magdalena would have realised that she was pregnant. One can only imagine what the knowledge that her mother would never see her grandchild would have done to Maria Magdalena's already damaged emotions.

Johann and Maria Magdalena van Beethoven's first child was baptised Ludwig Maria on 2 April 1769. One can envision *Kapellmeister* Beethoven's joy at the arrival of his first grandchild, augmented by the couple's decision to choose him as godfather, meaning that the child carried his name. For the couple, too, the arrival of a son after almost a year and a half of marriage must have been a cause of enormous family celebration, and one can imagine the stern grandfather melting towards the daughter-in-law he had not wanted to see become a member of the Beethoven family.

The infant Ludwig Maria van Beethoven died within a week of baptism. Even in an era when infant death was common, the loss of a child who carried so much hope for reconciliation must have been a catastrophe for the family. For Maria Magdalena it meant that she had been widowed and had lost two infants before she was twenty-three years of age.

Approximately a year later she fell pregnant again. As the months passed she must have been overwhelmed with trepidation about the child's survival. As on the previous two occasions she safely gave birth, and on 17 December 1770, the infant was baptised Ludwig after his grandfather, who was once again godfather. Like his grandfather, he was given the sole Christian name of Ludwig.

There were now two Ludwig van Beethovens in the family, and as each day passed the child grew stronger. Correspondingly there occurred a remarkable change in the demeanour of the elder Ludwig. He began to be drawn towards his daughter-in-law and soon the two had established a close and loving relationship. Unfortunately this was due at least partly to a shared disappointment in Johann.

As a boy Johann van Beethoven had shown considerable musical talent, to the extent that his father removed him from school and undertook his musical training himself (a pattern that was to be repeated when Johann, in turn, removed his son Ludwig from school to concentrate on music). He sang in the court chapel both as boy treble and after his voice had broken, and at the age of twenty-four, being proficient in singing as well as on the clavier and violin, he obtained salaried employment.

Three years later Johann was married, and things started to go downhill almost immediately. It is evident that he developed a taste for alcohol. He had no shortage of drinking companions. The fish dealer Klein lived across the street, and the two men would lounge in the window making faces at each other, prior to a night's drinking. The Fischers reported that Johann van Beethoven would spend many an evening in the tavern, often not arriving home until the middle of the night.

It cannot have helped that soon after Johann moved into his first marital home his father followed, taking an apartment just a few doors away in the same street. Ludwig van Beethoven senior was clearly a dominant, even domineering, figure, and was intolerant of his son's behaviour. He mocked him continuously. 'Johann *der Läufer*,' he called him. 'Johann the sprinter. Keep running, keep running. You will some day run to your final destination.'

It can't have been easy living up to his father's expectations, but whether his own inadequacies preceded his father's intolerance, or the other way around, it's impossible to say. Similarly, whether his penchant for alcohol was a cause of his father's disappointment in him, or a form of escapism from it, must also remain a matter for conjecture.

What is beyond doubt is that an event that shook the Beethoven family to its foundations offered Johann the opportunity to turn his life round. On Christmas Eve 1773 *Kapellmeister* Beethoven, who had suffered a stroke earlier in the year, died at the age of sixty-one. Johann saw himself as the natural successor and the next holder of the highest musical position in Bonn.

Unfortunately for him, he was unsuited for it in every respect. His dissolute habits were well known and unfitting to such a high office at court. There had also been a noticeable deterioration in his vocal skills, no doubt caused by alcohol, tobacco, and late nights. His skills on clavier and violin were not exceptional, and he had no compositions to his name, unlike other candidates for the office.

It is dangerous to apply modern-day sensibilities to events of more than two centuries ago, but certainly a reading of Johann's petition for the job as *Kapellmeister* suggests a confused, even negative, attitude:

> *Will your Electoral Grace be pleased to hear that my father has passed away from this world, to whom it was granted to serve His Electoral Grace(s) for 42 years, as* Kapellmeister *with great honour,* whose position I have been found capable of filling, *but nevertheless I would not venture to offer my capacity to Your Electoral Grace, but since the death of my father has left me in needy circumstances, my salary not sufficing, I am compelled to draw on the savings of my father ...* Your Electoral Grace is therefore humbly implored to make an allowance from the 400 rth now saved for an increase of my salary ... [my emphasis]

It hardly reads like an appropriate job application, seeming on the one hand to take it for granted that the job is his, and on the other pleading for a salary increase. In any event he did not get the job. There was only one *Kapellmeister* Beethoven.

—

Of crucial importance to the future development of his son is that these traumatic events were witnessed by the infant Ludwig van Beethoven. How much comprehension a child of three can have is impossible to determine, particularly at such a distance in time. But, with the proviso that this is largely conjecture, we might assume the infant would at least pick up signs of distress in his mother, and probably too be aware that it is his father's behaviour that is causing it.

Ludwig was one week past his third birthday when his grandfather died, and of this at least we can be sure beyond any doubt: the loss rocked him profoundly, and it is something he never truly came to terms with. He idolised—and idealised—his grandfather and spoke highly of him for the rest of his life. Certainly when his own musical talents began to emerge, he would quickly have become aware of his grandfather's considerable achievements, at the same time no doubt witnessing the decline in his father's.

Exactly how early Ludwig's musical talents began to emerge is not known, but by the age of four he was being taught clavier and violin by his father, and so some special talent in the child must by then have been evident. There is considerable anecdotal evidence that Johann drove Ludwig hard, and more than one witness reports seeing the small boy standing on a footstool in front of the clavier in tears. Others reported seeing the father using physical violence, even shutting the child up in the cellar. These accounts were given many years after the event, by which time Beethoven had become famous throughout Europe, so it is possible some exaggeration had crept in. We can, though, be relatively sure that at the very least Johann van Beethoven drove his son hard in the quest to develop his musical talent.

By 1776 Johann van Beethoven had moved his family back into the Fischer house on the Rheingasse, where he had lived with his father before marriage, this time into a spacious apartment on the second floor. There were to be later moves, but this was the house in which Ludwig van Beethoven spent the greater part of his youth, and where he felt most at home.

On 26 March 1778 there occurred a remarkable event in the early life of Ludwig van Beethoven, one that has given rise to much myth and speculation surrounding the actions of his father.

Johann staged a public concert featuring one of his singing pupils, and his son Ludwig. Here is the advertisement he put in the newspaper:

Today, 26 March 1778, in the musical concert room in the Sternengasse, the Electoral Court Tenorist, Beethoven, will have the honour to produce ... his little son of six years, [who will perform] various clavier concertos and trios ... Tickets may be had at the Akademiesaal ...

Do you spot the mistake, and, more importantly, is it deliberate? In March 1778 Ludwig van Beethoven was seven years and three months old. So why might Johann van Beethoven, on an important occasion such as this, have stated his son's age incorrectly?

There are two possible explanations, which I shall call the 'conspiracy theory' and the 'kind theory'. The conspiracy theory runs like this. Johann van Beethoven deliberately falsified his son's age because he wanted to make him appear younger than he was. This would make his musical skills all the more impressive, leading—Johann hoped—to favourable comparisons with the boy Mozart. It was well known that Mozart's father had taken him on tour as a child, to wide acclaim and the amassing of substantial payments. The fact that Ludwig's birth certificate had disappeared was no doubt because Johann had deliberately destroyed the evidence.

The kind theory absolves Johann from deliberate falsification. It points out that there was a general laxity in keeping family records at that time, that on no other known occasion did Johann make an error in his son's age, and that his own birth certificate had vanished, as well as his son's, pointing to his general carelessness with paperwork. On this occasion he simply made a mistake.

Knowing what we know of Johann van Beethoven, it is hard to be charitable, particularly in the light of the deliberate dishonesty that was to come a few years later. It is clear that he rec-ognised his son's remarkable talent very early, and the fact that he put him in front of a paying audience at such a tender age is evi-dence of his intention to earn money through him. We know that the Beethoven family was short of funds from Johann's impas-sioned plea to the Elector for an increase in salary. Even if he ex-aggerated the poverty, which is likely, it is still beyond doubt that they were not flush, and that this situation was compounded by Johann's profligate lifestyle.

I subscribe to the conspiracy theory. Is it really likely that a fa-ther would not know how old his oldest son was? If he was in doubt, wouldn't he have checked with his wife? Or if he didn't want to do that, he could have left the age out of the advertisement altogether. I think it is beyond reasonable doubt that Johann van Beethoven de-liberately falsified Ludwig's age to impress the audience all the more with his talent.

Future events lend weight to this. Beethoven appeared confused about his age for much of his life. His second published work (of which more later) contains the words on the title page, 'composed by Ludwig van Beethoven, aged eleven years'. It was 1783, and he was in fact twelve. Well into adulthood the confusion remained. In his twenties there is evidence that he believed he was two years older than he actually was. In his mid-thirties he clearly believed he was two years younger than he was. Living in Vienna, he asked friends back in Bonn to send him copies of his baptismal certificate, since he was considering marriage. When the first copy arrived, he refused to accept the date, claiming his friend had mistaken him for his elder brother Ludwig, who had died at a week old. The second copy also failed to convince him—he wrote '1772' on the back of it. This in spite of the fact that he must surely have surmised that if he really had been born in 1772, just one year before his beloved grandfather died, he would have had no memories of him at all.

Was he confused, delusional, or just not interested in the facts? Or did his father's falsification so affect him that he could never quite be confident of his age? We do not know the answer.

Rather more importantly for musical history, we have no idea of how that performance in the Sternengasse concert room went. We do not know what music the young Ludwig played, nor do we have any idea of whether it was successful or not, because no one wrote it up.

There is no evidence that Johann put on any more public performances, which suggests maybe that the receipts did not justify the effort. Soon after that recital, Johann did the best thing he could possibly do for his son: he put him into school. But it was not long before he then did the worst thing possible: he took him out of school to concentrate solely on music. This was in 1780 or 1781, when Ludwig was around ten years of age. For the rest of his life he suffered from an inadequate education. His handwriting was close to illegible, his punctuation and spelling poor, and he was useless with figures—there is evidence later on that he could not add up his household bills. In later life his signatures were often so erratic that future musicologists had trouble deciding whether some were authentic.

Until Johann took his young son out of school, Ludwig led what amounted to a normal childhood. There was a sandpit on the bank of the Rhine, and he and his two younger brothers often played in it. His childhood friend Gottfried Fischer reported that Ludwig and his brothers would steal eggs from the henhouse behind the Fischer house. Once, Frau Fischer caught Ludwig crawling through the fence into the henhouse.

'Hah,' she said, 'and what are you doing there, Ludwig?'

'My brother Caspar threw my handkerchief in here and I came to get it.'

'Yes, that may well account for the fact that I am getting so few eggs.'

'But Frau Fischer, the hens often hide their eggs, and there are foxes, they steal eggs too.'

'Yes, and I think you are one of those sly foxes, Ludwig.'

'Yes, I am a musical-note fox.'

'And an egg fox too!'

Fischer adds that the two brothers ran off laughing like rogues, Frau Fischer laughing with them, unable to find it in her heart to chastise them for their monkey tricks.

On another occasion, recounts Fischer, the Beethoven brothers spotted a cockerel that had flown out of the yard and onto the top of a barn in the Fischers' backyard. They dared each other to catch him. Together they coaxed him with bread, caught him, squeezed his throat so he could not crow. Then they ran back upstairs to the attic and laughed at their prank.

Fischer also recounts how Ludwig and his brother Caspar Carl would put a target on the garden wall of the house and shoot arrows at it. A bull's-eye would earn the marksman the promise of a small coin.

These events, with the dialogue, were recorded around sixty years after the event,[3] by which time Gottfried Fischer was aware of the fame attained by the child who had lived in his house, so there might be inaccuracies in them and the dialogue polished. But I believe that, whatever may have passed between Ludwig and Frau Fischer, or between the brothers and the cockerel, it is very unlikely that Fischer would have invented the entire scenarios.

I find it beguiling to think that the famous composer of the 'Choral' Symphony and *Fidelio* stole hens' eggs as a child.

This is all in stark contrast to Ludwig's brief spell as a schoolboy. The school's head described him as 'a shy and taciturn boy, the inevitable consequence of the life apart which he led, observing more and pondering more than he spoke'. When, later, musicologists and biographers sought out his schoolfellows, not one related anecdotes of playing games with him, or even described him as a friend. There was no talk of trips on the Rhine or rambles across the hills. As early as his schooldays, his prodigious talent for music set him apart.

This sense of apartness was compounded by Ludwig's physical appearance. His skin was dark and swarthy, unusual in northern Germany, and Fischer recounts that from childhood on he was nicknamed 'Der Spagnol' ('The Spaniard'). It is inevitable, given how children are, that Ludwig will have been teased at school about his appearance. It might be conjecture, but it is not difficult to imagine playground taunts.

This is made more likely by one highly distressing anecdote. One of his schoolfellows, who later rose to high office in local government and the law, relates that as a schoolboy 'Luis v. B. was distinguished by uncleanliness, negligence, etc.' and he attributes this to the fact that Ludwig's mother was already dead.

Maria Magdalena van Beethoven was far from dead. She in fact gave birth to a daughter in 1779, who died in the same year, and a son in 1781, who died two years later. The implication of this, and its effect on a ten-year-old boy, are dire. At its most basic it must mean that Frau van Beethoven was never seen either to drop her son off at school, or to pick him up later. If that is excusable on the basis that Ludwig was able to look after himself, it further suggests that nothing was known among the school community about his family. That implies no casual conversations, no playground chat, which in turn points to a lonely existence for Ludwig.

Compounding that is the starkness with which his schoolmate described Ludwig's appearance. To be in such a state of neglect suggests Ludwig was paid scant attention at home by his mother, if she allowed him to attend school unwashed and dishevelled.

Finally, with regard to this brief, but portentous, anecdote, one can hardly begin to imagine the effect on a ten-year-old boy of his schoolfellows believing his mother was dead, when he knew perfectly well she was not. Given his state of disarray, and the penchant of schoolchildren to pick on a less fortunate schoolmate, it is more than likely he was the butt of playground jokes and jibes. He might even have been taunted over the (mistaken) belief that his mother was dead. It certainly seems as if Ludwig did nothing to correct matters, which in itself is puzzling.

This is conjecture, and again the anecdote was related many years later. But, as with Fischer, it is unlikely to have been wholly invented, particularly since its author rose to become Electoral Councillor and President of the Landgericht, the state court.

All in all, detrimental though it might have been to Ludwig to end his school career so soon, he might himself have welcomed it, since he could at least escape from schoolfellows with whom he had nothing in common, and devote himself to music.

———

A year, or possibly more, before being taken out of school, Ludwig began music lessons.[4] If this was a good decision on the part of his father, it was rendered unhelpful by the fact that Johann chose unsuitable music teachers for him. The first was the venerable court organist Gilles van den Eeden, who had been good friends with *Kapellmeister* Beethoven, no doubt because of their shared Flemish heritage, and was witness at his friend's marriage. Van den Eeden was over seventy years of age and had been in court service for more than fifty years when he began to teach the young boy.

To suggest a clash of generations would be an understatement, and one can easily imagine Ludwig, even at such a tender age, impatient to move faster than the aged musician from another era was prepared to go.

Details of the instructions van den Eeden gave his young pupil are unclear, as are the exact dates between which he taught him.

What is certain, though, is that the arrangement, for whatever reason, did not last long, and Ludwig soon had a new teacher.

Tobias Pfeiffer was, by all accounts, an accomplished artist. He was also, as several contemporaries avow, something of an eccentric. Pianist, oboist, and flautist, he was also an actor and singer with the Grossmann and Helmuth theatre company, which accounts for his arrival in Bonn at the end of 1779. He took lodgings with the Beethoven family, and soon found himself employed to give music lessons to the young Ludwig.

He was highly accomplished on the flute, but apparently had little liking for it. Gottfried Fischer's sister Cäcilie recounts how when she asked him to play the flute, he replied, 'Oh, the flute. That instrument doesn't interest me. You waste your breath for other people, and I don't like that.' However, when he did play, with Ludwig accompanying him on the piano, the result was so beautiful that people stopped in the street outside to listen. Gottfried said he heard several people say they could listen to the music 'all day and all night'.

This anecdote is of some importance. It is the first evidence—albeit, like all the Fischer reminiscences, recalled decades after the event—of Ludwig van Beethoven performing on equal terms with an adult professional, and already establishing a reputation.

Unfortunately for the boy, though, Pfeiffer was an erratic teacher. After an evening's drinking with Johann, the two of them would arouse Ludwig late at night, drag him to the piano crying, and force him to play. Pfeiffer would then instruct him often until daylight. It does not take a lot to imagine the horror of being aroused from sleep, forced to play no doubt surrounded by alcohol fumes, and being generally bullied by two men, one your father, the other a musician whose eccentric behaviour was earning him enemies.

That eccentricity could be dangerous as well as harmless. When asked by Fischer senior, who lived on the floor below, to stop stamping up and down his room in heavy boots because it was keeping him awake at night, Pfeiffer agreed to remove one boot but not the other. On another occasion, when the barber came to tend to the men of the house, he said something to offend Pfeiffer, who picked him up bodily and threw him down the stairs, injuring him badly.

It was perhaps as much of a blessing for the people of Bonn, as for the young Ludwig, that Pfeiffer left Bonn with his theatre company after just three months.

—

We know from the records that Ludwig did not enter secondary school (Gymnasium) in the autumn of 1781. In mitigation of his father's behaviour, it should perhaps be pointed out that it was common practice for parents in Bonn to remove their children from the education system after primary, lower-grade, school, with a view to apprenticing them so they could begin to earn a living. It had happened to Johann himself, who left before secondary school to take up an appointment as court musician.

If Johann was thinking that this was an appropriate moment to test his young son's earning power, the perfect opportunity presented itself. Through a family connection in Holland, an invitation was made for the Beethovens to visit Rotterdam. Johann's court duties prevented him from going, but he sent his wife and son, with clear instructions that Ludwig should perform, and be remunerated for it.

This episode is rarely mentioned in biographies, for the obvious reason that very little is known about it, and what we do know—as with the Fischer anecdotes—was related by a neighbour many years after the event. But again, as with Fischer, it is the small telling detail that rings absolutely true. That detail in this case, I believe, throws a fascinating and intriguing light on the relationship between Ludwig and his mother.

The winter of 1781 began early with bitterly cold weather. Frau van Beethoven sat with her ten-year-old son on the deck of a sailing boat as it travelled down the Rhine towards Holland. Huddled against the wind, Ludwig became very cold. His mother coaxed him to lie on the bench, took his feet onto her lap, and rubbed them to try to keep them warm.

Could this be the same woman who allowed her son to turn up at school in such a dishevelled state that fellow schoolboys thought she was dead? If we believe the anecdotes, then there were clearly emotional complexities at work in the Beethoven family that we can only guess at.

Two years before the trip to Holland, Maria Magdalena had given birth to a baby girl who died before the end of the year. In the same year as the trip, she gave birth to a son. Would a mother leave her infant of less than a year to make the trip? What arrangements did she make for the child to be looked after? Could she have suffered from postnatal depression after the death of the baby girl? And what feelings of guilt awaited her when the baby boy she left behind died at the age of two?

Question after question, and we cannot answer any of them. But, as with the hens' eggs and the cockerel, I cannot help but be bewitched by the thought that, as titanic an artist as he was, Beethoven still got cold feet.

As for the trip, the hoped-for financial rewards were not forthcoming. The boy certainly played in the highest salons and was apparently showered with compliments, but little else. A performance before Prince Willem of Orange Nassau yielded a mere 63 florins. When his friend Gottfried Fischer asked him how it had gone, Ludwig replied, 'The Dutch are skinflints. I'll never go to Holland again.' And he didn't.

Johann also was making efforts to earn money through his son. When the Elector was absent from Bonn, and court musicians were free, Johann would take trips with his son into the countryside around Bonn and alongside both banks of the Rhine, visiting wealthy noblemen and persuading them to listen to Ludwig perform.

This afforded an opportunity not just for financial gain, but for father and son to develop a closer relationship. Although there is some evidence of the former, there is none of the latter. Neither these excursions nor the trip to Rotterdam appears to have brought the boy any closer to his parents. It is also fair to speculate that these trips, coupled with the Rotterdam experience, put him off performing 'to order' for life.

From Johann's point of view, if his son really was to be a source of income for the family, as young Wolfgang Amadeus had been for the Mozarts, then he needed to acquire more skills, and that meant finding another teacher.

Whether it was Johann, or the Elector himself, who took the next step is not clear. Whoever it was, a decision was made on Ludwig's behalf that changed his life. It was decided to employ a certain Christian Gottlob Neefe to teach Ludwig. A better man could not have been chosen. From the day he began lessons with Neefe, probably in 1781 at the age of ten, Ludwig van Beethoven began his life as a musician.

CHAPTER TWO

THE RIGHT TEACHER

THIS BOY COULD BECOME
A SECOND MOZART

THE SMALL TOWN OF BONN, ON THE WEST BANK of the Rhine, then as in more recent times, punched above its weight. Surprisingly chosen as the capital of the Federal Republic of Germany in 1949, it was, in Beethoven's lifetime, the unlikely seat of the Elector, who was also Archbishop of Cologne and Münster. It was a medieval Archbishop who selected Bonn for his residence, rather than the more obvious choice of Cologne, possibly for the reason that the mighty Rhine narrowed at this point and could be blocked, thus bestowing on Bonn a crucial strategic importance. In later centuries it endowed Bonn with a certain grandeur, more than a veneer of aristocracy, a degree of wealth and prosperity, which its rival towns on the Rhine—Cologne, Mainz, Coblenz—could only look at with envy. And for the people of Bonn—fewer than 10,000 according to a survey in 1789—it meant pleasant, well-tended surroundings and, more importantly, security and income. For a town with no manufacture or commerce, it was commonly stated that 'all Bonn was fed from the Elector's kitchen'.

Clemens August, who made his solemn entry into Bonn as Elector in 1724, endowed the town with a fine palace (now the University of Bonn) and an ornate Town Hall (today used for ceremonial functions—President Kennedy made a speech there in 1963). But, of more importance to our story, in 1733 he employed a Flemish immigrant by the name of Ludwig van Beethoven as court musician, and twenty-three years later his son Johann.

This Elector left his mark on Bonn in another way too. He danced himself to death, literally. Leaving Bonn to visit his family in Munich in early 1761, he was struck down with illness, and broke his journey to call on the hospitality of his fellow Elector in Ehrenbreitstein.[1] At dinner he was too ill to eat, but not it seems too poorly to take to the dance floor afterwards with the alluring Baroness von Waldendorf, sister of the Elector. She must have been exceedingly alluring, because he danced with her not once, or twice, but for 'eight or nine turns'. Other ladies, complaining of neglect, received their turn too. If his spirit was willing, his flesh could not withstand the exertion. He passed out on the dance floor, was carried to his room, and died the next day.

I recount this story, not just to raise a sympathetic smile, but because of the impact it, and subsequent events, had on the Beethoven family. Clemens August's successor as Elector, Maximilian Friedrich, had barely got his feet under the desk, as it were, when he received a petition from court bass singer Ludwig van Beethoven seeking elevation to the supreme musical position of *Kapellmeister*, the post being vacant following the death of the previous incumbent. The petition pleads with the Elector 'to grant me the justice of which I was deprived on the death of Your Highness's *antecessori* of blessed memory', which suggests the elder Beethoven had made moves—if not in a formal petition—to be appointed *Kapellmeister* before the previous Elector's untimely demise.

We can assume the death of Clemens August, and the manner of his passing, was the predominant topic of conversation at all levels among the populace of Bonn, with varying degrees of ribald observation. Certainly, at court level, it led to immediate jockeying for promotion, in particular among the court musicians, since the top job itself was vacant.

Beethoven senior's bold approach paid dividends. By an order of the Elector dated 16 July 1761, he was appointed *Kapellmeister*, with an increase in salary, though less than he might have expected due to the fact that he was not a composer. A little over two years later he managed to secure a permanent position at court for his son Johann, as tenor and violinist. Between them, father and son (not yet married) were earning a comfortable sum.

This was particularly fortunate, for under Maximilian Friedrich things changed for the burghers of Bonn. The Elector himself was an affable and kindly man, sharing with his predecessor a predilection for the fairer sex, and court entertainment carried on much as before. But his popularity with his people was in stark contrast to that of his First Minister. Count Kaspar Anton von Belderbusch had been instrumental in securing Maximilian Friedrich's election. In return he demanded—and was granted—unrivalled political power. On examining the exchequer and discovering the previous Elector's extravagance, he came down hard on all expenditure.

Practically overnight the good life in Bonn ended. People suddenly found themselves out of work, some even losing what had previously been considered a 'job for life' at the court. At all levels there was a financial crackdown. A visitor from England was somewhat horrified to find that at dinner with the Elector, 'no dessert wines were handed about, nor any foreign wines at all', which, while it might say as much about the travel writer Henry Swinburne as it does about the Elector, at least suggests a comfortable life was expected at court, if nowhere else.

The easygoing and even-tempered Elector was not one to stand up to his First Minister, which might have something to do with the fact that Belderbusch knew rather a lot about the Elector's private life. The two men shared a mistress, a certain Countess Caroline von Satzenhofen—who happened to be Abbess of a Benedictine nunnery close to Bonn!

Once again, this is likely to have been common knowledge, at least among court employees. It is inconceivable that there were not hushed whispers when the two men were seen together, and the fact that the Elector was as much liked as his First Minister was disliked might have had something to do with resentment at the fact that Belderbusch not only behaved as if he was Elector, but even enjoyed the services of the Elector's mistress.

This, then, was the Bonn that Ludwig van Beethoven was born into, a town that had seen more comfortable days, that was nominally ruled by an ineffective Elector and governed by a strict disciplinarian First Minister, but that still boasted an enviable artistic life, with a busy calendar of performances by court orchestra and theatre, and was a desirable location for touring theatrical companies. It was this reputation for the arts, particularly music, that brought the thirty-one-year-old composer, organist, and conductor, Christian Gottlob Neefe, to Bonn.

—

A combination of circumstances made Neefe the ideal teacher for the budding young musician, Ludwig van Beethoven. As a young man in Chemnitz in Saxony he had had serious disagreements with his father, who wanted him to follow his example and take up law. Under protest he enrolled at the University of Leipzig to study jurisprudence, but was so unhappy he apparently contemplated suicide. Against his father's wishes he gave up the law and turned to music. At the same time he immersed himself in the philosophy and ideals of the German Enlightenment, reading Gellert, Klopstock, and particularly the young Goethe.

Imagine the effect of this background on a ten-year-old boy. Ludwig's beloved grandfather was long dead, and he was watching his father descend into alcoholism and his parents' marriage come under increasing strain. Here was an adult who might well have poured out his troubles with his own father to young Ludwig, at the same time encouraging him to develop as a musician in the way he wanted, without reference to his father. He will also without doubt have filled the boy's head with radical, even revolutionary, ideas. This was the decade in which the Enlightenment was sweeping Europe, questioning the divine order of things, the God-given right of rulers to rule—ideals and philosophies that were to come to such a terrifying climax in France in just a few years' time.

Judging by an autobiographical tract he wrote in Bonn in 1782, at about the time (or shortly after) Ludwig became his pupil, Neefe believed strongly that sensual desire should be sublimated into art and the quest for ethical perfection. A more apt description of the adult Beethoven's ethics would be hard to find.

Of crucial importance, I believe, is the rarely stated fact that Neefe was a Protestant, and he had come to live in a Catholic town. True, Bonn was hardly a hive of subversive activity, but the fact that Neefe was a Protestant would certainly have been noted. He joined the local Order of Illuminati, nominally a nonsectarian organisation with branches throughout Europe, which attracted artists and literary figures such as Goethe. Members took a vow of secrecy and obedience to their superiors, and Neefe soon became one of its leaders. The movement began in Bavaria, and when it was suppressed there, the Bonn branch dissolved itself in favour of a less suspect body, called the Reading Society (*Lesegesellschaft*).

Neefe became a leading light in the Reading Society, and since his pupil was in his early teens at the time, it is not inconceivable he took him along to meetings. At any rate, it is hard to imagine a more intimate, even secretive, situation than a teacher and pupil alone in a room at the piano, and the young Ludwig would easily have come to admire the forward-thinking, radically minded, intensely musical Neefe. If evidence were needed, less than a decade later Ludwig wrote to Neefe from Vienna, rather formally, 'I thank you for the advice you have very often given me about making progress in my divine art. Should I ever become a great man, you too will have a share in my success.' I believe that the seeds of Beethoven's radicalism, both in music and in his personal and political beliefs, were sown in these early, impressionable years as Neefe's pupil.

On the death of old van den Eeden, court organist and Ludwig's first teacher, Neefe was appointed to succeed him. This was remarkable for someone who had not long since arrived in Bonn, and whose duties would require him to play at church services. It says something for the degree of religious tolerance in Bonn that Neefe's Protestant faith did not stand in his way.

The appointment gave Neefe status. Although one might suspect that his new court duties would leave him little time for instruction, Neefe was perceptive enough to recognise that his young pupil had extraordinary talents that needed nurturing. When he expressed this view, he was listened to, given his elevated position as court organist. This led to a significant development in the life of young Ludwig.

Shortly after getting the job of court organist, Neefe was committed to a lengthy absence from Bonn with the Grossmann and Helmuth company. He proposed that his young pupil should stand in for him, and play the organ at church services. Ludwig was just eleven years of age. The proposal was accepted, even if with raised eyebrows, and one can be sure that any doubts or misgivings were laid to rest when Ludwig's skill on the organ was heard.

Thanks to Neefe, Ludwig's talents were now beginning to be widely appreciated. Neefe did not stop there. It was fortunate for Ludwig that Neefe was a composer. It meant that when he expressed a desire to compose, very soon after beginning lessons, Neefe did not discourage him. A lesser teacher might well have advised him to learn to walk before he could run but, perhaps recognising something of his own early enthusiasm in the boy, he encouraged Ludwig.

It is probable Ludwig had begun making musical sketches even before beginning instruction with Neefe. Whether or not this was the case, or whether Neefe gave him direct advice on what to try his hand at, in 1782 Ludwig produced a composition for piano. It was a set of variations on a march by the recently deceased German composer Ernst Christoph Dressler. Ludwig probably wrote it during Neefe's absence. Again, a lesser teacher might have torn it to shreds, or at least criticised it heavily, even if constructively. What Neefe did, instead, was arrange to have it published.

Within a year or two of taking Ludwig on as a pupil, then, Neefe had given him the opportunity to play the organ at civic services and had arranged for the publication of his first work. Ludwig was not yet twelve years of age. Had Neefe then vanished from the scene, these services alone would have been enough to earn him his place in musical history. But there was more, much more, to come.

—

The marriage of Johann and Maria Magdalena was drifting perilously close to the rocks. Johann, loving his drink more and more, thought nothing of walking through Bonn gulping wine from a flask, unmindful of being seen. Gottfried Fischer gives graphic accounts of the strains in the marriage of the couple living in the apartment above him, and—again with the caveats that he was a child when witnessing what he describes and that he wrote down his memoirs around sixty years later—they have more than a ring of truth to them.

Maria Magadalena, berating her husband for drinking outside in the street, draws this response: 'It is such hot weather that I have to have a drink.'

She replies, 'That's true, but you have to have a drink even without the summer heat.'

He responds, 'You are right. I agree with you. Thank you. Tell me when it's time to eat and I'll come straight in.'

Gottfried recounts how Johann van Beethoven tried to plant a kiss on his sister Cäcilie, calling her 'our patroness of music'. She replied,

'I am not the sort of girl to go round kissing people, anyway you already have a wife, go and kiss her, not me.'

'You are a clever little witch,' said Johann. 'You know exactly what to say.'

According to Gottfried, Johann chanced his luck with Cäcilie again, some years later. He made a drunken lunge at her, she deflected him with a hearty push, he knocked over the oven, pulling the stove and stovepipe from the wall. According to Gottfried's memoirs, everyone (rather surprisingly) took it in good fun, including Johann, who said, 'That taught me a good lesson', and Maria Magdalena, who appears to have been in the room at the time, told Cäcilie, 'That was the right thing to do. That's how to handle him.'

The dialogue may be stilted, the reminiscences coloured with the passage of time. But at the very least what we have here is a musician employed at court descending into alcoholism, prone to making a fool of himself in private and public, uncaring of what this might be doing to his career and reputation.

From further anecdotal evidence it is clear that Maria Magdalena had long since given up on her husband. When he received his monthly salary, or payment from pupils, he would toss the bag of money into his wife's lap and say, 'There woman, manage with that.' This is stark evidence that Maria Magdalena was in charge of the family's finances, and her husband was acquiescent. According to Gottfried, after Maria Magdalena had the money safely in her hands, she would tease her husband about his drinking, saying, 'A man cannot be allowed to return home with *empty* hands.'

'Yes, *empty* hands!' One can imagine Johann staring dolefully at his empty hands.

'Yes, *so empty*,' says Maria, 'but I know how much you would like to fill them up with a full glass.'

'Yes, yes,' as a smug grin spreads across his face, 'the woman is right, she is always right.'

Once again, if the dialogue is contrived and exaggerated, it suggests that in the early stages of their marriage at least, before Johann's drinking had a fatal effect on his career, Maria Magdalena would be content to indulge her husband's habit as long as the money kept coming in.

But this was not to last. There is anecdotal evidence from several sources as to just how unhappy Maria Magdalena was. Gottfried quotes her saying to Cäcilie, 'If you want my advice, stay single, that's the secret to having a quiet, happy life. For what is marriage? A little joy, but then a chain of sorrows.' Cäcilie in her turn is quoted as saying that she had never seen Maria Magdalena laugh, that she was always serious. Another neighbour describes her as a 'quiet, suffering woman'. She was apparently not above losing her temper, and on occasion was able to give as good as she got.

An unhappy marriage, then, although certainly in the early years not one beyond repair. But as Johann's drinking took hold, it was to lead to a disastrous sequence of events that was to throw a heavy shadow over the Beethoven household.

This is the atmosphere in which young Ludwig van Beethoven grew up. According to Gottfried Fischer, Ludwig witnessed the conversation in which his mother described marriage as 'a chain of sorrows'. He will certainly have witnessed disagreements, even rows, between his parents, and will have become aware painfully early of his father's excessive drinking.

By the time he began lessons with Neefe, he was the eldest of three sons, there was an infant in the house who died at two years of age, and a daughter born five years later who died at the age of one.[2] This can only have contributed to the tensions in the marriage, and the difficult atmosphere in the apartment on the second floor of the house in the Rheingasse, which Gottfried Fischer so vividly describes.

But Ludwig had something that neither his brothers, nor anyone he knew, had. A means of escape. It must have been not just with a feeling of relief, but an overwhelming sense of excitement, that he set off each time for instruction with Neefe. An opportunity to enter the world of music, his world, where the conversation would be on a different plane from the mundanities of his home life and where, if they were discussed, they were no doubt dismissed with a wave of the hand as being too trivial to impinge on the higher calling of true art. Total escape, though, was not possible. At its most basic, Ludwig had to return to the apartment, to his mother's sadness and despair, his father's drunken antics, two younger brothers no doubt running riot, and a baby restless with ill-health.

Ludwig would not have been able to evade the knowledge that if his father's career were to implode, the full weight of caring for the family would fall on his shoulders, as the eldest son. This was customary in that era. Normally the eldest son would be apprenticed to the father's trade—as Gottfried Fischer was to his baker father—but this was not possible in Ludwig's case. He was training to be a musician, and he had not yet entered his teenage years. How on earth would he be able to earn a living as a musician at such a young age?

Once again, history—as well as a small, apprehensive boy—owes a debt of gratitude to Christian Gottlob Neefe.

—

In a remarkable leap of faith, Neefe wrote a piece for the *Magazin der Musik*, a musical publication owned by the German book dealer and writer on music, Carl Friedrich Cramer, in which he described the musical scene at the Elector's court in Bonn. It was published in the issue dated 2 March 1783, and is so prescient about his young pupil that the paragraph concerning him deserves to be quoted in full:

Louis van Betthoven [sic], *son of the above-mentioned tenor, a boy of eleven* [sic] *years and of most promising talent. He plays the clavier very skilfully and with power, sight-reads very well, and—to put it in a nutshell—he plays chiefly The Well-Tempered Clavier of Sebastian Bach, which Herr Neefe put into his hands. Whoever knows this collection of preludes and fugues in all the keys—which might almost be called the non plus ultra of our art—will know what this means. So far as his other duties have permitted, Herr Neefe has also given him instruction in thorough-bass.[3] He is now training him in composition, and in order to encourage him has had 9 variations on a March by Ernst Christoph Dressler published in Mannheim. This young genius deserves support so that he can travel. He would surely become a second Wolfgang Amadeus Mozart, if he were to continue as he has begun.*

This is an extraordinary endorsement. Here is a professional musician going public in print with the belief that his young pupil is a musician of genius, not just of genius but potentially the equal of Mozart. In more practical terms it gives us a wonderful insight into exactly what Ludwig was capable of. At the age of twelve, he was proficient in arguably J. S. Bach's greatest set of compositions for the keyboard, exploring all twenty-four keys, recognised at the time as some of the most difficult keyboard music ever written. There is many a professional who fails to master 'The 48'[4] in a lifetime. Neefe also—and this is startling evidence of his farsightedness—gives equal weight to the instruction he is giving Ludwig in composition.

The final two sentences stand alone as the first endorsement of Ludwig's skills to appear in print. Neefe's use of the word 'genius' and the name 'Mozart' could have made him a hostage to fortune, staking his reputation in print.[5] He clearly saw this as no risk, and history has most certainly vindicated him. Finally, I find it touchingly humble that Neefe is writing in the third person, almost as if to concentrate the reader's mind on Ludwig van Beethoven rather than himself.

Hardly had the piece been published before Neefe set about encouraging Ludwig in his next great enterprise—more composition. One begins to form the impression that Neefe believed there was nothing more he could teach the boy in terms of performance, that in fact Ludwig might already have been a better keyboard player than he himself was. What better course of action, then, than to encourage him in his desire to compose?

This might well have been linked to the two final sentences in that paragraph published in Cramer's magazine. In one sense they can be read as a generalised suggestion that Ludwig needed to broaden his horizons, so that he could become as good as Mozart. In another, more subtle reading, they are in effect a plea to the Elector, or failing him any moneyed aristocrat, to come up with the money that would enable Ludwig to travel to Vienna and study with Mozart.

This second reading is reinforced by the composition that Ludwig now produced. It was nothing less than a set of three full piano sonatas. If the *Dressler Variations* were impressive—the rapid runs in the final variation are intimidating even for a proficient player—the three piano sonatas are on a higher plane altogether. For a start it was extraordinarily bold and ambitious for a twelve-year-old to choose the sonata form, rather than something simpler such as a rondo, or minuet, or more variations. Secondly there are elements in all three compositions that point ahead to his more mature work. It has been convincingly argued that these three piano sonatas, although without opus numbers, should be included in Beethoven's total piano sonata output, so that we should talk of his thirty-five piano sonatas, rather than the more normal thirty-two. There might be several hundred recordings of the Beethoven piano sonatas by virtuosos over the last seventy or eighty years, but relatively few that include the first three.[6]

If Ludwig's choice of the sonata form was bold, the person to whom he chose to dedicate these first three sonatas showed a confidence bordering on arrogance. It was none other than the Elector himself, Maximilian Friedrich. And what a contrast to the dedication of the *Dressler Variations*. Those were dedicated to a noblewoman *'par un jeune amateur'*. The sonatas were a gift for a scion of the House of Habsburg, the most senior aristocrat in Bonn, and the letter accompanying the manuscript shows not a shred of self-doubt:

> *Having become acquainted so early with the gracious Muse who tuned my soul to pure harmonies, I learned to love her, and she, as it often seems to me, began to love me too ... Since then my Muse in hours of sacred inspiration has often whispered to me: 'Make the attempt, just put down on paper the harmonies of your soul!' ... I was almost too shy. But my Muse insisted—I obeyed and I composed.*
>
> *And now may I dare,* Most Excellent Lord!, *to lay the first fruits of my youthful work on the steps of your throne? ... Filled with this heartening confidence I venture to approach you with these youthful essays. Accept them as a pure sacrifice of childlike reverence and look upon them,* Most Illustrious Lord!, *and their young composer with favour.*

Even given the touching hint of shyness, these are hardly the words you would expect from a twelve-year-old, and there can be no doubt that Neefe played a significant role not just in the composition of the sonatas, but in the choice of dedicatee and wording of the accompanying letter. And why should Neefe encourage young Ludwig to make such a bold move? To convince the most powerful man in Bonn that this youthful genius deserves the kind of help that will enable him to travel, of course.

The ploy might well have succeeded, had Maximilian Friedrich not died less than six months later. Evidence of this is the fact that in

February 1784, two months before the Elector's death, Ludwig was appointed assistant organist to Neefe. His star was in the ascendant, but fate intervened.

First, in that month of February, the Rhine burst its banks. The situation was serious, with the quarter adjoining the river inundated. The Fischer house was on the Rheingasse, so named because it ran at right-angles down to the river, and the house was on the lower portion of the street. The waters quickly engulfed the lower floors, and Gottfried Fischer wrote in his memoir that Frau van Beethoven played a leading role in calming the panic and helping residents to safety, until she had to make her own escape over boards and down ladders. This is particularly heroic, given that she had three boys, aged thirteen, ten, and eight, to look after. Significantly, there is no mention of their father in this episode.

It was as the waters receded and the town was struggling to get back on its feet that the Elector died, replacing one form of disarray with another. The succession was immediate, since it was the custom for all Electors to have a co-adjutor, an appointed successor. In this case, the new Elector of Bonn and Archbishop of Cologne and Münster, was one Maximilian Franz.

As Ludwig had been fortunate in his teacher Neefe, he was just as fortunate in the chosen successor as Elector. The same cannot be said for his father. In fact the months following Maximilian Franz's accession were the most difficult the Beethoven family had had to face to date.

—

Max Franz, as he was familiarly known, was to play a crucial role in the development of young Ludwig van Beethoven as a composer, though it did not seem that way to start with. Endowed with an acute mind and a love of the arts, he did nothing to endear himself to his people. In fact his deportment and looks made him the butt of sarcastic humour. He was described as kindly, lazy, fond of a joke, honest, amiable, and affable. He had a debilitating limp, caused when he fell from his horse on campaign in Bavaria. That put paid to his short-lived military career, and so he followed the only other career path open to a member of the ruling Habsburgs: the church.

Installed in Bonn, sedentary and inactive, he quickly put on weight, and more and more weight, and was soon chronically obese, which did nothing to improve his reputation. But he had one attribute that stilled all seditious tongues. He was the youngest son of Empress Maria Theresa, and brother of the Holy Roman Emperor Joseph II. He was also brother of Marie Antoinette (Maria Antonia), wife of Louis XVI and Queen of France. In other words, he was a senior member of the most powerful ruling family in Continental Europe.

He used that power the moment he became Elector. He shut down the theatre company, depriving Neefe of a portion of his income, and ordered full and detailed reports into every aspect of government, including musical appointments and activities. The result of this investigation was to have profound implications for the Beethoven family.

Each and every court musician was investigated, and individual reports submitted. Of the three musicians directly relevant to our story, it was a disaster for Johann van Beethoven, a potential disaster for Neefe, and rather good news for young Ludwig. The reports have survived, and make compelling reading.

J. van Beethoven, age 44, born in Bonn, married, his wife is 32 years old, has three sons living in the electorate aged 13, 10 and 8 years, who are studying music. Has served 28 years, salary 315 fl.

Johann Beethoven has a very stale voice, has been long in the service, is very poor, of fair deportment and married.

Christ. Gottlob Neefe, aged 36, born at Chemnitz, married, his wife is 32, born at Gotha, has two daughters in the electorate aged 5 and 2, has served three years, was formerly Kapellmeister *with Seiler, salary 400 fl.*

Christian Neefe, organist, in my humble opinion might well be dismissed, inasmuch as he is not particularly versed on the organ. Moreover he is a foreigner, having nothing in his favour, and is of the Calvinist religion.

Ludwig van Beethoven, aged 13, born at Bonn, has served two years, no salary.

Ludwig van Betthoven [sic], *a son of the Betthoven sub No. 8, has no salary, but during the absence of the* Kapellmeister *Luchesy [Lucchesi] he played the organ, is of good capability, still young, of good and quiet deportment, and is poor.*

Johann van Beethoven's 'very stale voice' was tantamount to a death sentence on his career, though it was to be a few years before the axe fell. Neefe's Protestant religion is now counting against him. Young Ludwig, it seems, has a bright future. And also a problem. If Neefe is sacked, he is the obvious successor as court organist. One can imagine the boy was torn between his natural ambition and loyalty to his teacher.

The situation was resolved by a decision to keep Neefe on, but he found his salary slashed, with a good proportion of it going to his assistant. It is the first time Ludwig van Beethoven was paid for his services as a musician. He was thirteen years of age, and it was to be the first, and almost last, salaried position of his entire life. Maybe that was the stimulus for his next grand compositional project, nothing modest: a piano concerto. But, probably realising he was not ready, he abandoned it.[7]

Young Ludwig, now a teenager, was acquiring a confidence that saw him start to behave in ways that drew admiration and exasperation in equal measure. In Holy Week it was customary for a court singer to sing portions of the *Lamentations of Jeremiah* to Gregorian chant, accompanied on the piano. In 1785 the singer was the highly respected Ferdinand Heller, and the pianist Ludwig van Beethoven. A mischievous streak, hitherto largely hidden, emerged in Ludwig, who was piqued at Heller's self-confidence and tuneless singing.

On day two, he asked Heller for permission to try and throw him off the note by varying the piano accompaniment. Heller apparently readily agreed, stressing his experience against his accompanist's lack of it. In the service, Ludwig's fingers flew off in all directions, save for one finger which repeatedly struck the note that Heller should sing. Heller held his ground, but soon found the dazzling accompaniment too distracting. Towards the end of the passage, he lost the note completely.

Lacking a sense of humour, as well as the superior talent he believed he had, Heller entered a formal complaint against Ludwig with the Elector. Max Franz admonished Ludwig, but with a smile on his face, saying in future he had better stick to simple accompaniment. *Kapellmeister* Lucchesi, on the other hand, was a good enough musician to see that Ludwig's skill on the keyboard was a rather more important attribute than Heller's singing.

This anecdote was recorded by a young man who was to have the most profound influence on the life of Ludwig van Beethoven.

CHAPTER THREE

MEETING MOZART

WATCH OUT FOR THAT BOY

FRANZ WEGELER WAS FIVE YEARS OLDER THAN Ludwig, and it is not clear how and exactly when they became friends. It was certainly in the early years of 1780, when they were at opposite ends of their teenage years. How, though, is difficult to answer, because theirs was an unlikely friendship. They cannot have been school friends, given the age difference and that neither referred, in their writings or reported conversation, to their school years. Ludwig, we know, made few friends in his early years, having so little in common with other youngsters. If he looked up to the intelligent Wegeler as something of a role model, that does not explain what Wegeler saw in him. Musical talent, obviously, but again there is no evidence then or later that Wegeler had any particular interest in music—he himself admitted it—and it is unusual for teenagers to mix with youths several years younger than themselves.

There was no meeting of minds either, on intellectual matters. Ludwig was totally consumed with music, playing and composing. Wegeler, on the other hand, had scientific interests, and was to go on to qualify as a doctor. That they became close friends, though, is not in doubt, and it led Wegeler to publish, along with a future friend, his recollections of Ludwig in his Bonn years.[1] When, a little over a decade later, both were in Vienna, Wegeler wrote that 'hardly a day went by when we did not see one another'. That was clearly true in Bonn, too.

Wegeler instinctively knew how to handle the unpredictable youngster. He recalls in his memoirs how Ludwig developed an aversion to playing at social occasions, and he would often become angry when asked to do so. He would walk round to see Wegeler, gloomy and upset, complaining that he had been forced to play 'even if the blood burned under his fingernails'. Wegeler's tactic was to chat to him and amuse him to calm him down, until gradually a conversation would develop between them. When he judged the moment was right, Wegeler would walk to the writing table and tell his young friend that if he wished to continue the conversation, he had to sit on the chair in front of the piano facing outward. Soon the temptation to play became too strong; Ludwig would turn and play a few chords. Before long, he was turned fully round and then 'the most beautiful melodies would develop'.

Later, as Ludwig's skills improved, Wegeler took to leaving a blank piece of manuscript paper on a nearby stand, in the hope that Ludwig would cover it with notes. Instead he used to pick it up, fold it, and put it in his pocket. 'All I could do was laugh at myself,' writes Wegeler.

Ironically the most important service Franz Wegeler was to afford Ludwig did not come from Wegeler himself—instead it came from a family he introduced him to. The von Breunings were a respected and highly cultured family, prominent in court and social life in Bonn. One day some time around 1784, Wegeler, who was acquainted with the Breunings, suggested he take Ludwig along to meet them. It is not an exaggeration to say that this marked a turning point in the life of the teenage musician.

—

The Breunings were not simply well liked, but were owed a great deal of respect due to the fact that the head of the family, Court Councillor Emanuel Joseph von Breuning, had lost his life in a fire at the Electoral Palace. In determined and frantic efforts to save as many art treasures and papers as he could, Breuning had gone back into the blazing building one time too many, and died as the structure collapsed on him.

His widow, Helene, was left to bring up four children, ranging in age from six years to an infant of four months. Finances were not a problem, and the family lived in an imposing two-storey house with dormer windows and a gated front garden in the elegant Münsterplatz in Bonn.[2] There, Helene von Breuning was determined to give her children as cultured and varied an upbringing as possible.

One can well imagine the trepidation Ludwig felt as he stood at the gate of the Breuning house for the first time, particularly if his appearance was as haphazard as in his schooldays. True, he had by now performed in the salons of the nobility, and was not lacking in self-confidence, but I suspect there would have been more than a twinge of nerves as he walked through the gate for the first time, which liveried staff and the opulence within will have done nothing to dispel.

What might have persuaded Wegeler to introduce his undoubtedly rather gauche and socially inept friend to such a highborn and cultured family? The answer is obvious, even if it cannot be proved. Helene von Breuning had told young Wegeler she wanted her children to have piano lessons, and he replied that he knew just the fellow.

We can probably assume that she had seen Ludwig perform in a salon and been duly impressed, reasoning that his remarkable talent would compensate for any lack in social graces. She might also have calculated that her children would take more easily to a teenager than to an adult. Otherwise why should she not have chosen Christian Neefe, a much more highly qualified musician, for the role? Certainly he would have struggled to find the time, given his onerous court duties, but he certainly could have done with the extra income. We might even assume that he resented the fact that his young assistant was earning extra cash, though that can only be speculation.

Ludwig did more than teach piano to the Breuning children. He in effect grew up as part of the Breuning household, becoming almost a surrogate member of the family. Wegeler writes that not only did Ludwig spend the greater part of the day in the Breuning house, but many nights too. It was there, also, that he first became acquainted with German literature, especially poetry. It is beyond doubt that he will have been introduced to the works of the two emerging giants of German literature, Goethe and Schiller. Wegeler also tells us that he read Homer and Plutarch. He was trained too in social etiquette. He even went away on holiday with the family. Helene von Breuning clearly took him under her wing and made it her duty to fill in the gaps—academic and social—that early exit from school and singular devotion to music had caused.

At the same time, she was exceedingly tolerant of his sometimes wilful behaviour. He was also employed as piano teacher in a count's house directly across the square—quite possibly Helene von Breuning secured it for him—and when it was time for him to go to the count's house, she would be prepared for him to make excuses for not going, but insist he went. Then, when he left, she would remain in the doorway and watch him. Sometimes he would turn back immediately and say it was impossible to give a lesson that day, but tomorrow he would give two. Instead of scolding him, according to Wegeler, Helene would simply shrug her shoulders and say, 'He has his raptus again.' Wegeler does not elucidate on the word 'raptus', but it does not take much imagination to discern its meaning.

There is no doubt Ludwig was aware of just how kind and indulgent Helene von Breuning was towards him. Later in life he referred to the Breunings as guardian angels, and said of Helene, somewhat obscurely and with maybe a touch of arrogance, 'She understood how to keep the insects off the flowers.'

In a touching passage in his memoirs, Wegeler, who married the only Breuning daughter, Eleonore, describes how many years later he, his wife, and mother-in-law would get together and discuss the re-markable achievements of Europe's greatest living composer, and reminisce about how they remembered him as a gauche youth. Helene, then in her late seventies, was finding it difficult to recall the past, but still remembered young Ludwig with affection.

—

It is hardly surprising Ludwig escaped as often as he could to the cultured and affectionate surroundings of the Breuning household. Things at home were going from bad to worse. The unloved First Minister Count Belderbusch had died a few months after the death of his protector, Elector Maximilian Friedrich (a double blow for the Abbess). This led to a bizarre and ruinous course of action on the part of Johann van Beethoven.

He decided to put forward a claim on Belderbusch's estate, on the grounds that he had given several valuable gifts to the Count and his mistress, in return for which he had been promised promotion to *Kapellmeister*. To describe this course of action as 'bizarre' is an understatement. Johann was in effect saying Belderbusch had told him he could be bribed to give Johann the top musical job. Bribery might not have been entirely unknown in late eighteenth-century Europe, but to suggest the First Minister in a Habsburg principality who had made it his mission to end profligacy and introduce savings in the economy could be bribed to give an exalted position that was not actually in his gift to a mediocre musician who was known to like his alcohol is absurd.

It gets worse. At the bottom of the petition demanding that the Belderbusch heirs return the gifts, Johann forged the signature of a lawyer. The lawyer, one Nikolaus Phennings, swore in an affidavit, 'The above signature is not in my hand and I have not the slightest knowledge of this document, with all its vileness.'

The fraud quickly unravelled, and Johann was fortunate not to face legal action. What led Johann to embark on this doomed piece of folly is not known. Alcohol will have played its part, but this was more than a moment of madness. He must have thought about it over a period of days, even weeks. If anything, it is a sign of just how permanently addled his brain was.

His reputation, already low, now reached rock bottom. Not that it had far to travel to get there. Two years earlier, a court report on Ludwig's petition seeking appointment as assistant court organist stated, '… Your Grace has graciously provided for [Ludwig van Beethoven's] care and subsistence, his father no longer being able to do so …' Evidence that Johann remained of low standing, and was little more than a figure of ridicule, was to come on his death in 1792, when the Elector wrote to a court official, 'The revenues from the liquor excise have suffered a loss.'

Johann continued to earn a pittance, but Ludwig was in effect the family breadwinner. Given his father's alcoholism, he was also de facto head of the household. This was before he was midway through his teens. The pressure he was under must have been enormous. He held a salaried position at court, which demanded serious work. He was continuing instruction with Neefe. At home he was witnessing his father's increasing alcoholism and his mother's distress. This was made immeasurably worse by his mother's obviously declining health. She was showing all the signs of having contracted the deadly disease of consumption (tuberculosis).

And yet he found time to compose. He wrote a rondo, a song 'To an Infant' (possibly in the aftermath of his baby brother Franz Georg's death at the age of two), the aforementioned piano concerto, three piano quartets, and a trio for piano and wind.

In these early compositions the influence of one man above all others is evident: Wolfgang Amadeus Mozart. In musical circles in Bonn the extraordinary achievements of Mozart were well known. As soon as new works were published, they made their way to Bonn where they were eagerly seized on by the court musicians, and it is certain that in his lessons with Neefe, he and his teacher pored over the music, examining, deconstructing, and generally holding Mozart up as an example to be emulated.

Then there was a development that must have taken Ludwig's breath away. Four years after Neefe wrote in Cramer's *Magazin der Musik* that 'this young genius deserves support so that he can travel', it happened. How it happened, we do not know. Most likely Neefe approached the Elector directly. Maximilian Franz might have been becoming obese, his limp and the way he acquired it might have led to derisory comments, but he soon made his mark as an effective, and tolerant, ruler. He was an avid supporter of education and the arts, and over a period of time reopened the court theatre, maintained the court orchestra, and founded the University of Bonn. He would have heard young Ludwig play the organ at services, and he might well have heard him give recitals at the keyboard.

It might have been at Neefe's suggestion, or the Elector might well have made the decision himself. Either way, Ludwig's dream was about to come true. The Elector granted him leave of absence to travel to Vienna to meet Mozart, and agreed to cover the costs. It is beyond doubt that his father would have protested loudly. How could he possibly cope with the children, and a sick wife, if Ludwig was going to swan off to Vienna? But Ludwig had powerful support, and there was no stopping him.

In late March 1787, Ludwig van Beethoven, aged sixteen and a quarter, left Bonn and left his family to travel to the capital of the Holy Roman Empire, and the capital city of European music. Vienna.

—

When I first began researching Beethoven's life, and discovered that he and Mozart actually met, I expected to find page after page of information, documents, eye-witness accounts, letters, and so on.

And what is there? Nothing but secondary accounts. A single paragraph in a biography of Mozart written more than sixty years after Mozart's death (in fact, to coincide with the centenary of his birth), one inconclusive line in a Beethoven biography again written many years after his death, and a couple of anecdotes running to no more than a line or two each.

Why might this be, given that both composers were household names while still alive, and famous beyond words within a short time of their deaths? There really can be only one explanation, and that is that neither Mozart nor Beethoven spoke or wrote about their encounter, meaning we have no first-hand account of what happened. This alone raises more questions.

It is a similar case in the myriad of biographies of Beethoven. The encounter with Mozart barely rates more than a swift paragraph. I know of one biography, published in 2003, that does not mention the meeting at all. Their authors would no doubt justify this by pointing to the obvious: that, as with the trip to Rotterdam, we know virtually nothing. But I believe that a meeting between the two most revered, respected, admired, beloved composers in history deserves as close an examination as possible, with speculation allowed after that.

First, then, this is what we know.

On 1 April 1787 '*Herr Peethofen* [*sic*], *Musikus von Bonn bei Kölln*' arrived in Munich and checked into the tavern *Zum schwarzen Adler* [At the Black Eagle], according to the *Münchener Zeitung*. It appears either the newspaper knew about his musical prowess, or it did its homework while he was away, because when he checked into the same tavern on 25 April on his way home, it described him as '*Herr Peethoven* [*sic*], *Kurköllnischer Kammervirtuos von Bonn*' ('Piano virtuoso at the Electoral Court of Cologne from Bonn'). This is the furthest that word of his musical talent had spread to date.

He reached Vienna on Easter Eve, 7 April. We do not know where he stayed or how soon after arriving he met Mozart. All we know, from the Mozart biography,[3] is that Ludwig was taken to Mozart, who asked him to sit at the piano and play something. Ludwig did this, but Mozart was cool in his praise, saying he had obviously prepared a showpiece specially. Ludwig then asked Mozart to give him a theme that he could improvise on. Mozart did so, and Ludwig began to improvise. His playing became more and more elaborate, because he was inspired in the presence of the master musician whom he so greatly admired. Mozart became more and more impressed, and finally, without saying anything to Ludwig, went into the adjoining room where some friends were sitting, and said, 'Watch out for that boy, one day he will give the world something to talk about.'

That is the sum total of the most comprehensive second-hand account we have. We do not even know who recounted it, only that it could not have been either of the two principals, who had both been long dead. As far as other evidence goes, Beethoven's friend and helper Ferdinand Ries (who collaborated with Wegeler on their book of reminiscences) says Beethoven told him he regretted never hearing Mozart play, but Beethoven's pupil Carl Czerny claimed Beethoven did hear him, and described his playing as 'choppy' and 'unsmooth'.

As for Beethoven himself, it appears the only recorded reference to Mozart in conversation came late in life when his deafness led him to carry a notebook, so-called 'conversation books', for people to write down their questions. His nephew Karl wrote in one of these, 'You knew Mozart, where did you see him?' And in another conversation book a few years later, 'Was Mozart a good pianoforte player? It [the instrument] was then still in its infancy.'

Of course the utterly maddening, infuriating, frustrating fact is that Beethoven spoke rather than wrote his answer, so we have no idea of what he said.

Given how significant I believe this meeting, however brief, to be, I will now allow myself to put a few speculative clothes on the bare bones of what we know.

First, I believe Mozart was in no mood to see Ludwig. In fact it was the last thing he needed. His health was poor. Two and a half years earlier, at an opera in the Burgtheater (not one of his own) he was taken ill, 'sweated through all his clothes', caught a chill in the night air on the way home, began to vomit violently, and was diagnosed with rheumatic fever. His recovery was slow, and he was ill again in April 1787, the month young Beethoven came to visit.

His domestic life was in turmoil. With two small children, he had moved the family into a large apartment in the Grosse Schulerstrasse, where the rent was four times higher than in their previous apartment. He could not afford the rent, and at the time of Ludwig's visit, the family was in the throes of moving out to the suburbs.

On top of this he was worried about his father's health (Leopold Mozart was to die a little over a month later), and last but not least he was fully preoccupied with his new opera, *Don Giovanni*.

So when a sixteen-year-old boy was ushered into his apartment, presumably on the strength of a letter of introduction from Max Franz (who had met Mozart in Salzburg some years earlier),[4] he is unlikely to have welcomed him with open arms. One can imagine him looking the youth up and down, probably unimpressed with his attire, tousled hair with no wig or queue, the boy's Rhineland accent more guttural than he was used to in Vienna, and barking, 'Well, boy, they say you can play the piano. To me you look more like a street urchin than a musician. There's the piano, play something, and be quick about it.'

That is shameless fictionalising, I readily admit, but it gives a flavour of what I believe probably happened.

It is also more than likely that once Ludwig started improvising on the theme Mozart had given him, the older man became more and more impressed. The quote about 'watch[ing] out for that boy' is famous, and who knows how it might have become embellished in the years before it was written down? But we can safely say that Mozart was impressed with what he heard, almost certainly impressed enough to offer to take Ludwig on as a pupil.

We can make this assumption, I believe, because in the first place Mozart would have welcomed the chance to earn some extra cash, and Ludwig clearly had the Elector's financial backing, and also because he is likely to have recognised that the boy had pianistic skills well beyond his years, and this would have appealed to the virtuosic musician in Mozart. One other factor: Ludwig stayed in Vienna for almost two weeks. It was during this time, obviously, that he must have heard Mozart play. We can probably reconcile the evident contradiction between Ries and Czerny by assuming he heard Mozart play in private, but not in performance.

But the big question is: did Mozart give Ludwig lessons in the brief time he was in Vienna? That takes us back to the question I posed earlier. Given that Beethoven admired Mozart so much, performing his piano concertos on a number of occasions in Vienna, if he had received even a single lesson, would he not have trumpeted it for the rest of his life? And if Mozart was that impressed with Ludwig's playing, so much so that he immediately went into the adjoining room to tell friends, would he not have told more people, and wouldn't they also have told other people, particularly in the years following Mozart's death when Beethoven's fame was spreading across Europe?

Yet there is nothing. Even that is puzzling. If no lessons took place, you would expect even *that* fact to have been referred to by Beethoven later in life, in tones of regret.

So it remains something of a mystery. The only possible explanation I can think of—and I accept this is far fetched, even a little scurrilous—is that in both cases there were singular reputations to uphold. Mozart's family and friends did not want his legacy to be overshadowed by Beethoven, and Beethoven did not want to attribute any part of his genius to Mozart.

One last piece of speculation. What if the sixteen-year-old boy *had* taken lessons with Mozart? Might Mozart the perfectionist have smoothed off the rough edges, rounded the corners, tamed the wild spirit we know today? Impossible to answer. I suspect that could have been the case. Fiercely independent he might have been, but what sixteen-year-old boy would not have been susceptible to guidance from Europe's greatest living musician?

Enough conjecture. What we know for a fact is that within a short time of arriving in Vienna, Ludwig received word from his father that his mother was seriously ill, and that they feared for her life. He had no choice but to leave, which he did within the fortnight, arriving again at the *Zum schwarzen Adler* on 25 April.

On arriving home he was devastated to find his mother's consumption had advanced so far that she was in the terminal stages, and she died on 17 July.

If things were serious before he left for Vienna, they were critical now. He truly was head of the family, and the task of not only providing for the family, but trying to control the nominal head, Johann, fell squarely on his shoulders. There was no mother for him or his brothers to turn to when, later in the same year, their baby sister died.

The situation in the Beethoven household was indeed dire.

—

Not for the first time in his life, Ludwig benefited from an extraordinary stroke of good fortune. Just as Christian Neefe had been the perfect teacher to satisfy his musical ambitions, and Maximilian Franz the ideal Elector to further them, on or about 1 February 1788 there arrived in Bonn a certain Count Ferdinand Ernst Joseph Gabriel Waldstein und Wartenberg von Dux.

Count Waldstein, to give him his simple title, was a member of one of the most aristocratic families in the Habsburg Empire. His misfortune was to be the fourth son, and as such was allowed to play no role in the power politics at the Viennese court. After a couple of fruitless years in the military, he opted to join the Teutonic Order.[5] This led to him being summoned to Bonn by Maximilian Franz, who was Grand Master of the Order. There he was made a Knight on 17 June 1788.

Count Waldstein was in every sense Ludwig van Beethoven's most important patron in his teenage years. Max Franz might have subsidised Ludwig's abortive trip to Vienna and rubber-stamped his appointment as court organist, but his interest in music beyond that was not great. Waldstein, by contrast, was himself a dilettante pianist and composer, and had a deep love for the arts, in particular music. Wegeler, in his memoir, describes Waldstein as 'Beethoven's first, and in every respect most important, Maecenas'.

It is more than likely that Waldstein first encountered Ludwig at the Breunings' house, and heard him play. He immediately recognised an extraordinary talent, and decided to make it his mission to nurture it. He did more than that. From Wegeler we learn that he visited the Beethoven family in their new apartment in a rather fine house in the Wenzelgasse, which was in a better part of town than the Rheingasse down by the river. There, after the death of Maria Magdalena, they employed a housekeeper.

Wegeler leaves us in no doubt that Waldstein gave money to Ludwig on a number of occasions, always disguised as an advance from the Elector. The move to the Wenzelgasse certainly came before Waldstein's arrival in Bonn. One wonders how long the family would have been able to remain there, and employ a housekeeper, without Waldstein's help.

There now occurred a dramatic change in the Beethoven family's circumstances. It was almost certainly brought about by an incident as humiliating for Ludwig and his family as it is possible to imagine, and it is inconceivable Ludwig would have taken the step he did without advice and guidance from Waldstein, who had the Elector's ear.

Johann van Beethoven became so drunk in public that he was arrested. Ludwig had to go to the police station, where he argued furiously with the police, before obtaining his father's release.

It was, for Ludwig, the final blow. His father's reputation was ruined once and for all. Something needed to be done, action taken. Some time in the autumn of 1789 Ludwig petioned the Elector to dismiss his father from court service, and pay half his salary over to him. The Elector went further. He not only agreed to Ludwig's demands but ordered Johann to leave Bonn and go and live in exile in a village in the country.

In the event this latter demand was not enforced. Johann remained in the Wenzelgasse house until his death. It is probable Ludwig, having taken the action he did, felt the humiliation was enough. Financially, half his father's annual salary of 200 thalers was now paid to him. As further lessening of the humiliation, Johann continued to receive the other half, but quietly made it over to his son.

Ludwig was now, at the age of eighteen, no longer just the de facto head of the family, but *de jure* head as well, recognised as such by the Elector. It was a turning point. The pain of his father's degradation must have been difficult to bear, but it had been going on for some time, was no secret in Bonn, and Ludwig was now at last able to acknowledge it, to have no need any longer to make excuses. The formalising of his father's disgrace was, for him, in some sense a liberation.

That immediately proved itself in his musical activity. It led to a burst of creativity. The pieces poured out of him. Among them is the most significant work that he was to compose in his first twenty-two years, and it was brought about by an unexpected, and thoroughly sad, event in the Habsburg capital, Vienna.

On 20 February 1790, Emperor Joseph II, eldest son of the great

Empress Maria Theresa, died at the age of forty-nine. The Empire went into mourning. In Bonn, the remainder of the opera season was cancelled. The *Lesegesellschaft* met to discuss a way of marking the death, given that the Emperor was Max Franz's brother, and commissioned a young poet to write a text, which would subsequently be set to music. The text was duly delivered, and then the question arose of who should be asked to compose the memorial cantata.

The *Lesegesellschaft* had a number of names for consideration, all court musicians senior to Ludwig. But Waldstein was a member of the *Lesegesellschaft*, and he undoubtedly brought his influence to bear. The duty of commemorating the Emperor's death in music went to the nineteen-year-old Ludwig van Beethoven.

He certainly rose to the occasion. His *Cantata on the Death of Emperor Joseph II* is justifiably regarded as his first mature composition. For a start he is now working with full orchestral forces, solo singers, and chorus. If the work has an added dimension, it is surely because he had empathy with the subject matter.

Emperor Joseph had been a reformer. He made education compulsory for all boys and girls, and brought about the freedom of serfs throughout the Empire. He completely reformed the legal system, abolished brutal punishments for minor crimes, and abolished the death penalty except for serious crimes. He ran into opposition when he tried to reform the Catholic Church—that was an ambition too far.

Of greater significance to the higher levels of society in Vienna, he was an enthusiastic patron of the arts. He was known as the 'Musical King', and championed German culture. It was he who commissioned a German language opera from Mozart,[6] and he ended censorship of the press and the theatre. At the same time he was intolerant of opponents to his rule, encouraging his Chancellor to establish a network of informants. He has rather unkindly been called the creator of the secret police. He was, to use the language of historians, an 'enlightened despot'.

In Bonn, he was a popular figure, and not just because he was the elder brother of the Elector. His reforming ideas, his 'enlightened despotism', appealed to this cultured town, which was, in some sense, an outpost of the Empire, away from the court intrigue and rigidity of life in Vienna. Without a doubt his ideas would have been debated by the Illuminati and then the *Lesegesellschaft*, and it is beyond question that the Protestant Neefe would have lauded the Emperor's praises to his young pupil.

Ludwig would have appreciated the poet Severin Anton Averdonck's text too. Although the language is highly subtle and allusory, it is an unmistakable paean of praise to a reforming Emperor. Even if that is an exaggeration, it is undoubtedly how Ludwig would have seen it. Joseph's untimely and unexpected death would have come not just as a shock to the people of Bonn but, more than that, as very sad news indeed.

Ludwig captures this in the very first bar of his *Cantata*, a strikingly soft low note on strings, followed by a pause. The winds then echo this, followed again by a pause. Daring and original, he repeats the exchange more loudly, before leading into a fragmented mourning phrase on flute. After several more bars of fragmented, almost tortured phrases, the chorus enters with the single portentous word '*Todt*' ('Dead'). The listener is hooked from the very start.

There are also elements that he was to use later in more mature works. Several passages presage the 'Eroica' Symphony, and there is a striking oboe phrase, soaring above the rest of the orchestra, that was to reappear to dramatic effect in the dungeon scene in *Fidelio*. Beethoven knew better than to waste a good idea.

And, in this case, wasted is exactly what these extraordinarily original ideas would have been. The court orchestra in Bonn—particularly the winds—declared the piece unplayable, as it did with the sister piece that came a few months later, a *Cantata on the Elevation of Emperor Leopold II*. Neither piece was performed in Beethoven's lifetime. We do not know how the composer reacted to this rejection, but whatever he may have said, it was good practice for his later years. This might have been the first, but certainly was not the last, time in his life that musicians complained to him that his music was unplayable.

The following year another composition followed, and it could not have been more of a contrast to the two cantatas, for an extra-ordinary and at first sight incredible reason.

CHAPTER FOUR

WORD SPREADS

YOUNG BEETHOVEN
AS KITCHEN SCULLION

L UDWIG VAN BEETHOVEN THE COMPOSER HAD
come of age. More than that, he was an all-round musician, and was recognised as such. Assistant court organist
to Neefe, he also played viola in the court orchestra and he was the
composer of several works. The complexities of the cantatas might
have been regarded as unplayable, but for precisely that reason were
judged to be highly impressive. The commission alone gave him an
unrivalled reputation.

Given these factors, his decision regarding the next composition
seems all the more surprising. The idea was Count Waldstein's. As
a leading figure in Bonn, he was deputed to arrange a celebratory
occasion to mark the end of the operatic season and the beginning
of the annual Carnival in early March 1791. He decided to organise
a 'ballet' in one of the grander rooms of the Town Hall, to be preceded by a procession of the town's nobility dressed in traditional
German costume.

A ballet in the late eighteenth century meant in effect a series
of tableaux, men (it was rare for women to take part) assuming dramatic poses on stage. For this, music was required. Waldstein asked
Beethoven if he would compose it. We do not know if Beethoven received any money. It is more than likely that he did, and that it was
passed to him clandestinely, for Waldstein made another request:
that the music should be published under his name. And indeed it
was: *Musik zu einem Ritterballet* (*Music for a Ballet of the Knights*) by
Count Waldstein.

The event duly took place, and was a magnificent spectacle. Noblemen in medieval German costume, accompanied by their ladies —who, as one observer subtly put it, lost none of their charms by donning costumes of antiquity—processed across the square to the Town Hall, where in the Ridotto room more men in appropriate medieval costume took up poses from German folk legends.

We can get an idea of what this involved from the titles to the pieces composed by Beethoven: *March, German Song, Hunting Song, Love Song, War Dance, Drinking Song, German Song, Coda*. It must have been a picturesque spectacle, depicting the sort of Germanic legends a certain Richard Wagner would get hold of half a century or more later.

The music was acclaimed, later published, and attributed to Waldstein, and it stayed that way for the best part of a century, until musicologists established beyond doubt that it was composed by the nineteen-year-old Beethoven. In fact we should not be too shocked that the music was appropriated by Waldstein. Such behaviour was not all that uncommon in eighteenth-century Europe, the most notorious example being the composition, at about this very time, of the *Requiem* by Mozart, in the knowledge that it was to be presented as having been composed by Count Walsegg, the nobleman who commissioned it as a memorial to his wife.

The *Ritterballet*, to my knowledge, is never performed today, and is regarded as having no real significance, particularly when measured against the two cantatas that preceded it. But it does hold one distinction: it is the only composition for orchestra by Beethoven that was actually performed while he was living in Bonn.

—

There is a delightful anecdote about Beethoven that dates from around this time. It shows him in a very different light from that usually described by his contemporaries, and I cannot help believing (though there is no proof) that his unusual congeniality relates to a remarkable occurrence in December 1790, and what followed it.

The event itself happened many miles away, and did not concern Beethoven in any direct way. But indirectly it was to have the most profound musical influence on him imaginable. In September 1790 Prince Nikolaus Esterházy, great patron of the arts, died at his sumptuous palace at Esterháza. This led to freedom from a rigorous regime of musical servitude to which his composer-in-residence had been subjected for almost thirty years.

The composer was a certain Joseph Haydn, and he relished his sudden liberty. His name was well known in several European countries, and a friend of his, Johann Peter Salomon, who was a concert manager based in London, persuaded him to come to England. The two men could have chosen any one of half a dozen routes, but Salomon had been born in Bonn and had family there, and so they decided to stop off in Bonn.

This was another amazing stroke of good fortune for Bonn's young musical wunderkind, Ludwig van Beethoven. Haydn and his companion arrived in Bonn on Christmas Day 1790, and were scooped up by the musical establishment. Haydn gave his own account of what happened to an interviewer some years later. This is usually compressed into a few sentences by Beethoven biographers, but it offers such delightful insights into Haydn's character, as well as the behaviour of Bonn's senior musicians—including, without doubt, Beethoven—that it is worth recounting in some detail.

On Sunday, 26 December, Haydn and Salomon were invited to attend Mass in the court chapel. No sooner had they taken their seats than the first chords sounded, and Haydn immediately recognised one of his own works. He professed himself flattered but embarrassed. The Mass over, the two men were invited into the oratory, where they were surprised to find none other than the Elector himself, Max Franz, along with a group of Bonn's most prominent musicians.

The Elector took Haydn by the hand and presented him to the assembled company, with the words: 'Gentlemen, allow me to introduce you to the Haydn you all revere so highly.' The musicians gathered round the esteemed composer, who clearly enjoyed the adulation, but retained his natural modesty. This turned to genuine embarrassment when the Elector invited him to dinner.

The problem was Haydn and Salomon had not expected this, and had arranged for a small dinner to be served to them in their lodgings. They were committed, and it was too late to cancel. Haydn, by his own account, apologised profusely, explaining the problem, and the Elector accepted with good grace. After a suitable time, Haydn and Salomon returned to their lodgings. On entering the dining room, they discovered the small dinner had become a banquet, and there were around a dozen court musicians present. The Elector had organised a surprise party.

If Haydn, now nearly fifty-nine years of age, was feeling any weariness, he did not say, and it seems a convivial evening ensued. Was Beethoven in the company in the chapel oratory, and subsequently at Haydn's lodgings? We do not know. But I believe it is beyond doubt. He was not only Bonn's finest pianist, he was also far and away its most prolific composer, having written piano works, chamber works, ballet music, songs, not to mention two substantial cantatas commissioned by the *Lesegesellschaft*. To host a composer of the standing of Joseph Haydn in the small town of Bonn without introducing him to a homegrown young composer with an already outstanding reputation is, frankly, unthinkable.

I shall now shamelessly indulge in speculation, but in a way that is borne out a year and a half later when Beethoven's future musical course is decided in the most dramatic way. At the dinner, with musical conversation flowing easily and good food and wine being enjoyed, Haydn tells the company some home truths about being in the employ of Prince Esterházy, how he and his musicians were often treated no better than servants, made to wear uniforms, and eat in the kitchens with the staff. In return the musicians tell him about musical life in Bonn, and—singling out Beethoven—regale Haydn with tales of the two cantatas that were impossible to play.

Beethoven, probably with some pique, retaliates that the pieces were by no means impossible, all that was lacking was musicians sufficiently proficient to play them. Haydn then says, 'Look, it is a bit late now, and I have to leave early tomorrow, but I'll tell you what I'll do. On my return journey I'll make sure I come via Bonn, and I would very much like to look at the cantatas, see the manuscripts. Would that be all right?'

I confess the conversation and that last quote are drawn from my imagination, but in July 1792 that is *exactly* what happened, and it led to a life-changing decision for Beethoven. But that lies ahead.

—

To turn now to the anecdote that finds Beethoven in a particularly benign and cooperative mood. It was recounted nearly fifty years after the event, and the date is given as the summer of either 1790 or 1791. In the summer of 1790 Beethoven was at the height of his troubles over the cantatas. The musicians were refusing to perform the first, and he was about to embark on the second, which would meet a similar fate. In the summer of 1791, though, he was basking in the afterglow of having met the great Haydn, who had expressed a personal interest in his compositions. So let us place it at the later date.

Beethoven and a companion—likely to be either Wegeler or one of the Breuning sons—were walking in Godesberger Brunnen, a small village just outside Bonn renowned for its natural springs. They approached an older man—the source of the anecdote—and fell into conversation with him, during which he happened to remark that the church in the monastery at Marien-forst, in the woods behind Godesberg, had been repaired and ren-ovated, which was also true of the church organ, which was either entirely new or greatly improved. Beethoven's friend suggested that they go to the church, and that Beethoven should try out the new organ. The older man joined in, and soon they were urging him to play.

This is something Beethoven was by now used to. So virtuosic was he at the keyboard that he was forever being asked to demon-strate his skills. He quickly came to hate this, and in later years in Vienna, where the demands intensified as his fame spread, he would point blank refuse. On one occasion a titled lady went down on her knees in front of him in one of the most aristocratic salons in the city, and still he refused.

And on this occasion in Godesberg? 'His great good nature led him to grant our wish,' recalls the older man. The group walked to the church, but found it locked. Undeterred, they sought out the prior, who was very obliging and had the church unlocked. Beetho-ven went straight to the organ, tried it out, then asked his compan-ions to give him a theme. This they did, and Beethoven improvised on it. Then another theme, and another. Always Beethoven impro-vised, variations flowing out of him. His playing was such that 'it moved us profoundly', recalled the older man.

Then he adds—and this is what gives the whole story an extra layer of credibility, even poignancy—workmen who were clearing up the building debris outside the church laid down their tools and came into the church to listen 'with obvious pleasure'. That more than anything, I am convinced, is what will have persuaded Beetho-ven to play on and on. Here was an audience of genuine music-lovers who appreciated what he was doing, not a collection of aristocrats eager to be seen to be supporting the arts.

So why do I bother recounting this anecdote, when it first appeared in print almost two centuries ago, and rarely finds its way into modern biographies? Because this is the real Beethoven, not the permanently choleric and uncooperative Beethoven of myth.

—

Also rarely mentioned, or given no more than a passing reference, is a trip up the Rhine that Beethoven and around twenty-five members of the court orchestra took in the late summer of 1791. Rarely mentioned because it yielded nothing in terms of composition, but with regard to Beethoven's reputation as keyboard virtuoso it was to prove very important indeed. Also, as with the Godesberg anecdote, it shines a light into the character of the young man who was to go on to become such a titan in the world of music. So, with no apologies, I intend to recount it in detail.

The trip, which Beethoven was to remember fondly for the rest of his life as 'a fruitful source of loveliest visions', was occasioned by the fact that the Elector, Maximilian Franz, as Grand Master of the Teutonic Order, was due to attend a gathering of the Order's leadership in Bad Mergentheim, which was the official residence of the Grand Master. For his and his fellow Knights' amusement, he decided that the court orchestra should join him there for a full month. Beethoven was among those selected to go.

The spa town of Bad Mergentheim lies around two hundred miles southeast of Bonn, and by far the most comfortable and practical way to make the journey two centuries ago was by boat, first up the Rhine, then along its tributary the Main, and finally the smaller Tauber. It is apparent from the few details we know that the Bonn court orchestra was under no compulsion to reach Mergentheim in the shortest time possible, probably because the boat could make only slow progress sailing against the direction of the fast-flowing water.

There is no river in Europe richer in myths and legends than the Rhine, and the portion of it that the orchestra was about to travel on, the Middle Rhine from Bonn to Mainz, with its medieval castles standing guard over villages clustered on the waterfront, is the richest in its 760-mile length.[1] Anyone born and brought up on the banks of the Rhine, or close to it, learns of the legends from childhood, and passes them on to their children. We know from the Fischer memoir that there were two telescopes in the attic of the Fischer house, a small one and a large one, and that with them one could see twenty miles up river, to the hills of the Siebengebirge (Seven Mountains) stretching away from the river on the far bank. It was Ludwig's delight to go to the attic and gaze through the telescopes, Fischer recalls, because the Beethovens had a love for the Rhine.

It is therefore beyond doubt that Ludwig learned of the legends as a child. He would have heard of how the hills of the *Siebengebirge* were created by dwarves digging lakes and throwing the earth over their shoulders. And he would certainly have been familiar with the legend attached to the largest of the hills, the massive rock that stood—and stands—on the east bank of the Rhine about eight miles up river, and which he would have been able to see clearly through the telescope from the attic window.

The *Drachenfels* (Dragon Rock) is named for the fearsome dragon that inhabited a cave halfway up the rock, whose lust for human flesh was such that it could be sated only by the annual sacrifice of a virgin. So the heathen people of the right bank of the Rhine each year crossed the river to the Christian left bank to kidnap the intended sacrifice. One day into their midst on a snow-white charger there rode a young Teutonic hero by the name of Siegfried. Fortuitously he happened to arrive on the day the heathen warriors returned to their own left bank with a bound and trembling girl intended as the annual human sacrifice for the dragon.

When challenged by Siegfried, the heathens explained that without such a sacrifice the dragon would come down into their town and devour their children. Siegfried realised that only the death of the dragon would bring an end to this awful state of affairs. Clutching his invincible sword he climbed the rock, to be met by a startled dragon who had been expecting his yearly sacrifice. It reared up at the sight of Siegfried, blowing first smoke then two jets of fire from its nostrils. Siegfried struck its neck with his sword, but it merely glanced off the scaly armour-plating. But Siegfried saw that under the dragon's neck was a soft patch of skin. He swiftly gathered up as much dry brushwood as he could hold, and when the dragon again breathed fire at him, he thrust the bundle of brushwood into the dragon's jaws. The dry brittle wood immediately burst into flames. Roaring with pain and anger, the dragon lifted its head to shake the wood free. Its soft neck was exposed for an instant, and Siegfried rammed the sword home. The dragon fell to the ground, its blood draining fatally into the soil. The danger to the people was at last over.[2]

The yacht carrying the court musicians would have glided past the Drachenfels within an hour, or less, of setting off from Bonn, and I can picture them clustering onto the deck to gaze in awe at the Drachenfels, and its clearly visible cave, as the bass singer Joseph Lux—elected 'king' for the voyage—recounted the legend in tremulous tones. Is it too fanciful to imagine King Lux gazing with trepidation at the sopranos and mezzo-sopranos, urging the men to protect and shield them, as the yacht sailed past the rock?

Probably not, since before leaving Bonn the musicians had themselves held the joyful ritual of electing Lux 'Great King of the Journey'. He, in turn, then handed out duties to musicians whom he appointed senior members of his regal court, the tasks becoming more menial as he progressed to the junior ranks.

And who was youngest, and therefore most junior, of all? None other than Ludwig van Beethoven, who along with the slightly older cellist Bernhard Romberg, was appointed kitchen scullion. To me, the thought of the twenty-year-old Beethoven being given the lowliest of kitchen duties is one of the most enchanting images from his Bonn years.

The boat, with 'mast and sail, flat deck with railing, comfortable cabins with windows and furniture, generally in the style of a Dutch yacht',[3] made slow progress against the current, but it would not have been long before it approached another massive rock, even richer in legend than the Drachenfels, which towers several hundred feet above the river: the Loreley.

It is true that the legend of the maiden who inhabits the rock and lures sailors to their deaths with the sweetness of her song achieved global fame following the publication of a poem a decade or so after the Bonn musicians' boat trip, and its musical setting some years after that. But legends have swirled around the Loreley since medieval times, occasioned by the fact that at this point the Rhine bends and narrows alarmingly.[4]

The current flows fast, and lethal rocks—the *Sieben Jungfrauen* (Seven Virgins)—lie just below the surface, creating dangerous whirlpools. Many a vessel has come to grief here.[5] As with the Drachenfels story there are several versions of the legend, but the best-known one certain to have been familiar to the Bonn musicians recounts how the lovely maiden Loreley was engaged to be married to a sailor, but he deserted her. In her grief she threw herself from the top of the rock into the swirling waters below, and in revenge lures sailors with her beautiful singing, which turns to mocking laughter as their vessel breaks up on the rocks and they disappear into the depths.[6]

As with the Drachenfels, it is certain the Bonn musicians would have gathered on deck as their yacht passed the massive rock. It is said that if conditions are right, a sevenfold echo can be heard on the southern slope of the rock. I imagine King Lux commanding silence so the musicians could listen out for it. Was it sweet singing, or scornful laughter?

In Beethoven's day, the stretch of river to the south of the Loreley became even more treacherous, narrowing to little more than a gorge, with vicious cross-currents and lethal underwater rocks. Approaching Bingen, where the Rhine takes a sharp turn east, it reached its narrowest point and was unnavigable.[7]

For this reason the yacht docked on the east side of the river and the musicians had to leave it, climb up to the thickly wooded hill above the bend in the river, and join it again where it widens on the stretch towards Mainz. On the heights above the small town of Rüdesheim King Lux summoned his court, and there conferred promotions on those who had earned them.[8]

Step forward kitchen scullion Ludwig van Beethoven who, in recognition of his devotion to duty, was promoted to less menial tasks.[9] He must have performed extremely well, because King Lux presented him with a diploma confirming his promotion. Several threads cut from the yacht's rigging were attached to the document, and at the other end was a huge seal of pitch attached to the lid of a small box. The document folded neatly into the box. Beethoven treasured this, and kept it with him for many years after he moved to Vienna.

At Mainz, where the Rhine turns south, the musicians boarded another boat to take them east along the Main. An easy day's sailing—the Main was less turbulent and fast flowing than the Rhine—took them to Aschaffenburg, where the Elector of Mainz had his summer palace. Since their own Elector had put them under no pressure to reach Mergentheim, it was decided to make a stop in Aschaffenburg, and introduce Beethoven to one of Germany's most renowned and respected piano virtuosos, the Abbé Sterkel, who resided at the palace.

Two senior members of the orchestra took Beethoven, along with former kitchen scullion colleague Romberg, to meet the great musician, and the ensuing encounter has entered legend. The palace was an imposing four-sided structure encompassing a courtyard, standing on the banks of the Main, and it is likely that the Bonners—albeit familiar with palaces—were impressed.[10] It is also probable that Sterkel played on his great reputation, no doubt dropping into the conversation how pleasant it was to be resident at the palace itself, as befits a renowned musician.

After some polite conversation during which the visitors would surely have flattered Sterkel, they urged him to demonstrate his powers at the keyboard, and the Abbé it appears took little persuading. We do not know what he played, but we do know that Beethoven approached the piano and stood transfixed. He quite simply had never heard playing like it. Relating the story later, one of those present said that brilliant young virtuoso though Beethoven was, his playing was 'rude and hard', whereas Sterkel had a 'refined and cultivated' style, and his playing was 'in the highest degree light, graceful and pleasing'.

As the sole pianist in Bonn with virtuosic talent, it was the first time Beethoven had heard another pianist who even came close to his skills, and Sterkel's technique introduced him to a new world of grace and delicacy. He was seriously impressed, more than he had ever been before.

Sterkel finished his display to universal praise, and all eyes turned towards Beethoven—including those of Sterkel. They urged him to demonstrate his skills, but Beethoven demurred, muttering he would rather not under the circumstances. Sterkel seized the moment.

'Maybe the young gentleman from Bonn does not quite measure up to the reputation he seems to have established?'

It was, as Sterkel might well have reasoned it would be, a red rag to a bull. Seeing Beethoven's discomfort, he pressed harder. 'We have seen your latest publication, and I confess to being impressed with the complexity of the writing and the skills you require in the performer. In fact, dare I suggest, you demand more skills in the performer than maybe you yourself possess? I have an idea. Why do you not play the piece now, and put our suspicions to rest?'

Earlier in that same year Beethoven had composed a substantial piece, a set of no fewer than twenty-four variations on a theme by one Vincenzo Righini, a colleague of Sterkel in the service of the Elector of Mainz. For that reason the published work— Beethoven's first for seven years—had quickly found its way to Aschaffenburg.

Beethoven, clearly stung, his honour impugned and his ire aroused, said he would play. 'Give me the score.' Sterkel rifled through the sheet music on the piano, inside the stool, on nearby surfaces, but failed to find it. Undeterred, Beethoven began to play.

He played variation after variation, including some of the most technically demanding, from memory. Then, in the midst of playing, announcing he could not recall the remaining variations, he instantly improvised entirely new ones, of a complexity equal to the most difficult of those he had already played. To round things off, he imitated Sterkel's style of playing, exaggerating its lightness and refinement, making it appear 'almost ladylike', no doubt drawing discreet chuckles from those present.

We are not told of Sterkel's reaction, but this would not be the last time that Beethoven, his skills at the keyboard thrown into doubt, would embarrass his accuser with an unparalleled display of virtuosity.

As well as an illuminating tale regarding how easily Beethoven could be goaded into performing when his skills were impugned, this encounter in Aschaffenburg is important for another reason too. It provides evidence that, through publication, knowledge of his compositional skills had spread well beyond his hometown of Bonn. Now his virtuosity was certain to achieve a similar fame.

On arrival in Bad Mergentheim, the musicians from Bonn turned their minds to musical duties. On the orders of the Elector they were given quarters in the complex of buildings that housed the Teutonic Order, and no doubt appreciated the comfort and convenience this afforded. They had a busy schedule. There were performances in theatres, ornate halls and churches, on every day of the week. There were balls, concerts, operettas and plays. Added to this were lavish receptions and banquets, with musicians on hand to entertain guests. The Teutonic Knights—Count Waldstein attended for a period—were dressed in medieval finery of white cloaks.

On the Elector's name day he presented his Bonn musicians with a bag containing one thousand ducats. Beethoven's share amounted to around forty guilders.

We would know little more about the stay in Mergentheim, were it not for the diligence of a well-known composer of the time by the name of Karl Ludwig Junker. He visited Mergentheim and was warmly received by the Bonners. It says something of his perspicacity as music critic that he regarded the orchestra to be sufficiently accomplished to merit a lengthy report, which he published in a musical journal.

He praises the orchestra's 'surpassing excellence' in music of the utmost difficulty. He writes that the musicians were resplendent in red uniforms trimmed with gold. Beethoven played in the viola section, and it is a beguiling thought to imagine the young musician, so notoriously careless about his appearance in later years, sitting in resplendent uniform with his fellow players.

So far, so interesting, but little more than that. Indeed the name of Karl Ludwig Junker would be well and truly consigned to oblivion were it not for the paragraph that he wrote next. For reasons we do not know, he watched Beethoven improvise on the piano in a private room with no audience. More than that, Beethoven asked him for a theme, so that he could improvise on it. This is something Beethoven was consistently asked to do throughout his life, and (as I have noted earlier) he nearly always refused. On this occasion he obliged. Not only that, but he made an impression on Junker that led to a description possibly unique in all the thousands of words written by men and women who knew him. It is so extraordinary, it is worth quoting at length.

I heard also one of the greatest of pianists—the dear, good Be-thofen [sic] *... True he did not perform in public, probably the instrument here was not to his liking ... But what was infinitely preferable to me was that I heard him extemporise in private. Yes, I was even invited to propose a theme for him to vary ... The greatness of this amiable, light-hearted man, as a virtuoso, may in my opinion be safely estimated from his almost inexhaustible wealth of ideas, the altogether characteristic style of expression in his playing, and the great execution which he displays. I know, therefore, of not one thing that he lacks that is necessary to the greatness of the artist ... Bethofen, in addition to his execution, has greater clarity and weight of ideas than Vogler,[11] and more expression—in short his playing goes straight to the heart. Even the members of this remarkable orchestra are, without exception, his admirers, and are all ears when he plays. Yet he is exceedingly modest and free from all pretension. Had I agreed, as my friend Bethofen implored me, to stay another day in Mergentheim, I have no doubt he would have played to me for hours, and the day ... would have been transformed into a day of the highest bliss.*

This is on several levels a quite remarkable commentary. For a start here is a professional music-writer in his forties openly stating that Beethoven is a better keyboard player than the best he knows. Even if we might have expected that, it comes as a genuine shock—given what we know of Beethoven's notoriously unpredictable temperament—to learn that he is so popular with his musical colleagues. There is not one, according to Junker, who does not admire him and listen attentively when he plays. We have to deduce from this they liked him too. It comes shining through Junker's prose. Finally, what do we make of the words 'he is exceedingly modest and free from all pretension'? Well, the earliest and most authoritative of all Beethoven biographies, written by a man who interviewed many people who had known Beethoven, describes these words as 'utterly inexplicable'![12]

Certainly Junker was caught up in the moment.[13] But if Beethoven actually tried to persuade him to stay so he could play some more for him, the two men—a generation apart in age—must have got on exceedingly well. We cannot simply dismiss Junker's words as those of a sycophant. He observed the Bonn orchestra performing, witnessed their relationships, and was given a private recital by Beethoven.

My reading of this is that Beethoven, twenty years of age, was away from Bonn, away from the tensions of family, away from the confines of court, away from anyone—and any circumstance—that was not musical. He was in the company of musicians, making music. Nothing else. I do not find it in the least surprising that here, in Mergentheim, for the first time in his life we see Beethoven, the innate musician.[14]

One can almost feel his sense of despair when the time came to return to Bonn in late October 1791.

—

At one o'clock in the morning on 5 December 1791, an event occurred that went largely unnoticed in Vienna, that caused much sadness in musical circles in Bonn, that would have caused Beethoven considerable grief, and that is still being mourned today. Wolfgang Amadeus Mozart died at the age of thirty-five. It is not an exaggeration to say that Beethoven, who turned twenty-one less than two weeks later, was soon being talked of as Mozart's natural successor. As performer his virtuosity was unquestioned and unparalleled.[15] As composer he now had a substantial number of works, in a variety of genres, to his name.

One man recognised that more than any other. He was in London when the sad news reached him, but he kept his promise to pass through Bonn on his return to Vienna. In July 1792 Beethoven once again met Joseph Haydn, now Europe's unquestioned preeminent musician. Haydn was now sixty years of age, and a good enough musician to recognise that he belonged to an older generation and that new blood was needed. More than that, he was prepared to do something about it.

A breakfast meeting was arranged between Haydn and members of the court orchestra at Bad Godesberg, close to Bonn. Beethoven was present, and no doubt remembering Haydn's suggestion at their last meeting, had the manuscript of his *Cantata on the Death of Emperor Joseph II* with him. Haydn asked to see it. He studied several pages, finally confessing himself very impressed. He urged Beethoven to continue his studies.

The meeting is recounted by Wegeler, who frustratingly gives us no further detail. However, by the time Haydn left Bonn shortly after, there was a clear commitment that if Beethoven could find his way to Vienna, he, Haydn, would give him lessons. We do not know how this was viewed by the people around Beethoven, Count Waldstein, or Christian Neefe, or most importantly the Elector, who would not only have to give Beethoven permission to take leave of absence, but also subsidise the trip. It was summer, certainly, and court duties were light, but come autumn the new opera and theatre season would have to be prepared and then got under way. There was not much Beethoven could do in the few weeks before then. But if it was to be a longer stay, how likely was it that the Elector would grant leave of absence to a young man who had by now made himself such an indispensable member of musical life at court?

Not for the first time, extraneous events worked in Beethoven's favour, though he must have been the only resident of Bonn for whom this was true. In October 1792 the French Revolutionary Army invaded German territory and marched towards the Rhine. On the 22nd they took Mainz and headed north. The towns and cities of the lower Rhine were at their mercy. Those who could fled. It was decided that the Elector and his family should leave Bonn.

In the chaos of evacuation, the question of whether or not Beethoven should be allowed to go to Vienna paled somewhat. We do not know exactly what happened, but almost certainly Count Waldstein seized the moment to secure the Elector's agreement for Beethoven to go to Vienna, possibly for six months, maybe for a year.

Beethoven did not need telling twice. He immediately began making preparations. We do not know how he told his father, or what his father's reaction was. Probably he presented it as a fait accompli, in the knowledge that his two brothers, now in their mid- and late teens, would take over responsibility.

Before leaving, Beethoven made the rather charming decision— or maybe it was made for him—to fill an autograph book with messages from close friends. This book has survived, and is rather more surprising for what it does not contain than for what it does.

Only fourteen friends have signed it, none of them musical colleagues, many with names that do not feature in any of the literature. Christian Neefe did not sign it. It seems to give the lie to Junker's assessment of Beethoven's popularity among his fellow musicians. On the other hand, it is always possible that he had another book for musicians, or that shyness prevented him from approaching everyone he would have liked to.

One notable omission is Stephan von Breuning, one of Helene

von Breuning's sons to whom he had given piano lessons. With Stephan the young Beethoven had formed an even closer friendship than with Wegeler. The two youths—Beethoven was the elder by nearly four years—spent a lot of time together. Stephan appears to feature less in this period than Wegeler, by virtue of the fact that he did not write his reminiscences down. But the friendship with Stephan von Breuning was to be the closest, and longest lasting, of Beethoven's life. It was to last, literally, until Beethoven's death. Stephan was to follow Beethoven to Vienna, and his name will feature many more times in these pages. Why, then, is he absent from the autograph book? We do not know. It might be simply that he was away at the time, because Beethoven would be gone within days.

Stephan's sister Eleonore most certainly does feature in the autograph book, and thereby, I am convinced, hangs a tale. We are in the realms of conjecture now, but I make no apologies for what follows. It is a subject that has not been accorded much space by previous biographers, but I believe that to ignore it leaves us with an incomplete picture of an adolescent Beethoven.

Where are the young women in this narrative? Conspicuous by their absence. Girls do not feature greatly in Beethoven's pubescent years, but it was not, apparently, for want of trying. According to Wegeler, 'There never was a time when Beethoven was not in love, and that in the highest degree.' In this period, in his adolescence, as well as in his entire adult life, he would fall in love with females who were simply not available. It is a consistent pattern, to such an extent that you have to wonder if it was a deliberate course of action on his part, as if he was somehow fearful of the commitment it could lead to. But in the early years, this was clearly not the case. He was certainly more than anxious to have an amorous relationship.

There was a certain Jeanette d'Honrath, from Cologne, a friend of Eleonore who would come to Bonn and stay with her.

Wegeler describes her as 'a beautiful, vivacious blonde, of good education and amiable disposition, who enjoyed music greatly and possessed an agreeable voice'. She was clearly well aware of Beethoven's attraction to her, because she used to sing him a teasing little song, of which the words lamented her being separated from him, and being unable to prevent this, which was too hurtful for her poor heart. We do not know how Beethoven reacted to this. Suffice it to say she went off and married a soldier who later rose to the rank of field marshal.

Then one Fräulein von Westerholt, whom Beethoven took on as a pupil and with whom he fell in love with such a passion that Wegeler discreetly calls her just 'Fräulein von W.' and Romberg was telling tales of his friend's unrequited love forty years later. Fräulein von Westerholt became Frau von Bevervörde.

Beethoven and his friends frequented a tavern near the town hall in Bonn called the Zehrgarten, run by a certain Frau Koch, assisted by her beautiful daughter Babette. It is certain that Beethoven was attracted to her. Whether he tried to pursue this we do not know, but if he did he was clearly disappointed, since he wrote from Vienna shortly after arriving that he was hurt she hadn't replied to his letters.

It was around this time that an incident occurred that perhaps best—and most painfully—sums up Beethoven's lack of success with girls.

One evening he was in a restaurant with a number of the younger members of the court orchestra. There was a particularly attractive young waitress, and they persuaded her to tease Beethoven and flirt with him. This she did (we are not told how), and Beethoven reacted with 'repellent coldness'. They encouraged her to flirt more. Finally Beethoven lost patience and 'put an end to her importunities with a smart box on the ear'.[16]

This merits slightly closer examination. Why would his colleagues do this, if they did not already know of his gaucheness with

girls? Had some of them previously witnessed his attempts at se-
duction? If so, the attempts must have failed. Clearly alcohol was
flowing when they put the waitress up to her antics, but that would
simply have exaggerated what they all knew already—that Beethoven was pretty hopeless when it came to girls.

More importantly, can we really believe that a twenty- or twenty-
one-year-old Beethoven would strike a girl? Or is the teller of the
tale merely using a euphemism? We cannot be sure. But this was
clearly no simple prank. It was calculated to upset Beethoven, and
upset him it did. It must also have deepened a certain self-loathing
he is bound to have had over his inability to acquire a girlfriend.

Which leads us back to Eleonore von Breuning, Lorchen as she
was known, and the speculation I shall now indulge in. I am assuming that in order to have his autograph book signed, Beethoven
went to the Breuning house on the Münsterplatz with which he was
so familiar. He found Stephan out or away, but Lorchen was there,
alone. He asked her to sign his autograph book.

This she did, choosing to write three lines by the German poet
and philosopher Johann Gottfried Herder. They read:

> *Friendship with that which is good*
> *Grows like the evening shadows*
> *Until the sunshine of life finally sinks.*

She signed it: Bonn, 1 November 1792, your true friend Eleonore Breuning.

Hardly an overwhelming declaration of affection, in fact bordering on the formal. Compare this with a birthday card she presented him with one year earlier. Two four-line verses wishing him
happiness and long life, and in return asking from him, her piano
teacher, kindness, patience, and favour. She drew round the verses a
garland of flowers, and signed it with her pet name, Lorchen.

What had happened? I am convinced Beethoven fell in love with Lorchen very soon after beginning to teach her. I believe that, at some point in his teenage years, he expressed this to her, and that later—in between the birthday card and the autograph book—he put his feelings into action with an attempted kiss, which she rejected.

Now, alone in the house with her, about to leave for Vienna, he made—I believe—one more attempt to show his affection. I imagine he made an ungainly lunge at her, which she again rejected and which left her seriously upset.

How else to explain the language he used in a letter to her written a full year after arriving in Vienna?

> *Although it has been a year since you have heard from me, you have been constantly and most vividly in my thoughts, and very often I have conversed in spirit with you and your dear family, though frequently not as calmly as I should have wished. For whenever I did so I was always reminded of that unfortunate quarrel. My conduct at that time really was quite detestable. But what was done could not be undone. Oh, what I would give to be able to blot out of my life my behaviour at that time, behaviour which did me so little honour, and which was so out of character for me ... It is said that the sincerest repentance is only to be found when the criminal himself confesses his crime, and this is what I have wanted to do. So now let us draw a curtain over the whole affair.*

Eleonore, it seems, was prepared to forgive him, to an extent. She sent him a hand-knitted neckcloth (he had asked her to send him something made by her hands). But he is still tortured by guilt, no doubt made worse by the fact that he now knew that Eleonore had formed a close friendship with his friend Wegeler, and that the two would soon be married.

The beautiful neckcloth, your own handiwork, came as a lovely surprise to me ... But it also made me sad, awakening memories of things long past. Also your generous behaviour made me feel ashamed. Indeed I could hardly believe you would think me still worth remembering ... I beg you to believe, my friend *(please let me continue to call you friend), that I have suffered greatly, and am still suffering, from the loss of your friendship ... I know what I have lost and what you have meant to me. But if I were to attempt to fill this gap, I would have to recall scenes which you would not be happy to hear about, and I would not be happy to describe.*

I rest my case.

The most important entry in Beethoven's autograph book, without question, is that written by the man who had done more to further Beethoven's musical ambitions in Bonn than any other, Count Waldstein. In fact his entry has earned him a certain immortality. For the first time in Beethoven's life, his name is linked in writing with music's two greatest contemporary names (though the reference to Haydn is a trifle barbed).

Dear Beethowen! [sic]
You journey now to Vienna in fulfilment of your long frustrated wishes. The Genius of Mozart is still in mourning and she weeps for the death of her pupil. With the inexhaustible Haydn she has found refuge but no occupation. Through him she now wishes to be united with someone else. With persistent hard work you shall receive: Mozart's Spirit through Haydn's Hands.

———

Beethoven left Bonn at six o'clock on the morning of Friday, 2 November (the morning after the encounter with Eleonore von Breuning), carrying a large amount of musical scores, finished and unfinished, and little else. The journey was not without danger. At one point the coach driver whipped the horses into a gallop and drove right through the Hessian army.

The coach drove south along the river, turning east at Ehrenbreitstein, the hometown of Beethoven's mother. He would certainly have taken a last look at the Rhine, expecting to see it again in six months or a year.

He never saw the Rhine, or Bonn—or, indeed, Eleonore von Breuning—again.

CHAPTER FIVE

IMPRESSING THE VIENESE

BUT HAYDN FEELS THE WRATH OF AN ANGRY YOUNG MAN

V IENNA, CAPITAL CITY OF THE HOLY ROMAN Empire, seat of the Holy Roman Emperor, formal, correct, proper. Into its midst there arrived in November 1792 a young man just one month short of his twenty-second birthday, from Bonn in the Rhineland several hundred miles to the northwest, who had never worn a wig in his life, let alone a powdered one, whose clothes were ill fitting and in need of repair, and whose accent was rough and harsh on the sophisticated ears of the Viennese.

And what of the city in which he had arrived? At the crossroads of Continental Europe, Vienna could lay claim to being Europe's most exotic city. Less than a decade before Beethoven's arrival, a traveller had written that the streets of Vienna teemed with …

Hungarians in their close-fitting trousers, Poles with their flowing sleeves, Armenians and Moldavians with their half-Oriental costumes, Serbians with their twisted moustaches, Greeks smoking their long-stemmed pipes in the coffee-houses, bearded Muslims with broad knives in their belts, Polish Jews with their faces bearded and their hair twisted in knots, Bohemian peasants in their long boots, Hungarian and Transylvanian wagoners with sheepskin greatcoats, Croats with black tubs balanced on their heads.

And everywhere there was music. It went from the very highest social strata to the lowest. In the 1790s every member of the

Emperor's immediate family had taken music lessons and was proficient either on an instrument or in singing. The late Emperor himself was capable of directing an opera from the harpsichord, with his sisters singing the main parts and performing in the ballet sequence. There was a first-class court orchestra, court choir, and court opera company. The same traveller wrote:

> One cannot enter any fashionable house without hearing a duet, or trio, or finale from one of the Italian operas currently the rage being sung and played at the keyboard. Even shopkeepers and cellar-hands whistle the popular arias ... No place of refreshment, from the highest to the lowest, is without music. Bassoonists and clarinettists are as plentiful as blackberries, and in the suburbs at every turn one alights upon fresh carousing, fresh fiddling, fresh illuminations.

Vienna could lay claim to being the most easygoing, even frivolous, city in Europe (a mantle that Paris would assume in later decades), where enjoyment came before anything else. An English traveller wrote that 'good cheer is pursued here in every quarter, and mirth is worshipped in every form'.

A famous Viennese motto was that 'matters are desperate, but not serious'. There was street entertainment, dancing was everywhere, and cafés and *Weinstuben* were full late into the night. Prostitution was rife, and if the Emperor himself is to be believed, reached into every corner of the city. When it was proposed to him that brothels should be licensed, he replied, 'The walls would cost me nothing, but the expense of roofing would be ruinous, for a roof would have to be constructed over the whole city.'

Another British visitor neatly caught the twin themes that ran through Vienna, when he wrote, 'No city can at the same time present such a display of affected sanctity and real licentiousness.'

There was, however, a dark side to the city. Just as, a century later, the Viennese would waltz towards the oblivion of the First World War and the end of the seemingly indestructible Habsburg dynasty, so in the 1790s the carousing masked deep fear and tension. No one, though, could have foreseen that within a few short years the Holy Roman Empire and its Emperor would have been consigned to historical oblivion by a certain Napoleon Bonaparte.

Three years earlier the people of Paris had invaded the Bastille, and the French Revolution had begun. Three months before Beethoven's arrival in Vienna, the French King had been found guilty of treason, and would mount the scaffold in January of the following year. Before that year was out, his Queen would follow him. To the people of Vienna she was not Marie Antoinette, but Maria Antonia, youngest daughter of the 'mother' of their nation, the great Empress Maria Theresa, and they were aware of how she had been vilified by the French, who called her the 'Austrian whore'.

What had seemed impossible—the downfall of the oldest hereditary monarchy in Continental Europe—had happened. How safe was the Habsburg Emperor in Vienna? As the French Revolutionary Army under its inspired young commander began to rampage across Europe, the threat became ever more real. Time and again Austria entered into alliances with other European powers to take on Napoleon; time and again it suffered humiliating defeat. The old officer class of the Habsburg Empire, the cavalry still wielding lances, were no match for the revolutionary cannon of the French.

So outward frivolity masked an underlying tension. The least safe commodity in Vienna was words. Increasingly spies proliferated, ears pricked in cafés and taverns, and above all in the back of horse-drawn fiacres. And when words were dangerous, what was the commodity that was safest of all? Music. That is how Vienna became Europe's capital city of music.

Beethoven was to live in Vienna for just over thirty-four years until his death. For the first half of that time, roughly, Vienna was a city at almost permanent war; for the second half it was what today would be called a police state, as Foreign Minister and later Chancellor Metternich clamped down on political freedom.

Cataclysmic events were taking place across Europe. Beethoven absorbed the drama, the tension, the danger, and it all left its mark on his music.

—

Beethoven's life in Vienna began in the humblest of ways. He was given an attic room in a house owned by a Viennese aristocrat who was a distant relative of Count Waldstein. His name was Prince Karl Lichnowsky, and he was no ordinary aristocrat. He happened to be one of the wealthiest in the city, and one of the greatest patrons of the arts, in particular music. His salon was home to the leading artists of the day.

Initially, though, Beethoven was on his own. One can almost sense his loneliness—coupled undoubtedly with a feeling of freedom—as he made a shopping list days after his arrival: 'Wood, wig-maker, coffee ... overcoat, boots, shoes, piano desk, seal, writing desk ...'

He was aware too that he would have to cut a figure in keeping with the elevated class that he hoped to penetrate, but that his small allowance from the Elector would be sorely stretched. Another shopping list reads: 'Black silk stockings, 1 ducat. 1 pair winter silk stockings, 1 florin 40 kreutzers. Boots, 6 florins. Shoes, 1 florin, 30 kreutzers.' One suspects these domestic issues were a distraction from the real task at hand: to become a part of the sophisticated, very formal, very aristocratic, musical scene in Vienna.

He began lessons with Haydn immediately, and then six weeks after arriving he received the worst possible news from home—or what *should* have been the worst possible news. On 18 December his father died.

There is no reference to this sad event, as far as I can tell, in anything he said or wrote down at the time, and no indication of any inner struggle over whether he should return to Bonn for the funeral. Maybe the fact that central Europe was at war made the journey inadvisable. I suspect, though, it merely hardened his resolve to get on with his new life without interruption. He did not return. It was a symbolic putting of the past behind him. His new life as professional musician in Vienna had begun.

He most certainly threw himself into it. His musical life had three strands. He was studying intensively with Haydn; he was composing new works, and through Lichnowsky's contacts he was performing at salon soirées. This total immersion in musical activity alone made him something of a rarity in Vienna, but of the three pursuits the one that truly singled him out was salon performances.

There was an undercurrent of collective guilt among the city's aristocrats that the musical genius who had died so recently, the greatest musical genius the city, indeed Europe, had seen, had not been better looked after. It was as if there was an unspoken determination among them not to let that happen again. In one sense Beethoven made it rather easy for them. He was quite simply, even in his early twenties, a piano virtuoso unlike any this city had seen, not excepting Mozart. If Lichnowsky was the key that unlocked the doors to the highest salons in the land, once Beethoven sat at the piano, his extraordinary and boundless talent ensured he would be accepted in whatever company he mixed, however elevated.

Without Lichnowsky's patronage, it is doubtful any salon doors would have opened at all for the young man from Bonn. He simply did not look like a musician. He had no sophistication about him, no refinement, no air of the artist. Thayer describes him as:

Small, thin, dark-complexioned, pockmarked, dark-eyed ...
with looks of the Moor about him ... His front teeth protruded,

*owing to the extraordinary flatness of the roof of his mouth, and
this thrust out his lips. His nose, too, was rather broad and decid-
edly flattened, while his forehead was remarkably full and round
… in the words of Mähler, who twice painted his portrait, a 'bullet'.*

The word 'thin' is perhaps surprising, since all images of the
adult Beethoven show a powerful, stockily built figure. But this did
not come until later. Early portraits show none of the suppressed
power of his middle years.

Once his fame was established, the word most often used to describe him—and frequently used today—was 'leonine'. This implies
more than just a large powerful head and body. The lion is the king of
beasts, unchallengeable, undefeatable. He had, contemporaries noted,
a strong jaw, with a deep cleft in the chin, and he was powerfully built,
despite his short stature, with wide shoulders, strong hands with tufts
of hair on his fingers, which were short and thick.

His eyes were noticed and commented on. 'His eye is full of rude
energy,' wrote one observer. Another noted that 'his fiery eyes, though
small, are deep-set and unbelievably full of life'. Rossini recorded,
albeit when Beethoven was in his early fifties, that 'what no etch-
er's needle can express is the indefinable sadness spread over his features—while from under heavy eyebrows his eyes shine out as if from
caverns, and though small, seem to pierce one'.

He was, once he had become Vienna's preeminent musician, beyond trivial criticism for having wild hair, or being unshaven, or
wearing ill-fitting clothes, or even being ill-mannered. But in his
early years in Vienna, people were shocked by his sheer lack of physical grace, and were not afraid to say so.

One noblewoman wrote after encountering him, 'His entire deportment showed no signs of exterior polish. On the contrary he was lack-

ing in manners in both demeanour and behaviour.' Hardly the kind of appearance that would fit easily in the noblest salons of Vienna, particularly when coupled with his notoriously unkempt appearance (despite the shopping list). But the moment he sat at the piano, everything changed. In fact at that point his social gaucheness worked in his favour. It increased the admiration he was accorded. How could a man so clearly unsuited to the refined pursuit of the highest of the arts be such an accomplished practitioner of it?

Word, which began in the salon of Prince Lichnowsky, raced round the aristocracy of Vienna. The city had lost Mozart, but another young genius—a truly remarkable virtuoso who looked more like a street seller—had found his way to the city. The aristocrats, patrons of the arts, flocked to see and hear him.

—

'I took lessons from Haydn, but never learned anything from him.' Beethoven is quoted as saying this in later years by Ferdinand Ries in the memoir he cowrote with Wegeler. It was not as simple as that. In fact there is evidence Haydn worked hard to improve his pupil's knowledge of musical theory, particularly counterpoint. But it is true that the older man had a great deal of call on his time, not to mention his emotions.

He was deeply affected by the death of Mozart at such a young age, as well as the sudden death of another close friend. He was living through a disastrous marriage, openly writing in envy to a friend whose wife had died, 'Perhaps the time will come … when four eyes shall be closed … Two are closed, but the other two …', and was juggling two mistresses, a widow in London, and an Italian mezzo-soprano who had moved to Esterháza with her husband. On top of that there was the small matter of six new symphonies he was planning for a return trip to London.

So if he had less time to give than his pupil wanted, it was perhaps understandable. But Beethoven clearly bore a rather long-standing grudge against his teacher. Ries recounts that the reason for this was that Haydn, aware of just how promising Beethoven was, asked him to put on the title page of his first works—*any* first work—'Pupil of Haydn'. He might have understood his pupil's musical prowess, but this anecdote shows he was less understanding of Beethoven's character.

Beethoven refused point blank. This was more than a refusal, it was a gesture of defiance, an insult almost, to the older and much venerated composer. Haydn was to wreak small revenge before too long, but in early 1794 he unwittingly did Beethoven a great favour by leaving for London. It was a kind of liberation for the young man. There is some evidence that he took secret lessons with another composer, but of more importance is the fact that he began to compose in earnest.

He completed his first major work, a set of three piano trios which he would publish the following year as his opus 1. He wrote two full piano concertos, and began serious work on a set of three piano sonatas, which would become his opus 2. There were several other smaller works as well.

Beethoven had, by late 1794, been in Vienna for less than two years, yet he was already—at the age of just twenty-three—far and away the city's most accomplished all-round musician, performing regularly in salons and publishing substantial works. There was only one thing missing, and that was where Prince Lichnowsky came in.

Using his considerable influence, the Prince secured for Beethoven his first public performance. The venue was the highly prestigious Burgtheater, the largest and most important of the imperial court theatres, which stood adjacent to the Hofburg Palace, seat of the Emperor. Other works were to be performed, but the programme announced the performance of a piano concerto by Ludwig van Beethoven, who was also its composer. The last musician of consequence who had performed his own piano concertos in Vienna was Mozart.

Things did not go smoothly. In fact they could hardly have gone worse. Beethoven, all his life a chronic rewriter, completed the slow movement only two days before the concert. He was suffering from severe stomach pains and diarrhoea while he was composing. His old friend from Bonn, Franz Wegeler, now a qualified doctor, was in Vienna and did what he could with various potions. So tight was time that four copyists sat in the hallway making fair copies as Beethoven handed over barely decipherable manuscript sheets one by one. His notation was notoriously difficult to decipher at the best of times. The copyists are likely to have helped each other out with difficult passages, rather than risk the wrath of the ailing composer by querying what he had written.

Worse than this, at the rehearsal the following day, the eve of the performance, Beethoven discovered the piano was a semitone flat. With no apparent difficulty he transposed the piano part up a semitone, but it would have done nothing to improve his mood.

Frustratingly we have no eyewitness account of how the concert went. But the fact that it was repeated the following day suggests at worst a satisfactory performance, at best a success. Just as frustratingly, it is not known for certain which of his first two piano concertos Beethoven played.[1]

Extraordinarily, on the third night, at a concert arranged by Mozart's widow, Beethoven performed a Mozart piano concerto. Three concerts, on three consecutive nights, in front of a paying audience. Beethoven the performer had arrived.

Four months later, in what was turning into something of an *annus mirabilis* for Beethoven, his Op. 1 Piano Trios were published. Within a matter of weeks, Joseph Haydn returned from a triumphant London tour. Beethoven, putting aside any resentment he might have felt towards his erstwhile teacher, asked Lichnowsky to arrange a soirée at which he would perform the three piano trios in front of Haydn.

Haydn was now sixty-three years of age; he had been abroad for something over a year and a half, had performed, composed, been wined and dined and fêted practically every night. We can assume he was weary. We can also assume that musical friends had told him that the set of piano trios was enormously impressive. I do not think it is far-fetched to suggest that Haydn, as a musician, wanted to hear them, but that at the same time he was apprehensive. Would they represent such a major leap forward in composition that his own works would be rendered old-fashioned, out of date? He knew what his pupil was capable of. He probably feared the younger man would eclipse him.

The three works are substantial, grand and expansive, and in four movements each. They are almost pared-down symphonies. To hear all three in a single sitting makes for a lengthy, intense, evening—particularly for a man in his sixties for whom the previous eighteen months had been so demanding. There was the added element that Prince Lichnowsky had not done things by halves. He had invited the city's top music-lovers and artists. All knew and respected Haydn, all were keen to shake his hand, ask him about London ... and at the end of the evening ascertain his thoughts on Beethoven's piano trios.

None more so than their composer, who, no sooner had the final chord of the final movement of No. 3 sounded, leapt up from the piano and made straight for his teacher to ask his opinion.

This is where Haydn exacted revenge of a sort on the eager, and uncooperative, young man. He began by praising the works in a general sort of way, and then had the temerity, the gall, to suggest that No. 3 needed more work, and his advice to Beethoven was to revise it before sending it to the publisher.

One can imagine the collective gasp in the salon as all eyes turned to

Beethoven. If the guests were shocked, Beethoven was appalled. We-geler, who recounts the incident, states diplomatically that Beethoven was 'astonished', the more so since he considered No. 3 the strongest of the set. Wegeler, writing many years after the event, adds, 'In fact to this day it is always found to be the most pleasing, and has the greatest effect.' It is true to say that to *this day*, that is the case. Of the set of three piano trios, it is No. 3 that modern musicologists rate the strongest.

Wegeler does not recount how the frosty (heated?) encounter played out. But although the relationship between Haydn and Bee-thoven of teacher and pupil was effectively at an end, there is ample evidence that Beethoven did not lose respect for the older man. At a soirée at Prince Lichnowsky's only a matter of weeks later, Beethoven performed his new set of three piano sonatas before Haydn, and when they were published the following year, they were dedicated to him (though without any mention of 'Pupil of Haydn'!).

Then in December Haydn staged a public concert at which Bee-thoven performed one of his two piano concertos.[2] Whatever ten-sion there might have been between the two composers, it was clearly sublimated to the greater good of their art.

—

It is just as well that things were going well for Beethoven the musician, because for Beethoven the man they were not so good. An acquaintance from his Bonn years came to Vienna. She happened to be the 'beautiful, talented and accomplished' singer Magdalena Willman, who had been among the court musicians on the boat trip up the Rhine to Mergentheim just a few years before. Clearly Beethoven had admired her from afar on that sojourn, but there is no evidence he pursued matters then. He most certainly did now.

Magdalena was accompanied by her brother and his wife, and Beethoven renewed his friendship with the family. He does not appear to have given her piano lessons, but it is more than likely he accompanied her in salon recitals. He must have seen her on a number of occasions, because he fell head over heels in love with her, and wasted no time in proposing marriage.

She turned him down flat. We know no further details, except one. Her niece, interviewed by Thayer sixty-five years later, told him her father had often spoken of how the famous musician had once proposed marriage to his sister. Thayer asked her why Magdalena had turned him down. She hesitated a moment, then said, 'Because he was so ugly, and half crazy!'

For the niece—Thayer discreetly calls her 'Madame S.'—to know this detail so many years later suggests it was common currency at the time of the proposal. Even if Beethoven never heard such words, he is certain to have known that he was the butt of humour, even ridicule. Following on rejections by several women in Bonn, not to mention the humiliation by the waitress, this must have hurt his pride considerably. He would have been grateful he had music to turn to. There, no one could laugh at him.

Something else had happened, guaranteed to darken his mood. His brothers had left Bonn and come to join him in Vienna. Caspar Carl had arrived in May 1794, Nikolaus Johann at the very end of 1795. Beethoven had never been close to his brothers. They were talentless individuals, and he was a being apart. Nikolaus Johann had at least trained in pharmacy, and soon found employment in Vienna. Caspar Carl appears to have done nothing. He was in the dire position of having a mediocre musical talent. He attached himself to his elder brother, negotiating on his behalf with publishers, teaching, even doing a little composing himself. But the two did not get on, and there were frequent disagreements. Within a very few years things were to sour deeply between them.

Escape was at hand, in the best and most exciting form possible. Prince Lichnowsky decided that Beethoven should undertake a European tour, and he chose exactly the same itinerary he had undertaken with Mozart some years earlier: Prague, Dresden, Leipzig, and Berlin. In fact Lichnowsky, no doubt for business reasons, decided to accompany Beethoven no further than Prague, but he made sure through his contacts, no doubt gleaned on the earlier trip with Mozart, that his protégé would be well looked after.

That he most certainly was. In Prague, together with Lichnowsky, he was welcomed into the most noble salons. He performed, and composed several pieces. In Dresden he was received by the Elector of Saxony, who it appears persuaded him to give a solo recital for an hour and a half with no one present but the Elector himself. There is no record of his brief stay in Leipzig, but in Berlin, well, there is no other way to put this. He reached the top.

The King of Prussia, Friedrich Wilhelm II, personally received Beethoven, making him welcome at court. Beethoven was on his own, with nothing more than a letter of introduction, but it so happened the King was not merely a great lover of music, but a fine cellist. He very quickly recognised an extraordinary talent, and Beethoven more than reciprocated by composing several pieces for cello—two sonatas and two sets of variations—as well as other works too. The two sonatas were almost certainly too difficult for the King to play, but they were performed for him by a prominent cellist attached to the court, with Beethoven at the piano, and they would have no doubt inspired him to improve his skills. Beethoven curried more favour still by dedicating the two sonatas to the King.

Beethoven remained in Berlin for the best part of two months, and it is possible he began to tire of the attention and adulation. In later years his pupil Czerny recounted how, when Beethoven improvised at the piano, people in the salon would break into tears and loud sobs, so moved were they by what they heard. But at the end of the improvisation Beethoven would burst into loud laughter and chastise his audience. 'You are fools!' he would shout at them. 'Who can live with such spoiled children?' Czerny then adds, rather enigmatically, that Beethoven himself told him that it was for that reason he declined to accept an invitation the King of Prussia extended to him after one of his improvisations. He elaborates no further, but it is possible the King was offering him a permanent position at court.

It would seem, though, that if offence were intended, none was taken. On his departure Beethoven was presented with a gold snuff-box filled with coins by the King himself. This was not all he returned with. From Prague he had written to his brother Nikolaus Johann that he was earning considerable money, as well as winning friends and respect. He goes so far as to write that if his brother should need money, he could approach Prince Lichnowsky 'boldly, for he still owes me some.' It seems extraordinary that the Prince should owe Beethoven money, rather than the other way round, and it is impossible to know if this really was the case.

In the same letter Beethoven cannot resist a small word of advice from an older brother on matters of a private nature. 'I hope that you will enjoy living in Vienna more and more, but do be on your guard against the whole tribe of bad women.' This might be considered somewhat rich coming from someone who had received rejection after rejection from women. It could, on the other hand, be a veiled warning to take care when visiting prostitutes. This would suggest Beethoven had personal experience of this kind. Or the whole thing might have been a brother's jest to a brother. We have no way of knowing.

Of more significance is the fact that Beethoven was now known across central Europe. He mixed not only with aristocracy, but royalty too. He was lauded wherever he went. His talent was unquestioned, his virtuosity unchallenged. Added to this he had something few other virtuosos could offer: he was composing. Composition after composition flowed from him, in all genres, from the lightweight to the seriously heavy. Publishers were clamouring for new work. He had concertos under his belt, sonatas for a variety of instruments, trios, a quintet, a septet.

He was about to embark on a musical form considered the purest, and of which in later years he would prove to be master: the string quartet. There was one other form, considered the noblest and most elevated in all music, at which he had tried his hand, made many notes and sketches, but had not yet produced a complete work: the symphony. That was about to change.

In short, at the age of twenty-six, with a successful tour behind him, compositions to his name, a reputation already unrivalled in Vienna, he had achieved a golden start to what promised to be a long and glittering career.

What could possibly go wrong? Only the single most disastrous fate that could possibly befall a musician. When it started, how it started, is not known. All we know for certain is that in the summer of 1797 things go quiet. Beethoven attended a concert on 6 April, at which his Piano Quintet in E flat, Op. 16, was given its first performance. In the same month, bizarrely, a nobleman presented him with a horse as a thank you for the dedication of a composition to his wife. Beethoven apparently rode the animal just a few times before forgetting about it. The next positive occurrence is a letter Beethoven wrote, dated 1 October. Between the two dates, nothing.

There is anecdotal evidence that around this time Beethoven took a long walk, returned home sweating profusely, stripped to his underwear, opened all doors and windows, and stood in a chill draught. This led to the onset of serious illness.[3] No more is known. If it is true, it is likely that Beethoven closeted himself away. His old friend Dr. Wegeler had left Vienna, and he would have been reluctant to confide in anyone else.

More credible is an account written many years later by a surgeon who knew Beethoven, that the composer earlier in life—he did not specify when—'endured a frightful attack of typhus', and that this was the cause of the terrible fate that befell him.[4]

Beethoven was beginning to lose his hearing.

CHAPTER SIX

MY POOR HEARING HAUNTS ME

BUT THERE IS A 'DEAR CHARMING GIRL WHO LOVES ME'

F OR SOME TIME HE TRIED TO HIDE IT. THERE is no record of Beethoven consulting a doctor for another three years, possibly more. Undoubtedly there would have been more than an element of self-denial involved. It is easy to understand why he would refuse to accept that such an appalling fate had befallen him. Certainly to begin with he is likely to have expected it to clear, to wake up one morning and find it was nothing more than a blockage, and he could get on with his life.

Getting on with his life is what he did. He composed intensively, producing works of greater complexity than ever before. After a rather fraught creative process, he composed a set of six string quartets. His Piano Sonata in C minor, Op. 13, the 'Pathétique', was a huge leap forward from any previous piano sonata, by him or anybody else. And finally, somewhat late in life for a young prodigy, he completed his First Symphony. There were other smaller works too.

He was active on a social level as well. He met the French Ambassador in Vienna, the Napoleonic General Bernadotte (later to become King of Sweden). He gave a recital with the Italian double-bass virtuoso Domenico Dragonetti, impressed that Dragonetti was able to perform one of his cello sonatas on the double-bass.[1] He became closely acquainted with the pianist and composer Johann Baptist Cramer. Also during this time he met and corresponded with friends. There are countless notes to his good friend Nikolaus Zmeskall, some of them written with considerable humour, setting up drinking sessions at local taverns.

Nowhere, either in his own writing or reported speech, or in the memoirs of any of his friends, is there any mention that he might be having a problem with his hearing. This lends credence to the notion that he was in some sort of denial, or that he genuinely believed it was temporary and would pass. In the early stages of deafness it is not difficult to cover up problems—a slight leaning forward of the head, a quick look at the lips of the person talking, a request to repeat what was said, even joking about losing your hearing, or saying you really must get your ears syringed. Clearly, whatever problem Beethoven might have been having, it was not affecting his musical activities, and that was what mattered most.

This became very clear in two events in the first few months of 1800, one private, one public. Perhaps surprisingly it is the private event that did more to cement Beethoven's reputation. It has done more than that: it has entered legend.

It was customary at that time in Vienna for aristocrats to stage 'improvisation contests' in their salons. The way it would work was that two virtuosos, with their supporters, would meet in a salon, and display their skills before an audience. This would involve playing their own compositions, possibly with an ensemble, and then setting tasks for each other. One would play a theme he had invented, which the other could not possibly have heard before, and improvise on it. The other would then go to the piano and try to emulate this. Then this second virtuoso would set a theme of his own invention, and the first player would have to copy that. Often it would involve imitation. If one pianist had a particular style, the other would imitate it. It was an evening's entertainment in aristocratic Vienna.

Very soon after his arrival in Vienna, when aristocrats such as Lichnowsky realised what young Beethoven was capable of, they put him up against the local talent, and one by one he saw them off, at the same time steadily enhancing his reputation. Enter Daniel Steibelt, from Berlin, capital of Prussia, a renowned piano virtuoso with a fearsome reputation. Steibelt had stunned salon audiences in Berlin with his extraordinary virtuosity, enhanced by his trademark flourish, the *tremolando*.[2] Now on a tour of European capitals, he had arrived in Vienna to conquer that city's sophisticated musical cognoscenti. He brought with him something of a dashing reputation. He had been forced to join the Prussian army by his father, but had deserted to pursue a musical career.[3]

It seems some of Beethoven's friends went to hear Steibelt and were stunned at his virtuosity, to such an extent that they feared he might damage Beethoven's reputation. This is probably why Beethoven, by now sick of these showcase events designed solely for the amusement of aristocrats, agreed to go along to the home of Count von Fries. He decided that he would play his recently published Trio for piano, clarinet and cello, which he had dedicated to Prince Lichnowsky's mother-in-law.[4] Steibelt brought along four musicians to perform his Piano Quintet.

The company assembled, including no doubt Prince Lichnowsky and his family. Beethoven and his musicians played first. His Trio was perhaps a slightly odd choice, since the piano part does not call for a particularly high degree of virtuosity. The work is in three movements, is fairly straightforward, and the critics welcomed it as being more easily comprehensible than the earlier published Op. 1 Piano Trios. The final movement is a set of variations on a well-known theme from a comic opera which had recently played successfully in Vienna.

There was polite applause from the salon audience, including Steibelt, who had listened 'with a certain condescension', and made a show of complimenting Beethoven. He took his position, with his musicians, in front of the audience, confident his Quintet would put Beethoven's Trio in the shade and win the day. To make sure, he added some impressive (no doubt prepared) improvisation, and drew gasps from the audience with his audacious *tremolandos*.

At the end there was no doubt in anyone's mind who had put on the more impressive display. All eyes turned to Beethoven, who as was usual at these events had the 'right of reply'. Beethoven remained stubbornly in his seat and refused to play again. Steibelt had carried the day.

A week later it was decided to repeat the event, to stage a 'rematch'. Given that Beethoven had been reluctant to attend the earlier evening, we can only assume his blood was up. Steibelt's condescending behaviour, not to mention his ridiculously showy playing, had got under Beethoven's skin. He was out for revenge.

There must have been an air of tension and anticipation in Count Fries's salon on this second evening. Beethoven's unpredictable temperament was well known. Everybody knew he had been bested a week earlier, and they would have seen the flare in his eyes and the set of his jaw. This spelled trouble.

Steibelt went first this time. He performed another of his quintets, which again met with great approval. Then he once again improvised on the piano, in a way that put his previous performance in the shade. It was brilliant. But he made a mistake, a serious mistake. There were gasps from the audience as they realised he had chosen the theme from the final movement of Beethoven's own Trio, performed at the previous meeting, on which to improvise.

If the audience was shocked, Beethoven's friends were appalled. That was nothing to how Beethoven felt. This time he needed no encouragement. He got out of his seat, stormed to the front, and as he passed the music stands snatched up the cello part of Steibelt's Quintet. He sat roughly on the stool, all thoughts of salon etiquette gone, and made a show of putting the cello part on the piano stand *upside-down*.

He glared at the music, playing now to the audience, knowing he had everyone's attention, aware that the decisive moment in the 'Contest Beethoven v. Steibelt' had come. With one finger he hammered out a series of notes from the first bar of Steibelt's music. He made it sound exactly what it was: crude and unsophisticated. He then began to improvise. And boy, did he improvise. He imitated Steibelt's playing, he unpicked it and put it back together again, he played some *tremolandos*, emphasising their absurdity. He played in a way no salon audience had heard before, and that Steibelt could not have believed was humanly possible.

It is easy to picture that powerful head, hair untamed, clothes inappropriate, fingers moving in a blur, no doubt singing, shouting, quite possibly hurling insults at the Prussian, who was probably sitting, back erect, powdered wig in place, clothes perfectly fitting, fingers curling tighter and tighter, as he realised he was not just being outplayed, he was being humiliated—in front of the most sophisticated musical gathering in the most sophisticated musical city in Europe.

Steibelt did not sit that way for long. With Beethoven still playing, he rose from his chair and strode out of the salon. He made it clear he never wanted to meet Beethoven again, and that if ever he was invited to perform again in Vienna, he would do so only if Beethoven was not present. In fact he took even more drastic action than that. He abandoned his tour and returned to Berlin to nurse his wounds. Some years later he went to St. Petersburg and remained there for the rest of his life. He never returned to Vienna, and never met Beethoven again.

As for Beethoven, he was now—if there was any doubt before— the undisputed master of the keyboard in Vienna, if not Europe. Even Hummel, greatly admired, could not touch him. And following the drubbing of Steibelt, Beethoven was never again asked to take part in an improvisation contest. His position as Vienna's supreme piano virtuoso was established once and for all.

———

The public event that had a profound impact on Beethoven's life took place on 2 April 1800, and, if less dramatic than the Steibelt encounter, was of much more importance to Beethoven. It marked his coming of age as a composer, and we should remember that it was as aspiring composer that the young man had come to Vienna; it was as composer that he wanted to make his name, as composer that he wished to earn his place in musical history. Demonstrating his skills at the keyboard was merely the means to that end.

After much lobbying, and a little bit of bribery (the dedication of the two Piano Sonatas, Op. 14, to his wife), Baron von Braun, manager of the imperial court theatres, allowed Beethoven the use of the Burgtheater for a benefit concert, his first in Vienna. This favour was never granted lightly, since it involved no profit for the theatre— after expenses, all profit accrued to the composer—indeed a couple of years later Beethoven was to fall out with Braun when he refused a second benefit concert (despite further similar bribes).

A benefit concert was hard work. It was customary for the beneficiary to decide the programme, naturally, but also calculate ticket prices, and even sell them from his own home. It was his job to hire musicians, arrange rehearsals, have posters and flyers printed and arrange for their distribution. As near to a full house as possible was imperative. It was unusual for a benefit concert to provide much profit, even with a full house, but it was a way of attracting the critics' attention, and—it was hoped—approval. Reputations could be made, and the reverse. All in all, a benefit concert—and this would not be Beethoven's last—was a calculated risk, but on balance worth taking.

Interestingly Beethoven, aged twenty-nine and with his reputation as the city's supreme piano virtuoso unassailably established, still lacked the confidence to stage a concert of his works alone. And so, as well as his newly completed Septet, First Symphony, and piano concerto (it's not known which of the two), he programmed a Mozart symphony, and two pieces from Haydn's oratorio *The Creation*. For good measure he threw in what he knew he was best at, a guaranteed audience pleaser: 'Herr Ludwig van Beethoven will improvise on the pianoforte.' A long concert, but not unusually so for the time, which was programmed to start at 6:30 p.m.

It was not a success, or at the best had a mixed result. Again, not for the last time in his career, there were disagreements over who was to conduct, with Beethoven favouring one, but the orchestra refusing to play under him and preferring another. There was also clearly not enough rehearsal, since in the piano concerto, according to the *Allgemeine musikalische Zeitung*, 'the players did not bother to pay any attention to the soloist, and in the symphony they became so lax that no effort on the part of the conductor could drag any fire out of them, particularly the wind instruments'.[5]

Consolation of a sort was that the newspaper's critic thought the piano concerto had 'a great deal of taste and feeling', and that the symphony contained 'considerable art, novelty, and a wealth of ideas'. We do not know what the critic thought of the Septet, but according to Czerny it became so popular so fast that Beethoven could not bear to hear it!

Far from being discouraged, Beethoven threw himself into more composing. He embarked on another symphony (his Second), setting that aside to work on a commission for a ballet, *Die Geschöpfe des Prometheus* (*The Creatures of Prometheus*).[6] He also composed more piano sonatas and a violin sonata.

But there was no escaping the cloud hanging over him, the dreadful affliction that was beginning to affect every aspect of his life, which instead of improving or magically disappearing, was worsening. What should he do? What could be done?

—

Suddenly, unexpectedly, Beethoven' closest friend from his Bonn days, his childhood—even closer than Wegeler—Stephan von Breuning, arrived in Vienna. It was a sad development that brought him. Elector Maximilian Franz, who had made it possible for Beethoven to come to Vienna, was in ailing health, and the Teutonic Order con-sidered it prudent to appoint a successor, should the worst happen. This meant convening a Grand Chapter in Vienna. Stephan, now a qualified lawyer working for the Order, came to Vienna to attend the meeting. In the event he took a job at the War Ministry in Vi-enna and remained in the city for the rest of his life. He will feature many more times in these pages, as Beethoven's closest, and albeit with severe disruptions, most constant friend.

Although I can offer no proof of this, I believe it was Stephan's arrival in Vienna that unlocked Beethoven's denial of his deafness. At last there was someone he could confide in, and trust. If he told Stephan to say nothing to anyone, he could rely on Stephan to com-ply. I imagine the two old friends sitting up late into the night as Beethoven brings Stephan up to date on his musical activities, the concerts, salon recitals, the relative merits, pianistic and otherwise, of his young female pupils, and then pours his heart out over his encroaching deafness. I imagine Stephan's horror, no doubt diplo-matically concealed, and even discreet attempts to ascertain how bad the problem was by speaking ever more quietly. He would soon have realised that it was serious.

We know the two men were overjoyed to meet up again, and spent a lot of time together. In a letter dated 29 June 1801, Beethoven writes:

> *Steffen[7] Breuning is now in Vienna and we meet almost every day. It does me good to revive the old feelings of friendship. He re-ally has become an excellent, splendid fellow, who is well informed and who, like all of us more or less, has his heart in the right place.*

Ah yes, that letter. It can lay claim to being the most important letter Beethoven wrote among the thousands of letters and notes he wrote in his entire life, because as far as we know it was the first time Beethoven set down on paper that he was having a problem with his hearing.

It was written to Dr. Franz Wegeler. No surprise, then, that he chose to reveal this intimate detail to an old childhood friend who was now a qualified doctor. To begin with he beats about the bush a bit, writing about how much he would love to see Father Rhine again, talking about his earnings from composition, and concerts he has given and hopes to give. Then, out of the blue, without so much as a new paragraph, this:

> *But that jealous demon, my wretched health, has put a nasty spoke in my wheel, and it amounts to this, that for the last three years my hearing has become weaker and weaker.*

He then talks of his health in general, and absurd remedies various doctors have given him—evidence that he has at least begun seeking medical advice—which might have helped his diarrhoea and colic, but has done nothing to improve his hearing, as they assured him would happen.

Then, a few sentences later:

> *My ears continue to hum and buzz day and night. I must confess that I lead a miserable life. For almost two years I have ceased to attend any social functions, simply because I find it impossible to say to people: I am deaf. If I had any other profession I might be able to cope with my infirmity. But in my profession it is a terrible handicap ... As for the spoken voice, it is surprising that some people have never noticed my deafness. But since I have always been liable to fits of absent-mindedness, they attribute my hardness of hearing to that. Sometimes I can scarcely hear a person who speaks softly. I can hear sounds, it is true, but cannot make out the words.*

But if anyone shouts, I can't bear it. Heaven alone knows what is to become of me.

This is absolutely remarkable. For a start he gives a graphic description of his symptoms. Secondly he acknowledges how much more devastating this is for a musician than for anyone else. Thirdly, he provides evidence he has tried to conceal the problem, and—arguably most remarkable of all—he admits not only to absent-mindedness, but to the fact that everybody knows he's absent-minded!

Only in the privacy of a letter to an old and much trusted friend could we expect someone of Beethoven's character to pour his heart out like that. It is more than a *cri de cœur*, it is an act of self-confession.

Unsurprisingly he begs Wegeler to say nothing to anyone about his deafness, not even to Lorchen,[8] but urges him to write to the doctor he is currently seeing in Vienna. We do not know whether Wegeler did.

One other nice detail. Beethoven asks Wegeler to send the portrait of his grandfather, the *Kapellmeister*, to him in Vienna. This is the painting Beethoven knew as a child, and that his father pawned. This Wegeler did. Beethoven treasured it, and it hung on the wall of every apartment he lived in until his death.

We owe Wegeler an enormous debt of gratitude for preserving the letter. Sadly, Beethoven was not as careful with the letter that Wegeler wrote in reply. None survives. But we know he replied, because Beethoven wrote again to him five months later, and began by thanking him for his concern, and saying he was applying herbs to his belly, as Wegeler recommended.

This is another remarkable letter, for two very different reasons. First, taken with the earlier letter, it gives an extraordinary insight into just what the doctors in Vienna were putting him through. One prescribed cold baths, another warm baths. A third put almond oil in his ears, which made his hearing even worse. There was a suggestion that he try a new-fangled technique called Galvinism, though there is no evidence he actually did. The doctor who prescribed warm baths, a distinguished army surgeon, whose daughter Stephan von Breuning was to marry, then came up with something entirely novel.

He soaked the bark of the poisonous plant *Daphne mezereum* in water, strapped it to Beethoven's arms, and told him to allow the bark to dry. As it dried, it shrank, tightening the skin underneath and causing blisters to form. These the doctor lanced—to relieve Beethoven's deafness. It might have failed to achieve that (although Beethoven writes that he cannot deny the humming and buzzing in his ears was slightly less), but what it did do was cause Beethoven enormous pain in his arms, and make playing the piano impossible. He soon gave it—and the doctor—up.

The second reason this letter is important is that it contains a sentence so extraordinary, so unexpected, that you really do have to read it several times to make sure it says what you think it says. There he is, writing about his hearing problems again, when suddenly ...

> *My poor hearing haunted me everywhere like a ghost, and I avoided—all human society. I seemed to be a misanthrope, but I really am not one any longer. This change has been brought about by a dear charming girl who loves me and whom I love. After two years I am again enjoying a few blissful moments, and for the first time I feel that—marriage might bring me happiness. Unfortunately she is not of my class—and at the moment—I certainly could not marry—I really am far too busy bustling about ...*

Beethoven was in love! Despite all his problems, health and otherwise, the thought of marriage was on his mind, though the letter rambles on in some detail about his work and problems without mentioning love or marriage again.[9]

So who was the object of his affections, the young woman whom he considered below his class, and who he believed was as much in love with him as he was with her? The evidence points conclusively to one of his pupils, Countess Giulietta (Julia) Guicciardi, aged sixteen in 1801. His description of her as being beneath him socially seems somewhat disingenuous. Her father was a senior Austrian civil servant at the Austro-Bohemian court chancellery in Vienna, and her mother closely related to the aristocratic Hungarian family Brunsvik (who will feature again in these pages).

What certainly is true is that the Guicciardi family was not particularly well off, did not move in the same social strata as Beethoven's patrons, and would certainly have derived some cachet from the famous composer's obvious attraction to Julia. We know few details about the progress of the romance, or whether it really was a mutual attraction. But Thayer, who evidently spoke to people in Vienna who had direct knowledge, albeit many years after the event, states that it is his opinion that Beethoven went so far as to propose marriage, and that Julia was 'not indisposed' to accept it, that her mother was in favour of the match, but that her father forbade it on the grounds that Beethoven was

> *a man without rank, fortune, or permanent engagement; a man, too, of character and temperament so peculiar, and afflicted with the incipient stages of an infirmity which, if not arrested and cured, must deprive him of all hope of obtaining any high and remunerative official appointment, and at length compel him to abandon his career as the great pianoforte virtuoso.*

Another painful rejection, then, for Beethoven, no doubt made worse by the knowledge that his deafness lay behind it, and that his affliction was now common knowledge.

As for Julia, she went on to marry a mediocre musician by the name of Count Gallenberg, with whom she moved to Italy.[10] Her place in history is assured, though, through Beethoven's decision to dedicate his new piano sonata to her, a sonata published under the title 'Sonata quasi una fantasia', but known to us today—thanks to a music critic who compared it to the moon setting over Lake Lucerne—as the 'Moonlight' Sonata.

———

Once again Beethoven's deafness had stood in the way of his aspirations, in this case desires and longing of the most personal kind. How long would it be before this dreadful affliction began to affect his life's work, his *raison d'être*, his calling, the sole path he was capable of pursuing?

And then, in early 1802, one of his doctors, Dr. Johann Adam Schmidt, came up with the only sensible suggestion any doctor ever made to him. He advised Beethoven to get out of Vienna, to leave the dust and dirt and bustle of the city behind, to free his ears of the rasping jangle of carriage wheels grinding over uneven cobbles, to distance himself from the demands of publishers, to go somewhere where his hearing loss would not be an obvious problem, not lead to questioning and veiled comment. And also to allow him to put the pain of marital rejection behind him. In short, to rest, relax, and compose.

Dr. Schmidt had a friend who owned a small cottage for rent in a small village north of the city, known for its warm springs, its gently meandering stream, its woodland, its calm. The name of the village was Heiligenstadt.

CHAPTER SEVEN

ONLY MY ART HELD ME BACK

IN WHICH BEETHOVEN CONSIDERS SUICIDE

THE BEETHOVEN WHO ARRIVED IN HEILIGEN-STADT in April 1802 was a very different man from that of two years earlier. Then, he was the undisputed supreme piano virtuoso in the city; he had staged his first benefit concert, which even with mixed results established him firmly as the city's leading composer (a mantle the ageing Haydn was quite content to cede), and he was falling in love with a girl who appeared to be reciprocating his interest. There was a problem with his hearing, certainly, but several doctors were trying to tackle it, at the same time assuring him it was only a matter of time before the problem was solved.

Two years on, and Baron Braun had reneged on his promise of a second benefit concert (despite the inducement of more dedications), his amorous ambitions had been quashed, and his deafness was worse. In fact it had become so much worse that he had finally lost faith in his doctors, and now believed nothing would stop the deterioration. If the best that medicine could come up with was a recommendation to take a break, it showed there was nothing more that science could offer.

In one sense, getting away for a break was the last thing Beethoven needed. He would be on his own in a small cottage—no one to converse with, eat and drink with, step out to the tavern with. He would have hour upon hour in which to brood, which would lead him naturally to magnify his problems. If he arrived depressed, that was likely to become worse as the weeks passed.

On the other hand, Beethoven liked solitude. There are count-less anecdotes of how he would be oblivious to everything around him while composing, how his favourite activity was to walk for hours across country, beating time to imaginary sounds in his head, stopping to jot down thoughts on scraps of paper. If nothing else, he would have time to compose without distraction.

And compose he did. He brought his Second Symphony to fru-ition, and embarked on new piano sonatas and piano variations.[1] Also, Heiligenstadt was only an hour's carriage ride from the city—it was not unreasonable to expect visits from family and friends.

That is what happened. Brother Carl, who was now handling his elder brother's business affairs—upsetting publishers with de-mands for ever larger amounts of money—came to see Beethoven to discuss a commission for new piano sonatas from a Swiss publisher. And Ferdinand Ries had arrived in Vienna a few months earlier and was proving himself invaluable to Beethoven.

Ries was the son of the leader of the electoral orchestra in Bonn, Franz Ries, who had given Beethoven violin lessons. He was four-teen years younger than Beethoven, and as a tousle-haired boy had been sent by his father to the teenage Beethoven for piano lessons. Their friendship thus went back a long way, and only the age differ-ence prevented Ries being as close a friend to Beethoven as Wegeler and Stephan von Breuning.

With the French occupying the Rhineland, young men were be-ing enlisted to fight alongside the French. But Ries had a problem with vision in one eye, and needed to wear an eye patch. This ex-empted him from service.

Ries had shown remarkable musical talent very early in life, and his father sent him to Vienna in 1801 to further his career.[2] He wrote to Beethoven asking him to look out for his son. In the event Ries, who was totally dedicated to Beethoven, did far more for him, acting as secretary, helper, assistant, and endured all his moods and vicissitudes with patient good grace. His memoirs, written with Wegeler, provide unique insights into Beethoven. Indeed it is his report of one incident, which almost certainly took place in Heiligenstadt, that provides stark and graphic evidence of just how far Beethoven's deafness had progressed.

One beautiful morning, after breakfast, Beethoven suggested he and Ries take a walk in the surrounding countryside. At one point Ries drew Beethoven's attention to a shepherd in amongst the trees who was playing sweetly on a flute made from lilac wood. Beethoven could not hear him. They stayed in the same spot for half an hour, but still Beethoven could not hear the sounds of the flute. Ries remarks that Beethoven became extremely quiet and gloomy. He assured Beethoven that he couldn't hear the flute either (which wasn't true), but it did nothing to lift his mood.

Fleshing out the bare detail Ries gives us, we can imagine that both men could see the shepherd, that Beethoven strained to hear, changed his position, walked a bit nearer, retreated again, but after half an hour of this, still nothing. Ries writes that Breuning had told him in Vienna that Beethoven was having problems, but this was graphic evidence of the seriousness of it.

In a final line to the anecdote, Ries writes that when Beethoven was occasionally really happy, he could be almost boisterous, 'but this rarely happened'.

Ries must have worried about leaving Beethoven alone in the cottage, and probably tried to persuade him to return to the city. But Beethoven was staying put. At least Ries knew he was composing, so his creativity was not being affected by loneliness or worry over his hearing. Even if he had not been able to hear the shepherd, he was still able to hear the piano in his room and the sounds of music in his head.

Also Ries knew he was comfortable. The cottage had a house-keeper and daughter who between them provided Beethoven with all his meals, and kept his room tidy. The cottage was beautifully situated, with windows looking out on a stream, fields and woods in one direction, and towards St. Michael's Church in the other.³ Ries knew too that Beethoven paid frequent visits to the spa, basking in the natural warm waters that welled up from below. It might not help his deafness, but it would certainly improve his well-being.

Beethoven's stay was not planned with a definite departure date, but probably no one—himself included—expected him to stay beyond the summer. In the event he stayed a full six months, not leaving until mid-October. During the final few weeks an extraordinary change came over him.

As summer gave way to autumn and the evenings became longer, so Beethoven withdrew within himself. He carefully and methodically weighed up where he was in life, what was happening to him, what was likely to happen in the future. It resulted in a remarkable decision, one that he could have allowed to plunge him even further into despair. Instead, it had quite the opposite effect.

He decided, at the age of thirty-one and three-quarters, to write his Last Will and Testament.

This is such an extraordinary document, raising questions as well as answering them, that it merits close analysis. It is, for biographers, scholars, musicologists, indeed for any lover of Beethoven's music who wants to understand him better, the single most important piece of writing he ever produced that was not in the form of musical notes. Here it is in full:

For my brothers—Carl—and — Beethoven
Oh all you people who think and say that I am hostile to you, or that I am stubborn, or that I hate mankind, you do not realise the wrong that you do me. You think you understand, but you do not know the secret cause of my seeming that way. From my childhood on, my heart and mind were disposed only towards

tenderness and goodwill. I even knew I was destined to accomplish great deeds. But consider this: for the last six years I have suffered from a terrible condition, made worse by stupid doctors, yet hoping from one year to the next that it would improve, but finally realising that I'd been deceived, that I would have to face the prospect of <u>a lasting malady</u> (at least that it would take many years to be cured, or even that it might never be). Born with an ardent and lively temperament, from an early age I had to cut myself off from society in all its diversity and lead my own life. And if from time to time I wanted more than anything not to have to do that, oh how hard I had to fight against the dreadful consequences of my poor hearing. And I wasn't yet in a position where I could say to people: Speak louder, shout, for I am deaf. Ah, how could I possibly explain that I was deficient in the <u>one sense</u> that should have been more highly developed in me than anyone, a sense that I was once in full possession of, to an extent in fact that few in my profession are or ever were? Oh I cannot do it, so forgive me when you see me shrink back, although I really want to mingle with you. My misfortune is doubly bad, because through it people misjudge me. For me there can be no enjoyment in other men's company, no stimulating conversations or exchange of ideas. I must be totally alone, except in cases of the direst emergency. I must live like an exile. If I go near to a group of people I am overcome with anxiety, and I am frightened I will be put in a position where my condition will be noticed. And so I was told by my one sensible doctor to spend these few months in the country, to rest my hearing as much as possible. Occasionally—albeit against my natural disposition—I have wished to have company. I have on occasions yielded to the temptation. But what a humiliation when someone next to me heard a flute in the distance and I heard nothing, or someone <u>heard the shepherd sing</u>, and again I heard nothing. Such things have brought me near to despair. Only *a little more and I would even have ended my life. Only <u>my art</u>, that is all that held me back. It would have been impossible for me to leave this world until I had brought forth everything that was within me, and so I continued to eke out a miserable existence— truly miserable, my condition so sensitive, that a sudden change of mood could plunge me from happiness into despair—<u>Patience</u>— that is what I must now let guide me, and what I have let guide me—I hope above all that I will be resolute enough to wait until pitiless fate determines to break the thread. Maybe my health will improve, maybe not. Whatever, I am prepared. Already in my 28th year I was forced to accept my fate, and that is not easy, in fact it is harder for an artist than for anybody. Divine One, you alone can see into my innermost soul. You understand me, you know that I love my fellow men and want only to do good. Oh my friends, when you read this understand that you did me an injustice, and should there exist in the world any man as unfortunate as I, let him comfort himself in the knowledge that, as I have done, he too can accomplish everything that is within his power, and be elevated into the ranks of worthy artists and great men. To you my brothers—Carl—and — , as soon as I am dead ask Professor Schmidt in my name, assuming he is still living, to describe my illness to you, and attach this document to my medical history, so that after my death, people might begin to understand just a little about me. Also I declare you both as the heirs to my small fortune (if it can be called that). Divide it fairly, be good friends and help each other. You know that whatever you did against me I have long since forgiven. You my brother Carl have my special thanks for the proven devotion you have shown me, especially of late. My wish is that you may both have a better more carefree life than I had. Teach your children <u>Virtue</u>, for it alone can bring them happiness, not money, and I speak from experience. It was Virtue which lifted me up when I was wretched. I* owe it to Virtue, together with my art, that I did not end my own life. And so farewell and love one another. I thank all my friends, especially <u>Prince Lichnowsky and Professor Schmidt</u>. The instruments Prince L. gave me I wish to be kept by one of you. But do not quarrel over them, and if they can be of some use to you, go ahead and sell them. It makes me so happy to know I can help you, even from my grave—if that is to be the case, I would gladly hasten towards my death, and if it should come before I have been able to create all the art that I am capable of, then even given my harsh fate it will be too soon, and I will wish so much that it had come later—yet I shall still be satisfied, for will it not release me from my endless suffering? Come death when you will, I shall face you with courage. Farewell and forget me not when I am dead, for I deserve to be remembered, just as I so often remembered you during my life, and tried to make you happy: remain so—

Heiglnstadt [sic] Ludwig van Beethoven
on 6th October
1 8 0 2 [seal]

For my brothers Carl—and
To be read and executed after my death
Heiglnstadt [sic] on 10th October 1802—and so I bid thee farewell—with such sorrow—to think of the hope I had when I came here, that I might be cured even just very slightly—that hope I must now realise has abandoned me completely, as the leaves fall from the trees in autumn and fade away. Thus has—thus has my hope also withered, so that it is now no more than it was when I came here—but I will go on—even that Noble Courage—which so often inspired me in those beautiful days of summer—it has gone for ever—Oh Providence—let one last day of <u>pure joy</u> be granted me—for so long now the innermost echo of true joy has been denied me—Oh when—Oh when Oh Divine One—shall I

be able to share it again with Nature and Mankind,—Never?—
no—Oh that would be too cruel.[4]

The main body of the Will is written over two and a half pages, ending with signature and seal. The last part, beginning with instruction to his brothers, is written on the fourth page, but above the fold. It was clearly added as an afterthought, after he had finished and folded the document.

A straightforward Will, in one sense, leaving his effects to his brothers, but also a *cri de cœur*, full of self-pity one moment, defiance the next. Through it runs the single thread of his deafness. He has, finally, decided to confront it head on, to write about it, to think about it, to consider its effect on his artistic calling, to understand that for a musician it is a fatal defect. He talks about suicide, how he has considered it in the past but only his art held him back, how he holds it in reserve for the future. In his whole life, neither before or after, did he write a document of such intensely personal thoughts.

What, then, is it? One thing I am utterly convinced of: it is *not* is a suicide note. Yes, he talks about suicide, but he is clearly not about to commit it. His art, he says, saved him from taking his own life. 'Come death when you will, I shall face you with courage.' Not the words of a man about to take his own life. But they are the words of a man who might decide to take his own life one day. When might that be? When 'pitiless fate determines to break the thread'. And what might that mean? We have no clear answer, but I am convinced he is saying that when the day comes when he can no longer hear his own music, and to compose has become impossible, *if* that day ever comes, then he will take matters into his own hands and obtain release from his 'endless suffering'.

We know now, of course, that that day never came, that he continued to compose to within days of his death twenty-five years later. He struggled, certainly, but he was still able to compose. That points to two factors, one intangible, one more practical. The courage that he speaks of in his Will never left him, for which he, and generations of human beings, can be grateful. It further suggests that he never totally lost his hearing. Something always got through, however distorted, right to the end.

Some commentators have seen the first line of the postscript, 'and so I bid thee farewell', where he suddenly slips into the more familiar, and poetic, 'thee', as an announcement of intended suicide. But in the original German, just as in the English translation, this is entirely ambiguous. He could just as easily be referring to the village of Heiligenstadt, which is altogether less dramatic.

There are several other points of interest concerning what is known to history as the Heiligenstadt Testament. The first, and most evident, anomaly is that he does not write his brother Nikolaus Johann's name. Those spaces are there in the original document. In fact it applies to Carl too, though he filled in the name later (it fits oddly into the space). What could this mean? Plenty, or nothing.

To take the 'plenty' explanation first. Both Beethoven's brothers, when they came to Vienna, decided to be known by their second name, thus Caspar Carl became Carl, and Nikolaus Johann became Johann. Beethoven clearly did not like this. It represented a break with the past of which he did not approve. He might also have considered it pretentious, and there might have been a twinge of jealousy in that he had only one Christian name and so could not do likewise. Also, as elder brother and head of the family, they should have consulted him first. Either they failed to do so, or if they did they ignored his objections.

Why, then, was he ultimately able to bring himself to write Carl's name, but not Johann's? Because Johann was the name of their father—the man Beethoven considered ruined his childhood, who dragged him from bed on his drunken return from the tavern and forced him to play the piano, who abused him verbally and very probably physically too by rapping him across the knuckles when he played a wrong note, who as he descended into alcoholism brought shame upon the family, whom Beethoven as a teenager had to rescue once from police jail, who made his wife's life a misery, and from whom Beethoven had finally managed to escape, and whose death probably came as something of a relief to his eldest son.

And here was his youngest brother consciously adopting the father's name! Probably because he knew the pain it would cause his eldest brother, and be some sort of revenge against the sibling who had inherited all the talent.

Given Beethoven's fraught relationship with both brothers in the years to come, this explanation, dramatic, even incomprehensible though it might seem, is not all that far-fetched.

The far simpler explanation is that since Beethoven was aware his Will was a quasi-legal document, he was not sure how to address his brothers, and would leave Johann's name out until he took legal advice on his return to Vienna.

Given the family history, coupled with Beethoven's character, I believe it is not unreasonable to subscribe to the 'plenty' theory.

A further point of interest is that, by Beethoven's standards, the document is remarkably neatly written. The handwriting is quite precise, the lines narrowly but tidily spaced. On the first page, roughly A4 size, he fits in no fewer than forty-five lines, on the second page, forty-three. Despite the emotion of what he is writing, the stream of consciousness concerning intimate details of his life, the writing nowhere becomes ragged. It would be tempting to say he wrote it at several sittings, but the way the sentences flow into each other suggest a single sitting as far down as the signature. This is reinforced by the single date.

There are some ink blots at the top of page two, and one or two crossings out lower down both pages one and two, but nothing that would prevent this Will being accepted in law. It is, in fact, considerably neater than most of his musical manuscripts. He is clearly taking great care to make sure the document is legally valid.

It is very possible he tried out his wording first on other pieces of paper, and then copied them onto the final version. The punctuation, and individual sentences, suggest this. By contrast, the final paragraph on the folded page is redolent with dashes—nineteen in just fifteen lines, with only a handful of commas and no full stops—making it certain this was added at the last moment in a single unprepared sitting.

The final curiosity is that, on completing it, he folded the document twice, across the centre and then lengthways across the centre again, so that it was no wider than an envelope, and hid it. He not only hid it in his bag in Heiligenstadt, he hid it when he returned to Vienna, and kept it with him, hidden, for the rest of his life. He must have remembered it and seen it each time he moved apartment—more than sixty times, including summer sojourns, in the remaining years of his life—but he never told anybody about it, never consulted a lawyer about it, never attempted to have it enacted.

Now that really *is* curious.

These are all fascinating details, but ultimately they pale before the most important set of inferences the Heiligenstadt Testament allows us to make about Beethoven's life. He had, at last, come to terms with his deafness. He had confronted it, and in a sense defeated it. He was now in control of it, not the other way round. He also no longer cared for it to be kept a secret. His deafness was now part of him. It was what he was. He was also now in control of his life. He would choose to end it when he thought fit. He alone would make that decision.

God gets barely a look in. The closest he comes is in the sentence: 'Divine One, you alone can see into my innermost soul.' But the word he uses is *'Gottheit'*, which properly translates as 'Divinity'. It is more nebulous, ethereal, than 'God'. And in the postscript he refers only to 'Providence' (*Vorsehung*), which is a spiritual power rather than a deity, and again to *'Gottheit'*.

Beethoven has not only come to terms with, and therefore conquered, his deafness. He has taken control of his life. The Beethoven who arrived in Heiligenstadt six months earlier was to an extent a broken man. But the man who returned to the city had a new resolve. He still had much to give the world, and he was determined to go on doing that until it became impossible. He would no longer mourn for his loss of hearing. By writing the Testament he had buried it.

On returning to Vienna he said to Czerny, 'I am not very well satisfied with the work I have done thus far. From this day on I shall take a new way.'

And take a new way he most certainly did. He was about to embark on the richest period of his life, when the works that flowed from him were not just new, and different, but unlike anything any composer had written before. Not for nothing is it known as Beethoven's Heroic Period.

CHAPTER EIGHT

EGYPTIAN HIEROGLYPHICS

NAPOLEON IS NO MORE THAN 'A COMMON TYRANT'

B EETHOVEN, AGAINST ALL EXPECTATIONS— including his own—landed a job. In January 1803 he was appointed composer-in-residence at the Theater an der Wien, which, as the title implies, came with a small apartment in the theatre.

It's worth a brief detour to explain the background to this, particularly since it will introduce into the story—albeit briefly—one of those colourful figures that the world of the arts can occasionally throw up, and who, were it not for a fortunate set of circumstances, would have disappeared without trace. Instead they achieve a certain immortality.

Vienna, at the turn of the century, enjoyed an extremely healthy theatrical life. There were several theatres that came under imperial administration, headed by Baron von Braun; the most prestigious was the Burgtheater. There were also a number of independent theatres in direct competition with them, of which the most important (to our story as well) was the new Theater an der Wien.

Crucially, the Theater an der Wien—named for the small river that ran past it to the Danube Canal—stood outside the city wall, the Bastei. It was therefore suburban, which gave it an entirely different feel from the ambience of the imperial court theatres—more relaxed, more innovative, and favoured more by ordinary suburban people, rather than the nobility.[1] There were no purpose-built concert halls in Vienna as yet (London alone could boast that), and musicians had to compete with all other theatrical pursuits to secure a theatre—

which is why Beethoven failed to obtain the Burgtheater for his second benefit concert.

The Theater an der Wien was built in 1800–1801 as the result of an unlikely collaboration between a wealthy businessman and a thoroughly eccentric theatre director whose elaborate and expensive productions had led to huge debts, which cost him his job at his previous theatre. The two men needed to do something quickly to establish their theatre, and they hit on works by the Paris-based Italian composer Luigi Cherubini. Just as they began to taste success, Braun travelled to Paris and signed up Cherubini exclusively to the court theatres.

And then the eccentric theatre director made the second decision of genius in his career. The first, for which the world remembers him today, was to write the libretto for Mozart's *The Magic Flute*, playing Papageno in the premiere. The second was to engage Beethoven as composer-in-residence at the Theater an der Wien—all the greater stroke of genius since what he wanted was opera, and Beethoven had not as yet composed one.

Beethoven was about to embark on the most important creative period of his life to date, producing works that would echo down the centuries. To a large extent, we owe the somewhat carefree conditions in which he was able to do this to a man who was 'a strange compound of wit and absurdity, of poetic instinct and grotesque humour, of shrewd and profitable enterprise and lavish prodigality, who lived like a prince and was to die like a pauper'—but not before the name of Emmanuel Schikaneder became forever linked with two immortals of music.

—

There was a small downside to the accommodation in the Theater an der Wien that came with the job. Beethoven's brother Carl moved in with him. We do not know which of the two brothers was the instigator of this, but given Beethoven's antagonism towards both his brothers, it cannot have made for harmonious living. Carl was now more and more running his elder brother's business affairs, and making enemies in the process. He even managed to upset the publisher Simrock, a friend of Beethoven from his Bonn days, who described Carl's demands as 'impertinent and incorrigible'.

But whatever fraternal tension there might have been in the small apartment in the Theater an der Wien, there was no stopping Beethoven's creativity. He had now completed his Third Piano Concerto, and had composed an oratorio, *Christus am Ölberge* (*Christ on the Mount of Olives*).

An immediate bonus of his new job was a benefit concert on 5 April 1803 in the Theater an der Wien—a sort of public snub to Baron Braun and the imperial court theatres. This time he needed to do no persuading, no cajoling; the theatre was his, and he could perform any programme he wished. He did not hold back. He put together a programme so ambitious, with so little time to rehearse, it was almost doomed from the start. In fact, so ad hoc was the whole thing that the announcements in the press advertising the concert stated only that Beethoven would produce his *Christus am Ölberge*, the other pieces to be performed being announced later on posters.

No complete programme has survived, but we know that Beethoven intended giving his First Symphony, the premiere of his Second Symphony, the premiere of his Third Piano Concerto, and the premiere of his oratorio *Christus am Ölberge*. It is also highly likely he planned to interject some vocal pieces as well. Nothing if not ambitious. And, as was not unusual with Beethoven, preparations continued right up until the last minute.

On the morning of the concert, at around 5 a.m., he summoned Ries, who gives a compelling account of what he found. Beethoven was sitting up in bed, writing on separate sheets of manuscript paper. Ries asked him what it was he wanted. He replied that he was adding trombones to the score of *Christus am Ölberge*. Ries was dumbfounded. The final rehearsal was due to begin at 8 a.m. Though Ries does not say so, he must have remonstrated as tactfully as he could with Beethoven, pointing out that it was surely too late to add an entirely new instrumental section to the orchestra. For one thing, there was no time for the copyists to write out the parts, and in any case where on earth would they be able to find trombonists at three hours' notice so early in the morning?

Beethoven was adamant: he wanted trombonists, and I imagine Ries scouring the city at dawn to find them. Find them he did, and at the performance in the evening they played from Beethoven's hand-written manuscript sheets!

Before that there was the rehearsal, and it was, unsurprisingly, a disaster. Beethoven drove the musicians for hour after hour, until by 2:30 p.m. they were exhausted. Fortunately Prince Lichnowsky—possibly alerted by Ries, who sensed problems—attended the rehearsal from the start, and ordered bread and butter, cold meat and wine, to be brought in large baskets. He invited the musicians to help themselves which, according to Ries, they did 'with both hands', re-establishing good feelings—good enough, in fact, to risk one more rehearsal of the oratorio at Lichnowsky's urging.

The concert began at six o'clock, but threatened to be so long that several pieces were omitted. Definitely performed were the First and Second Symphonies, the Third Piano Concerto, and *Christus am Ölberge*.

The concert master of the theatre, Ignaz Seyfried, later wrote a fascinating account of the performance of the piano concerto, which gives a wonderful insight into the chaotic working mind of the towering genius that is Beethoven.

Beethoven asked Seyfried to turn the pages for him. But, 'as was so often the case', says Seyfried, Beethoven had not had time to put it all down on paper. Seyfried's blood ran cold when he looked at the piano part on the stand and saw almost nothing but empty sheets of paper. 'At the most on one page or the other a few Egyptian hieroglyphics which were wholly unintelligible to me, scribbled down to serve as clues for him ... He gave me a secret glance whenever he was at the end of one of the invisible passages, and my scarcely concealable anxiety not to miss the decisive moment amused him greatly, and he laughed heartily at the jovial supper which we ate afterwards.'

Which, if nothing else, demonstrates that Beethoven was capable of a sense of humour at least after the event. Seyfried lived with the memory for years to come. To this day I cannot hear the Third Piano Concerto without thinking of the hapless Seyfried and Beethoven's 'Egyptian hieroglyphics'.

The good humour at the post-concert supper probably dissipated when the reviews came out. The *Freymüthige* found the two symphonies, and certain passages in the oratorio, very beautiful, but thought the oratorio 'too long, too artificial in structure, and lacking expressiveness, especially in the vocal parts'. The *Zeitung für die elegante Welt* liked the First Symphony, but thought the Second strived too hard to be new and surprising. It also said Beethoven's performance of the Third Piano Concerto was 'not completely to the public's satisfaction'. But Ries would have been pleased to read that the paper particularly liked the Seraph's air in the *Christus*, with trombone accompaniment which 'in particular makes an excellent effect'.

Some concert-goers were harsher even than the critics, and prepared to say so publicly. Angry that the *Allgemeine musikalische Zeitung*, the most respected of the musical journals, described the *Christus am Ölberge* as having been received with 'extraordinary approval', even opining with remarkable foresight that Beethoven in time could 'effect a revolution in music like Mozart's', a correspondent wrote to the paper flatly contradicting this. 'In the interest of truth, I am obliged to contradict the report ... Beethoven's cantata did not please.'

Interestingly Beethoven himself somewhat rejected the oratorio and was later to make substantial changes to it. Possibly the criticism was offset by the fact that he made a clear profit of 1800 florins on the evening, a substantial sum. His residency at the Theater an der Wien had therefore got off to a solid financial start, even if the musical results were somewhat mixed.

—

Not one to learn from his mistakes, Beethoven again ran things very tight at a smaller-scale, but highly prestigious, recital just a few weeks later. A brilliant young violinist arrived in Vienna from England, by the name of George Bridgetower. Poor George Bridgetower. Rather like Schikaneder, his brush with the greatest living musician looked set to immortalise him too, but alas it was not to be.

Bridgetower, son of an African father and Polish (or German) mother, had established a fine reputation for himself, being employed by the Prince of Wales, and remaining in his employ when he succeeded to the throne as George IV. His letter of introduction on arriving in Vienna gained him access to the highest salons, and Prince Lichnowsky introduced him to Beethoven.

Beethoven heard Bridgetower play, almost certainly accompanying him on the piano, and was seriously impressed. A colleague of Beethoven, the Viennese violinist Ignaz Schuppanzigh (whose name will appear again in these pages), ran the summer series of concerts in the pavilion of the Augarten public park,[2] north of the city across the Danube Canal. The suggestion was made—it is not clear by whom, probably Schuppanzigh—that Beethoven should compose a new violin sonata, and he and Mr. Bridgetower would give it its premiere at the inaugural concert of the season on 22 May.

Beethoven agreed. Bridgetower, having probably been forewarned, panicked. He pressed Beethoven to finish the violin part in good time so he could practise it. There was less than a month to the concert, and as far as he knew nothing had yet been written. Beethoven, realising time was short, decided to take the final movement from a sonata he had composed the preceding year, and make it the final movement of the new sonata. That much at least Bridgetower was able to work on.

Beethoven set to work on the opening movement, beginning it with fiendishly difficult double-stopping across all four strings, possibly because Bridgetower had demonstrated he was capable of it. But the movement became ever longer and more complex. In a repeat of what had happened just before the benefit concert the preceding month, Beethoven summoned Ries at 4 a.m. and told him to copy out the violin part for the first movement.

It was clear that the second movement would not be ready in time, and the concert was put back two days, to 24 May. The Augarten concerts were held at 8 a.m. The night before, Beethoven was still writing out the second movement. It is probable Bridgetower, fearing his reputation was about to be torn to tatters, stood over Beethoven, rehearsing as he composed.

At the performance, in the first movement something quite extraordinary happened. In bar 18 of the *Presto,* Beethoven had written a huge arpeggio run just for the piano, up two octaves, down two octaves, up two octaves again, with a final leap from a top note to a bass note. During this virtuosic display, the violinist can do nothing but stand and watch. But Beethoven had marked the *Presto* to be repeated, and in the repeat, when it came to the run, Bridgetower watched Beethoven's fingers fly up and down the keyboard, then he fixed the violin under the chin, and imitated it on the violin.

Beethoven looked up at Bridgetower in utter astonishment. The audience must have held its breath as Beethoven leapt up from the piano stool, ran across to Bridgetower, hugged him, shouted, *'Noch einmal, mein lieber Bursch!'* ('Again, my dear fellow!'), ran back to the piano, played his run, then held down the sustaining key as Bridgetower again copied it on the violin.[3]

The audience was entirely won over, which was no bad thing since Bridgetower was compelled to play the second movement from Beethoven's hastily scribbled manuscript. This he achieved with success, and the third movement, the only movement that Bridgetower had had time to rehearse fully, was flawless.

The performance was a triumph, so much so that Beethoven dedicated the sonata there and then to the Englishman. Sadly for Bridgetower that is not the end of the story.

It might have been at the celebratory supper following the concert, or it might have been shortly afterwards, that Bridgetower made a mistake. He made the mistake of his life. He made an off-colour remark about a lady. Beethoven was appalled, utterly appalled, so much so that he withdrew the dedication from Bridgetower. Bridgetower tried to reason with him, no doubt arguing that it was just a joke, he hadn't meant anything bad by it. He might also have urged Beethoven's friends to intercede on his behalf. But it was no good. Beethoven's mind was made up. Nobody who could say such a thing was to have a Beethoven composition dedicated to him.

Soon afterwards Bridgetower left Vienna, and the two men never met again. Very many years later, Bridgetower was an old man living in poverty in Peckham, South London, where he was visited by a music researcher. He recounted the story of how he had lost the dedication of Beethoven's Violin Sonata through one off-colour remark which led to an altercation over a lady.

There are two sad codas to this story. Bridgetower died in poverty in a home for the destitute. We know this because the woman who witnessed his death signed the death certificate with a cross for her name. He is today buried in Kensal Green cemetery, west of London, his name forgotten to history.

After withdrawing the dedication, Beethoven sent the manuscript to a French violinist living in Paris by the name of Rudolphe Kreutzer, with a dedication to him. The sonata that bears his name, the 'Kreutzer' Sonata, is now acknowledged as the greatest violin sonata by Beethoven, or anyone. And do you know what Monsieur Kreutzer said when he received the manuscript and examined it? *'C'est impossible, c'est la musique du diable, on ne peut pas la jouer'*, and never once performed it in public, the sonata that bears his name.

Bridgetower lived with the knowledge of what he had lost for the rest of his life. Beethoven quickly forgot it. He was moving on to something on an altogether much larger scale.

—

First there was the matter of the opera he had without doubt committed himself to in order to secure the position of composer-in-residence. Schikaneder had just the thing: an opera based on Roman mythology to be entitled *Vestas Feuer* (*Vestal Flame*). He produced a libretto and gave it to Beethoven, who began work. He soon tired of it, finding the sentiments banal. 'Just picture a subject from ancient Rome—with language that comes out of the mouths of our local apple-women,' he wrote in a letter to a friend. There was no reasoning with Schikaneder, who was 'too infatuated with his own opinion' to allow anyone else to improve the libretto.

So Beethoven abandoned the project, a somewhat rash move since it was probable his job depended on producing an opera that Schikaneder could stage.[4] But he had other things on his mind. He had begun work on a new symphony, his Third. It was a symphony that would, quite simply, set music on a new course. It is a cliché, and usually an exaggeration, to say any one thing changed the course of any other thing. In this case it is true. Beethoven's Third Symphony changed the course of music. We are talking here about the 'Eroica'.

As always with Beethoven, ideas began with fragmentary sketches and jottings, but it seems he composed the 'Eroica' in an intensive three-month period in the summer of 1803. This is all the more remarkable in that the work is longer, and more complex, than any symphony hitherto written by anybody. The first movement alone runs to almost 700 bars, anything between fifteen and twenty minutes in performance.

I could spend the next chapter and a half examining the musicological innovations and surprises in the 'Eroica', from the utterly unexpected and startling opening two chords with the descent to C sharp in bar seven, the 'false' horn entry before the recapitulation in the first movement, to the strange decision to make the second movement a funeral march, labelling the third movement 'scherzo', literally 'joke', and borrowing the main theme of the final movement from the finale of his ballet *The Creatures of Prometheus*, composed nearly three years earlier. But true to my pledge to reach the music through the man rather than the man through the music, I will limit myself to aspects that throw light on Beethoven the man.

Beethoven himself was in no doubt he had composed something out of the ordinary, nor were those close to him. Shortly after completing it, but before orchestrating it, he played it on the piano to Ferdinand Ries. Ries wrote to Simrock that a full orchestral performance would make 'Heaven and Earth tremble'. Some months later Ries was at Beethoven's side as the orchestra rehearsed it for the first time. Ries states candidly that the rehearsal was 'horrible'. In bar 394, over extreme *pianissimo* (*ppp*) first and second violins, the lone horn enters with the opening motif, before the full orchestra crashes in *fortissimo* for the recapitulation.

Ries, assuming the horn player had mistimed his entry, said, 'Can't the damned horn player count? That sounded dreadful!' Beethoven looked witheringly at Ries and muttered that the horn player had played exactly what he had written. Ries looked embarrassed and kept quiet. He wrote later that he had come pretty close to receiving a box on the ear, and that Beethoven didn't forgive him for a long time. That horn entry has exercised musicologists and put the fear of God into horn-players ever since.

By far the most illuminating aspect of the 'Eroica', in so far as it throws light on Beethoven's character, is its dedication—or, rather, non-dedication. Beethoven had made no secret of his admiration for Napoleon Bonaparte, a man of the people who had risen through the ranks and was now, as First Consul, leading the people of France in a new era of liberty, equality and brotherhood, following the French Revolution. Indeed, he approved of events in France to such an extent that he had spoken openly of leaving the aristocratic stuffiness of Vienna for good and going to live in Paris.

Ferdinand Ries said Beethoven considered Napoleon as great as the greatest consuls of ancient Rome. This is conjecture, but I can see his friends telling him to keep his voice down in taverns and restaurants as he extolled the virtues of Napoleon and France, Austria's enemy, at the same time knowing that any spies or government agents who might be within earshot would know this was just the eccentric musician who was losing his hearing—he was no harm to anyone.

At what stage Beethoven linked his new symphony with Napoleon is not clear, but he undoubtedly had Napoleon in mind as he composed, because when he had completed the autograph manuscript, he had a fair copy made, which he intended forwarding to Paris through the French Embassy. Was it intended as a gift for Napoleon himself? We don't know, but it's quite possible, since Beethoven wrote at the top of the title page, 'Buonaparte', and at the extreme bottom, 'Luigi van Beethoven'.[5] He probably intended to write the title of the piece in the space between.

In late May 1804 Ferdinand Ries recounts how he went to see Beethoven and gave him the news that a few days earlier, on 20 May, Napoleon had proclaimed himself Emperor of France. Beethoven flew into a rage, shouted out, 'Is he then, too, nothing more than an ordinary human being? Now he, too, will trample on all the rights of man, and just satisfy his own ambition. He will exalt himself above all others and become a tyrant!' He stormed over to the table on which the fair copy of the 'Eroica' score lay, snatched up the title page, tore it in two, and threw it on the floor.

But he did not entirely let go of his admiration for Napoleon. The title page of the copyist's score reads: '*Sinfonia grande/intitolata Buonaparte/del Sigr/Louis van Beethoven*'. Still, though, he could allow his distaste for what Napoleon had done to overwhelm him. In a further fit of temper, he scratched out the name 'Buonaparte' with such force that there is a hole in the paper! And *still* he could not make up his mind. In faded pencil below his own name, he wrote '*geschrieben auf Bonaparte*' ('written on Bonaparte'). He really could not—and never did—make up his mind about the Corsican. What he most certainly *did* do, though, was abandon any serious desire to go and live in Paris.

—

If this behaviour conforms to the irascible Beethoven of legend, it can perhaps be mitigated slightly by the unfortunate turn of events that occurred at this time. The man Beethoven disliked so much, Baron Braun, fed up with the competition provided by the Theater an der Wien, bought it. In short order he sacked Schikaneder and terminated Beethoven's contract. With the loss of his job, the composer lost his apartment too.

Beethoven moved into an apartment in the same building as his good friend Stephan von Breuning, but Stephan suggested that he move in with him, to save rent. This Beethoven did. But Stephan soon had good reason to regret his offer. Apparently due notice had not been given to the previous landlord, thus incurring a penalty. At the dinner table in Stephan's apartment, Beethoven accused his friend of being entirely responsible. Stephan, appalled, defended himself. Beethoven, in a sudden overwhelming rage, stood up at the table, knocking over his chair, stormed out of the apartment, and went to live elsewhere.

There would, before too long, be a full reconciliation—Beethoven, as so often, having been utterly belligerent, was then overwhelming in his remorse—but it would not be the last time Beethoven would cause a severe rift with his long-suffering and loyal friend.

Beethoven's unpredictability was now well known among his circle, and on the whole they bore it with good grace since they recognised that a genius such as his could not come without flaws. But he most certainly did test their loyalty, and these were not just casual friends but people without whose help he could barely have survived.

Prince Lichnowsky had been paying Beethoven an annuity of 600 florins since 1800, purely out of the goodness of his heart. Ferdinand Ries was at Beethoven's beck and call, as we have seen, at all hours of the day and night. Perhaps two men who knew the composer so well were slightly foolish to have decided to play a practical joke on him, but that is what they did, and they suffered the consequences.

It seemed pretty harmless. Soon after completing the 'Eroica', Beethoven composed a mighty piano sonata, almost as if he needed to get back to the piano. For reasons that remain unclear, he dedicated it to his old patron from the Bonn days, Count Waldstein, so that it is known to posterity as the 'Waldstein' Sonata.[6] The original second movement of the sonata was considered too long, and after some persuading Beethoven agreed to remove it, publish it separately, and substitute a new, shorter, movement.

The original was published as an *Andante* in F. It became so universally popular that Beethoven himself christened it *'Andante favori'*, the title by which it became known, and remains known today. When Beethoven first played it for Ries, the younger man was so delighted with it he urged Beethoven to play it again. On his way home, Ries called in on Prince Lichnowsky to tell him of the 'new and glorious composition'. The Prince made him play it, and Ries did as best as he could from memory. As he played he remembered more passages, and the Prince made Ries teach it to him. Together the two men hatched an innocent little plot.

The following day Prince Lichnowsky called in on Beethoven and said he had composed something for piano that wasn't at all bad, and he would like Beethoven's opinion on it. Beethoven said gruffly he was not interested, but Lichnowsky took no notice, sat at the piano, and played a goodly portion of the *Andante*. He played on, fully expecting Beethoven to appreciate the joke.

He miscalculated. Beethoven was livid. He ordered Lichnowsky out of his apartment, and Ries reports that his extreme anger accounted for the fact that 'I never heard Beethoven play again'. This could well be the case. Several months later Beethoven still held a grudge against the hapless Ries, reducing him to tears in front of company. Not much later Ries left Vienna, and although he returned for a brief period a little later, another row blew up between them over something entirely different. None of this, though, was to stop Ries championing his master's music when he moved to London, as we shall learn. Beethoven's friends might have been few, but on the whole they were unswervingly loyal to him.

—

Baron Braun was having something of a midlife crisis. In late August 1804 he reinstated Beethoven at the Theater an der Wien. He probably realised he needed that opera Beethoven had pledged to write, and would certainly have known that after abandoning *Vestas Feuer*, Beethoven had begun to collaborate with a lawyer, who had a sideline in translating French plays into German, on Jean-Nicolas Bouilly's play *Léonore, ou L'Amour conjugal*.

The lawyer, Joseph Sonnleithner, was a member of a family well connected in music and theatre, and he and Beethoven had met. Beethoven quickly realised Sonnleithner was in a different league from Schikaneder, and the two men began to make progress on a new opera, based on Bouilly's play.

Beethoven revelled in Braun's discomfort, writing to Sonnleithner, 'I am used to the fact that [Braun] has nothing good to say about me—let it be—I shall never grovel—my world is elsewhere.'

To say that Beethoven was stretched would be an understatement. But he was stretched in exactly the way he loved. He was involved in rehearsals and first performances of his colossal 'Eroica' Symphony. He also composed another new piano sonata, which was his mightiest to date. It would become one of his best known and most loved, given a name by the publisher who recognised its unparalleled intensity, a name that would stick for all time: 'Appassionata'. And now, as if that was not enough, he was making huge progress on his first opera.

Something else was happening too, something that would have a profound effect on him. He was once again in love.

CHAPTER NINE

O, BELOVED J!

MUSICAL FAILURE, BUT WILL BEETHOVEN SUCCEED IN LOVE?

I T HAD BEGUN A LITTLE OVER FIVE YEARS EARLIER when, in May 1799, a Hungarian widow by the name of Anna Countess von Brunsvik brought two of her daughters to the Habsburg capital to introduce them into society, to develop their interest in the arts, and, possibly uppermost in her mind, to find them wealthy husbands.

We owe the elder daughter, Therese, a debt of gratitude for the comprehensive memoirs she wrote later in life, providing us with considerable insight into the on-off, and ultimately off, relationship between Beethoven and her sister Josephine.

A family friend advised the mother to ask Beethoven to give the two girls piano lessons, warned her that Beethoven was unlikely to respond to a letter, but that if she and her daughters were prepared to climb three flights of a narrow spiral staircase and knock on his door, they 'might have a chance'. This they did, and it is easy to see Beethoven, hitherto so unlucky in his relationships with women, being somewhat bowled over at the sight of a no doubt smartly at-tired and coiffed noblewoman and her two daughters, the younger of whom was by any standards very beautiful, calling to see him.

Whether the Countess's request for Beethoven to give her daugh-ters piano lessons was helped by the fact that they were cousins of Giulietta Guicciardi, or whether it was just that Beethoven saw this as an opportunity for an amorous relationship, we do not know. What is certain is that for a man who thoroughly hated teaching, he not only said yes, but took up the project with extraordinary zeal.

According to Therese, he came to the hotel where they were staying every day for sixteen days, and from twelve noon stayed not just for the allotted hour but often until four or five o'clock in the afternoon to give the girls lessons.

Unfortunately for Beethoven, the Brunsviks also met the owner of an art gallery by the name of Müller, who saw 'the incomparable beauty which lay hidden in Josephine as in a bud, and from the moment he set eyes on her he burned with a fierce passion'. This 'Müller' had a rather colourful past, having had to flee the country temporarily after a youthful duel, and changing his name to make good his escape. He might or might not have come clean about this to the Countess, but he certainly left her in no doubt of his passion for Josephine and his desire to marry her.

He would have impressed her, too, by claiming the Emperor, no less, as a personal friend, a claim he was able to prove when he went to the Emperor and asked for a pardon for his past misdemeanour. This was granted and his title returned to him, so that he could truthfully present himself to Countess Brunsvik as the highly eligible Count Joseph Deym. Since he was the owner of a renowned art gallery, famous for its wax portraits and copies of classical works of art, there was no doubt either about his wealth.

The Countess was suitably impressed, brushing aside any doubts over the fact that the Count was forty-seven years of age, her daughter Josephine just twenty. When one morning at the end of the Brunsviks' brief stay in Vienna, Count Deym called on the Countess, requesting a private talk, no one was in any doubt as to what it was about, nor of the outcome. Therese records that,

after a few minutes, Josephine was called into the room, and my mother introduced her to—Count Deym. 'Dear Josephine,' she said, 'you can make me and your sisters very happy!' After a painful pause a scarcely audible 'Yes' floated from her trembling lips—

and to this 'Yes' she was to sacrifice a whole lifetime's happiness, so nobly and with such courage. She had no idea what she was letting herself in for. Soon afterwards she threw her arms round my neck and shed a flood of tears.

Within weeks Deym and Josephine were married. Any hope Beethoven might have had of a relationship with his beautiful young pupil was dashed.

Soon after the marriage, Josephine and her mother were horrified to discover that Deym's supposed wealth was a lie. He was, in fact, heavily in debt. The deception might actually have been two-way. Deym blamed his financial problems on the fact that a promised dowry from the Brunsvik family had not materialised.

There was then something of a transformation of loyalties. The Countess, realising that the marriage offered neither social nor financial advantage, pressed for a separation. Her daughter reportedly had furious rows with her mother, refusing to break her marriage vows.

Within three years of marrying Deym, Josephine gave birth to three children and was pregnant with a fourth when, at the beginning of 1804, she was widowed. Deym contracted consumption and died. Josephine suddenly found herself with four infant children, an art gallery to administer, and the letting of eighty rooms owned by Deym to manage.

Josephine's mental health was, according to her sister, already fragile. Later in the year that Deym died, she began to have attacks of fever, which were particularly bad at night. 'Sometimes she laughed, sometimes she wept, after which she suffered from extreme fatigue.'

Beethoven, despite any disappointment over Josephine's marriage, remained close to the Brunsvik family, so must have been aware of the sad events that had overtaken Josephine. At the end of 1804, now reinstated at the Theater an der Wien and working hard on his opera, he decided to press his suit.

In the period 1804–1807 he wrote an extraordinary series of thirteen letters to Josephine Deym, which came to light only as recently as 1949, and were published in 1957. The majority of these letters are, quite simply, passionate declarations of love. The first letter to contain such language was written in the spring of 1805,[1] and suggests that his hand was forced.

In December 1804 Beethoven had composed a song entitled 'To Hope' ('An die Hoffnung'). Prince Lichnowsky saw the manuscript in Beethoven's apartment, and it appears Beethoven had written Josephine's name on the title page. Lichnowsky assured Beethoven he would remain tight-lipped. Beethoven relays this to Josephine in the letter, then writes:

> *Oh, beloved J, it is no desire for the opposite sex that draws me to you, no, it is just you, your whole self with all your individual qualities ... When I came to you—it was with the firm resolve not to let a single spark of love be kindled in me. But you have conquered me ... Long—long—long-lasting—may our love become—For it is so noble ... Oh you, you make me hope that your heart will long—beat for me—Mine can only—cease—to beat for you—when—it no longer beats—Beloved J ...*

This is an unequivocal declaration of love, such as Beethoven had never before put to paper, as far as we are aware. And certainly, to begin with, Beethoven had good cause to believe the love was mutual, even if Josephine was being slightly ambiguous. She replied:

> *You have long had my heart, dear Beethoven. If this assurance can give you joy, then receive it—from the purest heart ... You receive the greatest proof of my love [and] of my esteem through this confession, through this confidence! ... Do not tear my heart apart—do not try to persuade me further. I love you inexpressibly,*

as one gentle soul does another. Are you not capable of this cove-
nant? I am not receptive to other [forms of] love for the present …

If Beethoven took this as encouragement, one can hardly blame
him. It would appear he did, both in writing and probably in person,
because later in the year Josephine decided to end any ambiguity:

> *This favour that you granted me, the pleasure of your company,*
> *would have been the finest jewel in my life, if you could have loved*
> *me less sensually²—that I cannot satisfy this sensual love—does*
> *this make you angry with me—I would have to violate holy bonds*
> *if I were to give in to your desire.*

That is an unequivocal rejection of a physical relationship. More
than that, it could be read as a refusal of a proposal of marriage. In
her memoirs Therese wrote, 'Why did not my sister J, as the widow
Deym, accept [Beethoven] as her husband?'

Beethoven did not immediately give up. From later letters to Josephine, it appears he went to her house to try to see her, but was refused admittance by the servants, which he found humiliating. This
was enough to convince him that he was pursuing a lost cause. In the
final letter of the thirteen, he writes:

> *I thank you for still wishing to make it appear as if I were*
> *not entirely banished from your memory … You want me to tell*
> *you how I am. A more difficult question could not be put to me—*
> *and I prefer to leave it unanswered, rather than—to answer it too*
> *truthfully—All good wishes, dear J. As always, your Beethoven,*
> *who is eternally devoted to you.*

That 'eternal devotion' seems more like politeness, given what
comes before it. Josephine now leaves our story, but will come right

back into it when I discuss the identity of the Immortal Beloved, the one woman who as far as we know returned Beethoven's love.

—

There is an irony in the fact that in 1805, the year Beethoven was actively pursuing Josephine, he was hard at work on an opera that tells the story of how the love of a wife rescues her husband from certain death.

By the late summer of 1805 much of the work on *Leonore* had been done, but now the hard work began. Singers were hired, and although the females were adequate, some of the male singers were simply not up to the job. One in particular, chosen to sing the role of the prison governor Pizarro, had a high opinion of his own talent and told the company he believed there was no composer to touch his brother-in-law, Mozart. Beethoven decided to bring him down a peg by writing a truly tricky passage for him to sing. He found it impossible to master, dismissing it with contempt: 'My brother-in-law would never have written such damned nonsense.' It did not make for a happy company.

Rehearsals were difficult—as always with Beethoven performances—and he let small matters get to him. At one rehearsal the third bassoon failed to turn up. Beethoven was furious, and when Prince Lobkowitz made light of the matter, he felt the force of the composer's anger.[3]

A date was set for the first performance of the opera, Tuesday, 15 October 1805. Then things really *did* go wrong. The censor stepped in and banned it. The plot—a man falsely imprisoned by the prison governor who plots his murder, his life saved by his wife who disguises herself as a man to get work at the prison—was simply too political. Yes, the wrongdoer is hauled off to face justice at the order of the provincial governor, but in the contemporary climate it just wouldn't do. Couldn't Beethoven write operas like

Mozart and Cherubini, which by and large steered clear of political issues?

Beethoven, on the surface, was furious, but actually to an extent
the ban worked in his favour. The process of composition had been
enormously difficult, even by his standards. It had filled the equivalent
of over three sketchbooks (in contrast to the 'Eroica', which had filled
half of a single sketchbook), and had taken him longer than any other
work he had hitherto composed. In one sense that is not particularly
surprising. There is no musical genre that uses quite as many forces as
opera. He had written works for voices and orchestra—cantatas and
an oratorio—but in these works the singers are static. An opera demands drama, choreography, theatrical production, as well as singing.
There are also issues such as costumes and scenery, which one imagines Beethoven could hardly be bothered with.

There is something else too. Beethoven, by his own admission,
did not find it easy to compose for the human voice. He said that
when he heard sounds in his head, they were the sounds of the orchestra. Singers, from his day to ours, have complained about his
vocal composition, whether it be *Fidelio*, the *Missa Solemnis*, or the
Ninth Symphony. All make demands on the voice that are to an
extent not natural. As we shall see later, the premiere of the Ninth
Symphony nearly did not happen, at least in part because of a revolt
by the soloists who complained their parts were unsingable. Singers
who complain today are aware, at least, of the unquestioned genius
of Beethoven, and generally do their best to fulfil his demands. That
was not the case two centuries ago. It really is no surprise Beethoven
was never to write another opera.

So when the censor banned opening night, Beethoven realised it
gave him more time to work on the score and rehearse the singers
and orchestra. Sonnleithner the librettist, however, had friends in
high places, and a grovelling petition to the censor did the trick. The
ban was lifted.

Proof that the opera was nowhere near ready to be performed came with the decision to postpone opening night by five weeks, until 20 November. This could not have been a worse decision, due to circumstances totally outside the control of anyone in Vienna.

Earlier in the year Austria had joined a coalition to fight Napoleon. This was an annoying distraction from the French Emperor's principal aim, which was to invade Britain. But Austria was an enemy he could easily deal with, and he decided to do so. Abandoning his camp at Boulogne, he marched at the head of his army into Germany, crossed the Rhine, and then headed southeast towards the Danube. The Austrian army made a stand at Ulm in Bavaria, but on 20 October Napoleon swatted it aside and continued his march into Austria.

In Vienna there was total panic. Anyone who could left the city. This meant in effect the nobility, bankers, and wealthy merchants, those who had somewhere else to go, a residence in Bohemia or Hungary, perhaps, and who had the money and means to escape. Precisely the level of society in which Beethoven moved, those he could be certain would come to the Theater an der Wien to see his new opera.

By 10 November the French army had reached, and occupied, villages just a few miles west of Vienna. Three days later the vanguard of the army entered the city in battle order, flags flying, to the sound of martial music. Napoleon, to add insult to injury, made his headquarters in the Austrian Emperor's summer palace, Schönbrunn. The French had taken the capital of the Austrian Empire, with barely a shot fired.

Five days later Beethoven's new opera, *Leonore*, opened at the Theater an der Wien.[4] The timing was disastrous. The first act of the occupying French army was to close the gates of the city wall and put armed guards in place to prevent movement. This meant people from inside the city wall could not venture into the suburbs.

The sort of people who lived outside the city wall were not, on the whole, enthusiastic opera-goers, nor did they like the idea of going out after dark with French soldiers on patrol, and so Beethoven's opera opened on 20 November to a handful of his friends and an otherwise empty house.

The following night there were a few French soldiers in the audience, and on the third night a few more. It is hardly a surprise that the plot of the opera—which, as well as being a love story, extols the triumph of freedom over oppression—did not exactly appeal to the soldiers of an occupying army, and after just three performances the opera was shut down.

Given the difficult gestation period, the problems with rehearsals, the intervention of the censor, the delay of opening night, Beethoven was already drained. Three unsuccessful performances put the seal on a dreadful experience. And the opera was unsuccessful musically, too, and that will have hurt Beethoven all the more.

The *Freymüthige* critic wrote:

> *A new Beethoven opera has not pleased. It was performed only a few times, and after the first performance [the theatre] remained completely empty. Also the music was certainly way below the expectations of amateur and professional alike, the melodies, as well as the general character, much of which is somewhat false, lack that joyful, clear, magical impression of emotion which grips us so irresistibly in the works of Mozart and Cherubini. The music has some beautiful passages, but it is very far from being a perfect, or indeed even successful, work.*

The *Allgemeine musikalische Zeitung* was just as unforgiving:

> *Beethoven has sacrificed beauty so many times for the new and strange, and so this characteristic of newness and originality in*

creative ideas was expected from this first theatrical production of
his—and it is exactly these qualities that are the least in evidence.
Judged dispassionately and with an open mind, the whole piece is
marked neither by invention nor execution.

Beethoven had experienced his first unquestionable flop and, easy though it might be to blame the French, there was more to it than that. His opera had been judged to have failed artistically.

Now this was something that was not entirely new to Beethoven. His cantatas, back in his Bonn days, had been judged unplayable by the court orchestra, and earlier in the same year as *Leonore* was staged, 1805, the *Allgemeine musikalische Zeitung* had this to say about his Symphony No. 3, the 'Eroica':

> *This long composition, which is extremely difficult to perform,*
> *is in reality an enormously expanded, daring and wild fantasia.*
> *It lacks nothing in the way of startling and beautiful passages, in*
> *which we recognise the energetic and talented composer. But often*
> *it loses itself in lawlessness ... The reviewer belongs to Herr van*
> *Beethoven's sincerest admirers, but in this composition he must*
> *confess that he finds too much that is glaring and bizarre, which*
> *hinders greatly one's grasp of the whole, and a sense of unity is*
> *almost completely lost.*

Did Beethoven take criticism to heart? He most certainly did not. A reviewer's criticism or a musician's complaint was not enough to cause him to alter a single note. Which makes the next step in the difficult journey of his opera all the more remarkable.

Beethoven agreed to attend a meeting at the home of his patron Prince Lichnowsky, with singers who had taken part in the opera, and friends, to discuss ways of improving the score. This is unprecedented. The only possible explanation is that deep in his heart

Beethoven knew the opera was not right. But it is still remarkable that he was prepared to discuss this with other people, some of them nonmusicians, rather than repair to the privacy of his own apartment and work on it alone. This can be only because he did not feel comfortable with the operatic form, that he understood that opera, above all musical forms, was a collaborative enterprise. In short, he needed advice.

The Prince and the others must have been surprised that Beethoven agreed to the meeting, and if they expected it to be difficult, and Beethoven to be obstructive, they were not proved wrong. They obviously agreed in advance on the single most important improvement that needed to be made. The opera was in three acts, and the first act in particular was lengthy and failed to take the plot forward. The three acts needed to be fused into two. On top of that, several pieces needed to be cut entirely, and others reduced.

Lichnowsky's masterstroke was to have his wife, an extremely accomplished pianist, provide musical accompaniment, as every number in the opera was run through. The Princess, although only five years older than Beethoven, had taken a motherly interest in him when he first settled in Vienna, looking after him, making sure he was well housed and provided for. Beethoven knew he owed her an enormous debt. In recent years she had fallen into poor health, and had had both breasts removed. Although only forty years of age in 1805, she was extremely frail. In the last resort, Lichnowsky knew Beethoven would listen to his wife, even if to nobody else, and she, fine musician that she was, was as aware as everybody of the need for major alterations to be made to the opera.

That is, in essence, what happened, but not without considerable struggle. 'Not a note will I cut!' Beethoven kept shouting, as proposals for improvement were made. The entire opera was gone through, piece by piece, note by note, with frequent repetition. The group pleaded and cajoled; Beethoven resisted at every point.

It was well past midnight before the end was reached. Finally Lichnowsky, who had taken the lead throughout, said to Beethoven, 'And the revision? The cuts? Do you agree?' Everybody held their breath. Beethoven's voice was sombre. 'Do not make these demands,' he said. 'Not a single note will I cut.'

But there was no resistance in his voice, the fight had gone out of him, and those present could sense it. Lichnowsky said in a joyful voice that the meeting was over, the work done, there would be no more talk of it, and they would celebrate. He gave a signal, servants flung open the folding doors to the dining room, and everybody gratefully ate and drank.

As a nice coda to the evening, Joseph Röckel, the young tenor who was to take over the lead role of Florestan—and to whom we owe the eyewitness account of the whole proceedings—sat opposite Beethoven at the dining table. He was so ravenously hungry that he devoured his plate without pausing for breath. Beethoven pointed to the empty plate, smiled, and said, 'You gulped that down like a wolf—what have you eaten?'

Röckel replied that he was so famished he had not noticed what was on his plate.

'Hah!' said Beethoven. 'That is why you sang the part of Florestan, who is starving in the dungeon, so well tonight. It wasn't your voice or your head that was on fine form, but your stomach. So, just make sure you are starving before you go out on stage, and we can be sure of a successful performance!'

There was laughter, and relief, around the table. Beethoven's unusually jovial mood was evidence, to those who knew him, not only that he had not taken offence at the evening's proceedings, but that he would comply.

The net result was a reworked opera in two acts, with practically every piece shortened and an entire aria dropped. One other major change. Beethoven's oldest friend, Stephan von Breuning (with whom he was reconciled eighteen months after their falling out over accommodation) revised the libretto. This was a somewhat surprising decision, given that Stephan had no track record in such matters, and in a letter to Sonnleithner Beethoven disguised the fact that the inexperienced Stephan was now involved. The suggestion of involving Stephan might well have been made to soften Beethoven's opposition to the rewrite. If so, it worked.

The new version complete, it needed only the irascible and uncooperative Baron von Braun, director of the imperial court theatres, to be brought on side and offer a performance date. This was achieved, but Beethoven soon raised the Baron's ire by insisting on composing a new overture, and then repeatedly missing the deadline for its completion. January and February passed and they were into early March.

Braun finally lost patience. He offered Beethoven the night of Saturday, 29 March, in the Theater an der Wien, which he said was the best night of the season since it was the final night before the theatre closed for Holy Week. If the opera were not performed on that night, Braun threatened, it would not be performed at all. There was also the promise of one night (possibly two) after Holy Week. But there was a catch. Given the failure of the previous performances, Braun was prepared to offer Beethoven only a share of receipts, not a guaranteed fee. This could, of course, work to Beethoven's advantage if the theatre was full. Beethoven was in no position to argue.

Still Beethoven was late in delivering the final score, so that there was time for only two or three rehearsals with piano and only one with orchestra. Beethoven, possibly under instructions, stayed away. The rehearsals were directed by Ignaz 'Egyptian hieroglyphics' Seyfried, who also conducted at the performances.

The first performance on the 29th was not a complete success, the theatre again being almost empty. Beethoven complained that the chorus was 'full of blunders', and that the orchestra—particularly the wind (shades of the cantata problems)—ignored all the dynamic markings. 'Any pleasure one might get in composing departs when one hears one's music played like that!' he wrote.

The second performance, after Holy Week, on Thursday, 10 April, fared rather better. There was a larger audience, though the theatre was still not full. But it seems Baron Braun was prepared to make the theatre available for more performances. Beethoven, though, had other matters on his mind. He was convinced that his due receipts, based on the number of tickets sold, were larger than the Baron was prepared to pay him.

Young Röckel is again our witness to one of the most extraordinary episodes in Beethoven's life. It is as if all the resentment towards the Baron came pouring out in one tempestuous encounter.

On the day following the second performance, Beethoven stormed into the Baron's office and openly accused him of withholding his just receipts, of underpaying him. There was a violent row between the two men. Braun told Beethoven he was the only composer to whom he had ever offered a share of the profits, and if there had been a larger audience, he would have received more money. Beethoven accused Braun again of swindling him out of what he was owed. Braun pointed out that although the boxes and front-row seats had all been taken, the bulk of the cheaper seats remained empty.

As a *coup de grâce*, calculated to offend, Braun said that Mozart was always able to fill these cheaper seats with ordinary people, whereas Beethoven's music seemed to appeal only to the more cultured classes.

Beethoven, stunned and shocked at Braun's words, stormed up and down the office, then shouted, 'I do not write for the multitude— I write for the cultured!'

Braun, knowing he now had the upper hand, calmly replied, 'But the cultured alone do not fill our theatre. We need the multitude to bring in money, and since your music makes no concessions to the ordinary people, you only have yourself to blame for the fact that your takings are less than you hoped.'

Beethoven saw red. The unfavourable comparison with Mozart, then the insult to his music, was too much. 'Give me back my score!' he shouted. It was the Baron's turn to be stunned. Beethoven shouted again, 'I want my score. My score. Now!'

The Baron, possibly deciding to call Beethoven's bluff, pulled a bell-rope and a servant entered. 'Bring the score of yesterday's opera for this gentleman.'

The two men stood staring at each other until the servant returned with the score. Braun tried to calm matters. 'Look, I am sorry about all this, but I believe that on calmer reflection—'

Beethoven did not listen. He snatched the score from the servant's hand and stormed out of the office, down the stairs, and away.

Röckel entered a few moments later and Braun looked visibly shocked at what had happened. He had, in effect, lost the opera. 'Beethoven got over-excited,' he said to Röckel. 'You know him, he respects you, go after him, and see if you can get him to agree to give the score back. I want to put it on the stage again.'

Röckel concludes predictably, 'I hastened to follow the angry Master ... but all was in vain.'

It certainly was. Beethoven's opera did not see the light of day for another eight years, and then it was in a form substantially different yet again—a third version. Which does lead one to wonder whether the whole fracas over underpayment of box-office receipts was an elaborate charade engineered by Beethoven because deep down he knew, consciously or subconsciously, that his opera was still not right.

If that were so, he certainly did not regard it as a pressing matter that needed to be resolved. Or if he did, it was about to be supplanted by a crisis of a very different, and much more personal, kind.

Ludwig van Beethoven (1712–73). Beethoven's grandfather was the first musician in the family. This portrait shows him as court *Kapellmeister*. Beethoven had the portrait sent to him in Vienna and kept it for the rest of his life. (© Alfredo Dagli Orti/ The Art Archive/Corbis)

Beethoven's father, Johann van Beethoven (1739 or 1740–92), and his mother, Maria Magdalena née Keverich (1746–87). Johann was a tenor described in a court report as having 'a very stale voice'. At school Beethoven was so unkempt that his schoolmates assumed his mother was dead. These are the only known portraits of Beethoven's parents, and cannot be verified. (*left:* akg-images; *right:* © Bettmann/Corbis)

Count Waldstein was Beethoven's most important patron in his formative years in Bonn. A lover of the arts, he nourished Beethoven's talent and almost certainly provided financial support for the Beethoven family. He was the first to link Beethoven's name with Haydn and Mozart. Beethoven later dedicated his Piano Sonata Op. 53 to Waldstein.

Waldstein became obsessed with defeating Napoleon, and raised an army to do so. It bankrupted him. Beethoven dedicated the Piano Sonata in C, Op. 53 to him. (Courtesy of Chateau Duchcov-Dux/National Heritage Institut, Czech Republic. Photograph by Marta Pavlikova, 2012.)

By the turn of the nineteenth century, an unshakably roman-ticized image of Beethoven had taken hold. This is a lithograph by the German painter and sculptor Sascha Schneider purporting to show Beethoven performing the 'Moonlight' Sonata for Giulietta Guicciardi, to whom it is dedicated. (akg-images)

The autograph manuscript of the first page of the 3rd movement of the Piano Sonata Op. 27 No. 2, known now as the 'Moonlight' Sonata, which Beethoven dedicated to a 'dear charming girl who loves me and whom I love', Giulietta Guicciardi. (akg-images/ Beethoven-Haus Bonn)

The title page of the copyist's score of the 'Eroica' Symphony. The hole in the paper where Beethoven scratched out Napoleon's name can clearly be seen. At this stage the symphony was entitled 'Sinfonia Grande'. (Erich Lessing/Art Resource, NY)

Karl Lichnowsky (1756–1814). In every respect Beethoven's most important patron during his early years in Vienna. He gave Beethoven lodgings in his house and several of Beethoven's compositions were first performed at Lichnowsky's Friday concerts. (Getty Images)

Josephine Deym (née Brunsvik), whom Beethoven took on as a pupil and with whom he fell passionately in love. That love was unrequited, as a series of letters discovered as recently as 1949 show. Beethoven was devastated when she died at the age of only forty-two. (Beethoven-Haus Bonn)

Archduke Rudolph, the most supportive of Beethoven's patrons, both artistically and financially. In gratitude Beethoven dedicated far more compositions to Rudolph than to anyone else, including many of his greatest works. Rudolph was a fine composer and pianist in his own right. (Getty Images)

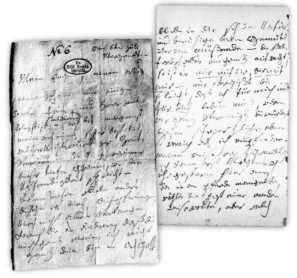

The first two pages of the letter Beethoven wrote in 1812 to the woman known as the 'Immortal Beloved', the only evidence we have that his love for a woman was ever reciprocated. The identity of the woman is still open to question. In the fifth and sixth lines of the second page, the words 'mir mit dir, dir mit mir' can be seen clearly underlined. (akg-images)

This miniature was found among Beethoven's effects after his death. Its identity is uncertain. It has been attributed to Antoine Brentano, a strong candidate for the Immortal Beloved. She was a woman who meant a great deal to Beethoven, since he kept the portrait hidden. (Beethoven-Haus Bonn)

The incident at Teplitz. Goethe on the left, top hat in hand, executes a low bow to the Emperor and Empress, leading Beethoven—who stomps by regardless—to accuse Goethe of fawning too much before the court. Archduke Rudolph, hat in hand, looks on in astonishment at Beethoven's behavior. (© Bettman/Corbis)

Amalie Sebald (1787–1846), a singer from Berlin, with whom Beethoven formed a flirtatious—albeit brief—relationship while unwell in Teplitz. Amalie brought him food, and he wrote her several affectionate notes. (akg-images)

Karl van Beethoven (1806–58), t composer's nephew and the sole Beethov of the succeeding generation. Beethov embarked on a lengthy, turbulent, a ultimately ruinous court case to exclu Karl's mother from the boy's upbringi Beethoven considered Karl to be his ov son, and encouraged the boy to call h 'Father'. (akg-images)

Beethoven in 1814, aged forty-three, in an engraving by Blasius Höfel, considered Beethoven's friends to be one of the best likenesses of him ever achieved. Unusually portraits of Beethoven, the dark complexion that led to his nickname 'The Spaniard' clearly evident. (De Agostini/Getty Images)

The artist Johann Nepomuk Hoechle was an admirer and contemporary of Beethoven's. This drawing was certainly done from observation, and bears out friends' testimony that Beethoven would walk out in all weathers. (akg-images)

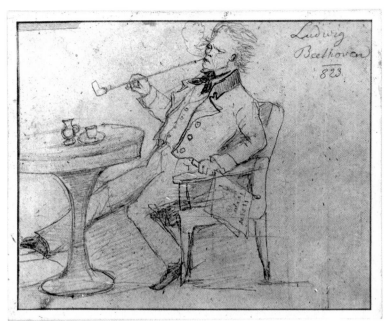

It was customary for taverns in Beethoven's day to have ready-filled pipes that customers could purchase along with their drink. We know from this sketch made in 1823 that Beethoven enjoyed smoking a pipe, particularly in his later years, 'sitting in a corner with closed eyes'. (Beethoven-Haus Bonn)

Karl van Beethoven in middle age. Karl left the army five years after his uncle's death, married, and had four daughters and a son, whom he named Ludwig. He briefly tried his hand at managing property, but was able to live comfortably on his inheritance from his uncles. He died at the age of fifty-two. (akg-images)

CHAPTER TEN

A DEEPLY IMMORAL WOMAN

BEETHOVEN HOLDS THE MOST
IMPORTANT CONCERT OF HIS LIFE,
AND IS OFFERED A JOB

REMARKABLY LITTLE IS KNOWN ABOUT BEETHO-VEN'S two brothers, other than information that links them directly to their famous brother. For one thing, we have practically no idea what they looked like. I can find no contemporary portrait of Carl, and the only physical description of him that I am aware of is terse and uncomplimentary, which is hardly surprising since it came from Carl Czerny, who hated him: 'Carl van Beethoven is small of stature, red-haired, ugly.'

There is, as far as I am aware, just one portrait of Johann, done when he was in his mid-sixties. It shows an extremely wide thin-lipped mouth, long prominent nose, and a right eye with severely drooping eyelid. There is no resemblance to his elder brother. Johann had at least one quality that Carl lacked. He had qualifications. He had trained and qualified as a pharmacist, and was later to buy a pharmacy in Linz and make a considerable amount of money. Not that this earned him his elder brother's respect. When Johann wrote a letter to him and signed it, 'From your brother Johann, Landowner', Beethoven signed his reply, 'From your brother Ludwig, Brain Owner'.

Carl, on the other hand, had nothing but his mediocre musical talent. On arrival in Vienna he managed to get a job as clerk in the Department of Finance, which left him time to handle his elder brother's business affairs. This he did aggressively, and Nikolaus Simrock was not the only publisher who regretted having to deal with him. Ferdinand Ries, who like Czerny couldn't stand Carl, wrote to Simrock that Carl 'for the sake of a single ducat breaks fifty promises, and as a result makes bitter enemies for his brother ... All the publishers here [in Vienna] fear him more than fire, for he is a terribly coarse man.'

When Breitkopf und Härtel, concerned that they might lose exclusive rights to a composition to rival publisher Artaria & Co., wrote blaming Beethoven for not respecting the exclusivity, Carl replied on his brother's behalf, 'You have written my brother a letter which might possibly be appropriate for a schoolboy, but not for an artist such as Beethoven.' Similarly, when the highly respected *Allgemeine musikalische Zeitung* criticised the oratorio *Christus am Ölberge*, Carl wrote to them that he found it 'remarkable that you should print such garbage in your journal'.

Beethoven himself, at least to begin with, appeared none too concerned about this. If anything he had some contempt himself for publishers and critics, and if his brother was upsetting them, maybe it was no more than they deserved. But the case against Carl was building, with publishers threatening to end relationships, and friends and colleagues warning Beethoven that Carl was seriously compromising his reputation.

If Beethoven was unsure what to do next, Carl solved it for him in the most dramatic way. He announced to his brother that he intended getting married, and that the object of his affections was a certain Johanna Reiss. If he had set out to upset his brother, he could not have chosen to do it in a more effective way.

Johanna Reiss was the daughter of a well-to-do Viennese upholsterer and his wife, who, it is fair to say, had something of a reputation, even in her youth. As a teenager she accused the family's housekeeper of stealing something she had herself taken. The case actually went to court before she was forced to admit her dishonesty, and she was fortunate no action was taken against her. A curious anecdote from her childhood might go some way towards explaining her behaviour. She apparently told her son in later years that every time she had wanted money her father had said, 'I won't give you any, but if you can take it without my knowledge you can keep it.' This tendency to dishonesty did not leave her after she married, as we shall see.

It is also probably true to say that her unfavourable reputation extended to her morals as well, though there is no direct evidence of this before her marriage. Certainly it became a real issue in later years—again, as we shall see—and, given Beethoven's vehement opposition to acquiring her as a sister-in-law, it is probably a fair assumption to make. As far as he was concerned, the fact that she was already three months pregnant with Carl's child before she married him was proof enough of that.

As head of the family, Beethoven no doubt tried everything he could to prevent the marriage, but it was to no avail. Carl married Johanna on 25 May 1806. Almost immediately he stopped acting as his brother's business manager—it is not clear whether this was his decision or Beethoven's. Little over three months later, on 4 September, the couple's son Karl, Beethoven's nephew, was born. This straightforward sequence of events was to have the most profound effect imaginable on Beethoven's life.

Beethoven's relationship with his sister-in-law began badly, and became progressively worse as the years passed. Approximately a decade later it was to lead to what can only be described as a catastrophic period in Beethoven's life. It is impossible, at a distance of two centuries, to understand fully the complexities that were at work. A modern-day psychiatrist would require many sessions with Beethoven on the couch to try to get to the bottom of just why he disliked Johanna so intensely. Was it to mask a hidden desire for her? Was it more simply that he was envious of his brother's success in finding a wife? Was it that he thought she was unworthy to carry the name 'Beethoven'? We cannot know. But the vitriol he would use towards her in later years, and the extraordinary actions he would take against her, will, I have no doubt, shock readers of this book as much as they shocked Beethoven's circle at the time.

What we can be in no doubt about is that, at the time of Carl's marriage, Beethoven's mental state was precarious. He was in despair over his opera—all that effort, years in fact, the struggle to compose, arguments, tension, postponements, the failure of the premiere, the rewrite, the final showdown with Braun—and now he had what he saw as a grave domestic crisis on his hands. And yet, paradox of paradoxes (no surprise with Beethoven), he was composing at a furious pace, and these were not small compositions.

The Russian Ambassador in Vienna, Count Razumovsky—an accomplished violinist who had formed his own quartet—commissioned three string quartets from Beethoven. There is evidence he actually began writing out the score of the first of these on the day after Carl married Johanna. He started serious work on a new symphony, his fourth; he was soon to complete a new piano concerto, again his fourth, and before the year was out he would compose a violin concerto. All these are gigantic works which are staples of the repertoire today.

How did he accomplish all this, given how difficult life was for him in Vienna? By leaving the city, and that was thanks to his great benefactor, Prince Lichnowsky. Lichnowsky could see the strain Beethoven was under, having himself lived through the trauma of *Leonore*, and being aware now of the tension between Beethoven and his newly wed brother. Lichnowsky had a country estate at Grätz near Troppau in Silesia,[1] and he suggested Beethoven come away with him and spend some weeks there.

Beethoven acquiesced, and the two men left Vienna in late August for a trip that would last longer than planned, that would have a profoundly beneficial effect on Beethoven's compositional process—and that would end in scenes of unbelievable trauma.

—

It began so well. Beethoven took his manuscripts with him; Lichnowsky promised him peace and quiet; he had his own quarters with piano, and he worked with renewed energy. Within days of arriving, he received news from Vienna that Johanna had given birth, and that he had a nephew called Karl. One can imagine that momentarily disturbing his peace of mind, but it certainly did not interrupt his compositional flow.

He was also in receptive enough frame of mind to agree to travel the short distance—thirty miles or so—with the Prince to the castle at Oberglogau of another nobleman by the name of Count Oppersdorff, no doubt tempted by the knowledge that the Count maintained his own orchestra. It is likely that Lichnowsky further sweetened the pill by telling Beethoven that the Count's orchestra had been rehearsing his Second Symphony and would perform it for him. This was a calculated risk, given the wrath the Prince had incurred over his *Andante favori* practical joke, but it seems all went well.

Beethoven, in fact, took a great liking to the Count, and was evidently so pleased with the performance of his symphony that he went on to assign the score of his soon-to-be-completed Fourth Symphony to the Count for six months' private use for 500 florins,[2] and promised to dedicate it to him on publication. Further proof of his unusually good relations with Oppersdorff came a year or so later when the Count was evidently so pleased with the Fourth Symphony that he offered Beethoven a further 500 florins for a new symphony, on the tacit understanding that he would receive the dedication of that too. Again Beethoven agreed, but when the new work was published Oppersdorff was somewhat disappointed to discover that he was not the dedicatee. And so he might be. It was Beethoven's Fifth.

But that is to leap ahead. Some weeks after the visit to Oberglogau the Count paid a return visit to Grätz. One evening Prince Lichnowsky entertained some French army officers to dinner. Both Beethoven and Oppersdorff were present. This was not a particularly tactful move. The French army still occupied Vienna—albeit peacefully—as well as large tracts of the Austro-Hungarian Empire, including Silesia. Lichnowsky must surely have known of Beethoven's fury at Napoleon declaring himself Emperor of France, and would certainly have heard Beethoven venting his fury at all things French. It is not beyond imagination that Lichnowsky, along with Beethoven's friends, would frequently have had to calm him down when spotting uniformed French soldiers in the streets of Vienna, as well as in cafés and restaurants.

It is therefore highly likely that Beethoven was a reluctant guest at the dinner, and is certain to have made his disapproval of the French clear, no doubt to the embarrassment of everyone at the table. Which makes what happened next even more inexplicable. The French officers, well aware of who Beethoven was, brushed aside any anti-French feeling he might have expressed, and asked him to play the piano for them. Beethoven was appalled. But the officers persisted, making frequent demands throughout the meal for Beethoven to play. More extraordinary still is that Lichnowsky not only made no attempt to defuse the situation but that he too urged Beethoven to play, no doubt hoping to bask in the reflected glory of having Europe's greatest virtuoso as a guest in his house, thereby currying favour with the French. Beethoven refused again and again, but neither the officers nor Lichnowsky would take no for an answer.

Finally Beethoven, his rage overflowing, stormed up from the table, hurled abuse at the company, and charged up to his room. There he bolted the door shut, while he hurriedly packed his clothes and gathered his manuscripts, stuffing them between folders. Lichnowsky was equally furious. He too hurried up the stairs, closely followed by Oppersdorff. Livid at finding the door bolted, he summoned servants, who forced the door open. Lichnowsky—all his pent-up frustration at Beethoven's always unpredictable behaviour boiling over—rushed in, Beethoven picked up a chair, and only Oppersdorff's timely intervention prevented serious damage and probable injury.

Oppersdorff persuaded Lichnowsky to leave Beethoven to work off his temper. Left alone, Beethoven scribbled a note on a scrap of paper: 'Prince, what you are, you are by accident of birth. What I am, I am through myself. There have been and will always be thousands of princes. There is only one Beethoven.'

Beethoven then grabbed his belongings and in the darkness of night left the house, and walked in the pouring rain to Troppau, which was several kilometres away. From there he took the first coach he could find back to Vienna.

Once back in the city, he climbed the three flights of stairs to his apartment. In the hall there stood a marble bust of Lichnowsky which the Prince himself had given him. Beethoven seized it and smashed it to the ground.

Now there are several versions of this story, none of them told by direct eyewitnesses, and I confess the one I have related is the most dramatic. But the source is Ferdinand Ries, who is reliable, and all the sources agree there was a violent confrontation between Beethoven and his patron. What is also true is that, soon after, Lichnowsky stopped his annuity payments to Beethoven. It is also a fact that the autograph manuscript of the 'Appassionata' Piano Sonata, one of the manuscripts Beethoven had under his arm, and which has survived, carries clearly visible water stains.[3]

There is evidence that the two men continued to meet, but less frequently, and there was a change in the relationship. Slowly Prince Lichnowsky, who had done so much for Beethoven, providing him with accommodation when he first arrived in Vienna, gaining access for him to the most elevated salons in the city, financing him, and just generally always being there for him, slipped out of Beethoven's life.

Later Beethoven, who rarely forgot a grudge, gave orders to his servant that Lichnowsky was not to be admitted to his apartment. Lichnowsky, hurt beyond measure but undeterred, would sit in the ante-room near the door, where Beethoven would not see him, listen to the glorious sounds coming from within, then leave as quietly as he had arrived, content that he had played a part in the development of such genius.

—

In the following months, at the same time as coming to terms with the failure of his intended relationship with Josephine Brunsvik, he composed the work that alone ensured his immortality, the Fifth Symphony. And as his fame increased, and his works became more magisterial, so his life seemed to do the opposite, lurching forward with no clear sense of purpose or direction.

Not that the fault for this was always entirely his. The imperial court theatres were in trouble, no doubt hit by the French occupation. The blame was laid firmly at the door of Baron von Braun, and he was forced to retire. Beethoven no doubt enjoyed a certain *Schadenfreude* at the downfall of his old foe, and was able to take heart in the fact that the administration was put in the hands of a committee of senior patrons of the arts, including Prince Lobkowitz, who had received the dedication of the 'Eroica' and the joint dedication of the Fifth Symphony.

Beethoven seized the moment and penned a long letter to the committee, in essence asking for full-time employment with a regular salary, and containing a none too veiled threat to leave Vienna if his request was refused.

His timing, from the committee's point of view, could not have been worse. In the first place they needed to turn the court theatres' finances round, which meant putting on popular performances. Comedies, for instance, were much cheaper to stage than orchestral concerts, with more direct appeal to a wider audience. Also, with his behaviour over *Leonore*, Beethoven had cemented his reputation for being supremely difficult to work with. No reply from the committee has survived—it is possible they did not accord him the courtesy of one.

It seems though that Beethoven was at least promised a benefit concert. A date was set for the spring of 1807, then cancelled. It was reset for the following December, and cancelled again.

The committee spent the best part of a year trying to reverse the fortunes of the imperial court theatres, before giving up and putting in a new director, one Joseph von Hartl. We do not know if Beethoven made a direct approach to the new man, but Hartl was clearly not in a position to make any promises.

In April 1808 Beethoven directed several of his works at a charity concert in the Theater an der Wien, and he was to do so again later in the year. This is as likely to have been a deliberate attempt to curry favour with Hartl as for any altruistic motive. He was no longer looking for employment, just a benefit concert, and he was certainly in a strong position to do so. He was by far Vienna's most productive and respected composer, even if he had his detractors. He was publishing substantial new works at a prolific rate, and was at the same time continuing to perform in the salons of the aristocracy.

But no benefit concert was forthcoming. All this, taken with the Josephine saga and Lichnowsky debacle, his brother's appalling choice of wife, not to mention the slow inexorable loss of his hearing, meant that by the spring of 1808 he had had enough of Vienna, of musical cabals, of personal problems. He wanted to leave, go somewhere new, start again. But the question was how to do it, and where to go. He could not in his wildest imagination have come even close to predicting from where possible salvation would come.

But, before that, he decided to get away just as far as a small village north of Vienna that he had visited before. He stayed in a different house this time, but once again the peace of Heiligenstadt was exactly what his jagged nerves needed. To say that the bucolic calm of fields and pastures, the birdcalls of summer, the gently rippling stream, a sudden summer storm, then blue skies again, inspired him creatively, would be only the slightest of understatements.

Inspiring too were the inns and taverns of the villages dotted among the foothills of the Vienna Woods, such as Grinzing, Nussdorf, Unterdöbling, many with their resident groups of musicians playing the stomping dances of the country folk. In one such tavern there was a band of seven musicians. Beethoven watched, entranced, as the musicians, drinks at their elbows, would frequently fall asleep, reawaken at just the right moment, play a few notes in the right key—if their instrument hadn't dropped to the floor—then fall asleep again.

For hour after hour he strode the open fields and wooded lower slopes of the Vienna Woods, sitting by the stream, allowing the summer rain to refresh him, always sketchbook and pencils in his pocket.

By the time he returned to Vienna he had created one of his great masterpieces, the only orchestral or instrumental work he ever composed in which he told us exactly what the music represented, what feelings it should inspire, what events it portrayed. The music is stress-free; it reflects the ordered calm of nature. The babbling stream ripples over stones and along grassy banks, the birdcalls of summer are there—nightingale, quail, cuckoo—the country folk gather for a rustic dance, the drunken second bassoon repeatedly falls asleep, waking just in time for his few notes, the dark clouds gather, unleashing a summer storm, and finally the shepherds give thanks for the return of blue skies. You can almost smell the wet grass.

'Awakening of happy feelings on arrival in the country', Beethoven labelled the first movement, and that set the tone for the whole. His Sixth Symphony could not have been more of a contrast to the one that preceded it. 'No one can love the country as much as I do,' he wrote in a letter a couple of years later. This symphony was his evocation of what he loved. He called it the 'Pastoral'.

—

No sooner did Beethoven arrive back in Vienna than the gloom descended on him again. No word of a benefit concert, and so no opportunity to present his new works to the public. His thoughts turned once again to leaving Vienna, going somewhere new, starting afresh. With perfect timing, an exquisite opportunity presented itself.

Beethoven was offered the job of *Kapellmeister* at Kassel, capital of the Kingdom of Westphalia, on an annual salary of 600 ducats. Or as Beethoven himself put it in a letter to a friend, 'I am to be paid handsomely—I have been asked to state how <u>many ducats</u> I should like to have ...'

What had happened was that the High Chamberlain at the Westphalian court, Count Friedrich Ludwig Waldburg-Capustigall, either by letter or in person, conveyed the offer of the job of *Kapellmeister* to Beethoven on behalf of His Majesty King Jérôme of Westphalia. Or to put it another way, the universally derided and despised youngest brother of Napoleon Bonaparte, who had been stuck on the throne of a fictitious kingdom his brother had carved from the states of northeast Germany and called Westphalia, wanted to bring a bit of culture to his court and someone had mentioned the name 'Beethoven' to him.

Whichever view you take—and Beethoven took the former—it was highly flattering, and the financial incentive seriously attractive. The duties, as spelled out by the Count, were light in the extreme: Beethoven was to play occasionally for the King, and conduct his infrequent concerts. Beyond that there were no obligations. He was to have a carriage permanently at his disposal. A further plus was that this was Germany. Kassel was around 160 miles from Bonn. Beethoven, in a sense, would be going home.

He sent word that he would accept, and a contract was prepared. What do you think happened then? The long-awaited benefit concert suddenly materialised. As if out of nowhere. Hartl told Beethoven he could have the Theater an der Wien for a benefit concert on 22 December 1808.

There was a catch. On the same night, the long-programmed concert to raise funds for the Musicians' Widows and Orphans Fund would take place in the prestigious Burgtheater. The city's best orchestral players had long since been hired. To make matters worse, the organisers of the charity concert, in league with Vienna's senior musician, *Kapellmeister* Salieri, threatened any Burgtheater musician who agreed to play for Beethoven with the sack.[4]

It was thus a motley selection of musicians, who well knew the reputation of the man they would be working with, who gathered for rehearsals at the Theater an der Wien. Not for the first time in Beethoven's life, a musical disaster threatened.

A musical disaster was what happened, yet this was to be the single most important concert of Beethoven's life. Just the kind of paradox with which Beethoven's life is replete.

—

The rehearsals went about as badly as it is possible for rehearsals to go, even by the standards of *Leonore*. The orchestral players, no doubt with the experience of *Leonore*, not to mention other encounters with Beethoven, decided to lay down ground rules. Beethoven would not be allowed to attend rehearsals, and furthermore should not conduct at the concert. Only section leaders would agree to talk to him, and if any disputes arose on which he was not prepared to give way, the players would walk out.

It seems they got their way over rehearsals. Beethoven was confined to a room at the back of the building, and the concert master Seyfried would come to him between pieces to get his view. Given that Beethoven's deafness was now serious, one can imagine how difficult this was for him. In effect he was unable to make constructive criticism—no doubt just what the players had aimed for—and clearly held back, possibly as a bargaining tool to ensure he conducted. He got his way at least on that.

When you look at the pieces Beethoven had programmed, you certainly feel a twinge of sympathy for the musicians. The concert was to be a gigantic undertaking, guaranteed to stretch the most accomplished instrumentalists, not to mention the inherent difficulties of working with this particular composer.

This is how the concert was advertised in the *Wiener Zeitung*:

On Thursday, December 22, 1808, Ludwig van Beethoven will have the honour to give a musical Academie *in the Theater-an-der-Wien. All the pieces are of his composition, entirely new, and not yet heard in public.*

FIRST PART:

1. *A Symphony, entitled: 'A Recollection of Country Life', in F major*
2. *Aria*
3. *Hymn with Latin text, composed in the church style with chorus and solos*
4. *Pianoforte Concerto played by himself*

SECOND PART:

1. *Grand Symphony in C minor*
2. *Holy, with Latin text composed in the church style, with chorus and solos*

3. *Fantasia for pianoforte alone*

4. *Fantasia for the pianoforte which ends with the gradual entrance of the entire orchestra and the introduction of choruses as a finale*

No fewer than eight pieces, with a total running time of around four hours, depending on how long item 3 in Part II was, an improvisation by Beethoven. Clearly the two showpieces were the new symphonies, one to begin each part of the concert. And just in case you are in any doubt, these are the 'Pastoral' to open the first part, the Fifth to open the second.

This concert, as scheduled, demanded musicianship of the very highest level from the orchestral players, superlative singing from a chorus, and an audience prepared to be patient and long suffering in the extreme. With the benefit of hindsight, we can envy the audience for being present at the first performance ever of three of Beethoven's greatest works, if we include the Piano Concerto, even if the musical demands outstripped the players' competence.

To flesh out the other pieces, the Aria was 'Ah! Perfido', composed for soprano and orchestra some years earlier; the Hymn was the *Gloria* from the Mass in C, composed the previous year; the Piano Concerto was to be the newly completed No. 4; the Holy was the *Sanctus* from the Mass in C, and the final Fantasia was the *Choral Fantasia*.

Two of these other pieces presented particular problems—in each case problems of Beethoven's own making. His preferred choice to sing the aria was the soprano who had created the title role in *Leonore*, Anna Milder-Hauptmann.[5] She accepted immediately, but 'an unlucky quarrel provoked by Beethoven' resulted in her refusing.[6] Several other sopranos were tried, but found wanting. Finally he engaged the sister-in-law of his friend Schuppanzigh the violinist, Josephine Killitschky, who was both young and inexperienced.

There was potentially a much larger problem with the final piece in the programme, the *Choral Fantasia*. This had only just been composed by Beethoven, and consisted of a long solo piano introduction, joined first by the orchestra, and then the chorus. In fact so recently had he composed it, that he had not written out the piano introduction. This meant, in effect, that the orchestra had no idea when to come in. One can imagine there was some rehearsal—Beethoven being permitted into the rehearsal room for this, at least—with Seyfried assuring the orchestra that if he could turn pages for Beethoven when confronted by nothing more than a few squiggles, he could be sure to lead them in at the right point.

These incidentals, certainly in Beethoven's eye, were merely irritants compared to the much larger issue of a successful performance of the pieces on which he knew his reputation hung, the two new symphonies.

As for the audience, they had something else to contend with too. It was a bitterly cold December evening, and the Theater an der Wien was unheated. With four hours of music to look forward to, it does not take much imagination to see them turning up in heavy coats, scarves, gloves, hats, possibly stamping their feet to keep warm and blowing into their hands. Not exactly conducive to a good evening's music-making.

Good was what it was not. Frustratingly there are no reviews of the concert—it's hard to understand why this is the case, other than the probability that the critics decided to cover the other concert that night in the Burgtheater—but several of Beethoven's friends and colleagues have left eyewitness accounts.

These accounts choose not to comment on the opening piece, the 'Pastoral', but I believe the audience will have been stunned by the birdcalls towards the close of the second movement. These are not incorporated into the music as other composers had done with birdcalls (notably Handel), but are stand-alone, and stand-out, solo passages for flute, oboe and clarinet.

Is it too much of an exaggeration to suggest that the birdcalls, which Beethoven repeats a few bars later, drew laughter from the audience? Possibly not, since the *Allgemeine musikalische Zeitung*, in a review of a performance of the 'Pastoral' only a few months later in the Gewandhaus in Leipzig, wrote elliptically of the birdcalls:

> *Even a few incidental imitations of certain little natural manifestations (especially towards the end), treated jokingly, can only be received with a benign smile even by those who otherwise dislike that kind of thing, because they are so aptly portrayed and, as previously stated, only introduced jokingly.*

The aria, which followed the 'Pastoral', we can assume was pretty dreadful. Thayer writes, albeit without attribution, that poor Josephine Killitschky was so nervous, and made even more so by the nervousness of her friends on her behalf, that when Beethoven led her on to the stage and let her hand go, she became overwhelmed with fright and 'made wretched work of the aria'.

We know nothing of how the *Gloria* from the Mass went, but the Fourth Piano Concerto, directed by Beethoven from the keyboard, has left us with an image of Beethoven that has lodged in legend and colored our thinking of him ever since.[7]

Early on in the first movement, at the first attacking passage, Beethoven apparently forgot he was the soloist, leapt up from the piano stool, and conducted the orchestra so vigorously, waving his arms so wide, that he knocked both candles from the music stand off the piano. The audience, not unreasonably, laughed. Beethoven saw this, lost his temper, and made the orchestra start again.

While the players rearranged their music, Seyfried hurriedly sent two choirboys on stage to stand either side of Beethoven with a candle. The boy on the right side stepped close to Beethoven so he could follow the piano part. At the same point in the first movement Bee-

thoven flung his arms out again, hitting the boy in the face and causing him to drop his candle. The other boy, seeing it coming, ducked.

'If the audience had laughed the first time, they now indulged
in a truly Bacchanalian riot,' Spohr wrote. 'Beethoven broke out in
such fury that when he struck the first chord of the solo he broke six
strings.'

And so Part I of this historic concert ended.

Again we know, frustratingly, nothing of how the Fifth Symphony
went, or the *Sanctus*, and we do not know any details of the piano improvisation. We most certainly do know what happened when it came
to the *Choral Fantasia*.[8]

Beethoven, it appears, had agreed to the dropping of a passage
that comes soon after the orchestra joins the piano, possibly as a
concession to the lateness of the hour and the chill in the theatre. But in performance he forgot this, and so while the orchestra
ploughed on, he played the repeat. This exposed the clarinettist,
who appeared—to Beethoven at least—to come in at the wrong
place.

Orchestra and soloist struggled to come together again, but it was
impossible: 'Like a runaway carriage going downhill, an overturn
was inevitable.' Beethoven leapt up from the piano in a fury, stormed
over to the orchestra and hurled insults at the players so loudly that
the audience heard every word. He stabbed at the music and demanded they start the piece again. Several musicians—including,
most probably, the offending clarinettist—stood and threatened to
leave the stage.

Maybe Beethoven mumbled an apology, or at least calmed down,
because eyewitnesses agree the piece started again (presumably from
the entrance of the orchestra) and this time went without a hitch.

The audience went home no doubt chilled to the bone, but content that as usual a concert by Beethoven did not disappoint, even
if for reasons unconnected with the supreme works they had just

heard. The orchestra seethed backstage afterwards, several of them swearing they would never play for Beethoven again.

Seyfried gives a rather nice coda:

> *At first Beethoven could not understand that he had in a manner humiliated the musicians ... But he readily and heartily begged the pardon of the orchestra for the humiliation to which he had subjected it, and was honest enough to spread the story himself and assume all responsibility for his own absence of mind.*

In circumstances, therefore, bordering on the bizarre, Beethoven had given the world his Sixth Symphony, the 'Pastoral'; his Fifth Symphony, and his Fourth Piano Concerto.

CHAPTER ELEVEN

UNDER CANNON FIRE

IN WHICH BEETHOVEN ONCE AGAIN TRIES HIS LUCK AT LOVE

BEETHOVEN LIVED IN SQUALOR. IF THAT SEEMS like an exaggeration for such a supreme artist, consider this description by a senior French army officer and diplomat[1] who visited him in his apartment only a few months after the benefit concert:

> *Imagine the dirtiest and most disorderly room possible. There were water stains on the floor, a rather ancient piano on which the dust struggled for supremacy with sheets of paper covered with handwritten or printed notes. Under the piano—I do not exaggerate—an unemptied chamber pot. Next to it, a small walnut table that had ink spilled on it, a large number of quills encrusted with ink ... and yet more music. The chairs nearly all had straw seats, and were covered with plates filled with the remains of last night's supper, as well as clothes.*

It was for precisely this reason that a certain member of the Habsburg royal family decided to take action when he heard of Beethoven's intention to leave Vienna for Kassel, coupled with the composer's deafness and a general lack of social awareness.

This was no ordinary member of Habsburg royalty; this was Archduke Rudolph, youngest brother of the Emperor, no less. Rudolph had one quality certain to endear himself to Beethoven, no obvious admirer of royalty. He was an extraordinarily gifted musician. He was an excellent pianist, and a talented composer too. Beethoven met him for the first time, probably at a soirée, around 1808 or possibly earlier, and agreed to give him tuition, both on piano and in composition. In fact he was the only person Beethoven ever took on as a pupil of composition, so Beethoven must have been seriously impressed.[2]

In a sense it is fair to say that Rudolph stepped into the vacuum left by Prince Lichnowsky, both artistically and financially. And even more than that. As an accomplished musician, he recognised Beethoven's genius and instinctively understood and forgave his shortcomings. As brother of the Emperor, he was able to gain access for Beethoven into the highest salons in the city. Lessons with Beethoven took place in Rudolph's private quarters in the Hofburg Palace, the seat of the Emperor, and so Beethoven was able to come and go as he pleased in the heart of the royal establishment.

Rudolph, although seventeen years younger than Beethoven, took it upon himself to be, in effect, Beethoven's guardian, to protect him as a supreme artist from the vicissitudes of life. A word from the Archduke would instantly smooth matters over, and Beethoven was most certainly not averse to dropping his patron's name when he needed to.

Rudolph was perfectly placed to help Beethoven. Poor health had prevented the Archduke from pursuing the military career his position fitted him for, so instead he had entered the Church and taken minor vows.[3] This meant he was domiciled in Vienna, free to indulge himself in the city's artistic activities.

It is certain that towards the end of 1808 Beethoven would have lost no time in telling Rudolph of the offer he had received from Kassel, and his intention of accepting it. Rudolph recognised immediately that the move would be a mistake for Beethoven, potentially a fatal one. People in Kassel did not know him; they would not understand his eccentricities, and would soon tire of making allowances for his increasing deafness.

But how to persuade him to remain in Vienna? What incentive could he offer? He came up with a brilliant solution. He called in two of the city's senior aristocrats, patrons of the arts, and together they offered Beethoven a lifetime annuity of 4000 florins on the sole condition that he agree to remain in Vienna, 'or some other town situated in the hereditary lands of His Austrian Imperial Majesty'. There were no other stipulations. He did not have to agree to compose, or perform, just remain where he could be looked after and protected.

It did not take much working out, even for Beethoven, to see that this was an offer he could not refuse. Despite having formally accepted the offer from Kassel, he thought nothing of pulling out, and agreed to Archduke Rudolph's proposal. Maybe with renewed peace of mind, he began work on a new composition. It was to be his Fifth Piano Concerto (named the 'Emperor' by the publisher, despite Beethoven's objections), his mightiest by far, and in gratitude he was to dedicate it to Rudolph, along with the Fourth, and several other works, including the monumental 'Hammerklavier' Piano Sonata and the *Missa Solemnis*. In fact, Rudolph was to receive more dedications from Beethoven than any other single individual, and we can say without hesitation that he deserved it.

The renewed peace of mind led to a development in another direction as well. It appears he was ready to chance his luck once again at love. Within days of signing the contract with Rudolph, he wrote to a young male friend in terms that were unusually light-hearted, with a touch of arrogance, and which give a nice insight into his priorities:

Now you can help me look for a wife. Indeed you might find some beautiful girl where you are at present [Freiburg], and one who perhaps now and then would grant a sigh to my harmonies ... If you do find one, however, she must be beautiful, for it is impossible for me to love anything that is not beautiful—or else I should have to love myself.

It was, apparently, less unusual than you might think for Beethoven to appreciate female beauty, and not always in the subtlest of ways. Ries wrote in his memoirs:

> *Beethoven very much enjoyed looking at women. Lovely, youthful faces particularly pleased him. If we passed a girl who could boast her share of charms, he would turn round and examine her through his glasses, then laugh or grin when he realised I was watching him. He often fell in love, but usually only for a short time. When once I teased him about his conquest of a certain beautiful lady, he confessed that she had captivated him more intensely and longer than any other—seven whole months.*

Ries frustratingly gives no clue as to who this 'certain beautiful lady' might be, and there is no indication that Beethoven had any particular woman in mind in his letter to his Freiburg friend.

If Beethoven had indeed found new peace of mind, with the annuity solving any financial problems and giving him freedom to compose as and when he liked, it was to be shattered once again—and this time it really was not his fault.

———

Austria had quite simply not learned from its mistakes. It declared war on France again. Napoleon, newly returned to Paris from Spain, decided once and for all to give Austria a hiding from which it would not recover. He left immediately to take command of his army in Germany,[4] and began his march on Vienna.

A few skirmishes out of the way, Napoleon advanced rapidly across Germany, into Austria, and east towards the imperial capital. In scenes similar to those of three and half years earlier, there was a mass exodus from the city, amid scenes of some panic as word spread that this time Napoleon was in no mood to be benevolent.

The exodus reached right to the top. On 4 May the Empress left Vienna with the royal family, including Archduke Rudolph. This had an unexpectedly beneficial—and indeed unusual—effect on Beethoven's musical output. He decided to compose a piano sonata to commemorate Rudolph's departure.

He initially composed only the first movement. It opens with three descending chords, over which Beethoven wrote, 'Le—be—wohl' ('Farewell'). He said he would write the second movement, entitled *Die Abwesenheit* (*Absence*), while Rudolph was absent from the city, and told him he would not compose the final movement, to be called *Das Wiedersehen* (*The Return*), until Rudolph's safe return to Vienna.[5]

Napoleon established his headquarters at Linz, less than a hundred miles in a straight line west of Vienna, and sent his commanders to the capital to demand its surrender. It was in Linz that Johann van Beethoven, a year before, had bought a pharmacy, and the ensuing conflict was to make his fortune, as well as earning him a lifetime's contempt for having, in effect, collaborated with the enemy.

The defence of the imperial capital was in the hands of sixteen thousand soldiers, bolstered by around a thousand students and artists, and an ill-equipped and under-trained civil militia, all under the command of a junior member of the royal family, Archduke Maximilian. The Emperor, from the safety of exile, ordered Maximilian to resist the French and defend the city at all costs. Thus Maximilian rejected the demand to surrender, effectively signing a suicide note for Vienna.

The French commanders unhurriedly set up their new short-barrelled howitzer cannon on rising ground in Spittelberg, a suburb a short distance west of the city wall, the Bastei. A day passed in quiet anticipation, the people of Vienna bracing themselves for what they knew was coming. A contemporary wrote that people milled around in the streets, swapping jokes and light-hearted banter to keep spirits up, and then when dusk fell retreated indoors, until no sound could be heard inside the city wall.

At nine o'clock on the evening of 9 May 1809, as daylight finally faded, twenty cannon opened fire. The bombardment continued through the night, pounding the inner city mercilessly. Any defence was rendered useless by the distance and range of the howitzers. The soldiers and militia had nothing to fight against except shells dropping onto them from the sky. Surrender was inevitable, and it was not long in coming. At half-past two the following afternoon the white flag was raised.

And where was the city's most famous resident, its leading artist, during this traumatic period? At home, in his apartment, which abutted the Bastei on the inner, city side and was therefore almost in direct line of fire.

Why Beethoven did not leave the city for the safety of the surrounding countryside, we do not know. It is even more incomprehensible given his penchant for rural calm, and his escape almost every summer to the peace of small villages. We can safely assume he had no shortage of offers. All the city's leading aristocrats left the city for the safety of their country estates, including Prince Lichnowsky. Did the Prince attempt to mend their relationship by suggesting Beethoven accompany him and his wife? We do not know.

Beethoven's brother Carl did not leave Vienna either, and we know from Ferdinand Ries that the two brothers had intimate contact at this time, despite the antagonism between them. Ries says in his memoirs that Beethoven was 'very frightened' by the bombardment of the city, and spent most of it in the cellar of his brother Carl's house, 'where he covered his head with pillows to shut out the sound of the cannon'. Carl and his family lived in an apartment building on the corner of Rauhensteingasse and Himmelpfortgasse close to St. Stephansdom in the heart of the city, and so they must all have been in extreme danger. This, added to Beethoven's overt contempt for Johanna and dislike for his brother, coupled with the presence of an infant not yet three years of age, must have made for a highly tense time.[6]

After the bombardment, Vienna was a changed city. Prices soared, to such an extent that copper coins were done away with. Food, bread in particular, became expensive—always guaranteed to upset the populace—and the French demanded huge sureties, requisitioned enormous amounts of supplies, and levied a tax on all property. Never was Beethoven more grateful for his annuity, from which he had begun to receive the first payments.

There was an added element, true of all military occupations. Foreign soldiers in uniform patrolled the streets, heaping humiliation on top of other hardships on the populace. If any resident of Vienna was likely to let resentment at this boil over, it was Beethoven. And he did. A young musical colleague reported that Beethoven, seeing a French officer in a coffee-house, shook his fist at him, and shouted, 'If I, as a general, knew as much about warfare as I, the composer, know of counterpoint, I'd be able to give you a lesson or two!' One imagines that from anyone else this would have led to immediate arrest, but not from the universally known, admired, eccentric, and harmless composer.

As a coda to the occupation, twenty days after the bombardment, quietly and practically unnoticed, the world lost one of its finest composers. Franz Joseph Haydn died at the age of seventy-seven.

—

Beethoven had more reason than the obvious to be grateful for his annuity payments. The mythical woman of his letter to Freiburg had materialised. He was once again in love, and this time he was determined to present himself as an irresistible catch, and that meant smartening up.

The lady in question was the eldest of two daughters of a family of Italian extraction by the name of Therese Malfatti. Her father had made his fortune in the silk trade, enough to branch out and establish his own sugar refinery, and owned a sumptuous house just off the fashionable Kärntnerstrasse, and a country estate in Walkersdorf about forty miles northwest of Vienna.

Therese was known to be a volatile, impetuous young lady— eighteen years of age in 1810—and was said by those who knew her to have more of the fiery Italian temperament in her than her slightly younger sister or any other family member.

Perhaps Beethoven's friends warned him of this, but if so he paid little heed. They might have pointed out to him too that he was about to turn forty years of age, and that Therese was therefore young enough to be his daughter. If they did, he again brushed it aside.

He no doubt saw himself as a prime catch. He could now—for the first time in his courting experiences—offer financial security, thanks to the annuity. He was a friend of the Emperor's brother, and could reasonably expect court engagements. Even if his compositions were not universally understood, they were accepted as masterworks, and brought him unrivalled recognition. More lucrative commissions were sure to come.

So, for the first time in his life, he paid exquisite attention to his appearance—even if he admitted he found it thoroughly alien to him. He wrote to one friend asking if he could borrow his mirror—'Mine is broken'—and to another, Ignaz Gleichenstein,[7] sending him 300 gulden, asking him to buy linen or Bengal cotton which the society tailor Joseph Lind would make into shirts for him, as well as at least half-a-dozen neckcloths.

Please do this at once, he added, 'since not only do I understand nothing whatever about such matters, but also such matters are profoundly distasteful to me.'

He was clearly in no doubt that Therese would agree to a marriage proposal, since he wrote to Wegeler asking him to send urgently his baptismal certificate, offering to pay all expenses, including Wegeler's travel from Koblenz (where he was now living with

Eleonore and their two children) to Bonn, and cautioning him not to confuse him with his elder brother Ludwig Maria, who had died at six days old.

Beethoven had been introduced to the Malfatti family by Gleichenstein, was instantly attracted to Therese, and soon began heaping lavish (and certainly exaggerated) praise on her piano skills, offering to give her lessons. Knowing as we do how Beethoven hated giving lessons, the attraction must have been very strong indeed.

It did wonders for his spirits. He sent Gleichenstein another 50 gulden for neckcloths, saying in the accompanying letter that he felt whatever wickedness people had inflicted on his soul 'could be cured by the Malfattis'. As evidence of his acceptance into the Malfatti household, he teased Gleichenstein in the letter that he, Gleichenstein, was not the only person the family dog Gigons was happy to see.[8]

To set the seal on his amorous intent, he did what only he could do, or at least with such a degree of prestige and kudos. He composed a piece of piano music for Therese, making it deliberately simple so that she could play it.[9] The clincher, as far as he was concerned.

But once again, as on every previous attempt at forming a lasting relationship with a woman, he was seriously misjudging the situation.

For a start, it seems Therese had given him no clear indication of her feelings. In repeated notes to Gleichenstein, he asked him—given his closeness to Therese's sister Netty—to try to find out whether he had reason to be optimistic that a marriage proposal might meet with a favourable response. Clearly his frustration was building. Therese was certainly flattered by the attention of Vienna's most famous musician,[10] and it was possible—given her flighty nature—that she flirted with him.

It is known she had other suitors at the time, and she might well have led Beethoven on, keen as she must have been to retain his friendship, even playing him off against the others. The point clearly came when he felt she was more than interested in him, and he decided to take things further.

Then it all went disastrously wrong. Exactly what happened we do not know, but we can surmise from surviving correspondence that Beethoven was at the Malfatti house, possibly alone with Therese, became drunk on very strong punch, and made a clumsy lunge at her. She was utterly appalled, and rejected him in no uncertain terms.

The family repaired to the estate in Walkersdorf and summoned Gleichenstein to join them. To him was given the unenviable task of writing to Beethoven to spell out the family's displeasure, and make it clear to him that they did not wish Beethoven to continue seeing their daughter in any capacity. The letter has not survived—who could blame Beethoven if he tore it up?—but his reply to Gleichenstein expressed his deep hurt: 'Your news has plunged me from the heights of the most sublime ecstasy down into the depths.' And the news that he was being barred even from continuing to give Therese piano lessons drew from him a sentence of extraordinary pathos, even self-pity: 'Am I then nothing more than a Music-Man for yourself or the others?'

Beethoven here uses the untranslatable German word *Musikus*, which carries a derisory, even insulting connotation. 'Mr. Music Man' might be the closest English rendition.

Beethoven wrote one final lengthy letter to Therese. He berates her gently for her flighty nature: 'Our fickle T who treats so lightheartedly all the affairs of life.' He confesses that he is leading a lonely and quiet life. He teases her about a theme he composed for her when they were together, inviting her to find its hidden meaning, but cautioning her in a painful reference to his own indiscretion: 'Work it out for yourself, but do not drink punch to help you.' He even—in shades of his *mea culpa* to Eleonore von Breuning nearly twenty years before—writes, 'Remember me and do so with pleasure—Forget my mad behaviour.'

Thus another amorous adventure ended in failure, and Therese passed out of Beethoven's life. But not out of musical history. For what was the piece of music he composed specially for her, that was undemanding enough for her to be able to play, and that was found in her effects after her death forty-one years later?

It is a small piece, and Beethoven gave it the innocuous title 'Bagatelle'. But it is what he wrote at the top of the title page that has exercised musicologists and scholars ever since. This is what he wrote: *'Für Elise am 27. April zur Erinnerung an L. V. Bthvn'* ('For Elise on 27 April to remind you of L. V. Bthvn').

The question is, who was Elise? One theory that gained acceptance was that Beethoven's handwriting was notoriously difficult to decipher, and that the publisher mistook 'Therese' for 'Elise'. But that stretches credulity—the two names do not resemble each other even closely. More likely is that Therese had the family nickname 'Elise'. Her sister Anna was known as 'Netty', and such nicknames were common practice.[11] Beethoven too had a propensity for giving people nicknames—there are numerous examples in his correspondence—so he might even have invented the name himself (though he does not use it in correspondence with her). Another possible explanation is that after the debacle of Lichnowsky spotting Josephine Brunsvik's name on the manuscript of the song 'An die Hoffnung', he deliberately disguised Therese's name. Or finally, maybe this is not the piece that he composed for her at all. He composed it for a woman named Elise about whom we know nothing, and she passed it on to Therese.

What we *do* know is that the Bagatelle known around the world today as 'Für Elise' is quite possibly the single best-known piece of piano music ever written by anyone,[12] and is beloved by under-talented pianists of all generations, who may well boast that they can play Beethoven. 'Für Elise' is what they play.

—

Did Beethoven finally, once and for all, abandon all hope of a relationship with a woman who might return his love? Most certainly not. We are now approaching the single closest and most intense relationship he was ever to have.

It did not result in marriage, it did not even last long. In fact we know far more about what did not happen than about what did. Most frustratingly of all, we do not know beyond doubt who the woman in question was. She is known to posterity simply as 'The Immortal Beloved'.

CHAPTER TWELVE

IMMORTAL BELOVED

'MY ANGEL, MY ALL, MY VERY SELF'

THIS IS WHAT WE KNOW BEYOND ANY DOUBT. On the morning of 6 July Beethoven, in a hotel in the Bohemian spa town of Teplitz[1], wrote a four-page letter to a woman. That same evening he added two and a half more pages. The following morning, 7 July, he completed page seven and added three more pages. The letter contains declarations of love throughout, which become extremely intense towards the end, and the letter closes with an unequivocal declaration of eternal, and mutual, love. This letter was found—as was the Heiligenstadt Testament—in his effects after his death.

Here it is in full:

6th July, morning

My angel, my all, my very self—only a few words today, and even with pencil—(with yours) only tomorrow will I know definitely about my lodgings, what an awful waste of time—Why this deep sorrow when necessity speaks—How else can our love endure except through sacrifices, through not demanding everything from one another? How can you alter the fact that you are not wholly mine, I not wholly thine—Oh, God.

Look to nature in all her beauty and let her calm your heart about what must be—Love demands everything and rightly so, and that can only mean <u>me with you and you with me</u>—you forget so *easily that I would have to live for myself and for you, only if we were completely united would you feel as little pain as I—*

My journey was terrible. I did not get here until 4 in the morning yesterday. Because they were short of horses the coach took a different route, but it was a dreadful road. At the one to last stage they warned me not to travel at night, that I would have to go through a dangerous forest, but that spurred me on—and I was wrong. The coach, of course, had to break down on the dreadful road.

Esterházy took the other more usual route and had the same trouble with 8 horses that I had with four. Yet to a certain extent I got pleasure as I always do when I overcome a problem—

Now swiftly from external matters to internal ones. We will surely see each other soon. There is no time now to tell you what I have been thinking about these last few days regarding my life— if our hearts were only united I would not have to have such thoughts. My soul is so full of things to tell you—Oh—There are times when words are simply no use—be cheerful—remain my only true darling, my all, as I am yours. The rest is for the gods to decree, what is to be for us and what should be—

your faithful
Ludwig

Monday evening on 6 July

You are suffering my most precious one—only now have I discovered that letters must be posted very early in the morning. Mondays—Thursdays—the only days when the mail-coach goes from here to K.—you are suffering—Oh, where I am you are with me, with me and I can talk to you—if only we could live together, what a life it is!!!! now!!!! without you—Pursued by the kindness of people here and there, which I think—which I no more want to deserve than do deserve—humility of a human towards humans—it pains me—and when I regard myself in relation to the universe, what I am and what is He—I weep when I think you will probably not receive the first news of me until Saturday—as much as you love me—I love you even more deeply—do not ever hide yourself from me—Goodnight—taking the baths has made me tired—Oh go with, go with—Oh, God—so near! so far! is our love not truly sent from Heaven? And is it not even as firm as the firmament of Heaven?

good [sic] *morning on 7 July—even lying in bed thoughts of you force themselves into my head, my Immortal Beloved, now and then happy, then again sad, in the hands of Fate, to see if it will heed us—I can only live with you wholly or not at all, yes, I have even decided to wander helplessly, until I can fly into your arms, and say that I have found my haven there, my soul embraced by you to be transported to the kingdom of spirits—yes, sadly that must come—you will accept it more readily, knowing I am true to you, that never can another woman possess my heart—never, never—Oh, God, why do we have to be so far apart from what we love? And yet my life in V. now is such a wretched existence— Your love makes me at once the happiest and unhappiest of men— at my time of life I need stability, calmness of life—can that exist in a relationship like ours?—Angel, I have just been told that the post leaves every day—and so I must close, so you can get the letter immediately—be calm, only through reflecting calmly about our existence can we reach our goal to live together—stay calm—love me—today—yesterday—what tearful longing for you—you—*

211

you—my Love—my all—Farewell—Love me still—never mis-judge the most faithful heart of your beloved

L.
eternally thine
eternally mine
eternally ours[2]

Now the questions begin. Let us start with the most mundane element, the date. That's clear enough, isn't it? No, it isn't. For a start you'll notice that although he is precise about the date and time, and in the second part the day, he does not give the year. During Beethoven's lifetime 6 July fell on a Monday in 1795, 1801, 1807, 1812, 1818. Nineteenth-century scholars could not agree on the year, and it was not until the twentieth century that 1812 became accepted, as far as I am aware, without question.

But here's something else to consider. Beethoven was notoriously unreliable when it came to dates. A huge number of his letters, including lengthy ones as opposed to mere notes, are undated. Scholars have since assigned dates to them all, but not with certainty. Yet here he is being precise even about the time of day. Why? There is no need for him to be so precise, since it is clear he and the woman were together possibly on the 5th, or shortly before, and she was aware of his travel plans. This attention to detail is totally unlike Beethoven.

Is he falsifying the date, and leaving the year out, deliberately, in case the letter falls into the wrong hands? It is certainly possible he feared the letter might go astray, since it is extraordinarily free of detail. For instance, nowhere does he use the woman's name, or even give her an initial. The only two initials are for place names. 'V' is clearly Vienna, and 'K' more than likely Karlsbad,[3] the only town beginning with 'K' within easy reach of Teplitz and which matches the times for the mail coach.

There is a further mystery in that the letter was found hidden in his desk after his death. This means he kept it with him for the rest of his life. He must surely have been reminded of it every time his desk was moved. There are two possible explanations: either he never sent it, or the woman received it and gave it back to him. The envelope has not survived; maybe there never was one, or maybe he kept it in a blank envelope after deciding not to send it. Certainly there are no stamps or sealing-wax marks on the letter. It is a reasonable assumption that he never sent it.

But if he was worried about the letter falling into the wrong hands, so worried even that he decided not to send it, why did he keep it? Simpler, surely, to destroy it, and thereby destroy the evidence.

Unless he *wanted* it to be found after his death, to show that he did have more success when it came to love than his friends gave him credit for. After all, it is very possible he wanted the Heiligenstadt Testament to be found so that the grief his deafness caused him would be there in writing.

One theory I am certain can be discounted, that the letter was an elaborate hoax by Beethoven, that no such woman, no such love affair existed. If you are going to set out to do that, would you really put in details of an uncomfortable coach ride, problems with finding a hotel room, complications over mailcoach timings?

And this is Beethoven, remember, who once said, 'I would rather write ten thousand musical notes than one letter of the alphabet.' No, it was not a hoax.

We can, I believe, be sure that there was a love affair between Beethoven and a woman, a mutual, reciprocal love affair. Was it consummated? The letter does not make it clear for certain one way or the other. Beethoven tentatively expresses the hope that the two might live together. Some researchers have taken this as evidence of a physical relationship, others have drawn the opposite conclusion. It is almost as if Beethoven is loath to commit to paper anything that is definitive.

But all these questions pale before the single most important question of all, which has been asked by every Beethoven biographer since the first almost two centuries ago; which has been answered in many different ways; which has been considered solved time and time again, but about which whole books continue to be published, films created, documentaries made, articles written.

Who was the woman? Who was Beethoven's Immortal Beloved?

—

I need first to sketch in a little background, before describing how events unfolded. The period following the rejection by Therese Malfatti proved to be difficult for Beethoven. His health was causing real problems. The perennial problems of colic and diarrhoea debilitated him. One can imagine that the trauma of yet another rejection aggravated things. So did something else beyond his control.

The Austrian economy was crippled by the effects of war. After the value of the currency became weaker and weaker, it was officially devalued in March 1811. This had the effect, not only of forcing prices to rocket, but of robbing Vienna's richest aristocrats overnight of their wealth. One, our old friend Prince Lobkowitz, dedicatee of several of Beethoven's most important compositions, was bankrupted and suffered the humiliation of having his estates seized.

Of direct relevance to our story is the fact that Lobkowitz was one of the two senior aristocrats who joined Archduke Rudolph in agreeing to pay Beethoven the annuity that kept him in Vienna. In September 1811, after only two years of payments, Lobkowitz was no longer able to continue.

It got worse for Beethoven. Two months after that, the other aristocrat who contributed to the annuity, Prince Kinsky, was thrown from his horse and killed. His payments too were halted, and Beethoven began a long-running dispute with his estate to try to get the payments continued.

As ever with Beethoven, there is a paradox. He continued to compose at a furious rate: the 'Archduke' Piano Trio, music for two plays, *König Stephan* and *Die Ruinen von Athen*, and most importantly the Seventh Symphony completed and the Eighth begun.

By the summer of 1812 he needed a break—in fact, *another* break. The previous summer he had visited the spa town of Teplitz, and decided to do the same again in 1812.

On either the evening of Sunday, 28 June, or the morning of Monday, the 29th, he left Vienna for Prague. He arrived in Prague on Wednesday, 1 July, and checked into the hotel *Zum schwarzen Ross* ('At the Black Steed'). The following day he attended a meeting regarding the Kinsky annuity. The day after that, the 3rd, he failed to keep an appointment scheduled for the evening. On Saturday, 4 July, before noon, he left Prague for Teplitz. He arrived in Teplitz at 4 a.m. after a difficult journey during which his carriage lost a wheel. He found a room at the hotel *Die goldene Sonne* ('The Golden Sun'). The next morning, Monday, 6 July, he began the letter to the Immortal Beloved. He added to it that evening, and again the following morning. Later that day he moved into the hotel *Zur Eiche* ('At the Oak Tree'), where he stayed for some weeks.

A close reading of the letter, fitting it into this time frame, indicates that Beethoven met the Immortal Beloved on Friday, 3 July, probably in the evening when he failed to keep a prearranged appointment. How long the two were together, whether they spent the night of the 3rd together, we do not know. After this, he left for Teplitz, and she left for Karlsbad. That they met cannot be in doubt—she gave him her pencil.

While we can be relatively certain of Beethoven's movements, therefore, through the evidence of hotel ledgers and police registers, the same is most certainly not true of the Immortal Beloved, for the simple reason that we are not sure what name we are looking for.

It is surely safe to assume the woman must be someone who was well known to Beethoven in Vienna. The passion in the letter is not credible if this is a woman he met in Prague and fell in love with on the same day (or the day after). It also would be entirely out of character for Beethoven to behave like that.

Only one name that Beethoven definitely knew appears in registers both in Prague and then Karlsbad on the right dates. Her name is Antonie Brentano, and the American musicologist and Beethoven biographer Maynard Solomon, in his exhaustive biography published in 1977,[4] came to the unequivocal conclusion that Antonie was the Immortal Beloved. He presented powerful evidence of an intimate friendship between them, regarding her presence in the two right locations at the right time as conclusive proof.

So certain was he that he wrote in the biography, 'The weight of the evidence in [Antonie Brentano's] favour is so powerful that it is not presumptuous to assert that the riddle of Beethoven's Immortal Beloved has now been solved.'

In that if nothing else, he was mistaken. Several names have been proposed since, some for the first time, some not, and in 2011 alone two full-length books were published arguing the case for different women.[5]

The argument *against* Antonie Brentano is that she was a married woman with children, and in fact was with her husband Franz and one of their children staying at the *Rothes Haus* ('Red House') hotel in Prague. Is it realistic to assume she would be able to absent herself from husband and child for a clandestine meeting with Beethoven, which might well have lasted for several hours, if not an entire night, and which was clearly emotionally fraught? And even if she had, would Beethoven, whose strong moral rectitude was beyond doubt, have entertained such a meeting with a woman who was a wife and mother?

For every argument, there is a counter-argument. For precisely that reason, it could be argued, he expressed himself so strongly in the letter, stating unequivocally that the love affair could not proceed, however much they both might wish it. There remains the question, though, of whether Antonie could have absented herself from her husband and daughter to pursue an affair, consummated or not.

The argument in favour of Antonie is further weakened by the fact that three weeks after arriving in Teplitz, Beethoven went to stay with Antonie and her husband and daughter in Karlsbad. Could that really have happened, all together under the same roof, if Beethoven and Antonie were desperately in love with each other and had met secretly in Prague?

After Beethoven left them in Karlsbad, he never met them again. But they stayed in touch, and Beethoven was to dedicate compositions to Antonie much later, very substantial compositions. There is also evidence that a decade later Franz Brentano advanced Beethoven a considerable sum of money when he was in need. If Franz knew Beethoven and his wife had had a love affair, his generosity is truly remarkable. If he never found out, he was at best naïve.

There can be no doubt that Beethoven was very close to the Brentanos, but under the circumstances outlined above—even given the fact that Antonie can without doubt be placed in Prague and Karlsbad on the right dates—I find it hard to believe he and Antonie were lovers, requited or unrequited.

Shortly after Solomon published his book, his arguments in favour of Antonie were challenged by one of Europe's leading musicologists and Beethoven scholars, the German Marie-Elisabeth Tellenbach. Her candidate is Josephine Brunsvik. In fact, despite recent arguments in favour of other women, it is fair to say that the two leading candidates for identification as the Immortal Beloved are Antonie Brentano and Josephine Brunsvik.

Tellenbach argues against Antonie for precisely the reasons I have outlined, that although she fits the facts, emotionally as wife and mother and in the company of husband and daughter, it is not realistic to postulate a love affair.

She puts powerful arguments in favour of Josephine, not least that the letters discovered after World War II prove beyond doubt that Beethoven was in love with her and asked for a physical relationship. There is also the song 'An die Hoffnung', the discovery of which by Lichnowsky led to such embarrassment for Beethoven.

But there are counter-arguments. Josephine remarried in February 1810. The marriage was disastrous, and her husband, Baron Stackelberg, an Estonian, was frequently absent from Vienna. Since there is no direct evidence that Josephine was in either Prague or Karlsbad on the relevant dates, it means she would have had to absent herself from Vienna for some weeks, travel between Vienna, Prague and Karlsbad, without being seen or reported by anyone. In other words, she would most probably have had to travel in disguise. For a married woman—happily married or not—this presents almost insurmountable practical problems.

Solomon argues that with Europe at war, travellers were compelled to register with the police when crossing borders. Therefore it is impossible for Josephine to have done this incognito. Tellenbach counters that Prague and Karlsbad were both within the Austrian Empire, and so registration was not compulsory. Who is right? We cannot say.

The emotional argument regarding Josephine can be seen in two ways. Would Beethoven, having been rejected by her while she was between marriages, want to rekindle his desires? Maybe, maybe not. Josephine was known to be emotionally unstable. How would this have affected Beethoven? It might have deterred him; it might have attracted him.

A further example of how intractable the arguments are is that it appears self-evident that the Immortal Beloved has to have been in

Karlsbad, following the tryst in Prague. Not necessarily. All that we need to be able to say is that Beethoven *believed* her to be in Karlsbad. She does not actually have to have been there. In fact, if at the last moment he realised that she was not where he thought she was, maybe that would explain why he did not send the letter. This weakens the case for Antonie, and strengthens it (possibly) for Josephine.

There is a poignant coda to the candidacies of Antonie and Josephine. Both gave birth eight to nine months after the Prague encounter.

Antonie gave birth to a son, Karl Josef, on 8 March 1813. At an early age Karl suffered partial paralysis of the legs. At the age of three he showed signs of severe mental illness, and suffered from seizures. Antonie took him to a succession of doctors, who could do nothing for him. In a letter Antonie wrote, 'Oh, when one has to drink such a bitter cup of sorrow daily, hourly, how can there remain a last bit of joy and strength?' Karl died at the age of thirty-seven.

Josephine gave birth to a daughter on 9 April 1813. She named her Minona. Minona remained unmarried and lived to the age of eighty-four, almost into the twentieth century. She inherited her aunt Therese's estate, including her papers and the diary she kept meticulously in which she wrote of her sister Josephine's attachment to Beethoven. But no letters which might throw light on the events of July 1812 have survived. This has led to speculation that Minona, who treasured the memory of her mother, destroyed any evidence of an affair between her mother and Beethoven, and with it evidence that she, Minona, might have been Beethoven's daughter.

It has been pointed out that Minona is Anonim spelled backwards, 'the child with no name'. There is a photograph of Minona taken in old age. She bears a striking resemblance to Beethoven, which proves nothing.

—

To return to the letter, the more intricately one examines it, the more unyielding it becomes. But I believe there is a danger. It is possible to *over*-analyse its meaning. Beethoven was never subtle with words. His many hundreds of letters exactly mirror his thoughts. For profundity of thought and emotion, listen to his music.

This is a love letter, written in the white heat of passion. It is as if he is barely pausing to think. Towards the end of the letter, his writing becomes more frantic, the words more widely spaced, the lines shorter. He is emotionally wrought, quite possibly in despair. Looking at the writing, it is entirely feasible that he has drunk several glasses of wine.

What I believe the letter gives us is unequivocal proof that Beethoven was in love with a woman, a woman who returned that love in equal measure—the only evidence we have in his whole life of his love being fully reciprocated. Yet he knew their love could not endure. Circumstances prevented it. *'I can only live with you wholly, or not at all.'* Why? Because she was married? Or because he knew he could never give himself to her in the way a husband should, because of the demands of his music?

One fact I can state with total certainty, without the slightest chance of contradiction. The arguments, theories, speculation will continue. If Beethoven's letters to Josephine were discovered as recently as the 1940s, who knows what other evidence is inside a shoebox in an attic somewhere in the world?

In fact some years ago I was approached by a young Frenchwoman who said just that—that her mother, who lived outside Paris, had a letter written by Beethoven which she kept in a shoebox in her attic. She said the handwriting had been authenticated as belonging to Beethoven, and the letter proved beyond doubt that Josephine Brunsvik was the Immortal Beloved. I arranged to meet her, but the meeting was cancelled by a family member.

It is quite possible that the woman who was Beethoven's Immortal Beloved is a woman as yet unknown to history. One day new evidence will emerge. It might be in my lifetime, though I rather doubt it.

—

But even in the calm of Bohemia, taking the waters and musing over a lost love, the outside world intruded on Beethoven, in the shape of his own family. It sent him into a spiral of despair. His youngest brother Johann, it seemed, had succeeded where he had failed. He had found himself a woman, and he intended marrying her.

Beethoven sent Johann an urgent message, saying in effect 'over my dead body', abandoned his stay in Bohemia, packed his things, and headed as fast as he could for Linz to confront his brother. He only hoped he wasn't too late.

CHAPTER THIRTEEN

AN UTTERLY UNTAMED PERSONALITY

BEETHOVEN TURNS AGAIN TO HIS 'POOR SHIPWRECKED OPERA'

B EFORE WE ACCOMPANY BEETHOVEN ON HIS mercy mission to Linz, something else happened in Teplitz that merits attention. In this small spa town in northwest Bohemia, the two greatest artists of the age met—and didn't like each other very much.

Beethoven had revered Johann Wolfgang von Goethe from his teenage years in Bonn, when he set some of Goethe's poems to music. More followed after the move to Vienna, and in 1810 he composed incidental music to Goethe's play *Egmont*. This was a commission from the Burgtheater, which wished to revive the play, and it appealed to Beethoven on two levels. The first was his admiration for Goethe; the second the subject matter of the play, which depicted the revolt of the Flemish hero Count Egmont against the Spanish occupier— thus appealing not just to Beethoven's innate belief in the triumph of freedom over oppression, but to his fondness for a true story that happened in the land of his fathers.

So pleased was he with his work, that he wrote to his publishers, Breitkopf und Härtel, in January 1812, asking them to forward the score to Goethe himself. Six months later Beethoven was in Teplitz, and found that Goethe was there too.

The two great artists met for the first time on 19 July, and what a contrasting pair they were. Goethe, elegant, sophisticated, at ease with aristocracy even royalty, at the height of his fame just a few years after the sensational success of the first part of his epic drama *Faust*; he was indisputably Germany's leading figure in poetry, drama, philosophy and science. Tutored privately from an early age, he was proficient in Latin, Greek, French, Italian, English and Hebrew, and had also been taught to dance, ride and fence. He was, in essence, Enlightenment man.

Well might Beethoven, albeit twenty-one years Goethe's junior, feel somewhat inadequate in the great man's company. He had his music, most certainly, but it was the only area in which he could claim any kind of ascendancy over Goethe.

At the time of their meeting, Goethe was sixty-three years of age, Beethoven forty-one. If opposites attract, they should have got on very well indeed, particularly since their different disciplines, combined with a substantial age difference, should have precluded any rivalry. And it seems, at first, there was indeed a mutual admiration.

After the first meeting, Goethe wrote to his wife, 'Never have I seen a more intensely focused, dynamic, or fervent artist.' Some days later Goethe called on Beethoven, and reported that he played the piano 'delightfully'.

But a famous anecdote shows an underlying tension. The two men were walking together, and the renowned Goethe attracted considerable attention. He found this irritating, and said so. Beethoven drily commented, 'Don't let it trouble Your Excellency; perhaps the greetings are intended for me.'

Then something really did go wrong between them. We do not know for certain what it was, but an incident occurred—highly embarrassing for Goethe—that might explain it.

Goethe and Beethoven were walking in the park behind the castle in the centre of Teplitz, when Goethe spotted the imperial royal family walking towards them. Goethe caught Beethoven's arm and said they must pay their respects. Goethe took his position to the side of the path, and as the Emperor and Empress passed, arm in arm, Goethe removed his hat, swept his arm to the side, and executed a deep bow.

Beethoven, appalled at Goethe's act of sycophancy, slammed his top hat down on the back of his head, held his hands tightly behind his back, and strode defiantly in the opposite direction.

Admittedly the source for this is Bettina Arnim, née Brentano, sister-in-law of Antonie, who is widely judged to have fabricated elements of her contacts with Beethoven, but it is highly unlikely she would have invented the whole episode—even if we allow her points of exaggeration—and the two protagonists seem to confirm in letters they wrote soon afterwards that something of the kind happened.[1]

Goethe wrote to a friend:

> *I made the acquaintance of Beethoven in Teplitz. His talent amazed me. However, unfortunately, he is an utterly untamed personality, not necessarily in the wrong if he regards the world as detestable, but certainly not making it any more pleasant either for himself or others by thinking so. On the other hand one certainly has to make allowances, indeed pity him, as he is losing his hearing, which perhaps has a less harmful effect on the musical part of his nature than the social. By nature rather reserved, he becomes doubly so because of this deficiency.*

Beethoven, by contrast, saw it—unsurprisingly—rather differently. He wrote to his publisher:

> *Goethe delights far too much in the atmosphere of the court, far more than is seemly for a poet. How can one really say very much about the ridiculous behaviour of virtuosi in this respect, when poets, who should be regarded as the leading teachers of the nation, can forget everything else when confronted by that glitter.*

If the two men were not unhappy to take leave of each other, it seems Beethoven's admiration for Goethe might have outweighed the playwright's for him. Some years later he set Goethe's poems 'Meeresstille' ('Calm Sea') and 'Glückliche Fahrt' ('Prosperous Voyage') to music, and sent the settings to Goethe. Receiving no acknowledgement, he wrote to Goethe almost a year later, referring first to 'the happy hours spent in your company' which he would never forget, then saying rather pointedly, 'I am now faced with the fact that I must remind you of my existence—I trust that you received the dedication to Your Excellency of *Meeresstille und glückliche Fahrt.*'

There is again no record of Goethe replying. But if his frustration with Goethe was causing him any anxiety, word from brother Johann of his impending marriage was more than enough to distract him. Beethoven decided to leave for Linz straight away; it was the worst decision he could have made.

——

Beethoven had been in Teplitz for more than two months, and it had been a difficult time for him. There was the emotional aftermath of the Immortal Beloved affair, as well as the obvious tensions surrounding his relationship with Goethe. He had not stayed still, travelling between Teplitz, Karlsbad and Franzensbad, to take different waters on doctors' orders. When he first arrived in Karlsbad, he had forgotten his passport, and the police made him return to Teplitz for it. He had also performed at a public concert.

In August the weather turned and autumn came early. It all caught up with him. Already in poor enough health to have contacted his doctor, in September he fell ill and was confined to bed. The presence of a pretty woman did much to raise his spirits. Amalie Sebald, a singer from Berlin, seventeen years Beethoven's junior, was in Teplitz with her mother. She took it upon herself to look after

Beethoven, well aware that she was tending to the needs of Europe's foremost musician.

She brought him cooked chicken and hot soup. He was flattered by her attention, and wrote her several flirtatious notes. But there was no suggestion that things went any further, and Amalie and her mother left after less than a fortnight.

Tired, unwell, and without doubt depressed—'I am writing to you from my bed. I must tell you that people in Austria no longer trust me completely, and no doubt they are right too,' he wrote to his publisher—he should have packed his things and returned to Vienna, where he could sleep in his own bed and be tended by his doctor.

Instead, spurred on by the news of Johann's intended marriage, he threw his things together and rushed south to the central Austrian town of Linz, via Prague and Budweis, to confront his brother. And confront him he did.

First he tried the straightforward approach of attempting to talk his brother out of marriage. Foremost in his mind was the fact that the object of his brother's affection was a woman by the name of Therese Obermeyer, whom Johann had taken on as his housekeeper. A housekeeper to be given the name of Beethoven? It was, to the head of the family, simply unthinkable. The other brother, Carl, had married an immoral woman, now Johann was intending to marry a domestic servant.

There was an oblique, and to Beethoven appalling, similarity in the circumstances of his two brothers. Whereas Johanna was already pregnant with Carl's child months before their marriage, Therese had an illegitimate daughter from a previous relationship.

Something else had happened in the Beethoven family that was an embarrassment by any standards. To Beethoven it was much, much more than that. Carl's wife Johanna had committed an act of extreme folly, which was to come back years later to haunt her.

A friend had asked her to look after a pearl necklace, valued at

20,000 florins, possibly because she was about to travel and wanted to ensure the necklace was safe. Johanna, it appears, hid the necklace and reported it stolen. It took the police five minutes to put two and two together. Johanna was arrested and put on trial for theft. She was found guilty and sentenced to the extraordinarily harsh punishment of a year's imprisonment. This was reduced to two months, then to one month, and finally to the relatively lenient sentence of one month's house arrest. But the damage was done. Johanna had a criminal record, and Beethoven was not to forget it.

His fire was up; he knew he had to take drastic action, but even Johann can hardly have been prepared for what happened next. Beethoven went to see the local bishop. We have no record of the conversation, but we can assume he told the bishop that since Therese had an illegitimate child, she was an immoral woman who could not be allowed to marry. The bishop no doubt asked whether either Therese or Johann had been married before, and on hearing that they had not, told Beethoven there was nothing to prevent the marriage.

We know Beethoven received no satisfaction from the bishop, because he then went to the local magistrates to ask for a ruling against the intended marriage. That must have failed too, because in what can only be described as an act of extreme desperation, he went to the police and demanded that they set a deadline for Therese to leave Linz, or face arrest. On what grounds is not clear, nor is the response of the police. But certainly no order was issued against Therese.

Johann, hardly surprisingly, was not simply shocked at his brother's behaviour, he was insulted and humiliated. Given Beethoven's actions, the whole town now knew of the family dispute. More than that, his intended wife saw her name being dragged through the mud. Illegitimate daughter she might have, but this she did not deserve.

According to Thayer, Johann decided to confront his brother. In the large room he had given him in his own house, he remonstrated with him, ordering him to keep his nose out of his affairs, to mind his own business. Instead of contrition over the extreme action he had taken, Beethoven argued back. Tempers flared and ... 'A scene ensued on which—let the curtain be drawn,' Thayer diplomatically writes.

There can be no doubt that the two brothers came to blows. Europe's most renowned musical genius scrapping with a leading citizen of Linz, his younger brother. It is not an edifying spectacle.

If anything, Beethoven's actions not only misfired, they were counter-productive. To retain any kind of dignity at all for either of them, Johann had no choice but to marry Therese, which he did on 8 November 1812.

—

It would be wrong to give the impression that this was a swift visit by Beethoven to Linz, during which he took frantic measures to try to prevent his brother marrying, then left having failed. Such was Beethoven's fame by now that he was unable to move entirely as he wished.

There was huge excitement in Linz at the arrival of such a famous figure. It is quite possible that Johann let it be known that his famous brother was on his way to come and stay with him, basking in the reflected glory he knew that would bring. Even if he had misgivings about the purpose of the visit, he would most likely not have let that stop him spreading the news.

Linz Cathedral[2] had its own *Kapellmeister*, a certain Franz Xaver Glöggl, who announced in his music journal, the *Linzer Musik-Zeitung*, the arrival of Beethoven on 5 October. He did not disguise his elation: 'We now have the long-desired pleasure of welcoming to our city the Orpheus and greatest composer of our time, Herr L. Van Beethoven, who arrived here a few days ago. If Apollo is

231

favorably disposed towards us, we shall also have an opportunity to admire his art.'

Glöggl in fact got less than he wanted, but was not entirely disappointed. Beethoven evidently took a liking to Glöggl, perhaps welcoming the company of another musician, and ate at Glöggl's house almost every day. Indeed relations between them must have been very warm indeed, for Glöggl dared to ask Beethoven to compose some funeral music, known as *Equale*, for trombones, and Beethoven agreed.[3]

Inevitably the nobility of Linz vied among themselves to hold soirées in Beethoven's honour. At one such occasion Beethoven's behaviour caused a mixture of consternation and amusement.

Beethoven, as guest of honour, was entertained to music by local musicians, and then some of his song settings were sung. After that his host, no doubt hoping the music had put him in benign mood, asked him if he would entertain the gathering to one of his famed improvisations on the piano. Beethoven refused.

There was some polite conversation, another attempt to cajole Beethoven into playing, then a general invitation for everyone to repair to the adjoining room where a table had been spread with food. The guests picked up a plate from the table by the door, and moved into the next room. Beethoven did not come with them. In fact he was nowhere to be seen. Some of the guests offered to go and look for him, but returned shaking their heads. Finally it was decided to sit at the table and eat.

Once the meal was firmly under way, sounds of the piano being played drifted in from the adjoining room. It was obviously Beethoven, but the guests were not quite sure what to do. They knew that if they all rushed in, he was likely to stop. At the same time, they could hardly continue eating and talking.

So, one by one, with extreme caution, they stepped quietly into the music room, aware they were witnessing something rare, which was to be savoured and treasured. Beethoven continued to play for the best part of an hour, exactly the sort of improvisation for which he was famous, but which he was by now so reluctant to provide.

Then, as suddenly as he had started, he stopped, realising that he had been invited to eat. He leapt up from the piano and, barely seeing anyone else in the room, dashed to the door, where he collided with the table and sent the china crashing to the floor.

There was nervous laughter, which quickly turned to relief, as the host smilingly escorted Beethoven to the dinner table.

—

Unbelievably, incredibly—but this is Beethoven, so maybe it is neither unbelievable nor incredible—while he was in Linz doing battle with his brother, his emotions in tatters, his health even if improved still fragile, his mood despondent, he completed his Eighth Symphony, his wittiest and most humorous symphony to date, replete with twists and turns, unconventional key changes and unexpected dynamics.

If this might be expected to lift his mood, it did not do so. He returned to Vienna in November after an absence of four months in a state bordering on despair. He wrote to Archduke Rudolph that he was 'ailing, although mentally, it is true, more than physically'. He began to keep a diary (*Tagebuch*), and the first entry, although undated, was probably written in November or December of 1812, and it indicates a tortured soul:

> *Submission, absolute submission to your fate, only this can give you the sacrifices—for the servitude—Oh hard struggle!—Do everything that still needs to be done to plan for the long journey. You must—yourself find everything that your dearest wish can offer, yet you must bend it to your will—Keep always of the same mind—*

*You may no longer be a man, not for yourself, only for others, for
you there is no longer any happiness except in yourself, in your
art*—Oh God, give me strength to conquer myself, nothing at all
must chain me to life—

Whatever internal traumas he was suffering, external events
could only worsen them. It was just days after returning to Vienna
that he heard that his benefactor Prince Kinsky, one of the three
signatories to the annuity contract, had fallen off his horse and died.
The payments were stopped and he began a protracted, and draining, fight with the Kinsky estate to get the payments reinstated.

More likely to hurt him emotionally, he returned to the city to
find that his brother Carl was seriously ill with tuberculosis, the disease that had killed their mother. In fact so grave was Carl's health
that in April 1813 he made a declaration in which he called on his
brother Ludwig to undertake sole guardianship of his son Karl. The
one-paragraph document was signed by Carl, Beethoven, and three
witnesses. It does not mention Johanna by name, but the obvious
effect of it would be to exclude Johanna from playing any part in the
upbringing of her son.

This, on the face of it, was an extraordinary decision. Exactly what
turned Carl against his wife is not known. Most certainly Beethoven
himself would have pressured his brother, and we might find it surprising with modern eyes that three witnesses were persuaded too. But
that was nothing compared with the turn of events that would follow.

In fact Carl's health improved in the following months, and the
declaration was not enacted, but it was a foretaste of what was to come.

—

Beethoven's behaviour in this period was giving his friends
cause for concern. He had given up caring about his appearance, or
even his hygiene. Restaurants—those that would admit him—kept

a solitary table at the back of the room, so that his eating habits did not deter other guests.

It is from this time that rumours began that he visited prostitutes regularly. There has been enormous controversy over this, derived from the fact that in notes and letters to his close friend Zmeskall there is nothing specific, but he uses oblique words and phrases that are capable of different interpretations. If he did visit prostitutes, as a single man in his forties it would certainly not be unusual, but for Beethoven the moralist it comes under the same category as conducting an affair with a married woman. It is possible, though highly unlikely.

That his emotions were in a dire state, though, is not in doubt. 'So many unfortunate incidents occurring one after the other have really driven me into an almost disordered state,' he wrote to Rudolph. Most important of all, he had composed nothing substantial, nor published anything for over a year.

More than anything it was his volatility, his unpredictability, that made him so difficult to be with, that made his friends, even his family, so reluctant to involve themselves with him. His brother Carl, even as his health was being sapped by tuberculosis, was not immune from his elder brother's wrath—or from the overwhelming remorse that followed it.

Carl, Johanna, and their six-year-old son Karl were at the dinner table some time in late 1812 or early 1813. Suddenly the door opened and Beethoven burst in. 'You thief! Where are my manuscripts?' Carl, physically weak, either denied he had taken anything, or told his brother he had no idea what he was talking about. A violent quarrel ensued, which threatened to come to blows, or possibly even did, since Karl recalled later that his mother had difficulty separating the two men. Carl tore himself away, with his wife's help, crossed the room, opened a drawer, took out the 'missing' manuscript pages, and threw them down in front of Beethoven.

Visible proof that his brother had not stolen the pages was enough to calm Beethoven down, who actually went so far as to apologise. In reality he had no choice, in the face of the evidence. But righteous indignation—quite possibly a culmination of smaller aggressive incidents—got the better of Carl, and he refused to be placated. He continued to hurl abuse at his elder brother, who rushed out of the room—leaving the offending manuscript pages behind. Carl continued to shout after him, saying he did not want that 'dragon' (*Drachen*) to set foot in his home again.

According to Karl, a short time after the incident he and his father were crossing a bridge over the Danube Canal, when by coincidence Beethoven was crossing in the opposite direction. Beethoven saw Carl, and gasped to see the physical deterioration in his brother. He threw his arms around Carl's neck and covered him in kisses with such passion that 'people stared in complete bewilderment'.

Beethoven's contrition might be commendable, but its excessiveness, and the fact that it was delivered so publicly, suggest a certain lack of proportion. However we look at it, we are left to struggle with the knowledge that one of the greatest artists who ever lived came to physical blows with both his brothers, and that in each case the dispute was entirely of his making.

—

Arguably Beethoven, in 1813, was at the lowest ebb in his life. A failed love affair, continuing ill-health, domestic tribulations, blocked creativity, worsening deafness … You begin to wonder how much more he could take, what might come along that might tip him over the edge. Those words at the end of his first entry in the *Tagebuch*—'nothing at all must chain me to life'—take on a truly ominous ring.

However, not for the first time in life external events came, obliquely, to his rescue, and once again they concerned the adventures of the

Corsican-born commander and Emperor who was rampaging across Europe at the head of the Continent's most powerful fighting force.

—

On 21 June 1813, Arthur Wellesley, at the head of 79,000 British, Portuguese and Spanish soldiers, routed the French army under King Joseph of Spain at the Battle of Vitoria. Joseph had been placed on the throne of Spain by his younger brother Napoleon Bonaparte three years earlier. The battle cost Joseph all his guns, supplies, treasure—and his kingdom. The loss of Spain was a devastating blow to the French Emperor, all the more so for coming less than a year after his own humiliation in Russia.

In Vienna there were wild scenes of jubilation on the streets, in the parks, along the high paths of the Bastei. No one doubted that this was the beginning of the end of Napoleonic hegemony in Europe. For a country whose army had suffered so often at the hands of Napoleon, whose capital city, seat of empire, had been shelled into surrender, it was a sweet moment.

To what did the people of Vienna turn to celebrate? Music, of course. And to whom? It was just what Beethoven needed. He gave two hugely successful concerts, at which he conducted the first public performances of his Seventh Symphony,[4] as well as the piece he had composed to celebrate the Battle of Vitoria, *Wellingtons[5] Sieg[6]* (*Wellington's Victory*). This was followed by a third concert, including again the Seventh Symphony, and the first performance of the Eighth.

And what did the Emperor and the ruling elite of Austria do to celebrate? What they had done many times before: declare war on France. This time Austria joined the allies in a new coalition, which resulted in Napoleon, at the head of 195,000 men, facing 365,000 Austrian, Prussian, Russian, and Swedish soldiers at the Battle of Leipzig, known as the Battle of the Nations.

Defeat for France was inevitable, though in the event French losses were nothing like as great as those of the allies, when considered proportionately. But defeat it was. The disastrous Russian adventure, the loss of Spain, now defeat on the battlefield—the Napoleonic era was nearing its end.

The allies followed up their victory by invading France in January 1814. Less than three months later Napoleon was deposed by the French Senate, forced to abdicate in favour of his son, and was exiled to the Mediterranean island of Elba.

The question was what to do now. It was decided that, with Napoleon Bonaparte finally defeated, a Congress of European leaders would be held to redraw the post-Napoleonic map of Europe. Where would this triumphal meeting be held? In the city that had so suffered at the hands of Napoleon and his army: Vienna.

It was actually by virtue of the successful concerts, not the decision to hold the Congress in Vienna (which came some months later), that the theatre directors decided to approach Beethoven and make a rather bold suggestion. Would he consider reviving his opera *Leonore*, which had been so ill-fated eight years earlier?

Perhaps to their surprise, he agreed, on condition that the libretto be extensively revised. His choice for this was a German-born playwright and librettist, Georg Friedrich Treitschke, whose work he admired. The directors agreed.

It really is remarkable—in a way that so often characterises Beethoven's life—that, despite the extreme depression into which he had sunk so recently, and considering the traumatic events that had surrounded the first two productions of his opera, he not only agreed to rework it, but did so with gusto, apparently establishing a comfortable working relationship with Treitschke.

Beethoven clearly gave Treitschke carte blanche, and even when they disagreed he allowed himself to be persuaded. Treitschke tightened up the first act, entirely rewriting the end, so that the prison governor's anger is a natural consequence of the prisoners being allowed out into the daylight, and his order that they return to their cells bringing the first act to a satisfying close.

But Treitschke's revisions to Act II were far more far-reaching. Beginning with Florestan's heart-rending cry from his dungeon, he rewrote Florestan's aria so that a man being starved to death experiences a last blaze of life before he dies. This met entirely with Beethoven's approval. Treitschke—earning our eternal gratitude—has left a riveting account of Beethoven in the white heat of inspiration:

> *What I now relate will live for ever in my memory. Beethoven came to me about seven o'clock in the evening. After we had discussed other things, he asked how matters stood with the aria. It was just finished; I handed it to him. He read it, ran up and down the room, muttered and growled, as was his habit instead of singing—and tore open the piano. My wife had often begged him to play, but in vain. Today he placed the text in front of him and began to play wonderful improvisations, which sadly no magic could cause to remain solid in the air. Out of them he seemed to conjure the motif of the aria. The hours passed, but Beethoven continued to improvise. Supper, which he had intended to share with us, was served, but he would not allow himself to be disturbed. Finally, at a late hour, he embraced me, and declining an invitation to eat, he hurried home. The next day the admirable composition was finished.*

This is quite possibly the only eyewitness account we have of Beethoven actually involved in the compositional process—I am not aware of any other. It is made all the more precious because the aria he composed that night and completed the following morning is the aria we know today. It is one of the most famous, and poignant, moments in all opera: Florestan, starving to death in the underground dungeon, lets out a piercing cry, followed by a lament, but now ending in a kind of trance, seeing a vision of his wife Leonore as an angel leading him to freedom in Heaven. Any operatic tenor will confirm what a challenge it is, beginning with the *crescendo* cry, going through an extensive range of emotions, and ending in an extremely high register—all sung from a lying and sitting position.

With his fine sense of theatricality, Treitschke moved the final scene into the town marketplace, in other words up into the daylight—both previous versions of the opera had taken place entirely in the dungeon. This allowed the rescue to be fully celebrated, for the reunited couple to sing a joyous duet accompanied by full chorus, as well as giving the psychologically satisfying transition from darkness into light.

It was as if, this time, Beethoven's opera was preordained to be a success. It went into rehearsal in April 1814, and was performed several times over the following weeks. Changes continued to be made, and on 18 July it was performed in its final version, the version we know today. Beethoven composed yet another overture, the fourth, crisper, more dramatic than its predecessors, and again that is the overture played today.

It had been around a decade in coming, and had caused Beethoven more pain and heartache than any other composition, but *Fidelio* was at last complete, and in a form he was satisfied with. Small wonder that when the organisers of the Congress of Vienna decided to arrange a gala evening for the crowned heads of Europe in September, they chose to stage *Fidelio*. Small wonder too that Beethoven henceforth turned his back on the operatic form, and never composed another.

Before we leave the Congress, which has entered history more for the entertainment it provided—'*le congrès ne marche pas, il danse*', with the Viennese amusing themselves in a new game of spotting the King or Prince hurrying through the streets at night in disguise on the way to his mistress—than any concrete political results, it had one more direct effect on Beethoven's musical output.

To honour the presence of so many crowned heads, he set absurd lyrics to music in a composition entitled 'Der glorreiche Augenblick' ('The Glorious Moment'). The piece has survived, is rarely played today, and is usually treated as an aberration.[7]

So why did he agree to set to music the simplistic words of a certain Alois Weissenbach, Professor of Surgery and Head Surgeon at St. John's Hospital in Salzburg? More than that, why did he invite Professor Weissenbach to call on him for breakfast, and greet him with a warm handshake and even a kiss? Because Professor Weissenbach was profoundly deaf. 'It was pitiful to hear them shout at each other,' wrote an eyewitness. I suspect it wasn't at all pitiful, and that they relished each other's company, two men barely able to hear a word the other said.

The frivolities and philandering were brought to a sudden end at the beginning of March 1815, when word reached Vienna that the unthinkable, the impossible, had occurred. Napoleon Bonaparte had escaped from Elba, landed in southern France, and was marching north, gathering an army around him.

But it is unlikely this impinged much on Beethoven. He had a far more serious problem to contend with, a crisis that had been in abeyance for two years, but that now returned with a vengeance.

CHAPTER FOURTEEN

INTO THE
WITNESS BOX

HOW THE SINGLE LETTER 'O'
RUINED BEETHOVEN'S LIFE

CARL VAN BEETHOVEN HAD FALLEN ILL again with tuberculosis, and this time it was clear to everybody that it was terminal. The ramifications of this, and what followed, were to have the most profound effect on Beethoven, indeed it is not an exaggeration to say that they were to affect him for the rest of his life.

It is possible to pinpoint the beginning of it to the exact day: 14 November 1815. Carl van Beethoven lay dying. He was forty-one years of age. On that day Beethoven went to see his brother. By chance, he discovered Carl's Will lying on a sideboard. He had not known either that the Will had been written or what its terms were.

He picked it up, read it—and Clause 5 hit him like a thunderbolt: 'Along with my wife I appoint my brother Ludwig van Beethoven co-guardian [of my son Karl].'

He angrily told his brother there and then that the Will could not stand as it was. It flatly contradicted the declaration of two and half years before, when the tuberculosis first took hold, which stated Carl's wish that, in the event of his death, his brother Ludwig should become Karl's guardian. He insisted that Clause 5 had to be changed. Carl acquiesced. He took a pen and crossed out the words 'Along with my wife' and 'co-'.

It must have been an extraordinary scene. Carl was less than twenty-four hours from death. One imagines him propped up in bed, his small frame ravaged by disease, his cheeks flushed in the characteristic sign of tuberculosis, probably racked by coughing, a handkerchief flecked with blood held to his lips, gazing in despair with feverish watery eyes ... as his brother strode across the end of his bed, waving his arms and ranting against Johanna.

Beethoven himself wrote of it later, in a memorandum to the Court of Appeal, in measured tones. Having discovered the Will and read it, he realised '[certain] passages had to be stricken out. This I had my brother bring about since I did not wish to be bound up in this with such a bad woman in a matter of such importance as the education of the child.' In reality one can only envision the vitriol he poured out to his dying brother against the woman he had loathed since the day he had set eyes on her—and, given her repu-tation, before. Clearly the passage of time had not exactly mellowed Beethoven's antagonism towards his sister-in-law.

Thanks to his timely arrival at his brother's bedside, however, he had averted disaster. Satisfied with his efforts, he left his brother, but not for long. Some sixth sense, possibly, caused him to return just an hour and a half later. If he had suspicions, they were justified. The Will had gone. There followed yet another confrontation between Beethoven and his dying brother. We do not know exactly what was said, but we know the circumstances, and I have therefore allowed myself to presume Beethoven's words.

'What has happened to it? Where is it? Who has taken it?' Bee-thoven demanded to know. Carl summoned his failing strength and told his brother—haltingly, no doubt, knowing even so close to death the torrent it would unleash—that something had been added to the Will, and he had been made to sign it.

'Was it to do with Karl?' Beethoven demanded. 'It was, wasn't it?' Carl must have made the smallest nod of his head he possibly could, as he said something. Beethoven wrote later in the memorandum that his brother begged him to hurry to the lawyer's office, recover the Will and bring it back so he could change it, 'because otherwise some great misunderstanding might arise therefrom'.

'Those were his very words,' Beethoven wrote. It seems unlikely. The probability is he dragged the name of the lawyer from Carl, or if Carl was too weak to give him details, searched the room and possibly other rooms too until he found the lawyer's name and address, and hurried off.

The lawyer's office was closed. Beethoven reported that the 'lawyer could not be found that day'. But it was a Tuesday, and the lawyer had clearly been involved in whatever alteration had been made to the Will only a short time earlier. He made repeated attempts to find him, but without success. It is probable the lawyer had simply gone home.

At five o'clock the following morning Carl died. When the Will was later read, the codicil that had been added during Beethoven's short absence from the room, which Carl had signed along with three witnesses, was as devastating as Beethoven had feared.

At its heart, surrounded by legal language, this crucial sentence:

> *I have found it necessary to add to my Will that I by no means desire that my son be taken away from his mother, but that he shall always ... remain with his mother, to which end his guardianship is to be exercised by her as well as my brother ... God permit them to be harmonious for the sake of my child's welfare. This is the last wish of the dying husband and brother.*

Carl cannot, in his worst fears, have imagined just how far his last wish would come from being realised.

—

Beethoven went on the attack. He decided to fight Johanna in every way he could, for as long as it took, whatever the cost, to exclude her from the guardianship of her son. It is difficult for us today, even at a distance of two centuries, to excuse him for what he did. His friends were equally appalled. There is virtually no mention of them in this period. It is likely they tried to broach the subject, tried to reason with him, to persuade him to drop legal action, felt the full force of his wrath, and retired from the scene.

What certainly lay behind Beethoven's determination, as well as his antipathy towards Johanna, was his unwavering belief that his nephew Karl would—alone—be 'Beethoven the musician' of the next generation. Alone, because Carl was now dead, Johann was trapped in a loveless marriage that had not produced children and was unlikely to do so, and he, Ludwig, knew he would never marry.

Karl, the sole child of the Beethoven brothers, was by now nine years old, with no evident interest in music and no obvious talent for it either. None of that altered his uncle's unswerving belief that Karl would carry the musical banner forward. And for that to happen, the boy had to be separated utterly from the malign influence of his mother so he could give himself wholly to his uncle, to his 'father'. But there was a hurdle in the way: Carl's Will. Beethoven knew he had, somehow, to get rid of it.

On 28 November, two weeks after Carl's death and one week after his Will was enacted, Beethoven appealed to the *Landrecht* to exclude Johanna from the guardianship of her son. It was a high-risk strategy. The *Landrecht* was the upper court, the court of the nobility. Only those of noble birth could have their cases heard there. Ordinary people, the 'lower classes', were obliged to use the lower court, the *Magistrat*. Beethoven was not of noble birth—far from it—but most people were not aware of this, or, more probably, in a city where everybody connected to the arts had noble rank of some kind or another, few thought to question it.

Though there is no direct evidence of this, it is more than likely that when Beethoven, as a young man of almost twenty-two years of age, arrived in Vienna from Bonn, he found himself mistakenly introduced as Ludwig *von* Beethoven, and it was therefore assumed he was a member of German aristocracy. It was an easy mistake to make: he was German, his prodigious musical talent saw him quickly taken up by the aristocratic patrons of the arts, so that he became a familiar figure in the highest salons. No doubt his very un-aristocratic mode of dress and demeanour was put down to the eccentricities of a musician. No one, therefore, thought it in any way inappropriate that Beethoven should take his case for guardianship of Karl to the court of the nobility, the *Landrecht*.

Beethoven appeared before the court on 13 December and declared that he could produce 'weighty reasons' for excluding Johanna from the guardianship of Karl. The court ordered him to do so within three days, or his case would fail. This is the moment when Johanna's folly regarding her friend's string of pearls came back to haunt her.

Beethoven applied to the City Magistrates for an official certificate detailing Johanna's conviction for embezzlement in 1811, which was to be the main plank of his argument that she was unfit to bring up her son. The Magistrates' office replied that it could not issue him personally with a copy of the judgment against Johanna, but that it would forward it direct to the *Landrecht* tribunal. This it did on 21 December.

To reinforce his case, Beethoven drew up a lengthy document outlining his argument and submitted it to the *Landrecht* on 20 December—technically the final day allowed to him by the court, given the intervening weekend. The document is written in another hand and signed by Beethoven, the assumption being that it was actually drafted by a lawyer. The key sentences state that the codicil in Carl's Will appointing his widow joint guardian of Karl was added 'when I was absent for an hour and a half, i.e. without my knowledge and behind my back', and that it can be proved easily that his dying brother added the codicil only 'because he was insistently urged to do so by his wife and was not in a condition to take an entirely free decision'.

In language clearly formulated by the lawyer, Beethoven declares he regards it as 'a sacred duty enjoined on my conscience not to abandon my rights to the guardianship … and shall make every effort to do whatever in my strongest conviction can contribute to and promote the true welfare as well as the moral and intellectual benefit of my nephew'.

On 9 January 1816 the *Landrecht* ruled in Beethoven's favour. Ten days later he appeared before the tribunal and 'vowed with solemn handgrasp' to perform his duties as Karl's sole guardian. On 2 February Karl, nine and a half years old, was taken from his mother.

Beethoven's first act as guardian was to put Karl into a local boarding school, away from the influence of his mother. But it was not to be as simple as that. Johanna made repeated attempts to see her son—on one occasion apparently disguising herself as a man to gain admittance.

Beethoven decided the headmaster needed to know exactly what kind of woman Johanna was, to ensure he would deny her access to her son, and wrote to him in extraordinarily defamatory terms:

> *Last night that Queen of the Night was at the Artists' Ball until 3 a.m. exposing not only her mental but also her bodily nakedness—it was whispered that she—was willing to hire herself—for 20 gulden! Oh horrible!*

You can almost sense Beethoven's reluctance to commit to paper his allegation that she was prostituting herself, and his satisfaction at being able to equate her with the duplicitous character from Mozart's *The Magic Flute*, one of his favourite operas. Since there is no evidence from anyone else at the Artists' Ball to corroborate Beethoven's accusations, we must assume either that he was inventing what he saw, or at best exaggerating. Perhaps she was being overtly flirtatious, which in Beethoven's eyes equated with what he described.

Beethoven angrily went back to court to take out an injunction forbidding Johanna from seeing her son. The court granted it, but with a proviso: Johanna could see Karl in his leisure hours, and only with Beethoven's consent.

It was an unhappy situation, exacerbated by events. Later in the year Karl complained of severe stomach pains and had to undergo a hernia operation, after which he needed to wear a truss. The trauma of this brought home to Beethoven just what he had taken on, and how unsuited he was to take on the role, not just of father, but mother as well. He practically said as much in the later memorandum to the Appeal Court:

> *I once in anger pulled my nephew from his chair, because he had done something very naughty. As he had to wear a truss permanently after his operation for hernia ... my action caused him some pain <u>in the most sensitive spot</u> when he had to turn round quickly.*

In the same document he impugns Johanna's character with potentially more devastating accusations than in the letter to the headmaster:

> *Immediately after my brother's death she began to have intimate relations with a lover, and her behaviour even shocked the modesty of her innocent son. She was to be seen in all the dance halls and at festivities, while her son went without the necessities of life and was left to fend for himself in the charge of some wretched maid of hers. What would have become of him if I had not looked after him?*

There is no evidence any of these accusations were true. This is a man clearly prepared to stop at nothing to get his way, even if it meant destroying a close family member.

Beethoven began to make plans to take Karl out of the boarding school and have him live with him, but it is perhaps another indication of his growing self-doubt that this did not happen for another sixteen months.

That self-doubt was accompanied by a raft of other emotions. Beethoven was clearly disturbed by what he was doing. There is evidence his conscience was troubling him. He wrote in his diary, 'My part, O lord, I have performed. It might have been possible without hurting the widow, but it was not so ... Bless my work, bless the widow! Why can I not wholly obey my heart and help her, the widow?'

One of the daughters of the boarding school headmaster quoted him in her diary as saying, 'What will people say? They will take me for a tyrant.'

Worse than anything, during the long-drawn-out legal process, Beethoven was composing—virtually—nothing. This period was to be the most barren, artistically, of his life.[1]

In the autumn of 1818, Johanna appealed twice to the *Landrecht* to reconsider its decision excluding her from her son's guardianship. She cited Beethoven's failings as guardian, as shown by the fact that Karl was expelled from another school his uncle had sent him to, and several instances of unruly behaviour that had been reported to her. No wonder, she told the court—he needed his mother's influence. She also argued that Beethoven's deafness seriously impeded his attempts at guardianship.

Beethoven, again with legal advice, submitted a document rebutting her arguments. On the question of his deafness, he wrote—to the surprise of his friends who surely must have made some pact to say nothing to contradict him:

Everybody who is closely acquainted with me knows only too well that all verbal communications between me and my nephew and other people are carried on with the greatest of ease and are by no means impeded by my indifferent hearing. Furthermore, my health has never been better ...

This at a time when, according to one eyewitness, people had to shout at Beethoven to make themselves understood, when he had begun to carry a notebook and pencil everywhere so people could write their questions down, and when in correspondence he frequently referred to his ill-health.

In an obvious boost to his self-confidence, and his belief that what he was doing was morally right, the *Landrecht* rejected both of Johanna's appeals.

By now Beethoven had taken Karl out of the boarding school to live with him. It was a fraught situation. Beethoven was aware of his eccentricities, but had never made any attempt to hide or adjust them in front of friends. With Karl it was different. He suspected Karl was ashamed to be seen out with him, because his clothes were always untidy and in need of repair.

He noted Karl's reluctance to eat in restaurants with him. Several of his favourite restaurants would keep a table apart for him and he knew why. But he could not adapt his behaviour and it undoubtedly worried him. There was also his deafness, and he was aware that Karl was frustrated at constantly having to repeat himself. Also Karl was still recovering from the painful hernia operation and still wearing a truss. Beethoven simply did not know how to handle such domestic issues.

Then, on 3 December 1818, Karl—a pawn hitherto in the prolonged battle between his mother and his uncle—took matters into his own hands. He ran away—to his mother. Beethoven was devastated. He hurried back to the boarding school whose headmaster he had befriended. The headmaster's daughter recorded in her diary, 'B. came in great excitement and sought counsel and help from my father, saying that Karl had run away! I recall that ... he cried out tearfully, "He is ashamed of me!"'

Beethoven went round to Johanna's apartment the next morning and demanded she return Karl in compliance with the court order. Johanna promised to do so that evening. But Beethoven feared she would spirit the boy away, and so he called the police. They reminded Johanna of her obligations, and she—one can only imagine with what degree of anguish and heartache—handed her son over to them.

Now Johanna herself took the initiative. She used the fact that Karl had run away from his uncle to be with her as reason to petition the *Landrecht* yet again to reconsider its exclusion of her from Karl's guardianship.

The court convened on 11 December and all three parties to the case—Karl, Johanna and Beethoven—gave evidence separately.

It must have been dreadfully intimidating for Karl, just twelve years of age, to stand in the dock and give evidence against his mother, which he knew he had to do because of the court order that favoured his uncle. His answers, as quoted in the court minutes, are nervous and anxious. He speaks highly of his uncle, and when asked if his uncle has ever maltreated him, replies that it happened only once, after the police had returned him from his mother, and his uncle threatened to throttle him. He admits to making disrespectful comments about his mother in the presence of his uncle, but he did this to please his uncle.

Johanna's testimony is calm and assured. Why else would her son come to her, if not because he did not like living with his uncle? She had indeed advised him to return, but he was reluctant to do so because he feared his uncle would punish him.

Her lawyer, a relation by marriage, presented a damning indictment of the Beethoven family. He said that the Beethoven brothers were eccentric men, so often at each other's throats that they were more enemies than friends. As for Johanna's late husband Carl, he was civil towards his elder brother only when he wanted money from him.

In what has to be the most extraordinarily condemnatory statement ever made in public about the great artist whose music will enrich humanity for all time, the lawyer said, 'Johanna van Beethoven's son Karl cannot be allowed to remain under the sole influence of his uncle and guardian, because of the danger that he will suffer physical and moral ruin.'

For good measure the lawyer added that he had himself observed that Karl had frostbitten hands and feet when he ran away to his mother, that he was wearing flimsy clothes in the depths of winter, and had clearly not taken a bath for a long time.

Then came an episode of high drama that would change Beethoven's life.

Johanna, it appears without appreciating the full implication of what she was saying, told the court she believed Beethoven intended sending Karl away to a private school outside Vienna. She, on the other hand, wanted him to go to the local public seminary, where he would mix with other boys and be in the familiar surroundings of the city. Furthermore, she had been assured there was a place available for him.

When it came to Beethoven's turn to enter the witness box, the court asked him why he was against sending Karl to the seminary. Beethoven replied that there were too many pupils there and the supervision would be inadequate.

Then the court, probably like Johanna unmindful of what they were about to unleash, asked him what plans he had for the boy's education. Beethoven's reply sank him. He said he would put Karl back into the boarding school for the winter, then send him to the private seminary in the town of Melk—adding, almost as an afterthought, that he would gladly send Karl to the Theresianum Academy 'if he were but of noble birth'.

The panel of judges must have sat aghast when they heard his words, then exchanged looks of incredulity with each other. One of the judges finally asked him the obvious question. Were he and his late brother then not members of the nobility? Clearly suspecting that they were not, the judge asked Beethoven if he was in possession of documents to prove he was of noble birth.

Beethoven had in the witness box with him his friend, the journalist and librettist Karl Joseph Bernard, to help him with his deafness. One can imagine Bernard, white-faced, turning to Beethoven and repeating the judge's question loudly into his ear, writing it down as well to make sure Beethoven understood it. And one can imagine Beethoven's shock, as he must have taken in the unbearable realisation that he had demolished his own case with a few unnecessary words.

Probably without waiting for Beethoven to prompt him, Bernard told the court that 'van' was a Dutch predicate that did not signify membership of the nobility, and that Beethoven did not possess any documents to prove the contrary.

The judges recalled Johanna and asked her if her husband Carl was of noble birth. Her answer was devastating: 'So the brothers said, and the documentary proof is in the possession of the oldest brother, the composer.'

Under oath Johanna was testifying that the Beethoven brothers claimed to be of noble birth, and Ludwig van Beethoven was in possession of the documents to prove it. Johanna's record for honesty, as a convicted thief, was not good, and it is certainly possible that she was lying.

But the judges of the *Landrecht* had no need to waste their time trying to establish the truth of the matter. Beethoven had admitted he did not have documentary proof of nobility, and that was enough to allow them to wash their hands of the matter. This was not a case for the *Landrecht*, and they referred it—no doubt with some relief—

to the *Magistrat*, the lower court, the court of the 'common people'.

It was, for Beethoven, much more than a disappointment; it was a public humiliation. In no time the news raced round Vienna. Beethoven, who counted the aristocracy among his friends, who could call on the Emperor's brother without so much as an appointment, who was lauded in the highest salons in the land ... was himself of no higher status than the ordinary people in the street.

There was another, more practical, reason for his distress. He knew perfectly well that the *Magistrat*, the lower court, was a champion of ordinary people, with a reputation for finding in their favour when they ran into trouble with the nobility. It was certain to take a dim view of the fact that he had taken his case to the court of the nobility when he was in fact on the same level before the law as any other common citizen.

His fears were well founded. The new year had barely begun when the *Magistrat* found against Beethoven, withdrew Karl from his guardianship, and returned him to his mother. Beethoven was devastated.

—

But Beethoven was not finished. He was determined to win this fight. It had been going on for more than three years, and he was in no mood to give up. Five times during the year 1819 he wrote to the *Magistrat* pleading with them to reconsider. Some of the letters were brief, some rambling. He received no reply.

Then, in the autumn of that year, Beethoven took on a new legal adviser, Johann Baptist Bach. In February 1820, with Bach's help, he drew up a lengthy document—the longest piece of writing in Beethoven's hand—divided into seven parts. It details every aspect of the case, and is unstinting in its characterisation of Johanna as a wicked and immoral woman, with a criminal record, with no education whatsoever, and utterly unsuited to bringing up her son.

Bach submitted the document, not to the *Magistrat*, but to the Court of Appeal, the highest court in the land. Three weeks later, on 8 April 1820, the court ruled in Beethoven's favour. Johanna made a direct appeal to the Emperor to intervene personally. He refused.

Finally, Beethoven had won. Karl was his. Johanna had lost. Was that not proof he had been right from the start? But what on earth could have brought about this extraordinary turnaround? We shall never know. One of Beethoven's friends had told him that the *Magistrat* was known to be corrupt, and if he had used bribery he would undoubtedly have won at that earlier stage. Might he have used bribery with the Court of Appeal? There is no evidence he did, but there wouldn't be, would there?

Karl was at last Beethoven's, at the end of a four-and-a-half-year struggle. But at what a cost. He was soon to fall seriously ill, and was never again to enjoy complete good health in the remaining six years of his life.

The court case he pursued so relentlessly against Johanna is an episode for which it is hard to forgive him. One of his modern biographers writes:

> *The lawsuit over his nephew brought out the worst in Beethoven's character, and during its course he exhibited self-righteousness, vindictiveness, unscrupulousness, lack of self-control, and a wholesale disregard for any point of view but his own.*[2]

Perhaps the most we can say is that the mind of a true genius is often found to be wanting in other areas; that the balance between different parts in the brain of a genius is not always as it should be. The genius might be supreme in the area of his genius, but in other areas—which to the non-genius may seem straightforward and obvious—he is left floundering.

But what is also clear is that Beethoven had a conscience. There is evidence even he knew deep down that what he was doing was wrong. There is the quotation already cited: 'What will people say? They will take me for a tyrant!' And in his diary he wrote, 'This one thing I clearly perceive: life may not be the greatest good there is, but the greatest evil is certainly guilt.'

A little later: 'It would have been impossible without hurting the widow's feelings, but it was not to be. Thou, almighty God, who seest into my heart, know that I have disregarded my own welfare for my dear Karl's sake, bless my work, bless the widow, why cannot I entirely follow my heart and from now—the widow—God, God, my refuge, my rock ...' Little wonder he suddenly enquired after Johanna's health when he heard she had been unwell, and offered her money.

What is truly extraordinary is that Johanna, despite all that Beethoven had inflicted on her, appears never to have written or spoken out against her brother-in-law during the rest of her long life, which outlived Beethoven's by forty-one years and ended in her early eighties. Nor is there any evidence that she ever tried to make money from her closeness to Beethoven—memoirs, reminiscences, what today's newspapers would call 'kiss and tell', of the great composer into whose family she married—despite ending her life in some degree of poverty.

It is all the more surprising given the macabre events that would befall her son Karl, for which his uncle was directly, if unwittingly, responsible.

A MUSICAL GIFT FROM LONDON

HOW ROSSINI FOUND BEETHOVEN 'DISORDERLY AND DIRTY'

BEETHOVEN'S HEALTH HAD CAUSED HIM PROBLEMS all his adult life, and it concerned his digestive system. He complained of bloated stomach, colic, diarrhoea, indigestion. Today he might well have been diagnosed with irritable bowel syndrome, or something similar. Certainly he did nothing to ease the problems. He drank excessively, mostly local red wine. He smoked a pipe when drinking in a tavern. (A pipe with its bowl filled with tobacco could be bought at the counter.)

His eating habits would appal any doctor—he ate irregularly, would miss dinner and get up in the night to eat, eat enormous quantities one day and practically nothing the next, sometimes devouring a meal so quickly it was bound to give him digestive problems. In a restaurant he was known on some occasions to skip a main course, on others to order two. Once, dissatisfied with the lamb chops put in front of him, he hurled the plate at the waiter, who reacted by pretending to enjoy the taste of the gravy as it trickled over his lips.

Eating for Beethoven was rarely a pleasure; it was simply a means to an end. Not that he was entirely unthinking when it came to food. He employed a cook, and sacked several for not cooking to his satisfaction. It appears he was not averse to trying his hand in the kitchen himself. He sent a note to a local fishmonger, undated but probably in 1822, enclosing 5 gulden, and requesting them 'most politely' to let him have 'a carp weighing 3 or 4 lbs, *or better still*, a pike of at least 3 lbs. If you have neither of these kinds of fish, then please send me some other fish of about the same weight.'

It is possible, of course, that he was ordering the fish on behalf of his cook. But we know for certain that he did on occasion cook, thanks to his musical colleague, and Egyptian-hieroglyphic page-turner Ignaz Seyfried, who relates that on one occasion, being without a cook, Beethoven decided to invite friends to supper and cook the meal himself. Their host greeted his guests wearing a blue apron and nightcap. After a wait of an hour and a half, Beethoven served up 'soup of the kind dished up to beggars, half-done beef, vegetables floating in a mixture of water and grease, and roast that seemed to have been smoked in the chimney'. Beethoven, alone, was proud of his efforts, and the situation for the guests was saved, says Seyfried, only by the 'unadulterated juice of the grape'.

Mercifully for Beethoven (and his friends), these occasions were rare, and for the most part he ate in restaurants or at friends' houses. But there is no denying his eating and drinking habits exacerbated whatever underlying health problems he had.

For one thing, he seems to have suffered from a painfully distended stomach. He wrote to his tailor, 'I need a new body belt. This one is no good, and owing to the sensitive condition of my abdomen it is quite impossible for me to go out without a strong protecting belt.'

The court case made matters far, far worse. From 1816, the year it took over his life, his health deteriorated and continued to do so. In October, the month after Karl's hernia operation, he wrote that he was suffering from 'a violent, feverish cold, so that I had to stay in bed for a very long time, and only after several months was I allowed to go out, even for a short while'. He details the treatment he was prescribed: six powders daily and six bowls of tea, a healing ointment to be rubbed into his skin three times a day, another medicine, and a tincture of which he was to swallow twelve spoonfuls daily.

None of it worked to his satisfaction, so he sacked his doctor. This was the estimable Dr. Malfatti, a relative of his former *inamorata*

Therese. He will make a dramatic reappearance in the final stages of Beethoven's life. A new doctor diagnosed severe catarrhal inflammation of the lungs and warned Beethoven he would be ill for a long time.

On top of all this, and far more detrimental to his well-being, was his deafness, which now, as he approached his fifties, was severe.

But, in late 1817, a totally unexpected event occurred that was to help him turn the corner. I say 'help', because it is not clear which came first, the unexpected help or his own decision to compose a major new work.

'Major' is an understatement. 'Monumental' is better. 'Gigantic' is not an overstatement.

Some time around late November or early December, Beethoven received a visit from a certain Thomas Broadwood Esq., of the London firm of piano manufacturers, John Broadwood & Sons. We do not know how the meeting came about—Thomas Broadwood was on a tour of European capitals, probably to secure orders—but it would undoubtedly have been set up by a musical colleague who suspected Beethoven might be interested.

Beethoven's style of playing had always been markedly different from that of other pianists. He held his hands flat over the keys, using the strength of his forearms and wrists to push his fingers, with little bend at the joint, into the keys. This contrasted starkly with the established style of playing, as used for instance by Hummel, hands arched high over the keys, fingers fully bent at the joint, giving a much more delicate style of playing.

Without doubt his deafness influenced his action, as he struggled more and more to hear what he was playing, and his compositions favoured it—it is hard to imagine a pianist such as Hummel giving necessary weight to the great opening chord of the 'Pathétique' Piano Sonata, for instance. It was known in Vienna that English pianos were built with a heavier action than those in Vienna and

Paris, and were thus more suited to Beethoven's style. At their meeting, Broadwood confirmed this, and in an extraordinary act of generosity—unwittingly earning his company, still going strong today, a place in musical history—he offered to send Beethoven a Broadwood concert grand as a gift from London.

He kept his promise. In late January 1818 Beethoven took delivery of a brand new six-octave grand piano, which was shipped from London to Trieste and then taken overland to Vienna. One can only begin to imagine Beethoven's excitement as he watched workmen break open the wooden shipping case reinforced with tin, at last leaving him alone to gaze at this wondrous gift.

The piano was built of Spanish mahogany with a solid steel frame, triple-stringed throughout, inlaid with marquetry and ormolu, the brass carrying-handles formed of laurel leaves. Engraved on the board above the keys were the words: Hoc Instrumentum est Thomae Broadwood (Londini) donum, propter Ingenium illustrissimi Beethoven. His own name was inscribed in ebony, alongside 'John Broadwood and Sons, Makers of Instruments to His Majesty and the Princesses. Great Pulteney Street. Golden Square. London.' To the right of the keyboard, in black ink, the signatures of five prominent musicians active in London—among them his old friend and pupil Ferdinand Ries.[1]

Beethoven expressed his unbounded gratitude in a letter to Broadwood written in excruciating French: 'Jamais je n'eprouvais pas un grand Plaisir de ce que me causa votre Annonce de l'arrivée de cette Piano, avec qui vous m'honorès de m'en faire present ...'

Immediately Beethoven set about—or continued—in earnest composing a new piano sonata, which was to be the longest, most complex, most profound sonata of any he had hitherto composed, or was ever to compose. He knew it. He told Czerny, 'I am writing a sonata now which is going to be my greatest.'

The finished work, which he completed in just a few months,

begins with a huge two-octave leap in the left hand, followed by seven *fortissimo* chords, with a deliberate discord in the fourth. This is Beethoven, pure Beethoven. He was composing again, and the works that were to follow the 'Hammerklavier'—the name given to the sonata by Beethoven, quite possibly in honour of his new instrument—the Piano Sonatas, Opp. 109, 110, 111, the *Diabelli Variations*, the *Missa Solemnis*, the Ninth Symphony, the Late Quartets, were to be his greatest body of work, indeed the greatest body of work any composer would ever produce.

But it was not straightforward. The 'Hammerklavier' was the single glorious exception to the barren years of the court case. In the final year of that lengthy trauma Beethoven began to compose the *Diabelli Variations*, but set them aside, unable to make progress. He promised a new sacred work to be performed at Archduke Rudolph's enthronement as Archbishop of Olmütz, and indeed began work on a setting of the Mass to be called *Missa Solemnis*, but did not complete it until two years after the enthronement.

Why these problems? Once again domestic issues were hindering his creative process. In late 1820, shortly after the Court of Appeal's final ruling in his favour over custody of Karl, he fell ill again. But this was nothing like his usual complaints. In fact so serious was it that in January 1821 the *Allgemeine musikalische Zeitung* went so far as to report: 'Herr von Beethofen [*sic*] has been sick with a rheumatic fever. All friends of true music and all admirers of his muse feared for him. But now he is on the road to recovery and is working actively.'

'All admirers feared for him ...' This is nothing less than a suggestion that Beethoven's life was in danger. *That* is how debilitating the whole protracted court case, and its concomitant problems, had become.

As for the second sentence of that report, the newspaper was either correct but the recovery did not last, or it was completely wrong.

Later in January the rheumatic fever took hold again, and Beethoven was ordered back to bed, where he remained for a full six weeks.

At his lowest ebb he received news that is certain to have saddened him greatly. Josephine Brunsvik, once the object of his affections, died at the tragically early age of forty-two after a long illness. Her sister wrote that she died of 'nervous consumption', and 'suffered from want, was lacking food and assistance of any kind'.

This is unlikely, given that Therese was with her at the end, but it points to a mental collapse as well as a physical deterioration. Word of Josephine's condition is bound to have reached Beethoven some time before, so he was not unprepared, but her death can only have exacerbated his own physical condition.

That is what happened. No sooner had the rheumatic fever passed than he fell ill again, this time with jaundice. It was one thing after another. He remained unwell throughout the summer and into autumn, only writing that in November he had begun to recover his health.

It did not last. He spent the entire first half of 1822 suffering from what he described as 'gout in the chest'. At his lowest ebb he received a visitor, and what might under different circumstances have been a remarkable, even fruitful, meeting, was anything but.

Vienna was experiencing something of a craze for the operas of a certain Italian composer by the name of Gioachino Rossini, who, keen to bask in the adulation of the musically sophisticated Viennese, came to the city on his honeymoon. Once there, he insisted on paying a visit to Beethoven, whom he greatly admired.

There are two versions of what happened. One says that Beethoven, known to be less than enthusiastic about Italian opera, twice refused to receive Rossini. Rossini himself, though, insisted he did indeed call on Beethoven, and gave a fascinating account of what happened when the two composers met.

As with so many stories and legends surrounding Beethoven,

Rossini's was given many years after the event—in this case nearly forty—and it is understandable that he would want to show the meeting in the best possible light. So there might well be exaggerations in his account, but—stripping it of its more obvious self-praise—it has the ring of truth in so many aspects that it is worth retelling.

Rossini was appalled at the squalor in which Beethoven lived. He described being ushered into an attic that was 'terribly disordered and dirty'. The ceiling had cracks through which the rainwater poured down 'in streams'.

Rossini says that Beethoven, after first ignoring him, then congratulated him, particularly on *The Barber of Seville*. One might expect Rossini to say this, knowing as he did late in life that *The Barber* was such a popular work. But he has a nice line in self-deprecation as well, not too proud to relate how Beethoven damned him with faint praise.

'Do not ever try your hand at anything but *opera buffa* [comic opera],' he quotes Beethoven as telling him. 'You would be doing violence to your destiny by wanting to succeed in a different genre. In *opera buffa* none can equal Italians. Your language and your temperament predispose you for it.'

Rossini describes how the meeting was necessarily short, since Beethoven was profoundly deaf, and neither understood the other's language.

That evening Rossini was guest at a gala dinner at the palace of the Austrian Chancellor, Prince Metternich. He relates how he berated the company, made up of court members and aristocracy, for allowing the 'greatest genius of the epoch' to live in such straitened conditions, and suggested the wealthy families of Vienna should contribute a small amount each to allow him to live in some degree of comfort.

His proposal, he relates, met with little support, the general reaction being that however much you tried to help Beethoven, he would ignore your goodwill and live exactly as he wished, in whatever degree of squalor that might be.

—

How starkly this account contrasts with the experience of another renowned composer, a Viennese, of a rather more shy disposition than the ebullient Rossini. In the same month as Rossini's visit, Franz Schubert published his *Eight Variations on a French Song* for piano four hands, with a dedication to Beethoven. He agonised over whether he should personally give a copy to Beethoven, considering his own compositions to be unworthy. Finally he plucked up the courage to do so, but when he went to Beethoven's lodgings the great man was out, so Schubert left it with the servant.

As far as is known, Schubert, whose admiration for Beethoven was such that on his deathbed he asked to be buried in a grave alongside Beethoven's, met him only once, when Beethoven was on his deathbed, though even this is not certain.[2]

It was probably in the autumn of this year, 1822, that an extraordinary event occurred that has become one of the legends surrounding Beethoven's life. It was related to Thayer, again some forty years after the event, by a lithographer named Blasius Höfel for whom Beethoven sat, so as with many other tales of eccentricity it might have become embellished over the years, but as with Rossini's account there is no reason to doubt its authenticity.

One autumn evening Höfel was enjoying an early-evening drink in the tavern *Zum Schleifen* ('At the Ribbon') in the Vienna suburb of Wiener Neustadt. Among the party was the local Commissioner of Police. It was already dark when a police constable came to the tavern to find the Commissioner.

'Sir,' said the constable, 'we have arrested someone for behaving in a suspicious manner. He won't be quiet. He keeps on yelling that he is Beethoven. But he's just a tramp. He's in a moth-eaten old coat, no hat. He has no identity papers, there's no way of finding out who he is. We're not sure what to do.'

'Keep him under arrest overnight,' replied the Commissioner. 'We'll speak to him in the morning and find out who he is.'

But it did not end there. As the Commissioner told Höfel later, at eleven o'clock that night he was woken at home by a policeman who told him the man in custody would not quieten down, was still yelling that he was Beethoven, and was demanding that Anton Herzog, Musical Director in Wiener Neustadt, be called in to identify him.

The Commissioner decided he had better investigate. He went to Herzog's house, woke him up, and asked him to accompany him to the police station. The Commissioner and Herzog were taken to the cell, and as soon as Herzog cast eyes on the tramp he exclaimed, 'That *is* Beethoven!'

The Commissioner, no doubt congratulating himself that he had taken the matter seriously, ordered Beethoven's immediate release. Herzog took him back to his own house, gave him the best room, assured him he would not be disturbed, and looked forward to seeing him for breakfast if he so wished, or if he preferred to sleep longer ...

The next day the local Mayor came to Herzog's house to apologise in person to the renowned composer for his treatment at the hands of an over-zealous police officer, gave Beethoven his best coat and the mayoral carriage to transport him home.

By then everyone knew what had happened. The day before Beethoven had got up early in the morning, put on his threadbare old coat, forgotten to take a hat, and set out for what he intended to be a short walk. He reached the towpath on the Danube Canal and followed it. He walked on for hours.

By late afternoon he ended up at the canal basin at the Ungertor, a considerable distance from the city. He was totally lost and disorientated, and in a pitiful state having had nothing to eat all day. In this condition, tired, drawn, hungry, in tattered old clothes, he was seen by local people looking in at the windows of houses. They became suspicious and called the police.

A constable approached him and told him he was arresting him for behaving suspiciously.

'But I am Beethoven.'

'Of course you are. Why not? I'll tell you what you are. You're a tramp, and that Beethoven is no tramp.' (*'Ein Lump sind Sie; so sieht der Beethoven nicht aus.'*)

—

And yet through all these traumas—ill-health, personal problems, one thing after another—he continued to compose. The *Missa Solemnis* was finally completed; he composed the three piano sonatas that were to be his last; he took up the *Diabelli Variations*[3] again, and he was making notes for further compositions.

Then, out of the blue, in November 1822, he received a letter from St. Petersburg. The writer of the letter was a Russian nobleman by the name of Nicolas Borisovich, Prince Galitzin, and the request he made of Beethoven—or, more accurately, Beethoven's positive response—has earned the Prince his place in musical history. He asked Beethoven if he would consent to compose one, two, or three new quartets, for which he would pay Beethoven whatever he, Beethoven, considered appropriate.

This was an unexpected stroke of luck for Beethoven, because in letters he wrote earlier in the year he said that he was considering composing string quartets, maybe as many as three. Now he could not only get on with composing them, he would be paid as well.

But once again—as with the *Diabelli Variations* and the *Missa Solemnis*—he put the quartets to one side, because quite simply he got a more attractive offer. There was another composition he had begun making sketches for in the autumn of the previous year. That's a slight understatement. You could say this was a composition that had been on his mind, and slowly germinating, since he briefly attended lectures on the German philosopher Immanuel Kant at the University of Bonn as a teenager, and acquired a volume of poetry by the German poet and playwright Friedrich Schiller.

He had kept that volume of poetry with him, always intending to set to music a poem that particularly appealed to him, 'An die Freude' ('Ode to Joy'). By 1822 he was beginning to think that maybe a symphony would be the appropriate way to go about it. No composer, not Mozart, Haydn, nor anyone else, had ever incorporated words—spoken or sung—into a symphony. If this was the way forward, then it was going to be a radical departure from any previous symphony, and from what a symphony was generally accepted to be.

The first indication that he intended writing a new symphony (though there is no indication yet that it would include voices), came in a letter he wrote to his friend and helper Ferdinand Ries, now based in London, on 6 July 1822: 'Have you any idea what fee the Harmony Society[4] would offer me for a grand symphony?'

Ries evidently replied with good news, because on 20 December, Beethoven wrote to Ries accepting the Society's relatively low offer of £50. There was history between Beethoven and the Philharmonic Society. In 1815 the Society had paid Beethoven 75 guineas for three overtures. He provided them with three overtures that had already been performed, whereas they were expecting new works, and the directors of the Society were disappointed with their quality.[5]

This time, therefore, the offer was just £50, and one suspects that even that amount was offered with some reluctance. They cannot have known that the work with which their name would forever be associated would redefine the symphony and represent the pinnacle of Beethoven's achievement.

—

It took Beethoven well over a year to bring his Ninth Symphony to fruition, the biggest problem being how to introduce the voices in the final movement. Aware of how ground-breaking this final movement would be, he sketched then rejected several ideas, before deciding to quote the theme from each of the preceding three movements, but rejecting it before it could be completed. A solo bass voice then articulates in words the desire to abandon these sounds in favour of more pleasing and joyful tones. The final movement therefore breaks free and takes flight. The mind of a genius at work.

By early 1824 the Ninth Symphony was complete. Now for the easy part: securing a theatre and date for the first performance. Easy, because word had spread in Vienna that its most celebrated composer was working intensively on a new symphony, his first for over ten years, and that it was going to be radically different. The theatre managers of Vienna were falling over themselves to win the concert for their theatre.

Easy? Nothing is ever easy where Beethoven is concerned. For reasons known only to him—possibly no more than a desire to spite the Viennese musical establishment—he decided he wanted his new symphony to be given its premiere in Berlin.

Berlin? That musical establishment was dumbstruck. Why Berlin? Their bewilderment was certainly laced with anger. Not only would it mean none of Vienna's musicians would be involved, but to add insult to injury it awarded the prize of a new Beethoven work to the capital of Prussia, a militaristic nation the Austrians at best treated with suspicion, at worst hated, whose army they had faced on the battlefield and would do again.

When they realised Beethoven was serious—the general manager of the Berlin Theatre was delighted to accept his proposal—they swallowed their pride and anger, and decided to write an open letter to their most famous musical son.

In wonderfully overblown language, no fewer than thirty illustrious musical names implored Beethoven, whose 'name and creations belong to all contemporaneous humanity and every country which opens a susceptible bosom to art', to recognise that 'it is Austria which is best entitled to claim him as her own', along with Mozart and Haydn, 'the sacred triad in which these names and yours glow as the symbol of the highest within the spiritual realm of tones [which] sprang from the soil of their fatherland'.

They continued:

> *We beg you to withhold no longer ... a performance of the latest masterwork of your hands ... We know that a new flower glows in the garland of your glorious, still unequalled symphonies ... Do not any longer disappoint the general expectations! ... Do not allow these, your latest offspring, some day to appear perhaps as foreigners in their place of birth, introduced perhaps by persons to whom you and your mind are alien! Appear soon among your friends, your admirers, your venerators!*

Well, Beethoven was as susceptible to flattery as any man. '[The letter] is very beautiful!—it rejoices me greatly!' he wrote.

That small hurdle cleared, the problems really now *did* start.

Beethoven insisted on making the final decision on every aspect of the concert—the venue, the time, the programme, selection of musicians and singers, copying of the musical parts, rehearsal timings, and even the price of seats. All of which would have been fine, if he had been able to make up his mind on any of it.

Time was running short. Spring would soon give way to summer, and the concert season end. It would take at least three weeks to prepare for the concert—rehearsals and posters printed—and the single most important decision had still not been taken. The venue.

The obvious choice was the Theater an der Wien, which had seen so many of Beethoven's works premiered. Baron Braun was long since gone, and the current manager, Count Palffy, was known to be enthusiastic about Beethoven's music. It would also be simpler and quicker to arrange dates with the Theater an der Wien than with the bureaucracy of the imperial court theatres.

But there was a problem. Beethoven loathed Palffy. It dated back some years, to when Beethoven was giving a recital in the salon of one of his patrons. Palffy was in the small audience, carrying on a conversation with a lady. Beethoven, having tried several times to silence him, finally stopped playing, shouted, 'I will not play for pigs!'—and stormed out.

It was probably in revenge that Beethoven now demanded a change of conductor and leader if the concert was to be held at the Theater an der Wien. Palffy was surprisingly accommodating. He agreed to allow Michael Umlauf to conduct, in place of the theatre's resident musical director, and Beethoven's friend Ignaz Schuppanzigh to lead instead of the resident leader. On top of that, Palffy offered Beethoven the theatre, staff, musicians, as many rehearsals as he wanted, at the price of a mere 1200 florins, allowing him to keep all profits.

It was a remarkably generous offer, and Beethoven's friends and colleagues were delighted that at least the problem over the venue had been resolved.

But Beethoven turned it down. Back to square one.

———

There was an underlying issue that was making matters infinitely more difficult than they needed to be. There were essentially two camps operating on Beethoven's behalf. The one that was negotiating with Palffy was made up of patrons and musicians. But Beethoven was convinced they were not to be trusted, so he authorised his brother Johann and nephew Karl to make secret overtures to other theatres—Johann, who had business experience but no knowledge of the world of music, and Karl, now aged seventeen, with no knowledge of anything.

The first group, after Beethoven's rejection of Palffy's offer, entered into talks with the manager of the Theater am Kärntnertor, one of the imperial court theatres. This prompted Palffy to improve his offer, dropping the price for the Theater an der Wien to 1000 florins. He also offered a selection of dates: 22, 23 and 24 March.

This time Beethoven agreed, no doubt to a collective sigh of relief from the first group. But unknown to them, Beethoven's brother and nephew were negotiating with a *third* theatre—a totally inappropriate venue, being more a hall than a theatre and seating only five hundred people.

Days, weeks, were passing, and nobody was getting anywhere. Finally, confronted with reality, Beethoven made the only sensible decision: he abandoned the concert. There would be no performance of his Ninth Symphony.

Then he changed his mind *again*. The concert would be held in the Kärntnertor (whose resident orchestra he had described not long before as being worse than a musical clock). Palffy made one last desperate bid. Beethoven could have the Wien for nothing. But this time Beethoven's mind was made up, and he did not change it again.

His Ninth Symphony would receive its premiere at the Kärntnertor on Friday, 7 May.

—

Now the soloists needed to be selected, and fast. The females were relatively straightforward. Everybody agreed on the soprano Henriette Sontag, and the contralto Karoline Unger. The men were more of a problem. The preferred tenor claimed the part was too low for his voice. The bass claimed the part was too high and impossibly hard.

Choices were finally made, singers selected, chorus members named, with an orchestral force of 24 violins, 10 violas, 12 cellos and basses, and double the number of woodwind. This, by the standards of the day, was an enormous line-up, but everybody understood that with this new symphony, they were dealing with something quite out of the ordinary.

Then Beethoven dropped a bombshell. He said he would conduct. Profoundly deaf, unable to hear normal conversation, unable to hear musical sounds, even with his ear to an ear trumpet held on the piano keys, he insisted on conducting the most complex and demanding score he had ever written.

Hurriedly a plan was put into operation—a cunning ruse. Yes, said the concert organisers, of course he would conduct, who else could possibly conduct such a work but its creator? Purely, though, as a back-up, for no other reason than to make sure everything went smoothly, Michael Umlauf would be on stage with him. Michael Umlauf, the well-known conductor. But don't worry, Herr Beethoven, he won't get in your way. Beethoven acquiesced.

Given the shortness of time, there could be only two full rehearsals. The first was a disaster, the second worse. The problem was the solo singers. They complained that their parts were simply impossible. They told Beethoven he did not understand the human voice.

Beethoven was in no mood to compromise. He told them to sing exactly what he had written. Karoline Unger, the contralto, threw a tantrum. To Beethoven's face, she called him 'a tyrant over all the vocal organs', and turning to her colleagues said, 'Well then, we must go on torturing ourselves in the name of God!'

The bass soloist went one further. At the last minute, declaring his part was impossibly high, he pulled out. He was replaced, probably, by a member of the chorus who was familiar with the part from rehearsals.

In secret the four soloists made a pact. At the concert they would not try for notes they were doubtful of reaching, and they simply would not sing impossibly difficult passages. Beethoven was deaf anyway, he wouldn't know.

The stage was set for a farcical first performance of the most important, demanding, complex, innovative work Beethoven had ever composed.

—

The Theater am Kärntnertor was almost full, which was gratifying, but it was the wrong audience. The concert season was all but over, and Vienna was basking in early-summer warmth. The nobility, aristocrats, patrons of the arts, had left the city for their country residences.

A genuine disappointment for Beethoven was that the royal box was empty. Beethoven had personally gone to the Hofburg Palace to invite members of the imperial royal family. His most loyal supporter, Archduke Rudolph, was away in Olmütz. Beethoven rather hoped the Emperor himself, with the Empress, would attend. But the empty royal box spoke of an unwillingness to be associated with disaster.

Beethoven's small circle of close friends was there. He no doubt watched with sadness as his old friend and drinking partner Nikolaus Zmeskall was carried to his seat on a sedan chair because of crippling gout that had left him bedridden.

We can assume a ripple of laughter (no need to stifle it, he can't hear), as Beethoven, a pace or two in front of Umlauf, walked to the stage and people noticed that he was wearing a green frock coat. Black was de rigueur, but Beethoven did not own the 'correct' garment. He was otherwise appropriately dressed: white cravat with waistcoat, black breeches, black silk stockings, and shoes with buckles.

Another ripple of expectant laughter, maybe even a gasp of anticipation, as Umlauf—unseen by Beethoven—made a sign of the cross over the players.

Beethoven took his place in front of the musicians, raised his arms and brought them down. To the side of him, and slightly behind,

Umlauf made sure he had their attention, raised his arms and he too brought them down.

The audience fell silent as the mysterious opening chords sounded, a floating cloud of sound, a sound world they had not heard before, yielding to huge affirmative chords from the whole orchestra. They watched, and listened, as Beethoven flailed with his arms to the sounds in his head, and Umlauf directed the musicians who were playing as if their lives depended on it.

The second movement took them completely by surprise, with its driving rhythm and totally unexpected solo section for timpani, rarely before accorded more than an accompanying role. The constantly repeated theme that emerges halfway through the movement is surely a foretaste of what is to come. By now the audience— sophisticated musically, even if not belonging to the aristocracy—knew they were experiencing something extraordinary.

The end of the second movement, quietly disintegrating before that theme is heard once more, but cut off this time, yielding to a series of final affirmative chords, brought them to their feet. The audience needed release, they needed to breathe. They leapt to their feet, shouting and applauding.

Beethoven continued to conduct the orchestra in his head. Umlauf turned to see the audience on its feet, shouts of *Encore! Encore!* reverberating around the hall. He made a judgement. He raised his arms for the third movement. The gentle chords from the wind calmed them, yielding to a theme of sublime gentleness on strings.

At the end of the third movement, Umlauf led swiftly into the huge discord that began the final movement, before cellos and basses gave their portentous sound to a hint of the great theme that was to come.

The bass singer was soon on his feet, and the words '*O Freunde, nicht diese Töne!*' rang out over the audience.

Umlauf, knowing now he and the musicians were creating something extraordinary, drove the pace on, players and singers performing as if somehow knowing this was a defining moment in the history of music.

Suddenly, it all stops, total silence. A small beat on bass drum and deep wind. Syncopated dotted rhythm. Martial music. Tenor summons all forces.

In unison, in harmony, faultlessly, the music drives to its conclusion. Umlauf held it all perfectly together, singers, chorus and orchestra giving the performance of their lives.

Again, just before the end, a tremendous slowing down, almost to a stop, before full forces drive to the final flourish.

Umlauf brought his arms down for the final great chord. It was over. The audience erupted, rose to their feet, cheered and shouted, handkerchiefs and hats waved in the air. *Beethoven! Beethoven! Beethoven!*

Umlauf looked to his side. Beethoven, oblivious to what was happening, continued to wave his arms, conducting the orchestra he was hearing in his head. Karoline Unger, the contralto who had so berated him in rehearsal, stepped forward. Gently she touched Beethoven on the shoulder, nodded encouragingly at the bewildered face, and turned him to face the cheering audience.

At that moment Beethoven knew the gift he had given to the world.

CHAPTER SIXTEEN

'I WANT TO BE A SOLDIER'

IN WHICH BEETHOVEN GETS DRUNK WITH FRIENDS

B EETHOVEN'S CREATIVE PROCESS WAS IN FULL
drive. Within a few weeks of the triumphant premier of
his Ninth Symphony, he began serious work on the Galitzin commission for three string quartets.

This would have been remarkable if he were a much younger
man in good health with no domestic problems to distract him.
On all counts this was untrue of Beethoven. First, the aftermath
of the Kärntnertor concert should have been a time to pause, take
stock, thank the team who had worked so hard to make it possible.
Instead Beethoven accused them of cheating him.

He summoned them to a lunch at the *Zum wilden Mann* ('At the
Sign of the Wild Man') restaurant in the Prater, and openly accused them of withholding receipts from him. They defended themselves, pointing out that in a highly unusual arrangement Beethov-
en's brother Johann and nephew Karl had actually been in charge of
financial arrangements for the concert at his insistence—Johann
overseeing expenses and payments, and Karl collecting audited
receipts from the box office.

Beethoven persisted, insisting he had been informed by an
'entirely credible source' that he had been cheated out of money that
was justly owed to him. His guests knew there was no reasoning with
him, made their excuses and left.

Just a few weeks after this Karl, a little short of his eighteenth
birthday, dropped a bombshell on his uncle. He was about to complete his first year as a student at the University of Vienna, studying

philosophy and languages. He knew how badly he was doing, so badly that he was certain to have to repeat the year's studies. He decided on a radical change of direction.

Clearly bracing himself for the storm he knew he was about to unleash, Karl wrote first in a conversation book how he would not do anything without his uncle's consent, then scribbled a lengthy preamble admitting his new choice of career was rather strange, 'not a *common* one'. Then the single word: Soldier.

Beethoven predictably exploded. Karl was the sole Beethoven of the next generation; he was an artist, and to him was accorded the highest privilege of bearing the name Beethoven. A couple of years earlier, Beethoven had instructed his pupil Czerny to give Karl piano lessons, and Czerny had reported back that the boy had no musical talent whatsoever. This did not deter Beethoven from the unshakeable conviction that Karl's destiny was as an artist. For the time being, though, Karl had no choice but to remain at university, but the seed had been sown. Almost inevitably it was not long before Beethoven fell ill again.

Extraordinarily, unbelievably, none of this hampered Beethoven's creativity, and by early the following year he had completed the first of the string quartets, Op. 127. Just as the three Piano Sonatas, opp. 109, 110, 111, had taken the piano sonata into new territory, the Ninth had redefined the symphony, Beethoven was now doing the same with the string quartet.

Neither he, nor anyone, had ever composed a string quartet comparable to Op. 127. The second movement was the longest he had written for string quartet. The demands on all players, particularly first violin, are extraordinary. All four players are required to play to the most exacting standards imaginable. The first violin has to execute leaps across the strings, perform demi-semiquaver runs, and stop almost off the fingerboard on the top E string. Key signatures change in mid-movement—no fewer than four times in the *Adagio*—with accidentals scattered like so much confetti.

A date for the first performance was set for 6 March 1825, on earlier assurances from Beethoven that the quartet would be ready in good time. It was not, of course, leaving the musicians less than two weeks' rehearsal for the most difficult piece of music they had ever been confronted with.

Shades, again, of the Ninth Symphony, but this time there was to be no happy outcome. The performance was a failure. Beethoven, now completely deaf, did not attend. His brother Johann, known as a musical ignoramus, did, and reported back to Beethoven that it was all the fault of the quartet leader, his old friend Ignaz Schuppanzigh. Johann said Schuppanzigh was tired from too much rehearsing, did not like the quartet anyway, and would rather not have been performing it.

The truth was that Schuppanzigh had been driven to his wits' end by Beethoven's delay in completing the piece, had indeed over-rehearsed to the point of fatigue, and would rather the date of the performance had been postponed.

Beethoven summoned his friend and blamed him entirely for the failure. Schuppanzigh stood his ground, probably intentionally angering Beethoven even more by telling him he could easily master the technical demands of the piece, but was having trouble arriving at its spirit.

It was no surprise that when the quartet was performed for a second time two weeks later, it was with a different first violinist. This time the performance was a triumph, and was repeated several times in the following days.

—

How did Beethoven react to all this tension? In the way he had done so often, with increasing frequency. He fell ill once again. This time, though, it was far more severe than before. He was suffering from his usual bad digestion and diarrhoea. He also complained of catarrh and frequent nose bleeds. Most ominously of all, he was spitting up blood.

His doctor, Anton Braunhofer—successor to the successor of Dr. Malfatti, both sacked—warned Beethoven that his condition was severe, and that he risked inflammation of the bowels and 'inflammatory attacks' if he did not strictly follow his advice, which was to consume no wine, coffee, spirits, or spices of any kind. He gave him a medicine to swallow as well.

He was strict with his obviously restive patient, writing in a conversation book:

I can assure you that all will turn out well, but you must be patient for a while yet. An illness cannot be cured in a day. I won't bother you much longer with medicine, but you will have to stick strictly to my dietary prescriptions, which won't cause you to starve.

It was summer, and Braunhofer's advice to Beethoven to leave the city concurred with his own desire to get away, and so he left once again for Baden. To begin with, the change of air did him good. Within a few days of arriving he wrote Braunhofer a letter describing his severe symptoms, but in the form of a humorous dialogue between a patient and his doctor.

As further evidence of his good humour, he added to the letter a small sixteen-bar canon, which he said he had written on a walk in the Helenenthal (Valley of Helen, west of Baden), on the 'second Anton's bridge'.

It is a beguiling image: the great composer in obviously bad health, but never too ill to pull a scrap of manuscript paper from his pocket and, perhaps leaning on a railing watching the stream rushing underneath the bridge, compose a piece of music.

The good humour, predictably, did not last. The weather was unseasonably cold. Beethoven complained in a note to Karl that it was so cold he could hardly move his fingers to write, adding that it was 'practically impossible to produce anything in this cold and utterly dismal climate'.

The obvious target was Braunhofer, whose remedies were showing no signs of working. He even blamed Braunhofer for not warning him to avoid asparagus, which gave him diarrhoea after he ate it at an inn in Baden. Beethoven took his health into his own hands. He began to drink wine again—white wine diluted with water to begin with, then straight wine—and coffee (instead of chocolate which Braunhofer had recommended as a substitute). He wrote to Karl that Braunhofer was 'narrow-minded and a fool with it'.

As a further sign of mental strain—or rather a continuing refusal to accept reality—in letters to Karl, he addressed him as 'Dear Son!' and signed the letter 'Your faithful father'. Karl had now left university and enrolled in a business school, with Beethoven's permission, probably as an attempt to induce him to forget a military career.

He visited Beethoven several times in Baden, but entries in conversation books show that his uncle's hold over him—Beethoven's refusal to countenance his wishes, his constant demands to know how Karl was spending his time, his continued refusal to allow Karl to see his mother, his belief that he really was Karl's father—was beginning to wear Karl down in a serious way. He was becoming something of a ticking time bomb.

—

And yet, and yet ... once again none of this was hindering Beethoven's creative process. Even before the unsuccessful first performance of the string quartet Op. 127, Beethoven had begun work on its successor, which would become Op. 132.[1] Now, in mid-May 1825, convalescing in Baden, he was about to write one of the most extraordinary of all his string quartet movements.

As if in final proof that Braunhofer was a fool, Beethoven's health suddenly took a turn for the better. The fact that he was now ignoring Braunhofer's advice, as well as having lost (probably purposefully) the medicine prescribed, was proof it had nothing to do with medical advice. No, it was divine intervention.

There are not many instances of Beethoven showing a religious side, but in his final years on occasion a degree of spirituality emerged. Now he put that to good use. He decided to compose the third movement of the string quartet as a personal offering of gratitude to God for his recovery from what he clearly believed was a life-threatening illness.

At the top of the movement he wrote: *Heiliger Dankgesang eines Genesenen an die Gottheit, in der lydischen Tonart* ('Sacred Song of Thanksgiving to the Deity from a Convalescent, in the Lydian Mode').

The Lydian Mode was an ancient musical form used in medieval church services, and in the first thirty bars of the movement Beethoven has the four strings play solid chords in perfect imitation of a church organ. It creates a most remarkable sound, and stands alone in all Beethoven's compositions for string quartet. It then gives way to a lively section marked *Neue Kraft fühlend* ('Feeling new strength'). Beethoven is describing his illness and recovery in music.

———

But matters with Karl were beginning to deteriorate. Word reached Beethoven—we don't know from whom—that Karl was disobeying the court order and secretly seeing his mother. Beethoven wrote to him from Baden, at *exactly* the time he was composing the *Heiliger Dankgesang*:

> *Until now it was only conjecture, though someone has indeed assured me that you have been seeing your mother in secret—Am I to experience once more this most abominable ingratitude?*

And again, ten days later, still bitter:

—*God is my witness, I dream only of being completely removed from you and that wretched brother and this horrible family who have been thrust upon me*—*May God grant my wishes. For I* <u>*can no longer trust you*</u>.

Unfortunately your father
or, better still, not your father

As soon as he had completed Op. 132, he began work on the third string quartet, Op. 130, and as with the *Heiliger Dankgesang*, once again his personal problems found their way directly into his composition. This time it was not his health, but his agony over his nephew Karl's behaviour.

The fifth (of six!) movements is as extraordinary in its way as the *Heiliger Dankgesang*. Beethoven called it *Cavatina*, a word usually applied to a simple, melodious, expressive air. In this case that is something of an understatement.

The first violin takes the melody, beginning with a deep B flat on the low G string, rising a sixth. It is a lift, marked *sotto voce*, which seems to take the soul with it. After a development, the first violin then falls a sixth. It is heartrending. When you believe Beethoven cannot increase the intensity any more, he writes *pianissimo* quavers for three strings, and then the first violin … weeps. I do not know any other way to describe it.

Beethoven wrote '*Beklemmt*' over the first violin part. It is difficult to convey the meaning with a single word. It means oppressed, anguished, tortured, overcome by grief and heartache. It is a unique passage in all Beethoven. The first violin climbs, in quavers and semiquavers, off the beat, almost every note an accidental, interspersed with rests, sighs, then falls an octave, exactly as you do when you sob, catch your breath, then weep. The first violin climbs again, with demi-semiquavers, before another fall, more sobs. The passage lasts for just six bars, before the opening theme, with its rising sixth, resumes.

It is small wonder Beethoven's friend Karl Holz, a violinist, said the *Cavatina* cost Beethoven tears in its writing, and Beethoven himself confessed that nothing he had written had so moved him and that just to hear it in his head brought him to tears.

There can, in my mind, be no doubt of the inspiration for this extraordinary writing. Beethoven realised—even if he would not admit it to himself—that he was losing Karl.

—

Beethoven broke off writing Op. 130 to return to Vienna to attend the first performance of the earlier quartet, Op. 132. Thanks to the presence of the English conductor Sir George Smart, we have a vivid account of what happened. And thanks to the Berlin music publisher Moritz Schlesinger, who arranged the performance, we have an equally vivid account of the merriment that followed.

Schlesinger was staying in the hotel *Zum wilden Mann* in the Kärntnerstrasse, and it was in an upstairs room that the four musicians, along with Beethoven, Karl, Schlesinger, Smart, and a prestigious gathering of academics, assembled.

It seems the quartet was performed twice. Smart reports that the room was hot and crowded, Beethoven took off his coat, and directed the performers. He could not hear, because of his deafness, but his eye told him that one *staccato* passage was incorrectly played. Beethoven took the violin from Karl Holz, who was second violin, and demonstrated how he wanted it played—but played it a quarter-tone flat!

This is a fascinating little detail. We know Beethoven took violin lessons from Ries's father Franz as a teenager in Bonn, but evidently did not reach a very high standard, and I am not aware of any other evidence of him playing violin in later years. The small audience must have looked on bewitched, to see the great composer, now profoundly deaf, in effect conducting his string quartet, even playing a passage.

Probably because of this interrupted first performance, the decision was made to play the quartet a second time—the full forty-five minutes—presumably without interruption. Smart tantalisingly reported only that those present paid Beethoven 'the greatest attention', as you would expect them to do.

After the audience had departed, Schlesinger ordered a meal and wine to be served in the private room for the small gathering of himself, Beethoven, Karl, and the musicians. Beethoven took out a conversation book, put it on the table, and almost all contributed to it—unusually, it includes a written comment by Beethoven himself. Thanks again to Schlesinger, the conversation book has survived, and it gives fascinating insight into a post-performance meal involving a great composer and his colleagues.

The remarks mostly are flippant comments by a group of men relaxing, and all the more intriguing for that. Schuppanzigh, who had played first violin, is frequently referred to as Falstaff, on account of his girth. Holz, whose name means 'wood' in German, which Beethoven punned on frequently in notes and letters, is called 'the wooden friend'.

The Italian double-bass virtuoso, Domenico Dragonetti, who had so impressed Beethoven many years earlier, apparently refused to attend the first performance of the Ninth Symphony in London, and receives a sound pasting from Holz: 'Dragonetti demanded too much money for his participation, and said Beethoven had written the entire Symphony *just for him*.'

One can imagine Beethoven reading this and laughing out loud at Dragonetti's presumption. The great Italian composer Cherubini—a very tall man, it seems—'has so much regard for a certain

Beethoven, that if one mentions his name, Cherubini grows even taller out of respect—' Beethoven is certain to have chuckled again.

The music publisher Tobias Haslinger (who was not present) is teased for having a name similar to the title of Handel's oratorio *Il Ritorno di Tobia*. Schlesinger says, 'I told Tobias today, Beethoven will immortalise you and the Paternostergässl [the street where the publishing house was located].'

Beethoven at this point reached forward for a pencil, and scribbled, 'Tobias confided in me today that you are also giving the Quartet to [the publisher] Steiner.'

It is not long before the men's writing becomes a little slapdash, and their words no doubt slurred, as the wine takes hold, and no surprise that a group of men becoming drunk start to talk in ribald terms about women.

SCHUPPANZIGH: I asked Czerny whether he had never fallen into a hole without hurting himself.
HOLZ: Also comical, like Falstaff.
SCHUPPANZIGH: A slovenly fellow. A whoremonger ... He is saying that Mozart drooled over [Barbara] Auernhammer's bosom, because she was the most delightful sweetie he could find.

Beethoven's reaction is not recorded. I can see much male laughter and joshing, the language becoming even cruder, for that reason not written down, and the great composer joining in the laughter as he drank more wine.

—

If that is how it was, it was a fleeting moment of joviality for Beethoven. He had a major domestic problem, one of his own making. Before leaving for Baden back in May, Beethoven had given notice on his Vienna flat, and done nothing about finding new lodgings. He left his brother Johann to clear his things out. He received the newspaper in Baden, and despite being fully occupied with the string quartets, found time to scour the columns for a vacant apartment. Whenever he found one, he summoned the hapless Karl down to Baden, gave him the details—or sent the details to him in Vienna—and told him to go and look, and let him know if it was suitable.

He found an apartment in the Ungargasse, told Karl to tip the caretaker to hold it for him, but it seems it came to nothing. He dispatched Karl to look at other apartments. There was evidently one that took Beethoven's fancy, over which Karl had evidently failed to act, because Beethoven sent him a note saying, 'The apartment was in the newspaper again on Tuesday. Was there really nothing you could have done, not even through someone else?'

To describe Beethoven's lifestyle as peripatetic is something of an understatement. In thirty-five years in Vienna he moved over thirty times, rarely staying at one address for more than a few months. If you include his lengthy summer stays away from Vienna, he had well over seventy addresses in all.

There were, certainly, instances of him being expelled from a lodging because of complaints from other residents about his habit of working through the night, pounding on the piano keys to try to hear his music, banging on the apartment walls. He had to leave one apartment after getting in a stonemason to knock a hole in a wall and install a window to give him a decent view, without permission from his landlord. Other residents demanded to know why they couldn't do the same. More often, though, he simply became restless and wanted a change of environment.

So when he vacated his apartment in May, nobody was surprised. Karl, though, clearly resented the constant summonses to Baden, and being given the onerous task of finding new lodgings for his uncle.

An apartment was found, possibly the one referred to by Beethoven in his petulant note to Karl. It was a four-room apartment with servants' quarters on the second floor of a large building that was once home to an order of Benedictine monks from Spain. It stood outside the Bastei and the largest room had two windows looking out across the green Glacis towards the city wall.

The apartment had one unexpected bonus. It was directly opposite another apartment block, the 'Rothes Haus' ('Red House'), where his old friend Stephan von Breuning lived, and where, many years before, Beethoven had briefly lived with him, an arrangement that had ended with the heated argument that had led to their estrangement.

Stephan lived there now with his wife and two children, and one day in August 1825, when Beethoven was in Vienna for the performance of his string quartet Op. 132, purely by chance—in an incident reminiscent of his reconciliation with his brother Carl some time before—Beethoven was walking along a street just outside the Bastei, head down, and probably quite literally bumped into Stephan and his young son Gerhard.

Gerhard, whose memoirs[2] written many years later provide a unique and intimate insight into Beethoven's last years, recounts that a joyful reunion took place, and good relations were once more finally restored between the two men whose friendship dated back to their childhood years.

Beethoven moved into the apartment in the Schwarzspanierhaus ('House of the Black-Robed Spaniard') in mid-October 1825. No one could have foreseen it, but it was to be his final home, and the place of his death.

—

His actual demise might not have been foreseeable, but there was no disguising his worsening, even pitiful, condition. His behaviour, too, although always eccentric, was now seriously worrying.

Karl resisted being seen out in the street with his uncle, who would wave his arms wildly while talking unnecessarily loudly, who couldn't hear what was said to him and insisted on being shouted at, whose clothes were inappropriate to the season—heavy coat in summer, lightly dressed in winter—and in need of repair. Street urchins would follow, and taunt him.

Stephan's wife related that Beethoven's animated gestures, his loud voice, his ringing laugh, and his indifference to whoever might be near by, made her ashamed to be seen out with him because people would take him for a madman.

Beethoven clearly took a liking to Constanze von Breuning, because he frequently invited her in for a coffee. She always politely declined, because—according to her son—she found his domestic habits rather unappealing. He had a habit of spitting; his clothes were dirty, and his behaviour extravagant. He was aware he was not overly attractive to the opposite sex, because he told her he longed for domestic happiness and greatly regretted that he had never found a wife.

Constanze had reason, even, to take exception to Beethoven's inappropriate behaviour. On one occasion she left the Rothes Haus for the rather long walk to take the waters at the Kaiserbad on the Danube. Beethoven—who might well have been watching through the windows on the back of his apartment—joined her, and insisted on accompanying her for the whole way.

She spent about an hour in the bathhouse, and was rather surprised to find Beethoven waiting for her outside to accompany her home. This would have been difficult for her, given Beethoven's eccentric and extravagant behaviour, if he had been an unknown individual, but it is true to say that he was the most famous man in Vienna. Important personages, musicians, admirers came from all over Europe in the hope of meeting him. One even came especially from Quebec. Beethoven was world famous. It is likely Constanze's walk to the baths and home again was constantly interrupted, to her embarrassment.

If his behaviour was becoming increasingly bizarre, his physical condition now shocked those who knew him. He was clearly unwell. His stomach was distended and his ankles swollen. He was, in late 1825, approaching his fifty-fifth birthday. Friends remarked that he suddenly looked much older and his complexion had become permanently sallow. We can assume that his old foes—indigestion, colic, irregular bowels—were causing him increasingly acute problems.

Though the disease was not understood at the time, and with the caveat that post-diagnosis, particularly at an interval of two centuries, is dangerous, it is probably true to say that Beethoven was suffering from terminal cirrhosis of the liver.

The person closest to him, who might be expected to care for him and tend to his needs, was his nephew, his 'son', Karl. But Beethoven had by now thoroughly alienated the young man, aged nineteen by the end of 1825.

It was nearly a decade since Karl had lost his father and the nightmare of the prolonged court case had begun. Ever since, he had witnessed the conflict between his uncle and his mother. He had been a pawn in their custody struggle. He had suffered physically with a hernia, and there were even reports of violence in the aftermath of his operation. Wearing a truss and in considerable pain, he had been forced by Beethoven to take a strenuous walk with him in the Helenenthal outside Baden.

Exhausted, bleeding from his wound, he had taken to his bed, where Beethoven had continued to berate him. He snapped, lashed out, cutting Beethoven's face.

When he had run away to his mother, Beethoven had called the police to have him returned. He was suffering frostbite at the time. In living with his uncle, in his early teens, he had had to survive in the domestic chaos that was Beethoven's life. One can only imagine what mealtimes were like, or when they were. Beethoven might have employed a cook, but none lasted long.

It was as if Beethoven refused to allow Karl to make a single decision for himself, not least over the matter of wanting to join the army. Karl had no desire to enrol in the university, no wish to go to business school, no ambition to learn music. He wanted to be a soldier. But Beethoven was not having it.

There was no let up. Summoned to Baden time and again, his life interfered with and his schedule disrupted, ordered to find lodgings; he was being used more and more by Beethoven to run his domestic affairs. His professional affairs too. Possibly as a further inducement to Karl to follow a musical career, or more likely simply because he was mistrustful of anyone outside immediate family, Beethoven asked Karl to write to publishers, copy musical parts, buy him essential equipment such as manuscript paper, quill pens and pencils.

If Karl had been ten years older, and his life free of tension, he might have relished living in the same apartment as the world's greatest composer, assisting him in practical matters. Instead he was turning into a bitter, pathetic, resentful young man. It is not an exaggeration to say Beethoven was destroying the person he loved most in the world.

We know now, at a distance of two hundred years, that Beethoven at this time was composing his greatest works, that this was no ordinary composer, this was one of the greatest creative geniuses who ever lived. It can be argued that allowances could be made for his behaviour.

But Karl did not see it that way. And things were about to get a great deal worse.

Beethoven wanted to know *exactly* what Karl was up to. He knew Karl was clandestinely seeing his mother, and he probably realised he was powerless to stop it. But what else was Karl spending his time doing? Beethoven had a weapon: he held the purse strings. He frequently gave Karl money—in fact he had gone out of his way to ensure legally that his estate in its entirety would go solely to Karl after his death. He wanted the boy to live comfortably, but to live according to *his*, Beethoven's, precepts.

So he took action. He asked his young friend, the violinist Karl Holz, who was only seven years older than Karl, to spy on him, and report back. Holz, it seems, not only saw nothing wrong in this, but pursued his instructions with some relish. We can, in this instance, be grateful for Beethoven's deafness, which necessitated the use of conversation books, for giving us a glimpse into these surreptitious activities.

Holz reported back to Beethoven:

> *I have lured [Karl] into going to a beer house with me, because I [wanted] to see if he drinks too much, but that does not appear to be the case. Now I will invite [him] at some point to play billiards, then I will be able to see immediately from how good he is whether he has been practising a lot—*

Holz, being that little bit older, took it upon himself to offer Karl a little moral advice:

> *I told him also that he is not supposed to go too often into the Josephstadt [suburb]*[3]—
> *His reason is that he goes because it doesn't cost him anything.*
> *I also told him that his uncle would be more inclined to give him money if [he] went to some concerts in the Burg[theater] a few times each month and listened to some classic pieces—*
> *I told him also that I would speak with you about this. He didn't want that.*

That last entry is particularly revelatory. If Karl had had any doubt that Holz had been put up to these social activities—drinking, playing billiards—by his uncle, he did not doubt it any longer. Holz had admitted it. *He didn't want that.* The fact that Karl does not want Beethoven to know whatever it was that Holz was referring to, shows the strain, and guilt Karl was living under.

He had been a preteen when all this had started. He was about to become an adult, and there had been no let up.

Karl had had enough. He made a fateful decision.

CHAPTER SEVENTEEN

TWO PISTOLS AND GUNPOWDER

AN INVITATION TO GET AWAY FROM IT ALL

Problems were once again mounting for Beethoven—over and above any issues with Karl. His health was deteriorating. It is truer to say that ill-health was constant, with occasional improvements, than that he kept falling ill. It was, as before, his usual complaints of indigestion and irregular bowels—severe diarrhoea would be followed by acute constipation. There was also a recurrence of the eye problems that had first surfaced nearly three years earlier, causing him to sit in a darkened room by day and put a bandage over his eyes at night. This time an eye lotion was prescribed. He complained, too, of back pain. There was also the swelling of his stomach and ankles, which was now very apparent and showed no signs of abating.

Dr. Braunhofer once more came onto the scene, and made his familiar recommendations of no coffee or wine, advised Beethoven to eat as much soup as he could, and prescribed small doses of quinine. Beethoven's health was poor enough for his friends to insist he stay indoors, follow the doctor's advice, and try to take things a little more easily.

Utterly extraordinary as it is to report (I know, I am repeating myself, but this is Beethoven), his appalling health did not stunt his creativity. That—again—is the smallest understatement. As his health plummeted, he began work on a new string quartet, which was to become Op. 131, and which musicologists today rate as the greatest of them all. He was to continue work on this quartet throughout the turbulent months that were to follow.

Propitiously, in March his health did seem to improve slightly, at just the time his String Quartet in B flat, Op. 130, was being rehearsed for its first performance. Schuppanzigh was back in favour, and led the quartet in the inaugural performance on 21 March 1826.

It was a qualified success, but very qualified. The second and fourth movements were liked enough to be repeated, but the final movement left the audience in a state of shock. This is the piece known today as the *Grosse Fuge* (*Great Fugue*). It is a massive fugue of 741 bars, which can take anything up to twenty minutes in performance, and leaves players and listeners drained.[1]

After the first performance, opinion was divided. There were those that said the movement was simply too long, too mighty, for what had gone before. They said the piece was substantial enough to be published separately, as a work in itself. Others—mostly Beethoven's friends—leapt to its defence, arguing it had been misunderstood and would be accepted after more hearings.

The publisher Matthias Artaria bravely approached Beethoven, and suggested he publish the *Grosse Fuge* separately, in a version for piano four hands, and that Beethoven compose a new final movement for the quartet.

Beethoven, predictably, would have none of it, and then, unpredictably, agreed. He even made the arrangement himself. For that reason—that Beethoven himself agreed to hive it away from Op. 130—the *Grosse Fuge* is most often performed today as a separate work, and the string quartet performed with the new final movement that Beethoven was to write later in the year.

What neither he, nor anybody else, could have foreseen, was that the new final movement was to be the last complete piece of music Beethoven was ever to compose. He wrote it fairly quickly in October and November of 1826, and it is uncharacteristically light, even to a degree optimistic.

This is all the more remarkable, given that Beethoven had just lived through what were undoubtedly the tensest, most traumatic, most numbingly dreadful four months of his life.

—

In the spring of 1826 matters with Karl came to a head. Karl asked his uncle for more money. Beethoven went round to his lodgings on a Sunday and confronted him. It appears there was a third, unidentified, person in the room. Beethoven demanded to see the receipt of payment to Karl's landlord Matthias Schlemmer for the previous month's rent. Karl said he had already given it to his uncle. Beethoven denied it. Karl then searched his room but could not find it. He wrote in Beethoven's conversation book that it would surely show up, and if it didn't Schlemmer could give him another one.

Beethoven evidently then demanded to know from Karl how he spent his money, because Karl wrote, 'I go out walking and have a drink and that sort of thing. I don't have any other expenses.'

There are no further entries in the conversation book, but we know that an angry scene ensued, because a few days later Beethoven again went round to Karl's lodgings, and Karl wrote:

> You accuse me of insolence if, after you've shouted at me for hours when I haven't deserved it, I can't just switch off the bitterness and pain you have caused me and become jovial. I am not the wastrel you accuse me of being. I can assure you that since that embarrassing scene in front of another person on Sunday, I have been so upset that everyone in the house has noticed it. I now know for certain that I gave you the receipt for the 80 florins I paid in May. I told you that on Sunday. I have searched my room and it is not there, so it has got to turn up.

Karl then told his uncle to leave him alone, because he had an inordinate amount of work to do for the upcoming exams. Beethoven accused him of appearing to have work to do only when he came to see him, and for being idle and dissolute for the rest of the time.

Karl denied it, and then in turn accused Beethoven of believing tittle-tattle and gossip from other people. It is not written down, but Karl then seems to have made some kind of dire threat.

Tempers were flaring on both sides. Karl suddenly exploded and grabbed his uncle by the chest. At that moment Holz came in, and separated them. We know this from an entry by Holz in the conversation book: 'I came in just as he took you by the chest.'

Beethoven was deeply upset, and spent a sleepless night. But by the next day he felt remorse and forgiveness. He wrote to Karl:

If for no other reason than I now know you obeyed me, all is forgiven and forgotten. I will tell you more when I see you. I have calmed down now. Do not think I have any other thought on my mind but your well-being. That is how you must judge my actions. Do not take any course of action which would cause you misery and put an early end to my life. I did not get to sleep until about 3 o'clock, for I was coughing the whole night. I embrace you with all my heart and I am convinced that soon you will no longer misjudge me. I understand why you did what you did yesterday. Come round to see me at 1 o'clock today without fail. Do not cause me any more sorrow and anxiety. For the moment, farewell!

Your loving and true Father

—

The reconciliation did not last long, mainly due to the efforts of a mediocre musician who had attached himself to Beethoven by the name of Anton Schindler.[2] This man, undoubtedly the most sycophantic of all Beethoven's admirers—Beethoven himself wrote, 'I have long found this importunate hanger-on Schindler most repulsive', and after Beethoven's death the German poet Heinrich Heine described Schindler as 'a black beanpole with horrible white tie and funereal expression who presents himself everywhere as *l'ami de Beethoven* and bores everyone to death with his fatuous chatter'— formed a dangerous aversion to Karl, for the sole reason that the youth was causing the great composer problems.

Schindler wrote in a conversation book of seeing Karl gambling with coachmen in coffee-houses, and of gambling with drinkers and cheating them out of money. He also wrote that Karl had said to his teachers, 'My uncle! I can do what I want with him. A little flattery and a few friendly gestures, and everything will be fine.' Holz didn't help, writing that Karl had said he could wrap his uncle round his finger.

Beethoven did not stop to ask how his confidants could have known these details. Instead it all fed his paranoia, and he took to going to the Polytechnic Institute at lunchtime to wait for his nephew and escort him home arm in arm.

Karl's behaviour, coupled with the build-up of threats, gossip, hints, and innuendo, led Beethoven to believe something dreadful was about to happen. If those close to him dismissed this as over-dramatic, he paid no attention. Why else would he personally turn up at the Institute to escort Karl home? No, some sixth sense told him to prepare for the worst.

—

He did not have long to wait. In the last days of July, when Karl should have been sitting exams at the Institute, he disappeared—but not before telling both Karl Holz and his landlord Schlemmer that he intended killing himself. He might have hinted that he was in possession of a pistol and gunpowder, hidden in his trunk, because after Holz reported the threat to Beethoven, Beethoven wrote in a conversation book, 'Trunk Karl'. The two words are written in a large scrawl, one underneath the other, on the top right-hand side of the page, the page then folded lengthways down the middle, as if as a sort of aide-memoire.

On Saturday, 5 August, Schlemmer went to see Beethoven and wrote in a conversation book:

> *I learned today that your nephew intended to shoot himself by next Sunday at the latest. All I could learn from him was that it was to do with debts he had accumulated from past misdeeds, though I cannot be certain of this as he would not tell me everything. I had a good search of his room, and found in his trunk a loaded pistol with bullets and gunpowder. I am telling you this so that you can take appropriate action as his father. I have the pistol safely locked away.*

If Beethoven had any suspicion that this was merely a melodramatic threat, since Karl had given enough hints to allow his plot to be foiled, he was swiftly disabused.

On the same day, Karl pawned his watch, and with the money bought two new pistols, bullets and gunpowder. He then took the coach south to Baden, one of his uncle's favourite locations, where Beethoven had spent many a summer, and Karl with him.

Karl checked into a boarding house for the night. The following morning he took one of his uncle's favourite walks, west out of the town towards Helenenthal. There he climbed a thickly wooded hill, on top of which stood the ruins of a medieval monastery, the Rauhenstein.

The derelict towers of the monastery today stretch up into the sky like broken fingers, as they did nearly two hundred years ago. Karl climbed into one of them, loaded the bullet into the first pistol, put it to his temple, and fired. The bullet missed. He loaded the second pistol, put it to his temple, and fired. The bullet tore across the skin, burning it and ripping it open, but failed to penetrate the skull.

Karl fell wounded to the ground, where he was later found by a hill walker. In pain but conscious, he asked to be taken ... to his mother.

—

Beethoven's world fell in. Not only had his nephew, his 'son', tried to kill himself, but he had then asked to be taken to his mother. Everything that Beethoven had fought for in that long exhausting court case—all the arguments, the successes, setbacks, and ultimate victory—had come to nothing. The wretched boy had cast it all aside, and in his moment of utmost desolation he had opted to be reunited with that immoral woman, his mother.

As soon as he heard what had happened, Beethoven went straight to Johanna's house. One can only imagine the frostiness between them, the tension in the air, as the two of them—mother and uncle—approached the bed on which lay the wounded Karl. Beethoven did not spare the boy. He berated him for what he had done. Karl wrote in a conversation book, 'Do not plague me with reproaches and lamentation. It's done. Later we can sort everything out.'

Beethoven asked, 'When did it happen?' It was Johanna—we can surmise cautioning her son not to strain himself by trying to write or speak—who wrote in the conversation book:

He has just come. The person who found him carried him down from a rock in Baden—I beg of you not to let the doctor make a report, or they will take him away from here at once, and we fear the worst.

Well might Johanna have been concerned. Attempted suicide was a crime. A doctor would be obliged to report it to the police, who would then take appropriate action. Beethoven was probably horrified to learn Johanna had already sent Karl Holz to get a doctor—she said she had no choice, since it seemed apparent from looking at Karl's wound that a bullet was lodged in his skull. There was no doubt some relief when Holz reported that the doctor was not at home.

Beethoven scribbled a quick note to Dr. Carl von Smetana, who had operated on Karl's hernia some years before, and who he believed could be relied on to be discreet.

Most honoured Herr von Smetana,

A great misfortune has happened, which Karl accidentally inflicted upon himself. I hope that he can still be saved, especially by you if you come quickly. Karl has a <u>bullet</u> in his head. How, you shall learn—But be quick, for God's sake, be quick.

Yours respectfully,
Beethoven

Beethoven gave the letter to Holz and told him to be quick, but he returned with the news that another doctor had already been called in—it is not clear by whom—by the name of Dögl. Holz carried a message from Smetana that Dögl was a capable doctor, and that he would not intervene unless Dögl wished to consult him professionally.

Karl—for once—took the initiative, and declared himself satisfied with Dögl, and announced that was the end of the matter.

Beethoven left, distraught in the belief that his nephew had a bullet lodged in his skull, and was hovering between life and death.

As soon as his uncle had left, Karl's frustration poured out: 'If only I never had to see him again! If only he would stop blaming me for everything!' He even threatened to tear the blood-soaked bandage off if another word was spoken to him about his uncle.

Again we know this from Holz, who stayed to explain the situation to Johanna and her son. He said it would be impossible to hide what had happened from the authorities. The police would have to be told, and it was better it came from him, rather than somebody else.

Holz duly went to the police and explained what had happened. He returned with the depressing, but expected, news that Karl would be severely reprimanded, that he would have to be taken to hospital for treatment, and while there be subject to religious instruction from a priest into the wrong of what he had done. Only when the authorities were satisfied that he had been morally corrected, and he was able to pass a 'complete examination in religious instruction', would he be released from surveillance—if, that is, he survived.

The following day, Monday, 7 August, the case was reported to the criminal court and placed under the jurisdiction of a magistrate. It was up to the magistrate to appoint a priest to carry out the religious instruction. The same day, Karl was removed from his mother's home and admitted to hospital.

Beethoven was crushed. It would be charitable to say that his concern was entirely for Karl, but that appears not to be the case. He was aware the incident left him publicly humiliated. Crossing the Glacis to his apartment, he bumped into Stephan von Breuning's wife Constanze, who described him to her husband as 'completely unnerved'.

'Do you know what has happened to me?' he said to her. 'My nephew Karl shot himself!'

'Is he dead?' she asked.

'No, he only grazed himself, he is still alive. There is hope that he can be saved. But the disgrace this has caused me—and I loved him so much.'

Vienna was awash with the story. Within hours it seemed the entire city knew. In cafés, restaurants, in the back of fiacres, on street corners, there was only one topic of conversation. *Have you heard what happened to the Great Deaf One? His nephew, his son, tried to kill himself! What will this do to him? This'll tip him over the edge* ...

It is not difficult to imagine the effect of this trauma on Beethoven, himself in failing health and not far from mental collapse. Even Schindler, rarely known to utter any words about his master not in the form of a hagiography, wrote later that the strain of it all 'bowed the proud figure of the composer', and that he soon looked like a man of seventy.

Gerhard von Breuning, in his memoir, wrote, 'The news was shattering to Beethoven. The pain he felt at this event was indescribable. He was crushed, like a father who has lost his beloved son.'

Again, though, Beethoven seems as much concerned about himself as he does his unfortunate nephew, and is far from forgiving over what has happened. An eyewitness account graphically illustrates this. Breuning recounts how a certain Ignaz Seng, assistant in the surgical division at Vienna General Hospital, was doing his rounds in the late summer of 1826. A man in a grey coat who had the appearance of a 'simple peasant' came up to him. The man asked in a dull tone, 'Are you Assistant Dr. Seng? The office referred me to you. Is my scoundrel of a nephew in your ward?'

Dr. Seng asked the name of the patient, and on being told it was Karl van Beethoven, he replied that yes, he was in a hospital ward, and he asked the man if he wanted to see him. Beethoven, realising that the doctor did not recognise him, said, 'I am Beethoven.'

As Dr. Seng led Beethoven upstairs, he was harangued by Beethoven, who said, 'The truth is, I do not want to see him. He does not deserve it. He has caused me too much trouble.' Seng relates how Beethoven continued talking about the dreadful thing his nephew had done, how he had spoiled him by being too kind to him, and so on.

Dr. Seng concludes his account—given verbally to Breuning—by saying the aspect that surprised him most about the whole encounter was the realisation that the plain individual he took to be a simple peasant was none other than 'the great Beethoven'. He promised the renowned composer that he would take the best possible care of the young man.

Karl spent a little over six weeks in hospital, and was discharged when his wound was considered to have healed sufficiently. In accordance with the law for would-be suicides, he was handed over to the police. In the afternoon, around three o'clock, a clergyman came to see him, examined him for evidence of improved morals and religious obedience, and wrote out an affidavit on his behalf.

That evening Karl's mother went to see him, and gave him a little money so he could send out for food. Johanna told Beethoven that Karl had to spend the night 'among common criminals and the scum of humanity ... without a bed'. Karl himself later told his uncle he was in total darkness during the evening, and couldn't sleep because of rats running around his cell. The following day a meal of meat was brought to him, but he was made to eat it without knife or fork, 'like an animal'.

It is possible there was a touch of exaggeration from both Karl and his mother, with the intention of making Beethoven feel guilty about his nephew's plight, because there now began something of a concerted campaign to persuade Beethoven to allow Karl to join the army. Stephan von Breuning wrote in a conversation book, 'A military life will be the best discipline for one who finds it hard to lead a purposeful life on his own. It will also teach him how to live on very little.'

Breuning also reminded Beethoven that through his position at the War Ministry he was on cordial terms with Field Marshal Joseph von Stutterheim, commander of the Eighth Moravian Infantry Regiment, and was sure he could persuade the Field Marshal to give

Karl a place in his regiment. Both Schindler and Holz added their weight to Breuning's argument.

Karl himself was keeping up the pressure on his uncle. Even while in hospital he wrote in a conversation book:

> *I still wish to pursue a military career, and if allowed to do so I would be very happy. I am convinced it is a way of life that would suit me and which would make me happy. So please do what you think best, and above all please see to it that I get away from here as soon as possible.*

This was a subtle approach by Karl, which he calculated would resonate with Beethoven, because there was the issue of where he should go when he was discharged. Beethoven was adamant that he should not spend even a single day with his mother, and he told Karl as much. To join the army and move away from Vienna would solve that problem at least, even if a military career ran totally counter to Beethoven's wishes.

But Karl, after his suicide attempt, was newly emboldened. Maybe it was the knowledge that other people—Breuning, Holz, Schindler—supported him. Maybe it was a compulsion not to allow his act of desperation to fade without any clear benefit to him. For the first time in his life, Karl was beginning to stand up to his overpowering uncle. He wrote in a conversation book in the hours after being taken to his mother, clearly moments after Beethoven had ranted against Johanna in her absence:

> *I do not want to hear anything that is derogatory to her. It is not for me to be her judge. If I were to spend even a little time here with her, it would only be small compensation for all that she has suffered on my account. You cannot say it will be harmful for me to be here, if for no other reason that I will only be here for a short time.*

And moments later:

> *Under no circumstances will I treat her with any more cold-*
> *ness than I have before, whatever words you may care to say on*
> *the subject.*

Karl also knew that he had his mother on his side regarding his desire to be a soldier.

> *[Given her support] all the less can I deny her wish to be with*
> *me, since I am not likely to see her again for some time. There is no*
> *reason why this shouldn't stop you and me from seeing each other*
> *as often as you wish.*

Beethoven was seriously outnumbered. Reluctantly, in effect abandoning his long-held ambition for Karl to become a musician, the 'Beethoven' of the next generation, he agreed to let Karl join the army.

Hard to believe, then, that while agonising over his nephew's future, he was able to turn his mind to loftier matters, namely the dedication of the Ninth Symphony to accompany its publication.

He had drawn up an astonishingly glittering list of possible dedicatees, with one much lowlier name, indicating possibly that he recognised the extraordinary worth of the work. Potential dedicatees were the King of Prussia, the King of France, Emperor Alexander of Russia ... and his old friend and helper Ferdinand Ries, currently residing in London.

In April 1823, a full year before the first performance, Beethoven had written to Ries promising him the dedication. A year later, according to an entry in a conversation book, Ries was still a candidate, although joined now by the other more illustrious names. It appears that Beethoven decided on the Russian Emperor, but Alexander inconveniently died in December 1825.

In the spring of 1826 Beethoven decided finally that the symphony should be dedicated to the King of Prussia. The presentation copy was ready by September, and Beethoven hand wrote the title page containing the dedication—at just the time he was wrestling with the humiliation over Karl's suicide attempt, visiting him in hospital, fraught with worry over his condition and what to do with him when he was released from hospital.

There was a cordial exchange of letters between Beethoven and the Prussian monarch, and with his gracious acceptance of the dedication King Friedrich Wilhelm III enclosed a diamond ring 'as a token of my sincere appreciation'.

The actual ring that Beethoven received turned out to be set with a stone of 'reddish' hue, according to Schindler, which the court jeweller valued at a measly 300 florins. Beethoven was insulted and angry, and wanted to send it straight back. He was dissuaded from doing so. It was never established whether the King had second thoughts, or whether the ring was stolen and substituted either in Berlin or Vienna.

—

While Karl was in hospital, Beethoven's brother Johann had suggested that when Karl had recovered sufficiently, Beethoven should bring him to the spacious, comfortable, quiet country estate he, Johann, had bought in Gneixendorf. Far from being grateful, Beethoven was appalled at the idea of spending any time with the brother he despised, and the woman he had tried to stop his brother marrying. To Johann's invitation he replied, 'I will not come. Your brother??????!!!! Ludwig.'

In late September, just days after Karl left hospital, Johann repeated the invitation, and this time there was a compelling reason to accept. Karl had a large visible scar on his temple where the bullet had torn open his skin. Stephan von Breuning was adamant that Karl could not go for interview with Field Marshal von Stutterheim until the scar was no longer visible, since the Field Marshal had told him he wanted there to be no mention of the affair.

It was therefore decided that Beethoven would take Karl to Gneixendorf for a short visit. It would allow the scar to heal, give time for his hair to grow long enough to cover it, as well as provide peace and relaxation after the trauma of the preceding weeks. It would also provide Beethoven himself with a much needed escape from the city, and might even have a beneficial effect on his health.

In the event the visit would last for a little over two months. It was to be fraught from the beginning, and by the time Beethoven returned to Vienna his health had collapsed completely, and he was only months from death.

CHAPTER EIGHTEEN

FRIGHTENING THE OXEN

'THE GREATEST COMPOSER OF THE CENTURY, AND YOU TREATED HIM LIKE A SERVANT!'

JOHANN VAN BEETHOVEN HAD LED SOMETHING of a charmed life. He had trained as a pharmacist and it had been his ambition early in life to acquire his own pharmacy, but he lacked the funds to make his dream a reality. In 1808, at the age of thirty-one, he scraped together enough money to buy a pharmacy in Linz, a city on the Danube around a hundred miles west of Vienna. With a down payment that left him practically penniless and a mortgage he could not afford, together with the expenses of the purchase and travel, he was barely able to afford the first payment.

The business yielded practically nothing, and rent from rooms in the house that he let out was small. Within months Johann was in danger of defaulting. In desperation he sold the iron gratings on the windows, but it was nowhere near enough to keep him going.

In an extraordinary stroke of luck, events over which he had no control played into his hands. The Continental blockade that Napoleon Bonaparte had imposed on British goods in 1806 caused the value of British merchandise to rise astronomically. It just so happened that all the jars and pots on the shelves of Johann's pharmacy were made of English tin. He sold them all, replaced them with earthenware, and was able to forestall his financial crisis.

Then just when things were beginning to look ominous for him once again, a second totally fortuitous chain of events came to his rescue. The French Emperor, exasperated at Austria's continuing attempts to defeat him on the battlefield, decided to put an end to this precocity once and for all, and invaded Austria. He marched northeast, with the capital Vienna in his sights. This time there was to be no triumphal procession into a subdued city. Vienna, and the Viennese, needed to be taught a lesson. Napoleon established a base at Linz, and it was there that the Revolutionary Army's quartermasters placed orders for the supply of medical equipment—medicines, bandages, splints, and so on.

Who won the contract? One Nikolaus Johann van Beethoven. It was the making of him. It brought him wealth beyond his dreams. It also sealed his unpopularity—hatred, even—with his fellow Austrians for collaborating with the enemy, a stigma that was to follow him for the rest of his life. He brushed that off, and began to live the life of a wealthy and successful businessman.

As wealthy men do he acquired a mistress, and in late 1812 he married her, as we have seen against his elder brother's violent protestations. He sold the pharmacy in December 1816, buying another on the opposite bank of the Danube. And of crucial importance to our story, in August 1819 he bought a country estate in Gneixendorf.

Gneixendorf is a village lying on high ground just north of the town of Krems—dominated then as now by a huge medieval monastery—which sits on the banks of the Danube roughly halfway between Vienna and Linz. It was there that Johann, with his wife and her illegitimate daughter, whom he had adopted, lived the life of a country squire, and to where he invited his brother and nephew in late September 1826.

—

Delighted, finally, at Ludwig's acceptance of his invitation, Johann sent a carriage and driver to Vienna, and at nine o'clock on the morning of Thursday, 28 September 1826, Ludwig and Karl left Vienna for the two-day journey to Gneixendorf.

There is no question that Johann was looking forward to the visit.

He gave his brother a small self-contained apartment of three rooms on the first floor of the southwest side of the house—a sundial on the outside wall testifying to the sunny aspect—and a personal manservant to tend to his needs.

The rooms consisted of bedroom, salon, and dining room. The salon, between the other two, had a mural of the River Rhine painted on its walls. Johann, homesick for the river on the banks of which he and his brothers had grown up in Bonn, commissioned an artist from his hometown to paint the mural to remind him of his youth.[1]

He was obviously keen to show off the trappings of success to his brother. He might not have been a musician, but through his business acumen he had acquired considerable wealth. He also no doubt wanted to demonstrate to his brother that any reservations he might have had about the marriage to Therese Obermeyer had been ill founded.

Seen from Ludwig's perspective, things were very different. In fact they could hardly have been worse. A figure, if not of fun, certainly of gossip and some derision in Vienna, his extraordinary musical accomplishments—this was little over two years since the premiere of the Ninth Symphony—were in danger of being subsumed by the drama over Karl. He had never got on with his brother Johann, and had contempt for Johann's wife, and so the prospect of a stay in their house must have filled him with foreboding. The attempted suicide of a close family member would put a strain on the most rational of people, but one can only imagine its effect on Beethoven's already precarious mental state. His physical condition was pitiful: his stomach was now so swollen that he wore a belt around it to restrain it, and his ankles and feet were swollen to such an extent that he was in constant pain.

Johann did not help matters by charging his brother a small rent. When it became clear that Beethoven and his nephew were intending to stay well beyond the original two weeks, Johann pointed out that this would incur costs, and it was reasonable to expect a small contribution. Beethoven reacted furiously, but must have had something of a change of heart at one point, because an entry by Johann in a conversation book suggests Beethoven was considering moving in permanently, with Johann actually encouraging him with descriptions of how beautiful Gneixendorf was in spring and summer.

The manservant, Michael Krenn, was interviewed—along with other residents of Gneixendorf—by Thayer nearly forty years later. These accounts, together with many entries in conversation books, make it possible to build a picture of the fraught two months that Beethoven and Karl spent at Johann's country estate.

It seems as if the first few weeks of the stay were actually beneficial to Beethoven. The countryside in late autumn appealed to him, and he took pleasure from long walks. The fresh air might have been responsible for a slight improvement in his eye condition. The daily regime was a relaxed one. Beethoven would get up at half-past five in the morning to work, then join the family for breakfast at seven o'clock, after which, notebook and pencil in pocket, he would take a long walk across the fields. Local people grew used to seeing the famous composer, oblivious to anything around him, striding purposefully, shouting out loud and waving his arms in the air. They described how suddenly, in full stride, he would slow down, then stop, take out his notebook and scribble something down. They knew better than to interrupt him.

Beethoven would return to the house for lunch at half-past twelve, then go to his room until around three o'clock. After that he would again take a long walk across the countryside, return for supper at half-past seven, go to his room to write till ten o'clock, then go to bed. There was a piano in his small salon, which he played—although only occasionally, according to Michael—but no one was allowed to go near him when he was in his rooms. There were certainly no recitals, or musical soirées. The atmosphere, at all times, was tense.

Michael, son of one of the vineyard workers, was clearly frightened out of his wits to be assigned to the famous, eccentric, unpredictable composer. If he was apprehensive about unwittingly upsetting his master, he had good cause to be. And yet, as he was to discover, Beethoven had an unexpected soft side too.

We do not know what age Michael was, but can assume he was in his mid-teens, because in the early part of the stay at least he reacted with youthful mirth to Beethoven's eccentricities.

At first the cook was assigned the task of making Beethoven's bed each morning and sweeping the floor of the bedroom. But one morning, while she was doing this with Michael also in the room, Beethoven sat at a table, gesticulating with his hands, beating time with his feet, muttering under his breath and singing out loud. She tried to ignore it, but finally could no longer contain herself and burst out laughing. Beethoven saw this, leapt up from the table, and drove her angrily out of the room.

Michael, equally struggling to restrain his laughter, tried to hurry out of the room too, but Beethoven held him back, gave him a few coins, and told him that, from now on, he should make the bed and clean the floor each day. Beethoven told him to come early to get it done. Michael found he had to knock a long time, and increasingly loudly—no doubt worrying about waking the household—before Beethoven finally opened the door.

It took the boy a long time to become accustomed to Beethoven sitting at the table, banging, beating, waving his arms and singing, and for some time at least he had to hurry from the room, undetected if possible, and burst into laughter out of sight and safely protected by Beethoven's deafness.

On one occasion he panicked when Beethoven returned from a walk and could not find his precious notebook. He set Michael the task of finding it. 'Michael, hurry up, look everywhere, hunt for my notebook. I must have it back, whatever it takes!' he quotes

Beethoven as saying. One can imagine the boy's relief when he found it, though he does not tell us where.

Beethoven—surprisingly, given his unsuccessful record with house servants—seemed to develop a liking for Michael, no doubt enhanced by the realisation of the boy's usefulness. He soon banned everybody from entering his rooms, with the exception of Michael. He instructed the boy to clean and tidy his rooms while he was out walking. On several occasions Michael found coins on the floor. He would gather them up, and when Beethoven returned hand them to him. Beethoven made Michael show him where he had found them, and then told the boy to keep them. This happened three or four times, but then stopped.[2]

Beethoven demonstrated—for him—exceptional loyalty to Michael when the boy's carelessness landed him in serious trouble. Therese gave him five florins with instructions to go into the village and buy fish and wine. Michael lost (or spent) the money. He returned to the house sullen and quiet. Therese asked him for the fish, and he confessed. Furious, she sacked him on the spot.

At dinner Beethoven asked where Michael was. Therese told him what had happened. Beethoven flew into a rage with her, gave her the five florins, and demanded she reinstate Michael—which she did.

After that there was clearly a bond between the composer and his manservant. From that point on, Beethoven refused to sit at the table for any meals with the family. He told Michael to bring his meals up to his apartment, and to prepare breakfast for him in his room. While eating, he would ask Michael to bring him up to date on what had been said around the table. He even let it be known that if he could, he would take Michael back to Vienna with him.

Beethoven was clearly undergoing some sort of mental collapse. Inside the house, his eccentricities, his unpredictability, were to some extent manageable—in fact, his desire to closet himself in his rooms and bar entry to everyone except Michael might even have been welcomed. But outside the house, his erratic behaviour could hardly go unnoticed.

Again, nearly forty years later, an elderly resident of Gneixendorf recounted how the first time he had seen Beethoven striding across the fields, arms waving, singing and shouting, he had taken him for a madman. Once he realised who he was, that he was in fact the brother of the estate's owner, he always greeted him politely, but his salutation was never reciprocated.

The same man, a farmer, recalled vividly how, before he knew who Beethoven was, he was driving a pair of young oxen from an outhouse towards Johann's manor house, when Beethoven approached, 'shouting and waving his arms in wild gesticulations'. He said he gestured to Beethoven to be a little quieter, but was met with a blank look. The oxen took fright, charged down a steep hill, hotly pursued by the farmer who with a Herculean effort managed to restrain them and get them back up the hill.

The drama was not over. Beethoven was still outside, striding along, shouting and gesticulating. The farmer, angry now, asked him again to be quiet. Again there was no response. The oxen panicked again, and this time charged straight for the house. Fortunately another man, employed on the farm, managed to stop them. Between them the two men calmed the beasts, while Beethoven strode off, oblivious to what had happened.

The farmer asked the other man if he knew who the fool was who had scared his oxen. On being told he was the landowner's brother, the farmer replied, 'Fine brother, that's all I can say.'

Two other reported incidents are evidence of Beethoven's precarious mental state. One day Johann decided to pay a visit to a friend of his, a doctor, who lived with his wife in a neighbouring village. He took his brother with him. Unfortunately the doctor was out on a house call, but his wife, flattered to have Gneixendorf's chief landowner in the house, poured him a glass of her husband's best wine and gave him delicacies to eat.

They were chatting convivially when the wife suddenly noticed a morose individual, sitting silently in the darkness on a bench by the stove. Taking the man for Johann's servant, she reached for a jug of rough open wine, poured a glass, and said, 'He shall have a drink too.'

Later that night, when the doctor returned home and his wife recounted the visit, he asked her some pertinent questions, then exclaimed, 'For goodness' sake, woman, what have you done? Do you have any idea who that was? The greatest composer of the century was in our house today, and you treated him like a servant!'

The anecdote is perhaps just as illuminating for the way it highlights the obviously frosty relationship between the two brothers—wouldn't you at least expect Johann to introduce his brother?—as it does Beethoven's anti-social behaviour.

The two brothers were together again when a similar occurrence happened. Johann took his brother with him when he went to call on a local government official to discuss some business. The official had his clerk with him. Johann sat opposite them, but Beethoven refused to move from the door, and stood there during the whole of the meeting, which took some time.

The official clearly treated the morose and silent Beethoven with enormous—albeit unreciprocated—respect throughout, because after the two brothers had left, he turned to his clerk and asked, 'Do you know who that man was who stood by the door?'

The clerk replied, 'Judging by the respect you showed towards him, sir, I would imagine him to be someone important. Otherwise I'd have taken him for an imbecile.'

Both stories are illuminating for showing that for those who did not know who Beethoven was, the figure he portrayed was about as diametrically removed from the genius we know him to be as it is possible to imagine.

Beethoven might have been fraught, tense, in ill-health, in pain, yet the eyewitness accounts of him waving his arms, singing and shouting—whether in the open countryside or at the table in his room—suggest musical ideas were forming in his mind. They were, but paradoxically—no surprise there—they were slightly at odds with his mental and physical state.

Two months before the trip to Gneixendorf, almost as soon as he had finished composing the String Quartet in C sharp minor, Op. 131, Beethoven had begun work on a new string quartet, which was to become Op. 135. Now, in Gneixendorf, sitting at a table in his small salon, a piano to the side, and no doubt gazing at the murals of the River Rhine, which he had once known so well, he worked on it for the whole of September and the first half of October—in other words, for the first half of his stay in Gneixendorf.

As I have already noted, the early part of the stay was relatively benign. Beethoven enjoyed the pleasant autumn weather, the long walks and fresh air. But things soon declined. He was difficult and uncooperative towards his brother and sister-in-law, constantly fretting over Karl and his bizarre decision to join the military, upsetting staff at the house and local people, and all the time struggling to cope with the terminal decline in his health.

One would have every reason, therefore, to expect the String Quartet in F, Op. 135, to be among his most dense, even impenetrable, works. It is quite the opposite. It is on a smaller scale than its immediate predecessors, and seemingly light years away from Op. 133, the *Grosse Fuge*. In places it is carefree, even witty. The third movement is relatively short, and there seems to be none of the 'angst' that characterises the earlier quartets, in particular the *Cavatina* of Op. 130.

Beethoven finished the new quartet by mid-October, and if his behaviour away from the composing table was erratic, when working at his music he was clear-minded and methodical enough to copy out all the parts himself, before dispatching Johann to Vienna with them to deliver to the publisher.

That task completed, Beethoven turned his attention to a new final movement for the String Quartet in B flat, Op. 130, to replace the *Grosse Fuge*. This coincided with a deterioration on many levels, and yet again—as with Op. 135—he worked rapidly, and after a few false starts completed the movement in around a month. Again like its predecessor there is a lightness to it, it is on a relatively small scale, and there is a pervading mood of optimism. All this in stark contrast to its creator.

Once the work was finished, Beethoven dispatched it to the publisher. It was to be the last complete piece of music he would ever compose.

—

The weather in Gneixendorf became increasingly cold as autumn gave way to winter, and Beethoven became a more and more uncooperative guest, frequently complaining about the food and the coldness and damp in his quarters. There was also a further deterioration in his relations with Karl.

We do not know exactly how the twenty-year-old Karl occupied himself during the stay in Gneixendorf. We can only assume he was somewhat bored. There was nothing for him to do in the country, and he probably yearned for the student life with his friends in Vienna. It appears he played four-hand pieces at the piano with his uncle, because Therese remarks on this and writes in a conversation book, 'Karl plays very well.'

But this belies the underlying, indeed overt, tension between nephew and uncle, 'son' and 'father'. Beethoven continued to try to control Karl's activities, as he had done in Vienna. Therese writes pointedly in a conversation book, 'Do not be concerned. He will certainly come home by 1 o'clock. It seems he has some of your rash blood. I have not found him angry. It is you that he loves, to the point of worship.'

Beethoven certainly used Karl. He sent him frequently to Krems for writing materials, a task Karl welcomed, taking advantage of it to go drinking and play billiards—no doubt incurring Therese's reassurance to Beethoven in the conversation book.

Karl made repeated entries in conversation books, not attempting to restrain his frustration, even anger, at Beethoven's controlling attitude to him, which had clearly not been mollified by the suicide attempt. On one day, undated, Karl wrote:

> *You ask me why I do not talk … Because I have had enough … Yours is the right to command, and I must endure it all … I can only regret that I can give no answer to anything you have said today, since I know of nothing better I can do than to listen and remain silent as is my duty. You must not consider this insolent.*

And on another, clearly in despair at Beethoven's suspicions:

> *Have you ever seen me speak a word? Not very likely, because I wasn't of a mind to speak at all. So nothing you have to say about intrigues even requires a rebuttal. Please, I beg of you, just leave me alone. If you want to leave, that's fine. If not, that's fine too. I only ask you once again to stop tormenting me as you do. In the end you may regret it, for I can take so much, but then it gets too much. You did the same thing to your brother today, completely without reason. You have to realise that other people are human beings too.*

Johann—a target as well, judging by Karl's words—was clearly growing weary of having his difficult brother as house guest. The original stay of two weeks seemed to be stretching out with no finite end. By late November Johann decided to do something about it. Again, clear evidence of the tension between the two brothers, so great that a rational discussion was out of the question, is demonstrated by the fact that Johann chose to write his brother a letter, despite the fact they were both living under the same roof.

He began by touching a nerve, pointing out that Karl had been in Gneixendorf for so long that he had given up doing anything constructive at all, and the longer he stayed the more difficult he would find it to get back to anything like a normal life. Tactfully he says both of them, as the boy's uncles, are to blame, but that it is Beethoven's duty to allow Karl to fulfil his dream of entering the army as soon as possible.

After a few discursive lines, he comes straight to the point: 'I think [your departure] ought to be <u>by next Monday</u>.'

Karl, concerned about the scar on his temple, was clearly brought into the conversation, and suggests a small delay in departure:

> *I cannot argue against it since we have been here longer than was planned. But <u>Breuning</u> himself has said that I cannot go to the Field Marshal until I am able to appear without any visible sign left of what happened to me, because he does not want the whole affair to be mentioned. This is almost accomplished now except for a little bit which really won't take much more time. Therefore I believe that we should stay until next week at the least. If I had hair ointment here then it would be unnecessary. Besides, the longer we remain here, the longer we can all be together. Once we return to Vienna, I will have to leave right away.*

Schindler (generally unreliable, but probably credible on this occasion) says Johann's forthright request to his brother to leave, and leave soon, upset Beethoven considerably, which probably accounted for Karl's rather diplomatic suggestion that they stay a little bit longer.

In any case there was a problem over transport. Johann, it appeared, had only one covered carriage (presumably the one he had sent to Vienna to pick up Beethoven and Karl two months earlier). It had recently been used to take Therese to and from Vienna, and Johann was planning to make a trip very soon.

It is likely that the brothers agreed on a date some time after the 'next Monday' referred to by Johann, which was 27 November, and after Johann's return from Vienna, which would mean the carriage was available. But an unexpected and dramatic turn of events brought the departure right forward.

On the night of Friday, 1 December, the two brothers had a blistering row. The subject, perhaps rather surprisingly, was Karl's future inheritance. Beethoven demanded of his brother that he make a new Will, cutting out his wife and her illegitimate daughter, and leaving everything to Karl. Johann refused point blank, and the brothers argued long and vociferously into the night.

Suddenly, in the early hours of the morning, Beethoven snapped. He had had enough. He said he and Karl would leave that instant, and he ordered Johann to get the carriage and a driver to take them back to Vienna.

Johann immediately saw the folly of this. He tried to reason with his brother that it was the middle of the night, it was bitterly cold, Beethoven was in no fit state with his poor health to undertake the journey without properly preparing himself, and so on.

Beethoven's mind was made up. He was leaving with Karl and leaving now. It was Johann's turn to snap. Two months of frustration and suppressed anger boiled up in him, and he exacted revenge by denying his brother the covered carriage. All he had, he said, was a rickety old open-top cart—impossible to make the two-day journey in.[3]

If he thought that would bring Beethoven to his senses, he miscalculated. *'Get it!'* was Beethoven's riposte.

Some time around three or four in the morning of Friday, 1 December, in the middle of a raw, damp, frosty, and bitterly cold night, Beethoven, dressed in entirely inadequate clothing, climbed into the open-top cart with his nephew Karl for the long journey back to Vienna.

They stayed the following night in a tavern on the north bank of the Danube river. The building was old and dilapidated, and Beethoven was given a room with no stove to heat it, and no shutters for the windows.

Towards midnight he broke out in a fever, accompanied by violent shaking, and a dry hacking cough that split his sides with pain. He was violently thirsty. He was given a glass of frozen water, which eased his thirst but increased the shivering.

At first light he stumbled outside, weak, exhausted, and barely able to stand. Uncomplaining, he allowed himself to be lifted into the cart, and it set off for Vienna. One imagines the landlord was grateful to get his guest off the premises without having a death on his hands.

Some time in the afternoon of Saturday, 2 December, Beethoven and his nephew arrived in Vienna. Beethoven could barely climb the stairs to his second-floor apartment in the Schwarzspanierhaus. He was still shivering from fever, had no strength, coughed at the smallest exertion, could scarcely walk on his swollen feet and ankles, and was in pain from his vastly distended stomach.

That he was close to death was not in doubt. The priority was to get a doctor as quickly as possible to try to ease his suffering. Easier said than done.

CHAPTER NINETEEN

TERMINALLY ILL

'HIS FACE WAS DAMP, HE SPAT BLOOD'

THE APARTMENT THAT BEETHOVEN MOVED into in the Schwarzspanierhaus almost a year before the trip to Gneixendorf was, by any standards, stylish, in modern parlance well appointed. Beethoven was notoriously uncaring about where he lived, and there is no evidence he appreciated how suitable this apartment was for his needs.

The building that housed it was impressive. Abutting a church, it looked across open ground, affording light and fresh air for the monks whose bedrooms were on the top floor. Once converted into apartments, it was one of Vienna's more desirable residences, outside the city wall and across the Glacis, away from the noise and dust of the inner city. Beethoven's apartment on the second floor took up much of the middle section of the building, five windows—two in the bedroom—ensuring good views, as well as daylight.[1]

The apartment was reached by a wide marble staircase. Immediately to the left a low wide door opened onto a spacious entrance hall.[2] Beethoven used the hall as a dining room. The portrait of his grandfather, the *Kapellmeister*, which his father had pawned and which he asked Wegeler to forward to him in Vienna, hung on a wall of this room.

From the hall, with all doors open, it was possible to see through all three of the front rooms. The first was the music room, with piles of disordered manuscripts and published music, which Stephan von Breuning named the 'junk room'. The next, the largest room in the apartment, with two windows facing out to the Glacis, contained two pianos—one given to Beethoven by the Viennese piano builder Conrad Graf,[3] the other the Broadwood shipped from London[4]—standing curve to curve with keyboards pointing in opposite directions. In the far right corner stood Beethoven's bed, next to it a small table with a bell for summoning his housekeeper, and a folded conversation book for friends to write their questions. The third room was the composition room, containing Beethoven's desk. The desk was angled so that, while working at it with all connecting doors open, Beethoven could see if any visitor came into the flat.

One other benefit, the Schwarzspanierhaus was directly across the road from the Rothes Haus, where his old friend Stephan von Breuning lived with his family. Under different circumstances, Beethoven could have looked forward to many years of relative comfort in this apartment, as he continued to compose.

—

The reality was different. Supporting his gravely ill uncle on that chill Saturday afternoon, Karl staggered through the music room, mindless of precious compositions being trampled underfoot, no doubt clumsily negotiating the pianos, until with relief he allowed Beethoven to collapse onto the bed. We can imagine him trying to arrange the pillows under Beethoven's head, swinging his legs onto the bed and removing his boots.

Being late on a Saturday in the depths of winter, Karl did not immediately send for medical help, and was no doubt gratified to find that the following morning Beethoven had regained some strength. He continued to improve—it is possible his housekeeper Rosalie, known as Sali, came to cook for him—and after a few days it was Beethoven himself who decided on action.

He told Karl he wanted to pen some letters, but lacking the strength he would dictate them for Karl to write. The first was a short one-paragraph letter to his young friend and helper Karl 'Wooden' Holz. He explained that he had been taken ill and had confined himself to bed, and he asked Holz to call on him.

At that point he motioned for Karl to pass him the pen and paper, and underneath the letter he scribbled a four-bar canon on the words: *'Wir irren allesamt, nur alle irren anderst.'* ('We all err, but each one errs differently.')

They were the last musical notes he was to write.

The next letter was altogether different, very long and personal, to his old friends Franz and Eleonore Wegeler. They had written to him almost a year before, Wegeler addressing him as 'My dear old Louis!'; Eleonore beginning her letter more formally with 'For so long a time dear Beethoven!'

It is strange that Beethoven should choose this moment, a year later, to respond—or maybe it is not so strange. Both Wegeler and his wife separately implored Beethoven to make a return trip to Bonn and the Rhineland. He does not refer to this in his reply, but his words suggest little sign of a realisation that time for him was short:

> *If I let my Muse sleep, it is so that she may reawaken with renewed strength. I hope still to bring some great works into the world and then as an old child end my earthly course amongst kindly people … The beginning has now been made and soon you will get another letter, and the more often you write to me, the more pleasure you will give me …*

Holz came quickly in response to the letter, and on Beethoven's instructions set about trying to find a doctor. It was now that Beethoven's cavalier attitude to his doctors over the years came back to haunt him.

The first doctor to be contacted was Dr. Braunhofer, he of 'no coffee or alcohol'. He said he could not come, because he lived too far away and the journey at that time of year would be too arduous. It is more than likely that his past knowledge of Beethoven's health was enough to tell him that the illness was terminal, and he did not want to be in charge of the composer at his death.

The next doctor approached was Dr. Staudenheim, summarily sacked by Beethoven some years before. He said he would come, but did not do so. A third doctor was himself sick and unable to attend.

Finally Holz suggested a certain Dr. Andreas Wawruch, Director of the Medical Clinic in Vienna and Professor of Pathology at Vienna General Hospital. Holz told Beethoven Wawruch was regarded as one of the ablest physicians in Vienna, and was also a keen music-lover, an admirer of Beethoven's compositions, and a competent cellist.

Beethoven did not demur; Wawruch agreed to attend, and so on 5 December he came to the Schwarzspanierhaus to care for a man he had never examined before, who was clearly terminally ill, and who was the most renowned and revered musician in Europe. It is to his eternal credit that Wawruch, knowing there was only one possible outcome, cared for his patient with kindness and diligence to the end, and left us a remarkable account of the final illness and its treatment.

On first meeting Beethoven, Wawruch wrote in a conversation book, 'One who greatly reveres your name will do everything possible to give you speedy relief. Prof. Wawruch.' Examination, given Beethoven's deafness, was not easy, and so Wawruch dictated questions for Karl to write down.[5]

Wawruch wrote up a report of the first few days that he treated Beethoven, and it makes difficult reading:

> *I found Beethoven afflicted with serious symptoms of inflammation of the lungs. His face was damp, he spat blood, his breathing so irregular that it threatened suffocation, and a stitch in the*

side so painful that it made lying on the back a torment. A strong counter-treatment for inflammation soon brought the desired relief. His constitution triumphed, and by a fortunate outcome he was freed from apparent mortal danger. On the fifth day he was able, in a sitting position, to tell me, amid profound emotion, of the discomforts which he had suffered. On the seventh day he felt considerably better, so that he was able to get out of bed, walk about, read and write.

Wawruch visited Beethoven every day from 5 to 14 December, one day coming twice, but on the eighth day there was a dramatic deterioration. Wawruch wrote it up fully, and it merits quoting. Buried in his text is the suggestion of a furious row between Beethoven and Karl. Conversation book entries point to Beethoven accusing Karl of vacillating over his decision to join the military, and Karl arguing vociferously to the contrary. If these exchanges are what caused the crisis, it is evidence of the deterioration in Beethoven's condition, and his inability any longer to cope with emotional crisis.

On the eighth day I was considerably alarmed. I visited him in the morning and found him in great distress and jaundiced all over his body. A dreadful attack of vomiting and diarrhoea had threatened his life in the preceding night. A violent rage, a great grief caused by sustained ingratitude and undeserved humiliation, was the cause of this mighty explosion. Trembling and shivering, he was bent double because of the pains which raged in his liver and intestines, and his feet, which had been moderately bloated, were now massively swollen. From this time on dropsy developed, the passing of urine became more difficult, the liver showed plain indication of hard nodules, and there was an increase in jaundice. Gentle persuasion from his friends calmed the mental tempest, and the forgiving man forgot all the humiliation which had been put upon him. But the disease moved onward with gigantic strides. Already in the third week he threatened to suffocate in the night. The enormous accumulation of fluid in his abdomen demanded speedy relief, and I found myself compelled to advise tapping in order to guard against the danger of his stomach bursting.

Things were critical. Beethoven's abdomen had swollen so much that Wawruch actually feared it would explode, and the only possible solution was to puncture it and drain it manually, a risky and painful procedure.

In the meantime, as Wawruch suggests, Beethoven's spirits were being kept up by friends, in particular by a thirteen-year-old boy named Gerhard von Breuning, son of his old friend Stephan. Beethoven instantly took to the boy, nicknaming him 'Hosenknopf' ('Trouser Button').[6] Gerhard frequently brought Beethoven soup made by his mother, and visited the composer every day either before, or after, school.

Wawruch took a second opinion, consulting Dr. Staudenheim, who had failed to visit as promised earlier, but who now examined Beethoven and concurred with the decision to drain the abdomen.

Only then was Beethoven told. Wawruch reported that 'after a few moments of serious thought, he gave his consent'.

To perform the risky procedure Wawruch brought in Dr. Johann Seibert, chief surgeon at Vienna General Hospital.

On Wednesday, 20 December, with Wawruch, nephew Karl and brother Johann in attendance, the procedure was performed. Dr. Seibert pierced Beethoven's side with the tube, and immediately fluid gushed out. Relief was instantaneous, even bringing humour from the patient: 'Professor, you remind me of Moses striking the rock with his staff.'

There were clearly smiling faces all round at the obvious relief

Beethoven experienced. Wawruch quickly scribbled a series of questions and advice in a conversation book: 'Do you feel better? … Was it painful? … If you feel unwell you must tell me … [In English:] God save you … Lukewarm almond milk … Are you beginning to feel pain now? … Keep lying quietly on your side … We shall soon measure off the fluid … Five and a half measures were removed … I hope you will be able to sleep more peacefully tonight … You behaved like a brave knight.'

Shortly after the procedure the wound in Beethoven's side became infected, but it does not seem to have caused him much of a problem, and in any case his mood was considerably lightened by the arrival from a London admirer of a forty-volume edition of the works of Handel, whom he immediately declared to be 'the greatest, ablest composer that ever lived. I can still learn from him.'

With Beethoven bedridden, Karl went about his business of joining the army. He underwent a medical examination, and in the days following Christmas kitted himself out with uniforms, an overcoat and sabre.

On 2 January 1827, Karl bade farewell to his uncle, and embarked on the two-day journey to join his regiment in Iglau.[7] There is no record of what was said between them, no conversation book entry. He never saw his uncle again.

The following day Beethoven wrote to his lawyer declaring that Karl, 'my beloved nephew', should be the sole heir to all his property, including 'seven bank shares and whatever cash may be available'.

—

The relief from the draining of fluid was temporary. Beethoven's abdomen began to fill again. Wawruch believed a second procedure was necessary, but Seibert was reluctant, possibly because of the infected wound and an unwillingness to create a second puncture.

Beethoven, in a predictable pattern, was losing confidence in

Wawruch. According to young Gerhard, when Wawruch's name was mentioned, Beethoven turned his face to the wall and exclaimed, 'The man's an ass.' But all around him urged him not to give up on the physician. Schindler wrote in a conversation book, 'He understands his profession, everybody knows that, and he is right in considering your well-being paramount.'

Gerhard, meanwhile, was taking an early interest in the career he was to follow, writing in a conversation book, 'How are you? ... Has your belly become smaller? ... You are supposed to perspire more ... How was your enema?' It is likely the dying composer was more willing to discuss his condition with Trouser Button than with a doctor in whom he was losing faith.

On Monday, 8 January, Dr. Seibert repeated the procedure. There were no complications; the surgeon managed to draw off more fluid than before, and was pleased to find that it was clearer than the first time.

Three days later a meeting of doctors took place, with an interesting and somewhat unexpected addition to their number. As well as Wawruch, Staudenheim and Braunhofer, who had also now agreed to attend, there was present a name from Beethoven's past, Dr. Johann Malfatti, uncle of Beethoven's one-time *inamorata* Therese Malfatti, and summarily dismissed by him ten years previously.

Schindler claims credit for the reconciliation, even saying he had to use all his powers of persuasion on Dr. Malfatti, whose initial reaction was to say that as Beethoven was a master of harmony, 'so must I also live in harmony with my colleagues'.

But he was persuaded, and it seems the doctors were perfectly happy to involve him, all the more so since Beethoven too seemed pleased to see him and patch things up.

He was even more pleased with Dr. Malfatti's recommendation. In effect Malfatti made it clear to the other doctors that the one thing that would bring Beethoven relief was alcohol. He was dying, and there was nothing any of them could do to stop that. So why not at least allow him to alleviate the pain by drinking alcohol? Furthermore, since Beethoven was suffering attacks that caused his skin to burn and brought him out in running sweat, why not make the drinks ice cold?

He prescribed an end to the medicines Beethoven was taking—'75 bottles plus powder,' wrote Schindler later with, no doubt, more than a touch of exaggeration—no intake for Beethoven other than frozen alcoholic fruit punch, accompanied by rubbing of the abdomen with blocks of iced water. He assured his colleagues he had thus completely cured another patient with a similar illness.

The doctors, no doubt assisted by Beethoven's willingness, concurred. As with the first abdominal procedure, the effect was instantaneous. Even Wawruch was stunned. 'I must confess that the treatment produced excellent results for a few days at least,' he wrote.

Beethoven felt himself so refreshed by the ice with alcoholic contents, that already in the first night he slept quietly throughout the night and began to perspire freely. He grew cheerful and was full of witty comments, and even dreamed of being able to complete the oratorio 'Saul and David'[8] which he had begun.

But, again as with the abdominal draining, the relief was temporary, only this time it was largely Beethoven's fault. He liked drinking the punch so much that he drank more and more of it. In fact he repeatedly drank himself into a stupor. This did wonders for his mental state, successfully taking his mind off his dreadful illness, but had the opposite effect on his body.

Wawruch reported that the spirits soon caused a violent pressure of blood on the brain. Beethoven became comatose; his breathing was noisy and laboured as it would be if he was drunk; he began to slur his speech and talk nonsense, and occasionally, Wawruch noted, inflammatory pains in the throat were accompanied by hoarseness and even an inability to speak. His behaviour became more uncontrollable, and when the effect of the ice-cold drink caused havoc with his bowels, bringing on colic and diarrhoea, it was time 'to deprive him of this precious refreshment'.

Malfatti had another idea, and it was possibly the most bizarre of all the remedies inflicted on the dying composer. He was made to take a 'sweat bath'. Jugs filled with hot water were placed in a bath and covered thickly with birch leaves. Beethoven—removed from his bed with enormous difficulty—was made to sit on the heated bed of leaves, and his body covered with a sheet up to the neck. The aim, said Malfatti, was to soften the skin and allow perspiration to flow freely.

The effect was disastrous. Beethoven's body absorbed the moisture 'like a block of salt', wrote Gerhard later, causing swelling all round. It became clear a third procedure to drain fluid from the abdomen would be required, even though the wound in Beethoven's side had not healed from the last puncture.

Dr. Seibert carried out a third draining on 2 February, and the bath treatment was abandoned.

—

There was now a steady stream of visitors—friends and musical colleagues—anxious to see the great composer before it was too late. His old friend and drinking partner, Nikolaus Zmeskall, bedridden with gout, sent him greetings in a note. Beethoven himself, as if acknowledging time was short, dictated a number of letters.

Pleading financial hardship, as well as ill-health, he wrote to Sir George Smart in London asking the Philharmonic Society of London to make good their offer of payment for a future concert. They responded with a gift of £100, knowing full well the promised concert would never happen.

On a lighter note, he wrote to the publisher Schott of Mainz asking them to send him 'some very good old Rhine wine', which was unobtainable in Vienna.

Schuppanzigh and Linke, who had performed the Late Quartets, came to see him. Moritz Lichnowsky, brother of his great patron, came. Gleichenstein brought his wife, sister of Therese Malfatti, who was disappointed that Beethoven did not recognise her, and their son.

Diabelli, for whom Beethoven had written the great set of piano variations, brought him a print he had published of Haydn's birthplace in Rohrau. Beethoven showed it to Trouser Button Gerhard, and said, 'Look, I got this today. See what a little house it is, and in it such a great man was born.'

Baron Pasqualati, in whose building on the Mölkerbastei Beethoven had lodged longer than anywhere else, sent provisions, including champagne, wine—and stewed apples, pears and peaches, which the composer particularly liked.

Three men called to see him, and when they sent word in to ask which of them Beethoven would care to see first, the answer came straight back 'Let Schubert come first.'[9] Earlier, Beethoven had said of the Viennese composer, who was to die so young, just twenty months after Beethoven, 'That man has the divine spark'.

—

As soon as the third procedure was carried out on Beethoven's abdomen, the swelling began again. There was no hesitation this time. On 27 February Dr. Seibert inserted the tube into Beethoven's side for a fourth time. It seems that now everybody had given up hope, the medical team included.

Gerhard wrote that as the fluid flowed from Beethoven's body, it was allowed to run onto the floor and halfway across the room. In the conversation books there is mention of saturated bedclothes, and a suggestion by one of the doctors that an oilcloth be procured and spread on top of the mattress.

Beethoven, finally, accepted that the end was near, and went into a deep depression. Dr. Wawruch wrote later, 'No words of mine could brace him up, and when I promised him that he would certainly get better when the warm weather of spring arrived, he simply answered with a smile, "My day's work is finished. If there were a physician who could help me, 'his name shall be called Wonderful!'"' The allusion to Handel's *Messiah* was not lost on Wawruch.

On 23 March Johann Nepomuk Hummel, once Beethoven's rival in improvisation contests, arrived from Weimar with his wife and a musical colleague, Ferdinand Hiller. They found Beethoven, as Hiller wrote later, lying 'weak and miserable, sighing deeply at intervals. Not a word fell from his lips. Sweat stood upon his forehead.'

Hummel's wife took out her fine white linen handkerchief and wiped Beethoven's face several times. Hiller wrote, 'Never shall I forget the grateful glance with which his broken eye looked upon her.'

Beethoven had one final onerous task, to append a codicil and signature to his Will, leaving his entire estate to Karl, which for some reason had not been done earlier. It was a difficult and laborious task. He tried several times to write his name correctly, but each time misspelling his surname—once he left out an 'h', the next time an 'e'.

Finally, in despair, and declaring he would not repeat it again, he wrote, 'luwig van Beethoven'.

When it was over, he turned to the small group gathered, and said, '*Plaudite, amici, comedia finita est.*' ('Applaud, my friends, the comedy is over.')

Beethoven received the last rites. The following day, 24 March, the wine shipment from Schott arrived. He said, 'Pity, pity, too late.'

They were his final words.

While he could still swallow, a taste of the wine was put on his lips, but in the evening of the 24th he sank into a coma.

Gerhard von Breuning later wrote a graphic and deeply moving account of Beethoven's final forty-eight hours:

> *His delirium intensified with every sign of the death agony. This was at five in the afternoon, March 24th, 1827 ... On the next day and the day after that the powerful man lay there unconscious, breathing heavily with a clearly audible rattle in the throat. His powerful frame and undamaged lungs fought like giants against approaching death. It was a fearful sight. Although we knew that the poor man was suffering no more, it was appalling to see this noble being so irrevocably disappearing and beyond all further communication. On 25th March it was not expected that he would survive the night, but on the 26th we found him still alive—breathing, if that was possible, even more laboriously than before. March 26th, 1827, was the sad day of Beethoven's death.*

In the late afternoon of 26 March, a storm blew up over Vienna. Gerhard described it as very violent, with driving snow and hail—unusual for late March.

There was a small group by Beethoven's bedside, but there is confusion over who exactly was there. One of those present, composer and pianist Anselm Hüttenbrenner, said later that Beethoven's sister-in-law, Karl's mother Johanna, was present. This is extremely unlikely, since she herself complained later that she had received no news of Beethoven's final illness until it was all over. Most likely the sole female present was the housekeeper Sali.

Beethoven's brother Johann was certainly there, and it was probable that Stephan von Breuning and Schindler were also present, though they left some time in the afternoon to choose a burial site. The portrait painter Joseph Teltscher was making a drawing of

Beethoven, though he left the room when Stephan remonstrated with him. Gerhard, Trouser Button, left at a quarter past five to attend a lesson.

At around a quarter to six, there was an enormous clap of thunder, which startled everyone present. Beethoven opened his eyes, lifted his right hand, and looked up for several seconds with fist clenched, as if he wanted to say, 'Inimical powers, I defy you! Away with you! God is with me! Courage, soldiers! Forward! Trust in me! Victory is assured!' We owe this legendary, but exaggerated, account of Beethoven's last moments to Hüttenbrenner. If there is truth in it, the clenching of the fist was probably a muscle spasm brought on by the disease that almost certainly killed Beethoven, cirrhosis of the liver. But the legends had begun, within moments of his death.

What is fact is that at 6 p.m. on 26 March 1827—at the age of fifty-six years and three months, and exactly forty-nine years to the hour and the day since he had first walked out to perform in public—the greatest composer the world had known died.

CHAPTER TWENTY

THE LAST MASTER

'HE WAS AN ARTIST, BUT A MAN AS WELL'

THE DAY AFTER BEETHOVEN'S DEATH, WITH his body still on the deathbed, Stephan von Breuning, Johann van Beethoven, and Anton Schindler carried out a comprehensive search of the apartment to try to find the seven bank shares Beethoven had left in his Will to Karl. They could not be found. Johann was angry, and suggested either that they had never existed or that Stephan and Schindler had hidden them. Breuning was distressed at this insinuation, and left.

He returned later, and asked Karl Holz to come as well. He asked Holz if Beethoven had a secret hiding place where he kept valuable documents. Holz said yes, there was a secret drawer in the writing desk. He went to it, and pulled out a protruding nail. The secret drawer fell out. Inside it were the bank shares, the letter to the Immortal Beloved, and no doubt to everybody's surprise a miniature portrait of Josephine Brunsvik.[1]

Later that day a post-mortem was performed by the pathologist Dr. Johann Wagner. He made an incision across the front of Beethoven's forehead, lifted the top of his skull, and sawed out the temporal bones and auditory nerves. These were placed in a sealed jar of preserving fluid, which was held in the coroner's office for many years, before disappearing.

On examination of the auditory nerves, Dr. Wagner found them to be 'shrivelled and lacking nerve impulses, with the arteries dilated to the size of a crow quill and covered in cartilage'.

Dr. Wagner found Beethoven's liver to be 'shrunk up to half its proper volume, of a leathery consistence and greenish-blue colour, beset with knots the size of a bean on its tuberculated surface as well as in its substance. All its vessels were very much narrowed and bloodless.' In the cavity of the abdomen he found four quarts of an opaque greyish-brown liquid. The stomach and bowels were greatly distended with air, and both kidneys contained a thick brown fluid. The body in general was 'much emaciated'.

With all the danger inherent in attempting to make a diagnosis two centuries after the event, a modern reading of Dr. Wagner's meticulous and carefully worded post-mortem report suggests the cause of Beethoven's death was alcohol-induced cirrhosis of the liver.

The following day there was a steady stream of visitors to the death chamber, many of whom cut off a lock of Beethoven's hair as a keepsake. Gerhard von Breuning, lamenting that his father had not allowed him to do this for himself until the body was ready to be placed into the coffin, found that by then there was no hair left to cut off, though that is likely to be an exaggeration.

Beethoven had remained unshaven during his final illness, and his beard had grown thick. A barber was brought in to shave his face, telling those present that he would dispose of the razor as it was customary not to re-use a razor that had shaved a corpse.

The weather was warm and springlike on 29 March 1827, encouraging those who might have been in any doubt to come out and witness the elaborate ceremonial. There was plenty of opportunity to do so. The funeral procession would wind its way northwest out of the city to the small village of Währing, after stopping for a Funeral Mass at the Church of the Holy Trinity. Vienna had never seen a funeral of such extended pomp and grandeur, not even for a Holy Roman Emperor.

The church was a mere five hundred paces from the Schwarzspanierhaus, but it took the procession more than an hour and a half to cover the short distance. As the cortege processed, a brass band played the funeral march from Beethoven's Piano Sonata Op. 26. On the steps of the church there was such a crush that soldiers had to keep order. Official mourners, risking exclusion, had to point to the crepe bands on their hats to gain entry.

The interior of the church was bathed in candlelight, all three altars, wall brackets and chandeliers flickering. Ignaz Seyfried had arranged two of the Trombone Equali that Beethoven had written on that fraught visit to his brother Johann in Linz, for voices, and these were now sung, accompanied by trombones. This was followed by the Funeral Mass.

The cortege then resumed its slow processional progress northwest out of the city. The route was on a steady upward incline, causing the four horses to take the strain, and bringing laboured breathing to musicians, pallbearers and crowds. It passed along the Währing stream and into the small parish church.

There, once again, the Equali were played and sung. After another Funeral Mass the coffin left the church, carried this time on the shoulders of a bearer party, and followed by the chief mourners, augmented by schoolchildren and the poor from the local almshouse. Bells rang out.

There was a downward slope to the small cemetery, and at the entrance gates the bearers laid the coffin down.

This was an unscheduled change of plan. The leading playwright of the day, Franz Grillparzer, had written a funeral oration to be declaimed at Beethoven's graveside by the foremost tragedian of the day, Heinrich Anschütz, as the coffin was lowered.[2] However, strict religious law forbade the declamation of any text that was not sacred on consecrated ground. And so Anschütz read the oration over the coffin at the gates.

Grillparzer described Beethoven, amidst lengthy and florid language, as 'The Last Master, the tuneful heir of Bach and Handel, Mozart and Haydn's immortal fame…He was an artist, but a man as well ... Thus he was, thus he died, thus he will live to the end of time.'

The coffin was shouldered again, and carried to the open grave that abutted the outer wall of the small cemetery. The pallbearers stood around the grave with lighted torches. The coffin was lowered, and three garlands of laurel leaves were placed onto it. The priests consecrated the grave and gave Beethoven a final blessing. The pallbearers each threw a handful of earth onto the coffin, and then extinguished their torches.

—

Little of the dignity that characterised his funeral was accorded to the great composer in the months following his death. In early April, in the same room in which he died, his personal effects were auctioned. According to Gerhard von Breuning, who attended with his father, 'a miserable collection of old-clothes dealers had found their way in, and the articles that came under the hammer were tugged this way and that, the pieces of furniture pushed and thumped, everything disarranged and soiled'.

On 5 November, Beethoven's musical effects, including sketches in his own hand, autographs of printed works, original manuscripts and copied parts, were auctioned in rooms in the Kohlmarkt. The total intake was 1140 florins and 18 kreuzer. Beethoven's total estate, including cash, bank shares and personal effects, was valued at 9885 florins and 13 kreuzer (approximately £1000, or slightly under).

Just over a year and a half after Beethoven's death, Franz Schubert—one of those pallbearers who had accompanied the coffin and stood at the graveside with lighted torch—was buried alongside the man he admired so much.

In October 1863, the bodies of both Beethoven and Schubert were exhumed, their skeletons cleaned and reburied in lead coffins.

During this process, Beethoven's skull was given to Gerhard von Breuning—by now a qualified doctor—for safekeeping. He kept it on the table by his bed, 'proudly watching over that head from whose mouth, in years gone by, I had so often heard the living word!'

Before reburial a team of physicians compared Beethoven's skull with Schubert's, noting that Beethoven's was 'compact and thick', whereas Schubert's was 'fine and feminine'.

In June 1888, when the decision was made to close the cemetery at Währing, the bodies of Beethoven and Schubert were again exhumed and removed to the recently opened Zentralfriedhof, Vienna's main cemetery to the south of the city, where they lie today still side by side in the musicians' quarter.[3]

—

It is perhaps fitting that the wreaths placed on Beethoven's coffin were made of laurel leaves—since ancient time the symbol of achievement and success, of mystical powers and immortality. The legends surrounding this greatest of artists began with that raised fist on his deathbed, and continue to this day.

Most enduring is the image we have come to know of the leonine head, fixed and determined gaze, a huge sculpted figure in stone or bronze, determination in eyes and pose. In short, an image befitting the music.

In the years following his death, there was a campaign to have a monument to him erected in his hometown, Bonn. Largely due to the efforts—and financial contribution—of Franz Liszt, this was finally achieved in August 1845.

A massive bronze statue, designed by an almost unknown sculptor, Ernst Julius Hähnel, showed Beethoven, one leg in front of the other, both feet planted firmly on the ground, holding a pen in his lowered right hand and a notebook in his left, standing upright and staring ahead, brow knitted and features concentrating, abundantly thick hair framing his head.

The statue was placed at the top end of the Münsterplatz, where it stands today, a little way in front of the house of Count von Fürstenburg, where the boy Beethoven used to go to give piano lessons, when he was not having a 'raptus'.[4] A balcony was erected in front of the house for the guests of honour to witness the unveiling.

All Bonn turned out for the event. The small town on the Rhine had never seen anything like it. The guests of honour were no lesser figures than Queen Victoria and Prince Albert of Britain, King Friedrich Wilhelm and Queen Elizabeth of Prussia, and Archduke Friedrich of Austria.

The ceremony began with a speech from the Music Director at the university of Bonn, at the end of which, to the beating of drums, ringing of bells, firing of cannon, the statue was unveiled—and found to be facing down the square, its back to the guests of honour. Embarrassment all round.

Beethoven's music continues to resonate with each new generation. The opening motif of the Fifth Symphony was used as a single drumbeat in clandestine BBC broadcasts to the Free French under Nazi occupation. When the Berlin Wall fell in 1989, the first concert to be given in unified Berlin was the music of Beethoven. The European Union chose the theme of the final movement of the Ninth Symphony as its anthem.

Beethoven's music will, quite simply, endure for ever and all time. Hence the dedication of this book.

POSTSCRIPT

KARL VAN BEETHOVEN, ALTHOUGH HE MUST have been kept informed of his uncle's demise and would certainly have been allowed compassionate leave to attend the funeral, did not do so. He left the army in 1832 and married in the same year. He had four daughters and a son, whom he named Ludwig. That son had a son, who died childless. Karl died at the age of fifty-two of liver disease.

Johann van Beethoven lived prosperously on the proceeds of his pharmacy business for the rest of his life. He frequently attended concert performances of his brother's music, always sitting in the front row, according to Gerhard von Breuning, 'all got up in a blue frock-coat with white vest, loudly shrieking Bravos from his big mouth at the end of every piece, beating his bony white-gloved hands together importantly'. He was, wrote Gerhard with some malice, 'as preposterous after his brother's death as he had been contemptible during his brother's life'. Johann died at the age of seventy-one.

Johanna van Beethoven outlived her husband by more than fifty years, and her brother-in-law, with whom she had such a volatile relationship, by forty-one years. She died in some poverty at the age of eighty-two. I am not aware that she ever, either in writing or interview, uttered a hostile opinion or critical word about Beethoven.

Stephan von Breuning, Beethoven's lifelong and most loyal friend, already in poor health in 1826, never recovered it, and died barely two months after Beethoven at the age of fifty-two. His son, Dr. Gerhard von Breuning, attributed his father's early death to the trauma of caring for Beethoven in his final illness, and the distress of overseeing the disposal of his effects.

Ferdinand Ries, who made his home in London and did so much to further Beethoven's reputation in Britain, accumulated considerable wealth from composition and teaching, but lost much of it when the London bank in which he had invested failed. He moved with his family to Germany, but died after a short illness at the age of fifty-three.

Franz and Eleonore Wegeler returned to Bonn from Koblenz in 1837, and sat with Helene von Breuning reminiscing about the young Beethoven they had known, although 'Frau Breuning had to be largely left out of these discussions, her mind having become feeble with age'. She was eighty-seven at the time. Wegeler was eighty-three when he died; Eleonore died at seventy.

Antonie Brentano, candidate for the Immortal Beloved, had eleven grandchildren and thirteen great-grandchildren. At the age of forty-six she began to note down the names of her friends who had died. The first entry read: Beethoven, 26 March 1827. She died at the age of eighty-eight.

Archduke Rudolph, Beethoven's greatest patron and a composer in his own right, suffered a fatal stroke when he was only forty-three. In accordance with his wishes, his heart was removed from his body and placed in a niche in the walls of the Cathedral of St. Wenceslas in Olmütz. His body lies with other members of the Habsburg dynasty in the family crypt in Vienna.

—

This book, as I said in the Preface, is for lovers of Beethoven's music rather than academics, and so I have not crowded the narrative with source references. The musicologists know where the source material is.

For those who want to read further, the essential biography remains Thayer's *Life of Beethoven*, revised and edited by Elliott Forbes. It is a weighty tome, and there is a lot in it that the average reader might want to skip, but it is the biography which all subsequent biographers acknowledge, since it is the result of interviews carried out by Thayer with people who actually knew Beethoven.

Two contemporary books providing unique and first-hand insights are *Remembering Beethoven* by Franz Wegeler and Ferdinand Ries, and *From the House of the Black-Robed Spaniard* by Gerhard von Breuning.

The American musicologists Maynard Solomon and Lewis Lockwood have both written comprehensive biographies of Beethoven, though some of Solomon's theories—particularly with regard to identifying the Immortal Beloved—have been superseded, and Lockwood openly acknowledges that in his portrait the music looms larger than the life.

The Beethoven Compendium, A Guide to Beethoven's Life and Music, edited by the British musicologist Professor Barry Cooper of Manchester University, is an invaluable guide to all aspects of Beethoven's life, music, and the times in which he lived. Similarly, Professor Cooper's *Beethoven*, in the Master Musicians series, is a comprehensive and accessible account of the life, seamlessly integrating the music, though a knowledge of music and ability to read it is useful.

There are hundreds of books, if not thousands, but you would be hard-pressed to find one which does not contain musical examples, notes on staves. My belief that there are many lovers of Beethoven's music who cannot read a note of music, and have no desire to do so, was a spur to writing this book.

As with books, there are hundreds, if not thousands, of recordings of his works. I am regularly asked, in person or in letters or emails to Classic FM, to recommend recordings. It is, of course, impossible. It depends on how you like your Beethoven. Authentic or modern instruments? Chamber ensemble or full symphony orchestra? Rigid adherence or flexible approach?

I have dozens of recordings of a single work. I suspect most people will want just one. Pick from these:

SYMPHONIES: Toscanini for hard driving speeds, Furtwängler for more flexibility. Riccardo Chailly and the Leipzig Gewandhaus for the modern symphony orchestra in all its glory. Emmanuel Krivine and La Chambre Philharmonique for authentic chamber-sized ensemble. Nikolaus Harnoncourt and the Chamber Orchestra of Europe.

PIANO CONCERTOS: Howard Shelley and the Orchestra of Opera North, with bonus of Choral Fantasia and Triple Concerto. Pierre-Laurent Aimard with Nikolaus Harnoncourt and the Chamber Orchestra of Europe. Paul Lewis with Jirí Belohlávek and the BBC Symphony Orchestra.

STRING QUARTETS: The Lindsays, in the earlier of their two sets, recorded in the late 1970s, passion suffusing every note. The Endellion String Quartet more recently, using the edition prepared by the Beethoven scholar and editor Jonathan Del Mar. The Busch Quartet for something different—recorded in the 1930s, with a veil of hiss, the benefit of hindsight pouring the forthcoming tragedy of Europe into every note.

PIANO SONATAS: Daniel Barenboim for modern virtuosity on a concert grand. Paul Lewis for a young virtuoso's freshness. I still love the Hungarian pianist Jenö Jandó on Naxos, recorded in 1988 in Budapest in what sounds like a bare-walled studio with a single microphone. Beethoven can sometimes be over-sanitised. Not here. For authenticity, eccentricity, and that hiss again, Artur Schnabel. As this book goes to the printer, the French pianist Jean-Efflam Bavouzet has issued the first of a complete set, as has the young Korean pianist HJ Lim.

FIDELIO: Christa Ludwig and Jon Vickers, with the Philharmonia Chorus and Orchestra under Otto Klemperer. Never bettered. More recently, Claudio Abbado with the Lucerne Festival Orchestra, Nikolaus Harnoncourt with the Chamber Orchestra of Europe.

MY DESERT ISLAND DISC: Piano Sonata Op. 110, recorded by Jörg Demus on Beethoven's last piano, the Graf. Close your eyes and imagine ...

ACKNOWLEDGMENTS

I T WAS DARREN HENLEY, MANAGING DIRECTOR of Classic FM, who picked up the telephone in the summer of 2010 and gave me a new career in radio. And it was Darren who, when I told him I had embarked on a biography of Beethoven, said immediately he wanted it to be a Classic FM publication.

He introduced me to Lorne Forsyth, Chairman of Elliott & Thompson, Classic FM's publisher, and Olivia Bays, Publisher at Elliott & Thompson. Both were excited at the prospect of a new, full-length biography of the great artist, and encouraged me from our first meeting.

Olivia was a knowledgeable and sympathetic editor, infinitely patient with my corrections and amendments, and long suffering to a fault with the many changes of mind over the front cover. She is one of the few people I have ever worked with who responds as rapidly to emails as I do myself—exactly what a writer with more than forty years of journalism behind him is used to and needs.

I am grateful to Jennie Condell and James Collins at Elliott & Thompson for tracking down all the illustrations I asked for, and for making my own photographs look far more professional than they originally were.

The most important Beethoven research centre outside Europe is the American Beethoven Society at San José State University in California. I have been a member for many years. I have lauded the efficiency and dedication of the Society in previous publications on Beethoven. I once needed the words to an obscure musical jest by Beethoven. It was on my fax from San José within twenty four hours. My grateful thanks, once again, to Director William Meredith and Curator Patricia Stroh.

Thanks too to Boris Goyke at the Beethoven-Haus in Bonn, and Marian Hochel, Director of Chateau Duchcov-Dux in the Czech Republic, for their help in tracking down rare material.

Finally—and most importantly, for without her encouragement from the day I first said I was undertaking this enormous project, I might have fallen at the first of many hurdles—my eternal thanks to Nula.

NOTES

[1] The newssheet *Der Sammler* estimated the number at 10,000; Gerhard von Breuning in *Aus dem Schwarzspanierhaus* at 20,000.

CHAPTER ONE: THE SPANIARD

[1] Prince-Electors were senior members of the Holy Roman Empire who had a direct role in electing the Holy Roman Emperor, head of the Habsburg Empire, whose seat was in Vienna.

[2] In a bizarre turn of events almost a decade later, Johann and Maria Magdalena van Beethoven took out a suit against the Ehrenbreitstein court bailiff, who was related by marriage to Maria Magdalena and who was the guardian of her mother's estate, accusing him of stealing the old lady's savings. The suit was thrown out.

[3] Gottfried Fischer, *Aufzeichnungen über Beethovens Jugend (Notes on Beethoven's Youth)*.

[4] It is impossible to be precise. The chronology of Beethoven's early years, as with the date of his birth, is uncertain.

CHAPTER TWO: THE RIGHT TEACHER

[1] The Elector whose valet Maria Magdalena would marry some two years later.

[2] Together with the daughter who was born and died in 1779, and the eldest son, Ludwig Maria who died at a week, this means that in her first ten years of marriage to Johann, Maria Magdalena gave birth seven times—eight times in all, including the infant she bore her first husband.

[3] The harmonic embellishment of the bass line.

[4] The twenty-four keys in major and minor.

[5] Neefe's assessment of Mozart is remarkable too, given that the composer was still only twenty-seven years of age, and had not yet composed many of his finest works.

[6] A critical edition of the thirty-five Piano Sonatas published in 2007 by Britain's leading Beethoven scholar, professor Barry Cooper of Manchester University, was the first modern edition to include all thirty-five sonatas as a set.

369

[7] The piano part, and some orchestral passages, have survived.

CHAPTER THREE: MEETING MOZART

[1] Franz Wegeler and Ferdinand Ries, *Biographische Notizen über Ludwig van Beethoven*. As with Gottfried Fischer's memoirs, this account was written several decades after the event, but both Wegeler and his collaborator were educated to a much higher level than Fischer, and their accounts are regarded as largely reliable.

[2] Where today a huge bronze statue of Beethoven stands.

[3] Otto Jahn, *W. A. Mozart* (1856).

[4] He tried to persuade Mozart to come to Bonn as *Kapellmeister*. Mozart turned him down, saying he was too busy with his new opera, *Le nozze di Figaro*. How different the history of music might have been had he accepted!

[5] A prestigious—but by the nineteenth century largely ceremonial—body of German knights formed in the Middle Ages to protect and help German Christians making pilgrimages to the Holy Land.

[6] *Die Entführung aus dem Serail (The Abduction from the Seraglio)*, which occasioned the famous story that when the Emperor heard it, he said to Mozart, 'That is too fine for my ears—there are too many notes', to which Mozart replied, 'There are just as many notes as there should be.'

CHAPTER FOUR: WORD SPREADS

[1] The Middle Rhine was declared a UNESCO World Heritage Site in 2002.

[2] In another version of the legend, the chosen virgin stood naked and trembling in the mouth of the cave, suddenly holding the crucifix round her neck up to the dragon, which took fright, reared, and plunged into the swirling waters below—all without Siegfried's assistance.

[3] This description dates from around ten years earlier, but reflects the kind of vessel that plied the Rhine.

[4] The legend that treasure was cast into the Rhine was taken and used by Richard Wagner in his epic sequence of operas, *Der Ring des Nibelungen.*

[5] As recently as January 2011 a barge carrying 2400 tonnes of sulphuric acid capsized close to the Loreley, blocking the river. Two crew members lost their lives.

[6] Today there are markers in the river to indicate the treacherous shallows, and Rhine pleasure-boats helpfully play a tenor voice singing the song of the Loreley—words by Heinrich Heine, music by Friedrich Silcher—as the

boat passes the rock. A statue of Loreley, naked and with her legs enticingly entwined, stands on an island in the river just north of the rock, and a rather unprepossessing statue of her sits outside the tourist centre on the summit of the rock, mercifully not visible from the river below.

7 It was not until a century or so later that a navigable passage was blasted out of the rock.

8 One of the most picturesque towns on the Rhine, Rüdesheim is famous today (though postdating the Bonn musicians' trip by a century) for its production of Asbach Uralt brandy.

9 We do not know what rank he was promoted to. Waiter?

10 The palace was almost completely destroyed during the Second World War, but has been faithfully restored. Even today it is impressive, and is likely to have been much more so when Beethoven and his colleagues saw it.

11 A Mannheim pianist, regarded as the finest virtuoso of his generation.

12 Alexander Wheelock Thayer, *The Life of Ludwig van Beethoven.*

13 The orchestra apparently rehearsed one of the two cantatas Beethoven had composed following the death of the Emperor, and given that they considered both unplayable, it is pos-

sible there might have been a little tension in the air.

14 Bad Mergentheim, proud of its young visitor, today holds a regular Beethoven Festival, and conducts walking tours of locations and buildings dating back two centuries.

15 In later years he would be regarded in Vienna as a finer piano virtuoso than Mozart.

16 Thayer (see above), who recounts this, does not name his source(s).

CHAPTER FIVE: IMPRESSING THE VIENNESE

1 The concerto we know as 'No. 1' was in fact the second he composed, and the one we know as 'No. 2' the first, so named because they were published in that order.

2 Again, it is not certain which of the two he performed.

3 The source is thought to be Beethoven's friend Nikolaus Zmeskall, but it is second hand, unverifiable, and gives the date of 1796, which, given that Beethoven was in Berlin, seems impossible.

4 'Typhus' in German translates today as 'typhoid fever'. We cannot be sure what range of complaints the word covered two centuries ago, hence it is impossible to be precise about what illness Beethoven suffered.

1 Dragonetti was unusually tall, and had an extra tall double-bass specially made for him, with just three strings. It hangs on a wall today in the Victoria and Albert Museum in London.

2 The rapid alternation of notes to create tension and drive, honed to perfection a century or more later with the piano accompaniment to silent movies.

3 In his lifetime he would compose several ballets and operas, eight piano concertos, and nearly five hundred chamber works.

4 Countess Marie Wilhelmine von Thun, who on one occasion got on bended knee to beg Beethoven to play for her. He refused.

5 It was the wind players in Bonn who considered the two cantatas unplayable. What was it about nineteenth-century wind players?

6 There was some disappointment that the expected lead female dancer was replaced, after causing a stir the previous time she appeared with her 'lavish display of the Venus-like graces and charms of her exquisite form'. She wore a flesh-coloured costume, which gave the impression she was naked.

7 Diminutive of Stephan.

8 Eleonore von Breuning, shortly to become Wegeler's wife.

9 It does contain one memorable passage, beloved of biographers when describing Beethoven's character: 'I will seize Fate by the throat—I shall not allow it to bend or crush me completely.'

10 Gallenberg turned out to be impotent. For this reason he allowed Julia to take a lover, Count von Schulenburg, with whom she had one illegitimate son and four illegitimate daughters. For this information I am indebted to Lady Pia Chelwood, née von Roretz, who is the great-great-granddaughter of the illegitimate son of Julia and Schulenburg. Lady Chelwood, born into Austrian nobility whose family seat is at Breiteneich in Austria, is widow of the former Conservative MP Sir Tufton Beamish, later Lord Chelwood, and currently resides in East Sussex. She has in her home a marble bust of Julia sculpted from life.

1 It has been suggested that the opening four notes of the Piano Variations, Op. 35, are taken from the first bar of Steibelt's music, when turned upside-down!

2 Ries went on to become an admired musical administrator, and as composer he wrote dozens of pieces, including symphonies, piano concertos, oratorios, and chamber pieces, none of which has remained in the repertoire.

3 A statue of Beethoven today stands outside St. Michael's Church.

4 My translation.

CHAPTER EIGHT: EGYPTIAN HIEROGLYPHICS

1 It remains thus today, staging mainly musicals, although it is no longer suburban and the Wien now runs several metres below the street. The fruit and vegetable market that lined the river bank opposite the theatre two centuries ago is now a covered market, offering everything from fruit and vegetables to fast food and clothing.

2 Today the pavilion, bearing a plaque stating that Mozart, Beethoven, and Schubert all performed there, is a porcelain factory.

3 This improvisation by Bridgetower did not survive in the published version of the sonata.

4 He completed one scene, the last section of which he adapted later as the great love duet in Act II of *Fidelio*, 'O namenlose Freude'.

5 Beethoven frequently wrote his forename both in French, 'Louis', and Italian, 'Luigi'.

6 Waldstein became obsessed with defeating Napoleon, and raised an army to do so. It bankrupted him. It was reported he was in Vienna in 1805 in disguise to escape his creditors. It was possibly on hearing this that Beethoven dedicated the Piano Sonata in C, Op. 53, to him. There is no evidence the two men met.

CHAPTER NINE: O, BELOVED J

1 All thirteen letters, with one exception, are undated, but I am following the accepted dates attributed by modern scholarship.

2 The German word Josephine uses is *sinnlich*, which translates as either 'sensual' or 'sensuous'.

3 Like Lichnowsky, Lobkowitz was a great supporter of Beethoven; he received the dedication of the 'Eroica' after Beethoven decided against Napoleon.

4 There are conflicting reports as to whether the opera opened as *Leonore* or *Fidelio*. Certainly it was to become *Fidelio*, and it is generally accepted that at this stage it was called *Leonore*.

CHAPTER TEN: A DEEPLY IMMORAL WOMAN

1 Now Opava, near the border between the Czech Republic and Poland.

2 It was common practice, before publication, for a work to be sold to a patron for a limited period of time for exclusive use.

3 The autograph manuscript is today in the Bibliothèque Nationale de France, in Paris.

4 Beethoven made this claim in a letter to his publisher the following January. It is unlikely his suspicions were founded.

5 Described by Haydn, endearingly, as having 'a voice like a house'.

6 They evidently made it up later, since Milder went on to sing the role of Leonore in the revamped *Fidelio* some years later.

7 The account that follows was given by the composer Louis Spohr in his memoirs published fifty years later, and he attributes it to Seyfried. Given the passage of time, and the fact that it is second hand, it is not impossible that some elements are exaggerated.

8 There are several eyewitness accounts, which I have amalgamated to give a clear narrative.

CHAPTER ELEVEN: UNDER CANNON FIRE

1 An interesting comment on the unpredictability of Beethoven's likes and dislikes is that he welcomed this particular French officer, Baron de Trémont, whom he had never met before, into his apartment, despite his antagonism towards the French officers at Lichnowsky's Silesian estate.

2 Recordings of Rudolph's piano and chamber works are available on CD today, but are rarely performed.

3 A similar set of circumstances to Beethoven's royal patron in Bonn, Archduke Maximilian Franz.

4 Fatefully giving Arthur Wellesley, the future Duke of Wellington, the opportunity to gain a firm foothold in Portugal, which would ultimately lead to French defeat in Spain.

5 This he did, Rudolph returning to Vienna in late January of the following year, and the complete sonata is regarded as one of Beethoven's finest. When it was published in 1811 as Op. 81a, the publisher decided to give it a French name, 'Les Adieux', by which it is known today. Beethoven preferred to call it 'Das Lebewohl'.

6 Recent scholarship has suggested that this incident happened in the aftermath of the bombardment, when Napoleon ordered the demolition of part of the Bastei. If that is the case, the element of danger would have gone, but not the family antagonism.

7 It was to Gleichenstein that Beethoven had written in Freiburg asking him to find a 'beautiful girl'.

Gleichenstein, a young musician who helped Beethoven in much the same way as Ries, was to marry Therese's sister Netty, who outlived him by forty years.

8 One of only two references in all Beethoven's letters and papers to domestic pets.

9 Thus not repeating the mistake he had made with the Piano Sonata in C sharp minor, Op. 27 No. 2, 'Moonlight', dedicated to Giulietta Guicciardi, the third movement of which is beyond the reach of any but highly accomplished pianists.

10 In old age she boasted she had been Beethoven's pupil.

11 Josephine Brunsvik was known to her sisters as Pepi or Pipschen.

12 In the 1990s it was the most downloaded mobile-phone ringtone in the world.

CHAPTER TWELVE:
IMMORTAL BELOVED

1 Today Bad Teplice in the Czech Republic.

2 My translation.

3 Today Karlovy Vary, in the Czech Republic.

4 Maynard Solomon, *Beethoven* (Schirmer Books, New York, 1977; rev. edn, 1998).

5 Edward Walden, *Beethoven's Immortal Beloved: Solving the Mystery* (Scarecrow Press, 2011). In a forensic examination appropriate for a trained lawyer, Walden argues the case for Bettina Brentano, whose half-brother Franz was Antonie's husband. John Klapproth, *Beethoven's Only Beloved, Josephine!* (private publication, 2011). Klapproth, a German-born government official living in New Zealand, rehearses well-worn, albeit powerful, arguments in favour of Josephine Brunsvik.

CHAPTER THIRTEEN: AN UTTERLY
UNTAMED PERSONALITY

1 In the Schlosspark in Bad Teplice there is today a small monument by the side of the path, and a plaque set into the path, commemorating the incident.

2 Anton Bruckner was later to be organist at Linz Cathedral from 1856 to 1868.

3 Beethoven composed three short pieces for four trombones (*equale* signifying a piece for equal, or similar, instruments). Two of them, adapted for four male voices, were sung at the composer's funeral.

4 The composer Louis Spohr, playing in the violin section of the orchestra, has left a vivid description of Beethoven conducting at these concerts: 'When a *sforzando* occurred,

he tore his arms which were crossed across his chest with great vehemence asunder. At *piano* he crouched down lower and lower to indicate the degree of softness. When a *crescendo* entered he gradually rose again, and at the entrance of the *forte* he jumped into the air. Sometimes he shouted to strengthen the *forte* ... It was obvious that the poor man could no longer hear the *piano* passages of his own music.'

5 Arthur Wellesley was not, in fact, elevated to the dukedom until the following year.

6 Beethoven composed it, remarkably, for the Panharmonicon, a mechanical instrument that reproduced the sounds of the orchestra, invented by Johann Nepomuk Mälzel, known to musical history as the inventor of the metronome. So successful was it that, at Mälzel's suggestion, he orchestrated it.

7 Sample verse: 'And Wellington, the Spanish horde/Battled against with trust in the Lord/And at Vitoria struck them he/Till home with shame they had to flee.'

CHAPTER FOURTEEN:
INTO THE WITNESS BOX

1 With one major exception, of which more later.

2 Martin Cooper, **Beethoven: The Last Decade 1817–1827** (Oxford University Press, 1970).

CHAPTER FIFTEEN:
THE MUSICAL GIFT FROM LONDON

1 Some years after Beethoven's death the piano was presented to his great admirer Franz Liszt, who is reported never to have played it, judging himself unfit to touch the keys played by Beethoven. Later Liszt presented it to the Hungarian National Museum in Budapest, where it stands, fully restored, today.

2 This deathbed wish was granted, and further honoured when both bodies were exhumed and moved to the Musicians' Quarter in Vienna's Zentralfriedhof, where they lie just a few feet from each other today.

3 The music publisher Anton Diabelli, an accomplished amateur pianist, had composed a simple waltz, and asked fifty composers to compose a single variation on it. Beethoven at first refused, considering it demeaning, but eventually wrote thirty-three variations, creating his greatest set of piano variations.

4 The Philharmonic Society of London.

5 The three overtures were **Die Ruinen von Athen (The Ruins of Athens), Zur Namensfeier (Name Day), and König Stephan (King Stephen)**.

CHAPTER SIXTEEN:
'I WANT TO BE A SOLDIER'

[1] None of the Late Quartets (nor any of the final three piano sonatas) were given names, and their opus numbers are nonsequential, due to their publication dates. The order of composition was Op. 127, Op. 132, Op. 130, Op. 133 *(Grosse Fuge)*, Op. 131, Op. 135.

[2] *Aus dem Schwarzspanierhaus (From the House of the Black-Robed Spaniard)*

[3] A red-light district of Vienna.

CHAPTER SEVENTEEN: TWO PISTOLS
AND GUNPOWDER

[1] I once heard a performance of the *Grosse Fuge* by the Lindsay Quartet at the Wigmore Hall in London. At the end the leader, Peter Cropper, his shirt soaked with sweat, stood, and had to steady himself on the chair. His face was grey and he was close to collapse.

[2] Schindler made himself indispensable to Beethoven in the final period of the composer's life. After Beethoven's death, Schindler regarded himself as 'keeper of the flame'. He was Beethoven's earliest major biographer, but deliberately falsified facts to enhance Beethoven's image. He forged conversation-book entries to give the impression he had known Beethoven for much longer than he in reality had, and modern scholarship has established that around a hundred and fifty of his entries in the conversation books were made after Beethoven's death.

CHAPTER EIGHTEEN:
FRIGHTENING THE OXEN

[1] Johann's house still exists, is privately owned, and the small self-contained apartment in which Beethoven stayed is perfectly preserved. All the furniture is either genuine, or of the period. The murals of the Rhine are as vibrant today as they were when Beethoven saw them. The stove in the bedroom, the current owner told me when I visited, is the actual stove Beethoven filled with wood.

[2] It would be nice to date the *Rondo a capriccio*, Op. 129, 'The Rage over the Lost Penny', to around this time. Although it was found, incomplete, after Beethoven's death, the evidence suggests it dates from much earlier.

[3] Beethoven later described it to his doctor as a milk wagon (*Milchwagen*). It might well have been, or Beethoven might have been being deliberately pejorative.

CHAPTER NINETEEN: TERMINALLY ILL

[1] Despite protestations from around the world, the building was pulled down in early 1904, after a small

ceremony held on 15 November 1903 in the rooms once occupied by Beethoven.

2 The door has been preserved, and is today in the museum that occupies the apartment that Beethoven lived in longer than anywhere else, in the Pasqualatihaus on the Mölkerbastei.

3 Currently in the Beethoven Haus in Bonn, its keyboard protected by a Perspex cover. It was last used for a recording of the Piano Sonata in A flat, Op. 110, and the Bagatelles, Op. 126, by the Austrian pianist Jörg Demus in 1967—'the last time its voice was heard', as I was told when I visited.

4 Now in the Hungarian National Museum in Budapest

5 Several pages of the relevant conversation book are missing, presumably removed and destroyed by Schindler as too intrusive for public knowledge.

6 The same Gerhard von Breuning who left an invaluable record of Beethoven's final years in his book *Aus dem Schwarzspanierhaus*, and would in adult life become a distinguished physician.

7 Today Jihlava in the Czech Republic.

8 While we may trust Wawruch on medical matters, he is not so reliable when it comes to music. Beethoven never worked on such an oratorio— but Handel did, and given Beethoven had the forty-volume set of Handel's works, it is likely Wawruch confused the two.

9 There is no corroborating evidence that this meeting took place. If it did, it would be the only meeting—as far as we know—between the two great composers.

CHAPTER TWENTY: THE LAST MASTER

1 The Heiligenstadt Testament, which must have been secreted in the same drawer for many years, was found among Beethoven's papers.

2 Both Grillparzer and Anschütz had been known to Beethoven personally.

3 Währing is today a suburb of Vienna. The former cemetery is a small park, with tennis courts, named Schubertpark. The original graves with headstones of the two composers are still there.

4 The building is now the post office headquarters.

INDEX

3/05

‖‖‖‖‖‖‖‖‖‖‖‖‖‖‖‖‖‖‖‖‖‖‖‖
W9-BRP-724

MAGICAL

MYSTERY

TOURS

tony bramwell

with Rosemary Kingsland

MAGICAL MYSTERY TOURS

my life with the Beatles

thomas dunne books

st. martin's press

New York

THOMAS DUNNE BOOKS.
An imprint of St. Martin's Press.

MAGICAL MYSTERY TOURS. Copyright © 2005 by Tony Bramwell and
Rosemary Kingsland. All rights reserved. Printed in the United
States of America. No part of this book may be used or reproduced in
any manner whatsoever without written permission except in the
case of brief quotations embodied in critical articles or reviews. For
information, address St. Martin's Press, 175 Fifth Avenue, New York,
N.Y. 10010.

www.stmartins.com

Design by Kathryn Parise

LIBRARY OF CONGRESS CATALOGING-IN-PUBLICATION DATA

Bramwell, Tony.
    Magical mystery tours : my life with the Beatles / Tony Bramwell with Rosemary Kingsland.—1st ed.
        p.   cm.
    ISBN 0-312-33043-X
    EAN 978-0312-33043-9
    1. Beatles.   2. Rock musicians—England—Biography.   3. Bramwell, Tony—Friends and associates.
  I. Kingsland, Rosemary, 1941–   II. Title.
ML421.B4B73   2004
782.42166'092'3—dc22
[B]   2004056113

First Edition: April 2005

10 9 8 7 6 5 4 3 2 1

To my family and friends, with love

In memory of Roger Houghton.
Always courteous, kind and thoughtful,
he was one of the publishing world's true gentlemen.

MAGICAL

MYSTERY

TOURS

prologue

It was a snowy night on December 27, 1960, when I got ready to go to a concert at Litherland Town Hall. I was on Christmas holidays from school and looking forward to seeing a new group that had been advertised on fliers glued to lampposts and hoardings. They were billed as THE BEATLES! and it said they were DIRECT FROM HAMBURG! Everybody in Liverpool knew that Gerry and the Pacemakers had just gone to Hamburg—as had the Silver Beetles—a place that sounded incredibly exotic to a young lad like me. But the fliers gave us no reason to think anything other than that these Beatles were a German group, and we presumed they were.

The number 81 double-decker bus, which made a stop at Litherland Town Hall, started in our suburb of Speke and went round a whole ring in Liverpool to the far side. I got on it that cold night at my local bus stop in Hunts Cross and, as usual, ran upstairs to sit right at the front. To my surprise, there was my old friend George Harrison, with his guitar next to him. He must have gotten on at his stop. I knew George well. I just hadn't seen him for a few months, not since the days when he was a delivery boy on Saturday mornings for one of our local butchers, E. R. Hughes, who had a shop in Hunts Cross. They supplied George—the future vegetarian—with a big old bike, a rattling, black boneshaker that had originated before WW I. It had a large basket on the front, which George would fill with meat so he could deliver all the local orders, including my mum's. He'd stop at our house for a bit of gossip, or a cup of tea and a slice of cake, and we'd discuss all the latest records. After work, George would come by occasionally to borrow records from me, or from a guy round the corner named Maurice Daniels, a drummer in a skiffle group. I used to lend Maurice records and he would lend his to George and so on, all of us swapping and sharing and talking records. Seven inches of black plastic with a hole in the middle. Life, magic.

Then, one day, George Harrison sort of disappeared. Time went by. Now, here he was again, on the 81 double-decker bus, wearing blue jeans and a black leather jacket. I felt suitably impressed and somewhat gauche in my smart little suit and tie. When George saw me, he grinned that lopsided smile of his.

"Hi, Tone, how are you?"

"Where you going, George?" I asked, and sat down next to him.

"Litherland Town Hall," he told me. "We're playing there tonight."

That's when it slowly dawned on me. George Harrison was one of those DIRECT FROM HAMBURG BEATLES!

"*You're* the German group?" I asked, amazed.

George nodded. "Direct from Liverpool!" he said.

I jangled the five bob in my pocket and thought, *Hey, I can almost buy a new record with this.* I looked down at George's guitar.

"Can I carry your guitar for you, George? So I can get in free?"

"Of course you can," George said.

As the bus rumbled along, George and I chatted about this and that. But looking back on it now, it was a strangely moving moment, riding on the top deck of a double-decker bus, with a Beatle on his way to the first-ever Beatles gig in Liverpool. We could never have guessed in our wildest dreams, as we handed over our thruppences to the conductor, what was in store for George Harrison in terms of fame, wealth and adulation. But on that chilly night in Liverpool, that ocean of success still lay ahead in the distant future. If we had had a crystal ball instead of George's guitar in a battered black case up there in the front of the bus, we might have seen huge stadiums filled with screaming fans across America, the snow-capped peaks of the Himalayas, movie stars and yachts, and bowing to the queen at Buckingham Palace. The list is almost endless.

But we saw none of that, George and I. We were just a couple of teenagers with our whole lives ahead of us, chatting about girls and records as we rode the bus around Liverpool two days after Christmas. The whole town was glowing with magic and celebration. As we looked at the lights and the sparkling trees in people's windows, we had no notion that soon every day would seem like Christmas. That within two or three years our bomb-ravaged Liverpool would become famous around the world.

The number 81 was as familiar to us as fish and chips. George's dad, Harry, was a driver on the 81 route. I don't know if he was our driver that night, but we would often see him sitting up front in his worn serge uniform with the cap. He always had a smile and a wave for us, and often we didn't have to pay. The idea that one day we would move away, and that vast estates in the country, ranches in America, apartments in New York and French chateaux would be home to my old mates would have seemed crazy. The idea that the River Mersey—just another muddy old river—would soon lend its name to Merseybeat, a bona fide genre in the history of music, would have made us laugh. We had no concept that Strawberry Fields, a wildflower wilderness where we hung out and played as kids, would be forever enshrined in millions of hearts. How could we have guessed that the name would be borrowed as a place of remembrance and pilgrimage in New York, to use John's word—*forever?*

We had no clue that quiet night, riding the familiar old bus route, George and I, that we were about to go from the simple to the symphonic, with hometown places like Penny Lane and its rich, evocative characters living in, and living on, in the hearts of generations as if Shakespeare had set a play there. The idea that the humble, everyday goings-on in a scruffy Liverpool street could be set in sound and song was as far away as getting to heaven, which, according to Eddie Cochran, just took three steps. But then he wasn't talking about barbers and firemen and bankers. He was talking about girls, and girls and music were all we ever talked of.

At the town hall, I carried George's guitar and walked with him through the stage door, then I wandered off to hang out in the hall to wait with the audience for the Beatles to appear. The hall was a smallish room, with a small stage and a few seats along the walls. A large glitter ball spun slowly in the middle of the ceiling, throwing dazzling patterns of light on dancers, walls and floor.

Legend has it the place was packed; it wasn't, but the fans who had braved the freezing snow to get there made up for it in noise. The Beatles ran on stage, wearing jeans and leather jackets and pointy-toed cowboy boots, hair a bit looser than the old DA, but still flicked back and greased. There was John Lennon—our local juvenile delinquent—and my old cycling pal, Paul McCartney. Chas Newby, John's friend from art school, was on bass that night because Stuart Sutcliffe, their original bass player, had decided to stay behind in Hamburg with his German girlfriend. Seated at the back on drums was Pete Best, the mean and moody one who made all the girls swoon. We all had his mum, Mo Best, to thank for opening the Casbah, one of the best clubs ever, in the basement of her rambling old house.

Despite their new name, to me, John and Paul were still the Quarrymen, the skiffle group who played the village halls doing their "Rock Island Line," Lonnie Donegan stuff, their "Cumberland Gap," "Don't You Rock Me Daddy-O" stuff. They'd gone a bit rock 'n' roll with the Silver Beetles before they'd gone off to the trenches and we'd lost touch. Now, suddenly, they were a proper beat group with George and Pete Best, who I'd last seen around with the Blackjacks.

The Beatles were pretty good that night, tight and full of energy. Hamburg had made them grow up. They were told to *mach shau* in the clubs they played there and were almost literally thrown to the lions, being ordered to play for eight hours nonstop before a baying crowd that seemed to consist largely of drunken sailors who wanted to fight. If they stopped making a show of it bottles flew at the stage and there was a punch-up equivalent to any in a Western movie.

On stage that long-ago night in 1960 the audience seemed to sense that the Beatles were different from the other Liverpool bands. They seemed more aware, they had an edge, you felt they were dangerous. Part of the mystique was that they were different. You could jive when they played R&B, or Elvis hits—even though they changed the rhythm, which was confusing—but it was almost impossible to dance when they played their own songs. It was totally the wrong rhythm, so we'd just cluster around the stage and watch.

Despite the so-so attendance that December night, it was a great show. But no one screamed. (Girls didn't start screaming en masse until the spring of 1963 when the Beatles exploded out of Liverpool with an energy that had never been known before.) In those early days the girls just sat by the stage and drooled. Where the lads in the audience were concerned, there was too much unrequited testosterone flying around. To compensate, after a gig they got into fights. It was pell-mell bedlam—one of the reasons why, traditionally, pop bands were banned from posh venues—while the girls would go off arm in arm in giggling groups to their homes.

I waited while Brian Kelly, the promoter who had organized the gig, paid the Beatles. He counted it into their hands, and then they went into a huddle while they split it between them—twenty-four shillings each. Brian said they'd gone down so well, he'd like to book them again. By the time we got outside, the crowds had thinned and the bus stop was almost empty. The Beatles were on a high, laughing and talking excitedly about how now that they were back and with bookings to look forward to, things were looking up.

We grew cold waiting at the bus stop and we stamped our feet and turned up the collars of our jackets. None of us had gloves, and I remember how cold my hands were, carrying George's guitar. We were glad to jump into the warm, smoky fug of the last bus home. Talking and laughing, we stumbled upstairs to the front where the panorama of the snowy streets and Christmas lights spread wide. The Beatles were still up, adrenaline still pumping, as they discussed the wild time they'd had in Germany. To them, I was a new audience, albeit of just one.

I asked, "What's it like being back?"

"Fucking fabulous!" John replied.

Paul said, "It's great to have a hot bath at home, instead of washing in a cracked old sink in the Top Ten Club toilets."

I think they were glad to be back so they could have a rest, eat familiar food, take regular baths and get their laundry done. They acted like hardened rock 'n' rollers, but at heart they were middle-class boys who liked home, friends and family.

The bus trundled past Heyman's Green, where the Casbah Club was—Pete Best's stop—into Childwall and posh Queen's Drive, home to Brian Epstein from the record shop where we all bought our records. John and Paul got off, leaving just George and me.

Sometimes I wonder if I could ever have imagined, from those days of catching buses to gigs, that ordinary places in the center of Liverpool would become iconic images known the world over. That John and Paul would turn our childhood haunts into songs that one day I would help to capture on film. The idea that one day I would work for them, tour with them and promote their records didn't seem real. The idea that I would go from handing them their modest pay packets on a Friday night, to reading on one of Paul's bank statements two years later the dizzy figure of one million pounds—six zeros—seemed utterly preposterous.

I smile. I really do. I catch myself doing it. Remembering how, just after we decamped to London, by February 1967 when I was still twenty, I was directing the symphonic "A Day in the Life" on 35 mm film, the kind used for Hollywood movies. Mick Jagger, Keith Richards and Donovan took turns with handheld cameras. That night at Abbey Road, a producer named George Martin would instruct the orchestra thus: "Start quiet, end loud."

On a quiet December night six years earlier I had only carried George's guitar into Litherland Town Hall so that I could get in free to a Beatles gig, well before their lives got loud.

When I started to work on this book, just like those haunting words that open Daphne du Maurier's novel—"Last night I dreamt I went to Manderlay again"—I dreamed I was in Liverpool again. In sleep, I went back in time to that faraway night on the 81 bus riding home with the Beatles through the empty streets. We were all having a wonderful time, but when I looked at the reflection in the bus window, John and George weren't there. But somehow they felt close, as they and all the Beatles always do with me, and outside the window, snowflakes whirled and all the fairy lights on all the Christmas trees along the route blended into one.

PART I

Liverpool

1940–1963

1

Liverpool, the grimy northern town that John, Paul, George, Ringo and I were born and grew up in, was a dynamic port full of sea shanties, sailors and music. The ancient town had long been a melting pot of musical influences and traditions. Jazz, soul, blues, Irish music, sea shanties, folk and pop all blended from a dozen directions to create a unique sound. African music was introduced when the port became a center for the slave trade in the early eighteenth century. Scandinavian sailors, selling whale oil and salt cod, brought in a tradition of music that went back far beyond the Vikings and influenced all Celtic music. In fact, the slang word for a Liverpool citizen was "Scouse," the name of the cheap and popular Norwegian sailors' stew, made of vegetables and ships' biscuits with whatever scraps of meat or fish were available. Scouse was what poor people crowded into dockside slums ate as their main meal, and Scousers were what they became. (All the Beatles considered themselves Scousers, rather than the more grandiose Liverpudlians.)

Most importantly for the tradition of music along Merseyside, Liverpool was the gateway to England from Ireland. This was the route by which many Irish immigrants came when escaping poverty or famine, the largest influx being in the 1840s during the Great Famine when over a million shipped across to Liverpool alone, swelling a population that previously had been a mere ten thousand or so. By the turn of the century, Liverpool had the largest Irish population of any English town. Irish music, with the sound of the fiddle, Uilleann pipes, tin whistle, a handheld drum called a bodran and Celtic harmonies, could be heard in almost every home and bar, particularly among the dockside slums.

The transatlantic shipping trade took Liverpool music to the eastern seaboard of the United States and, significantly, brought it back, changed, enlivened and made more commercial with the emergence of pop records. In fact, like sailors, the music shipped in and out on almost every tide. By World War II, when American soldiers and airmen were stationed at huge bases in Merseyside, the exchange of music was well established. In the wartime years, GIs brought all the top hits of the 1940s, with stars like Frank Sinatra, Bing Crosby, Judy Garland, Doris Day and Ella Fitzgerald—but also Tommy Dorsey, Glenn Miller, Western Swing music from Texas and folk heroes like Woody Guthrie. After the war, merchant seamen and ships' stewards, like John Lennon's recalcitrant father, Fred, continued to bring in the latest American records.

The boys who became the Beatles were born during the Second World War when bombs were raining down. I was born at the end. But for all of us it was a period of great change, deprivation and excitement. Our lives were influenced by the widespread ruin and by the lean times and hard rationing that followed.

Liverpool was a target for enemy planes because it was the main receiving port for vital war supplies from America. Night after night, while people ran for the Anderson shelters, the drone of the Junkers 88s and Dornier bombers would get louder, searchlights speared into the black sky and antiaircraft guns started firing. At times, all the sky would be brightly illuminated with radiant but deadly chandelier flares that slowly drifted down on their parachutes. With the docks, shipping, factories and railways lit up by flares, the German bombs would begin to fall. The worst period of all was during the so-called Liverpool Blitz, which started on May Day—May 1, 1941—and lasted for seven consecutive days and nights. It was the heaviest bombing of the war in Britain outside London. Bombs hit a munitions ship on the night of May 4, causing the greatest explosion ever heard in Liverpool. Three thousand people were killed and eleven thousand homes completely destroyed that week alone. The Mersey estuary was so clogged from shore to shore with smoking, ruined ships that nothing could leave or enter. Seventy percent of the housing was destroyed. The relentless bombing, the grinding poverty and the overcrowding forged a ruined city of such squalor and citizens of such courage that after the war, there was only one way to go and that was up: to rebuild, expand and start over.

This abrasive and energetic northern port was where I was born and brought up because my mother, a wealthy beauty who resembled Merle Oberon, had eloped with a seaside snapper, one of those smooth professional photographers who haunt sea fronts and parades with a suave line in chat and oodles of charm. She had slender shapely legs and an hourglass figure and he chased her, pursued her to distraction, courted and caught her. Her parents had fifty thousand kinds of fits, but it was too late: they were married without the family's blessing or permission. Mother was a Ferguson-Warner, one of a dynasty of cotton traders whose family seat was a grand mansion at High Lane overlooking the Peak District outside Manchester. Her slide down the social scale after she ran off with my father was rapid. "You've married beneath yourself," some in her family declared, looking down their noses.

When war broke out my father got a job in Liverpool, in one of the new factories surrounding Speke Airfield, assembling those Lancaster bombers. My mother followed him. By then she had been forgiven by her family, who provided her with enough money to buy a house in Hillfoot Avenue, Hunts Cross. She hadn't been there long before my father was called up into the army and disappeared to the war. Neatly summing up their doomed relationship, Mum told me later that every time he came home on leave she got pregnant. Shortly after my birth in 1946 my charming but feckless father didn't bother to come home anymore and they were divorced. I didn't miss what I had never known and was happy enough.

When I was growing up, Hunts Cross was still pretty rural, surrounded by golf courses and plenty of other open places for a boy to run wild in. Young Paul McCartney lived close by in Speke, in a small house in the vast social housing projects—known in England as "council estates"—on Western Avenue provided by the local public services because his mother, a midwife and a district nurse, needed to live within the community she served. When Paul was nine, they moved to Ardwick Road, to another house on the same council estate. Mary McCartney was a pleasant and popular figure locally. Having a nurse live nearby was a plus and many mothers made it a point to become friends with her. We went to different primary schools (Paul to Stockton Wood and I to Kingsthorne). We were four years apart in age, but as far as we were concerned, the age difference didn't seem to matter. Paul was always just "around," part of our ever-expanding gang of small boys running around with short trousers and muddy knees in and out of various degrees of fun and mischief. It didn't seem to matter that we lived in posh Hunts Cross and Paul lived in poor Speke, where all those factories were. He was a nice polite boy and my mother liked him.

When I was about five, the eight-year-old George Harrison also moved to Speke from central Liverpool, where he and his family had been crowded into a two-up two-down terraced dwelling with an outside toilet. (Until he moved near us George and John Lennon had gone to the same primary school in Penny Lane, but, with the three-year difference in their ages, John was in a senior class and George in a junior one and they scarcely noticed each other. However, George's mum and John's Aunt Mimi were acquainted.) One day someone in our gang turned up at our house with George. He was very shy. He sat at the table and said nothing, just nodded when Mum asked if he was hungry. Mum never minded our friends coming round without notice. There was always plenty of plain food—bread and butter and jam sandwiches (known as jam butties) and some kind of knock-up cake. Or Mum would bring us spam sandwiches out in the garden. Afterward, we ran around and just played.

George's house was in a cul de sac called Upton Green, in the next street from Paul. It wasn't long before they met each other and realized that they were part of "our gang."

My best friend, a boy the same age as I, was the son of my mother's closest friend, Sonny, a woman she had known since childhood. Sonny married a musician named Hal Christie, but being a polite boy, I always called them Mr. and Mrs. Christie. They performed in cabaret at places like the Savoy Hotel in London. The boy's name, my best friend, was Jim Christie. Years later, he would live with John Lennon's former wife, Cynthia.

Jim, George, Paul, Tony, Chris, Barry. It didn't matter who it was, or even what the age difference was, we were always in and out of each other's homes, sometimes being offered jam butties and lemonade, sometimes a big plate of fried chips. Ketchup was never an option. We always had salt and vinegar. We all used to go cycling down Dungeon Lane to the Cast Iron Shore along the muddy banks of the Mersey, where gang fights were often going on. We'd watch and egg the big boys on, without getting involved ourselves. If things got too bloody, we'd jump on our bikes and spin off to Woolton Woods where there was a fantastic arboretum of rare trees, or to Camphill, part of an old Roman settlement, or to Strawberry Fields behind John Lennon's house. Or we'd go to Halewood, one of the little linked villages spread out along the banks of the Mersey, still surrounded by hay meadows.

There was so much to do. Our gang would build haystacks into castles and camps to defend, all the wonderful things young kids do. We'd go to Bluebell Woods and do bike scrambling, or explore the grounds of ancient Speke Hall, a fantasy black-and-white Tudor building straight out of the history books. We built camps within the dense rhododendron shrubberies and thick yew hedges of the hall and played war games or cowboys and Indians. We filled up our days, late into dusk until we were dragged home to supper and bed. There was none of this watching TV endlessly, or playing computer games, or moaning we were bored. We were too busy and far too active.

But one bit of mischief we got into went too far and almost killed the lot of us, including George Harrison. It started when we found some unexploded shells in a field near the airport. Someone said they came from ack-ack guns, left behind by troops guarding the airfield. These shells were a glorious find. We gathered them up and decided that we were the Resistance, fighting the Nazis. One of the forbidden places where we played was among the wartime pillboxes still guarding the main railway line that linked Liverpool with London. We got onto the tracks and followed a deserted branch line until we came to a tunnel. It was the very spot for a bit of sabotage.

Our worst crime to date had been placing pennies on the lines to watch train wheels flatten them. Once, we'd been caught and dragged home by the police to the wrath of our parents. But having an armful of live shells was far worse. Hell, this was *dangerous!* I looked at George. Our eyes met—his were wide and dark—with fear? Would one of us be the first to break and run? Of course not. We dug a huge hole and, brave little buggers that we were, we made a big bomb, packing in the explosives—any one of which could have blown us to kingdom come. We lit the fuse and ran for it. With a dull roar, the stonework crumbled and a huge hole appeared in the bridge.

Awestruck, we stared. Bloody hell, we'd done it! Suddenly the enormity of our crime sunk in and we fled. For days afterward, we waited for the heavy hand of the law to descend. How long could you be sent to prison for such a heinous crime? We were scared witless.

Apart from that one lapse, we were good kids, not malicious or into wrecking things. There should be many more dramatic incidents to remember, but fortunately, given the war zone we grew up in, there weren't—though there were stories of boys being blown up along the shore, where unexploded bombs and land mines were fenced off by miles of barbed wire, marked by notices with skull and crossbones in red. Paul had played down there and been beaten up by some bigger kids who had stolen his watch. One boy lived in the house behind him, so he was easy to find. He was hauled off and taken to court. Paul told us that the offender was sent to Borstal, the place where bad boys went. Would that happen to us? We trembled. Nothing happened and eventually we forgot about it.

From the earliest age, we were mad about music. On Saturday evenings, we would slick down our hair with Brylcreem or water and pedal off past Dungeon Lane to Halewood, where a youth club was held in the village hall. We'd play Ping-Pong or listen to our own records on the portable Dansette, while the vicar did his best to jolly us along.

When Paul was thirteen his family moved to Allerton, a district that was slightly closer to Liverpool. It was still within half a mile of Hunts Cross, on the other side of Allerton Golf Course, a distance that could be covered in five minutes on a bicycle, so we didn't lose touch. John Lennon lived on the third side of the golf course in a respectable middle-class house on Menlove Avenue with his Aunt Mimi and Uncle George. He and Paul had many mutual friends, who along the chain, were mutual friends with George and me.

Unknown to John, his runaway mother, Julia, also lived facing the golf course within a stone's throw of Paul, in a new council house in Blomfield Road with her lover and their daughters, John's younger half sisters. Paul's mother knew Julia and her daughters well and would often stop for a chat. The bus was another link. The number 72 was the one that went to downtown via Strawberry Fields and Penny Lane to the smart shopping area around Princes Street, before turning around at the Pierhead Terminal. George's mum, my mum, Julia and Paul's mum, in that order, would often get on along the route. They all knew each other by sight and would sit down in adjoining seats to gossip.

It was all a pattern of events and place-names which didn't seem at all important then, but years later gained a great deal of significance in songs and among millions of fans worldwide when the various homes the Beatles had lived in became shrines.

When they were older, my brothers and George got part-time jobs, which was wonderful because it meant they could buy more records. I was heavily into records, spending all my pocket money on buying whatever I could lay my hands on, from Buddy Holly, the Everlys, Carl Perkins, to Elvis. The record lending circle continued. I'd lend them to George and George would pass them on to Paul, who had just started at the Institute, the famous Liverpool grammar school. In turn, Paul lent records to George, and when George, our butcher's delivery boy, came in with our order he'd leave his battered bike leaning up against the hedge, often with the basket full of deliveries still to be made. Mum would offer him a drink or a sandwich. Then there'd be a new record to listen to, or a band to discuss and he'd forget the time. Mum would say, "What about that meat, son? It'll go off—it's in the sun!" and he would grin and off he'd pedal to finish his deliveries.

I had quite an advantage over the other boys where music was concerned. My mother had a friend who worked at the Adelphi Hotel, the place where anyone who was famous stayed when they came to Liverpool. Through this friend I was given complimentary tickets to as many shows as I cared to see at the Empire. I was taken backstage and met my hero, Roy Rogers, when I was eight. He did some special lariat tricks just for a small boy, and sang "Happy Trails"—but the icing on the cake was seeing Trigger being taken up the wide sweeping stairs of the hotel and being put to bed in a grand suite. It was a stunt of course: he was actually bedded down in one of the garages, which they turned into a stable for him.

Joe Brown, Marty Wilde, Gene Vincent, Eddie Cochran, Billy Fury, Georgie Fame, Tommy Steele: I saw them all. The best show was Duane Eddy and the Rebel Rousers with Emile Ford and the Checkmates and special guest, Bobby Darin in a tuxedo. I'd never seen anyone in a real tuxedo singing rock 'n' roll. When he came out and conducted the orchestra I thought it was pure show biz. I went every single night for a week. I was hooked; music became my first love.

As we grew older, like seeds blown in the wind, our little gang was dispersed to different schools, not necessarily to those closest to our homes, but with so many new estates, schools filled up really fast and you had to go where you could. Instead of splitting us up, this dandelion scattering widened our social circle. John Lennon wasn't in our cycling gang, although he had a bike, but he was the same age as my brother, Barry, so he came into our lives. Suddenly, he was just there and it seemed he'd always been a part of our consciousness. He and Paul knew each other years before they "officially" met.

Paul and George were bright kids and went on to the Institute, one of the best grammar schools in England. A boy named Neil Aspinall was also in Paul's class. George, who was nine months younger, was in the class below them. John went to Quarry Bank High School while I went to Hillfoot Hey Grammar School for Boys in Hunts Cross. It made no difference which schools we attended, because this invisible network kept us in touch. As we grew into our teenage years, the news on the grapevine would be about places to go to meet girls and listen to music. We'd hear that there'd be a gig, or a barn dance or a party, and we'd be there, catching up on more news and gossip.

2

Because they came from Liverpool, most people think of John and Paul as "English." In fact, their roots were Irish and they thought of themselves as Irish. Music was in their blood. John's great-grandfather was a famous singer in Ireland. His grandfather, John "Jack" Lennon, was born in Dublin in 1858 and he was a traveling minstrel. His grandmother was a Maguire. However, his mother's side of the family, though Celtic, was Welsh. Their name was Stanley and there was a Victorian street named after them, Stanley Street, in Liverpool city center.

Paul was Irish on both sides, his father from the Scotch-Irish McCartney clan and his mother being a Mohin or Mohan of County Monaghan in northwest Ireland. They embraced all forms of music, and went round to the pub on most evenings to listen to a live band, or to join in with a singsong—that usually continued back in their homes when the pubs closed. Paul's dad, James "Jim" McCartney, played trumpet in a jazz band. They had a piano in the living room and all the children were encouraged to learn an instrument.

But tragedy hit the McCartney family when Paul's mother, Mary, a lovely woman, died of breast cancer in October 1956. Paul was only fourteen. He always felt terribly guilty because he and his brother, Michael, had been away, staying with an uncle and aunt across the Mersey when she had died. When he returned, she wasn't there anymore. It was as if they hadn't said good-bye. He came from a large, close-knit family, with lots of relatives, music and spirit, but his mother's death left a huge gap.

"I miss her, the house feels empty," Paul said. He didn't say much more than that, but at times he looked lost and quite vulnerable. It was round about then that you would often see him bicycling off to the woods and fields, or along the shore, with binoculars, to watch birds for hours on his own. My father had kept on walking after the war, but being too young to remember him, I was used to just Mum looking after us and couldn't imagine how I'd feel if anything happened to her. Like Paul, I'd probably want to be on my own as well.

Music helped Paul compensate for his loss and he threw himself into it. In Liverpool, skiffle was more trad, like the Jim Mac Jazz Band, Paul's dad's old band. He wouldn't give Paul piano lessons himself (he'd say you have to learn properly) but Paul watched and picked it up by ear. He did have a few formal lessons, which bored him with the repetitious chords and homework. The first songs he played were "Red Red Robin" and "Carolina Moon." His dad bought him a trumpet for his fourteenth birthday, so Paul's early influence was trad jazz. Then when Cliff Richard came along with the Shadows it was all electric guitars and a wonderful, spine-tingling twangy sound.

Paul wanted to sing too, and you couldn't do that with a trumpet stuck in your mouth. He asked his dad if he could swap his trumpet for a guitar and came home with an acoustic Zenith, worth about fifteen pounds. He had found his forte—but the problem was, he couldn't figure out how to play it. At the time, he didn't realize it was because he was left-handed. He said that when he saw a picture of Slim Whitman, who was also left-handed, that he realized what the problem was. Copying the picture, Paul restrung his guitar "upside down." He couldn't reverse the top fret, known as the nut, so he glued on a matchstick to make a new notch for the thickest strings. Even then, he was clumsy and still couldn't play a chord. Things looked up a few mornings later on the number 72 bus to school, when he discovered that George could play guitar. Well, he could knock out a few chords and soon he could "pick" a bit too.

George's dad had been in the merchant navy during the war and played the guitar. He brought back some unusual records from the U.S., like Hoagy Carmichael and Jimmy Rodgers, which they'd listen to on the wooden record player he also fetched home from New York. It had removable needles. I can remember seeing it in their house, long after we all had Dansettes.

George always said his very first memory was listening to "One Meatball" by

Josh White. His parents were always having singsongs downstairs with neighbors and friends after the pub on the corner closed. From his bedroom, he'd hear them sing and play. There'd be Bing Crosby and early Music Hall songs on the wireless. His next influences were Big Bill Broonzy and Slim Whitman, so he was always immersed in some fairly esoteric types of music. When he was twelve or thirteen and attending the Institute, he heard that an old friend from Dovedale Primary wanted to sell his Egmond guitar for three pounds ten shillings. This was a lot of money for a cheap old Spanish, but George's mum gave him the cash and he went around and got it.

To us, this was sensational. George had his own guitar! It was really cool. He was serious about learning to play it. It came with a manual and his dad helped him a bit to learn from it, but George soon got so good, he went on to lessons from a man who lived above a liquor store. The teacher was getting on a bit in years and knew all the old songs of the twenties and thirties. We were further stunned when George showed us how he could play a little of the Django Reinhardt and Stephane Grapelli styles. That was real picking!

Out of the traditional airs of Ireland, jazz and blues, and jump-started with American pop records, there was an explosion in skiffle and pop groups in Liverpool, particularly in Speke, from around 1957. None of us had been anywhere at the time and we didn't know that Liverpool was different, that this explosion wasn't happening as quickly in the rest of Britain. We could feel the buzz in the air. My mum came from a cosmopolitan background. Her family mixed socially with people like the bandleader Jack Hylton, and Hutch—Leslie Hutchinson— who had been Cole Porter's lover. She wasn't too fond of Elvis, but she liked Cliff and Buddy Holly and often popped into North End Music Store—run by a young man named Brian Epstein—when she was in town and bought us the latest record.

Sinatra gave way to Elvis and Eddie Cochran, though to some extent, the different musical genres overlapped. At number three on the charts when the year began was Frankie Vaughan with his cover version of a song called "Garden of Eden." This song, which was not a strong piece of songwriting, was interesting because it was covered by no less than three variety style artists. However, Frankie, who was Jewish and looked Italian, prevailed, probably because he had better management and TV exposure thanks to the leading TV boss, Lew Grade, nee Gradzinski (who would later buy the Beatles' song catalog). Frankie had the number one with it, beating out the challenge of the other three. But a fourth challenger, who had also tried to make a break with the same song and got nowhere at all, was a Jewish crooner, a balding guy who had changed his name from Richard Leon Vapnick to Dick James. Later, he and Lew Grade would enter the Beatles' lives in a big way.

Yes, 1957 had started with a hangover from 1956 and good-looking, smarmy crooners like Guy Mitchell, Johnny Ray and Frankie Vaughan at numbers one, two and three. Guy was "Singing the Blues," Johnny Ray was at number two, having hit the top over Christmas with "Just Walking in the Rain." By February, Buddy Holly and the Crickets would blow people away with "That'll Be the Day," but skiffle was still big. Lonnie Donegan had five hits that year, mostly with American folk-blues things like "Cumberland Gap" and "I'm a Gamblin' Man."

Soon there was a new pop music show on television called *The Six-Five Special.* Looking back it was a very sad program, though now it would probably have a certain kitsch appeal. It had a lousy theme song done by, as I remember, Don Lang and his Frantic Five, but it was on the BBC on Saturday night about six P.M. prime time. Television was shut down after the nine o'clock news, then it was cocoa and bed for the good folk. But despite this, the early legendary Mersey Sound was gradually evolving in the bedrooms of cramped houses in back streets, where young men like George, John and Paul were practicing their craft on cheap instruments. No one really taught them. They copied each other and watched carefully when pop bands played on television. I think Paul got hold of a copy of Bert Weedon's how-to guitar book, *Play in a Day*, which practically became a bible.

Poor old Bert—whom I came to meet—was the butt of many jokes among musicians over the years, but he had a great sense of humor. He'd give new members of a pickup band a lovely bound copy of the sheet music they were to play. "Here," he'd say, "use this." When they opened it, all it said inside was "Everything's in G and Go Man Go!"

We were part of a wide circle of bands in our age group, in their late teens or early twenties. Billy Fury was one of my brother Barry's best friends, though his career didn't take off until he went to London, like Georgie Fame, another northern lad, who started out a weaver in the cotton mills. People like Gerry and the Pacemakers, Billy J. Kramer, the Fourmost, the Merseybeats, the Swinging Blue Jeans and a drummer named Pete Best started making names for themselves locally, playing in places like St. Barnabas Hall in Penny Lane, Bootle and Aintree Institutes, Knotty Ash Village Hall, or workingmen's social clubs, like the British Railways Social Club where Gerry played quite often.

The big halls and ballrooms didn't allow beat groups in until the Beatles made it, though, because beat groups were considered the lowest of the low. Gerry came from Garston, a rough, slummy district. I knew him well because his girlfriend, Pauline, lived a few doors away from us and Pauline's mum was friends with my mum. Gerry's band was much in demand, playing every night of the week. During the day he worked hard on the railways with his dad, which goes to show that back then even a "successful" band didn't make much money. What drove them to play was pure love of music.

In March of 1957, when he was still sixteen, John formed his skiffle group, first named the Black Jacks, but changed after about a week to the Quarrymen after his school. Soon, a lad named Ivan Vaughn, who was in Paul's class at school, joined them on the tea-chest bass. A few months later, on June 22, 1957, a big street party was held to celebrate the 550th anniversary of King John's presentation of the Royal Charter to Liverpool, and the Quarrymen played their first gig on the back of an old coal lorry parked in Rosebery Street in the center of town. I was eleven. A huge crowd of us went, kids and parents, catching the 72 bus downtown to join in the activities and watch the lads play. According to John—when we reminisced years later—they were paid the princely sum of "Sweet fuck-all."

It was just as well that they didn't have to wait for their money because we saw a crowd of Teds arrive at the end of Rosebery Street, bent on a fight. Liverpool was a tough city. Some Teds had flick knives and razors and even meat cleavers hidden away under their drape jackets. They studded their belts with heavy washers that they would file razor-sharp and use as weapons; they inserted razor blades under their lapels, so that if you grabbed them your fingers were badly cut. They would kick someone's head in with their pointed steel-capped shoes. There were terrible gangs with names like the "Bath Hall Bloods" that would roam around and terrify the living daylights out of us. You would definitely cross the road if you saw them coming. Even their girlfriends, known as Judies, were feared. There was bad blood between the Teds and John. Of course we discussed it—why John? I think it was because there was something about the way John looked and stood and even walked that spelled sex and trouble. He was also very shortsighted but wouldn't wear his glasses, so it looked as if he was arrogantly outstaring people. The Teds thought he was giving their girls the eye and they weren't having any of that.

Another reason the Teds picked on John and were always beating him up was because he dressed like them, but didn't live the life or fight the fights. He just walked the walk. They also despised the fact that he came from a middle-class home and went to a grammar school, while they were genuinely tough working-class navvys working on the roads, or in factories.

John, perhaps unintentionally, was a genuine misfit. George was just a bit of a Ted too, but a lot of guys were. At least, they dressed up and had attitude, but in a fairly mild way. It was the rebellious look rather than the violence that appealed. However, things escalated and John became a marked man. The Teds all knew him. They seemed to recognize him at a hundred paces.

That day, the crowd split as the Teds shoved their way through. The Quarrymen spotted the gang, but continued playing to the end of the song. We were all on tenterhooks, convinced that there would be a bloodbath. Leaving it almost too late, I saw John and the lads grab their equipment and climb off the parked lorry, through the open window of the house behind—number 84, the home of Mrs. Roberts, one of the event's organizers. We kids were in awe. John was quite a hero because of his incredibly cool appearance and daring exploits and here was another one being acted out before our eyes. After the Teds had slunk off out of hearing, we cheered like mad. Mrs. Roberts gave the Quarrymen a nice tea with scones and sandwiches until it was safe to leave via the back alley.

They had enormous stamina, as did most of the fledgling groups. None of them had any money, and a car or van to get them about was usually out of the question. They went to gigs by public transport—even the drummer had to drag his cumbersome gear behind him. A few groups had what they grandly referred to as "managers"—older pals, dads or brothers, who would sometimes arrange the bookings, but they were never managers in the proper sense. Very few of them had phones and often they would pedal around to fix things on their bicycles. But, despite all the logistical difficulties, by August, the Quarrymen had graduated to their first-ever gig at the Cavern Club, which at that time was a jazz cellar. I wasn't around: I was spending the summer at the seaside with my aunties as usual. Paul was at Boy Scout camp and George was at Butlin's holiday camp with his family.

A few weeks after the coal lorry episode, the Quarrymen did a skiffle gig at Wilson Hall. Afterward, John and Pete Shotton were riding the bus home when a gang of Teds caught sight of John on the top deck at the front. They gave chase and leapt on at the next stop. They weren't after Pete and he ducked out of sight down behind a seat. John fought his way through the the confined space and fell down the stairs. The Teds dashed after him and jumped off the bus, believing that their quarry had escaped down the street. Pete sat there, fearing the worst, but when he went downstairs at his stop to get off, he saw John sitting very still and very quietly between two fat women. When John and Pete got off the bus they swung down the road, laughing, and the story became a sort of legend to us boys.

But it wasn't a game. When the Silver Beetles played at a hall in the rural Cheshire village of Neston, on the far side of the Mersey from Liverpool, a teenage boy was trampled to death in a surge of Teds toward the stage and once again the band had to fight their way out to escape through the emergency doors. Paul and George were both beaten up one night at the Hambleton Hall in Huyton; and John was always being battered. Rough areas like Litherland, Bootle and Garston were the heartlands of the Teds' domains, where they ruled supreme. For a long time, these thugs were an ugly British phenomenon. They dressed nattily but they were dangerous and we tried not to go anywhere near them.

John was okay, considered crazy maybe, but not violent. While the rest of us were still at the average schoolboy stage, John Lennon was something else. Not only was he considered a juvenile delinquent, but he had a propensity for wreaking havoc, all in the name of angst and art. "If you hang out with that John Lennon," mums—including mine—would warn their sons, "you'll get into trouble!" In fact, everybody probably did think that John was headed for Borstal, or even jail, and he did little to improve his image.

I can still see John to this day, in his Quarryman period, summer of 1957, sitting on the roof of Halewood Village Hall where our youth club was run, flames shooting up, smoke swirling all around him. We kids were wide-eyed, watching, waiting for the roof to fall in and John to be fried to a crisp—while the vicar was demanding ladders and buckets of water and shouting at John to come down. Soon there was a large crowd, with John the focus of attention. When the fire engines showed up, John started a kind of pyromaniacal dance on the roof, cackling his head off. Of course, he had started the fire. John was always starting something— and that was his fascination for us. He was the rebel we longed to be. We could count on John putting on a good show, something we could later laugh about among ourselves. We just never knew what he would do next.

At a young age John saw and heard things that nobody else did. Voices in his head and faces reflected in mirrors would talk to him. It was a bit like *Snow White*, where the wicked queen would stare into the magic mirror and ask, "Mirror, mirror on the wall, who is the fairest one of all?" People were always talking about John. He was a born leader, a wild, yet charismatic boy, and the stories spread through a mixture of rumor, gossip and even John's own mumblings. At times, he spoke in riddles, his conversation disjointed and almost incomprehensible, and when you were totally confused, he would laugh and go off on a tangent or say something really wise or witty or sarcastic. You never knew if he was telling the truth, and it didn't much matter. He was simply mesmerizing.

Everyone had their stories about him, in awe because he seemed to know so much about so many things and was almost fearless. Pete Shotton had his stories, Ivan Vaughan had his stories—we all had our stories. In later years when we grew close, John told me how he used to think he was going crazy. At home he said he would gaze into the mirror and ask when he would become rich and famous. "Soon John, soon," the mirror would seductively reply. The visions were huge and all-encompassing and instilled in John the absolute conviction of his own greatness. He often said he was different from the rest of us—probably from another planet. I used to sometimes see him staring into the mirror in dressing rooms when he combed his quiff and there was something different about his expression. The other lads would preen and fix their hair without thought, like we all did, but John would seem to go into a trance. Then he'd shake himself out of it. He was like the Fonz before the Fonz existed.

He could well have been psychic, or even the genius he was later thought to be, but to adults he was always just a pain in the arse at that time. He portrayed himself as a natural rebel, but I think he was quite unhappy. In fact, you could never really get close to John. Even when he was talking to you there was always a sense of isolation, a cutoff point beyond which he didn't go, and you didn't go.

His sense of isolation originated because his parents had split up when John was five and he was never told whether they were alive or dead. His Aunt Mimi and Uncle George—who owned a dairy—brought him up quite strictly. When John discovered that his mother lived within half a mile of him on the other side of the golf course, a few hundred yards from the McCartney's, he was shocked.

John got into the habit of dropping by Julia's house so he could spend some time in a rowdy, happy-go-lucky family atmosphere he missed, and at the same time, get to know his two younger half sisters, Julia and Jacqui. When he realized the extent of her natural talents, John almost hero-worshipped his mother. She was a brilliant pianist with a lovely voice and she taught John to play banjo, having been taught by his wayward father, Fred—who in turn had been taught by his own father. John's Irish grandfather had been a professional in a black-and-white minstrel show traveling around America. As well as the piano and the banjo, Julia could play the harmonium and the harmonica. She could sing, paint and act—all abilities that John discovered he shared. The banjo seemed to give John direction in life and he practiced all the time, imagining that he would become the next George Formby, a music hall star. (I don't know if George copied John, but he also loved George Formby and in turn, George would teach his son, Dhani, the ukulele.) It's all a wonderful legacy of passed-down music and humor.

But guitars were cooler and John wanted one. When he was fourteen he saw an advertisement for a guitar costing ten quid by mail order in *Reveille,* a trashy weekly newspaper. It was a Spanish-style flat-topped acoustic Gallotone Champion guitar made by the Gallo Company of South Africa and "guaranteed not to split." Julia gave him the money and John sent away for it, giving her address because he knew Mimi would disapprove. (There is an interesting story connected with Gallo, which was a small family-run company. Years later, when the boys formed Apple Records they didn't always distribute through EMI around the world but did a country-by-country deal. At the time, there were embargoes on trading with South Africa due to their apartheid laws, but, believing that music crossed class, color and creed and that there were no barriers in the music world, illegal as it was, Ron Kass flew out and did a deal with Peter Gallo to distribute Apple records. Uniquely—something that happened nowhere else in the world— Gallo was allowed to put their own local bands—in Swahili or whatever—on the Apple label. These South African Apple records are as rare as hen's teeth and very few collectors even know of their existence. A further footnote: Peter Gallo comes to London every year and we always meet up for a drink.)

John still didn't know how to play his Gallotone properly, and Julia tuned it in the banjo way. She also encouraged John and his friends to come round and make music. Colin Hanton, Eric Griffiths, Rod Davies, Pete Shotton and Len Garry were all teenage boys who had improvised skiffle instruments, like a washboard from one of their garden sheds, and a tea-chest bass strung with or-dinary string tied to a broom handle. Their favorite place to play was the bath-room for its good echo. It was discussed when they were playing their gigs.

"It doesn't sound the same without the echo," John would often complain, and the lads in the group would discuss how they could obtain the effect in a vil-lage hall or workingmen's club. Of course it was impossible in those days.

In the middle of 1957 skiffle and the Rock Island Line segued into Bill Haley's rockabilly-based "Rock Around the Clock," which segued into "Jailhouse Rock." Rock 'n' roll had arrived. Among the hip youth, tight jeans and a quiff replaced flannel bags and a short back-and-sides. I was cool; I dressed in all the latest gear, from jeans to leathers, and followed the trend with my hairstyle. In one respect, I was different from many local lads, because as soon as I got into long pants, I was also into suits, nicely ironed shirts and ties.

At the age of fourteen George formed the Rebels with one of his brothers and a few mates from school. (After the Egmond split George bought a Hofner Pres-ident, which he sold to Ray Ennis of the Swinging Blue Jeans. And later, in Hamburg, he bought a Hofner Club 40, like John's.) Not long after the Rebels formed, the news went out that they were playing at the British Legion Club in Speke! It sounded so unlikely that we rushed around on our bikes to have a look. But it was true. The Rebels had gone to audition but since nobody else had shown up, they got the gig. It wasn't so funny when they had to play all night and their tender fingers, unused to playing so much, started to crack and bleed. Sore or not, proud as Punch, George waved the ten-bob note they had been paid—between about six of them. Next morning, he was still full of it and told Paul on the school bus about their triumphant debut.

The very next night, Paul showed up at George's house with his Zenith. They dug out the guitar manual that had come with George's cheap guitar and started strumming. By the end of the evening Paul had learned two chords and could play and sing "Don't You Rock Me Daddy-O," while George's long-suffering but good-natured family sat there and passed the occasional comment.

♏

Dressed in a too-large, draped, white sports jacket and skintight black trousers that he'd taken in himself, Paul did some pretty fancy playing the day he offi-cially met John at a church fete in a field next to St. Peter's Parish Church in the village of Woolton, half a mile to the north of us. It was in July, shortly before school broke up for the summer of 1957. On the posters that were pinned up everywhere we read that the Quarrymen were playing at the fete, which was to crown the Rose Queen. There would be floats and games and live music, and po-lice dogs would be put through their paces, so my brothers and George and I and a few of our mates jumped on our bicycles and made our way there, throwing our bikes in the hedge.

Paul had been dragged along by Ivan Vaughn, his friend from school, who said he would introduce him to the Quarrymen—which explains why Paul had dressed so carefully. He intended to make an impression. The first half of the Quarrymen's show was on a stage outdoors. Aunt Mimi turned up and was star-tled to see John in his Teddy Boy outfit of skintight jeans, long jacket and boot-lace tie. He started singing, "Mimi's coming, oh, oh, Mimi's coming down the path." Not many people in the audience realized that John was improvising.

The band's evening session was to be held in the church hall, and they car-ried all their instruments there and set up for later. When John went for a break, encouraged by Pete Shotton, Paul picked up John's guitar and played a few chords. Baffled, he realized it was tuned all wrong. Quickly Paul changed it from the banjo tuning. He played and sang "Long Tall Sally" and then launched into a virtuoso version of 'Twenty Flight Rock" when John returned. It was a long song, with many verses and a chorus that was similar to "Rock Around the Clock," but Paul seemed to know it all the way through. To John, this was an achievement, given that he never seemed to know all the words of the songs he sang and always improvised wildly. Not that many people noticed; they were too busy jiving and twisting away.

I was roaming around the fete with George and the lads when we heard the sound of the guitar coming from the church hall. We wandered over and saw Lennon looming over Paul in his owlish, shortsighted way, trying to make out the notes Paul was playing.

"He stank of beer," Paul said. "I didn't look up because I had to concentrate on where my fingers went, and at first I thought he was some drunken old git."

Despite this going down as the legendary "first meeting" in the Beatles iconography, Paul and John already knew each other. They had mutual friends; their mothers had been acquainted and they'd seen each other "around," in the way we all had for years. However, I think this was the moment when they became really "aware" of each other, through a mutual interest in music. They started chatting and Paul offered to write out the lyrics to a couple of verses of "Twenty Flight Rock." John, being John, was his usual sarky self, but Paul shrugged it off. Most Liverpudlians had taken a master class in sarcasm. Paul scribbled out the words on the back of a program and handed them over. John barely glanced at them, but he did stuff the program into his pocket.

When John had heard Paul sing he recognized that there was something about his voice that would harmonize perfectly with his own. But he wasn't going to tell that to this cocky, young, fifteen-year-old with short back-and-sides—and his guitar! And the little bastard had taken the liberty of tuning it up. Later, this became George's job.

Encouraged by Ivan Vaughan, Paul kept turning up with his own guitar and hanging out around them after school. If they were rehearsing, he'd join in. He'd sing a bit, tune John's guitar, or play something during a break so they could hear how good he was. However, John kept resolutely ignoring him. After a couple of weeks of brooding about this young whippersnapper who was almost as good as he himself was—better in fact, because he could play *real* guitar, not banjo-style—John finally relented and decided to ask him to join his group, but in his own way.

A couple of evenings later, Paul was riding his bicycle home across Allerton Golf Course when he bumped into Pete Shotton. "John said you can join us if you want," Pete offered casually.

"Yeah, okay," Paul said, equally casually. But he flew home like the wind and grabbed his guitar, playing in a frenzy, daydreaming about being in a real group, one that got bookings and was sometimes paid. Best of all was the thought he might soon be up on a stage—something Paul never got tired of. To celebrate, he lost his virginity that evening—and then told his mates. The news flew around. "Hey, guess what? Paul's shagged a girl!" There wasn't much that happened that we didn't hear about.

🎤

John suffered from dyslexia, but he was good at art and was always doodling in notebooks. Students were required to attend school until the age of sixteen, but most youngsters who left school at that age didn't have much of a future. Mimi discussed the options with John's headmaster and it was decided that he might do well at art school. The head wrote a special letter of recommendation and John was accepted at Liverpool School of Art in the autumn term of 1957 shortly before his seventeenth birthday.

Conveniently, the art school was right next door to the Institute where Paul was a student. Elvis and rock 'n' roll were considered very uncool by the art students, but John didn't care what they thought. He and Paul met up all the time in the adjoining graveyard during their lunch breaks and jammed. As the weather grew colder, they would regularly bunk off to practice and write what would become "the songs." It was Paul who showed John how to play chords properly, instead of banjo chords, which were all John knew. I think John was quite defensive when he realized that through much of his "career" with the Quarrymen, he had been playing two-fingered banjo chords on a guitar. The thought was tempered by the fact that nobody had noticed. John once told me, "Only that fookin' McCartney sussed me out. I love him, but he's such a good musician, I could kill him."

Suddenly, John, Paul and George desperately wanted to learn how to play properly and well. When Paul got a handle on a new chord he showed George or John; or if George suddenly grasped something new, excitedly, he would whiz around to show Paul, who in turn showed John. Sometimes John and Paul went to Julia's house, but mostly they wrote in Paul's house, which was empty during the day. (Paul's dad said they were always starving and consumed mountains of baked beans on toast.) They listened to records and learned to play all the songs recorded by their American heroes, as well as standard skiffle tunes by Lonnie Donegan and Johnny Duncan. They copped from Eddie Cochran and Buddy Holly and soon, apart from their own songs, they had a huge repertoire.

Their own songs were born on scraps of paper and in exercise books. When they weren't playing, they were constantly writing in every spare moment. I remember these numerous bits of paper well. It seemed as if everywhere John and Paul went—later on it was in vans and tour buses, hotel rooms and cafes—these scraps of paper were always floating around. They were stuffed into their pockets or guitar cases. Often, they were simply abandoned. Later, they were sometimes tidied up by hotel maids and thrown away. How I wish I had collected them together, but they were just random words and half sentences, scribblings that had little bearing on the songs that emerged. By the time they cracked it, they had more than enough material for their first albums.

Throughout the autumn of 1957 John let Paul perform at a few casual gigs, but it wasn't until January of 1958 that he admitted Paul was good enough to play on their second Cavern gig. I heard all about it from an excited George, who thought the world of John and followed him around almost everywhere. George was in the Rebels with his chums, but it was not like being in a real group, a serious group.

To George, the Quarrymen instantly represented the big time. They were becoming the better of the bands in our small area, although at the time they weren't as famous locally as the Sunnyside Skiffle Group. John and Paul had a strange fascination with handicapped people and it so happened that the guy who played the tea-chest bass for Sunnyside was Nicky Cuff, a midget who lived around the corner from us. He stood on top of the actual tea chest to play, which cracked up John and Paul, but they didn't laugh so hard when Sunnyside won the "Search for a Star" competitions, and the Quarrymen—who had temporarily named themselves "Johnny and the Moondogs"—lost out. After winning a competition at the Empire Theater in Manchester, Sunnyside got to play at Sunday Night at the London Palladium, which was just sensational. But locally the Quarrymen were catching up fast and got good, proper gigs every two weeks. George told me that he had begged John to let him join the band, like Paul.

"What did he say?" I asked.

"He told me to fuck off," George said. Then he grinned that wide smile which lit up his whole face. "But I'm not going to give in."

So George continued to follow John everywhere. He even sidled up to audaciously invite him to the pictures, and got the usual response he had come to expect from his hero: "Fuck off!" But finally he succeeded in his mission just a month later after a gig when the Quarrymen had played at the Morgue Skiffle Cellar, which was run by another pal, Alan Cadwell and his Texans (Ringo Starr was to join the Texans a few weeks later). It was all happening!

On a freezing March night George and I hung around the Morgue afterward and jumped on the last bus with the lads. Upstairs was almost empty and George, who had lugged his guitar along, suddenly launched into the instrumental, "Raunchy."

Paul, who was in on George's determination to join them, winked and said to John, "See, he can play it, and he can play it all the way through!" Joe Cool just hunched into his jacket and gazed into space. But a couple of days later when they were writing a song, Paul said casually, "What do you think of George?" John nodded and said, "Yeah, he's great"—and that was it. George was in.

3

No sooner was John getting to know his mother when, in the summer of 1958, she was run over and killed yards away from Mimi's house by a speeding policeman who was late for work. Another policeman came to the door and broke the news. In a rare display of emotion, John once told me he was gutted.

Julia's death threw him completely off the rails. He was just seventeen years old and, to his mind, an orphan. He became more bitter and cynical, his behavior even more bizarre, although he was at art school where strange behavior was often the norm. Stories filtered back to us about how John was. Our parents would comment, "Poor boy, he's taking it hard." He would sit in the windows of an upstairs hall, knees hunched to his chest and stare into space—what shell-shocked troops called the "thousand yard stare"—apparently not hearing when he was spoken to. He talked to himself. Ranted when walking along, so people steered clear of him. He started fights, blindly, lashing out at his best friends. Arms and legs flying, he had to be held back but, frenzied, he would break free and run off. Girlfriends complained that he screamed at them and sometimes hit them in the face for no reason. His anguish was so great that he even tried to run off to sea. But Mimi found out he'd signed up with the Seaman's Union and dragged him back.

Maybe it would have been better if John hadn't felt so rejected by both his parents, but no one had ever told him that his father had once come back for his family after the war and discovered that John and Julia were living with another man. The adults had an argument and Fred left. (Years later, a deeply kept family secret was to emerge. John's half sisters learned that after Fred disappeared the first time, in June 1945 their mother had a daughter, Victoria, by another man, a Welsh soldier named Taffy Williams. This was quite a scandal and John's grandfather, "Plops" Stanley, who had taken in Julia and young John to live at the family home in Penny Lane, insisted that the baby be given away for adoption. Julia went on to meet someone else by whom she had two daughters, someone who didn't get on with John, so she gave John to her sister, Mimi. But by then, "Plops" was dead, so she could do as she liked.)

There was something else besides the music that connected John and Paul, almost in a spiritual way. The loss of their mothers had an enormous emotional impact that they bottled up and couldn't discuss with anyone. In quieter moments, they sometimes shared their feelings, not in words, but on an intuitive level, something they couldn't do with their other friends. I only came to recognize how this was years later because Liverpool kids were tough. Even middle-class ones, as we in our little clique mostly were, would have been embarrassed to show our feelings, certainly not to each other. We had an expression, "Don't get real on me, man," which meant, "Keep your feelings to yourself." It was all bottled inside and we just grew up and got on with life. Sometimes, this made for a brittle shell and, as in John's case, a ruthless and cynical edge.

Paul missed his mother so much that the first song he wrote, when he was fourteen, "I Lost My Little Girl," was really about her. At the time, he said he didn't appreciate that it was about his mother. Lots of teenagers, filled with angst and change, moodily wrote poetry; it was unusual to write songs. Although Paul was impressed by a song that his dad had written, Jim McCartney dismissed his own efforts. When praised, he said, "I didn't write it, I just made it up," a sentiment that left a crucial impression on Paul, making him believe that songs had no real monetary value. Both he and John were to pay dearly for this mistake. (In 1968, Paul was to write a poignant song, "Lady Madonna," which was also about his mother. Although the song was very upbeat and rocky with elements of both New Orleans and Big Band jazz, it had a motherly image that was to be a recurrent theme in Paul's work, in his dreams and in his unconscious desire to find the ideal woman to replace her.)

I think John, Paul and George first took themselves seriously as a band and grew almost zealous in their passion to make music when Buddy Holly and the Crickets came to Liverpool and rocked our socks off at the Philharmonic Hall. In a strange preview of my future job, assessing songs as a record promoter, I had just won a competition in the *New Musical Express* where you had to predict the next week's top three chart records. My selection wasn't just potluck; I had used judgment. The prize was to see Buddy Holly and to meet him and the Crickets at the Philharmonic Hall.

I'd already seen Gene Vincent and Eddie Cochran when they were on tour, so I was well into all the American pop stuff. But Buddy Holly was my idol and Mum had already bought tickets, so I got to go twice. It was fantastic. It was the first time that a rock and roll show had been allowed at the Philharmonic Hall instead of the Liverpool Empire. Buddy Holly and the Crickets were so loud that I think the management started to have second thoughts. We kids loved it, singing and shouting our heads off. Of course, the Quarrymen went, with George, Paul and John. Afterward, I came in for a lot of stick and a few envious comments because during the intermission I was taken backstage and introduced to Buddy and the two Crickets, Jerry and Joe, and to the compere, Des O'Connor. Predictably, this made for a bit of a buzz at school. I was now "Tony who had been taken to meet Buddy Holly and the Crickets—and he saw both shows!" It was like I was suddenly famous, and in a way, I was.

The show inspired the Quarrymen to greater heights. They decided to go after a record deal though they went about it in the way that all hopeful kids do, by cutting a cheap demo and lending it to all their mates to play to death. George was full of this "first single," which he brought around for us to hear. It was amateur and pretty awful, scratchy and quite raucous, a 78 shellac demo they'd had made in a back bedroom of Percy Phillips, a man they knew who cut demos on just about the only record pressing machine in Liverpool—at 38 Kensington Road. But still, it was "Oh wow!" as we crowded around the record player. This was a *real record,* and scratchy or not, it sounded authentic, like the beginning of something. They did Buddy Holly's "That'll Be the Day" and "In Spite of All the Danger," with John singing lead on both songs. We were very impressed as George enthused about making records and getting a deal.

"How will you do that?" I asked.

"John is going to send this to a deejay he knows and see if he'll play it on his show," George said confidently. "Then someone will hear it and we'll get discovered."

We all knew about being discovered, like Elvis. Being discovered was how the system worked. My brothers and I passed the shellac flimsy to each other, handling it as if it were pure gold, hardly noticing the pasted-on handwritten white label. This was rock 'n' roll—show biz! We must have listened to it twenty times over a couple of hours, singing along to the songs, while George bathed in the glow of our admiration and the beckoning fame, which was just around the corner.

Eventually, Mum came in from the kitchen where she'd been making tea and with good humor said, couldn't we listen to something else?

"How much did this cost, George?" I asked, lifting it off the turntable and fingering it like an icon.

"One pound," George said. It seemed a huge amount. For me, it would have been two whole weeks of newspaper round earnings—and that made it all the more awesome. He giggled as he said that when they went to get it cut, they had only been able to scrape seventeen shillings together and had to go back the next day with another three bob which they'd somehow managed to scrounge before Percy let them take the demo away.

"Can we keep it until tomorrow?" I asked.

"Yeah, but don't give it to anyone else," George said, "or John'll kill me."

I was so in love with it that I played it over and over until Mum was fed up. I took it back to George and it was passed around the circle again like a well-thumbed library book until it was worn out. They never did get a deejay to play it and eventually Paul kept it and put it away. (A few years later he had some personal copies made at EMI, though the quality was very poor. They were eventually issued as part of the first *Beatles Anthology* compilation. To this day he still has the original and the copies locked away among his possessions.)

◆

But on February 3, 1959, Buddy Holly was dead in a plane crash, the legendary "day the music died." This tragedy made a huge impression on me, because I was the boy who had *met Buddy Holly*—and we all went into mourning. He was the best. Our reaction was, "Oh God, it can't be true."

He looked like an ordinary person—he was real. Unlike other big American performers, he didn't wear gold lamé or flashy clothes, which many of the groups in Liverpool copied. They dressed in horrible gold Lurex or lamé (like Rory Storm), Day-Glo pink or in white tuxedos that they thought were oh so cool but which cost the earth to dry-clean, so consequently were always pretty grubby.

The pre-Beatles, while starting out in long drape jackets and bootlace ties like most of the other skifflers (and they all went to the same shoe store to buy identical black-and-white two-tone loafers that all the bands wore), developed into Brando-type scruffs in leather jackets and skintight jeans, standing out a mile from what was expected from stage performers. When John started at art school he got all Left Bank poetical for a while and he influenced his bandmates to don black polo sweaters and black or charcoal gray cords with Norfolk-style tweed jackets with patch pockets. Uniquely, John also had dark green cords. Our footwear was winklepickers with Cuban heels until after Hamburg, when the Beatles returned with cowboy boots with decorative tops that they'd tuck their jeans into. (When John and Paul passed through London on their way back from Hamburg in 1961, they saw Chelsea boots in Annello and Davide in Drury Lane and were smitten. There were two versions, one with a Cuban heel, which became the famous Beatle boots; the other a kind of Shakespearean theatrical style—like Tom Jones's Spanish flamencos and P. J. Proby's big buckle variation.)

In contrast to all this stagy flamboyance was Buddy Holly. We all respected him because he looked modest. He wore ordinary suits and had big glasses, like John. He was a regular guy and yet he had all these wonderful songs and he played a guitar. This might sound obvious, but until he came along, most singers just sang, backed by a cabaret type of band. He had the best records, the best songs. Hell, he was one of us, he *belonged* to us. We had seen him in the flesh. I had met him! I only wish he had lived to meet the Beatles in 1963 or 1964.

John decided to rename the Quarrymen the Beetles, in honor of Buddy Holly's backing band, the Crickets. When he announced this after a gig, George—who I was closest to at the time—and I were agog, though we tried to act cool. It was a fitting tribute and everyone nodded solemnly. In any case, they'd grown away from being the Quarrymen, high school kids, and most of the original members were gone. I remember turning my hand over and looking at my palm in awe. This was the hand that had shaken Buddy Holly's. Sadly, I'd washed it a thousand times since then, but it had still been in direct contact. It was all connected—*we* were all connected.

However, along the route to their metamorphosis as the Beatles, the lads tried out many names, meanwhile still often being called the Quarrymen by long-standing fans. First John went for "Long John Silver and the Beetles," a combination of John's name and Long John Silver of the book, *Treasure Island.* John liked it, but a couple of the others thought it made him too important. However, John got his own way, as John usually did at the time. It was compressed to the Silver Beetles, the name they used for some months until they met Royston Ellis, a young English beat poet. In one of those plays on words that John and Paul liked so much, they invented the Beatals, as in "beat alls". According to Royston

Ellis this was his idea. But in an era when a lot can happen in a day, especially in a young man's mind, I don't think it was long before they were dithering again between names.

Without being aware of it, we were all natural street poets, goofing off with invented words and using figures of speech that were exclusively Liverpudlian. John and Paul's interest in word plays and doubles entrendres was focused when Royston Ellis gave a recital at Liverpool University. John, who was into new, different and bizarre, wasn't backward in getting to know the off-the-wall poet. They were the same age and recognized in each other a kindred spirit. They went back to some sleazy student flat where they spent the night doing some kind of drugs and "sharing" a willing girl named Pam. According to John, for some strange and perhaps kinky reason, she was wrapped in polythene, unusual night attire that piqued his curiosity so much that he wrote a song about her: "Polythene Pam." That same night Royston Ellis showed John how to get high by deep breathing the Benzedrine-soaked strips taken from inside a Vick's inhaler and it quickly went around the scene that this was a cheap and easy way of getting a buzz.

Pot wasn't all that cool. A few people smoked the occasional joint but it was purple hearts and black bombers that were mostly eaten to keep you awake and dancing. They were about sixpence each if bought singly, or a hundred for a pound in those golden days when there were 240 of those big round brass pennies to a pound. Purple hearts and black bombers (Durophet) and the like were mostly slimming pills that had a stimulating effect—a big one! They came from British Drug Houses, a local factory on the outskirts of Speke, where people were always breaking in and stealing sacks of the things, enough to keep you going for months. With a name like that, it was a bit of a magnet. We used to joke that they handed maps out around the pubs and gigs. I still have my old address book dating from my late teens and there, in black and white, is the address (but not the phone number) of the dealer everyone used—the one I went to for the Beatles when they were on the road and had to keep going: a guy we called Tex. By appointment, supplier of purple hearts, Benzedrine, black bombers and prellies to the Liverpool music scene. The lack of a telephone number wasn't unusual. Phone lines were like gold dust and were often shared. They were called "party lines" and in Tex's case, this would have been true.

I remember the gossip at school when George, Paul and John, having dropped the Beatals and reverted back to the Silver Beetles, were booked by a brash young impresario named Larry Parnes and disappeared up to Scotland to back Johnny Gentle in a rough dance hall where night after night they were pelted with beer bottles by Neanderthals on the old electric soup, who fell out of the balconies and despite broken limbs, continued to fight. Paul had bunked off just before he had been due to sit his "O levels" by telling his dad that he had two weeks off school to revise for his exams. When the news got out where he really was, our parents served it up as a warning about how important exams were and how Paul McCartney's future prospects were ruined. It looked like our mums and dads were finally proved right over all their dire predictions when John stunned us all by getting his photograph into the *Sunday People,* a lurid national newspaper, with the caption: "The Beatnik Horror, for though they don't know it they are on the road to hell."

The scandal—which John laughed hysterically over—came about because their first manager, bearded Allan Williams, who wore a top hat and ran the Jacaranda coffee bar in town, decided to open a strip club that he called the New Cabaret Artists Club. For his opening act he hired a stripper called Janice and sent some photographs of her backing band, the Silver Beetles, to the nationals as publicity. These photos showed John and Stuart Sutcliffe in their incredibly messy student flat. When it came to the actual performance, Janice, it seemed, could only strip to esoteric music like Beethoven and the Spanish Fire Dance. She handed John her sheet music, which he peered at short-sightedly and dismissed. Instead, dressed in poncy little lilac jackets, they played their own contorted arrangement of "The Harry Lime Theme" while Janice struggled to strip in time to it, front stage. At the end of the act, she turned around all out of breath, in all her naked full-frontal glory, while the boys, especially seventeen-year-old George, turned pink, then red, then grinned in unison. The bartender, a West Indian named Lord Woodbine, roared with laughter and rattled the ice in the cocktail shaker.

Allan tried anything that was different, including putting in an incredible, shiny, all-chrome, genuine Rock-Ola jukebox full of real American records! We gazed in awe then almost swooned when Little Richard then Chuck and Fats belted out. Crikey! This was magic. We loved American records because English records were such crap. We were snobbish about Cliff and Marty Wilde, Mark Wynter and Malcolm Earl, a dire balladeer who sang songs like "St. Teresa of the Roses" (his son started the Hard Rock Café and Planet Hollywood). From the bottom of our boots up we felt that American music was the genuine article. It was as if the U.S. was our spiritual home.

When everyone else was listening to skiffle or jazz, Allan installed a Jamaican steel band in his cellar. He didn't seem bothered about making money and let kids sit about all day with a cup of cold coffee. He even turned a blind eye when they topped up the coffee with spirits. Then from a German sailor who dropped by the Jacaranda Allan heard about the hot music scene in Hamburg.

He also heard that a drummer named Ringo Starr—whom we had seen around, and whose real name was Richard Starkey—had zoomed off to France with Rory. Allan went to Hamburg himself and talked to a few people, including Bruno Koschmeider, who owned the Kaiserkeller. He found that Bruno wasn't interested at first in any group from Liverpool, a place he had never heard of, and Allan returned home, down but not defeated. He knew something was going on, but unfortunately, by now everyone was hanging out at another cellar club that had been up and running since August 29, 1959, where the Beatles played on the opening night, and on every Saturday until October 10.

The Casbah had been set up initially as a den for her sons by Mona Best in the big basement of their rambling Victorian house on the far side of Liverpool. The house looked mysterious, like something out of a gothic novel, surrounded as it was by a thick stone wall and hidden away behind a high hedge of over-grown rhododendrons. It looked nothing like a teenage hangout that really rocked seven nights a week. It was considered really cool that Mona had bought the huge, nine-bedroom house from her winnings on the Grand National. She had pawned her jewelry from India and put the lot on a horse that had romped home.

Everyone loved Mo, who was a right bundle of fun and supercharged energy. When she saw how fast the news traveled about the ad hoc club in her base-ment, she decided to make it more commercial. It would be a place where groups could play and teenagers hang out. You went down a few steps from the outside to the cellar, which was about the size of two average living rooms—about twenty feet by twenty feet, barely room for fifty or sixty people. We all pitched in and painted the brick walls black, and then I think John came up with the idea of purple luminous paint. Inspired, we slapped it on, on top of the black. The walls glowed eerily, as if we were in a space ship floating through the galaxy with a couple of naked ultraviolet lights that dangled down on twisted electrical cord. Of course, Lennon loved it.

There was no stage, no real furniture. Mo went out to a sale with Neil As-pinall and returned in the van with some benches, the kind you might have in a park or school, with plain backs. There were a couple of chairs and a space in the middle where people shuffled about. The space was so small there was no room for gyrations. To this day, I remember the smell. It stank of sweat and old coal dust and of the girls' Nuit de Paris perfume and most of all, of Woodbines, cheap tarry cigarettes that came in a light green packet with swirly brown writ-ing and the illustration of bindweed. You could even buy five Woodbines in a soft packet identical to the ones that held ten or twenty, but made of paper in-stead of card. Even cheaper were Dominos, which you could buy singly, in those little white paper bags that loose candy was sold in by the ounce from jars at the sweet shop. We drank warm Coca-Cola and dined on crusty cheddar cheese rolls with slices of raw onion that were made in the kitchen upstairs—and cleared your sinuses like film cleaner. No pot was allowed nor alcohol. Mo could sniff both out a mile away and she strictly enforced the rules.

The sound was swamping. It was loud and all around us and seemed to vibrate with Lennon's glowing purple walls, making them pulse in a psychedelic way. Some groups still played skiffle, but the Silver Beetles rocked with all their favorite standards from the States, big hits like Buddy Holly's "Rave On" and "It Doesn't Matter Anymore," Eddie Cochran's "Summertime Blues" and "Come on Everybody," and Elvis's "Jailhouse Rock" and "One Night." No one did songs like the Silver Beetles. They were fab and—to coin a phrase—they started to attract a following.

We were all out by 10:30 though, in time to catch the last number 81 buses home toward Bootle or Speke. If we missed the bus it was a seven- or eight-mile walk. For some reason, those who had motorbikes didn't ride them to gigs, simply because you couldn't dress stylishly or hang out afterward and girls didn't want to go on them in case they were thought of as Judies. Another important consideration was that you might arrive smelling of oil and with your hair blown to pieces, when your quiff took ages to do. We'd slather on Brylcreem or Trugel, then comb it through and spend hours shaping it just so in a DA at the back, teasing the highest peak possible at the front before it flopped over and looked silly. Our hero was Kookie in *77 Sunset Strip*—"Kookie, Kookie, lend me your comb."

So there would be this natural curfew of 10:30, starting with a scramble to help the band pack up their gear, and we would all make a rush for the bus stops on opposite sides of the road, depending on which direction you were going. We would laugh and talk, still high on adrenaline and unrequited passion. It was fabulous.

But even though I was constantly around him, I felt I hardly knew Pete Best, although I used to go to a lot of gigs that his mother organized. He got a reputation as being mysterious, but he was probably just surly and introspective, or perhaps he was permanently depressed. Some people give out energy, others suck it in like a black hole. Maybe it wasn't his fault, but Pete was the latter. He had a steady girlfriend from when he was young and never really mixed with anyone, never came out much. You could say I knew his mother better; everyone did. She had quite a little circuit of venues, all local clubs and halls, such as the Casbah Club, Knotty Ash Village Hall and Hambleton Hall. All of them were run by Pete's delightful mum.

I never wonder if I could have had a bash at all that fame and glory. I'd never bothered to pick up a guitar because I had lost part of one finger in a freak accident with my own mailbox (although if someone had told me that losing a couple of fingers hadn't affected Django Rheinhardt I'd have probably given it a whirl). I was still nuts over music and was now old enough to be allowed out at night. The music scene in Liverpool was incredible at the time. It was unique, though it was probably much the same across the country, but to a lesser extent, in the days when there was no television as such. In fact, once upon a time, TV started at six P.M. and ended at nine because sets had to be switched off to let them cool down. Falling asleep in front of the TV could be as dangerous as smoking in bed. It was even joked that it was probably the reason why they played "God Save the Queen" after the last program—so you'd have to stand up.

Entertainment outside the home was important. However, I still think Liverpool had more buzz, more energy—more happening—than other towns. Perhaps it was because there were lots of Americans, because it was a seaport, and there was a postwar explosion of baby boomers. Live bands and groups played in clubs, ballrooms, village halls and workingmen's clubs. Every single Burton shop (stores that sold mass-market men's clothing) had a ballroom upstairs on the first floor. The back rooms of most pubs were venues for live music and there were hundreds of cabaret clubs which put on jazz, swing and comedy acts.

It is said that there were some three hundred bands and groups in Liverpool alone, but it wouldn't surprise me if there had been more. You couldn't walk down a street in any part of town without hearing music coming out from somewhere or the ground vibrating from frantic drumming and even more frantic dancing. Illegally using my school bus pass, I started to go to all the little ballrooms to watch the local groups. Among dozens, I often went to went to listen to the Alligators, the Delcardos, the Dominators, Ricky and the Red Streaks (not a great band, though Paul later borrowed their name as a joke pseudonym for Wings when he was doing his Back-to-Basics tour). There were Rory Storm and the Hurricanes, Gerry and the Pacemakers, the (Swinging) Blue Jeans, and Johnny Sandon and the Remo Four. The Remo Four were the best group to see because they could do all the Shadows' music, as well as Johnny doing all the country songs, which I thought was a really good combination. (The Shadows were like the Ventures, an American instrumental group.) The Remo Four's lead guitarist, Colin Manley, was the only one in Liverpool with a proper £150 worth of red Fender Stratocaster. There were no girls at all in the groups. There were only Cilla and Beryl Marsden, who used to just get up and sing. Sometimes they were invited to do guest spots. Not until Beryl went to London and joined Shotgun Express with Rod Stewart and Long John Baldry did she get taken seriously, while Cilla's eventual path to fame as Cilla Black was being discovered by Brian Epstein.

I got to know quite a few of the guys in the bands and, being a broke kid, wasn't always able to come up with the half a crown or three shillings entry fee. I would meet up with them after school or wherever and ask if I could carry their guitars in or help with their amps.

Yes, I was an early roadie, particularly for Gerry and the Pacemakers, until they suddenly disappeared off to Hamburg.

We knew Allan Williams saw something in the Silver Beetles, and he had been busy. He'd been down to London looking for work for them, where he bumped into Bruno Koschmeider again, this time in the Two I's coffee bar. Bruno had discounted Liverpool as a pool of talent, but went to London looking for acts to take back to Germany. This time, Allan got through to him and as soon as he returned to Liverpool, he told the Silver Beetles that he had a booking at the Kaiserkeller but they needed to sort out a proper, full-time drummer, not someone they picked up at the very last moment. (As last resorts at various times, they had even hired a Salvation Army drummer and a bent-kneed old geezer who only knew the "Gay Gordons" and the "Death March" from being the drummer in a military pipe band.)

Pete Best looked like a real rock star with his dark good looks, his leather jackets and tight jeans and his Elvis quiff, which had earned him a huge following. The band decided that if anyone could help them succeed in virgin territory, it was Pete. They dangled the bait of Hamburg, and that was all it took to steal Pete away from the Blackjacks, the group he was drumming for. They were all set, and off they went. Their lineup was John, Paul, George, Stuart Sutcliffe (a fragile-looking art student in John's year) on a bass he was still learning to play and had bought from the proceeds of a big art prize he had won—and Pete Best. For Pete, it was the worst thing that could have happened, because it ended up breaking his heart.

So it was just after the Christmas of 1960 when I read in the *Liverpool Echo* that a new band called "The Beatles" were appearing direct from Germany at Litherland Town Hall on December 27, with Bob Wooler, a young Liverpool deejay, acting as master of ceremonies. I decided to go—and found myself on top of that number 81 double-decker bus with George, on his way to that first real Beatles gig. From then on I was sort of known as "George's mate."

For me things had really changed while they'd been away in Hamburg. I'd grown tall, filled out. It's amazing what a year or so can do in the life of a boy. I went from being a scruffy little kid far beneath John's dignity to notice, to a bona fide teenager of fifteen with an opinion and a Brylcreem quiff.

"You can carry my fucking guitar too if you like!" John would say to me, in a way that only John could do.

They were so successful that night that the promoter, Brian Kelly, booked them for thirty-six gigs, starting with another one a week later at Litherland Town Hall on January 5. They haggled hard and their fee was upped to seven pounds ten shillings. Chas Newby, the bass player who temporarily replaced Stuart Sutcliffe, dropped out in order to return to art school, so that gave the remaining four Beatles the princely sum of thirty-seven shillings and sixpence each. It was those gigs that firmly established them as a charismatic group with a growing army of besotted fans. In a year I went to about three hundred Beatles gigs, from one end of the Mersey to another. I never stopped.

4

None of them had regular day jobs, but officially the Beatles were now professional musicians. Gigging was what they earned their money from, even though they were always flat broke. Their organization and timekeeping was still a bit shambolic because finding transport was always hit-and-miss to start with, and they had no roadies. In fact, I was *the* roadie, the one and only. If they were going to Manchester for instance, it was like, "Hey, let's get George's mate to help us with the gear, eh?"

Neil Aspinall was an early member of our little clique who also helped out. He was six months younger than Paul and had been in his class at the Liverpool Institute. (George was a year below them but he and Paul used to go home on the bus together, so they became friends, despite the age difference—which incidentally, was always with them. Right to the end, Paul always saw George as "our kid.")

Neil was training to be an accountant with a mail-order correspondence course, though his heart was in rock 'n' roll. Somehow he managed to lay his hands on eighty pounds to buy a van, a little Bedford, then he got an old Thames van, followed by a succession of crap vans which were always breaking down and off we'd go, with Neil driving, hoping that we would get to the gig on time, if at all. It was all very hairy and exciting. He was living with the Best family in the big Victorian house above the Casbah Club and he and Pete would go straight home with the gear so it would be locked up safely, while the rest of us bad people would stay out and go to all-night drinking clubs like the Blue Angel (known as "The Blue") or to one of the Chinese caffs, the kind of place where they probably had heroin and hookahs in the back room behind a bead curtain, the kind of place where if they'd *had* heroin and hookahs, John would have been in like a shot because he was always like a moth dicing with flames: he *wanted* to get burned. We felt it was very daring to drink Scotch and Coke or occasionally, rum and black, which I think was introduced to Liverpool by sailors. People thought we only drank Scotch and Coke to be pretentious when we came to London and hung out at the Scotch of St. James's, but we were into it long before. I'm not sure where it started. I could even have introduced it to our group, from the American family who were our neighbors in Hunts Cross.

The Macmillans lived four doors away from us. Charlie Macmillan was a captain in the USAF, at Burtonwood, one of the huge air bases along the Mersey. He was a nice man, who would bring home the latest American comics and records—ones we couldn't get in England, including some obscure labels and artists we'd never heard of—to be shared by his kids and my brothers and me (and of course these records would be passed along the grapevine to George, Paul and John). There'd be chocolate and bubble gum during the years when such things were seriously rationed in Britain and almost impossible to get, and endless supplies of Coca-Cola, all from the PX stores. In the summer, the Macmillans would have barbecues in their garden and as well as friends from the base; they'd ask the neighbors. I can remember the big bottles of Scotch and the cases of Coke and even ice—which was in short supply among most Brits in the fifties and even sixties—that went to make these exotic American drinks. I can still hear the ice tinkling in the glass and the smell of newly mown grass mingling with meat sizzling on the outdoor grill. To me, Scotch and Coke seemed terribly grown-up and exotic—but then, I was growing up fast and sprouted several inches in a year, so I looked older than I was.

📫

It was during this period that I got a part-time job working on a farm. It all came about because I had a pony that I kept in a field on the outskirts of Hunts Cross. Sometimes, I'd help the farmer feed the animals, or with mucking out, or with the hay, all of which I loved, so when the opportunity came to work on a larger farm near Halewood, I grabbed it. I wasn't paid a lot, about ten bob a week, but it was fun. The farm was owned by Frank Parker, a very forward-looking man. He had dairy cows and fields of vegetables, wheat and hay, and all the latest equipment to service it, from electronic milking parlors to pea-podding and fast-freezing machinery for packs of garden peas that he supplied to the first super-markets. It was my job to feed the hens twice a day. I'd rush over there on my bicycle before school in the morning, pour out the split peas, wheat and linseed and do the same again after school. On weekends and during the summer holi-days I was there from dawn to dusk. I drove the tractors and baled the hay and anything else that had to be done. It became my ambition to be a farmer and I applied to agricultural college, which you could go to before university age. Part of this was my passion for driving. I loved handling the farm machinery, espe-cially riding around on the tractors, and despite my youth and marked lack of a license, had first got into motorbikes when I was twelve or thirteen. One pound would buy an old wreck from a junkyard and our gang would fix them, get spares, and make them go, then we'd race around farm fields.

As we got older we were more biker rockers than Hell's Angels. We were a gang of my brothers and friends from school, just kids together, hanging out on the corner on our bikes, looking cool, eyeing the girls. We had some exciting times. On weekends or during holidays, we'd roar down to the docks and take the ferry across the Mersey to seaside places like New Brighton or Hoylake. Sometimes, we'd go into North Wales for the day, or to Rhyl, where my auntie's house was.

None of the Beatles had motorbikes. George hated them—though he was once photographed on one—but I'd offer to give him lifts to gigs and rehearsals and he'd reluctantly get on the back. We didn't wear helmets. They were sissy things. One rainy day I had a bad crash down by the docks, where railway lines and tram tracks crossed old cobbles. A car came out of a side road and in avoid-ing it, I skidded on the wet cobbles and my wheel got stuck in a track. I was in the hospital for weeks with broken elbows, a broken leg and a fractured skull.

It seemed a strange life I was leading, on the one hand at school, playing sports, riding my pony, working on the farm, being healthy and outdoors, and on the other, holed up in smoky dungeons and dance halls, drinking Scotch and Coke. Girls came into it too, but I was still young and not a sex fiend like John and Paul. On the whole, not many girls my age went all the way. They had a dreadful fear of pregnancy. We had our own fears too, the horror of getting a girl in trouble and having to leave school and get married. So it was more a matter of walking them home and hoping they would let you get away with something forbidden. I was still very shy, so for me at least that something was not much to shout about.

🎸

John's first serious girlfriend, Linda—known as Louie—came from Allerton like John. They were dating before he met Cynthia and I got to see him hanging out with her quite a lot. She was a pretty girl but John dumped her when he went to art school. Paul's girl, Dorothy Rohne, lasted longer. She even moved into a bedsit next to Cynthia and the two shared more than rollers, stockings and coffee. It seemed to me that they shared their fears and dreams over these two wild youths they were trying to tame and snare.

George's very first girlfriend was Iris Caldwell, when he was fourteen and she was twelve. She used to stuff her bra with cottonwool, and all the lads fancied her, but George was her sweetheart. They didn't do much more than play kissing games in the living room of the family home in Broadgreen Road. As with Mo Best, Vi Caldwell—"Ma"—was the attraction. She would welcome all the local kids in and make chip butties or bacon sandwiches for them at any hour of the night. Her home became our teenage hangout. Iris's brother Alan, of the Texans, became Rory Storm of the Hurricanes. He even changed their address to Broadgreen Road, Stormsville.

Paul also started going out with Iris in 1961 when he spotted her all grown up and stunning, twisting energetically away at the Tower Ballroom where the Beatles were booked. She was working there as a professional dancer, glamorously fetched out in black fishnets and stilettos. I'd often stop to chat with her when I went to the Tower because we'd known each other for ages. But when Paul saw her, he couldn't take his eyes off her. When he asked her out, she said, "Don't you recognize me? I'm Iris Caldwell." They dated on and off for a couple of years, finally breaking up when he went to London and fell for Jane Asher. Iris married Shane Fenton—who became glam rocker, Alvin Stardust.

I suspect George was a virgin before he went to Hamburg, but he certainly wasn't when they returned. Like all the Beatles, who were considered sex machines by this time, whether they were or not, George could pull women by the time they returned. However, he was always very insecure and shy, and it took him ages to make a move. John was also very shy, but he was loud and aggressive to make up for it and girls just flocked to him. Later, it didn't seem to matter that he and Ringo couldn't drive. In fact, they didn't get licenses for years, but it didn't stop either of them. With or without a license, John was a dreadful driver. And he refused to wear his glasses, which made it worse. George pulled his first real bird when he was eighteen, during one of the breaks from Hamburg. She was a strawberry blonde called Bernadette O'Farrell, a real stunner to look at, and a very nice girl into the bargain, the kind of girl you really could take home to meet your mum. We were all amazed because back then everybody wanted a girlfriend who looked like Brigitte Bardot, and lucky old George had landed a Bardot lookalike. None of us knew how he had done it because he wasn't what you would call good at chatting girls up. He was a dark horse, more laid back and less pushy than the others, but I suspect the real reason he snapped up Bernadette from right under their noses was that he was the only one back then with a driver's license. Long after George moved on and left her behind, Bernadette remained a loyal Beatle fan. For years she ran the Beatles Museum in Liverpool until the National Trust bought it out.

⋙

Pete Best became a kind of manager for the Beatles simply because the Bests had a telephone and someone was always around to take a message. Most of our families had telephones by the early 1960s, but they were so expensive, teenagers weren't encouraged to use them. Generally, if we wanted to get in touch with our mates we'd cycle round, or send a message via someone else who said they'd pass it on, or I would zoom round on my motorbike. In order to get bookings further afield, or to be booked, a manned telephone was a necessity. John, who always saw himself as the nominal leader of the group, couldn't take messages at the scruffy little bedsit he was now sharing with Cynthia Powell, his unlikely girlfriend. She was also an unlikely art student.

I knew Cyn as well as it was possible to know her, given how shy she was. She'd be at all the Beatles gigs, sitting at the back or to one side, sipping a drink and not talking to anyone. People said that John was wildly jealous, but it never occurred to me that he was. I'd nod and say something to Cyn, and she'd smile, and that would be about it. She was like a nervous fluffy Angora rabbit around John. Nicely brought up and sweetly pretty, she wore the standard middle-class uniform of twinsets and pearls. When she fell hard for John, daringly she bleached her hair blond and did it like Bardot—and she looked stunning. She switched to the Paris Left Bank look of big sweaters and fishnet stockings but her amazing new look didn't seem to lend her much confidence. With the change in her appearance, there also came an unexpected and tragic change in her circumstances. Her father died of cancer and her newly widowed mother, finding it hard to make ends meet, rented out their comfortable family home in posh Hoylake and went to Canada to become a nanny.

⋙

The Beatles returned to Germany in April 1961 to play at the Top Ten Club. Technically homeless and on holiday from art school, in June Cynthia and Dorothy Rhone, Paul's current girlfriend, went to Hamburg. John and Cyn stayed with Astrid and Stuart, while Paul and Dot moved into a bungalow by the docks, owned by Rosa, the obliging cleaning lady at the Indra nightclub where they played. Cynthia was stunned by the dangerous life the Beatles were living, with drugs and fights every night in the clubs, a new world that she didn't find that exciting, although she tried to fit in for John's sake.

On her return to Liverpool, Cynthia braved the dragon's lair to move in with Mimi. This was surprising and, not unsurprisingly, didn't work out. Mimi was too house-proud, too possessive of John to share him. In tears after a particularly snappy outburst from Mimi, Cynthia fled, to rent a squalid little bedsit close in the city center, which no amount of scrubbing and painting improved. Not that John cared when he returned from Germany in early July. Having a free central place to stay complete with resident blow-up sex doll and slave amused him, because Hamburg had changed the Beatles yet again and given them a sexual as well as a musical edge. (After Hamburg, Paul went round to see Dot and said they were through. She said he told her, "There are too many girls out there to be faithful to just one." In floods of tears, Dot moved out and disappeared from our lives.)

They were lean and wore skintight leathers. Astrid, Stuart's German girl-friend, tried to give them all a new Continental hairstyle, a casual preppy look, very different from their former greased-back Eddie Cochran DA, but Stuart was the only one brave enough to have the full floppy bang over the eyes. George and Paul went halfway, while John would only allow Astrid to trim it a bit. Only Pete held out and totally refused to abandon his beloved greaser look. It wasn't until almost a year later, when John blew the one hundred pounds he got for his twenty-first birthday to treat himself and Paul to a two-week trip to Paris that he saw the new style out in force among the French youth and dragged Paul off with him to have it done. When they returned with the new French look that Astrid had been so keen on, George immediately copied them, and before long, so did I. It was a boyish, fresh clean style that bounced up and down when the boys leapt about the stage. It seems odd, looking back, how individual that style looked to us then. We didn't know it then, but it was to become world-famous as the Beatles' look.

Long before the rest of England—or the world—Liverpool boys took to this new style in a big way. It was so easy. We washed our hair every day and just shook it dry. There was no more Brylcreem, no more preening for ages. Before, when we'd gone to the swimming baths, for example (where a horrible greasy scum used to float on the surface), afterward, we used to squirt a blob of white glop from the dispenser at the side of the pool and spend half an hour sculpting the works of art on our heads. With the Beatles' cut we were freed from all that. It might not seem a big deal, but was in fact a revolution.

Another more subtle revolution—one the fans didn't appear to notice—was that the Beatles started to wear makeup on stage. At first, it was to hide their spots. After all, George especially was still a spotty teenager, but they all flared up from time to time, as most teenage boys did. I can remember standing in dressing rooms as they stared into the mirror and poked and squeezed their spots, sometimes in unison. At times, spots became boils that looked pretty gruesome after being stabbed at with dirty fingernails. We used some horrible stuff that used to sting, dabbing it on with cotton wool, but the spots still rose to torment us, mini-volcanoes. It was hell to shave and frequently spots of blood marked white collars and torn-off scraps of paper stuck to faces. No wonder that black polo-necked sweaters became so popular.

The Beatles were a bit sheepish when the Max Factor Panstick and eyeshadow was produced, but they got over that by joking about it, strictly among themselves. I can't remember who started using it first. Probably George, because he had the worst skin problems. I can remember John and Paul goofing about, acting feminine and camp as they applied the makeup. They would pretend to apply lipstick, pursing out their lips and blowing kisses, but it was just camp playing about.

That spring and summer of 1961 girls quite literally seemed to fall at the Beatles' feet. Perhaps it was a kind of mass hysteria that was catching. Although the real shrieking didn't start until later, at the Cavern and other venues girls would gaze adoringly at them, then collapse onto their knees right at the front of the stage, clutching their heads and moaning. They were like this for no other band and it took everyone by surprise. The girls split up into factions of camp followers with very unfeminine names like the Cement Mixers and the Bulldogs, and like the Teddy Boy gangs they'd fight ferociously behind the scenes. They could be terrifying. The Beatles thought it was amusing.

Pete Best's girlfriend was one of the girls who used to get up and dance the twist in the Cavern. The lads would do Joey Dee and the Starlighter's song, "Peppermint Twist," and there would be Pete's girlfriend right up front, twisting away in a frenzy with Priscilla White, whose flaming red hair was lit up like a beacon under the lights. The two girls would even get up on the stage and twist like egg whisks. It has always been said that Priscilla was discovered by Brian, twisting and singing away at the Cavern, but this happened far more modestly at the Blue when she asked Bill Harry, a friend of John Lennon's, to introduce her. Bill got her name wrong and introduced her as Cilla Black, which stuck, and she became one of the first of the big girl singers to emerge in the sixties. She was wonderful, but she only had eyes for her Bobby, whom she married and remained true to for forty years until his death.

The Cavern was down in the cellars of some of Liverpool's oldest warehouses, built in the seventeenth century around an impressive inland pool, or natural harbor, in a bend of the Mersey. Over the centuries, the pool had been filled in and the warehouses ended up in the heart of the booming city. Somehow the Cavern cellars survived right through the war when they had been used as air-raid shelters, and in the 1950s they were used as a jazz club, until skiffle took over. The surrounding streets were still cobbled, the pavements steep and narrow. Often, when the Beatles arrived, they would have a swift black and tan (bitter and light ale) in the Grapes—an ancient inn that had stood there for some three hundred years—then they'd swing down the street to the club, while a swathe of teens parted to let them through. (When they became popular a buzz would rise—"It's them! It's them!" all along the sidewalk, where kids were lined up waiting to go in.)

I was too young for the Grapes, but I'd go ahead to help set up their gear. You'd go down eighteen dangerous stone steps, worn away from centuries of porters carrying foodstuffs up and down to be stored in the cellars. Music would already be blasting out from the turntable operated by Bob Wooler, the resident deejay, who was more grandly called the *compere*, or the master of ceremonies. The bouncer, Paddy Delaney, would look at your membership card, then you'd sign in and pay a shilling to Ray McFall at the little desk. After the first time, they recognized me as being with the Beatles and I didn't have to pay again. Once you passed through the door, off to the left was a little counter where you could buy hot dogs and the ubiquitous cheese rolls with a slice of raw Spanish onion washed down by Coke. Or you'd be served some variety of hot Heinz soup. With a nod to the majority of Irish Catholics in Liverpool, it was always tomato, pea or asparagus on Fridays.

The cellars consisted of three parallel barrel vaults, or tunnels, about a hundred feet long and ten feet wide. At intervals, connecting the vaults, were low archways, maybe about six feet wide. Off to the right was the first dark tunnel, with benches around the walls. The middle tunnel had about ten rows of bench seats (like joined-up dining chairs) facing a small stage that was about eight feet deep by ten feet across. A cramped little dressing room, known by the musicians as a "drezzy," was just off the stage on the left-hand side, which you got to by going through an arch into the third tunnel. The turntable and PA controls were back there, as well as a cloakroom and the dreadful toilets, with a primitive trough set into the floor and just a single-seated cubicle.

The floor was concrete, painted a bright cardinal red with heavy-duty floor

paint, until it got worn away by hundreds of dancing feet that raised a low car-
cinogenic cloud as they shuffled through cigarette stubs and ash. It was swept
out daily, but it was all back again the next night. The walls, which were curved,
were lime-washed a vile hospital green and the ceiling was bright orange. I don't
know if it was deliberately made to resemble the Irish flag, or if they just used
leftover distemper. At any rate, whatever it was, it was poor quality and rubbed
off and flaked if you leaned against it.

The lighting was almost nonexistent, and what there was had to compete with
the thick fug of cigarette smoke. Two small spotlights with bare lightbulbs were
halfway down the middle arch, focused on the stage; the rest was in darkness.
Apart from those who wanted to sit and watch the band, everyone else would
pack into the first and third arches and do the Cavern stomp, a sort of loose jive,
holding hands, because there was no room to move. There was no spinning or
twirling, no tossing your partner in the air. It was almost zomboid. In time, this
shuffle became known as the Shake. When the band was hopping you'd see
heads poking through the first and third arches, jostling for space to see what
was going on in the middle.

When the Beatles ran down the steps and arrived in the cellars, they would
hang onto each other's waists, heads down, and snake their way through the
crowd in the famous "Cavern Conga"—the humorous nickname it was given by
Cavern regulars, who would egg them through with cheers and a typically rowdy
Scouser welcome—until they reached the stage and could disappear into the
drezzy to hang up their coats. I'd have helped set up the drums and the guitars
and the show would start, usually with the lads chatting to the audience as they
picked up their instruments and did a bit of tuning. Bob Wooler would get a few
words in, trying to introduce the numbers—though often he was humorously
shouted down—and then it was off and running.

Everyone loved it when the Beatles did the "Pinwheel Twist," which Paul
had written. Pete Best used to leave his drums and dance right up front, while
Paul—who seemed able to play every instrument—would play the drums. The
girls would go wild over Pete, who looked like a dark-haired version of James
Dean. They'd crowd the stage and sigh in unison, grab their hair and pretend to
swoon. Maybe some of them did swoon: there was precious little air down there.

Cynthia used to come in and stand at the back with a couple of friends from
art school. Only a handful of us knew that she was John's girlfriend and she gave
nothing away. She looked quite stunning with her long blond hair, Bardot-style
sloppy joes and pedal pushers. (Boys used to call them pram pushers.) When I
went back to get a cheese roll, I'd stop and chat with her and nod to her girlfriends. It was all very casual. (It was round about then that I acquired the

nickname of Measles. I think John originated it, because I was everywhere, seen at all the gigs. He told me once that I'd probably been to more clubs than anyone else he knew.)

Cynthia would say, "Hi, Measles. How's it going?"

"Fine," I'd say. "How are you, Cyn?"

It was all very proper and formal, like our dress. Liverpool was a very Catholic area and boys weren't allowed to wear jeans down in the Cavern. Jeans were considered workingmen's gear. Instead, most of us wore Bohemian student gear consisting of polo sweaters and cords. I always wore snappy little suits, nice shirts and ties, a habit I got into down the years. I found that dressed like that I could blend in and get into most places.

Paul's dad, Jim, was a regular visitor to the Cavern. He knew it well. He had often played down there when it was a jazz club. After Mary died, Jim used to do all the shopping and cooking, but he never got home before Paul so often he'd go out during his lunch break to the greengrocer's and the butcher's to buy the makings for the McCartney evening meal at Forthlin Road, then he'd pop down to the Cavern, where the Beatles would be thrashing away onstage. Paddy Delaney, the doorman, would be standing outside in his evening dress in the daytime and he'd say, "Hello, Mr. Mac. How you doin' then? Good crowd in today." And Jim would stand and have the *craic*—the Irish word for "gossip"—before going on down the steps, to push his way through the crowd and plunk a load of pork chops wrapped in white paper on the edge of the stage. Paul would smile but keep playing "I Saw Her Standing There," or whatever. If he were on a break, Jim would say to him, "When you get home, son, put these on regulo five about half-four and they'll be lovely by the time I get in." It was a strange arrangement, but it worked—when Paul remembered.

The Cavern was baking when full and cold when empty. Overall, with the paint peeling and hanging off the damp walls, the whole place had a dank, musty smell of mold, cigarette smoke, pee and the raw bleach that they used to swab it all down. When you came out, you smelled of it.

The Beatles still weren't what we called pop stars. They were just scallywags who played the Cavern who the girls were wild over, though they didn't scream until Beatlemania. They cheered and clapped and shook their heads. Mostly they sat on the edge of the stage and worshipped. There was no special back entrance, no escape route for a band to leave by after a gig. At the end of a show we would break down the gear and then it was a matter of heads down as the Beatles ploughed their way through the crush and up the stairs.

I particularly remember a gig at Litherland Town Hall on October 19, 1961, when it suddenly dawned on me that the Beatles were big. You could see it from the reaction of the fans, from the crowds that mobbed in, by the excited chatter. The show was combined into a supergig with Gerry and the Pacemakers and other groups. The others played what was on the charts, but the Beatles concentrated on rock 'n' roll and rhythm and blues, which gave them a real edge. They closed with "What'd I Say," which they played for a long time. Everyone joined in, shouting their heads off. It was fantastic. We jived and twisted the night away in a frenzy. For me, it marked the moment when they really arrived.

There was a definite buzz even before the Beatles were discovered by a local Liverpool would-be impresario named Brian Epstein and hit the headlines. Bill Harry was a student at Liverpool Art School and a friend of John's. Bill's girlfriend at the time was an attractive girl named Virginia, with big bouffant hair, a great jiver. Bill latched onto the fact that something was happening and after a couple of years of making notes on everything and everyone he launched his tatty little roneo'd magazine, *Mersey Beat,* and he sold it for about fourpence through Brian Epstein's family-owned record store, or at the doors of ballrooms. It carried ads for NEMS, which was the grooviest record store; reviews by Brian Epstein; stories about Rory Sullivan and Johnny Conscience, or Cass and the Casanovas, musicians you never heard of again; some freebie small ads, like the Merseybeats are looking for a new bass player; and, most important, a gig guide of who was playing where and when. It became obligatory to have your own copy. Later, after Brian bought *Music Echo* (to be incorporated into *Disc,* the first magazine to award discs for best-selling records) Bill Harry claimed the title *Mersey Beat* as his own invention and registered it as a trademark.

Brian's personal taste in music was fairly universal. He liked all types of pop and classical, though he could be eclectic. I remember that he was keen on Pierre Boulez, a classical piano player who also composed some very avant-garde pieces. Boulez became conductor of the BBC Symphony Orchestra and the New York Philharmonic. Despite being heavily into the latest trends, Brian still had no idea of what was happening within a stone's throw of his record store until the day a lad came in and asked for a copy of a folk song by the Beat Brothers, "My Bonnie (Lies Over the Ocean)."

When the salesman who served him confessed himself baffled, Brian was called over. He had always stressed that if a customer requested a record they didn't have, then he would order a copy. A search through his catalogues didn't uncover the Beat Brothers, but he did find a version recorded in Hamburg on Polydor by a minor British pop star named Tony Sheridan. The flip side was "When the Saints Go Marching In."

The youth who had made the inquiry—Raymond Jones—informed Brian that Bob Wooler, a local disc jockey and promoter, was playing the record to death on the club circuit. (Despite rumors to the contrary, Raymond Jones existed: not only had I seen him around, but a photograph of him was published in Bob's 1962 biography.) Brian discovered that the "Beat Brothers" were the backing band for Tony Sheridan on the record. Stuart Sutcliffe, who was still in Hamburg, had sent over some copies to George, who had handed one to Bob Wooler on the top of a bus on their way to a gig. Then a steady trickle of fans—mostly girls—started to come in asking for "My Bonnie," which made Brian curious. He was always interested in what people wanted, no matter how obscure. He would often stop and chat to his regulars—including me—to find out what we were listening to.

When I walked in the next Saturday, Brian asked me if I had heard of that record. "Yeah," I said casually. "I've got a copy at home." Now Brian sat up and took notice. He knew me because I was always hanging out, going through the racks in one of the record shops which he had set up within his parents' big furniture stores. Despite my youth, I seemed to know a lot about records. Brian really cared about the customer and about music, and he always had a great selection of new records as well as some interesting older ones. Unlike other owners, he would buy at least one or two of every record issued that week, not just the ones played on the radio or heavily promoted. The archives he built up in this way of rare, little-known records, was remarkable.

"So who exactly are these Beat Brothers?" Brian asked me, puzzled.

"They're my old mates, the Beatles," I said. I didn't tell him that the boys had laughed about how in Germany the label had refused to credit them as the "Beatles" because it sounded too much like a slang word from north German ports, "peedles": a penis—an accidental joke they all, particularly John, appreciated.

When I told Brian that the Beatles were regulars down in the Cavern, which was a few hundred yards from his record store in some old wine cellars beneath a warehouse on Mathew Street, he picked up the telephone in his businesslike way to ask for VIP admission—as if they gave a toss about VIPs. The day he went, November 9, 1961, was to prove very important in the history of pop music.

*

The story of how Brian dropped in at the Cavern and, spoiled for choice, fell in love at first sight with each of the Beatles in turn, is too well documented to repeat here in great detail.

At the start of the session, Bob Wooler had announced, "Mr. Showbiz himself will be coming by shortly!" There were a few raucous catcalls and whistles and then the Beatles launched into another number.

I was there as usual, standing at the back. None of us knew what Brian wanted, or what he expected. I don't think he himself had a clue either, at least not before he walked down the steps and in through the door. He'd told me that he just wanted to check it out for himself, to meet and talk to the boys.

However modestly he later described it on radio and in press interviews, for Brian it was an earth-moving, life-changing moment. The hot, squalid and smelly interconnecting cellars were heaving with shop and office workers and students, mostly girls. As soon as he saw the Beatles through a haze of smoke and sweat, Brian had eyes for nothing else. He was fascinated by their outfits of skintight black leather jeans and zip-fronted black leather bomber jackets, and instantly smitten by the sound they made.

Bob Wooler introduced him: "We are honored to have Mr. Epstein of NEMS, Liverpool's largest record store here this afternoon."

Sticking out like a sore thumb in his pin-striped suit and immaculate white shirt, Brian, who was only twenty-seven but appeared much older because of the formal way he dressed, smiled and blushed to a chorus of catcalls and cheers. At the end of the session he pushed his way through the crush to introduce himself to the Beatles in the drezzy.

George looked him up and down and asked sarcastically, "What brings Mr. Epstein here?"

Brian stammered that he wanted to import two hundred copies of "My Bonnie."

The Beatles grinned sardonically, nodded their heads and, embarrassed, Brian asked if they could go and have a drink. As they trooped out to go across the road to the Grapes, John winked at me. I was dying to go, but I was too young. Instead, I cleared off home. I heard from George, who was pretty casual about it, that they didn't discuss anything important. It was just chat about music and their aspirations. The question of management didn't even come up, though Brian must have started mulling it over almost immediately.

More than anything else, he had fallen in love, not only with the Beatles, but also with the sexual immediacy of live performances. From the moment of that "Road to Damascus" experience, he wanted to be part of that exciting, throbbing, underground world. He returned time and time again, standing quietly in the background and then, after the show, coming forward to brave jibes and sarcasm from George and John. He met Neil Aspinall, Pete Best's quiet friend, who humped their gear and guarded the van. He made inquiries from Bob Wooler, he quizzed record reps, he took advice from his family solicitor, he drank coffee in the Jacaranda and stupidly asked their dumped manager, Allan Williams, how to go about managing them. "Don't touch 'em with a fucking bargepole," Allan is reported to have replied. "They're poison. Anyway, you can't get them a record deal, because they're already signed up to Bert Kaempfert at Polydor in Germany."

All the opinions offered to Brian were negative but he ignored them. For Brian, managing a beat group—as they were then called—promised something that running the record store did not: an escape from crushing boredom.

The topic of conversation was often this wealthy young businessman who was so interested in the Beatles. At the Casbah, Mona Best—who in fact had made the original telephone call that got them their residency at the Cavern—often sarcastically asked what Mr. Epstein had said about his intentions, in a way that suggested it would come to nothing. She felt protective of the group, which she always referred to as "Pete's group," not seeming to notice how much it irritated the others. But it was only because Mona thought of it as her son's group that they got use of a van, a telephone and elegant, brainy Neil to drive them around.

His homework done and his mind made up, Brian arranged a meeting with the Beatles just before Christmas, on December 6, 1961. None of the Beatles took him seriously enough to arrive on time. A stickler for punctuality, Brian was driven almost to distraction before three Beatles wandered in late to his offices, while Paul almost didn't come at all. He had gone home after their lunchtime session at the Cavern and was wallowing in a bathtub well over an hour past the appointed time. Uncharacteristically, Brian kept his cool and when the meeting finally got off the ground two hours late—with a very clean and cheeky Paul now in attendance—Brian almost promised to love, honor and obey them. Astonishingly for someone who didn't know what he was talking about and who had no prior experience in show business (beyond an abortive year as a student at RADA, the Royal Academy of Dramatic Art in London), he said he would get a release from Bert Kaempfert; he would double whatever they were getting from local gigs; he would book them in at major venues further afield; and he would get them a record deal on a major label.

The Beatles looked at each other, shrugged, and in his deadpan way, John held out his hand and said, "Right, where's the contract? I'll sign it."

"My solicitor will draw a fair one up," Brian said smoothly, not revealing how fast his heart was beating beneath his handmade Turnbull and Asser shirt and plain silk tie. (In fact, Brian did have a standard industry contract in his desk drawer, one he had gone out of his way to get ahold of, but some time later, when working on his memoirs in Devon, he admitted that he felt it was too one-sided in his favor, even in an era when musicians were considered scum.) He stood up and shook their hands. "Meanwhile, before you sign with me, to show my good faith, I'll prove to you what I can do."

Afterward I heard about it because they all joked about the meeting, particularly about how Paul wouldn't get out of the bath for Brian Epstein. The details were related over and over again until everyone knew the sequence of events as if it had happened to them.

Brian immediately wrote to someone named Disker, who wrote a music column that reviewed records in the *Liverpool Echo,* the city's daily evening newspaper. He told him all about the Beatles and their growing following of clamoring fans. To Brian's surprise, the letter he received by return post was postmarked London and written on Decca Records' distinctive notepaper. Disker turned out to be Tony Barrow, whose day job was to write sleeve notes for Decca albums. He also moonlighted as a freelance journalist under a nom de plume. Coming originally from Liverpool, he knew what NEMS was and had heard—vaguely—of the Beatles.

Brian put in a trunk call to him at once and they arranged to meet in London to "listen to a record by the Beatles." For Brian, the meeting was initially disappointing. Disker refused to review Brian's record, a poor-quality acetate of a performance at the Cavern, because it wasn't a bona fide record available for sale in shops. No record deal—no review, was his rule. But, even as Brian was returning depressed on the train to Liverpool, Tony Barrow was ensuring that Dick Rowe, head of A & R (artists and repertoire) at Decca, had been informed that the owner of an important store in Liverpool that sold hundreds of their records would appreciate an appointment to pitch a new group he was managing.

News traveled fast that Decca in London was sending a scout to the Cavern to check out the Beatles. It was Wednesday, December 13, 1961, just a week after Brian's meeting with the Beatles in his offices, so things had moved fast. The day before the great man's visit, Bob Wooler had announced that a talent scout was coming up from London, and asked us—the usual Cavern crowd—to be keen and enthusiastic. "Give it your best," he said. "Get everyone to come and put on a big show for our lads."

Brian anguished a bit about what the boys should wear. He personally loved the whole skintight black leather jeans and jacket look, so he suggested that, plus black T-shirts. The Beatles were tickled, because that was what they often wore anyway, along with their winklepickers. But Brian had the last word: "Make sure your shoes are clean. People notice, you know."

John thought this was hilarious. "We're just a bunch o'greasers, you know, Brian," he said. "Scruffs. Dunno if you can clean us up much."

I think that the others did clean their shoes, but John didn't. However, their moptop hair was clean and shining; only Pete stuck to the old rock 'n' roll DA. I don't think he ever changed it.

There were only two trains a day between Liverpool and London at the time, one in the morning and one in the evening. The scout, Mike Smith, an assistant A & R man from Decca, took the sleeper, checked into a hotel in Lime Street and then came to the Cavern for the lunchtime and evening shows. He didn't introduce himself, neither did he stick out like a sore thumb, but everyone still knew. There was an undercurrent of curiosity and excitement. By then, we'd all been primed. Fans and friends crammed into the cellar to ensure the two best shows ever. The Beatles leaped about, rocked like dervishes and gave it plenty of *wellie,* as we say up north.

Mike Smith wasn't knocked out, but he was impressed enough to tell his boss that he should audition the group. This was arranged for New Year's Day 1962, one of the coldest winters on record. While Brian traveled southward in the comfort of a heated railway carriage, Neil drove the boys down the day before in the back of a freezing van through a snowstorm. The uncomfortable journey took ten hours and they arrived battered, cold and hoarse. After they had settled into their modest hotel off Russell Square, they roamed around a snowed-in city that soon lived up to expectations when a drug dealer accosted them in the street and offered to sell them some pot. They ran a mile. (As a matter of fact, this was the only thing about their entire trip that I heard about on their return, and it was George who told me, "It was just like Hamburg, Tone.")

The next day, they fumbled through fifteen songs, chosen by Brian to reflect their full repertoire, and that was it. Dick Rowe said he would let them know.

Returning home, cold and depressed, the Beatles crouched in the back of the freezing van and brooded. They brooded because they felt the studio environment didn't allow them to shine, they said that Brian's choice of songs was wrong—only three of which were Lennon-McCartney numbers—and they had been dismissed with little comment or clue as to Dick Rowe's overall impression. Brian, on the other hand, smoking a cigarette in the comfort of the train, was upbeat and confident. Had they known that Dick Rowe intended auditioning another group, Brian Poole and the Tremeloes, before making up his mind, they would have been even more nervous.

No one said a word about what had happened on their return. It wasn't the sort of thing they would brag about, as if talking about it would bring them bad luck. If anything, they acted as if it was not going to happen. In fact, on their immediate return there was a general air of gloom about them, so much so that nobody dared ask them how it went. However, on the way to a gig in the new year there was a bit of a postmortem. I heard John mumble something about the choice of songs being wrong. Paul said they were in the studio just over an hour, during which time they recorded fifteen songs. "It was too rushed," he said. George was embarrassed over his rendition of the "Sheik of Araby." Paul did "Besame Mucho" at Brian's insistence. He muttered that it was a silly ballad. "We should have just done our own stuff," he said. "It's what we're all about, and at least it's different."

Despite this, Tony Barrow certainly thought they were in. Writing as Disker in the *Liverpool Echo* almost a month later, on January 27, he reported: "Latest episode in the success story of Liverpool's instrumental group, The Beatles: Commenting upon the outfit's recent recording test, Decca disc producer Mike Smith tells me that he thinks The Beatles are great. He has a continuous tape of their audition performances that runs for over thirty minutes and he is convinced that his label will be able to put The Beatles to good use. I'll be keeping you posted. . . ."

This little write-up was what Brian was waiting for to finally convince the boys that he was the right manager for them. By now he had what he believed to be a fair contract drawn up; he had been around to talk to Paul and George's parents and had even braved Mimi's skepticism, winning her over with a mixture of charm, earnestness and flattery, first having taken care to park his big, shiny car in the drive of course, where she could see it. Then he went to the Casbah where they were playing that night, had a word with Mo Best, and got them all to sign on the dotted line. The only one who didn't sign was Brian himself. Perhaps he was flustered and forgot. Personally, I think he didn't want to be that committed. He said a gentleman's word was binding. On another occasion, he told me that the contract wasn't worth the paper it was printed on, but I didn't know what he meant.

He was right. It didn't matter. The contract wasn't legal, anyway, because Paul and George were both under twenty-one.

🐾

In those days the whole pop music industry was all hit-and-miss—just like the early TV show, *Juke Box Jury*—and to a certain extent it probably still is. It's something I beat the drum a bit over, but these days, when the head honchos at the music-industry conglomerates listen they don't hear hit or miss, great songs or great music: all they hear is *product*. When the Beatles were at their peak, records had to sell in the half millions before they hit the top ten, where often they stayed for weeks. Today a record just has to sell a few thousand before it charts. Most of them fade unmemorably, as fast as melting snow.

The apocryphal legend that much-maligned Dick Rowe of Decca screwed up by uttering one short comment never made much sense to me. He reputedly stated that guitar groups "are going out of fashion" when he famously turned the Beatles down in favor of Brian Poole and the Tremeloes. That quote, which followed poor Dick around to the day he died and even beyond the grave, was unlikely. At the time of the Beatles' audition in January 1962, Decca Records had decided to sign only one of the two groups they had under consideration, and they signed the Trems—a guitar group. They signed them instead of the Beatles simply because the Trems lived closer. They came from just down the road in Dagenham, Essex—just outside London—which was a great deal more convenient for meetings and rehearsals than Liverpool. Just as Allan Williams had found a couple of years earlier when he had tried to persuade Bruno Koschmeider to book the Beatles, most blinkered London-based record executives dismissed the rest of the country. The idea that a hot group could come from the bleak north, where any telephone call was long distance and usually subject to numerous delays, was unthinkable.

For a long time we fondly thought Brian was brilliant, but the reality was he had huge gaps in his knowledge of how the industry worked. Andrew Loog Oldham, later to manage the Stones, and a youngster who hustled the Beatles press-agent gig out of Brian Epstein when he was still only eighteen years old, neatly summed up this attitude. Barely out of the famous public school where he'd been educated, he was an enthusiastic amateur in love with pop. When asked how he came to get the influential job of press agent to the Beatles, he said, "Because I asked."

Andrew was in Birmingham at the taping of the TV show, *Thank Your Lucky Stars,* while repping Jet Harris and Tony Meehan—the ex-Shadows—who were massive. The Beatles did "Please Please Me" and Andrew couldn't believe how powerful it was. He went over to John Lennon and told him he was very good and was amused when John instantly agreed with him: "I know."

Andrew said, "So I asked him who repped them and he pointed over his shoulder to this straight, public school–looking guy in a suit, overcoat and paisley scarf who was chatting in a corner to Ringo." It was Brian Epstein, who, to Andrew, seemed a most unlikely manager. However, he approached him and Brian instantly hired him as the Beatles' press agent.

No, guitar groups being on the way out doesn't play. The Trems had three guitars—just like the Beatles. If anything, guitar groups were coming in. The only real difference was that the Trems had Brian Poole out front with no instrument. "And that's how it should be. Just like Cliff Richard and the Shadows," said Brian Poole's mum in a newspaper interview. A year later, despite scoring a three-week number one with "Do You Love Me" and a top five hit with a cover of "Twist and Shout!" Decca dumped the Trems. Mike Smith, the producer at Decca who liked the Beatles, went with the Trems to CBS (now Sony), where they were very successful.

The Dick Rowe legend seems to have originated with a letter written by Len Wood, managing director of EMI, on December 17, 1963, to a journalist, explaining how the Beatles ended up with them. He states: "Dick Rowe's . . . reaction was that electric guitars were now 'old hat' and he was not interested in the Beatles." Well, if Dick Rowe did say that, it's possible he was thinking of the huge success of "Telstar" with its wonderful quirky production and use of electric organ; but, two years on, and secondhand at that, did Len Wood make this up as a good story?

Everyone seemed to be in a quandary over this guitar group business. We all wondered—which Beatle should be the leader? Who would be out front? John or Paul? Even George Harrison was a possibility. It didn't take us too long to figure out what we all knew anyway: they were indivisible.

🎸

Before Brian even got to see George Martin, he had spent several months growing ever more despondent, being turned down by all the big labels in London, including Philips/Fontana, CBS, Pye and Polydor (U.K.). He always sat the Beatles down in a local milk bar on his return from London to tell them frankly what had happened. He tried to remain positive during these postmortems, even when they started muttering among themselves that quite possibly he was all frock and no knickers. This is a northern expression, which means all show. In Brian's case, it hit home and he was deeply upset.

Annoyed because she felt she'd been sidelined in favor of "a queer Jew boy," Indian-born Mo Best told Neil Aspinall that the boys had better watch their arses. Rumors had flown around ever since Brian had made a misjudgment and been beaten up by a queer-basher he had tried to pick up in Liverpool. Normally, Brian would prowl further afield to Manchester or Southport with friends like Peter Brown, who he had brought in to manage a new NEMS shop. But sometimes, fueled by amphetamines, Brian liked the risk of risk itself. He was a gambler.

After mentally playing eeny-meeny-miney-mo in his mind with the Beatles, wondering which one he could truly fall in love with, with his inbuilt sense of masochism, Brian had settled on John as the object of his adoration. John was angry, he was given to fits of violence, had a cruel tongue and knew how to play

Brian, how to bring him to the brink of hopeful anticipation—then destroy him with a word. Even in my youthful naiveté, I had noticed that Brian would rarely look John in the face, that he would glance down and flush while John looked at him with a tight, wolfish grin.

Brian, who lived very comfortably with his parents in one of Liverpool's wealthier suburbs less than a mile from Mimi's home, secretly rented a small love nest on Falkner Street in the city center. It wasn't long before we found out about it. It became the in-joke to ask, "Has he asked you up there yet?" But despite the gossip and innuendo that swirled about him, with the exception of John, we were always very courteous to Brian. At first, until we got to know him, we formally called him Mr. Epstein, then it was Brian. The Beatles called him Eppy when they discussed him among themselves, as in "Will Eppy go along with this or that?" Or, "Where's Eppy?" Despite the superficial respect—and there was always respect—it didn't stop the nudge-nudge giggling type of gossip.

When George went to Brian's home—not to the flat but to his mother Queenie's house—and spent the day there, everyone was smirking and saying, "Oooh, George has been there *all day!* What do you think they've been up to?" When we saw George, he was mercilessly teased. Now George always appeared quiet and laid back, but he had quite a temper. He flew off the handle, snarled that he and Brian just talked and he wouldn't discuss it. Eventually we shut up about it.

5

Even though Brian had been unable to land a record deal, in April 1962 he issued a press release that grandly stated that he had arranged a European tour for the Beatles. In fact, it was a six-week season back in the trenches of Hamburg's notorious Star Club. To make a splash, the boys flew from Liverpool Airport at Speke. In those early days of flying, very few people that we knew ever flew anywhere, so this was pretty special, if hair-raising. The local airline had the wonderful name of StarDust, or Starlight Airlines, run by a Mr. Wilson, who made a fortune as a rag-and-bone man. It became a running joke that his planes, old Dakotas, were made from bits of scrap iron. People used to laugh that they'd fall apart, and it really did happen. Once, when we took off from Speke, the door fell off into the River Mersey. Everyone was terrified, waiting to be sucked out of the door. (When telling this story later, John used to say that it was a window that fell out; it wasn't. It was a door.)

The night before they went to Germany, they had a farewell gig in the Cavern. It was one of the most crowded nights ever, one of the best I can remember. On the actual question of "going to Germany" not a lot was said. The Beatles were very cagey; people *were* very cagey back then. There were no farewell hugs and kisses, no tears, no fare-thee-wells. So many things were private and left unsaid. It was just "See ya," and that was it. (Which makes the screaming, shrieking, sobbing, dawn of Beatlemania that was about to break all the more re-markable.)

Paul and John left together, but George wasn't well and left the next day, ac-companied by Brian, who returned a week later. They arrived in Hamburg to the news that Stuart Sutcliffe had died of a brain hemorrhage, and they were devas-tated, especially John. Stuart had been his best friend. The news traveled back to Liverpool. He was our age and people our age just didn't die of strokes. At the time, nobody knew the reason for Stuart's death, though he had suffered from terrible headaches for a long time. An autopsy requested by his mother would re-veal an old depression in his skull. It was likely that a brutal kicking in the head by a Teddy Boy gang in 1959 had fractured his skull. The Silver Beetles had been ambushed by Teds in the carpark of Litherland Town Hall. The lads had scattered and run for it, but Stuart, who was slight and pretty, was caught and kicked into unconsciousness by steel-capped boots.

John had gone back for him later when the coast was clear and found him unconscious, his head bloody. He managed to get him home, but Stuart said he didn't want a fuss and didn't go to a doctor or report it to the police. It was after that that his headaches and depressed moods started. I was shocked by his death though not as deeply affected as the Beatles. Offstage and on, I had seen Stuart around, but still didn't know him that well. The last time I had seen him had been at one of the Beatles gigs at the Cavern, when he and Astrid, who was over from Germany visiting, stood at the back with me, listening to the music. They were quiet and entirely wrapped up in each other, each of them standing out because of their fine-boned almost ethereal beauty.

I was busy with farm work and exams at school, but still dropped by the NEMS store on Saturday afternoons to listen to records and gossip. Brian liked to use people he trusted as sounding boards and even though I was just a record-crazy kid who dropped in to his record stores, who happened to be a friend of all the Beatles, and who happened to act as an unpaid gofer, in no way at all was I a close confidant of his. Consequently, although he appeared happy to talk about records and technical stuff, Brian didn't tell me that he had almost run out of op-tions—why would he?

But in Hunts Cross, some weeks after the Decca audition, we were still agog for news, and we pestered George to find out more. He told us that a letter from Decca, turning them down, was burning a hole in the desk drawer where Brian had concealed it. It preyed on Brian's mind until eventually he steeled himself to tell the boys they'd been rejected. He looked so ill that they were surprisingly philosophical, perhaps to make him feel better. "Never mind, Brian," John said, displaying a rare degree of sympathy. "There's more companies you can go to. At least now we've got a decent bit of tape you can play to other people."

Brian hated to lose and refused to give in, so it was in an edgy mood that he went down to London in May 1962. He went to Decca again and tried to get them to see sense. Instead, he ended up losing his temper. So did they. Words were exchanged. Everyone knows how Brian got in the final word before he stormed out: "My boys will be bigger than Elvis Presley," he said. Naturally, the Decca executives laughed, but not for long.

Everyone also heard the details of how after a restless night, Brian decided that he would finance a record himself, selling it through his stores. Accordingly, he set off to discuss this; but the producer he'd chosen was late and, running on speed, Brian stormed off yet again. Two abortive meetings later with two more labels, Brian was panicking. He had schlepped up and down from Liverpool to London some twenty times, like Twenty-Flight Rock. He was tired and there was almost nowhere left to try.

It was in an even more depressed and desperate mood that he made his way to Oxford Street, where he met up with Bob Boast, manager of the big HMV record shop. He had met Bob the previous year, before he had even known the Beatles existed, when he had been on a retail-management course run by Deutsche Grammophon in Hamburg. After apologizing that he couldn't make an introduction to anyone really useful, Bob suggested that Brian cut some acetates instead of lugging the cumbersome reel-to-reels about. Brian at once agreed and Bob led Brian upstairs to the small EMI public studio, where he passed him over to the in-house engineer, Jim Foy.

While the 78s were being cut the engineer remarked that some of the tunes sounded fresh and original. "Yes, they have never been heard before," Brian said. "They were written by Mr. Lennon and Mr. McCartney of the Beatles."

Foy smiled at the formality, but on learning that they didn't have a music publisher, he suggested that Brian play the discs to Ardmore & Beechwood, EMI's publishing company, which very conveniently was on the top floor of the same building. Within five minutes, the publishing general manager, Sid Colman, had come downstairs to the studio and was listening to these original songs.

"Yes, I like them," Sid Colman said. "We'd be interested in discussing the publishing."

Despite his careful research, this was the first time that Brian had come across the concept of song publishing. He nodded cautiously. He needed time to think, to do more research. To gain time, he said that he was more interested in a record deal for his boys.

"Have you been to Parlophone?" Sid Colman asked, mentioning a small EMI label.

Brian had been to two of EMI's prestigious labels: Columbia, which had Cliff Richard and the Shadows, and HMV, which had Johnny Kidd and the Pirates, one of the most influential groups in England at the time, but he hadn't considered EMI's Parlophone label, which was better known for its comedy records. In fact, Parlophone was home to Adam Faith, who was a huge pop star, but that appeared to be a gap in Brian's knowledge. He felt he had no options left and arranged an appointment with George Martin, who was head of A & R for Parlophone. After George listened to the newly cut discs, he didn't say yes or no, only that he would let Brian know and that seemed to be that. Disappointed, Brian returned home to Liverpool. Nearly three months later, on May 9, at his own instigation, Brian returned to London, where he met George Martin at EMI's famed Abbey Road Studios. Whatever else happened during that meeting, an appointment was set up for George to meet the Beatles in person and audition them on June 6.

After the meeting, Brian sent two telegrams. One was to the Beatles who were still in Hamburg, which read: CONGRATULATIONS BOYS. EMI REQUEST RECORDING SESSION. PLEASE REHEARSE NEW MATERIAL.

The other telegram went to Bill Harry at *Mersey Beat* magazine in Liverpool and read: HAVE SECURED CONTRACT FOR BEATLES TO RECORDED [*sic*] FOR EMI ON PARLAPHONE [*sic*] LABEL 1ST RECORDING DATE SET FOR JUNE 6TH—BRIAN EPSTEIN.

♛

From that point, a mystery evolved that has never been properly explained. Was it an audition—or was it a proper recording session? In other words, had Brian procured a record contract for his protégés?

The big mystery is that exceptionally and against all EMI policy—indeed, against his own policy—George Martin did put the wheels in motion to offer the Beatles a recording contract on May 18. This was typed, forward-dated to June 4 and sent to Brian for his signature. Brian signed it in record time and it was back on George's desk on June 5—all before George Martin had set eyes on the Beatles or had them in the studio.

"Don't be late!" he told Brian, confirming the details of the June 6 session.

Legends and myths are strange and moveable things. The press always says that as far as the public is concerned, when it comes to a toss-up between truth and myth, always print the myth. It's safer! But on that date with destiny was George Martin *auditioning* four "berks" from Liverpool, nothing more, nothing less, as he said? Or—as the paperwork says—was he *recording* John, Paul, George and Pete for a bona fide forthcoming record release?

Perhaps it will remain a mystery, for Brian is dead. To this day Sir George Martin insists that the June 6 date was an audition. Despite what anybody says, Brian was worldly enough to offer bribes and pay off people. He was pragmatic and he had done it before, when he'd been blackmailed and threatened because of ill-judged homosexual liaisons. Living on the edge as he did, Brian was always a contradiction. He was a fiercely loyal and honorable friend to those he loved, and ruthless toward those he despised. He was shy to the point of blushing and stammering, and theatrical to the point of ranting and frothing at the mouth. He considered investments carefully but was an addicted gambler. Above all, he had learned to do what had to be done and loved the rush it gave him.

6

On the blistering hot and thundery night of June 9, 1962, the Beatles returned to the Cavern and a heroes' welcome. There was a party atmosphere all
day in Mathew Street with long queues of giggling fans sitting along the curb or
on the steps leading into different premises as they chatted together or listened
to music from their portable radios. Local workers had seen nothing like it and
wondered what was going on. When the boys eventually arrived, with just me
and Neil to look after them, a tidal wave of screaming girls surged toward us and
we barely made it intact down the worn stones steps into the depths of the shad-
owy cellars.

A packed crowd of nine hundred somehow squeezed into the club that night
and for the following days when the Beatles were booked solidly, twice a day.
Some of the best "Cavern" gigs I can remember weren't actually in the Cavern
itself but on ferries crossing the Mersey. Or rather, they were so-called riverboat
shuffles which put out to sea on the *Royal Iris*, which was also known as "The
Fish and Chips Boat." The shuffles been running for some years, billed as dance
cruises, but the first one with the Beatles playing had been the previous year, on
Friday night, August 25, 1961, when they supported jazzman, Acker Bilk,
whose big hit, "Stranger on the Shore," was still in the top ten after about six
months. As usual, I helped carry their gear and got aboard free. The engines

would race and we'd pull away from the docks, heading out downstream past New Brighton, to Liverpool Bay and into the full swell of the waves.

The second shuffle, again with Acker Bilk, was a year later on Friday, July 6, 1962, shortly after the Beatles' triumphant return to Liverpool. This time we went all the way to the Isle of Man, a voyage that was several hours of unmitigated music, dancing and vomiting. Pizzas and hamburgers hadn't yet crossed the Atlantic; tomato ketchup and Coca-Cola were rare commodities. The standard fare was fish and chips cooked in lard and served up in greasy newspaper wrappings, liberally swamped with salt and malt vinegar and washed down with warm beer or lemonade.

We went on many more shuffles, once with Johnny Kidd and the Pirates—who looked fantastic, their matelot-striped pirates' gear and deep-cuffed sea boots in keeping with the riverboat theme. I can still smell the salty, oily, greasy smell, and feel my stomach heave as on those hot summer nights when we hit the choppy cross-currents of the Irish Sea. Everyone would be dancing away in a frenzy, the band would be playing—looking green—and the first passengers would be off to throw up in the gullies. A few minutes later, they'd be lurching about almost upright again, grinning at their heroism, swigging beer and ready to heave again. Everyone was seasick: me, the lads—all of us. Ringo, who was the worst one with his delicate stomach, would drop his drumsticks first and then rush for the side where he'd retch until he was able to return to the fray. Then it was the turn of John, Paul and George. Only Acker Bilk seemed able to keep going, despite the amount of cider he drank. It was awful, but fun.

When Eppy, or "Brian," as I always called him to his face, signed the Beatles, he started looking around to build up a small and loyal team to look after "his boys," as he called them. He had already taken to Neil Aspinall because they were close in age and background. Neil was tidy, respectably dressed and, when he qualified, would have a proper career as an accountant—but it wasn't as much fun as being around a band. So it wasn't long before Neil dumped his accountancy course and went to work for Brian as the Beatles' road manager. No one knew then how long the Beatles might last and pop bands were notoriously ephemeral. Apart from John, who had been convinced almost since birth that he was destined for fame, Brian was the only one who realized that things were about to go big very quickly. Even though he would often remark that pop fans were very fickle, in his heart—and fueled by large quantities of speed—he was exhilarated by what was happening. With remarkable vision, he would also convince Mal Evans, the part-time bouncer at the Cavern, that being a roadie for NEMS was a solid career, one with a real future.

I had left school that June of 1962 and started a draftsman's course at the local Ford plant. One evening I was helping out at a Beatles' gig in Liverpool when Brian came up to me and said, in his very public-school voice, "Tony, how much do they pay you at Ford motor cars?"

"Five guineas, Brian," I told him.

"Hmmm, yes, I see," said Brian. "Well, if I paid you ten guineas a week would you come and work for me? You can carry on what you're doing with the boys and when you're not doing that, you would work for me in the offices at NEMS."

"I don't know if I can, Brian," I said. "The music business is a bit dodgy really. Working at Ford is a career." It amazes me now that at such a tender age I was thinking along those lines. I suppose I was reflecting what everyone's dad thought, and what my mum had drummed into my head. A career was very important when so many people were out of work. I was sixteen years old and I had just left school with a clutch of O levels. I still wanted to go to agricultural college and had applied, but Mum wanted me to go to university, though I wasn't old enough. We decided that I would make up my mind when I was seventeen or eighteen, and meanwhile I would get some work experience. Ford Motor Company hired me as a trainee draftsman and sent me to North East Liverpool Technical College to study to be a layout inspector, one of those people in clean white overalls who check all the blueprints for the designs of the new cars—which were made on the factory floor by workers in blue overalls. However, shortly after I started, I had another accident and broke a finger in a door so I couldn't draw. I was getting sick pay of five guineas a week—five pounds and five shillings—which was a great deal more than my pocket money had been, so I was quite content.

I told Brian all this and he mulled it over in his friendly schoolmaster way, before coming up with a sort of contingency plan. "Well, if it all goes wrong you can work in one of the record shops. How about that?"

"Well I dunno," I told him. "I'll have to ask me mum."

"Tell her to come to see me," said Brian. "I'll be glad to talk to her."

My mum knew that Brian was Mr. Epstein, and that despite his youth, he was respected in Liverpool, and a man of his word. So she went along to the store and, as promised, he showed her around the office, all the while explaining to her the kind of work I would be doing. With his frankness and charm he persuaded her that this was a proper business on a proper footing and I wouldn't be selling my soul to the devil.

"If it doesn't work out, he can leave anytime he wants," Brian said. "He can always return to Ford, I'm sure they would be pleased to give him his position back. I'd have a word with them. But, as far as I am concerned Tony has a job with me for as long as he wants it."

That was the sort of man Brian was, a stickler for doing the right thing, for keeping his word. Mum left his offices content to let me start a career in "artiste's management," as Brian earnestly referred to it. Over the years Brian and my mum got to be quite close and he always referred to her as a lovely woman.

To illustrate how close we were as a group of friends and families, my mum knitted the Beatles the famous long black scarves that they wore on the front cover of the "Twist and Shout" EP. The Beatles had originally bought similar black scarves in Hamburg, which they wore with their very uncool long black leather overcoats. (We said they looked like the Gestapo!) I don't know what happened to those scarves—probably they were nicked by fans—but the lads were attached to them. They must have said something around Mum, because the next thing was she got out her knitting needles and balls of black wool, and started knitting away. My Auntie Margaret from Rhyl even got in on the act. She crocheted the Beatles a set of very colorful waistcoats.

I went to work for Brian just after the Beatles had landed their first recording contract and before "Love Me Do" was released. It was the calm before the storm, a time when none of us (except John, of course) were really quite sure how things would pan out. It became one of my jobs to take the boys' money to them on Fridays. I would ride the train all over the country to wherever they were playing and hang out for the weekend. If they played close to home, in Manchester for example, we would go for the evening and come home after the gig.

Despite rumors about what went on, I never saw a single orgy in those early days on the road. I was still an innocent kid who went to bed relatively early, if I wasn't going out, that is. I certainly hadn't been to Germany where it had been girls, girls, girls. On their return from Hamburg Paul said, "It was a sex shock . . . suddenly you'd have a girlfriend who was a stripper. If you had hardly ever had sex in your life before, this was fairly formidable. We got a swift baptism of fire into the sex scene. We got our education in Hamburg." They described how George lost his virginity in the squalid room they all shared while they pretended to be asleep. Paul said he had once walked in on John and seen a bottom bobbing up and down with a girl underneath him. It was very teenage and unself-conscious.

It would be remarkable after such experiences if the boys suddenly became Puritans back in England—and they didn't—but despite later legends to the contrary, and even according to the Beatles' own vamped-up recollections, for a long time English girls didn't throw themselves at pop stars. The Pill didn't exist, free sex meant pregnancy and shame. Girls hadn't yet learned to be tough groupies, though pretty soon the thunderbolt would hit with a bang as loud as an atom bomb exploding among the nation's teenagers. When sexual mores did change, it was with breathtaking speed. Within six months it went from, "No-no-no, I'm a good girl I am," to "Yeah, okay. Your place or mine?"

The bookings continued, at first mostly around the Liverpool and Merseyside area. Nearly every day there were two lunchtime sessions and usually one at a different venue in the evening, when they would play two hours nonstop. The lads had hardly any time off, and few real holidays until they broke up some years later. But despite all this frantic activity and a nice regular income— which thanks to Brian's efforts on their behalf, was more than they had ever earned before—the Beatles kept asking, "Hey, what about our record? When are we going to make it?"

Unfortunately, Brian didn't have an answer. Then he got a call from George Martin, one that perhaps didn't surprise him. George said he wanted to fix a recording session without Pete Best, who would have to be replaced by a session drummer. It's the accepted story that Pete couldn't hold a steady beat. After forty years, Pete Best himself says he has never got to the bottom of it. He says he never did believe that he wasn't good enough because clearly he had been good enough for two years, and there'd never been any complaints about the style of drumming he'd named "atom beat." (What's more, Brian even offered to form another group around him and said he would promote him heavily.)

Thus it was, pale-faced and tense, that Brian sat at his desk and gazed into space on August 16, 1962. John had just sprung on him the depressing news that Cynthia was pregnant and they had to get married. This wasn't in Brian's plans for the group nor in his private dreams for John, but meanwhile, his first onerous task was to fire Pete Best. Despite Pete's belief that things were fine and dandy, they hadn't been good for some time. The rest of the group had given him several clues about the way things were heading by frequently keeping him in the dark and not giving him tidbits of news as they came in. Even back in January they had decided not to mention to Pete that Decca had turned them down, but none of them had it in them to come out into the open and tell him to go.

I was around them as they passed the buck back and forth to each other. "You tell him—no, you tell him!" Nobody asked my opinion, but neither did they conceal it, and I could see that it was an issue. Finally, they told Brian it was his job as their manager. Glad to get that piece of dirty work out of the way, John telephoned Ringo Starr at Butlin's Holiday Camp where he was doing a season with Rory Storm and the Hurricanes, to ask if he would join the Beatles. Ringo was ready to move on and agreed at once.

Brian put in a call to the Best's rambling Victorian home and early on the following Saturday morning Pete was on his way into the center of Liverpool, driven by Neil Aspinall. When he went upstairs to Brian's office, instead of going with him, unusually Neil elected to lurk outside in the car. For some reason Pete thought Brian merely wanted to discuss bookings with him. This might have been the case once when Pete was responsible for most of the Beatles bookings in the pre-Brian era, but hadn't been so for a long time. They chatted a little until, running out of reasons to delay the words, white-faced and anguished Brian blurted: "The boys want you out of the group. They don't think you're a good enough drummer."

Pete told Neil that when he heard those words, he felt sick. He couldn't at first understand that he was being sacked. Cutting through his bewilderment, the phone on Brian's desk rang. It was Paul, asking if Brian had done the deed. Quickly, Brian said, "I can't talk now. Peter's here with me in the office."

Carefully, Brian didn't mention that while Ringo had already accepted John's offer to join the Beatles, he'd said he couldn't leave Rory Storm for another three days. He asked Pete to stay on for the next couple of dates. Pete was so numbed by such treachery that he agreed to continue until he was replaced. When Brian stood up to see Pete out, he said that he would be happy to build another group around him.

Outside on the pavement, Pete told Neil Aspinall what had just happened, then took himself off to drown his misery in the Grapes. By the end of the afternoon, drunk and embittered by their treachery, he decided to cut himself off altogether from the Beatles and in fact never played with them again. Pete was so upset that in the pub he gave a blow-by-blow account of his conversation with Brian to whoever would listen, and in no time, it was general knowledge in the street. The grapevine system was so remarkable that there were few secrets in Liverpool and the Grapes—hangout of so many musicians—was one of the last places that anyone with a secret to keep would have chosen to go. By the time I heard it officially, I could have quoted the scene in Brian's office, chapter and verse.

Left to his own devices, Neil returned to Mo Best to break the news to her. The situation between Neil and Mo and the Bests was rather complex. Neil had lived with John and Mo Best and their two sons, Pete and Rory, for some time. The previous month, on July 21, Mo had given birth to a third son, a baby boy she named Roag. It was an open secret that Neil was Roag's father.

It had caused some dismay among fans and musicians alike when after three years, giving no real reason, Mo closed down the Casbah Club at the end of June. We had all—the Beatles, including me—helped paint the walls of the scruffy old cellar when it first opened back in 1959 and the Beatles had played their final gig there on June 24, 1962. Everyone felt the Casbah was their club, a place where they could hang out.

Neil now found himself in the horns of a dilemma: who should he remain loyal to—Pete or the Beatles? He said he tried to do both. Pete didn't play out the last few bookings and Johnny Hutch of the Big Three stood in on drums. Meanwhile, Neil continued acting as roadie for the Beatles, but when Ringo started, Neil refused to set up the drums for some weeks. Often that task fell to me when I was there. Nobody had said very much, but it was clear that there had been an amputation and a falling out. The whisper that was going the rounds was that Neil had already split up with Mo and so would find Pete's presence awkward.

The Casbah was closed but I saw Pete around. He buttonholed me because he knew I was close to the Beatles and Brian, and complained about what he perceived as being stabbed in the back.

"I can play as well as Ringo," he said. "Brian even offered to put a band around me, so I can't be that bad, can I?"

I was uncomfortable and sort of shuffled about and listened. When Pete asked me if I knew what they'd been saying about him and if I'd heard why he'd been sacked, all I could say was, "I dunno."

The truth about Pete Best's firing is probably quite simple. The Beatles just didn't like him and said so to each other and in front of me. He wasn't as quick and sharp and funny as they were. Both Paul and John said he wasn't one of them, that he wasn't "studenty" or intellectual. He tended to be sullen and morose. Pete told me that he had hated it in Germany. He moaned all the time and he didn't hang out with them in Liverpool. He used to stay at home and snog on the sofa with his girlfriend while his mum was out and about, the life and soul of every party from one end of the Mersey to the other. Even after he joined the Beatles, while they hung out and wound down with a few drinks, Pete would go home with his girl after the gig. He wasn't really a joiner. I'm sure that was more of a problem than his suggested lack of talent. In all the years I had been around him, I didn't feel I knew him—nobody did. Ringo, on the other hand, was laid back and easy to get on with. He was funny and outgoing and he fitted in. The Beatles had known him in Hamburg, they'd seen him around on the scene and he had even stood in on drums a couple of times when Pete, who was often ill, didn't show up.

♛

Ringo was older than the others and held in awe, always so self-contained and cool the way he dressed, in leather or sharp suits, rings on every finger, his gold chains, his flashy cars. When nobody else had two brass farthings to rub together, Ringo had money in his pocket and all the right gear. He came from the Dingle, the dockside slums of Liverpool. A succession of childhood illnesses put him into the hospital for over a year. With little formal schooling, he fell behind in reading and writing and never caught up. As a kid he'd had to run with some pretty dangerous Teddy Boy gangs in order to survive—as he said, "We had to. You needed the protection." He'd been beaten up many times, too. Despite this, he was droll and laid back. He joked that he only joined the Beatles because they offered him five pounds a week more than Rory Storm—or was it ten? "Five!" the others would chorus whenever Ringo brought it up in interviews. Then he'd say, "Well, where is it then? Let's be having it. Who's got me five pounds?"

An important point where Brian was concerned was that, unlike Pete, Ringo was willing to dress like the Beatles and have his huge Teddy Boy quiff cut off. What no one anticipated was the fans' outrage when they found out that Pete had been dumped. They adored him, he was their own "mean, moody and magnificent" local hero. America had Elvis—Liverpool had Pete Best.

The fans kicked up a huge fuss and for a while it looked as if a huge mistake had been made. People were openly saying that it was Pete who had made the Beatles, not John, Paul or George, and Mona Best was delighted. She got on the phone and tried to drum up even more support in the press. Factions formed; hundreds of girls marched in the streets waving placards. They massed outside NEMS offices and chanted: *"Pete forever, Ringo never!"*

Brian and I and some of the other staff, like Alistair Taylor, would stand at the window and look down, stepping back a little so we couldn't be seen—or, as Brian said, in case a stone was thrown—and listen to the outrage. Brian always looked very worried. He would bite his lip and wonder if he had done the right thing.

"They really seem to like Pete, you know," he said. "Suppose they all turn on the Beatles?"

"No, they won't do that," Alistair said. "Let them march. They're enjoying themselves. Anyway, it's good publicity."

He was right. The newspapers were filled with it, and it seemed to stimulate even more controversy. Fights broke out, the Beatles were assaulted on stage and dragged into the audience, George got a black eye and Ringo had to run for his life and be protected from a baying mob. John gloried in the rough and tumble. It was like the old days in Hamburg, though none of us in the "inner circle"—or the Beatles themselves—expected this violent reaction. Things stayed at boiling point for a long time and Brian remained very anxious.

The heat was taken out only when the Beatles had their first hit in December and took off in the rest of the country. No one had heard of Pete outside of Liverpool. The drummer who was up there on the posters, on television and on the front pages of the national newspapers would be Ringo.

Unexpectedly, I came to have a lot in common with Ringo, because our girl-friends were best friends, both of them closer in age to me. Maureen Cox, who became Ringo's wife, had started out dating Rory Storm's guitarist, "Johnny Guitar." It wasn't long before this girl, who was small like Ringo, with jet-black hair, a heavy fringe and heavily kohled eyes, switched her allegiance to the Beatles. She and her mate, Lorraine Flyte, used to sit right on the edge of the stage at the Cavern, and in all that sea of faces, Ringo spotted pretty, bouffant-haired Maureen and fancied her immediately. Not all the fights between fans were over Pete's sacking. Many were between girls who had been scrapping for some time over the individual Beatles with whom they were "in lurve."

Ringo and Maureen—we called her Mitch—had to pretend that they didn't know each other. Giggling conspiratorially, Lorraine would help Mitch hide under a blanket in the back of Ringo's car and wait for him to come out during a break. When Ringo drove away after a concert, he would wait until they were several blocks away before Maureen would crawl into the front seat. But one night, a fan spotted Ringo getting into his car and chased him down the road. She managed to open the car door and saw Maureen. She dragged her out, scratching and kicking her on the cobbles of Mathew Street. In no time, a dozen girls surrounded them.

Suddenly being a Beatle girlfriend went from exciting and fun to a potential nightmare. All this was a shock to Maureen. She was a convent girl who had gone on to work in a hairdresser's with the unlikely name of Ashley du Pre; she was barely sixteen and still lived at home. Her parents insisted that she was al-

ways in before midnight—ten minutes to twelve, to be exact—not easy when
your boyfriend was a Beatle who didn't finish work until nearly dawn. Mostly,
they dated in the afternoon on Mitch's days off and pretended that they didn't
know each other in the Cavern.

Maureen's friend, Lorraine Flyte, who was also sixteen like me, became my
girlfriend and in turn, I came to know Mitch quite well. Often, Mitch, Lorraine
and I would hang out together on Sundays, go to the movies or walk in the park,
while Ringo—or Richie, as we all still called him—slept. I was the amiable lad
the girls asked to go shopping with them on their days off. When we saw posters
advertising a Beatles gig, or an article about them in a newspaper or a magazine,
Mitch would often giggle and say she had to keep pinching herself.

"I can't believe I'm a Beatle's girlfriend," she would say. "But I know he'll
get bored with me."

"'Course he won't," Lorraine would say. "Richie's all right."

Sometimes Mitch would comment that her parents weren't that happy with
the situation. "They say he's too old for me," she confided. "They say older boys
get girls like me into trouble and then dump them."

"Well, they only get you into trouble if you let them," Lorraine would say.
Then they'd look at each other and burst into laughter.

Ringo used to keep Mitch very secret partly for her own safety, and partly because Brian had impressed on them that all the Beatles had to pretend they were
some kind of celibate boy monks. Brian was very earnest about this. He would
repeatedly insist, "You belong to every girl fan in England."

Such sentiments made the boys uncomfortable, but they accepted that Brian
was right. Preserving their private lives from the fans, from the press and from
Brian himself became a conspiracy we all invested in. Ringo said, "It's like the
bloody Secret Service," but he went along with playing cloak and dagger with
Mitch, and Lorraine and I went along with helping them.

Lorraine lived in Wango Lane, which ran along one side of Aintree Racecourse, where the Grand National was run. With Mitch, we even watched the
race from Lorraine's bedroom window, while drinking warm cherry-ade from
bottles with straws and eating crisps. It was great fun, hanging out of the window
and cheering the horses on, though we weren't really close enough to see very
much in detail. We didn't even make a bet.

(Years after this episode, in 1967, Paul McCartney was to record a song with
his brother, Mike McGear—who was in the Scaffold—called "Thank U Very
Much for the Aintree Iron." This was the shape of the racetrack itself, like an
old-fashioned smoothing iron that you heated in the coals; and of course people
like Mo Best with big winnings on the Grand National had much to thank it for.

When Paul asked me to make a film based on the song, I remembered that fun day with Ringo, Mo and Lorraine and I got the Scaffold to mime the song at Liverpool Football ground, with the entire terrace strangely known as the Kop—behind one of the goals—singing away. I can't remember it ever being used, another lost film that will be rediscovered someday.)

▀

John's romantic entanglement with Cynthia became serious when she got pregnant, though how she was so sure, so soon, was puzzling. Judging by the timing—based on John's presence in Liverpool—she couldn't have been more than a week or two gone at the most when she broke the news to John. John was dismayed but bowed to the inevitable, though not as dismayed as Mimi—or Brian. This wasn't in Brian's plans for the boys at all—a Beatle had to be footloose and fancy free and available. Brian had very quickly seen huge value in the hordes of fans who followed the Beatles, in the blossoming fan clubs and fanzine newsletters, and once again, he trotted out his homily: "You belong to every girl fan in England." On the other hand, he agreed that the Beatles' image had to be "nice" and he didn't want any bad press.

Brian arranged the wedding ceremony at the registry office, with a simple chicken meal to follow in an ordinary café where he hoped nobody would notice them. To Brian's intense irritation—John found it hilarious—it was lunchtime and they had to stand in a queue for twenty minutes until a table became free, but Brian didn't want to make a fuss in case they drew attention to themselves. In fact, hardly anyone knew John was married. For a long time it was a secret that really didn't leak out beyond our immediate circle, unlike most other "secrets" in Liverpool.

John spent his wedding night in Chester, playing at the Riverpark Ballroom. Although the whole affair was very private and had been hushed up, at one point John did say that he hadn't really wanted to get married and felt pushed into it. (He even had another regular girlfriend he was besotted with, Ida Holly, whom he had met at the Blue, not to mention a string of one-night stands. I don't know if John knew it, but luscious Ida went out with me too.)

No, wedded bliss was not John's scene at all. "Christ," he said after the gig in Chester, as we were packing up, "I can't believe I went through with it."

Mimi was too angry to go to the wedding and turned her back on her beloved John for months. Brian decided that the squalid little student bedsit so lovingly prepared by Cynthia for John wasn't a good image for one of his precious Beatles, let alone a newly married couple. Instead, he gave them the keys to the little love nest in Falkner Street—that *he* once had lovingly prepared in his mind for John—hoping nobody would spot John coming and going and connect him with the pregnant young blond woman who lived there. I'm sure it was all very complicated for him—but I'm sure he also loved being mother hen.

▄

Finally, Brian got that recording date from George Martin, along with a song on an acetate disc that George wanted them to learn: "How Do You Do It," which was published by Dick James. There was an immediate argument when Brian called the boys in to play it to them. Neither John nor Paul would even consider it, having decided right from the start that they wanted to record their own compositions.

"It's a nice song, please give it a chance," Brian pleaded, not wanting to upset George Martin.

"Bollocks, tell him to stuff it up his arse," John snarled.

Earnestly, Brian assured them it was for their own good and making waves wouldn't help their career. "We can discuss it with George Martin when we're in London," he said. "Don't make him think you're difficult. We can work it out when we're actually in the studio. Making waves now could be most undiplomatic."

John told him to fuck off, stalked out and Brian sighed, looking down at his lily-white, beautifully manicured hands. "John can be so difficult."

With his usual tact, Paul said, "John will be okay. We'll learn the song and work it out later."

A week later, they were back in London, re-recording their material—this time, without the despised "How Do You Do It," which (ably demonstrating Paul's idea of "working it out") they had sung so boringly straight that George threw up his hands, grimaced and agreed to drop it. Much to their chagrin—and Brian's delight because by then he had signed up Gerry Marsden—it went on to be a huge number-one hit for Gerry and the Pacemakers.

In the studio, Ringo was depressed because George Martin had brought in Andy White, a top session drummer. Ringo, ever the consummate pro, didn't throw a wobbler. However, when the single was released, "Love Me Do" was the A side and "PS I Love You" was the flip side (with the standby drummer), so Ringo's honor was 50 percent intact.

▄

I happened to be in NEMS record store when the records were shipped early in October and was amazed to see carton after carton of the virgin single unloaded into Brian's stockrooms, all ten thousand of them. "They'll soon go," Brian said defensively and immediately got his team on a campaign to help ensure that they did.

I thought the actual real live record of "Love Me Do" was quite wonderful. "My Bonnie" had been a disappointment. It didn't sound like them. It was an old song, and they'd only sung backing. Apart from the acetate demos that you couldn't buy, until that point nothing at all had been recorded with the Beatles. They were a live band, without a record. Suddenly, they were authentic. They had a record! It was amazing. Even better was that these were their own songs that they'd been playing for about a year. I'd heard it a million times before but now it sounded authentic and different. "Love Me Do" was tremendous, every harmony, every note. You could sing along to it as well, something we didn't much do when they played live.

I can still remember the first time I heard it on radio one evening. Radio Luxembourg—208—was "our" station because it played practically all night and you could listen to it in bed. I turned it up really loud and shouted at everyone—Mum and my brothers—to come and listen. We sat there with big grins on our faces, and when it ended, I wished we could hear it again—on air, that is, because naturally, I had a copy of the record. I think everyone in Liverpool did. (I never bought a Beatles record. I was given every single one.)

We put it on the Dansette and listened to it over and over until it was almost worn out like that first flimsy acetate. I felt I had been on the journey with them every step of the way and was very proud. We all were. Mum didn't even tell us to turn it off. And then we heard it on the radio again and again. I knew then that it would happen for them. Oddly enough, it seemed to change things. Before, they were "our" boys, our mates. Now they seemed to gain in stature, to become someone we were sharing with the world. I know that I personally never treated them any differently, but many people did.

Paul even said it once. "It's not the same anymore. When I walk into a room of old friends and even family, there's a kind of shyness, a distance. I just want to shout, 'It's me—Paul!'"

Three days later, on Saturday, October 6, the day after the record's official release, Brian celebrated by formally signing a new management contract with the Beatles, one that no longer embarrassingly included Pete Best. This time, Brian remembered to sign it: or perhaps he hadn't forgotten before. Who knows?

Everyone, especially a primed network of fans, wrote and telephoned radio stations, disc jockeys and the press. Even our mums and girlfriends were roped in to write hundreds of letters. Everywhere the Beatles played, the machine swung into action, pestering radio stations, demanding the record at local record shops—and when it crept onto the charts at number forty-nine, we all went wild.

Brian walked around beaming. The running joke was that probably his mum, Queenie, had bought all the ten thousand copies and stacked them in her drawing room. Even though it didn't get anywhere near the number-one spot, peaking at seventeen on December 27, George Martin was very pleased. By then, the Beatles had started appearing on national television and had made national popularity polls in magazines like the *New Musical Express*.

The Beatles had one more booking to fulfill, made before their growing fame. It was in Hamburg again, the city that had been their testing ground. Without that grueling apprenticeship, they would not have been as tight nor as good. As if going into training to take on the world, they returned to the Star Club just before Christmas, but they were tired and jaded with an old scene that seemed light years removed from where they were now. But by the time they returned to England, when I saw them next in the New Year, they were ready for anything.

7

Before real fame hit, the Beatles did summer gigs, a week here and there at seaside resorts, a mix of a week at Southport, then a one-night stand in Aberdeen, a Sunday in Torquay and a week in Great Yarmouth or Bournemouth. My job description at that time was what you might call a "clerk" to Brian, but a lot of the time, if the gig were in Merseyside, I'd be off with them in the van at lunchtime to wherever the gig was and afterward we'd come home. If they went further afield, on weekends I'd take them their pay packets and stay over.

Their first van was the secondhand Bedford provided by Neil. It had two bench seats and was pretty basic. Neil would drive, with John often sitting up front with him. We'd push the other bench seat forward to make room for all the gear and then basically sit on it and be bounced around. It didn't make for a great deal of comfort, but we were used to it. Sometimes, when we were really tired, we'd try to find space on the floor and curl around the equipment and each other, lying on our coats, but it was a crush. Mostly, we'd talk or play cards on an amp.

If John and Paul were in the mood for writing songs, Paul might sit up front with John and they'd get engrossed, or they'd sit in the back and go into a huddle scribbling in their old exercise books and maybe one of them would pick a few notes on a guitar. I know I heard dozens of songs emerge while we were on the road, but none of them were ever finished—it was all bits and pieces, written down and polished later. Sometimes, John or Paul would wake up in the middle of the night; the last verse had come to them. Often we wouldn't hear a finished version until later, sometimes a lot later, perhaps when they were in the studio, short of a song for a new album. Then one of the exercise books would be dredged up and the pages thumbed through while John or Paul said, "What about this?"—and one of them would sing a few lines.

I can't say that at the time this "songwriting" was filled with earth-shattering, iconic moments. It didn't dawn on any of us, and certainly not on me, that in years to come each and every one of the songs would be deconstructed and analyzed, the stuff of theses. Sometimes a situation or a name would be the inspiration, but often the song was pure invention, its genesis just an idle notion, pure imagination. None of us, including John and Paul, took them seriously, probably because it came easily to them. It even took Brian a long time to realize that these scribblings were valuable. They were old-fashioned songwriters in their approach, writing wherever they happened to be, whether in the back of a van or a hotel room. They had nobody to clue them in about the song business. They didn't have a Brill Building as support. If only they'd had a manual, the songwriting equivalent of Bert Weedon's *Play in a Day* guitar book to teach them that "the song you do belongs to you," and that writing songs was a bona fide job, perhaps they would not have given so much away.

When bookings took them further afield, Brian invested in a brand new van. The Commer had better suspension and wasn't as prone to breaking down, but it still wasn't any bigger and only fractionally more comfortable than the old Bedford. Unremarkably, given the distances we traveled nearly every day, in all weather, we had quite a few crashes. But, remarkably, none of us were ever hurt. George—who had a license—once was driving the van in thick snow, heading home from Hull. Just outside Goole, he skidded on the icy road alongside a canal and we ended up on an embankment. As usual, no one was hurt and we eventually set off again. Another time, John, who didn't have a license and was blind as a bat, especially at night, wanted to drive. We were in North Wales, heading up the Horseshoe Pass, just above Llangollen. Back then, the road was dangerously narrow and steep. It zigzagged in a series of loops and Z-bends up the sides of an almost sheer slate cliff that marked one side of the River Dee. Suddenly, John lost control. We spun about a bit and for a moment I thought we were going right over the edge, but John managed to turn the wheel and we ended up on the moorland side, in the heather. No one ever mentioned it again, but that could have been the end of the Beatles.

A more dramatic event, though one that didn't involve an accident, was when the Beatles were appearing at the Royal Pavilion in Bath. Now, Bath is a very beautiful town, filled with classical Georgian buildings that lend it an air of elegance and style, and of all the places that we went, it was the last place we thought we would suffer from vandalism. Perhaps it was a few disgruntled boyfriends of some of the girls who were screaming their heads off—but the van was vandalized. The headlights and the mirrors were smashed, the panels battered and the windows shattered. However, we had to get back to Liverpool with the equipment for another gig. It was night and dark, too late even to consider renting another van or taking a train.

The police were wonderful. An inspector said, "We'll get you back home, boys." And he did. He laid on a police escort before and behind us, with lights flashing. We turned on the indicator lights that gave a little light, and headed out driving blind for some two hundred miles, with the wind whistling in, and squinting into the darkness. But the inspector was true to his word—he did get us home.

Much of the time, like homing pigeons, we traveled back and forth from gigs, always returning to Liverpool. Those days when the boys had a gig at home were wonderful because we could stay in bed all day. Staying in one place for a week was a real luxury. When the lads were away I'd usually be based in Liverpool doing whatever Brian wanted. When I did travel with the lads, after shows we would perhaps go off to the Wimpy bar for a hamburger and chips. Then we would go back to the hotel bar, drink some Scotch and Coke and go to bed when the bar closed. We hardly ever "made the scene." In fact, what scene? There weren't any "scenes" to make, no clubs to go clubbing at. The only after-hours joints were the odd casinos. They were private, and we didn't gamble anyway.

We never knew where to go to amuse ourselves outside Liverpool. Before the Beatles, Britain was severely monotone. It wasn't like America. Our outlook was restricted. Most English movies were austere kitchen-sink dramas, like our way of life. The feel of them was black and white like the TV. The Movietone newsreel at the cinema was in black and white. Clothes were drab. You weren't supposed to enjoy yourself. Just occasionally if there was somebody that we knew in the town where we were, we would maybe go and visit them and have a couple of light ales and listen to some records. But it wasn't Hamburg where the Beatles played into the early hours and took a load of speed, drank beer and chased girls. All England was closed by ten o'clock. If we were away from our familiar haunts in Liverpool it was all, "Get on stage. Yeah! Yeah! Yeah! 'Twist and Shout,' shake your moptop, run out the door. Then Wimpy and chips and good night Fab Four, see you in the morning." (On second thought, it was bloody great!)

Strange though it may seem now, despite the fans and the growing press, the Beatles' private lives were very normal—even provincial. Take George, for example. One of his regular activities on a day off was to take me and my mum out for a drive on a Sunday afternoon in his new car. George was the Beatle Mum was closest to. She adored him. Shortly after "Love Me Do" was launched, the Harrisons were able to afford to move just round the corner from us in Hunts Cross. Their new house was modern and slightly more upmarket than the previous one. It became well known when the fans started flocking there. The Harrisons welcomed them all in and the fans fitted right in with the family. Some of them took over the kitchen and made bacon butties or cooked beans on toast for everyone. Mrs. Harrison used to laugh when she recounted to my mum how the fans loved to do her housework. "They're busy little bees and tell me to put my feet up and read a magazine. They like ironing George's shirts best of all," she said with a smile. In fact, shortly, there were to be so many fan letters that both of George's parents would sit up all night answering them.

With money coming in from bookings, George bought his first car, a hot off the production line dark blue Ford Anglia with a sloping back windscreen— probably made at the local Ford factory at which I no longer worked. Until then, Ringo had been the only Beatle with a car. His was a very gaudy Standard Vanguard, sprayed bright orange, with railway track–type massive girders welded on like a stock car. With its blown exhaust and souped-up engine, it sounded like a tank coming down the road. I can still visualize Ringo, looking slightly manic and goggle-eyed behind the steering wheel.

George's new car was sedate in comparison. It became well known because it appeared in many of the early photographs. I can remember the first time that George zoomed around to our house in it, a big smile pinned to his face. He honked the horn and Mum and I came running out.

"Get in, Mrs. Bramwell," he shouted. "I'm taking you for a spin!"

We climbed in, and off we went on what was to be the first of many Sunday afternoon drives. It was the kind of thing that families did back then, going for a drive after lunch on a Sunday and stopping off at some quaint little old-world teashop for a pot of tea and a few sticky buns. We would go to little landmarks like the famed Transporter Bridge at Runcorn, or to local beauty spots like Frodsham, where there were sandstone crags you could scramble up. Sometimes we went to the medieval black-and-white Tudor town of Chester, which on a Sunday was mostly shut up. We were quite happy to stroll around window-shopping and then have tea in a cobwebby little teashop down a cobbled alley, or we'd go to Chester Zoo, one of George's favorite destinations, not far from the stately pile owned by the teenage Duke of Westminster.

To give an idea just how provincial it all was, Arthur Howes, the agent who did all the Beatles' early tours, was based in Peterborough. Americans have a rude phrase for such rural locations, but I'll just say it was a little place in the middle of nowhere. In the early days Brian was so troubled by his lack of management experience that he was always thinking of taking on a partner—almost any partner would have done, as long as he appeared to know what he was doing. The partners Brian needed were Lew and Leslie Grade and Bernard Delfont, a cartel who practically ran the British entertainment industry. They owned ATV (Associated Television Corporation), the biggest independent station, and a host of dance halls and theaters. They had even offered to sign up the Beatles to their agency for 10 percent, leaving Brian 15 percent but, apart from the loss in his earnings, Brian didn't trust them.

He'd pluck other names out of the air. "What about Larry Parnes?" he asked me.

It was Larry Parnes who had booked the fledgling Beatles to back Johnny Gentle in Scotland. He had the opportunity of managing them then, but had turned them down because it was said he didn't think Stuart Sutcliffe could play. He was right, he couldn't, but if Larry couldn't see beyond that he shouldn't have been in the business. Parnes was famous for his campness, his aggressive ways, his admitted dirty dealings and for getting into show business by accident. He was running his own clothes shops from the age of seventeen, until the night in a London nightclub when he won a whisky drinking contest and got so drunk he invested all his money in a loss-making West End play, *The House of Shame.* Stuck with an unpromising show that none of the papers would review, Parnes changed its name to *Women of the Streets* and made the female cast dress as hookers and parade outside the theater during the intermission. They were promptly arrested, the story was splashed in all the newspapers, and the show sold out.

From there, Parnes dumped the clothing shops and hustled around, booking every unknown cod Elvis lookalike he could lay his hands on, changing their names to the likes of Billy Fury and Marty Wilde.

I think perhaps Brian admired Parnes's ruthless energy, his in-your-face rudeness and the fact that their backgrounds in trade at least were similar. He said, "A fellow like Larry Parnes who knows his way around is what we need. What do you think, Tony?"

I was barely seventeen and didn't know what to think. I would nod and say, "You know what's best, Brian."

The trouble was, for a long time Brian didn't know what was best. He might have given the appearance of being coolly in control, but he was floundering all the way to the top. It caused him great angst. He often used to turn up at a Beatles gig in his Ford Zephyr Zodiac, wearing an expensive suit and a silk tie and smile and frown and watch and worry and wonder if he was doing the right thing or whether the real professionals were just laughing at him. In the end a partner really didn't matter because it turned out that nobody else knew what was going on either. That kind of woolly thinking stayed with him, and us, throughout the early days—luckily. Sometimes not knowing enough can allow you to think you can achieve anything.

One of Brian's big industry mistakes was approaching Dick James, an ex-crooner, to discuss the Beatles' publishing. "Love Me Do" and "PS I love You," the Beatles' first record, was on Parlophone and, before Brian was sure what "music publishing" meant (he thought it meant printing up sheet music, such as the music he sold in his stores) the publishing had been given to Ardmore and Beechwood. Both Parlophone and A & B were EMI subsidiaries. Brian still didn't know that publishing potentially represented millions of pounds, dollars, marks and yen collected from around the world. Publishing wasn't just pages of printed sheet music anymore, it was royalties from the song, from the record and from radio plays. In the latter case, the Performing Rights Society (PRS) collected royalties in the U.K. and the American Society of Composers and Publishers (ASCAP) collected royalties in the U.S. and passed them on.

Brian wasn't happy with A & B. He decided to shop around a bit before he offered the rest of the Beatles' publishing to them. He asked George Martin who else there was. George wasn't supposed to send people to their rivals, but he suggested Dick James. He had produced "Garden of Eden," Dick James's hit record on Parlophone, which had gone to number eighteen in the charts. Dick was not anyone's idea of a pop star. His only other claim to fame so far had been singing the theme song (also produced by George) to the popular television serial *Robin Hood* on ITV. He was Brian's age but was stout and balding and looked far older. He had finally seen the writing on the wall and knocked his abortive quest for pop fame on the head in order to become a music publisher. He had opened a small walk-up office on Tin Pan Alley (Denmark Street) on the corner of the Charing Cross Road and, for his first deal, had signed up none other than George Martin with an instrumental called "Double Scotch": No. 001 in his catalogue. Now he was twiddling his thumbs, waiting for someone else, someone big, to walk up the stairs.

George said, "Dick James is hungry and will work hard for you." Then he picked up the phone and made an appointment for Brian to meet him the next morning after he had been to A & B. Brian went to A & B on time, but the manager, Syd Coleman, was late and the door remained locked. After waiting for half an hour, Brian was extremely angry and stormed off. He went straight along Oxford Street to Denmark Street and arrived half an hour early for his appointment with Dick James. Brian was pleased to find him already in, seated at his desk and looking busy. Perhaps this was the kind of man he could do business with.

It's said that the devil not only has a silver tongue, but that he also comes in many disguises. It is also said that he has all the best tunes—and he got 'em when nobody was looking. Dick already had a cunning plan to land this Liverpool sardine seated before him. He took Brian's acetate and played "Please Please Me" and his mouth fell open theatrically. Think Jack Benny playing a music publisher for the cameras. "This is wonderful, a number-one hit," he enthused. "I can get your boys on TV."

Now it was time for Brian's mouth to fall open, because Dick had seen him coming and set up an ambush at the end of the alley in the shape of a phone call to Philip Jones, a producer friend of his, in charge of *Thank Your Lucky Stars*, a big pop music TV show. The producer agreed at once to have the Beatles on. This would be their first time on national TV and as Dick had intended, Brian was very impressed with the bait. The fish was hooked.

Dick opened his palms and said earnestly, "We'd like to publish. Have you got anymore good tunes?"

Brian, still with the mind-set of publishing meaning sheet music, and who had never heard of the monies that came back from deejays' needle time from all the broadcasts in all the gin joints in all the world, agreed that indeed his boys had several good tunes. The deal they discussed was remarkable, given that highway robbery was not on Brian's agenda. They would set up Northern Songs, 49 percent of which would be split between John, Paul (20 percent each) and Brian (9 percent), while Dick James and his silent partner, a city accountant named Charles Silver, would get 51 percent—after taking 10 percent off the top for administration. Today, publishers pay songwriters millions for their publishing. In that sleazy little office in Tin Pan Alley, Brian agreed to sell out the Beatles' early catalogue for nothing, and what's more, he didn't go away and ask for advice before agreeing to the terms. He blindly believed everything that Dick James told him and thought he was lucky to have found him.

At the end of the long meeting, Dick said, "Did you eat yet?" and they went off to lunch in Soho.

"Please Please Me" was released in January 1963 and was a number-one hit. A few weeks later, on the evening of February 22, a strange cloak-and-dagger scene took place in Brian's Falkner Street flat between John, Paul and

Brian and Dick James, who had gone up to Liverpool for the day. Brian described Dick to the boys as "an expert in the business." Paul and John didn't have a clue about the hidden fortune that was to be found in songs. Like Paul's dad, who actually had composed a song but didn't take it seriously, they were happy to sing them. They had no idea that by so casually giving away 51 percent of their copyrights they were about to make someone incredibly wealthy—wealthy beyond his wildest dreams. Within eighteen months, Dick James would go from a tiny walk-up in Tin Pan Alley to an entire block on New Oxford Street.

As the Beatles themselves readily admitted, such was their utter faith in Brian that they never read a single contract he gave them to sign. That evening with Dick James, Paul and John were tired and running late to play at the Oasis Club in Manchester, so they signed, shook hands all round and left almost on the run to join us there, where I had already set up the equipment in readiness. The deejay for the evening was Dave Travis and he spun discs and kept the chat going until the boys arrived.

There is a strange little postscript to the "Please Please Me" story. Norman Smith, the engineer at Abbey Road who had been so taken with the Beatles when they first recorded there, had a great sense of humor. It amused him that Decca had foolishly turned them down. He decided to play a mischievous little trick after they had their first number-one hit. "I couldn't resist it," he said, his eyes twinkling when he recounted the story. After the Beatles had recorded "Please Please Me" but before it was released, Norman had made up a name and sent a tape to Decca with a letter, asking for a deal. Once again, they turned down the Beatles.

"What did they say?" I asked him.

He smiled. "Just two words: 'No thanks.' But I don't think their executives ever listened to the radio. They hadn't a clue." Norman went on to engineer thirteen number-one hits for the Beatles. As a further postscript, some years later, when his fiftieth birthday was approaching, surprising everyone, he suddenly made up his mind to achieve a long-held ambition. Yes, Norman—whom John used to call "Normal" and Paul called "2-DBs" after decibels—who had engineered so many hits for others, and who had even produced Pink Floyd, decided to be a pop star. He composed a song, threw up his prestigious position as head of Parlophone and changed his name from Norman to "Hurricane" Smith. His first song reached number two in the U.K., but his second one, "Oh Babe, What Do You Say," knocked Elton John off the top of the U.S. charts. The icing on the cake was to be on the *Tonight Show with Johnny Carson* on his fiftieth birthday. It was a remarkable achievement, but Norman was always full of surprises.

When they weren't actually touring, the Beatles were able to maintain a little privacy. By the time they went into the studios to make their second album, *With the Beatles,* only a few hardcore fans camped outside. Even when they went into that first season of summer gigs at seaside resorts where they stayed in the same place for a week, it was still relatively peaceful. The idea of staying in one place during a nice English summer was great! We were like kids on holiday at Blackpool or Rhyl, paddling in the sea or swimming, strolling through town in late afternoon, eyeing the girls, going into arcades and playing pinball or shooting for a stuffed toy on the target range. In Jersey, local fans clustered at the theater, but mostly left the Beatles alone during the day. The momentum was moving up a couple of gears, but the period of hiding in hotel rooms and assuming disguises every second of every day hadn't yet arrived. Even running down the street to escape was still exhilarating and different. We just didn't know how different it was to become. Mostly I remember how we all looked at each other and started laughing over nothing because life was so bizarre, so surreal. We would run along the beach and jump into the surf, laughing. It was crazy, blissful, a summer in a long dream.

As time and their fame started to spread their freedom became restricted. It became impossible for them to escape, so most of the time they sat on the balconies of their hotel rooms, feet up on the railings, shades on, chatting about nothing very much. Weston Super Mare, scene of the famous photographs where they were snapped running and jumping along the beach in Victorian striped swimsuits, was a snatched moment of escapist fun.

In the early days, Neil Aspinall drove and acted as roadie, until it became obvious that just one man out on the road with them wasn't enough to control the increasingly hysterical crowds of girls, so Mal Evans drove the van with all the equipment and Neil drove the estate car in which the boys now traveled directly to gigs, or sometimes there was a tour bus. The tour bus was great because we had fun on it. It was like being in our own little space capsule, all friends together with a shared interest, surging from place to place with twenty or thirty musicians, a moveable feast that changed almost by the week. We'd play cards and sing songs in the back. Ringo was a great card player and generally won, but if money were bet, it was only pennies. It was like being on permanent holiday, broken each evening with a show.

The Beatles' very first proper U.K. theater tour—as in seated auditoriums— wasn't until January of 1963, supporting Helen Shapiro and Kenny Lynch.

Mostly, the venues were local ABCs and Gaumonts, places big enough to hold the anticipated crowds. On that first series of tours, there'd be Helen, the Shadows, Billy J. Kramer, the Dakotas and Billie Davis—a cute sixteen-year-old, managed by Stigwood, whose big hit "Tell Him" was in the top ten on the charts. The Beatles knew Billie from an early *Top of the Pops* and had fancied her then. On the tour all four of them—and I—pounced on Billie with lust in our minds and took bets on who would pull her. It became the tour mantra: "Who's going to pull Billie Davis?" But Billie was madly in love with Jet Harris at the time and managed to evade our embarrassing pick-up lines.

The next tour of twenty-four dates started almost immediately, with Tommy Roe and Chris Montez. "Please Please Me" had been huge but there was still no real hint of the hysteria that was to come. That happened about the time of the third tour—the Roy Orbison tour—which was in May and June of 1963. Brian didn't allow the Beatles any respite. Between January and April 1963 he packed in three major tours. It was a very tight, exhausting schedule, but Brian was right to push so hard.

Hysteria was a phenomenon that came from nowhere and shocked everyone with its power. Girls had screamed before, over Tommy Steele and Cliff Richard, and danced in the aisles to Jerry Lee Lewis, but it was different, more intense with the Beatles. The screaming had started on the first tour, with sporadic outbursts, but they were, after all, pop concerts. By the second tour, the girls screamed a little more, but it wasn't until the third tour that they had learned to scream in earnest. To see three thousand almost deranged girls heading your way was quite terrifying.

By the start of the third tour Roy Orbison had damaged his eyes and started wearing the dark glasses that became his trademark. The Beatles had released their third single, "From Me to You," and they closed the first half of the concert. Brian's new group, Gerry and the Pacemakers, opened the second half with "How Do You Do It," which was top of the hit parade; then poor Roy Orbison had to follow as top of the bill. His act was all huge ballads, but he quickly found that you could not follow a screaming mass of hysterical Beatles fans with ballads and when the fans began to go seriously wild, he was screamed off the stage. After four or five days the running order was changed so that Orbison closed the first half and the Beatles closed the second half as top of the bill. Roy was relieved, annoyed and bemused, but he didn't throw a tantrum. He was superb, an absolute Southern gentleman. Even on the coach he would stand until everyone had sat down. He'd been around long enough to have seen it all. He just bowed to the inevitable and got on with the show. A lovely man.

The dream of being able to stroll through a seaside town and paddle in the sea unmolested ended when "She Loves You" came out. Then it all went ballistic. Beatlemania had arrived and it was scary. There was little to compare it to for the English press, except royal weddings and funerals, or the Cup Final. Still, that didn't matter. They went at it as if they'd been waiting. The Beatles were front-page news every day for days and weeks on end. It was coats-over-the-head time. The police had to be notified when they were due to arrive in a town—or even if they were just going to be anywhere at all as a group. Official protection suddenly happened wherever they went, or there would be rioting. There was no option. At the very least they could be stripped naked and knocked unconscious with the sheer weight of numbers, or, worse, scalped.

Celebrity security hadn't been invented yet and no one knew how to deal with all this mania. Even at Cup Finals—the British version of the Superbowl—all they'd ever needed was a handful of police and the St. John's Ambulance Brigade, both of which were now hopelessly inadequate in the face of the new fan. Suddenly the boys were coming up with funny disguises, like Peter Sellers in an Inspector Clouseau film, to fool the fans.

The Beatles were now unstoppable. They got too big for a tour bus and had to be chauffeur-driven separately because the moment the coach was seen all hell broke loose. By the end of the so-called Roy Orbison tour it was screaming bedlam, even though the scenes of over fifty thousand screaming fans amassed together in the giant stadiums across the United States were still before them. The tour bus, with THE BEATLES written on the front like a destination, was constantly besieged. I can remember sitting inside, overwhelmed by the sheer mass of bodies and the screaming mouths.

You could only get so close to an entrance to a theater—there would still be several yards of pavement to cross. The Beatles would psyche themselves up and take deep breaths before plunging into the frantic mob. They went past the joking stage of the early days when they compared it to a rugger scrum. To even open the door and run out became brave and foolhardy. In the end, the bus was mothballed, or used as a decoy. For the Beatles, even limousines were too vulnerable. They would arrive at gigs in police black Marias and ambulances and make a run for it as if in a hundred-yard dash with determined fans streaming in their wake.

The disguises were necessary, but because it had never happened before the papers made a big feature of it. What would they show up in next? Disguised as what? The stories wrote themselves. Tradesmen with any kind of uniform doing their own everyday quiet minding-their-own-business thing anywhere near a

Beatles concert were immediately under suspicion. They were leapt on, stripped. Was Paul underneath? Don't ask! Get his clothes off! If it's not Paul, Ringo might be in there. Oh, no! It really is a policeman. Most took it in good heart. After all, who gets manhandled by a gang of delirious young girls every day?

As if attacked by a virus that changed their moral standards, teenage girls wanted sex with the Beatles and they didn't care how they got it. When they tried to grab a live one, crawl through windows or hide in wardrobes, they were sorted out by Mal and Neil Aspinall like M&M's, to be sampled and tasted first. Brian—who *was* puritanical where his protégés were concerned—would have had a fit had he only known, but he was kept totally in the dark.

Big Mal was a demon for sex. His stamina would have been remarkable in a harem. In the flat, sooty back streets of Birmingham or Manchester, he was a stud straight from the *Kama Sutra*. Like sacrificial virgins, a lot of the girls willingly accepted that they would have to do it with Mal to get to John, Paul, George or Ringo, and Mal knew it. Meanwhile at the hotel I would sleep blissfully on, tucked up in my little solitary bed and only hear about the goings on later from one of the boys, in the general chat and larking about in a hundred different dressing rooms.

Looking back, it's no good saying we had no idea of the full extent of the frenzy surrounding them, because as I've said, what was there to compare it to? People had heard about the "Bobbysoxers" who screamed at Sinatra or the scenes at Elvis gigs, but that was America where everything was always bigger, wilder, different. Nobody had ever witnessed that kind of thing in the United Kingdom or knew what to expect nor how to deal with it.

After all, their first real theater gig, back in the autumn of '62, had been that show in the one-horse town of Peterborough, supporting Frank Ifield, an Australian yodeller. The Beatles went on, did their little set. Nothing. Hardly a ripple. They didn't mean anything to the audience. Polite applause. They came off, got in the van, went home. There were no reviews, no comments. In their wildest dreams they couldn't have anticipated the difference those six short months would make to the rest of their lives.

PART II

London

1963–1966

8

As soon as the money started rolling in from nonstop touring in
England—frequently cash stuffed in brown bags—Brian grasped his dream
with both hands and opened offices in London in a bohemian (and relatively
cheap) theater district, at 13 Monmouth Street, Covent Garden. These offices
were small, with one purpose only: NEMS's footprint in the capital. The day he
walked in and claimed the offices, he appeared calm, but inwardly he was
delirious with joy as he stood looking out of the window, contemplating the birth
of his new empire in the capital. I think this was the moment he knew he had finally succeeded at something. During that transitional period, I spent all my
time either with Brian in Liverpool and London, or traveling on the road with the
Beatles.

For some months, the London offices were used mainly as a press office and
for the promotions staff, like Tony Barrow and Tony Calder. Andrew Loog Oldham also worked there for a while until the Stones, whom he managed, took off.
Things were going so well that Brian got big offices in Argyle Street, next door to
the London Palladium. As a kid, the biggest show ever on TV was *Sunday Night
at the London Palladium*. For a star being on it was important; being next door
wasn't bad either.

Brian made an announcement in the Liverpool press that NEMS was basically

moving shop to London and, very properly, he called us in one at a time to personally ask those he'd selected if they'd like to make the big move down south with
him and the Beatles. He chose me and the switchboard girl, Laurie McCaffrey,
and the accountant, who was a southerner. We were excited and all agreed to go.
Then Brian called everybody together to announce who was going, and who would
be staying to hold the fort in Liverpool.

We moved to London on a Friday and opened up the following Monday morning. It was as simple and as quick as that. Switchboard Laurie had such a good
voice, a wonderful deep Irish-Liverpudlian brogue. She was the first voice that
people heard when they called. Brian always said she was virtually irreplaceable. She was one who stayed on, all the way through Apple. Later, she was a big
success as one of the first people to do voice-overs for Capital Radio, as well as
their in-house ads.

At first, we were quite homesick. We found Londoners hard to get along
with. They saw us as Scousers and wacks and witty scallywags, speaking a
strange lingo that nobody seemed to understand. Silly expressions such as
"fab gear" went over their heads, which was hardly surprising since much of
the time we were just speaking our own rubbish to communicate. Otherwise,
we might just as well have been from Iceland. It wasn't until we had been living in London for about six months that I started being able to talk to people
about normal things. In the 1960s, Britain was very regional. The BBC was
very upper class, very London and county, definitely not provincial. People
hadn't really started to travel, not as we know it now. We had only one real mo-
torway, the M1, which just about reached Birmingham from London. After
that, it was all two lanes, not that it really mattered since few of our parents
had cars.

Paul bought the first car in his family, but not until after he'd moved to London. Liverpool was the back of beyond, even to Londoners, a place sung about
in sailors' folk songs and sea shanties, like "The Leaving of Liverpool" and the
one about Maggie May, the Liverpool sailors' trollop. (Not the Maggie May whom
Rod Stewart had in a tent at the first Glastonbury pop festival!) Brummie, Scotland, Wales and the West Country were all the stuff of comedy. The lower
classes were still only one step up from the peasants, the rabble, the mob. The
sixties' revolution hadn't started yet, so Lord knows what the rest of the world
made of it all. I suppose that the novelty of it was part and parcel of the whole
Beatles, Merseyside, Liverpool success story. It might have only been rock 'n'
roll and silly pop music, but it came at exactly the right time. Pot and the Pill
went hand in glove. If the Beatles hadn't happened, I don't think the Pill would
have been so widely used and accepted so fast. There would have been some

kind of social embarrassment or embargo, which would have slowed down the pace of change. All this came about after we arrived in London. Looking back, the Beatles triggered a massive social and sexual revolution.

Brian's early acts, quickly following on the heels of him signing the Beatles, were old friends of ours, all from Liverpool. Gerry and the Pacemakers, Billy J. Kramer, Cilla, the Fourmost, Tommy Quickly and the Remo Four were the first to sign to NEMS at the beginning of 1963. Endless hits seemed to explode out of them that year alone. The Beatles had four, and the others had a couple each. It was astonishing, a hit factory—and I'm not talking a few thousand records that would represent a hit today, but millions.

Brian gloried in it all. He loved the hands-on element of booking his acts, negotiating the fees and making the arrangements. I think it made it all seem real to him, fielding the phone calls and answering all the inquiries like: "We want Gerry and the Pacemakers next Friday in Wigan; how much is it going to cost us?" But as so much started to happen, he could no longer do it. Once he was settled at the new NEMS he head-hunted various agents from other agencies to look after particular artists. He got Bernard Lee from the Grade Organization, and some people from Rik Gunnell's office. Unusually, he paid these agents a wage instead of a commission.

It was now my job to go out on the road with whoever was touring. I was constantly on the move, acting like another pair of hands for Brian. In fact, that was how he introduced me: "This is Tony—he's my second pair of hands."

Just after we moved to Argyle Street a show was put on at the Palladium with the Fourmost, Cilla, Tommy Cooper and Frankie Vaughn, all NEMS acts. It was supposed to be a sort of interim show between the end of the summer season and the start of Christmas Pantomime, but it was such a success that it ran right through from March until December. I would pop next door to the Palladium in the evenings and learn stagecraft, lighting and rigging. I picked up all the knowledge, which was to come in handy when Brian bought the Saville Theater a couple of years down the road.

After the show I'd go to the Shakespeare's Head at the top of Carnaby Street with Tommy Cooper, who was known for his stage outfit of dinner jacket and a red fez. Tommy, one of the best-loved comic magicians in Britain, loved a drink but he wasn't allowed to have one before he went on. So he was watched very carefully. Sometimes he managed to get off the leash and slipped away to sink a few. Everybody could tell because he was larger than life, his show a little wilder, his laughter more manic, and his famous red fez more likely to slip down over his eye. One evening, the "boy" went by, shouting, "Three minutes, Mr. Cooper!" Nothing. Tommy was missing and people were in a panic.

He was discovered in a different pub than his usual haunt, playing darts and drinking port and brandy mixed. He was out of it, but brought back to the theater in time for his spot, given coffee and fanned with a towel. He usually set up his props himself before he went on but that night he couldn't get it together so a stagehand had to do it. This poor guy tried to follow Tommy's instructions but didn't get it right. One of the props was a wicket fence, about thigh-height, with a gate in the middle that opened inward. The stagehand set the fence up back to front so the gate opened out. When it was time, the curtain came up, Tommy took a deep breath, strode out and opened the gate to walk through it. Of course it didn't open but Tommy's momentum kept him going and he went headfirst over the gate, landed on the stage in a heap, rolled over and sat up looking out past the footlights. The audience went wild. They just howled with laughter. They thought it was part of his shtick, and the more he tried to get up the more they laughed. Like any great comedian, he responded to the audience and was never funnier. When he came off he said: "I think I might keep that in." Then he rubbed his back, had second thoughts and said: "No! Where's that stagehand? I'll kill him!"

Until the Beatles officially moved away from Liverpool, they and Neil, Mal and I were installed in the President, an unassuming hotel in Russell Square. Initially Brian also stayed at a hotel—a different one—but ultimately his lifestyle demanded privacy and he looked around for a place of his own. Perhaps it was the proximity of Harrods that attracted him to the modestly small though expensive flat in Whaddon House, a modern block in Lowndes Square, just behind the famous store in Knightsbridge. It was convenient to the tube, but Brian never traveled anywhere by tube. No, he bought himself a magnificent customized red Rolls Royce with monogrammed fittings and hired a driver, Reg, a rough and ready Cockney he fancied. He commissioned (for the cost of a country house) a top decorator to design a stark black-and-white theme for his flat, with fitted white carpets and black leather furniture. Lonnie, a black butler, was hired to cook meals and valet Brian's extensive wardrobe. Finally emancipated from Queenie's suffocating bosom, Brian was living the louche life he had always yearned for.

He has been described as being a country bumpkin, arriving in London as green as grass; but in fact he knew his way about. He believed that manners maketh the man, that the façade of dressing well and living a rich and luxurious lifestyle was not only the right way to go, but it would keep him out of trouble. It was this careful attention to detail, the posh speaking voice he had honed at boarding school, and his general courtesy that made the people he came to deal with in business think he was upper crust. In those days before a general breakdown in class structure, this was important and gained him respect and an air of authority. Because of this cultured veneer, no one guessed the doubts constantly gnawing away within him about his own ability, or questioned his decisions—some of which were to prove very damaging.

I liked and admired Brian enormously and in many ways was in awe of him. What he had achieved in a few months seemed little short of miraculous. Even the normally cynical Beatles were astonished. George had even said in an interview, and meant it, "Without Brian we'd be nowhere." They all believed that and until his death blindly went along with whatever he suggested. It never occurred to them to question or debate his decisions. Even when, for example, with their growing fame and box office pull, they could have gone out for bigger fees, if Brian had confirmed a booking months previously for next to nothing, he insisted on sticking to the deal. "A gentleman never reneges on a promise," he would say, noting how important it was to be known as a fair dealer. Through his fairness and honesty Brian broke the mold, the image of the crooked and devious manager.

And regarding his homosexuality, if he tried to hit on me, I never noticed. I think he was too wrapped up with his obsession for John. This had come to a head, but not peaked, during a strange little interlude that had taken place at the end of April 1963.

On April 8, in Liverpool, Cynthia had given birth to a baby boy, named Julian after John's mother, Julia. John wasn't there for the birth. The Beatles were in London, doing live radio and TV, as well as a concert. The popular legend is that it was a full week before John managed to sneak into the hospital, but we were in Liverpool on the ninth and tenth and he went to see the baby then, wearing as a disguise a silly hat and his heavy black "Buddy Holly" spectacles that made him look older than his years, more like a university professor. The glasses worked as a disguise because for ages, until he gained in confidence, he never wore them in public and people didn't recognize him in them. (Paul's regular disguise was a droopy stick-on Mexican mustache from a costume shop and a flat workman's cap.)

The previous year John had said it felt weird "walking about married." He had cringed at the thought of his mates seeing him with his pregnant wife and now he was embarrassed to be a dad. It made him feel old and settled down. To him marriage and parenthood and a baby pushed about in a pram represented everything he loathed—or more likely, was scared to death of. Later he would change, but perhaps it was because he was determined to show he was still a rebel that John did one of the most outlandish things he could think of. Almost three weeks after the birth of his son—whom he had seen only a couple of times by then—he agreed to go to Spain with Brian on a private holiday, while the other three Beatles flew to the Canaries for their spring break. I don't think John told Cynthia what he was doing—he rarely told her anything—and he certainly wouldn't have asked her permission. When she found out, she dissolved in tears, but she was scared of John and said nothing. To say we were astonished is an understatement. Much has been made of this trip. It was sun, sand and sea— but was it also sex?

John himself said he finally allowed Brian to make love to him "to get it out of the way." Those who knew John well, who had known him for years, don't believe it for a moment. John was aggressively heterosexual and had never given a hint that he was anything but. If it had been George, we might have believed it. George could act camp and had many homosexual friends, but John loved to say things to shock, and his sly statement was probably just another in a long line of such provocative statements. In fact, it was more in character for John to taunt Brian with promises during those long hot nights in Barcelona than to succumb. Equally, it was in Brian's masochistic nature to enjoy being tormented, then perhaps to rush off in search of a young bullfighter. Brian adored bullfighters so much, he ended up sponsoring one. (And I think Brian would have confided in somebody if it had happened.)

After Julian's birth, Cynthia left Brian's flat in Falkner Street and moved in with Mimi again, to endure a miserable and cowed existence, avoiding Mimi's sharp tongue and trying to keep the baby—who was a "screamer"—from disturbing the lodgers by sticking him in his pram at the end of the garden where he shrieked away unheard, while John spent most of his time on the road or in London staying in hotels. The next time he saw Cynthia was at Paul's twenty-first birthday party in June, which, because so many fans were camped outside Paul's family home, was quietly organized elsewhere. A big marquee was set up in the back garden of one of Paul's aunts who lived across the Mersey from Liverpool and invitations were secretly sent out.

Despite the tours and the mob scenes, there was still a sense of innocence and "Is this really happening to us?" about their fame. Paul was delighted when the Shadows turned up at the party, even though his hero, Jet Harris, had left the band by then and wasn't there. (Bruce and Hank were, and, I think, Brian "Liquorice" Locking, the replacement bass player.) Paul often said that if it weren't for Jet Harris, who had been the original bass player in the Shadows, he would never have picked up a guitar in the first place as a kid.

"I can't believe it," Paul said, shaking his head. Then, as he considered, he said almost shyly with a toothy grin, "But we're sort of like one of them now, aren't we?"

"Yeah, only bigger," I said. Paul looked at me doubtfully, as if I was pulling his leg. It still didn't seem real to him that *they* were the biggest names in the United Kingdom—and shortly would be the biggest names in the entire world.

John said, as if surprised, "Hey, you're right, we're part of this now!" The thought made him and Paul laugh wildly, because it really did still seem a dream. That night everyone drank too much, especially John. Bob Wooler taunted him over his holiday in Spain with Brian, said he was a queer, and John saw red. He assaulted Bob, breaking his ribs and ending up with a bloody nose himself. Brian settled the case out of court for two hundred pounds—a large sum, equal to the amount the Beatles were currently getting between them for a big theater booking.

Cynthia's woes accumulated when her mother heard of John's success. She flew back from Canada to also move in with Mimi. Yes, it was a disaster. Unable to return to the family home in Hoylake that they had shared in happier times before Cynthia's father had died because it was still rented out, Cynthia, her mother and Julian rented a shabby little bedsit in Liverpool at five pounds a week. It simply didn't occur to Cynthia that as the wife of a pop star who was earning a fortune she could have asked for a beautiful house with a garden and a nanny for the baby. Neither did it occur to John, who was incredibly selfish, to ensure that she was comfortable.

The women were left behind in Liverpool, but with the rest of us in London, Brian rented an expensive though sparsely furnished flat in Green Street, Mayfair, behind Oxford Street, for the Beatles. A bleak, soulless place, it had beds but little else. I could never find anywhere to sit and the kitchen was always as bare as Mother Hubbard's cupboard. They hated it so much, feeling quite the little boys lost and alone, that Brian moved them into a flat underneath his own penthouse in Knightsbridge. I rented a bedsit in Bayswater, a cosmopolitan district just north of Hyde Park, which was more a place to sleep and keep my clothes than a home. This didn't bother me. I was never in.

Being around the Beatles meant I didn't have to pay for very much. Accommodation, food and drink were freely offered wherever I went, Brian was generous with expenses and I spent most of my wages—by now upped to fifteen pounds a week—on clothes. I bought several good suits, about thirty pairs of jeans and a remarkable sixty shirts, so many that I could wear two a day if I wanted without going to the Laundromat for a month. Pure luxury. Things seemed cheaper then, or perhaps it was just relative. The Beatles' suits cost twenty pounds and their famous made-to-measure Beatle boots from Anello and Davide in Leicester Square were an outrageous seven pounds—which will now only get you three pints of beer.

Weekends in London could be boring. Work stopped on Friday night and the West End was dead, with few people, no traffic, shops that closed half days on Saturday and even the cafes closed. Sometimes on a Friday night I would take the tube up to Edgware where the main road north began and hitch a ride home to Liverpool to see Mum and all my mates and be there in about four hours for nothing.

Once down in London we were to find there were even more drugs, so easily available that we didn't think they were illegal. They were sold openly at clubs such as the Scene in Soho, where people like Georgie Fame played. Certainly, to us, "wacky backy" was a naughty, but not an illegal thing to do. And while I personally didn't use it, preferring to be more alert than dozy—my opinion—all four of the Beatles fell on pot like rabbits in a field of lettuce.

They'd never wanted to use it in Liverpool, but being new boys down south, perhaps they wanted to show that they were cool. They had a lot of energy and braggadocio, but underneath it, not a lot of confidence at first. Despite their time in Germany and all the gigs, they still felt out of their depth with more sophisticated, worldly people. It didn't dawn on them for a long time that they were really cool, that just being seen with them was cool. Their shyness and early diffidence was part of their charm and why journalists took to them and rarely wrote a bad thing about them. Girl reporters in particular were very protective of them. I remember the girls at *Fab* magazine in particular. *Fab* was influential, but tight. Their girl reporters were so poor they could barely eat because *Fab* wouldn't pay their expenses. If interviews went on late, as they often did because the girls were pretty and the pop stars they interviewed were good fun, they ended up missing the last tube or bus home and slept on the floor or in our bathtubs.

It had been drummed into us all by Brian—the Beatles themselves, as well as the staff—that we were never to give interviews to the press, nor answer their questions when waylaid. If we had stepped outside the line, Brian would have gone through the roof. The girl reporters were fine and knew how to keep secrets. If they hadn't, they knew they would have been permanently blacklisted. There were two male journalists in particular we could trust: Don Short, who did showbiz for the *Daily Mirror*, and Mike Housego, who I think was at the *Daily Sketch*. They used to travel with us, drink with us and crashed out on many a hotel room carpet. We could tell them anything, and true to their word, they printed the official releases allowed out of the office by Brian. In exchange, they—especially Don—got a huge amount of special access and "scoops." (The system worked: there wouldn't be a whiff of scandal until 1967.)

🐦

We started to make friends and "date chicks," particularly the long-legged, blond Scandinavian lookalikes who were running around London in droves. Everyone was convinced that we were into orgies, but I didn't see one. Plenty of sex, yes, but not a bona fide orgy. The darker, harder-edged rockers who followed—like the Stones—experimented with bizarre sex and every drug known to man, embracing every aspect of a new creed that said, "If it feels good, *do it!*" but everybody—including the Beatles, me and all our friends—jumped in and out of bed with London girls in the most normal heterosexual way. Sometimes, we'd find ourselves in bed with two girls at a time, and think, "This is *it!* Thank you God!" We believed we were really living it up when the reality was, we hadn't a clue.

🐦

Our favorite haunt in the early days was a tall townhouse in Gunterstone Road, West Kensington, which had been divided up into bedsits, one to each floor. We—the Beatles, the Stones, I and others—were drawn to it like moths to a flame. It seemed to be bursting at the seams not only with some of the most gorgeous girls in London, but with musicians. The Moody Blues lived there. Angie King, who married Eric Burdon of the Animals, shared a flat with Cathy Etchingham (Jimi Hendrix's girl) and Ronnie, who would eventually become Zoot Money's wife. A lovely girl named Marie was George's girlfriend for a while before she married Justin Hayward. Billie Davis lived next door, in the same house as Brian Jones of the Stones. All the girls worked in the "in" clubs like the Speakeasy or the Bag O'Nails. A few were models or aspiring actresses.

Gunterstone Road was very free and open. John and Ringo would drop in all the time, because essentially they were without a woman in London. Brian still insisted that they had to keep Cynthia and Maureen dark secrets in Liverpool. John and Ringo, therefore, acted as if they were footloose and fancy free, which—thanks Brian!—they rather liked. Also regular visitors were Jimi Hendrix, Brian Jones and Paul, before he met Jane Asher. Separately, or together in a crowd, we would drop in at all hours. It was great fun, a nonstop party, where we drank slightly fizzy pink Mateus Rose—the nicely shaped bottle you could stick a candle in for a bit of atmosphere—or spirits from a few miniatures that the girls had purloined from the clubs. Whatever the hour, someone was always at home, the jar of Nescafé always available, and the bag of sugar open with a sticky spoon stuck in it.

There were three girls in particular, waitresses at the Speakeasy, who seemed to be the most fun and drew us like magnets. It wasn't just that they were pretty and sexy—they were all that—we just liked to be there. For the Beatles it was a lot more welcoming than the austere discomfort of the flat that Eppy had rented for them. At the end of a hard night's clubbing we would wind up back at Gunterstone Road and crash out in bed with some girl or another, it didn't seem to matter who, while they, bless their hearts, loved us all equally and impartially. If several boys dropped by, sweetly they moved over in bed to make room for us, then snuggled up in a warm embrace.

When our same laddish crowd discovered the Ada Foster School for Drama in Golders Green, it was as if we'd found the big pot of honey. It was like that famous line in Paul Simon's song that refers to "The Greta Garbo Home for Wayward Boys and Girls," only ten times better—and all ours for the taking. We called it the Ada Foster School for Dirty Little Slappers. There were hundreds of lovely horny little nymphets. Several of them were in Dick Lester's film, *The Knack*. They were also invited to pad out (as a fake audience) the TV shows on which the Beatles appeared, like *Ready Steady Go*, the BBC's *Beat Room*, and *Search for a Star*. Some of them were even known as the Cuddle Pups—precursors of the delectable Pan's People, the all-girl dancing group that had every boy in England drooling—not to mention their dads.

Six of them lived together in a flat on the Fulham Road. "No! Don't bother to get up!" we'd say when we went in to collect them for a date. It was like a sinful St. Trinian's up there, pure giggling delight, all neat in black stockings. I had a girl from Ada Foster's who was in *A Hard Day's Night*. One? Who am I kidding? I had a lot of girlfriends from Ada Foster's over the early years. In fact, now that I think about it, I should have just gotten a flat near there. See Golders Green and die happy. Everyone had girls from Ada Foster's. They were the original all-singing, all-dancing, all-acting, all f-f-f-fucking ambitious, the lot of them. Nothing wrong with that, they had fun and we had fun.

My address book was a cornucopia of hot numbers. I had all of the Beatles' numbers and addresses from the year dot—with the old ones crossed out and new ones added since we were all constantly moving—and it was stuffed full of the girls from Ada Foster's. It was, "Help! . . . I need somebody. Help! Not just anybody. Help! You know I need someone . . . Call Ada Foster's now. . . ."

John or George or Paul would say, "Christ knows what they do to graduate."

"They marry someone rich, like you," was my reply.

Presumably the girls got their diploma from Ada, did the secret handshake like some Willie-and-the-hand-jive thing and shacked up with a rock star or a celeb. Ada's girls got to be in all the Beatles' films. They would brazenly court and spark and flash anyone who they thought might get them a break. Nothing wrong with that either. Pattie Boyd was from there and she was okay. It was probably because George knew so much about Ada's girls that he grew so obsessively jealous over Pattie from the moment he met her. She was a lovely lady, or, more to the point a "lovely Layla," as Eric Clapton wrote about her when he came to steal her from George.

9

In the spring of 1963, Paul embarked on a five-year on-again off-again affair with seventeen-year-old Jane Asher, a stunning titian-haired daughter of a Wimpole Street surgeon. They already had a nodding acquaintance from their times when the Beatles appeared and Jane was a regular panelist on *Juke Box Jury*, a top-rated TV show which awarded a bellhop's ding! for a hit, and a silly car hooter for a miss on that week's pop releases, but they weren't formally introduced until they met backstage at a Beatles' concert at the Albert Hall on April 18, 1963 when Jane was asked to interview the Beatles by the *Radio Times*. Paul was impressed by her . . . professionalism. That evening, both George and Paul made a play for the fine-boned young beauty, but it soon became apparent that she was smiling mostly at Paul. He was so entranced with her style and breeding that to the surprise of everyone there, he made no attempt to put the make on her. Jane was an up-and-coming young actress, as much a catch in her field as Paul was in his. They soon made an attractive and hip young couple and were invited everywhere.

I wasn't surprised when Paul moved in with the Asher family in their big, friendly—though grand—house in Wimpole Street, just off Oxford Street, London's main shopping district. At first he seemed more in love with Jane's intellect and her fabulous family than he was with her. Dr. Asher, a physician, had identified and named Munchausen's syndrome, but could talk in a warm and understandable way on any topic under the sun, despite suffering from severe bouts of depression. All three children were a delight—bright, smart, attractive and funny—but it was obvious that Paul adored Jane's mother, Margaret, often praising her high energy levels, her great cooking and her motherliness. I often popped in to see Paul and was treated like another son, so I understood the family's appeal. Margaret was a lovely and vivacious woman, who managed to fit in running a large and happy home with a job as a professor of music. Breakfast was a big deal for her. She always insisted that everybody who was there sat down properly even if you had a hangover and couldn't eat anything. It was an arresting scene, with Dr. Asher sitting there with his black hair and the rest of the family, Mrs. Asher included, as carrot-topped as a row of marigolds.

Officially, Paul was still the most eligible bachelor in the world. He was Paul McCartney, and while he could set seventy thousand women alight, he wasn't free; he was with Jane Asher, prim little actress, into Shakespeare and all that gear, though the fans didn't know it for some time. They would have been very surprised if they knew that Paul was living with Jane, not in Jane's bedroom as her live-in lover, but almost as another brother. He slept up in the attic in a tiny garret room next door to Jane's brother Peter.

Peter Asher had already started the folk duo, Peter and Gordon, while he and Gordon Waller were still schoolboys at Westminster, the famous public school. Imagine: it's 1963, you're Peter of Peter and Gordon. You're upper class but you want to be a pop star. You don't really look like a pop star with your red hair and your round face and your old-fashioned glasses, but then your sister goes out with Paul McCartney who moves into the house and gives you a hit song to sing ("World Without Love") which goes straight to the top of the charts in the U.K. and the States. Talk about good fortune. Gordon and I often went out for a beer and a bit of a laugh. Despite attending such a posh school, he was something of a rough diamond and good company.

Just across the street was the house where the artist Magritte once lived. The walls of the Asher home were covered with paintings and prints of the works of many artists, including Magritte, who was often discussed at family dinners. Paul became very curious about his work. This interest was to lead to him becoming a serious collector of art, and also to being an accomplished painter in his own right. Perhaps buried in that interest was an envy and admiration of John's artistic ability. They were equals in music, but to Paul, who had dropped out of high school with no qualifications. John's role as an art student had always given him an edge. John never stopped drawing from the time he left art school. He filled books with doodles and cartoons, and wrote short stories and poems as well as songs. His letters were works of art, with amusing sketches and plays on words. Many survive, but boxes full just disappeared over the years. Paul didn't have a similar interest, so to him Jane gave him an entrée into a different kind of creativity. She could offer him art, an intellectual family atmosphere and an introduction to a world he had not known existed.

Paul came of age through the Ashers. He delighted in going to tea with Jane's numerous aunts in their solid London homes. He found particular pleasure in visiting an ancient maiden aunt of Jane's in Westminster, between Buckingham Palace and the Houses of Parliament. They would be let in by a maid in a black frock and a little apron with a starched cap, and served a proper English tea from a large Georgian silver tray, with cucumber sandwiches and slices of caraway seed cake. Another aunt lived in a genteel manor house in the country, the kind of place where dogs lounged before the fire and horses were saddled up in the cobbled stable yard. Visits to the Asher's gentrified friends in the country introduced Paul to wood-paneled libraries and literary books placed next to his bed to read. Paul had read "good" books at school, but not with much interest. This was a very different world from a council estate in Liverpool. It was the world of the country-house set, one of breeding and style.

It was a world I happened to have grown up in during my holidays with my mother's family, so I understood what Paul was talking about when he said he was flattered that his hosts thought he was the kind of young man who read good books. For the first time ever, he started to read seriously and with real enjoyment. Crucially, he could go to all these places without ever tripping over a fan.

From Peter's window overlooking Wimpole Street, Paul could gaze down on the girl fans who started camping out day and night, even on the doorstep, once they discovered where he was. Dr. Asher would often go out and ask them to clear a path so his patients could come in. Feeling sorry for Paul, he also devised an escape route over the rooftops, into a retired colonel's flat, and out through a distant neighbor's back door. It always baffled the fans but they never figured it out. (Five years later Dr. Asher committed suicide for a reason known only to himself.)

When Brian, who always did the right thing, learned from somewhere about the conditions Cynthia had been living in, he was very worried. "I don't think John sees how it looks," he said. "If the papers find out that he is married with a baby son and then they find out that his wife and son are living in a slum in Liverpool while John is in a luxury flat in London, it could cause a great scandal. She'll have to come to London and I'll find them something nice."

John wasn't all that happy with his bachelor freedom being curtailed. He pointed out that recently Cynthia and her mum had moved back to the family home in Hoylake, a nice middle-class district where Cynthia had been brought up, but Brian was insistent she'd been practically hung out to dry. The boys were his family and by extension so were Cynthia and John's son. Before he could do anything, the cat was out of the bag. One morning Brian opened his daily newspaper and saw photographs of "Beatles' wife" Cynthia pushing a baby to the shops in a big Silver Cross pram. Instantly, Brian arranged a delayed honeymoon in Paris for John and Cynthia and on their return, flew them to London for official photographs that would present this happy and ideal family group to the world.

As he snapped away, the Beatles' photographer, Bob Freeman, mentioned that a top-floor flat was available above his own flat not far from Brian's block at Emperor's Gate in Knightsbridge. John had so little interest in where they lived that he took the flat sight unseen in November 1963, while Cynthia returned home to pack up and fetch Julian. Very quickly she discovered that having a baby and a large pram on the fourth floor of a building with no lift was a mistake, that living in the heart of London with fans camping on her doorstep was a bigger mistake, but she stuck it out for nine exhausting months. During the months they lived in London she and John did go out around town, but Cynthia always felt out of her depth.

Ringo continued to share the apartment with George—with whom he got on remarkably well—for another year, while sneaking Mitch down for covert weekends. When their affair got more serious, she left Liverpool altogether and moved in with him in the ground floor and basement of an elegant Georgian town house in Montagu Square he took on a long lease. They were in a nice little clique, close to Neil Aspinall who was sharing a flat with Mal Evans in Montagu Mews, and near Wimpole Street where Paul lived with the Ashers.

<hr />

There was so much demand for the Beatles that, as well as releasing a Christmas record exclusively for the burgeoning fan club, Brian decided to put on a Christmas show at the Finsbury Park Astoria in December of 1963. I was drafted to organize it. It was a pop concert with a selection of Brian's acts, including Cilla, the Fourmost, Billy J. Kramer and Rolf Harris, who all came on for a few minutes each. The Beatles put on a musical skit, which Brian devised, but they ad-libbed wildly. It was fun, being around them while the crazy and over-the-top ideas were bounced back and forth between them. It ended up a kind of cod *Perils of Pauline*. Paul was the hero in a flat cap and red suspenders, John the villain, with a huge villainous mustache, top hat and cape. George was the heroine in a spotted headscarf, who was tied down by John on the railway line (the audience went wild and wolf-whistled pretty George like crazy). I can't remember what part Ringo played. Probably the landlord, the sheriff of Nottingham or the girl's father. It was all very loose with a great deal of ad-libbing when they forgot their lines or what part they were each playing.

We did two special northern previews of the show—without the skit or the costumes—at the Gaumont Cinema in Bradford, and Liverpool Empire on December 22. Then we shot down to London and opened on Christmas Eve. Late that night—the twenty-fourth—Brian arranged for us all to fly home to Liverpool for Christmas Day, but we had to be back for Boxing Day, the twenty-sixth, for another two weeks. It was grueling—but just as we arrived in London and got to the theater, we heard that "I Want to Hold Your Hand" had gone to number one in the U.K.

We were still pretty hungover from the previous day, stuffed full of home cooking and worn out—but we raised the roof, or at least, the dressing-room roof, while Brian sat in the corner like a benign fairy godmother and beamed.

▼

As soon as the show ended, the Beatles did a booking for *Sunday Night at the London Palladium*, where they met Alma Cogan, who was to become a good friend. The next day, they flew to Paris for a three-week booking at the Olympia. It was cold and foggy when they arrived, they were tired, and only a handful of teenagers turned up at Le Bourget—a sign of the chilly welcome Parisians were to bestow on the Beatles. Overall, a general air of gloom cast a damper on their mood. John made a few of his usual sarcastic comments, within Brian's hearing. Brian shot him a glance, but didn't say anything, perhaps hoping that none of the fans could hear, or speak English—a pretty safe bet, back then.

The crowd at the Olympia was mostly middle-aged and stuffy, though, to Ringo's embarrassment, a wildly cheering gay contingent turned up and whooped for him. He sat behind his drums and bashfully shook his Beatle mop, looking dazed.

Don Short covered the Paris booking for his paper and described it to me when we met up for a drink on his return. I knew Paris because when I was a teenager, I had gone on a walking holiday around France with my Bohemian and eccentric aunt—a sort of *Travels with My Aunt*. In Paris, we'd been caught up in the Algerian crisis and the students' riots. We were arrested and, incredibly, thrown into the Bastille.

"The Bastille sounds much like the George V," Don commented, referring to the grand hotel they stayed in. "The suites were great gilded rooms you could get lost in with ceilings so high you couldn't see up that far. The bathrooms were echoing limestone caves, all ancient white marble and sinks as big as baths, and a bathtub in the middle as big as the *Titanic*."

He told me that the lads went back to their suite after a performance at the Olympia and got changed into pajamas and dressing gowns. They were sitting around having a nightcap, when Brian walked in with a cable, his face wreathed in smiles.

"Boys, you're number one in the U.S. charts," he announced.

"I Want to Hold Your Hand" had jumped from number forty-three to the pole position within days of going on sale.

Harry Benson, a photographer on the *Independent* who happened to be there, suggested they have a pillow fight to celebrate, to give him something interesting to snap. "That's the stupidest thing I've heard," sneered John. Harry, who was more used to dealing with politicians than pop stars, subsided in some embarrassment.

Then, Don said, "What d'you know, next moment, biff! John's got a pillow in his hand and he's whacked Paul around the back of the head. Paul's drink goes flying. Then they're all up on this huge Empire bed, bashing at each other with pillows. Harry was right—it made a great photograph."

The celebrations continued when another telegram arrived confirming their booking on *Ed Sullivan* and Brian was so ecstatic that he stuck a potty on his head during supper. Sat there, looking silly. However, topping the charts in America was enormously important to him. He had always told me that if they could get into the U.S. they'd break the world. He brooded long and hard about how to do it. In a way, it was a catch-22. He couldn't get a big tour there without a big chart success, which so far had eluded them, and everyone said they'd never get charted unless they went. He said that opening in some little venue like the American equivalent of the Cavern or the Casbah was out of the question. They had to make a huge splash, be noticed. And the only way was coast-to-coast TV. In Brian's eyes, the top show was *Ed Sullivan*—but for months, throughout 1963 he couldn't even get a look in. The U.K. newspapers did it for him when headlines splashed that magic word: "Beatlemania."

Armed with a stack of newspapers, Brian had flown to New York for talks with the *Ed Sullivan* people, almost twisting their arms to get the promise of a booking "if they chart well." No wonder he had sat in the starchy George V hotel in January of 1964 with a potty on his head. He must have felt potty with delirium and relief.

Three days after they closed in Paris, they were winging their way to

New York and the pop-music history books were being rewritten. Their arrival at the newly named Kennedy Airport, to the screams of thousands of hysterical fans, startled them. The Beatles—who like most of us in Liverpool, had been in love with all things American since childhood—couldn't believe that this welcome was for them, four Scousers from Liverpool. John loved it, but summed it up when he remarked, "Why do they want us? Don't they have enough stars of their own?" I don't think John would have asked that question had he known that in New York alone, "I Want to Hold Your Hand" was selling ten thousand copies an hour.

But, here they finally were, in their spiritual home, and ready to *"make a show"* with all the verve of their Hamburg days. They appeared on the *Ed Sullivan Show* twice, first in New York on February 9 (when the highest viewing figures of over 23 million was achieved) and then at Miami Beach on the 16th, when over 22 million switched on. To appear on such an iconic show, twice within a week, was remarkable and broke them in the States and the world.

I didn't go. Brian had left me behind to help take care of his other people like Gerry and Cilla and to be there if he telephoned with an urgent request. Daily, I would open the newspapers and read the latest on their exploits. It was stunning that so much of earth shattering (to us at least) import was going on halfway around the world, and we knew only what we read in the papers, along with the rest of England. None of it seemed real: they could have been on Mars.

The Beatles didn't top the bill on their second appearance on the *Ed Sullivan Show* (on Sunday, February 16, at the Deauville Hotel, Miami Beach), that honor going to Mitzi Gaynor, the very cute singing and dancing star of *There's No Business Like Show Business* and *South Pacific*. Afterward, they hung out in Miami, but didn't get in much sight-seeing because of the furor their presence caused.

On their return to London on Saturday, February 22, Brian had arranged a huge press conference at Heathrow Airport. They were on television, on radio and on the Pathe News at cinemas. I didn't see them in person that day, nor on the next, a Sunday, when they went straight into the ABC studios at Teddington, to rehearse all day for an evening performance of *Big Night Out* before a live audience. They spent Monday sleeping because on Tuesday they were up bright and early and at Abbey Road first thing in the morning—George Harrison's twenty-first birthday—recording their next single: "Can't Buy Me Love" and the B side, "You Can't Do That." In the afternoon, they recorded the first two tracks for the LP that was to be released as the soundtrack for their first film: *A Hard Day's Night*, which they would start shooting in just six days time. With a break of a day to record a second bank-holiday special show for the BBC at their studios in Piccadilly, almost the entire soundtrack was done in three days.

I dropped in at Abbey Road briefly, waved to the boys when I went in and chatted with them during a break, all very low-key. I knew they hated too much attention—they got more than enough of that from the gushing wives of mayors and town councilors. The idolatry of fans and press alike wore them out. They liked things relaxed and normal among friends, so we said, "Hi, how's it going?" cracked a couple of jokes, I said "Happy birthday" to George, the others ribbed him a bit, and that was about it. I don't think we even touched on America. Already, the huge impact of America seemed a million miles behind them.

By then, they'd lived through a couple of years of stardom in England. They'd grown used to being too big to go to pubs, to hang out as a group. Oddly enough, I got the impression that America was just one more "big experience" in hundreds of big experiences. If it weren't for the crowds of fans hanging out by the railings outside Abbey Road and trying to break in, everything would have seemed normal. They were back in their familiar surroundings, doing what they had done nonstop for the past few years: working their asses off. I don't say that cynically. I don't think anyone worked as hard as the Beatles. But they played hard too, a lot of which was done very strictly among friends and peers and in private. At all costs Brian's lovable moptop image still had to be maintained.

John was probably the first one to break the mold—but then, we all knew he just wasn't moptop material. In the spring of 1964, P. J. Proby, a Texan rocker from a wealthy oil and banking background, who looked and sounded like Elvis, was invited to appear on the first big Beatles TV show, *Around the Beatles*. Beyond his obvious talent, John was almost hypnotically fascinated by P. J's demonic, destructive nature. P. J. was like John's dark twin, a man who quickly found his way into the wilder circles and excesses of London society. He was a Jack Black man, lots of it, but John wasn't. To Cynthia's dismay, John started to hang out with the lean Texan who dressed like a cowboy during the day and in velvets, ruffled pirate shirts and buckled shoes by night. P. J. had charted in the top ten with hits like "Hold Me" and "Somewhere" and "Maria" from *West Side Story*—but ironically, not with the song John and Paul wrote for him, "That Means A Lot."

One evening they met up at the Ad Lib. P. J. just cruised through the booze, but John got hammered. P. J. roared with laughter when he told me the details of how the evening went from there, how Cynthia miserably trailed in their wake, begging John to take her home when they went on to a party in a basement apartment of a redbrick Victorian mansion block in Bayswater, where I had my bedsit. Cyn was horrified when she realized that many couples—some of them titled—were into voyeuristic sex, while others were watching a blue movie. John was passed a massive reefer and took a deep, chest-convulsing drag. He passed it to Cynthia and she declined, so he took another drag. Poor John. Tough nut and Joe Cool felt waves of nausea sweeping over him and rushed to the bathroom, where he threw up into the large white bathtub. As Rod Stewart used to say to his drunken girlfriends, it was "homey time." (And this was still several months away from the hot August night when Bob Dylan would be famously credited with turning the Beatles on, in a New York hotel.)

The deal for *A Hard Day's Night*, a poor one by financial standards, had been put together by Brian with United Artists, using Richard Lester, an unknown commercials director and written by Liverpool playwright, Alun Owen. By the time they returned from triumphantly breaking America, they could have asked for a much higher fee than twenty-five thousand pounds between them, but Brian never reneged on a deal.

At the time, he was privately mortified because, through lack of experience, he had agreed to 7.5 percent of the producer's net when UA had been willing to go to 25 percent. He never publicly showed his embarrassment with poor deals, but one could tell something wasn't right because inside, he anguished. Chewed his knuckles and grew pale.

Their records were selling in the millions. "She Loves You" had hit the number-one spot in the U.K. and the U.S. "I Want to Hold Your Hand" had a million advance orders, something that had never happened before. By April 1964 they had the first five slots in the *Billboard* charts—something else that had never happened before and probably never will again.

They had written hits for the Stones, Billy J. Kramer, Cilla Black and a host of other top acts. There were merchandising deals, concerts, films. Money was flooding in so fast, and not just for the Beatles: Brian started signing up more acts and setting up limited companies by the dozen. Unable to keep on top of it, he consumed Benzedrine in ever-larger quantities in order to stay awake and focused. When things got to be too much he rushed off to Crockfords or any of the other high-stakes, discreet, private gaming establishments in Mayfair he had started to frequent. Next day, he would be at his desk, immaculately presented, not a hair out of place. On the surface he remained calm and pleasantly courteous, outwardly he gave no clue as to the turmoil in his mind. Except for rare occasions when he let his guard down, Brian remained an enigma.

Until we moved to London it didn't occur to us that promoting records was a branch of the industry, because we hadn't seen it done as such. In Liverpool, we'd sit in the office and put the records in stiff envelopes and mail them off with a little newsletter to all the main BBC offices in Manchester or Scotland. Gradually, we spread our net and we'd send them to all the places where we had troops stationed, like Cologne, Aden, Cyprus, Hong Kong, Malta and Gibraltar for broadcasting on the British Forces radio stations. As for the TV shows of the time, Dick James had his connection with the producer Philip Jones at *Thank Your Lucky Stars,* and he also had a thing with Robin Nash, who did *Juke Box Jury.* Up north we had friends at Granada TV because we often did live slots. I knew the *Top of the Pops* crowd because at the time it was done in a church hall outside of Manchester. I'd go with all our people who were booked that week. We'd fly up, do the show, stay the night and fly back the next day. *TOTP* moved to London about 1967–1968, but by then, we supplied our own videos.

Before I was asked by Brian to "Pop along to a deejay or two," there was virtually nowhere to promote a record. Only the *Light Program* at the BBC played popular music. In fact on the BBC, which was supposed to be impartial, you could only get played on some lunchtime programs, *Saturday Club* or *Easybeat* on Sunday morning. It was the Dark Ages. Most teenagers listened to Radio Luxembourg, but their programs were sponsored by record companies who insisted on a playlist of their own records. Obviously it did work, but while it was very popular, it was also very restrictive. Some programs were sponsored by Horlicks, by American evangelists, or by sweets companies like Spangles. But then again there were only about ten records released per week in those days. That was the entire industry.

It was probably about the time of "Help," or maybe "I Feel Fine," possibly even "Ticket to Ride," when I went into the BBC and actually said the words: "Will you play this record?" I have to say that whichever record it was that I had in my sweaty mitt, it wasn't an enormously difficult mission. Asking producers if they wanted the new Beatles record to put on their turntable was like asking them if they would like a bucket of free gin and tonic. By that time I knew a lot of the people from going along with the Beatles to live sessions for *Saturday Club* or *Easybeat,* or for specials like *Pop Go the Beatles.* Any spare minute the Beatles had, they would be asked to do something for the Beeb so I got to know everybody. I knew the Rons, and the Brians, and the Bernies—all the producers.

When the pirate stations started up, it was like opening a whole new world for promotion. They played nonstop pop, whereas the BBC still had only a few selective programs on which pop music was allowed. It was difficult to be friends with both and not seem to be full of glee at Auntie Beeb's predicament. A fine balancing act was called for. We were feeding the pirates while we were also still exploiting the BBC. Some wanted us to choose sides, but for most people at the BBC it was a wake-up call. Its ruling board of governors had dragged their feet for too long and now the public—who, after all, paid for the BBC in the first place—wanted something back. This finally led to a big change: customer's choice. Of course the government tried to take the easy way out and sink the pirate ships instead of competing with them. The Labour government under Comrade Wilson and the Postmaster General, John Stonehouse, went for the pirates.

We used to meet up with the pirate deejays when they were ashore and ply them with rum and records. Sometimes we would even charter a little boat at Southend, Harwich, Margate or Frinton and go out to the ships, laden down with booze, which was thoroughly illegal. Apparently, giving aid and succor to pirate radio ships was punishable by imprisonment. We didn't care. We were like BumBoats bobbing around on the waves with the latest Fab Four records. It was such fun in those days.

I was on some of the *Hard Day's Night* shoots in the West End. At the Scala Theater I organized the hundreds of screaming fans, who were in fact students from the Central School of Speech and Drama and of course, Ada Foster, and were paid the extras' rate. Some of them were also paid to chase the Beatles along the Marylebone Road and Charlotte Street while the cameras rolled, but it was hardly necessary. Real fans came in the thousands, called by the jungle telegraph, and the police went potty. My job was to be there and attend to whatever was required. There wasn't much I could do, apart from rustle up lunch for the Beatles, pick up their suits and keep hold of their guitars to make sure they weren't stolen. It was bedlam. I don't think Dick Lester had a clue what was going on—nobody did. It was impossible to keep control of the script (what script?) or even control of the shoot. In the end, it was a happening and filmed as such.

Meanwhile, the accountants had seen a vast flood of money cascading in from records, tours, films and merchandise and suddenly they woke up to the fact that this was serious. Brian's golden geese weren't going to stop laying in the near future. But, just in case the money did stop rolling in, they advised the Beatles to invest in property. Bricks and mortar, they said, was solid. Brian wanted the Beatles to live in St. George's Hill, Weybridge, a secure, private estate in Surrey, near James Isherwood, their accountant and a partner in Northern Songs. This way, he felt, business could be conducted conveniently and discreetly. Apart from Paul—who was having none of it—the others were more than willing to comply with establishing a kind of "Beatles' enclave" in the countryside within striking distance of each other and London. But none of them seemed to believe that this was real, that they could afford such palatial properties.

George spotted Pattie Boyd on the very first day of shooting *A Hard Day's Night* and was instantly smitten. Her part in the film was small. She hadn't done a great deal of film work and was working as a model, but she was cute and very pretty, like a baby doll, with long blond hair and big blue eyes. Amused, we all watched George follow her around like a puppy, repeatedly asking her out. She said she was engaged, but, just like when he wanted to join the group and John kept telling him to go away, he wouldn't give in. Day after day, ignoring teasing from his compadres (who fancied her themselves) he banged the gong until she agreed. As she herself said, she would have been a fool not to date a Beatle, given the chance.

Like a bowerbird, George decided he would show her the nest he wanted to put her in. He went house hunting and in record time, came up with Kinfauns, a modern ranch-type of bungalow with spacious grounds on the Claremont Estate at Esher, not far from Weybridge. This was within the envelope of the area where Brian had ordained the Beatles should live, close to John's Kenwood—a mock-Tudor monstrosity—and Ringo's Sunny Heights, a large but cozier thirties house.

By the time Pattie had finished wandering dreamily through rooms that George said would be hers to decorate and furnish in any way she chose, she had made up her mind. For a girl who looked like a doll, playing with a real doll's house—and to be sharing it with one of the world's most attractive and eligible young men—was a fantasy, let alone for a girl who was only eighteen.

After the first flush of being seen with everyone, everywhere, as soon as they moved into the country with their women, the Beatles became quite reclusive. They didn't hang out on the scene, and didn't really know many musicians, not on a personal, friendship level. Their lives remained concentrated on the four of them and their small circle. Also, their domestic arrangements were very tight. George, normally the most private of people, became wildly jealous and possessive over Pattie. He holed up in Esher when they were married and would come into town only for recording sessions. He became very private and didn't go boogalooing a lot, unlike Pattie who wanted to have fun—lots of it.

It was unfortunate that she was a flirt. I'd often be at a club and there she would be, surrounded by any number of the dozen virile young rock and rollers. She was a successful model, mixing with the likes of David Bailey and the artsy-fartsy, feather-boas, Vogue-Tiffin & Foale-Biba crowd. She'd turn up at the Speakeasy with this camp entourage and we would stop and chat. I never asked her where George was, because we all knew that he was at home. If anybody did ask, she'd make that little moue and giggle, as if to say, "Poor George, he doesn't understand me. I just want to have fun." But she was never mean about it or spiteful. She was just so young and not ready to settle down in suburbia.

Sometimes, when we were in the studio, George didn't seem to care who heard him anguishing, tearfully begging her to come home. It was embarrassing having to listen to this. And it was even more embarrassing for me to see George, my old Liverpool mate who'd always had all the girls looking at him with big calf eyes since he'd been about twelve, on the end of the telephone, acting like a lovesick calf himself, as he pleaded with Pattie on the bar phone at whatever club she happened to be. Pattie was so beautiful. She was his first big love and he couldn't stand the pain. In the end, being excessively worshipped, and being the worshipper, were too much for both of them—she wasn't for him. She ran off with Eric Clapton, who had gotten ready for Pattie by taking out one of her sisters (who later came to work for the Apple Boutique when it opened). Oddly enough, George and Eric stayed good friends.

Paul and Jane were like two lovebirds but they didn't really mix with the others at all. Ringo and Maureen were two lovebirds who went dancing, George and Pattie were two lovebirds though only one of whom went dancing, and John and Cyn were like two "used to be lovebirds" who never did very much together at all, especially after she became a mum. The idea of everybody—the four couples—going over to Ringo's, or George's, for dinner, just didn't happen.

John's circle consisted of peculiar people and a few rock stars, while Ringo's clique was much more showbiz than the others, because he was the most show-bizzy of all of them, mixing with a different, more adult set from the rest of the Beatles. He and Maureen would go places, driven by their driver, Alan. They loved to dance, or they would go to the cinema and on then on to clubs, like the Crazy Elephant, or Dolly's, where they would do the Madison. Often, they met up with Cilla and her husband, Bobby, who also loved dancing, or Richard Burton and Liz Taylor, who were great mates of theirs and always dropped in on Ringo and Maureen when they were in England. Maurice Gibb and Lulu were also neighbors and regular dinner guests.

Paul and Jane went to the theater a lot with a young crowd, but in a way, Paul was more open. He mixed with literally anyone, but preferred mainly artistic people. Unlike Jane, who was into dinner parties, he liked to go to the pub as well. If he were about we'd go to the Green Man on Riding House Street, which he loved. It was behind Wigmore Street, not far from the BBC, and in those days run by a batty Viennese woman. It was a proper pub but unusually for the middle of the West End of London it had sawdust on the floor, bar billiards, darts, a pinball table and an old piano and it served wonderful pub food that's going out of fashion now because of the "Hygiene Squad," as Monty Python called the food police. We loved their cheese and onion pie (now called quiche) served with baked beans, their shepherd's pie and chips and crusty baked bread. Before he met Linda and they became vegetarians, Paul lapped up everything. The landlady made great Vienna schnitzel, which she served with a couple of dollops of mashed potatoes and great gravy. Wonderful!

We liked to go to the Champion just across Wigmore Street and down from the Green Man. We'd play spoof, a game involving guessing how many coins your opponent had in his closed fist. Sometimes we'd spend the day playing nine-card brag and drinking good ice-cold lager, which came in tins, rare in those days. Often Alice Cooper would come along and play when he was in London, or Allan Clarke from the Hollies and Mike Appleton, the producer from the BBC's *Old Grey Whistle Test,* would join in. We only put in a pittance, perhaps a sixpence a throw, but because you needed a lot of the cards to get out and win, by the time someone did there would be a huge amount of cash in the middle. Each hand ended up with more than a week's wages. Winners would fill their boots up. Alice loved it. He used to come straight there if he was in the U.K. He was used to drinking at least a case of canned beer every day anyway. Later he told me with a big smile that when he took to playing golf with Paul Newman, they had a case of Bud each and the greens got watered even when it didn't rain.

We sat in the Green Man pub one wet day in midsummer, Paul and I, talking about life in general, as we often did, about rainy-day things and about how certain things can shape your life. Our conversations were always about films, the news, music—a lot about music. The charts in *New Musical Express,* new records, gossip about the Stones or Elvis. Paul loved Elvis. He'd discuss how the awful movies he made, and the fact that he did no concerts after the army, ruined his career. He didn't think much of the colonel, who Paul thought was a destructive monster. Paul was fond of Brian and thought he was the best possible manager: one who was courteous, who didn't interfere with their private lives, but achieved all he said he would do. He never criticized him—none of us did.

Brian was a god. (It was only later that the façade cracked a bit, but even then we loved him. He was like family, and you accept your family for what they are and forgive them most anything.)

Some conversations and moods stick with you. I remember that rainy day going to the Green Man and can still smell that unique scent of hot, wet pavement. The pub door was propped open and we watched the rain pour down outside, bouncing up off dusty flagstones, gurgling into gutters. When we'd come in the door Paul had treated everybody to a bit of Buddy Holly's "Rainin' in My Heart" while we were served. He got a round of applause, took a bow, got high on it as usual—Paul loves to perform live—and he started ribbing me about Buddy Holly.

Looking around at a handful of regulars, Paul told everybody I'd met him. He digressed a little from the truth (Paul and John were always making such digressions) by saying that I'd won this competition to meet Buddy in *Housewives Weekly* by correctly guessing the name of Cliff Richard's cat, or by making up a little rhyme about Bisto gravy.

I started to laugh. When he sat down, Paul grinned and said, "Sorry about that."

I said, "No you're not. You're always doing it. And it was the name of Cliff's budgie, not his cat."

Paul asked me again about the competition that I'd entered that won me a trip backstage at Liverpool Empire to meet Buddy Holly and the Crickets. He was always asking me to name the three top records from that week I won—again—and about meeting Buddy. Paul had been there that day with our whole gang, but he'd not gone backstage, and to him it was the big thing. When he was a kid, Paul often hung around the stage door of the Empire when the Americans came to town. Like a lot of kids he collected autographs but, in a nice way, I knew he was a little bit jealous that I'd met Buddy Holly and now Buddy was dead and he'd never get to hang out with him. In fairness, he was nuts about Buddy and so was I.

"So what was Buddy like then, Tone?"

"I've told you a million times," I said.

"It should have been me that met him, you know, not you. So come on, tell me again. And then tell me what's your favorite Buddy song. And what did he look like? And what were the Crickets like? I wanna know everything 'cos you might have missed something. Me? I wouldn't have missed anything."

"Well, you know . . . he was just very polite. "True Love Ways" is my fave song and he looked just like his photographs. So did the Crickets."

"Yeah. Hell, you're a lucky bastard." Paul shoveled a ton of shepherd's pie

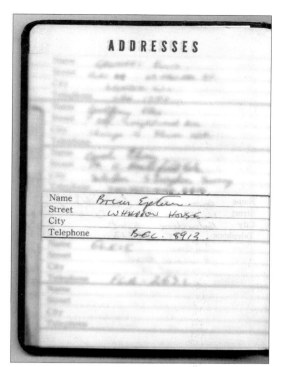

Name Brian Epstein.
Street WHADDON HOUSE
City
Telephone BEL. 8913.

THE FOLLOWING SIX IMAGES:
Six pages from my first address book in Liverpool and then London, featuring Brian Epstein, George, John, Paul (at the Ashers' home on Wimpole Street), and Ringo. Note how my writing changed from its schoolboy neatness back in the Liverpool days to more of a scrawl as I grew older and we moved down south, where so much was happening. John's Kenwood address is of particular interest. It contains the cryptic "Mr Pilgrim," which was the secret code name to which he answered.

Name George Harrison,
Street 174 Mackets Lane. Woolton.
City Liverpool 25.
Telephone GAT. 4595. + ~~——~~

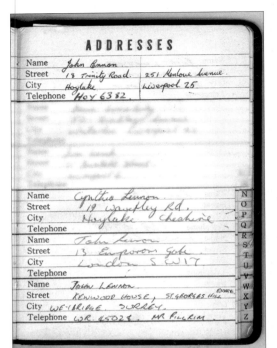

ADDRESSES

Name John Lennon
Street 18 Trinity Road.   251 Menlove Avenue.
City Hoylake   Liverpool. 25
Telephone Hoy 6382.

Name Cynthia Lennon.
Street 19 Waverley Rd.
City Hoylake   Cheshire
Telephone

Name John Lennon
Street 13 Emperors Gate
City London S.W.7
Telephone

Name JOHN LENNON.
Street KENWOOD HOUSE, ST. GEORGES HILL ESTATE
City WEYBRIDGE. SURREY.
Telephone WR 45023. MR PILGRIM.

N O P Q R S T U V W X Y Z

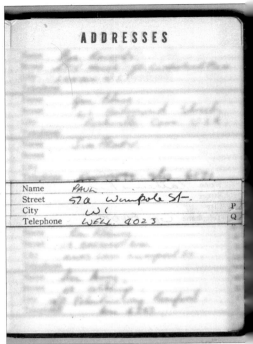

ADDRESSES

Name PAUL
Street 57a Wimpole St—
City W.1
Telephone WELL. 9023

P Q

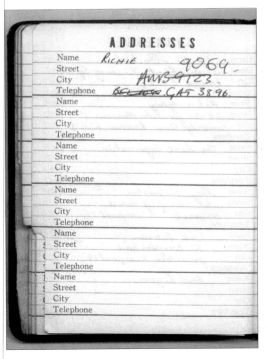

ADDRESSES

Name RICHIE   9069
Street
City   AUB 9723.
Telephone BELFAST GAT 3896.

Name
Street
City
Telephone

Name
Street
City
Telephone

Name
Street
City
Telephone

Name
Street
City
Telephone

Name
Street
City
Telephone

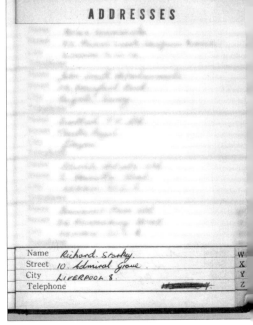

ADDRESSES

Name Richard Starkey.
Street 10 Admiral Grove.
City LIVERPOOL 8.
Telephone

W X Y Z

ABOVE: That's me with John, just before a show in Wolverhamton, autumn of 1963. There aren't many photos of John wearing glasses in those early days. CREDIT: Leslie Bryce. Used by permission of Sean O'Mahony.

RIGHT: Me ... taken by a *Top of the Pops* photographer, Harry Goodwin, in a little studio at the BBC when I was there in 1965 with the Beatles. CREDIT: H. Goodwin

ABOVE: Director Franco Zefferelli, in white turtleneck, discussing Apple financing for *Romeo and Juliet* in the reception room at Abbey Road with John and Paul. Many directors looking for the Beatles' involvement in movie projects, including Jean Luc Goddard, used to drop in and sit under the EMI dog. Goddard hung around for months and in the end asked the Stones to do "Sympathy for the Devil" instead. CREDIT: Tony Bramwell. Used by permission of London Features International Ltd.

This is me with Pattie Harrison and Tony King, standing around in hippie kaftans at the "All You Need Is Love" session. At the time Tony worked for the Stones. He enjoyed himself with us so much this day he came to work for Apple, then for John. Currently, he is Mick Jagger's assistant. CREDIT: Rex USA

That's me in the middle, in a sandwich board, at the "All You Need Is Love" session. It seemed a bright idea to put "Love" in different languages—English, Russian, French and Spanish. You can just see Paul, George and Ringo in the background in front of all the flowers. CREDIT: Rex USA

Again, at the "All You Need Is Love" session. I always feel a bit nostalgic when I look at this because it was the last-ever photograph taken of Brian, on June 25, 1967. He died eight weeks later, on August 27. He looks happy and relaxed here, appearing for once without a tie, in an open-neck shirt and a custom-made black velvet blazer with silk braid trim. Peter Brown (and, for some reason, a toy duck) are behind Brian. Getting in the mood, I'm wearing a necklace of hippie Krishna bells. CREDIT: Rex USA

The "All You Need Is Love" performance was filmed during the *Sgt. Pepper* sessions. That's me leaning forward and listening intently to Paul at the piano. He's in a very colorful hand-painted shirt that has the words from the single on the back. Ringo, seated to the right, is wearing a velvet suit. CREDIT: Rex USA

I thought it would make a good photo to line up the Beatles against a wall with Stan Gortikov, head of Capitol Records, in the middle. This was in the penthouse suite at the Royal Lancaster Hotel during the launch of the *White Album*. CREDIT: Tony Bramwell. Used by permission of London Features International Ltd.

into his mouth, washed it down with half a pint of beer. "I'm fookin' starving, me," he said. Paul was always starving. Even though he had a housekeeper and Jane also cooked when she was around, he never seemed to get enough to eat at home. Usually, he'd get caught up with something and forget.

I knew he'd reverted to being the kid from Liverpool hanging around the Empire in the cold, thinking about a fish-and-chips supper. He said, "I was going to eat last night in this casino, but I got me usual thirty quids' worth of chips and then for some stupid fookin' reason I started winning at this thing called thirty-six to one and I don't even know how it works! I ended up winning a lot of money. I took it all outside and distributed it to homeless people and—"

I said, "There aren't any homeless people in Mayfair at four A.M."

"Yeah, there are, too. Anyway, I never got around to dinner and I was too late for breakfast. Hey, did I tell you I met the Crew Cuts outside the Empire once?"

I nodded. "Many times."

He grinned. "They did that song, 'Earth Angel.' Remember that one?"

I said, "It's a corny song. Why don't you do 'True Love Ways'?"

Paul nodded. "Nah, I like 'Earth Angel.' John says I won't be told anything. Did you know he said that about me? He's been putting this rumor round the office saying I'm a know-all and an arrogant bastard." Paul was teasing. Our conversations were always a mixture of mocking throwaway lines and serious music discussion. The two often merged into the other, and only someone who understood would know what we were talking about.

Paul said, "John's only the rhythm guitarist, yer know. I taught him everything he knows, yer know. He were rubbish when I found him. Playin' on the back of a lorry outside the church hall, he were."

Paul might have suddenly gotten all Northern, but the pub door was propped open and outside it was raining even harder on streets that were paved in gold for us, especially for the Beatles. It was like we still couldn't believe life had moved so fast, so we clung onto memories of our younger days—and how odd that thought was, when I was still just eighteen and they were still barely twenty.

There was something about London's streets when it rained that smelled and felt good. The cobbles in Liverpool have a different smell, of the salt sea that was close and blew a fine mist over everything, diesel from the trains and trams that ran over the cobbles and coal dust. The smell of the suburbs where we were brought up was different again, probably a mix of farmland and factory and the river constantly flowing by.

Paul said, "Hey, you know it's funny about the photo thing."

"What photo thing?"

"You said Buddy and the Crickets looked just like a photo. Right? Well, when I first saw them early photos of Elvis I was knocked for six. He ruined me at school, yer know? Yeah, academically speaking." Paul was beginning to enjoy himself. He loved the pubs, sitting there while it rained too hard to go anywhere. I knew we were in for the day.

I said, "So tell me, maestro. How did these pictures of Elvis ruin you at school?"

"Because the pictures looked just like the records sounded. All moody and great, yer know? I wanted to be him. I did! I would have had me hair done like him but we could only afford one haircut and it was me brother Mike's turn. Hey, you don't know what it's like bein' a kid from a council estate, do you, Tone? Privileged you were, just like that fookin' Lennon. He doesn't get me to tune up his guitar anymore. He gets George to do it."

"George does it properly."

The class thing was a favorite ribbing theme of Paul's, even though he had taken to hanging out with the nobs far quicker than any of us. Even so, he could be very funny when he got going.

"If I'd have met Buddy Holly I would have—"

"You'd have tried to sell him a song."

Paul's face lit up. "Yeah, I would've, wouldn't I? Can you imagine, Buddy Holly singing something I wrote?"

Paul went over and sat down at the old piano. I still thought he was going to play "Earth Angel," but he played "True Love Ways." It was absolute magic. We stayed all afternoon.

Many years later Paul bought the whole Buddy Holly song catalogue. So here's a rainy day thought: isn't it strange that Paul owns all Buddy's songs but not all of his own?

🎸

During 1964 and 1965, as the months of our new life "down south" progressed, John and Cynthia grew more reclusive. Cynthia's mother came down from Liverpool and attempted to live with them, but John thwarted that by buying her a bungalow down the road. She still spent every day at their home, and John was forced to give her huge sums so she would go away and shop for antiques. "It gets her out of me hair, Tone," he'd say. "Hey up! It's money well spent. I can't stand her."

John was so nervous of strangers catching him on the phone that you had to use a code name to get through. It's in my old phone book: "Mr. Pilgrim: Weybridge 45028." Sometimes I'd put on a funny *Goon Show* voice like Bluebottle and said, "Hello, it's Min, is that Mr. Pilgrim?"

John would brighten up. "Hello Tone, what's up?"

But he came to hate the huge house, which was decorated in a stark modern style—at odds with its fake-Tudor exterior—by the same trendy interior decorator Brian had used for his apartment. The man charged a king's ransom to make it look chilly and cold. Cynthia was frankly threatened by its haughty glamour and craved John to herself in a cozy domestic environment. Mostly, he spent his time in the attic, in music rooms painted entirely in black or red, where he had a vast array of musical instruments, jukeboxes and pinball machines. He also had a train set that ran from room to room. When he came down from his dark eyrie like a bat blinded by the light, he and Cynthia ignored the rest of the palatial, echoing rooms and holed up in a cramped sun lounge off the kitchen. The kitchen was filled with so many gadgets that Cynthia was in terror of them. She didn't know how any of them worked and treated them as if they were bad genies hiding behind doors ready to jump out and attack her.

John kept a big box on a convenient shelf filled with pot. He often stayed stoned or dropped acid, something else that terrified Cynthia. She had been persuaded to drop acid at a dinner party where she, John, George and Pattie had been introduced to it, and had such a bad trip that she wouldn't use it again. She was convinced that sooner or later John would literally lose his mind, that his brain cells would melt and dribble out through his nose. The way in which he lay for hours on a wicker sofa in the sun lounge sleeping or gazing into the sky ignoring her and Julian convinced her that the rot had already started. She would hover helplessly over him, telling him to stop, watching him like a hawk in case he died—all of which wound him up, pissed him off, made him even more paranoid.

Kenwood became a prison. John was bored and lonely, rarely speaking a word to Cynthia, sneering at her mother and looking for ways to escape. I was a regular choice of playmate and co-conspirator. Every two weeks or so, he would come into London and get totally out of it. He would spend nights in the clubs or sleep in the back of the Roller, which would be parked behind the offices in St. James Yard. He would start these little adventures by suddenly arriving at my desk in the NEMS office, where he'd kind of hover.

"Hi, Tone, what're you doing?"

"Whatever you want, John."

"Let's go round," he would say, meaning he wanted to do the rounds. We never walked anywhere. Bill or Anthony would chauffeur us in the Rolls Royce, the Princess or the Mercedes, one of the half-dozen cars Eppy kept as runabouts.

John was now on the loose, looking for his fortnightly fix of freedom. We would start off at the pub at the top of Carnaby Street, have a couple of drinks, then it would be, "Where next?"

I became his tour guide, but I have to say that I always thoroughly enjoyed these outings. At least, I enjoyed the first few hours or so. The talk was good, the ideas a mile a minute. People gravitated toward John the moment we went in a door, genuinely pleased to see him. John was one of us, one of them, one of the lads. He was funny, as well as being irreverent and totally insecure. Despite being a brilliant songwriter, John wasn't as deep as people thought he was, but he was an original.

If it was still early, we'd go to our regular pubs, or we'd go to the movies in Leicester Square until midnight. "C'mon, let's go to a club, Tone," John would say at this point. That would be when my heart sank into my suede chukka boots because John was a notoriously lousy drinker. Two of anything was his limit, but he always demanded large Scotches and Coke. When the first drink hit the back of his throat and his eyes rolled back in his head, I knew we were in for a great deal of silliness. If I was lucky, John might fall asleep in the back of a car, either to sleep it off in the yard behind or to be quickly driven back to Weybridge, hauled out and handed over to Cynthia to be put to bed.

Sometimes if John fancied it we used to go out and drop in unannounced on Mick Jagger and Keith Richards in their squalid little flat, and brighten up their monochrome existence at their place up on, believe it or not, Shoot-up Hill, near Kilburn, a very Irish part of London. I liked going out to that part of town because I was infatuated with a girl who lived just up the road from the two Stones. I thought, great, because when they all get so stoned that they won't notice I could nip out and go and see her, maybe stay the night. Sometimes I was gone for a couple of hours and they never missed me.

On the way up to Kilburn in the limo, John got onto the subject of country music, a topic that often came up. The Beatles' recording engineer, Norman Smith, had been winding John up—which wasn't too hard—telling him to keep the hits coming or he'd be on the EMI scrap heap. As an example of how quickly things could change, Norman told John about when he was asked to record Frank Ifield's big hit, "I Remember You," which came just in time to stop EMI from dropping Frank for being a no-hit turkey. The Beatles had toured with Frank, an amiable Australian. Harmonica had figured prominently on "I Remember You."

"If you're in need of a quick hit, John," teased Norman, "there's no better way than with a country song and a blast or two of the old sea-salt harmonica."

John said, "No, we write our own stuff, Normal, you know that." But just the same, John loved country music.

The Beatles had also toured with Bruce "Hey Baby" Channel who brought harmonica player Delbert McClinton along. In the limo purring up Shoot-up Hill, John mused, "Normal's fookin' right, Tone. That song we did on *Ed Sulli-van*. 'Act Naturally'? That's a Buck Owens song for Christ's sake and about as country and western as you can get. And people love it." He was working up a head of steam, but enjoying every minute. The Stones, whose case he was look-ing forward to getting on, had a smash number one with Bobby Womack's song, "It's All Over Now." They were supposed to be part of all this big so-called blues explosion that was going on, but there was a lot of country blues about as well, and a lot of straight country which nobody bothered to mention. Country was considered hick and uncool. But in Liverpool one of our favorite local bands had been Johnny Sandon and the Remo Four whose set consisted of instrumen-tal hits—like Shadows' stuff—and Johnny did a lot of country.

By now we had arrived at Mick and Keef's flat, in one of those tall, flat-fronted, redbrick terraced houses with a few steps up. It was owned by an Indian man, and I think the rent was ten or fifteen pounds a week. By this time the Stones had taken off with a bang and were very successful, so this was cheap living—but they were rarely there and just wanted a private scruffy place to crash or to bring birds back to. They were either on the road, or at home with their mums and dads. Yes, like our Liverpool gang who felt homesick for ages after heading south, and returned home at every opportunity, the Stones were as sentimental as they come and homebodies at heart. After months on the road, sleeping in a succession of strange places, they loved getting into their child-hood suburban beds and waking up to the smell of their mums frying breakfast—or even bringing them early morning cups of tea with digestive biscuits to dunk. Instead of having their boys lug their laundry to a Laundromat, the generic rock star "Mum" would do it in the old kitchen boiler and hang it outside on the washing line, so it would smell of fresh air.

The shared hall in Kilburn was as scruffy as any other unloved and little-used areas in bedsit land. It was a place to park bicycles and collect the post. Steep stairs led up to the two or three flats above. I call them flats but they were really glorified bedsits. Mick and Keith's pad was on the first floor. There were two bedrooms, a kitchenette, a bathroom and a living room all carved out of the two rooms that had originally been on that landing. The living room furniture was awful. It consisted of modern G-plan beech tables, chairs and sideboard and ghastly uncut moquette sofa and chairs in a kind of sludgy green-brown. I also have a vague recollection of net drapes and chintz curtains strung out over the windows on wires. (It was nothing like the exotic rooms Keith later deco-rated with scarves and velvet wall hangings.)

We'd just slob out on the furniture, legs dangling over the arms or up on the

G-plan coffee table with spiky legs, while Mick or Keef would pour us generous dollops of Scotch and Coke (there was never any ice; in fact, there wasn't even a refrigerator) in regular tumblers, none of which matched and we'd talk about music.

"Hey Mick! How's it goin' then? Listen. I've decided that your smash hit, 'All Over Now' is straight country," John said as soon as Mick opened the door.

Mick grinned. "Course it is. Come in. Sit down, have a drink."

"Yeah," said Keef, trying in vain to sit up. "We used to play with Cyril Davies at the Marquee or somewhere, didn't we Mick?" He didn't wait for an answer. "Cyril did this song called 'Chicago Calling.' Great song. And another harmonica thing called 'Country Line Special.' " He paused and lit a cigarette with a twinkle in his eye. "Course, he could actually play it, not like you and Lips here. He played it properly did Cyril. Is he still alive? Mick?"

"Don't ask me, you cheeky bastard. I'm a pop star now."

Warming to the theme, John said, "I like a bit o' country, I do." Sipping his warm Scotch and Coke, he said, "If you lot ain't got any money, I'll lend you fifty quid so's you can get a fridge." Nobody bothered to answer because John never had any money on him. He said, "So the Stones have gone country, have they?" He picked up a guitar, began to play the opening riff to "It's All Over Now," and launched into as much as he knew of the song. It was obvious he liked it but took time out to mimic Mick's antics on stage, which amused Keef no end.

Keef finally managed to sit up straight, leaned over and literally wrestled his guitar back from John. "Country is cool. We've been experimenting. Taking a bit o' straight country and giving it a bit of an' offbeat."

A lot later, when we got up to leave, John said, "Can I tell the boys that you've gone cowboy and are no longer a threat?"

Keef said, "Tell 'em what you like, but you ain't seen nothing yet."

Mick had the last word as we went out the door, but Mick often did. "I always thought 'Love Me Do' was a bit country. All that harmonica. Did Delbert teach you all that stuff?"

A couple of years later, a piece of harmonica-driven music called "Stone Fox Chase" was used as the theme tune for the Old Grey Whistle Test, a great, somewhat cultish music program on BBC TV. The name of the program originated from the "Old Greys," who swept up at EMI's pressing plant where folklore had it that if the Old Greys could hum a new song, it was a hit. "Stone Fox Chase" was by an obscure Nashville band called Area Code 615, the area code for Middle Tennessee. Paul recorded in Nashville many years after that, and stayed at the Loveless Motel—deep in the heart of the Tennessee countryside—that was famed for its sausages and grits.

♈

Another day, John and I were sitting in the Shakespeare's Head in Carnaby Street when John said, "Come on, Tone, let's go and see if Mick and Keef are in." But this particular night they were all so stoned chez Stones that John and I had a few Scotch and Cokes and left. John was always pretty merry after two drinks and it was getting late. I never knew what he wanted to do until he said. Maybe he would want to go somewhere else, do something else. With him it really was the Magical Mystery Tour. As we left the Stones' pad I realized neither of us had any money for the return cab into the West End. We got on the tube at Kilburn and at first, alone in a carriage we reminisced about our life and how fast things had changed.

Back in 1957, like rock 'n' roll, John was about to grow up fast and acquire some attitude. I was ten, a well-behaved schoolboy, but as the Everly Brothers began a run of nineteen hits with the fantastic "Bye Bye Love," I'd gotten seriously with it. The Everlys strummed their acoustic guitars like there was no tomorrow, and hit the kind of raucous bittersweet harmonies I realized later that only kin or family seem able to achieve. They were copied by everyone from John and Paul to Simon and Garfunkel—who were called Tom and Jerry at that time and barely known.

On the truly raucous wrong side of the tracks, Elvis was "All Shook Up," and Little Richard was screaming about this sexy chick called "Long Tall Sally." John told me during one inebriated trip around the London Underground that when he first heard it he was in hog heaven. "See," he mumbled, "it's got a John." I knew what he meant. The John in "Long Tall Sally" was an Uncle John.

In that strange, twilight mood when anything makes sense, we debated whether the line about Sally being built sweet and being everything that Uncle John would need, had started out not as an Uncle John, but as an "Ev'ry John." Sally sounded like one bad girl, and as Dolly Parton said when her ma pointed out the bad, painted, red-lipped and rouged girls in town, and called them trash, "Ma, I *wanna* be like them trashy girls."

The Fabs had their share of trashy girls in song. They were amused by that sort of smut. She's a "big" teaser in "Day Tripper" was not the word they sung when they rehearsed it. I think what John was really saying in his insecure, introspective mood was that most of the records that came out in 1957 had become iconic. He was wondering if the songs he and Paul wrote would ever achieve that cult status.

"Dunno, John," I said, and fell asleep. In the morning we ended up at the end of the line where all the trains went to sleep in sidings after a long day. If a train cleaner found us and threw us out, we'd find a café and have breakfast if I had any money—John never carried any. But a week or so later, there he'd be again, by my desk, hovering.

"Hi, Tone. What're you doing?"

"Whatever you want, John."

10

I don't think Brian ever slept. At a period when the sky was the limit in the music industry in the U.K., he worked overtime to catch up with America, his wonderfully fertile mind continuously thinking up innovative ideas and then worrying about them—laying out a business scenario, then agonizing over whether it was smart or foolhardy. Some of his best deals came about when he discovered that Equity and work laws insisted that no British act or musician could perform in America unless an American act appeared in the U.K. It was tit for tat. Brian immediately saw a way he could use the leverage of his booming stable of talent to make money promoting American groups.

Through NEMS, in January 1964, Brian bought an off-the-shelf company named Suba Films, which I virtually ran. It was way ahead of its time, the only independent company in England making music videos. I learned my craft from the best, like veteran television producer Vyvienne Moynihan, and top pop producer Jack Good, who produced the successful *Six-Five-Special* and the innovative *Ready Steady Go*, as well as the Beatles' first TV spectacular, *This Is the Beatles*. Brian always tried to get the best. He hired Vyvienne, who worked for Rediffusion, the first independent TV station in England, as a consultant, to help put packages together and read scripts to see if any had potential as vehicles for the Beatles to star in. She took a shine to me and often asked me to the

Rediffusion studios to direct the odd number on *Ready Steady Go*. She would be on hand to show me the ropes.

There was a folk boom going on, so the New Christy Minstrels with Barry McGuire and Kenny Rogers was Brian's first exchange (or reverse) band that came over. To satisfy government requirements, all we had to do was to book them for one night at somewhere like the Scotch of St. James, the hot new club in town. But I also worked quite hard to launch their careers in the U.K., with some success. I found that American stars were treated with awe and respect, almost hero-worshipped. As Jack Good had found with P. J. Proby (an American who was practically unknown in the States), all you had to do was say the magic words "Top American singing sensation" to break them in the U.K.

Quickly, Brian gained confidence and organized some wonderful exchanges. We'd sit and discuss who was big, who we wanted to meet. It was like being able to pick the best candy in the candy store.

"What about the blues?" I said one day. The Beatles and the Animals were into the blues; the Yardbirds with Eric Clapton (the best blues guitarist outside Chicago) had made the blues into a white art form after the Stones had reinvented them. The blues were very much a "now" genre among real musicians.

Brian's training in his record stores ensured that he knew all the names and he knew who sold, even those on a cult level. When I mentioned a few of my favorites, acts I knew the Beatles were into as well, he nodded. "Good, very good. Let's arrange it."

So the greatest blues stars in the world, black performers like Chuck Berry, Muddy Waters and Fats Domino came over and were feted as heroes, great originals. (This was before Stevie Wonder and Otis Redding really took off.) When Ray Charles, a blind black man with an unbelievably soulful voice and a drug habit to match, came over to appear on television in July 1964, he was considered the "king"—and I was given the job of looking after him. It was a huge honor. The title of the show, *The Man They Called Genius*, summed up how Ray was regarded.

Rediffusion was one of the oddest places I have ever been. Everyone who worked there was ex-admiralty. Probably someone hired all his mates when they closed down a submarine base after the war. Or maybe they had all been in the Naval Intelligence film unit, with Ian Fleming and Graham Greene. They even called the executive floor "The Bridge," where pink gins flowed like water from a tap. It was as if the government had said, "Right, you chaps, set up this TV company as a front for MI5."

The offices and basement studios were in Rediffusion House, on the corner of Kingsway and the Aldwych. I'd been going there regularly for some time, but it wasn't until the Ray Charles's episode that I came across the entertainment suite, known as the "Green Room." I learned that they had green rooms on ships for the crew to relax in—no doubt painted a Ministry of Works green—but Rediffusion's green room had a long bar and was full of people. Despite the overwhelming "shipshape and piped aboard" feel, the atmosphere was as jolly as a sailor's hornpipe, so much so that when we did the top new teen pop show, *Ready Steady Go*, I was allowed to operate one of the big cameras, as if I were taking my turn on the firing range. This week: "The Rolling Stones"; next week: *Sink the Bismarck* and *The Cruel Sea*. As I considered this, it occurred to me that Billy J. Kramer's backing group, the Dakotas, had recorded the theme song from *The Cruel Sea*. It made the top ten in August 1963.

Everyone was in awe when Ray Charles walked in. He had presence. He was big, wore shades, and had a grin fixed on his face as if in on a secret only he knew about. During rehearsals—and there were days of rehearsals—practically everyone in the building and possibly the Aldwych, where the rival BBC had offices, came by to stare at him. He had his own minder, an American from Tangerine Records who must have been suffering from jet lag. He was tired and couldn't cope. It was obvious that he needed help with this brilliant but erratic star he was assigned to look after.

The TV critic Elkan Allen, who was head of light entertainment at Rediffusion, said, in his posh, plummy voice, "Tony, will you look after our Ray Charles for us in the afternoon, you know, between takes?"

"Sure," I said. "I'd be delighted."

"He's a blind chap," Elkan continued.

"Yes, I know," I said.

"Well, he's in the Green Room," Elkan added. "Keep an eye on him."

Sure enough, that was where I found Ray Charles, the center of attention, consuming cucumber sandwiches and drinking pink gins with gusto.

"Have a sandwich," Ray offered, after I had introduced myself. "And some of this pink stuff that tastes like shampoo. Not that I can see the color, but they tell me it's pink. Bottoms up, old chap." He'd gotten into the naval lingo, as well as the gin, very quickly. "Plymouth Ho! Down the hatch!" he shouted, tipping down another half pint of pink gin.

We sat down for an hour or so and I must admit that after a while, it didn't matter what color the gin was. By then, probably my eyes matched it and no doubt, so too did Ray Charles's, behind those dark glasses. I don't know when I noticed that he had disappeared. At first, I was quite relaxed as I sauntered about looking for him. He must be in his dressing room. No. In the head? No. Is he in makeup? The sound booth? We searched the whole building, offices, cupboards, the roof. He was nowhere to be found. He had slipped the net entirely.

People started panicking. "We're on air!" That was when Elkan's mellifluous tones deserted him.

"We've got to do this bloody program!" Elkan shouted. "He's gone AWOL. Get the press gang! Track him down. I'll have him in the brig next time, not the bloody Green Room."

What nobody actually said, but everybody thought, was that Ray Charles was a junkie. He had been busted for heroin a couple of times—he'd even written a song called "Busted"—and they were terrified that he would be busted again while in Rediffusion's care. Even a sympathetic judge in the U.S. had warned Ray that "next time" meant prison. He'd leaned over the bench and said, "Blind or not, Ray, I can't help you. One more bust and you're penitentiary bound." Meanwhile, he's on the lam in London.

Some of the others expected to find him dead, and said so. We searched again, combing every possible corner. Finally, they had to postpone the taping. A day or so later, Ray was run to earth in the Waldorf Hotel, just across the way. This wasn't the hotel where he was staying. We had already looked *there*. To this day I don't know how it happened that a crazy, doped-up hooker, who may have had friends with her, had managed to breach the security of the Green Room, Ray's minder and me—all of us *sighted* human beings—long enough to haul a blind man off for drugs and nookie. When we finally found Ray Charles, he was lying on the bed, pumped full of whatever drug he'd been given, with a big smile on his face. I just shook my head. I couldn't help but smile.

"Can you imagine?" I said to Jack Good. "The blind junkie in Kingsway, singing "Busted Again" to a gin-soaked barroom queen. It's like a documentary all on its own, Jack."

"My dear boy," said Jack. "Mr. Charles probably wanted a little fresh air to clear his head. The pink gins Rediffusion serves up are pure rocket fuel. He probably asked, 'Where am I?' and they said, 'The Waldorf.' To a black American, that's like saying you've made it."

<hr/>

I started to get more and more into television, mostly with the exchange bands, devising shows for them and handling the deals. For me, it was a fast track to an exciting new medium. Very few of us, including those who worked full-time for the BBC and independent television, had any real idea what we were doing, but that didn't seem to worry us at all. Nine months after I was first involved with television, Dick Clark telephoned me from Hollywood.

"Can you give us some segments for *Where the Action Is?*" he asked.

I had never heard of it. "No problem," I said, writing the name down. "What exactly do you have in mind?"

"We were thinking of fifteen-minute slots each week on the British scene. *Action* is the top U.S. pop show so you'll get plenty of exposure."

"Sure, we can do that," I said, resolving to ask Jack Good, who recently had returned from a year in Hollywood and was producing *Shindig*, a show that was quickly overtaking Dick's, for advice. Not only did Jack clue me in, but he asked if we could do clips for *Shindig* as well.

I hired space in what is now the Nikon Building, and for two days a week turned it into the Warham Green TV Studios. We got stars like Sandie Shaw, the Walker Brothers, Donovan, Gerry and the Pacemakers, Freddie and the Dreamers, the Moodies, the Small Faces, the Yardbirds—whoever had a record on the charts that week.

We got a little mobile video unit and were off and running. Videotape was brand new, the equipment heavy and chunky and the videocassettes like suitcases, but I learned how to use it in order to produce and direct as if I'd done it all my life. We worked in studios, or on the Embankment, or outside the Festival Hall or in the Albert Hall, drawing small clusters of interested onlookers who thought we were shooting movies. We could have shot movies, we could have made *Gone with the Wind*, that's how confident we were. It was truly wonderful, thinking up ideas and just doing it, not worrying about that negative word "can't." We could and did. We had a ball going to all the events and being a part of them as our cameras turned.

Freshly shaved and shampooed at his barber's, Trumpers, looking a real toff for his television appearances, Brian would go: "And now here we are by the River Thames. Direct from London it's the Yardbirds singing their latest hit, 'Good Morning Little Schoolgirl.'"

Then he'd stand aside and look puzzled as they launched into the raunchy little number with its amusing but smutty lyrics. We'd shoot it and off it would go on the plane to America where it was converted into NTSC format and inserted into *Shindig* or *Where the Action Is*. We used to do loads of clips in an eight-hour day, at a total cost of about one thousand dollars. Brian would get two hundred and fifty dollars per clip. The Americans really took to them, especially Dick Clark. It would have been incredibly lucrative if Brian had had any idea about what to ask for the clip, but even at two hundred and fifty dollars each, it still made a lot of money. A few months later, *Hullabaloo*, another American pop show, was launched and we supplied them with segments as well. As we gained in experience and enterprise, we went on to make entire programs for American television, such as, *Where the Action Is,* specials and *The English Scene.*

It was a magic time, very cutting edge for a twenty-one-year-old to be involved in during the swinging sixties. We started to have fun making classic little documentaries, shooting everything from the Richmond R&B Festival with the Animals, Long John Baldry's Steam Packet, The Who, Rod Stewart and the Stones to Gerry Marsden's *Ferry Across the Mersey,* a marvelous little film that showed what Liverpool and the Mersey Sound was all about. It was released in the States through United Artists, a company that Brian and the Beatles developed a special relationship with. It was the kind of film the Beatles would have liked to appear in because Liverpool remained very close to their hearts. It was the place to which we all returned like salmon, year after year for Christmas.

Tragically, very few of these original videos exist. We had no idea that at some stage in the future they would be pop history. Gold dust. When they were finished with, they were wiped and reused.

11

Brian's place down in the country in Rushlake Green, Sussex, was a joke around the office because its address was Black Boys Lane. All the papers grandly called it "Brian Epstein's country mansion," but Kingsley Hill was more a big cottage with roses round the door and some very nice grounds. It had been the secret retreat where Churchill met with his chiefs of staff during the war. Brian got up to a lot of nonsense down there, of course. Rent boys. Pills. Acid. Apart from the paranoia caused by drugs, Brian was deeply troubled. He was always in terror that one of his rent boys would spill the beans, but he was secure to some extent because "buggery" was still illegal, punishable with a very long prison sentence. Therefore, he believed that his rent boys wouldn't talk or they, too, would get sent down. But rent boys were often used by the police to turn Queen's Evidence against clients—immunity—and Brian often had to pay large sums to blackmailers. Guilt-ridden, always fearful that his understanding mother would one day open the newspaper and read some shocking exposé about her son, everything got on top of him. Brian couldn't cope. The odd nervous breakdown was followed by visits to the Priory, an exclusive private clinic just outside of London where film stars and sheiks went.

I don't know what Brian got up to sexually. As far as I was concerned, he was camp, but not depraved, as were many men in his immediate social circle. He was modest compared with his close chum, Lionel Bart, the camp writer and composer of the West End smash hit, *Oliver*. Brian had first known Lionel—who was born Lionel Begleiter in Bart's hospital—through the Tommy Steele connection. Lionel was in Tommy's skiffle group, the Cavemen, and had co-written their big hit "Rock with the Cavemen" with Mike Pratt, star of *Randall & Hopkirk* (deceased). With Mike, he had also written "Butterfingers" for Tommy Steele, and Cliff Richard's number-one hit, "Living Doll," as well as big themes like "From Russia with Love." For a man who couldn't read or write music and hummed the tunes into a tape recorder, it was remarkable that one or another of his songs were in the top twenty for three years and he won more Ivor Novello awards than any other songwriter. Brian had given him the idea for his last hot stage show, *Maggie May,* which was set in Liverpool. They had so much in common, they could have been brothers had it not been for the fact that Brian was middle class and posh and Lionel an unrepentant Cockney. When he wrote "Fings Ain't Wot They Used T'Be," it was the way he spoke.

Lionel had two houses: the so-called Grand House, behind the ABC in the Fulham Road, and a mews pied-a-terre behind South Ken Station. The Grand House was exactly that, stylish and elegant, a place to entertain in a formal way. The mews pad was like a debauched miniature chateau. It was small, yes, but every inch reflected sybaritic bad taste. No space was wasted, which was more than could be said for the guests. There were two-way mirrors everywhere, the toilet was a king-sized throne. It was a crushed-velvet Sodom and Gomorrah. Satin and silk orgies were going on all about you. Celebs and TV stars were being shagged in the corner as you walked in a room. Blowjobs in the kitchen. It was all going on, day after day, every night of the week when Lionel wasn't writing or rehearsing, and sometimes while he was. Brian's homes weren't like that. They were discreetly tasteful, everything just so. While things could be pretty wild down in darkest Sussex, you'd never stumble into an orgy in Brian's London home. Even if he had the odd guardsman or rent boy overnight, you'd never find a thing out of place in the morning. When his mother and father, Queenie and Harry, used to come down from Liverpool to visit with their son, they always stayed at the Carlton Tower, just around the corner from Brian's home, not in case they saw something, but because there simply wasn't enough room at his London place.

🦅

Brian was coming up to his thirtieth birthday, long past the age at which a nice Jewish boy was to be married. His family back in Liverpool started to put the pressure on. They were Jewish, traditional. Both his parents said they wanted to see him settled down with children before they died, so he looked around for a potential bride. She had to be Jewish, of course. That's when he went to one of Alma Cogan's little soirees with the Beatles, met her mum, Fay, and for the first time he looked at Alma with marriage in mind. He knew her reasonably well. We had all met her shortly after everybody came down from Liverpool, when she appeared with the Beatles on *Sunday Night at the London Palladium*. Two years older than Brian, she seemed ideally suited to be his wife. She was intelligent, attractive and funny, and in her private life dressed well and conducted herself demurely. She was a nice girl, nicely brought up and still lived with her mother and sister, Sandra, in a flat in Kensington High Street. Added to this, she was wealthy and successful in her own right. Most of all, she was Jewish.

Alma wasn't one to go out and about. She didn't hang out, or lig. She used to go to Danny La Rue's club occasionally where Danny, the kitsch queen of transvestites, reigned supreme. That was the sort of camp showbiz place that Alma favored when she did go out on the town, flaunting her trademark style of huge bouffant frocks with up to two hundred and fifty yards of net in the underskirts and a beehive so high Noel Coward had once asked her to remove her hat. She didn't go to parties. Instead she hosted "at-homes" that were lavishly catered. At one end of the big room would be a table groaning with a magnificent buffet and at the other end would be the piano and a radiogram. The furnishings were contemporary, very chichi, with settees that had that kind of squared-off look that wasn't very comfortable to sit on, though as I remember it, there were a couple of squashy armchairs you could relax in. Mostly we sprawled on the carpet. It was the kind of place where anyone, whatever their status, felt entirely at ease.

You could drop in to have a cup of tea anytime with the Cogans, but their proper parties were more formal and there was always a telephoned invitation. Brian discovered that John and Paul were regular and frequent visitors to the flat and he instantly asked to be put on the guest list.

"Of course, darling," Alma said, and after that Brian was always at these intimate showbiz parties. Guests were a mixture of up-and-coming young British stars like Michael Caine, Peter Cook and Dudley Moore and older, established stars, like Richard Burton, Liz Taylor, Bob Hope, Judy Garland, Peter Sellers, Dirk Bogarde, Cary Grant, Danny Kaye and Sammy Davis Jr.—the list is endless—they were all invited and dropped in when they were in town. I can remember people like Ethel Merman giving us amazing impromptu concerts. Sometimes Sinatra and Sammy would camp it up, while Dud played the piano. It was fabulous. I was always bumping into Sammy around London, particularly at a pub on Bruton Street, Mayfair. We'd drink his favorite brew, Guinness, and talk films.

At Alma's, innocent games like charades were played, or there would be singsongs at the piano. Alma used to say that some of the best concerts never to see the light of day happened in her living room, but such events were never recorded: cameras, journalists and tape recorders were strictly banned after a wire was discovered attached to a microphone, snaking down from the flat above—although often on a summer's night passersby on the busy pavements below would hear the music floating though the open windows.

At the legendary party Alma gave for Ethel Merman, pop legends like the Stones, Cliff Richard, Bobby Vee, Gene Pitney and of course the Beatles jostled with established icons like Chuck Berry. Paul sat on the floor at the feet of Noel Coward, quietly absorbing the scintillating conversation. For once, he was struck dumb when the Maestro said, "Young man, be satirical."

Brian was bowled over by this plethora of talent and wit and put a great deal of effort into being charming to Fay, a woman who insisted on smoking cheroots and wearing dark glasses in a room dimly lit by red lampshades.

The friendly family atmosphere and privacy allowed John and Paul to relax and be themselves. They started calling Alma's mother "Mrs. Macogie." Paul developed a slight crush on Sandra, Alma's younger sister, and started dropping in unannounced on his own. So too did John. After all, Alma had been a big star when the Beatles were nobody. Affectionately, John called her "Sara Sequin." It was a bit like musical chairs—as Paul left, John would pop in, but the Cogans took it in their stride and Mrs. Macogie produced another pot of tea and another plate of sandwiches.

Brian decided on a discreet courtship and arrived regularly to take afternoon tea with Alma and Mrs. Cogan, after which he would hurry away to Sussex with his male friends. He also had this thing about gambling which, strangely enough, none of us picked up on. Secretly, he went to heavy gambling clubs like Crockfords and lost huge amounts. We would have been startled had we known this, and certainly Alma would have been disapproving, perhaps more than about the homosexuality.

But, ultimately, Brian dithered about so much that Alma lost patience with him. She suddenly announced that she was going to marry someone else, a dark-haired good-looking chap who was Brian's double. Brian Morris was suitably Jewish and the owner of the Ad Lib. He was also the nephew of Al Burnett, who owned the Stork Club and had good showbiz contacts. Alma, Brian Morris, Ringo and Mo became close friends and I would often bump into them at the Ad Lib.

"I can't think what she sees in him," Brian complained almost snippishly. Now that he had lost the perfect woman, he convinced himself that he was brokenhearted, but I detected a slight air of relief, the hope that his mother would ease off. However, she didn't blame Alma and the pressure was soon back on. This time, Brian's attention alighted on a completely different woman: Marianne Faithful. Her mother was Baroness Eva Erisso of the von Sacher-Masoch family, with castles and dungeons and a history, an Austrian dynasty that Brian found infinitely intriguing and instantly identified with. Marianne's great-uncle, Count von Sacher-Masoch—after whom the word "masochistic" derived—had written the notorious *Venus in Furs,* and her father, Dr. Glynn Faithfull (Marianne dropped an L) had been a major in British Intelligence and worked as a secret agent. Oddly enough, he also invented a "sexual frigidity" machine, and after the war he had set up a progressive school, where the pupils didn't have to do anything they didn't want to do—in great contrast to his own daughter's formal education in a convent.

Marianne was fey and exceptionally beautiful, with probably the most luscious lips in London. She had been strictly educated, but under the surface she was Bohemian and believed in free love. She hadn't yet started her infamous and long, passionate affair with Mick Jagger but, unknown to Brian, was having affairs with the likes of Gene Pitney and a host of others. Brian didn't realize how promiscuous Marianne was because she had the face and the deportment of an angel. To him, she was a virginal schoolgirl and he appeared to romantically imagine that all he would ever have to do in the bedroom would be to brush her golden hair and lay out a Victorian nightgown.

The baroness had come to see him at his office with Marianne in tow, to ask if Brian would represent her. I knew Marianne, of course, and we smiled at each other as she walked in, looking demure, as if butter wouldn't melt in her mouth. Brian was making up his mind about signing Marianne when two things happened. The first was that Andrew Loog Oldham snatched her from under his nose and signed her up himself; the second more crucial event where Brian's wedding plans were concerned was that with no warning she suddenly married John Dunbar, a slightly built intellectual type who was an old friend and schoolmate of Peter Asher. As always, Brian mourned the loss and sought solace in Sussex. I had no idea if he had ever had normal hetero sex. No woman ever dragged him off to bed that I ever witnessed, but he did adore them. He loved everything that was feminine about them. He loved their clothes, their hair, their makeup, their perfume. He enjoyed sending everyone vast bouquets of flowers and carefully chosen gifts. I think he probably did ask Alma and Marianne to marry him but I don't know if he would ever have actually gone through with it had they accepted. Whenever things got raunchy and out of hand around us, he would make his excuses and leave. At times, he almost ran.

A combination of overwork in Brian's public life and overindulgence in sex and drugs in his very private life inside the closet led to his life careening out of control. We all knew it because of his erratic behavior, his mood swings, from euphoria to hysteria and, more frequently, to downright temper tantrums. Tormented and ill, once more he admitted himself to the Priory for a rest and to dry out. The problem was, he couldn't let go long enough to do any good. Daily, he'd check out for a party or an opening, or to have tea with Ringo, then be driven back to the clinic at dawn, using it as a hotel that came with doctors and nurses.

One major problem that had troubled Brian for years was the lawsuit he had initiated in an attempt to reclaim the Beatles' merchandising rights. It troubled him not only because so much money had been lost—about £100 million, if his own estimates are correct—but chiefly because it showed up his own incompetence. When the Beatles had first been launched upon the world, none of us had any idea what merchandising sales represented, least of all Brian. He should have had an inkling because he was, after all, in retail. During the first tour, when I saw how girls rushed at the boys and tried to grab anything as souvenirs, I can remember tentatively suggesting to Brian that if we printed up some T-shirts we could make a few bob on the side. Brian was doubtful because he somehow thought it would detract from the Beatles' image if they didn't sell— and if they did sell, it might look like barrow-boy tactics, but in the end he agreed as long as they were "nice."

However, after the Beatles had appeared on *Sunday Night at the London Palladium* in 1963 we were besieged by requests from manufacturers who wanted to sell everything from Beatle balloons and belts to mugs and dolls and even some dreadful black nylon wigs that would scare the horses. Brian was concerned that poor-quality items, dolls that split and trays that rusted, would be very bad for his boys' image, but he caved in under an avalanche of offers. Tentatively, he decided that he would accept a few of the better-quality items, and some deals were struck. The T-shirts were just the beginning. Brian didn't know how much to charge for royalties on posters, Beatles dolls, mugs—for the whole range of commercial merchandise.

Ultimately, it became too time-consuming for us to sort through all the samples and do the paperwork. John used to pop in from time to time and take a few prototypes home with him for Julian, or even for his own attic playrooms, but he was the only one who took any interest in the mass of stuff and eventually, Brian asked our lawyer, David Jacobs, to find someone to take it all off his hands. David came up with Nicky Byrne, a young man in the Chelsea set, on the basis that he gave fabulous parties and his wife ran a fashionable boutique, so he knew a little about sales. Nicky thought it might be fun to be involved with the Beatles. He agreed at once and asked five friends, also in their twenties, who also had no experience, to come in as partners. Two companies were set up: an off-the-shelf one named Stramsact in the U.K. and Seltaeb—Beatles spelled backward—in the U.S. For some unearthly reason when Nicky suggested a split of 90 percent for his company and 10 percent to the Beatles, David Jacobs agreed without quibble. If he had known that Elvis Presley's merchandising was earning an estimated $20 million a year he would surely have kicked himself. But he didn't know because he didn't bother to research. He agreed to the unequal terms and Brian signed the astonishing contract.

Nicky Byrne didn't even have to do very much to earn the vast sums that were soon to come his way. He didn't have to chase deals, he didn't have to beg. In fact, he had to fend off the manufacturers waving open checkbooks. All he had to do was what Brian had tired of doing: look at a vast mountain of Beatles' prototype merchandising, select some and negotiate terms. Things went so well that Nicky moved to New York to run Seltaeb, leaving his partners to handle Europe. When Brian arrived in New York with the Beatles to do the *Ed Sullivan Show*, Nicky gave him a check for $9,700. To give an idea of what this represented, the Beatles' fee for one *Ed Sullivan* appearance was $2,400. Brian was pleased with what appeared a substantial sum until Nicky casually informed him that $9,700 was just 10 percent of what he had earned in a few weeks after expenses.

Weakly, Brian said, "You mean Seltaeb has earned one hundred thousand dollars?"

"Yes, isn't it great?" Nicky enthused. He said that in three days alone they had sold a million T-shirts and had orders for half a million Beatle dolls—the list of the deals was long and there was the rest of the world to consider. When he added that Columbia Pictures Corporation had offered half a million dollars for his share of the company, plus Ferraris for all the partners, Brian nearly swooned. From that point on he determined to get it all back. He initiated legal proceedings in the U.S. through Nat Weiss and in the U.K. through David Jacobs, the lawyer who had been foolish enough to agree to the deal in the first place. The case was to drag on for years and was ultimately concluded with a small settlement to Nicky Byrne and the Beatles' merchandising rights back.

But the thing that really twisted Brian's heart and gave him no peace was that his contract with the Beatles was coming up for renewal. There had been several disagreements over finances and the contracts—some quite heated because John could be very spiteful. I think that John, egged on by Paul, who had rapidly become very aware of the business side of things, was beginning to realize that

Brian had *everything*, that it was all in his name or locked into his companies. In real terms, the Beatles had very little in their own names except numerous headaches in the shape of ill-thought-out enterprises that were a huge drain.

When John learned that Brian was even considering selling them—the *Beatles!*—to Robert Stigwood, he was outraged. He and Brian had stand-up screaming matches over this. John would storm off, or Eppy would run away. He'd flee in his Roller, driving off in a hurry, looking white and ill.

I don't know if it was the drugs or the rows he'd had with John that upset him the most. I do know he was deeply depressed each time he checked himself into the Priory and underwent treatment by a psychiatrist. Perhaps the psychotherapy, however scrappy, helped because when Ernest Hecht at Sovereign Press— quirkily, the English publisher of *Venus in Furs*—asked him to write his memoirs, Brian was thrilled. He was very artistic and had gone to acting school briefly, so writing his autobiography—as well as being therapeutic—was a way for him to shine center stage and at the same time, take his mind off his pressing problems.

"I told Ernest Hecht that no one would be interested in what I had to say about my life, but he convinced me that they would be. What do you think?" he asked me when he outlined his plans.

"I'd read it, Brian," I said, wondering what on earth he would find to write about. The truth would be too shocking. Casually, out of politeness, I asked what it was to be entitled.

Brian smiled, almost wistfully. *"A Cellar Full of Noise,"* he said. "After the Cavern. What do you think, Tony?"

I thought it was an odd title, but nodded and kept my counsel. Brian was depressed enough without me adding to it. "You'll sell a million copies, Brian," I said. In fact, I really did think it. An insight into the private way the Beatles lived, thought and worked, by their *Svengali?* Not to mention insights into his own *modus operandi?* That was dynamite, or so it seemed. But around the office Brian's book was soon referred to as *A Cellar Full of Boys.*

"I've decided to work on it down in Devon," Brian said. "Yes, I need to get right away from London, but not so far away that I'm out of touch, you understand." He had come over all artistic. He paused. "And I might discover a few new bands down there." Then he paused again and I knew he had something more to add. I waited. "You don't think John will think I'm raining on his parade, do you?" he asked hesitantly.

I knew at once what he meant. John's first book, *In His Own Write*, had been published a couple of weeks earlier, by Cape. It was due to be published in America the following month, then the rest of the world. We had all gone to a party in Cape's Georgian offices in Bedford Square, the heart of bookish Bloomsbury, to celebrate the book's launch. Their walls were lined with books, books were piled high everywhere. It was like an incense-laden temple, reeking of books and beeswax. We soaked up the literary atmosphere. It was different from anything else we had experienced, different from records and clubs and studios. John, of course, was the star. He'd experienced the adulation of thousands everywhere he went, but I could see this was different.

Now I said, "Oh, I don't know, Brian. John wouldn't give a toss. He'd be the first to tell you to put pen to paper."

"Yes, you're right," Brian said, visibly relieved. He grasped his book contract with relief and delight and put plans into motion immediately by hiring an old friend, a journalist from Liverpool. Derek Taylor had been one of the first to review the Beatles after Brian had signed them up. Derek also ghosted a national newspaper column for George Harrison and could do shorthand, so he was Brian's obvious choice for the task. Appointing Derek as his personal assistant (later, he became the Beatles' press officer), they left London together, seated in the back of Brian's carmine-red Roller. I waved them off, not believing for a moment that Brian would be able to switch off for long.

Arriving at Torquay, they checked into the Imperial Hotel, taking a magnificent suite on the first floor, which overlooked the promenade and provided wonderful views of the sea. Here, Brian began to dictate his life story. This went on for about two weeks, while Brian told Derek Taylor everything. That is to say, Brian told Derek a sanitized version of everything.

After a couple of weeks of intensive dictation, broken by lavish meals, the odd massage and manicure and afternoon promenades along the sea front, Brian grew bored writing his memoirs. I was surprised he had lasted as long as two weeks and I was expecting his call.

"Come on down, Tony," he said. "I thought we might swan around a bit, looking for the odd band."

"Good idea, Brian," I said. Privately I thought, *he means looking for the odd boy*, but again, didn't say anything. We did have a couple of groups playing in that part of the country, so that was the start. We would drop in on them. One group was called the Rustics; the other was the Silkie, who were quite good, but they didn't set the world on fire.*

I took the train from Paddington and on the way down to Devon, recalled that

---

*As I write this forty years later, there's a poster on the notice board at the village bus stop in rural Devon, where I live with my wife and two teenage sons. It's an advertisement for a gig by the Silkie—subject to the new village hall being built in time.

the Beatles had actually produced the Silkie doing "You've Got to Hide Your Love Away," and had played on it too. The Rustics disappeared. As a matter of fact, way back in the early days when the Beatles had played Torquay, they had also stayed at the Imperial. I remember because John got drunk and threw up in the cocktail bar. We had been in Llandudno the day before, then driven down to Torquay, via Birmingham where we stopped to do *Thank Your Lucky Stars* at the ATV studios. In Torquay we did two shows. That was four hundred miles and three shows in a single day, before there were any motorways, apart from the one hundred-mile stretch between Birmingham and London. The next day it got worse. We went from Torquay to London for another TV show, then straight back the same winding roads to Bournemouth, for a week's residency at the Palace Theater. Bad food, too much to drink, bumpy roads and exhaustion led to many vomiting episodes, some more public than others.

When I arrived in the suite, Brian looked subdued and Derek looked fed up. Derek got up, nodded at me and went out for a long walk. I asked Brian how the book was going. "Very well, thank you Tony," he said. But his expression said, "Not as well as I had hoped." He asked me how John's literary luncheon had gone. I knew he meant the prestigious publishing lunch at Foyles, the famous bookshop in the Charing Cross Road, where John had been the guest of honor a few days ago.

"I think it went very well," I said. "John stood up, sat down and everyone clapped."

"Really? What did he say?"

"Not a lot. I think he said, 'Thanks for asking me.'" Somehow the press had translated John's mumbling into the obscure acknowledgment, "Thank you. You've got a lucky face." I didn't tell Brian that John was tripping at the time and that Foyle's could have been Santa's grotto, or the moon.

I think Brian wanted someone different to talk to, a change of pace. Perhaps he intended to confide in me since we had been close for many years. But he was very subdued and didn't say much. He was a very private man. I don't think anybody could ever really fathom what he was thinking. It came as something of a surprise when he told me why he was tense.

Drumming his fingers on a table, he said, "What do you think, Tony? Do you think this beat-group bubble is about to burst? It's driving me to distraction, you know. Everybody is thinking that this can't go on forever, that it's suddenly going to stop."

He was right. That's just what everybody was thinking, including all those at the office who weren't too drunk or stoned to think at all. For instance, Ringo was already making plans to open up a hairdresser's shop or two.

"Ladies' salons, like Mr. Teezie Weezie Raymond," Ringo said. "I've got a bit of a name, so I should do okay out of this, don't you think, Tone?" he asked, his gold rings flashing as he snipped away with imaginary scissors in the air.

"Oh, I think they might remember you, Ringo," I said.

John and Paul also had a Plan B to fall back on, one that involved music. They always thought they could be commissioned songwriters, backroom boys down in Tin Pan Alley. Before Lennon-McCartney, and before Rodgers and Hammerstein, most of the British public didn't concern themselves with where songs came from. They could have been plucked off trees, for all they knew or cared. John and Paul changed all that. Songs became almost as important as the singer. Songs became hot currency, and song catalogues became worth hundreds of millions.

🎤

I remember a conversation I once had with John, who, some time after he and Paul had signed the lion's share of their copyrights away for no apparent reason or obvious benefit, had suddenly realized that songs, as in music publishing and copyright of same, were worth a great deal of money. Neither John nor Paul had understood the concept of "owning" a song. You could own a guitar or a house, but how could you own something you sang into thin air? But somewhere along the line, the word "royalties" and the idea of a song catalogue had attracted John's attention. (This was years before Michael Jackson spent $47.5 million on buying the ATV song catalogue. Included in this 1985 sale was the Beatles' Northern Songs catalogue, sold by Dick James. Ten years later, in 1995, Michael Jackson was paid $95 million to merge the rights he owned with Sony Music Publishing.)

John was quite surprised when the whole "song" thing dawned on him. I mentioned that many performers didn't write their own material, they got them from song pluggers. There were two kinds of song pluggers: ones who plugged songs to the deejays on the radio to get airplay; and pluggers who worked for music publishers and pitched the songs which professional songwriters wrote.

"You mean some groups *buy* songs?" John said, in some amazement.

"No, well, um, yes, sort of," I answered, having done some research into the matter. "It's a little bit more complicated than that, but not much. For instance, every time a record is played on the radio anywhere in the world, the *songwriter* gets a fee, which is collected by such organizations as the Performing Rights Society. The performers get their royalties mainly from the sales of the records. If they sing their own songs, then they get the lot—or would, if they haven't signed their copyrights away." The fact that John and Paul had signed theirs away hovered in the air, unspoken. John considered for a moment or two.

"And the *songwriter* gets royalties from the records sold as well?"

"Yeah, something like that," I replied, not sure of the exact figures, the "split" so to speak, nor how it all worked. This was new to all of us. John gazed into space and I expected some deep revelation.

"So if all this ends, Tone, I could make a living writing songs. What do you reckon?" he asked, in John-type naïveté. In other words, if this Beatle bubble should burst, can I still survive? *Good God*, I thought, *he still doesn't get it!*

"I don't see why not, John," was all I said.

Despite their obvious ability to put a song together with the greatest of ease and have a hit with it, it still rankled the Beatles and Brian that Decca Records had turned them down, proving that failure was always a specter looming over their shoulders. So they were especially delighted when the Stones covered "I Wanna Be Your Man" and had a hit—on Decca Records.

Sometimes John and Paul's throwaway songs became unexpected hits. "Bad to Me," "Do You Want to Know a Secret" and "Little Children," for example, songs they had knocked off quickly and didn't think were much good, were given by Brian to Billy J. Kramer to record and were monster hits. Paul liked the idea of being a Sammy Cahn and writing songs specifically for artists. He wrote "Step Inside Love" especially for Cilla, and "World Without Love" for Peter and Gordon. But John became a pest where songs were concerned. Once he realized he could make money as a songwriter, he thought anything he'd written should be recorded.

"Brian," he would shout. "Get Billy to record this song . . . Brian, get the Fourmost to record 'Hello Little Girl' . . ."

The thing is, of course he was right. Even their cast-off songs stood out like gold from what was being written for other artists by other songwriters, but John's attitude irritated Paul. He used to say to John, "You want everyone to bloody record anything you've bloody well written."

John shrugged. "And what's wrong with that?" He came across as the leader of the group, and the wildest, but he wasn't very wild. He was quite conservative in many respects. He was the first to start worrying about money. The more they had, the more he worried it would suddenly vanish. Mick Jagger was worse. When we went to see him and Keith, Mick would always be on about money. But then, he had studied at the London School of Economics and could count. I came across this dichotomy all the time. Pink Floyd would discuss Frank Lloyd Wright, rococo and Albert Speer on a plane, while the bass player in T. Rex did the *Telegraph* crossword in twelve minutes.

Meanwhile, down in Torquay, Brian explained his fears carefully to me, then he sighed, fighting against the confessional mode psychotherapy at the Priory and writing his memoirs had invoked. His biggest problem, perhaps his only real problem, was that he was homosexual in a still very unenlightened era. It kept getting in the way. Whenever he sat down for a meeting with heavyweights like Sir Joseph Lockwood at EMI, or whoever, he felt they all knew.

"They're talking behind my back, Tony," Brian said. "They don't respect me." He felt this lack of respect would rebound on his position in deal-making. Also, if he did see someone he fancied, someone he met on a business footing, he was never quite sure how to approach him to show his personal interest. "I mean, suppose they are offended and turn me down? How can I look them in the face again? It makes for bad business."

I knew he meant that if he asked a man out and his overtures were rejected, how could he continue on a business level with him? It was a difficult one. I was embarrassed by this unusual confidence, and tried to make light of it. "It's the same when you ask a girl out," I said encouragingly. "It's not really a big deal if she turns you down." But inside I knew that homosexuality was a very big deal and Brian was right to be so concerned. He might be arrested and sent to jail, or he might be sectioned, locked away in a mental institution. The angst Brian must have gone through was terrible, and looking back I can remember him looking off sometimes, deep in thought. Troubled, frowning. I felt a great deal of pity and sympathy for him.

I believe that Brian's paranoia over the Beatles' contract and his heavy use of drugs led him to think that it was only a matter of time before everything came tumbling down and he would be left standing in the ruins, with people pointing their fingers like kids in a playground. He certainly thought that music was cyclical, and in fact, he was quite right. But he didn't grasp—none of us did at the time—that the Beatles had achieved an extraordinary and almost unique iconic status and would never fade. But his fears were partly why he was always on the lookout for new bands, new groups, new soloists, new God-knows-what. By being so damn good the Beatles had started a big industry, made it unstoppable, whereas starting over with another band might not be easy or might not succeed. Brian continually said that teenagers were very fickle. The audience would change.

However, I don't want to give the impression that Brian was short of a bob or two, or worried about money. He might have been worried about the Beatles and a host of other personal matters, but not about his own business interests. John was serious about reducing Brian's commission from 25 percent to 10 percent because the group didn't tour or gig anymore, but it wouldn't have mattered to Brian's personal wealth. By then NEMS Enterprises was the biggest entertainment organization in the world.

I am sure that all Brian's motives were heavily influenced by his feelings for John. Though his feelings were mixed and confused, he was Brian's favorite Beatle. John was the witty one, he put himself forward. John was strong. Brian adored him and he so wanted John to love him back, and I think John did, but drew the line.

"You know, Tony, I quite see the boys' dilemma," Brian said to me, in his soft voice. "It *is* a bit pointless paying agency commission when there is no agency work."

"It sounds as if you have made up your mind," I told him. "John will be pleased."

"Oh yes," Brian said, "John must always be pleased."

12

During the time Brian spent in Torquay writing his memoirs, he contemplated a new project. "I'm going to open a theater with Brian Matthew," he told me. Brian Matthew was a popular radio and TV presenter, who, like Brian, had been at RADA. He went on to host *Saturday Club* and *Thank Your Lucky Stars* for BBC radio. He would even eventually go on to win the 1987 Pulitzer Publishing Award for the *Round Midnight* program, which he presented on the BBC.

"A theater, Brian?" I asked. "Sounds good."

"Yes, it will be. We're building it in Bromley. It will be a repertory theater, a place where we can try out our own shows before transferring them to the West End. Do you like the name, the Pilgrim?"

I said, "What, like John's alias? Mr. Pilgrim?"

Brian smiled enigmatically. "No, after the Pilgrims' Way."

He told me that the famous road, immortalized by Geoffrey Chaucer in *The Canterbury Tales,* had wound through the quiet Kentish town of Bromley on its way from London to Canterbury. He was very enthusiastic and put his usual energy into the project. Given the number of balls that Brian juggled it was remarkable that he didn't break down from nervous exhaustion more frequently.

In the first four months of that year alone, just on the business front he had taken "I Want to Hold Your Hand" to number one in the U.S. charts, set up Suba

Films, produced numerous pop videos, launched Cilla Black on her first U.K. tour, produced "Ferry Across the Mersey," romanced Alma Cogan, launched the Beatles in the U.S. with a ten-day tour, two *Ed Sullivan* shows and the front cover of *Newsweek*, produced the movie, *A Hard Day's Night*, moved NEMS to grander offices near the London Palladium, attended an awards ceremony at which the Beatles won five Ivor Novello Awards, been profiled himself by *Panorama* on BBC TV, written his autobiography, launched Peter and Gordon, made plans to open his own theater—and it was still only the end of April.

Happy as sandboys, the two Brians would disappear down to Kent where they held discussions with planners and architects. One day when I popped into the office, Brian looked despondent. "The Pilgrim Theater is not to be," he told me. "We have been refused planning permission."

"Did they say why?" I asked.

Brian shook his head. "We told them that we were going to put on plays and nice little musicals, but I don't think they believed us. I think they thought we might put the Beatles on and have riots in their nice middle-class town."

"Well, you can always open another theater somewhere else," I said.

Brian looked at me thoughtfully. He didn't comment. A year was to pass before he did anything about it.

A Hard Day's Night had barely been released at a royal charity premier— attended by Princess Margaret and Lord Snowdon and a host of celebrities— when Bud Ornstein, European head of production for United Artists, casually let slip to Brian that the two million soundtrack-album sales in 1964 alone had paid for the entire cost of the film. Brian was not happy when he realized that he had given away all soundtrack rights to United Artists. He had also locked the Beatles into two more films for UA. Brooding about it, he confided in Bud that he wanted to make full-length features himself, where all the income would be his. Bud instantly resigned from UA in order to set up Pickfair Films with Brian.

The Beatles' next film for UA, *Help!* was already being scripted for shooting the following spring in the Bahamas. The Bahamas were chosen because Brian wanted to set up a company there as a tax shelter. The third film in the agreement would be shot at the end of 1965. Meanwhile, Brian decided that he could put the wheels in motion for a Beatles/Pickfair film. But finding the right vehicle wasn't easy. They came up with a Western. It was canceled. Plans for *Help!* continued.

While his corporate life went three steps forward and two steps back, Brian also spent time on his private affairs. For some time he had considered that his modern flat in Knightsbridge didn't offer him enough privacy. Besides, he was bored with its bleak modernity. For a Christmas present to himself in December of 1964 he bought a Regency house of doll's-house proportions in Chapel Street, Belgravia, and furnished it tastefully with antiques. Personally, I thought it was too small. Compared with what he could have afforded, it was a narrow sliver of a building in a terraced row of similar houses and had too few rooms. In the basement were the servants' quarters, where his housekeeper and chauffeur lived. There was a little kitchen and a small lounge, his bedroom and his home office. He often threw quite lavish parties and they were always cramped. When he wasn't there, I used to go round and romance his secretary, Joanne Peterson (nee Newfield), who later married Colin, the original drummer in the Bee Gees. Lulu—who was married to Maurice Gibb, one of the Bee Gees—and Joanne were best friends. On one not-too-memorable occasion we went on a pub and club crawl. I got smashed and while Lulu bombed down the street in her Mini, I hung out of the window, chucking up. Both girls thought it was hilarious and told everyone.

We used to go drinking at Dehams in Dean Street, the Marquis of Granby on the corner of Shaftesbury Avenue, or when all the pirate radio stations got proper offices in Curzon Street, we'd go to the pubs up there and hang out with the disc jockeys who were on shore leave. In the evening we'd sometimes go to the Pheasantry, and there would be lovely Julie Felix. David Frost would be there, and quite often Eric Clapton. I don't think I went anywhere back then without seeing someone I knew in each and every watering hole.

My life was very relaxed and open, and quite different from Brian's or even the Beatles'. They tended to be more cautious about where they went, especially together, while Brian, when he wasn't out and about with his public face at some premier or another, was very private. However, Brian and I did go out together fairly frequently, not on a social level as such, but to check out talent. I was the scout, and if I thought someone worth signing up, Brian would pop along to have a look. Generally speaking, he trusted my ability but he could be perverse, as in the case of a young singer-songwriter, Paul Simon.

Paul, who had his first album with Art Garfunkel in 1964, still couldn't even get arrested in America and had made his way to Europe to play in the small folk clubs of Paris and around England. He was so settled in that he'd gotten a flat in London and a nice girlfriend named Kathy—as in "Kathy's Song"—who he always missed badly when he caught a train out of town to play at small folk cellars. It was one early morning on the bleak station at Widnes while he waited for the milk train back to London that he wrote "Homeward Bound."

I saw him playing at a folk club called Les Cousins, in Wardour Street, and thought he was rather good. In fact, I thought he was great. This was during the time of Bob Dylan and Donovan and Cat Stevens. Les Cousins was one of those Soho-type places where you didn't *go;* instead, you popped in for a drink. But on this occasion, I popped in and stayed awhile. The next morning, I was in the office and chatting to Brian when he asked, "Have you seen anything interesting recently?" I told him I had.

"Yes, there's a great folk singer in Les Cousins, called Paul Simon."

So I took Brian along to the club that evening, to watch Paul's show. Brian wasn't very impressed. "He's a bit small and Jewish-looking," he said. "Not real pop star material. I don't think the mass audience would go for him. Let's have another bottle, what do you say?"

I argued a bit—not about the wine but about Paul Simon. You didn't argue with Brian. He could be very stubborn and made up his mind quickly when it came to business.

🚩

Brian went on holiday with Lionel Bart to the South of France early in 1965, where they ran into James Baldwin. Apart from having homosexuality in common, all three of them instantly clicked on a friendship level. I don't know if it was this auspicious meeting of minds that reminded Brian of his dream of owning a theater, but on his return he put the wheels in motion to become a shareholder of the Saville. In October he produced his first play, *Amen Corner* by James Baldwin.

Brian had such an air of pride about him as he seated his guests—Dusty Springfield, Sir Joseph Lockwood, Lionel Bart, Andrew Oldham, Walter Shenson and Dick James—in the royal box, that he positively glowed. At the reception held afterward, you could see that there was a deep affinity between Brian and the openly gay black American writer. Baldwin had already published his seminal work, *Go Tell It on the Mountain,* to great acclaim and *Giovanni's Room* to great approbation. *Giovanni's Room,* which told the story of an anguished white homosexual, shockingly highlighted the themes of interracial relationships and sexuality. He was savaged by the critics and condemned by the black community. Escaping from prejudice and a hostile environment, Baldwin went to live abroad, first to Paris and Istanbul and, currently, the South of France, where he learned to be himself, and where he met Brian.

Back in London, Brian, who was still locked in the closet, was mesmerized like a bird confronted by a snake by Baldwin's satirical and self-deprecating use of terms like, "well, speaking as a faggot." Fascinated and admiring, but not enough to do it himself. When directed by Baldwin to be honest and brave, to openly confront his sexuality, Brian lamely said, "Well, this is London, of course, not Paris."

That autumn, Lionel Bart was busy with rehearsals for his newest musical, *Twang!* The title was dreadful enough and caused endless titters in the office, but the show was a complete disaster. Lionel had been so generous with friends and hangers-on when he was in the money, that he'd habitually kept a large bowl filled with one thousand pounds in crisp notes on his mantelpiece for anyone who was short to help themselves, which cheerfully and quite ungratefully, they did. Now, when he turned to friends to prop up *Twang!* very few came forward.

Privately, Brian helped, until there came a time when he had to say no. Desperate, facing bankruptcy, Lionel did the silliest thing in his life: he sold his copyright to *Oliver* and to all his future works and poured the cash into the doomed show until there was nothing left. The show bombed and Lionel declared bankruptcy. He lost his lavish homes and his sybaritic lifestyle. The eventual film version of *Oliver* was a massive hit. The album made many millions more. Lionel didn't see a penny from any of it and he became an alcoholic.

As he had done with pop management, starting with one group and then moving to two, then seeing the sky as the limit, Brian put on *A Smashing Day* written by Alan Plater at the Arts Theater, starring Hywel Bennett. It was the only thing he ever directed and he only did so because the assigned director, John Fernald, was taken ill. The play itself consisted of a couple of buskers who told a little story between scenes as a kind of musical thread. Brian told me to go out and find someone to play the buskers. At his suggestion, I came up with two kids from RADA, Robert Powell and Ben Kingsley, the latter of whom played guitar. Nobody could have guessed that many years later a bald version of Ben would win an Oscar for *Gandhi* and Robert would play Jesus in Lew Grade's huge TV series, *Jesus of Nazareth.* After the play we would go across the road to the Pickwick Club, which was owned by Harry Secombe, Lesley Bricusse and Anthony Newley, to listen to the Peddlers, or Paddy, Klaus and Gibson. It was a nice theatrical place to go. Members of our unofficial Glee Club would stay up all night with friends like Peter Noone who was "Herman" of Herman's Hermits, Chris Cooke, who was Lulu's roadie, Bob Farmer, editor of *Disc* Magazine, a whole crowd from the *New Musical Express*—including staff writers Richard Green *and* Norrie Drummond—and a giggle-gaggle of young female writers from *Fab.*

These were great times. At dawn, someone would say, "Let's go down to Brighton for the weekend," and off we'd go. Herman, who could be seen on TOTP looking like the kid next door, singing "Mrs. Brown You've Got a Lovely

Daughter," was a juicer. He had a great sense of humor and a serious booze problem—which many of us had at the time, though none of us realized this about ourselves. At one time he was almost as big in the States as the Beatles were. He earned a great deal of money and was fairly discreet about it; but the pop star who earned more money than anyone apart from the Beatles was Dave Clark, of the Dave Clark Five. Financially, he was very astute, far smarter than Brian, and without a doubt far smarter than the Beatles, who left it all up to Brian. Dave left it up to no one. He owned everything, from his copyrights to his production company. He paid the band wages and the rest was all his. He was one of the first artists to come up with a lease-tape deal, whereby he fully owned and leased out the product on a one-off basis to his record label. If Brian, who usually tried to think of everything first, had thought of *that*, the Beatles would have been richer than anyone in the universe. Again!

Clarky's first major purchase was the entire building in Curzon Street, Mayfair, which contained the Curzon Cinema, a very valuable property. He knocked several flats together into a penthouse duplex and that's where he still lives, with his original DC5 60s E-type Jaguar in the garage and all the toys that pop stars are supposed to have but rarely do. If there was a button or a switch that operated something automatically, Clarky had it, and what's more, he knew how to work it. A massive TV screen years before anyone else, noise-activated lights, clap your hands and the curtains closed. His girlfriends were some of the most beautiful girls in town.

Unlike Herman, Dave rarely drank, but when we dropped in he'd fill tumblers to the brim with Scotch or vodka. After that, it was literally a matter of surviving. I'd lie back in this state-of-the-art splendor and contemplate how very different it was from the early days in Liverpool when Clarky, who had been a film extra and stuntman, used to send Christmas cards to us at the NEMS offices, hoping to get noticed by Brian and signed up.

By the Christmas of 1965, with Lionel's *Twang!* still a recent enough nightmare to be an example of something to avoid, Brian put on a season of dear old uncontroversial Gilbert and Sullivan at the Saville, which did very well. I got to stay in the Savoy Hotel with the D'Oyly Carte Company for months on end. Looking after them all was a small price to pay for the convenience of living in luxury in the heart of the West End. I used to meet with them at the American Bar at eleven o'clock each evening for cocktails, with a carnation in the top pocket, de rigeur for Bridget D'Oyly Carte. It was wonderful fun and I adored it at first, but you can only go through their catalogue so many times before you knew it back to front and were sick and tired of it and bored with being de rigeur. Cilla did a cabaret season at the Savoy during the time I was there, and as a nightcap, I would drop in on her show and meet many people I knew. I had become a boulevardier, and it was fun.

At the other end of the Burlington Bertie scene, Don Arden was also around and rapidly gaining a reputation of being the British Al Capone. He even delighted in being a cliché of the old-time vaudevillehood and would relish telling stories of how he used to enforce his position through threats. Born Harry Levy in the East End of London in a tough world between the wars, he'd started in vaudeville at the age of thirteen and clawed his way up and out. His first success was as British tour promoter to Little Richard and Gene Vincent. Don and Gene fell out to the extent that Gene used to replace the words "our souls" in one of his songs, with "arseholes" and dedicate it on stage to Don. Next Don became agent to the Animals. It wasn't long before the joke went round that it was hard to tell who was the wilder—Don or the group. I was around the Animals a lot because of my close friendship with Brian "Chas" Chandler, their bass player. Aggressively, Don built up a big roster of acts, by which time he had an international rep as a heavy. Everything was cleared through Don, or else.

Three years earlier, the Beatles had been second on the bill to Little Richard at the New Brighton Tower Ballroom, just outside Liverpool. It was Brian's biggest venture, a five-and-a-half-hour, twelve-act presentation and very important for the Beatles, because it was the first time they had appeared on the same bill as a big American star. They loved Little Richard, despite the fact that he could be a bit weird and a bit of a prima donna. I was there that night when I saw "a look" pass between him and Brian, a kind of recognition. Nothing was said, everything was cool. Don frowned, but he didn't work it out because he didn't understand the subtleties of gayness. He thought something secret was going on, that Brian was trying to lure Little Richard away to sign with him. Don didn't understand someone like Brian at all. Brian would never dream of luring anyone away from their agency, unless sorely tried. But that's the way Don always thought. He once broke Robert Stigwood's desk with a single blow with a giant ashtray, and then hung him out of the third floor window of his office when he thought Stiggy was trying to steal the Small Faces. Describing the scene with the relish of a Capone, Don chuckled, "I went along to nail him to his chair, but I thought he was gonna have a heart attack, so I got him some fresh air."

In New Brighton that night, Don started an argument with Brian over Little Richard. In fact he went crazy. Brian didn't respond. He just stood, quietly gazing into space and when Don had run out of steam, Brian said quite mildly, "I will be calling your employers on Monday and demand that they terminate your employment." This was Brian's sophisticated version of today's, "Your ass is grass."

Still, it stopped Don dead in his tracks. He said he'd been all over the world and nobody had ever talked to him like that. *Politely.* He was even more incensed, when Brian actually did book Little Richard a couple of weeks later at the Liverpool Empire. Craig Douglas, Jet Harris and the Beatles were also on the bill. I remember that it was a Sunday, the day when by law performers couldn't wear any kind of a costume—and the original design of their trendy jackets was considered "costume." So everyone took off their jackets and went onstage in their shirtsleeves. The Beatles wore new shirts bought especially by Brian. They were pink.

Don eventually became very powerful. Along the early way he managed acts like Dave Berry and the Cruisers, and repped Chuck Berry. He was also very go ahead. He went to the States when nobody else did, tracked down the artists that he knew would fill concert halls and theaters and said to them, "Trust me. I'll look after you," and remarkably, it all worked well. He had some interesting people working for him, people who would sometimes be described as "having no thought before the deed, and no remorse ipso facto." They would walk up to someone and smack them. No warning. Just *whack!* He employed ex-bouncers from the old Star Club in Hamburg, men like Horst Fascher (a fan and friend of the Beatles) who, when he wasn't sleeping over as a guest of the Bundespolizei would fly over and smack people on Don's behalf.

To bring the story full circle, or at least back to the Savoy, Don also looked after Jayne Mansfield. I was at the Savoy having a drink with Don and some of his lads when I glanced up and there she was in one of those famous crocheted dresses and big wigs. Even in that sophisticated establishment, full of international stars, people were turning and staring and she smiled and glowed, doing a Monroe number. I think she was over to do the Batley Variety Club and Caesar's Palace. I couldn't imagine what she did onstage, but I presumed it was some kind of Marilyn Monroe, sex bomb "I wanna be loved by you"–type performance.

Jayne and Micky Hargitay had already split up, so when she took a shine to me and came on over, I smiled back at her, all kinds of fantasies happening, when she suddenly produced a baby from almost thin air. She handed it to me and said sweetly, "You look a kind young man. Would you mind holding Mariska for me while I do a photo shoot?"

There I was, suave old me, sitting at the bar in the Savoy Hotel, a foggy day in London Town, raincoat over my shoulder, drinking a martini—and bouncing Jayne's cute eighteen-month-old baby girl up and down and making goo-goo noises at her. Afterward, we all went off by taxi to Carnaby Street for a bit of shopping and some more drinks. A few months later Jayne was killed in a car crash. Her children, asleep in the back, survived. Mariska Hargitay grew up to become the beautiful detective from *Law and Order: Special Victims Unit.*

🎤

I'm not sure where Brian got the idea—perhaps it was simply his usual flair for the obvious—but he had the notion of using the dead Sunday, when the Saville, like all theaters, was normally closed, to put on special events. To my astonishment, he called me into his office and said, "Tony, you're in charge of these new Sunday shows."

"I've never done theater," I said cautiously.

Brian waved it away. "They'll just be pop concerts and so forth," he said. "You can handle it."

Brian's faith in my ability was remarkable, and I don't think I ever let him down. If he said I could do something, I found that I could. In reality, it was just like when we brought over all our favorite American singers for the exchange deal. I learned to direct shows with artists like the Four Tops, Pink Floyd, Little Richard and Cream and many more. Many people said they envied me working with so many sensational and iconic stars, but oddly enough, I didn't feel any different. Lucky, yes, but essentially, it was my job; I was paid to do it, so I got on with it. I have never been awe-inspired by fame—except when I met people I personally idolized, usually Americans like Chuck Berry and Jerry Lee Lewis. There were perks of course, like lunches, dinners and staying in nice hotels. The biggest perk was getting to know these living legends, often as friends, and talking music.

Of the British stars, I thought the Shadows were pretty cool, but I was never in awe of the other Liverpool groups. It was their job to be pop stars. I had grown up with them and we were fast mates. At the end of the day, they were just normal people.

One of Brian's favorite songs at the time was "Baby I Need Your Loving," by the Four Tops. He thought it would be wonderful to bring them over to open the new Sunday shows at the Saville. We paid them twelve thousand dollars, as well as airfares and hotels. Rehearsals were expensive, three days with a big orchestra at the Saville to get the whole Motown sound as near as possible. We ordered a special backdrop, with an American flag painted slightly out of focus. The whole thing at first appeared ridiculous because our total expenses were about thirty grand, against a maximum door of twelve hundred pounds, at one pound a ticket, but Brian liked to make lavish statements, and it was the grand opening. Once again he struck lucky. Their song "Reach Out I'll Be There" went to number one in the U.K. and Europe that weekend and we sold out. There was dancing in the aisles, a wonderful atmosphere, which didn't please the Lord Chamberlain's department. They tried to close us down for having dancing in a West End theater on a Sunday night. We would have lost our license before we had even started. Our lawyers put up a good fight, and we got reprimanded, but our license wasn't revoked.

It was almost uneconomically possible to make money at the Saville, even though Brian managed to extend his license to two shows on a Sunday. But I don't think he cared about anything other than having his own theater, where he could sit in the Royal Box and survey his domain. The Royal Box was decorated very tastefully and instead of chairs, contained sofas covered in zebra skin. Behind was a little anteroom for discreet suppers, stocked with drink. It had its own private entrance from the street and was a fun place to entertain his chums. The Beatles liked it because they could slip in and out, unnoticed.

Brian had an almost uncanny sense of timing. In addition to their appearances at the Saville, he had already cleverly negotiated with Motown to get the Four Tops for a full European tour for two months at a sensible fee. To compare, he paid Jimi Hendrix seventy-five pounds a night, Cream one hundred pounds and the Who got fifty pounds between them.

I wouldn't exactly call it moonlighting, but I got involved in many other projects while working for Brian. Often, these projects were sparked off during the long and winding pub crawling sessions with the likes of Peter Noone and Radio Caroline deejays. We'd start off in the Coal Hole in the Strand, then head for the Red Lion in Charles Street and, if it were a Friday afternoon, carry on cruising the pubs and clubs for full daytime drinking right through to Monday. Our endurance was amazing. On one lost weekend, Peter got me involved in working on a musical version of *The Canterville Ghost* by Oscar Wilde, produced by ABC television in America. It was a concept that sounded like a disaster about to happen, but everyone pressed on with it. Burt Shevelove, who wrote *A Funny Thing Happened on the Way to the Forum* for Frankie Howerd, was brought in to write the script and direct. The story was about an American family who buys an old castle and a ghost who doesn't like being interrupted and gives them all a hard time. Michael Redgrave played the ghost. Frankie Howerd, Douglas Fairbanks Jr. and my old chum, Peter Noone, were also in the cast.

We filmed it all in Allington Castle, near Maidstone in Kent, where Henry VIII used to have secret trysts with Anne Boleyn before they married. Eventually the home to an order of Carmelite monks, it was a perfect location that rattled with its own ghosts and clanking irons—not to mention monks, who lurked about beneath their cowls, keeping a watchful eye on us, but managing to look very creepy. Peter Noone didn't take it at all seriously. He spent most of his time fooling around, trying to scare the girls, trying to get a rise out of the monks and trying to find where they'd hidden their supplies of vintage claret and brandy, which he was convinced that all monks kept stocked in liberal quantities.

We stayed at a mini motel on the old Dover Road that probably had more than a few ghosts of its own. We partied till dawn and none of us slept. The combination of Michael Redgrave, a classical actor, piratical Douglas Fairbanks—both of them suave men of the world—and Frankie Howerd, a bawdy, earthy and wildly funny, though lugubrious comic, would never be repeated again on this planet. They fed off of each other and kept themselves and us entertained for hours. I wish I could say that I can remember some of their lines, but I'd drunk too much. We were so worn out that during the day in the monastery, members of the cast and crew kept disappearing into the cells to snatch some sleep and search parties had to hunt them down when they were needed for a scene. It was all great fun, but not surprisingly, when eventually the film was aired, the critics were brutal.

🐦

We had been making our videos for America for some time, when we decided to make straight promos, or promotional clips as they were called in those days. It started because it was impossible for the Beatles to go out to TV studios without a mob looking for them and, more to the point, without a strong-arm mob hired to protect them. A network of fans, almost all girls, kept a tight watch on Beatles' activities. They'd beat some kind of jungle drum at the slightest movement. "A Beatle's about! Quick, be there!" and fans would flood in from every direction, by bus, tube and on foot.

Paul was the only London Beatle, so the GHQ of this network first started in Wimpole Street, outside the Asher's home and continued outside the gates of his big Georgian house at Cavendish Road, where he and Jane moved in the summer of 1966. And that's where the girls who watched Paul lived, and I mean *lived*. They took up residence on the pavement, with sleeping bags and primus stoves. Lord only knows where they performed their ablutions. They were so faithful, so permanently there, they became known as the "Apple Scruffs."

Paul's house was also handy for Abbey Road, which was conveniently within sight across the famous zebra crossing. The scruffs once spent every night for five months sleeping on the pavement outside the studios when the Fabs were making an album. The fans-in-chief were named Big Sue, Little Sue, Gayleen, Margo, Willie and Knickers, and they had their sources. One of these sources was probably, and for the most part unwittingly, Rosie, Paul's housekeeper.

When Rosie went out or went shopping these girls used to go into Paul's house. They found out how to kick the security gate just right so it opened, like the Fonz would kick a jukebox to get it to play a song. They had watched and knew which flowerpot Paul hid the door key under and in they'd go. Then they'd help out by answering the phone. They'd tidy up by throwing out some of Paul's clothes, which they kept and took turns wearing.

When Paul came home he would get annoyed but they would weep and tell him that "rotten" Mal Evans had thrown them down the steps of Abbey Road. Or they'd console him by giving him a monkey, which bit him immediately. Or by taking him to the back of his house and improving his security clampdown by showing him where they clung from the wall that completely surrounded the property so they could see him sitting on the loo.

"The wall's eight-foot high," Paul said in a mixture of exasperation and admiration. "They hang from it by their fingertips until their arms come out of their sockets, then another girl takes over."

I shook my head. "Why don't you hire them as security?"

Paul grew quite fond of the girls. Even when he stood talking to them while they were wearing his jacket, or his trousers, he found it amusing. He called them "The Eyes and Ears of the World," and laughed affectionately; but George swore at them. The girls complained that he would push them out of the way or try to tread on their toes on purpose, which was his sense of humor, but they said they still loved him. George was also bad with photographers, journalists and TV people. He used to put on a schoolboy grin and try to trip people up by sticking his leg out. No wonder he loved Monty Python and was to finance their movies.

Wherever the Beatles were going to be, the network knew beforehand and arrived en masse. The police were fed up with being stretched to the limit and complained. It became so unsafe for them to go anywhere officially as a group, that we decided to do our own promo clips and just send them out. A good idea said everybody.

John said, "It's great isn't it, Tone? Just think, we won't be hanging around at the BBC for hours on end when we could be sitting at home quietly taking our drugs."

So we went in secret to Twickenham Studios on a single day in November 1965 and made promos for "Help!" "I Feel Fine," "We Can Work It Out," "Day Tripper," and "Ticket to Ride" . . . bang bang bang. It seemed so easy. I sort of produced and directed them. I say "sort of" because there was never a script or format. It was all put together on the spot. "Right boys, what shall we do? Try standing there, Paul, okay?"

This was the real origin of the pop video format—and where would MTV be today without it? I don't want to make a big thing of it because it was very loose back then and production and directorial "credits" for videos didn't seem that important. I got paid my wages anyway. Paul and I edited the stuff together. He really loved film and everything to do with film and so took to video and television very fast, and we would work on many more videos down the years to come.

At Twickenham we shot up to three versions of each promo and simply sent copies of the best, free of charge, to every TV station the Beatles had ever been on. But it was too "expensive," so we were told. When EMI called and complained that we had spent a total of seven hundred and fifty pounds, we fell about the office laughing. Their accounts' office said it was far too much. I said, "Hold on, I'll just go and I'll check the figures," and left the accountant holding the phone while we all went to the pub. When we came back an hour later he was still holding on.

I picked up the phone and said, "The paperwork needs more analysis. We've decided to call in the Beatles to discuss it with Sir Joe. Yes, that's right, as soon as I put down the phone I'm going to call their drivers to pick them up and when they get here they'll . . ."

"No!" he yelped, "Don't do that!"

My next foray into editing was on something very hush-hush and far more expensive. It came about after the Beatles' third American tour in August 1965. The first "tour" had been when they went to appear on the *Ed Sullivan Show,* when they had fitted in a concert at the Washington Coliseum and two concerts at the hallowed Carnegie Hall. It had hardly been a tour in the wider sense and they were more awestruck that they had been the first pop group ever to be allowed into Carnegie Hall. So in awe that for the first time their courage almost failed. George told me once, "Carnegie Hall is where real musicians play, philharmonics and symphonies, not people like us. We somehow thought we'd get struck dead by lightning when we walked onto that stage."

The tour in August 1964 was far more extensive and lasted a month. It was like a whistle-stop coast-to-coast jamboree during a presidential election. Brian hired a Lear jet and they flew around the United States with a large entourage of journalists and snappers. The third tour, in August of the following year, lasted two weeks, with an equally crowded schedule. I didn't go on either one, because with Brian away for so long, he wanted me there to "take care of business" for him, which was the phrase he loved, from the moment he'd heard Colonel Parker use it when they met.

Probably the most important concert of the 1965 tour was at Shea Stadium on Sunday, August 15. Shea Stadium in Queens is home to the New York Mets baseball team, an arena more suited to sports than to a live concert. Fifty-five thousand, six hundred fans poured in through the turnstiles, a world record for a pop concert. The Beatles flew by helicopter to the roof of the nearby World's Fair building, then traveled in a Wells Fargo armored truck to the stadium, sprinting down the player's tunnel to the stage.

The noise from the fans was deafening. It remained at fever pitch throughout the concert, which was unfortunate, given that it was to be turned into a film due to be broadcast later around the world. The *Ed Sullivan* production team filmed the entire thing, using twelve cameras. However, less attention was paid to the sound. My part in the experience came about some five months later, in London, when the finished film arrived at NEMS offices in London on a cold January morning in 1966.

Brian buzzed me and I went into his office. "The Shea Stadium master has come from the *Ed Sullivan* people," he said. "Can you book a viewing theater so we can watch it?"

I booked a theater in Wardour Street for the afternoon and Brian and I went along, firmly clutching the film so nobody would steal it. When it was put in the projector, we settled down on one of the wide, plushy seats and the lights went down. Fifty-four minutes later, when the lights came up, we sat in silence for a few moments, then we both reached for our cigarettes and simultaneously lit up.

"What do you think?" Brian asked.

"Not good, Brian," I said.

He took another puff. "I agree. We can't allow it to go out like that. Do you think you can fix it, Tony?"

"I'll try," I said.

In every industry on this earth there is a stock phrase. A little saying that passes for an explanation so that a work-in-progress can move on without workers and supervisors standing around and agonizing. In the music industry that phrase is, "Don't worry. We'll fix it in the mix." This is a real Alfred E. Neuman, "What me worry?" *MAD* magazine approach if there ever was one, but we are all entitled to hope.

When the Beatles first started recording, there was no mixing of tracks. It went down in mono on a tape machine called a BTR and what was recorded was basically what you got. It could of course be sweetened by judicious placing of microphones, use of tone controls—then called knobs—and some echo, but the executive staff at EMI and Abbey Road, for all their faults and their military approach, would always insist that if it couldn't be done properly, it didn't get done at all. They did not have packets of magic powder full of Stardust labeled, "For the use of: sprinkle with care!" and they knew it. The Beatles' original audition at EMI was almost canceled because the amps were of such poor quality they crackled, hissed and popped. The engineer, Norman Smith, managed to solder something together to get them to work, a mixture of skill and good luck.

Now, three and a half years on from that audition George Martin and I sat at CTS (Cine Tele Sound), postsynch studios in Kensington Gardens Square, in Bayswater, and watched the Shea Stadium footage. The visuals were good but the sound was awful. The Beatles' own amps were top of the line, but still not powerful enough. To compound the problems, they couldn't hear themselves against the noise of the crowd and were out of tune and out of time. When we finished watching, George said, "Oh dear."

I said, "You're right. The pictures are good, but the soundtrack sucks. We could redo the music sound to picture and synch it." It was standard movie technique to "loop" actors' dialogue if, for instance, the wind on the set or a passing plane drowned out their voices.

I knew that George was thinking. But would EMI permit this? It was one thing for a concert to be filmed live, it was another thing for the Beatles to go into the studio and cut new tracks. In simple terms, it raised thorny issues about the Beatles' exclusive recording contract with EMI. We talked it quietly through. I said, "If we take this problem to EMI, they will agonize for months and the BBC want to broadcast it on the first of March. The other thing is, even if we do redo it, no one must know. This is being sold as an 'original soundtrack.'"

George Martin was always pragmatic. If a thing needed to be done, it got done. "Right," he said. "There might be union problems too. They are making a big issue over miming and dubbing live performances."

I must admit I was a bit surprised that he had gone to the heart of the problem so quickly, and didn't refuse to take a risk, because I always saw him as very establishment. He had patrician good looks—in fact, at the fancy dress parties, which were quite the craze then, he and his wife, Judy, always dressed up as Prince Philip and the queen, and looked every inch the part. I had always liked and admired him very much. He was very gentle, well-read and knowledgeable, not a snob in any way despite running an important record label, and had a keen sense of humor. Now, I warmed to him.

We arranged a date for the Beatles to come in and a schedule to work from. I stressed that no one must know, and it was all very hush-hush, which intrigued them. It was a strange period in their lives. They had played their last live U.K. concerts three weeks earlier, in early December, although it wasn't advertised as such. For the concert at the Empire Theater in Liverpool alone, forty thousand fans applied for tickets, against two houses of two thousand five hundred seats each house. Other concerts took them across England, ending at the Capitol Cinema in Cardiff, Wales, on December 12, 1965. As usual, you couldn't hear the Beatles through the screaming of the fans.

As John said afterward in some disgust, "I reckon we could send out four waxwork dummies of ourselves and that would satisfy the crowds. Beatles concerts are nothing to do with music anymore. They're just bloody tribal rites."

Since then, unusual for them, the Beatles had done nothing very much beyond visiting friends and catching up with their social life. The last time they had been in the studio was just before Christmas, in October and November, when for the first time, they worked all night to complete their new album, *Rubber Soul*.

As they filed into CTS with their instruments, I said, "Don't forget, act naturally." They were amused. This was the title of one of Ringo's songs in the Shea Stadium set.

"So what's this all about, Tone?" Ringo asked.

"You have to lay down a new soundtrack, sound to picture," I said. I explained the problems and they were quick to grasp what had to be done, and why it had to be secret. "If anyone asks, the story is that the soundtrack has been sweetened," I said, adding, "think 'Honey Pie.' "

"Sounds like 'money pie' to me," said John.

We re-recorded all the songs for the final version of the film, close-synching it all carefully to match the picture, frame by frame. Ringo didn't sing at all in the overdubs, because "Act Naturally" was impossible to do again to picture. It was recorded again later at Abbey Road and issued as a single. George's "Everybody's Trying to Be My Baby" and Paul's "She's a Woman" were bad visually and orally and were cut altogether. We ran out of time to do John's "Twist and Shout," because postsynching is a very boring and time-consuming process and John was fed up with the time it was taking.

"I've got a party to go to," he said.

George Martin and Paul thought we should try to carry on and tried to persuade him to stay, but he was adamant and left to go to one of P. J. Proby's wild events in Chelsea. The others shrugged, packed up their gear and left as well. George Martin and I stayed to dub a few more things. I enjoyed spending time with him because he really was very pleasant and easy to work with. We found the final tapes of the Beatles at Hollywood Bowl concert from the year before and overdubbed some of the audience's screaming in the right places. The film ended up forty-eight minutes long, cut by eight minutes and I took it to the labs for processing.

When the Beatles came to view the finished work, they were amazed by the quality of the film. It was very pretty, with lots of edited-in footage of them in the helicopter, flying over New York on the way to Shea, and them backstage chatting. The sound was brilliant. The synchs and overdubs, seamless. We never told the *Ed Sullivan* people, or anyone else.

The Beatles didn't want to continue with live concerts, and even though they moaned a bit, Brian had set up several dates that they had to fulfill. The first, in June 1966 were three days in Germany. It would be their first visit to Hamburg, where once they were nobodies, in three and a half years. Many old friends were there to meet them at the railway station on their arrival: Astrid, Bert Kaempfert and even Bettina, the generous barmaid from the Star Club, who had been so kind to them when they were starving kids. Afterward, with Astrid, John and Paul slipped away and visited old haunts.

On June 30 they arrived in Japan. The trip really stood out because the Japanese government spent Tokyo's entire police budget for a year in just one day on security. Police stood shoulder to shoulder all the way from the airport to the Hilton Hotel in Tokyo, where they stayed, and the security continued at the five shows at the Nippon Budokan, with one policeman to every three fans. There was a great deal of protest over using the Budokan for pop concerts, the first time it had ever been used in such a way. Many of the older generation were outraged. It was a sacred place, more usually used for martial arts displays. Later, in the 1970 and 1980s, everybody did a "Live at the Budokan" album.

The Philippines, the next leg of the tour, was a disaster. To start with, the Philippine press thought their attitude to questions at press conferences was too flippant and therefore insulting. John's response in private was to call them "the flippin' Fillies." Their biggest faux pas was not to take morning coffee with Imelda Marcos, the president, and their three young children, who it was reported were avid Beatles' fans. Apparently, unknown to the Beatles, the *Manila Times* had informed their readers that the Beatles had invited the Marcos family to be guests of honor at the concerts and would also go to the palace to pay a courtesy call.

The entire family, government ministers, friends and staff waited at the palace, while the Beatles remained in bed and refused to get up when a limousine was sent for them. They said they weren't aware of the arrangement. The citizens were furious over this slur against Imelda, especially when the *Manila Times* ran the headline: IMELDA STOOD UP! Brian tried to apologize in a TV interview, but strangely, static interfered with the broadcast, stopping only when he stopped talking.

Bomb threats were received and the concert fees were frozen. Worse, all security was withdrawn and the Beatles were chased to the airport by a howling mob. At the airport, the electricity was cut off to the escalators and the Beatles had to carry their luggage up two flights of stairs. At the top, the mob caught up with them. Paul raced out of their reach to Customs, but the others were shoved to the floor and kicked while they tried to crawl out of harm's way. Brian got the brunt of the assault. He ended up bruised and battered and scared out of his wits.

They flew to Delhi for a little R & R, and swore they would never go abroad again. On their return home, still nervous from the memory of the Filipino disaster, Brian told me, "I have never been so frightened in my life. Being assaulted by one person is one thing, but this was a howling mob of about two hundred. I really did think I would be killed."

Someone has to get the blame for a cock-up, and someone did, fairly or not. Vic Lewis was the Far East booker for NEMS and he came in for a great deal of ribbing. In hindsight, the Beatles could joke about it. Paul told me how he had escaped security at the Tokyo Hilton. The cordon was so tight, that even when the others snuck out, the police caught them and returned them to their suite. "I stuck the old fake mustache and big glasses on," Paul said, "and wandered around sight-seeing." He had even gone shopping for gifts, including lots of happi coats—Westerners call them happy coats. These were wide-sleeved short kimonos with various patterns on them. Paul gave me a couple. I wore them all the time at home because they were very comfortable and easy to wear. I wish I still had them.

▼▼▼

Despite saying that they would never go abroad again, another American tour had been booked for August 1966. The Beatles were bored and restless and said they wished they didn't have to go, but the tour was almost canceled for a different reason than their boredom. A few months earlier, on March 4, John had given an interview to Maureen Cleave, a bright young reporter on the *Evening Standard* and a good friend of all of us from our first days in London. It was a thoughtful piece, written with Easter in mind, with John in one of his more introspective moods.

"What do you think of the church and God?" Maureen asked.

John said, "Christianity will go. It will vanish and shrink. . . . We're more popular than Jesus now; I don't know which will go first—rock 'n' roll or Christianity."

I remember reading the *Standard* and being interested in John's comments, which to me seemed typical John. I certainly didn't read anything into it, and by the next day, the article was forgotten about and the newspapers were wrapping fish and chips. However, a few months later on the eve of the Beatles' new U.S. tour, *Datebook*, an important American magazine that obviously had been biding its time, saw fit to reprint the article under the inflammatory headline: WE'RE MORE POPULAR THAN JESUS. All hell broke loose around the world, particularly in the southern U.S. There were public burnings of the Beatles' records and merchandise, radio stations refused to play their music; they were demonized. Even the Vatican's opinion: "John's remarks were made off-handedly and not impiously," didn't stop the furor.

If Brian was alarmed, John was scared. He hadn't meant to unleash the wrath of the godly against the Beatles and popular music. He meant what he said seriously enough, and if anything it was a condemnation of popular culture, and not an antireligious comment. John and Brian flew over to America to try to straighten it out. Brian gave a formal, scripted conference and later, John met the press for a question-and-answer session. He shouldered all the blame and gave his first press conference, in which his tone was muted and sincere. He ended up by saying, "Sorry, folks."

His apology was accepted, and the tour went ahead. However, many venues failed to sell out and sales were down. Their final concert, at Candlestick Park in San Francisco, before a crowd of twenty-five thousand, was the last Beatles concert anywhere in the world. "Long Tall Sally" was the last song they sang that night. It represented a great deal to them all, and their mood was very down and thoughtful when they returned to England.

PART III

1966–1967

13

An artist of mass destruction named Yoko Ono was heading toward London from New York early in September 1966. We weren't aware of it at the time—no one was—but she should have come with a warning stuck to her, like a cigarette packet, because gradually, inch by inch she intruded into our lives. She was connected to a New York conceptual art movement called Fluxus. Through her somewhat startling interactive shows, particularly "Cut Piece," staged at Carnegie Hall, in which she invited people to cut bits off her clothing with scissors, and another one, "Bag Piece," in which she sat silently in a big laundry sack for a very long time, she had drawn some modest attention to herself in some of New York's arty circles. This led to her being invited to London and the Edinburgh Festival for the Destruction in Art Symposium, organized in part by Barry Miles, one of John Dunbar's friends. Accompanied by her three-year-old daughter, Kyoko, and her second husband, Tony Cox, they traveled by the cheapest method, taking a freighter from Canada. Tony Cox had a gallery in New York called IsReal. In Yoko's case, nothing was real, but plenty to get hung about, as John once wrote. What you got with Yoko was never what you expected, an image she enjoyed reinforcing by appearing to be very mysterious, dressed in black, most of her face hidden behind a dense curtain of frizzy hair.

In London, she was introduced to metropolitan arty groups and managed to get quite a lot of reviews of her strange work in the *Daily Telegraph. The Financial Times* called her work "uplifting." The *FT* also mentioned that Yoko's father was a very wealthy Japanese banker, based in New York. There was even a very brief clip of Yoko's work on an arts program on the BBC. Inauspiciously, John and Cynthia caught it while watching television at home in the sunroom one evening. John frowned and, as he told me a week or so later when we discussed her, he'd commented, "The woman's a raving nutter."

Perhaps, but she was closing in on our innocence. NEMS managed Scaffold, the strange Liverpudlian poetry, song and humor trio, which consisted of the poet, Roger McGough, the comedian, John Gorman, and Paul's brother, Mike McGear. They had couple of whacko hits, with songs like "Lily the Pink" and "Thank U Very Much for the Aintree Iron." It was weird stuff, but sold well. They always did a full season at the Traverse Theater during the Edinburgh Festival, so Brian and I would go up to see them and also to keep an eye out for talent. Then Brian would have a couple of joints and book everything in sight. Shortly after she had arrived from New York, that summer Yoko went to the Edinburgh Festival with the Destruction in Art Symposium. Brian drifted off on his own and accidentally caught part of her show. He showed me a catalogue and mentioned that he had seen a very boring show by an unusual Japanese woman.

"What kind of paintings?" I asked, assuming that was what he was talking about.

"Oh, no, paintings I understand," Brian said. "Sculpture I understand. But I'm not sure I understand someone who sits inside a bag onstage and does nothing at all for a long time, but then, I didn't stay long. Two or three minutes perhaps." He looked a bit vague. "The thing is, I might have said I'd book her at the Saville."

"Oh dear," I said, as Brian sighed.

Shortly after that, Paul dropped by my desk, looking a little fed up. "Look, Tone, do us a favor, will you?

I said jokingly, "What do you want now?" Paul managed a grin.

"There's this woman, a Japanese artist—" he started. It seemed Paul had first become aware of the woman at an event of performance art he had attended at the Royal Academy during his increasing forays into the avant-garde scene. Then, she started coming round to his house. Paul said, "She's very pushy. She keeps making demands as if she has a right. First it was for old song lyrics, then it was money to put on an exhibition at an art gallery."

"Throw her out," I advised. "Get Mal to do whatever Mal does."

"Well, she's a bit persistent. She wants the lyrics to butter up John Cage, she says his hobby is collecting musical manuscripts. She didn't seem to understand that we don't have full scores." Paul and John couldn't read or write music and scrawled their songs on the backs of any scrap of paper on hand.

"Ignore her," I advised again. "She'll get the message."

"She said she'd tried John, 'cos he's been to art school and all that. She'd left a message but he hadn't called her back. Look, the thing is, she says she's a friend of Miles and John Dunbar, and she also said she met Brian at Edinburgh and he said he'd book her at the Saville."

It all came back. I said, "Ah, yes. Well, what do you want me to do?"

"Oh, I don't know. She's quite arty and sort of sings a bit and stuff. She said she wouldn't mind being put on at the Saville. Remind Brian, will you?" Pleased that he had done what he had obviously promised her he would do, Paul moved on to more interesting topics.

Duly, I met with Yoko to discuss her show. She said she'd done a few gigs at places like Middle Earth and been accepted, had gone down well even. To my mind, Middle Earth was generally filled with like-minded prats looking for "something." Quite what they were looking for I didn't know. It was spiritual maybe, but it wasn't art. However, London was very experimental at the time and we didn't want to lag behind.

We had to keep the theater open all the time, to keep the central heating going and help defray the staff's wages. As a result, we would always have something on every day of the week that punters would buy tickets for. Brian would meet people and enthusiastically book them, no matter how nutty they were. I never knew what or who to expect next. Feeling as deranged as the Mad Hatter, I'd sit in the office and wait to see who would come in through the door. There'd be the Tribal Dancers of Kalahari, or the Bearded Ladies Jazz Quartet, or the Circular Knitting Machine Moog-Madness Motherfuckers. A secretary would buzz us: "Mr. Hitler's in reception"—"Send him up!" We'd have all kinds, all shapes, sizes and persuasions—and then we had Yoko Ono.

We agreed to put her on during an artists' night, with a troupe called the Flux Partners, printed a few posters advertising her as avant-garde. Who were we, to know what was good and what was pseudo? Were we artistics or Philistines? She asked for the stage to be completely covered in black cloth, both the floor and backdrop and we stationed a few stepladders around, so the tiny audience who had been curious enough to buy tickets could go up and down them, thinking such deep thoughts as, "I'm climbing a stepladder to heaven."

At the start of her show, a small, round black spider that blended in with the blackout material we had draped everywhere ran almost invisibly across the stage on all fours. It was Yoko. To set an example, Yoko climbed a ladder herself, and then she climbed down. Then she wailed a bit while moving around like one of those stop-motion figures on *South Park*. I couldn't believe my ears. I really do believe that she thought rock and roll was simply people screaming their heads off. Finally, she brought out a chair and sat on it impassively, holding out a pair of scissors for her piece de resistance, the much-reprised performance of "Cut Piece." The scissors were wired for sound, so every cut had a horrific, almost animal sound, like a beast crunching into its human prey. The audience was very uneasy by this brutal aural and visual display of what suddenly seemed like a real assault on a woman. With the final snip, Yoko was left naked on stage, seated pallid in the spotlight, with droopy tits. People stirred uncomfortably in their seats, a few giggled, nobody clapped. The bloody place was obviously filled with Philistines.

I stood watching from the back with Brian, who had popped in briefly, as he always did. Full frontal nudes were illegal in public, and the fact that it was a Sunday compounded the crime. Brian was stunned, much concerned that he would be arrested for pornography. "I don't think we'd better put her on again," he said, visibly shaken.

Brian was upset at the time because the Beatles had told him they had played their last public fandango, they would never appear on stage as a group again. But, most of all, he was upset over Alma Cogan, who had just died of leukemia. It didn't seem real that someone we knew so well, someone in our own age group, could become terminally ill. From the time she was diagnosed, she went downhill very fast. A friend, Terry Ryan, a film student, who lived in South Kensington just around the corner from Alma's flat, described how sometimes late at night in the weeks leading up to her death, like a frail shadow, Alma would slip into a nearby wine cellar where he would be with friends from the film school. Wrapped in a fur coat, even in late summer, she sat huddled at the back on her own, slowly sipping a glass of wine. "She looked so sad, so utterly alone," he said. "I often thought I should go over and speak to her, but as with many people who are dying, what do you say? 'How's it going?'"

♔

Even though Brian told me that we weren't to book Yoko again, she was there among us and wasn't going to go away. John might not have returned her telephone calls, but she was fighting a determined campaign and was gradually closing in on him. In October, the radical new underground newspaper the *International Times* ("IT") was launched with a huge Middle Earth concert at the Roundhouse with Pink Floyd and the Soft Machine. Miles was involved with that as well and Paul put money into it. The Roundhouse was a former train engine workshop with a central turntable where engines would shunt in and be turned around to shunt out again. It was cold, poorly lit and filthy, but so packed, no one noticed. That night, in the middle of a set by Soft Machine, Yoko grabbed attention through another Fluxus-style happening. She got someone to turn out the lights, and through the total blackout darkness her amplified voice instructed everyone to touch the person next to them. You could hear giggles and squeals from the audience as a few people complied. The lights came back on, Yoko was thrown off the stage and Soft Machine continued. Paul was there, dressed as an Arab. I went, dressed as myself. I often went to such events, dressed as myself, on the lookout for talent for the Saville. Paul and I drifted around a bit but it was so noisy, you could never hold a conversation. Afterward, Paul mentioned the event to John, who looked wistful, as if he was missing all the fun, in exile out at Weybridge.

Soon Yoko would meet John in person. Dr. Asher and Paul had financed John Dunbar and Peter Asher, enabling them to set up Indica, their little art gallery-cum-bookshop, in commercial premises at Mason's Yard in St. James. They decided that they would paint the basement white and hold art exhibitions in it. Through her sponsor, Barry Miles, Yoko finally got her foot through the door into the world of the Beatles by getting Dunbar and Peter to stage her show, "Unfinished Paintings and Objects" as their opening exhibition. Yoko hadn't made any of these herself. Instead, she got some art students from the Royal Academy to do so. After she had finished arranging the sparse objects—an apple on a stand with a hefty price ticket, a couple of her empty sacks lying on the floor, a plank with nails half hammered in—Yoko turned to Dunbar and, apparently thinking on her feet, invented, "John Lennon said he might come to the exhibition. Why not ask him to a private preview? He's a millionaire, he might buy something."

Dunbar did telephone, and John agreed that he might drop in on the way to the studio next day. Everyone imagined that John was living in a whirlwind of fun, but he felt isolated and was often quite bored and lonely. Quite simply, he didn't get many invitations from close friends or people he knew and could trust. When Dunbar called, it could well have been the only invitation John got all week.

The following day, the man himself drifted down the stairs to the basement. He later told me about what he saw, which bemused but did not amuse him. As an art student, he had seen tons of this kind of what I call intellectual fakery and, in John's words, "didn't dig it." The story is now legend of how he stood hesitantly and glanced across at where Yoko and a couple of others sat cross-legged on the floor, stitching the sacks like jailbirds. John himself said he was on the point of leaving when Yoko jumped up and placed herself between him and the stairs. She asked who he was.

John stared. Amazed, Dunbar said, "It's John Lennon, of course."

Yoko shrugged. She said, "Oh," as if she had never heard the name before. I think, when the story went the rounds that John must have been the only person in London who didn't hear it.

She handed him a small card. It said, "Breathe." John peered at it short-sightedly, then took a couple of breaths and handed the card back. Once again he turned to leave, but he wasn't quick enough. Yoko got inside his guard. She took his arm and guided him to one of her stepladders, which had been painted white and positioned in the center of the room. "This is Ceiling Painting," she said.

"Yeah?" John peered upward. He couldn't see a painting. All he could see was a framed pane fastened horizontally against the ceiling; it appeared to be blank. Dangling from the frame was a small magnifying glass on a chain. Suddenly curious, John climbed up, picked up the magnifying glass and looked through it. On a postage stamp–sized card in the center of the frame he saw three miniature block letters: YES. Swaying giddily on the ladder with his head bent backward, he felt spacey. He gazed at the word for several seconds.

Back down, Yoko took his arm again and guided him to the plank, labeled HAMMER A NAIL IN. He picked up the hammer that was provided. Yoko quickly said, "You can't do that until the exhibition opens."

Dunbar said, "Oh, go on, let him. He might not come back tomorrow."

"Very well. You may hammer one nail in, for five shillings," Yoko agreed.

John, who never carried a scrap of change, reached into his pocket. "Imaginary money for an imaginary nail," he said. Yoko smiled faintly.

John said to me later, "That was when we clicked. I saw what she was about, and she saw what I was about. And the 'yes' on the ceiling. It was like, affirmative, none of these negative vibes I keep getting off people."

It was hardly surprising that John felt some kind of electricity; but it was probably the air crackling with Yoko's desperation. She needed to hook a big fish. Since arriving in England, she had thrown herself into a fervor of Fluxus-style self-promotion and networking, but none of it earned any money. After outstaying their welcome in the homes of a series of acquaintances who had put them up, before losing patience and evicting them, she and her husband were broke, now living hand to mouth in a large empty flat they couldn't afford. A similar history of evictions and moonlight flits had ensured that she had nowhere to return to in New York—apart from her parents' home where her husband wasn't welcome. To me, that says it all, because parents always go that extra mile. She urgently needed a wealthy patron. She had already tried other wealthy men like Paul and Brian, who derided her work. I don't know who else she had hit on, but miraculously, karma put John in her sights at exactly the right moment, when her female intuition told her he was looking for something, even if he didn't know it. It would become clear that she didn't intend to let him escape.

When John said he was late for the studio, Yoko clutched him tighter by the arm and coyly lisped, "Take me with you!"

However, John was used to women hitting on him and Yoko was skinny, plain and older than he was. She didn't look anything like his dream babe, Brigitte Bardot. There was no earthly reason why he should be attracted to Yoko and told me—and also Cynthia—that he wasn't. He pulled free and ran up the stairs, pursued by Yoko. His black Mini Cooper with tinted windows was waiting. John jumped in, slammed the door and the car took off. If his driver, Les Anthony, hadn't been so quick on the getaway, John said she would have jumped in with him. As the Mini shot out of Mason's Yard, Yoko stood on the cobbles staring after it.

🎸

Yoko had been building up a network of mutual contacts, most of them owners of art galleries, like one of Brian's intimates, Robert Fraser. Another was a slightly built Greek, Alexis Mardas, who had been working as a television repairman until he drifted into John Dunbar's circle. In much the same way as someone might say, "I don't have to do this, I'm a brain surgeon you know," Alex really wasn't a career television repairman. He was the highly educated son of a major in the Greek secret police. The young physics student was making his way around the world when, unfortunately, he was stranded in London because, so he said, his passport had been stolen and his visa had expired.

Alex and Dunbar decided to go into business making kinetic light sculptures, something the physics student found very easy to do. Some of his more way-out ideas, like hanging a sun from the sky, never worked and never would, but the concept alone earned him the name, "Magic Alex." To John, he was like a magician of olden times, someone who could make new suns shine and new moons revolve. In a remarkably short time, he became one of John's best friends, constantly down in Kenwood with his glowing boxes of tricks. To me, Alex was a fake, someone who could convince the bare-assed emperor that he was wearing clothes. I will always remember the twelve empty boxes he made for George. They contained nothing and didn't actually do anything, but George told John that they contained some kind of light ray that could recognize bad vibes. "Really? I'll have some of those," said John. "Yeah, me too. In fact, I'll have two dozen. Put 'em on my bill," said Ringo who was the most cynical of all the Beatles. Alex produced dozens and in all seriousness, they were lined up in key points around the Beatles' homes, where, as far as I could tell, they continued to do nothing at all.

One would have expected that it would have been John at galleries and events, but it was Paul who was immersing himself in all things weird, wonderful and new. Paul was also experimenting with electronic music. *The London Times* had said the Beatles were bigger than Beethoven, so immediately, the Beatles delighted in putting themselves in a pun: "Beat-hoven"; but it was Paul who sat in the music room at the top of his house and used some of the electronic gadgetry he'd bought in a trawl around London, creating a Stockhausen sound of layers of Beatles overlaid on Beethoven.

When John came up to town and saw what Paul was up to, the old sense of competition kicked in and he started dropping by galleries as well. In this way, he came to bump into Yoko again, and made a point of ignoring her. I got the impression that John actively disliked her. He told me he thought she was incredibly pushy; perhaps he was afraid that she might grab his arm again and squeak, "Take me with you!" If I were standing about with him, Yoko would come up to me and say something in her high little girl's voice, perhaps hoping to get John to notice her, perhaps hoping that I would suggest putting her on at the Saville again, but I didn't like her either and made it plain. John would walk off to talk to someone else, while she stared after him. In those days, Yoko was always staring after John.

14

There was no doubt that many people, particularly John, were suspicious when, early in January 1967, NEMS and Robert Stigwood's management amalgamated. Stigwood was made a joint managing director of NEMS with Brian; however, without actually lying, Brian managed to somehow convince the Beatles that this was a boardroom arrangement and Stigwood had no power. Stigwood was someone else who had a nickname. It was Robert to his face and "Stiggie" behind his back. Rumors spread that Brian was about to sell the Beatles. He was often seen in a huddle with Stiggie in clubs such as the Bag O'Nails, the new place to be. He always denied these rumors; he even pointed out that the previous year a story had been published about Paul and John meeting secretly with the Stone's voracious manager, New Yorker Allen Klein, which patently had never happened and was a Klein publicity leak—probably planted by Andrew Loog Oldham in the growing sense of competitiveness between the Stones and the Beatles as they jockeyed for place at the top of the charts.

But with the public announcement of an amalgamation between NEMS and Stigwood, it seemed the rumors could be true. At the very least, something was afoot. Mostly what was afoot was that Brian was seriously ill and desperately sought to escape from the circus of his own creation. He couldn't sleep, he was taking too many drugs, a soldier he had picked up had broken the banisters in his house and stolen his gold watch, and he felt as if he were slowly going mad. In a desperate attempt to regain control, or to run away—and perhaps the two were mutually compatible in his case—he made up his mind to change his life. It seemed a huge and daunting step, given the network of companies, clients, and complicated international activities he masterminded with a small staff of ten. In that year alone, just the Beatles' record sales had turned over two hundred million pounds. The royalties—the income generated from any number of deals—were funneled through our cramped offices in Argyll Street. Brian wasn't too troubled about abandoning most of his pop star clients or numerous business interests, but he was tormented by the idea of letting down his beloved Cilla and the Beatles, particularly John. He underwent deep sleep therapies at the Priory, being put under for days at a time with heavy drugs.

It was during this confused and disjointed period, when his tormented mind would give him no rest, that Brian suddenly made up his mind to secretly sell a controlling interest in NEMS to Stiggie and his partner, David Shaw, for half a million pounds. They had until September 1967 to find the money. Considering that the previous year he had been offered $3 million for the Beatles to appear in two just concerts and $20 million to "buy" them out by a consortium of American businessmen, it was an incredibly small sum. It was also badly thought out because Stiggie was an undischarged bankrupt in his homeland of Australia. The previous summer, Shaw had also been publicly named in a big bond-washing scandal. However, desperate to escape, Brian just wanted enough money to live in reasonable comfort in Spain and manage a few bullfighters.

Not only did he already manage one bullfighter, an Englishman named Henry Higgins, but he had spent several weeks in Spain, making a film about him. He had even asked me to make a film there, *Feria de Seville*. It had originally been Brian's intention to make this himself, but he was too ill. Instead, I went and had a wonderful time, shooting one of the big religious festivals, complete with blood and gore, horns and tambourines, candles, Madonnas and pretty girls.

Although far less than he could have gotten for the sale of NEMS on the open market, in 1967 half a million pounds was still a very large sum of money. Brian believed it would be sufficient. In the end, although it was legally complex, he tempered the deal by deciding that he couldn't let his protégés down: he would retain exclusive management rights over Cilla and the Beatles. Part of this decision was based on the fact that in the new nine-year record contract he had recently negotiated with EMI for the Beatles, he had written in 25 percent for himself. Regardless of whether he managed the Beatles or not, he would still get 25 percent of their earnings from record sales for nine years. This subtlety had somehow escaped the Beatles, but it bothered Brian. It gnawed at his conscience because in his heart he knew he had conned them. This is probably why he decided to keep them back from the NEMS deal with Stigwood, so he couldn't be accused of cynically exploiting them—which he was.

I had gotten to know Stiggie quite well because I was the one who promoted the groups he managed, such as Cream and the Bee Gees. I even saw more of Stiggie than I intended. One afternoon Chas Chandler and I were walking back to the offices from the BBC in Portland Place, when we passed Stigwood's luxury home and decided to pop in for a drink. The front door was never locked (few doors were at the time) and we walked along the hall to the living room, the door to which stood wide open. Directly in front of us was a big pouffe upon which a sexual act was taking place between Stiggie and a soon-to-be pop star who wanted to be managed by him. Chas and I backed out and crept away, closing the door very quietly behind us. In the street we laughed like lunatics.

While Rome burned and Brian was deranged, business back at the office continued as usual. Thinking we were inventing the wheel, we started experimenting with our promo videos, making them more complex by acting out the story of whatever song was about to be released. We had no format to follow. Our creative efforts were the precursors of the modern-day storyboarded video, every one a nice little mini movie. We didn't know we were giving birth to a new industry. Brian loved all this stuff and would discuss it endlessly, asking how it was going, dropping by to watch. "Penny Lane" and "Strawberry Fields Forever" were the first really creative ones, then some of the *Sgt. Pepper* songs were done shortly after. After some experimentation, we shot them on film because we'd done "Paperback Writer" and "Rain" on the first color videotape when it came out, but the tape was still very unstable. One of the plusses of this new format was that you could rewind and shoot again, but if you did that a couple of times it just shredded, which was useless for editing and you'd end up with a truckload of damaged tape. We did shoot them on video first, but as a standby we shot them again on film and transferred them to video.

They were beautifully done. I got in Peter Goldman, an avant-garde Swedish TV director, for "Penny Lane" and "Strawberry Fields." Michael Lindsey-Hogg did the Beatle shots in "Paperback Writer" and "Rain," which were filmed in Chiswick House in London. "Strawberry Fields" was filmed at Knole Park, which surrounded the stately home of the same name, at Sevenoaks in Kent. Knole was a perfect location and we used Bright's Hotel, an old-fashioned solid former inn on the old coaching road in the heart of Sevenoaks, as our base during filming. Peter and I, as well as the small crew, stayed there, but the Beatles were doing their usual twenty things a day, and stayed in town. They came and went as needed, whisked down in one of the limousines.

During a break from filming, John and I were strolling back to Bright's for a pot of tea and a sticky bun, when John spotted Ye Olde Antiques Shop on the High Street next door to the hotel.

"Hey, let's go in here," he said. John loved junk shops and church sales and bazaars and was always picking up junk to cram into his overdecorated house, perhaps to compensate for what he called its posh look. He forged in ahead of me and we started to browse.

"Hey, Tone, what do you think of this?" he called from the depths of the dark interior. I ambled over. John was holding up a small circus poster mounted on a board. It had subtle colors and a nice old-fashioned typeface that read: FOR THE BENEFIT OF MR. KITE. He liked quirky things like that.

I nodded. "It'll look good on your kitchen wall next to the milk safe."

John grinned. The idea appealed to him. But I think more than that, he was already getting the idea for a song. He paid a couple of pounds and carried it back to his limo. I was in the studio a few months later during the *Sgt. Pepper's Lonely Hearts Club Band* sessions, while everyone sat around for endless days getting stoned, while he wrote the song. It was indeed a flash of brilliance, pure John. All he did was virtually lift the words from the poster and then put them to a tune. It was a pretty nifty two-quid's worth.

The establishment, or atmosphere, shots for "Strawberry Fields Forever" and "Penny Lane" were done separately up in Liverpool in and around the actual places described: the barber's shop, the man from the bank and the fire station with the clean machine. The entire lot was done in two days. We all had a great deal of fun, in marked contrast to the almost oppressive atmosphere at the office. It seemed to me that there was just too much money to handle, too much business to take care of. Even though the Beatles had given up concerts and touring that year, the money from the record sales alone was like an unstoppable avalanche. It might have been only on paper, but it had to be dealt with, taxes had to be paid, legal ways of hiding it devised. I believe it was around this time that Brian reputedly hid vast sums in Swiss banking accounts. If he did—and he could have forgotten about them—they have never been found.

As a retreat away from it all, Paul had bought a near-derelict farm in western Scotland, overlooking the Isle of Skye and the Mull of Kintyre, where he could live the simple life. John promptly bought an Irish island and floated a gypsy-hued caravan across the sea to live in while building the house of his dreams, which never got built—something else that never happened. It was while Paul was at High Cross farm, watching the rain drip through a hole in the roof, that he first got the idea for "Fixing a Hole." He went on to write it in his psychedelic den at Cavendish Road. While it was memorable to hear Paul come up with the lyrics, that's not what I remember most about that night. Something else is foremost in my mind, further proof that the Beatles, in those early days, were naive boys when it came to money. Gradually the den had filled up that night until there were half a dozen musicians and friends, all hanging out, all doing our peace and love thing. As the hours passed, everyone grew hungry.

"Tone, do you mind popping out to get us a load of tandoori curry?" Paul asked.

"No problem," I said. Since I assumed the guys down at the local curry house were not likely to let me have a take-away on credit, I added, "Have you got any cash?"

"Yes, I've got a bit," Paul said. He pulled open the door of a little safe in the corner of his den and the accumulation of years of little blue Kalamazoo pay packets fell out, one after the other, tumbling onto the floor. There were a couple of hundred of them; the kind with holes punched in them so you could see the folded notes inside. He'd get home on a Friday and throw another one in the safe (which wasn't locked anyway) with all the other packets. It was as if he'd done a wages snatch, hiding it all until the heat went down and the gang would come around for the split.

"Here," Paul said, handing me one of the unopened packets. "That should cover it."

"Paul, have you any idea how much is in this pay packet?" I asked, out of curiosity, as I opened it. I pulled out some folded five-pound notes and a few coins.

"Course not, not the foggiest," Paul said, smiling and stealing a quick look.

"It's fifty pounds plus small change. You've even got a pay slip," I said, as I unfolded it.

"Let's have a look," Paul said. I handed it over and he started to laugh because it was so ludicrous, given the amount of money they actually spent.

I was now on a thousand a year and also had a pay slip—a genuine one, with my taxes deducted. It occurred to me that I was ligging around London, having a great time and spending, one way or another, ten times that. Paul, and George, to a lesser extent, were always quoting how much their dads earned.

Shortly after the pay packet incident, I again discussed the cost of living with Paul. He seemed to think that whatever his dad earned was a benchmark for honest wages.

"I think me dad's on about six quïd a week," Paul said, "and if that's what me dad gets, it must be about right."

"Brian pays me tons more than that, Paul," I said. His response was that if that was what Brian paid me, then *that* must be right, too. It never dawned on him that, ultimately, the four Beatles paid for everything and everyone in the organization. It was as if it was all Brian's money and wasn't he a fine and generous chap for settling all their bills without being pissed off?

The fast pace of the money machine became too much even for Brian Epstein's quick mind to fathom. In Britain there were no so-called showbiz lawyers who could handle what was happening in the sixties pop explosion. They were all old-school solicitors like Lord Goodman, dealing with such matters as divorce and the odd libel action and disgraced politician. None of them had studied what was already happening in the States. Before the Beatles, no British band had toured the U.S. in the way that American artists had always come to Europe. In fact, as a nation, the British (known then as "the English") went nowhere beyond these shores unless they were Burton and Taylor, or aristocracy with a villa in the South of France. Package tours to Spain were in their infancy. The English stayed at home, consumed loads of chips fried in lard—which still cooks it best, according to top chefs—and paddled in the freezing seas at Frinton or Rhyl in sleeveless Fair Isle sweaters and with handkerchiefs knotted on their heads. Avocado pears, garlic and lager were disgusting foreign gunk and you bought olive oil in little bottles at the chemist to use for medicinal purposes, like cleaning your ears. Little wonder then that words such as *songwriters* and *copyright* and *royalties* and the entire jargon of the *music industry* were almost foreign words to the lawyers of London Town. Little wonder that the Beatles sold their "recorded performances on record" to EMI for next to nothing. Little wonder that valuable rights were virtually given away, willy-nilly.

Many years later, when Paul was negotiating his own record deal with EMI, he demanded something like 27 percent on his future record sales, remembering how EMI had originally stitched them up for one old penny (less than half a new pence) per record divided among the five of them (including Brian Epstein) when a single retailed at six shillings and fourpence (thirty-seven and a half new pence).

᙮

The Beatles went from being broke to being incredibly rich and not really knowing it. One day, almost idly, while we were chatting, Paul opened an envelope from Barclays Bank at St. John's Wood, his local branch. He was about to toss it to one side, as all the Beatles did with most "bits of paper." Suddenly, his attention was caught and he gazed at the statement with the strangest look on his face.

"Here, have a look at this, Tone," he said, handing the statement to me with a deadpan expression. I took the piece of paper and read the writing at the top: *Paul McCartney, Esq. Current account.* My eyes traveled downward and focused on the figure in the final column. Then on the load of zeroes after it. Dosh, real dosh.

"Fuckin' hell! A million pounds!" I exclaimed. It just didn't seem real. "You're a millionaire!"

Paul took the statement back and gazed, as if mesmerized. He started to giggle nervously, out of sheer panic, I think. It was as if he felt he was dreaming and would wake up. It was "Nudge nudge, wink wink, I've done it! I'm a fucking millionaire!" But in his eyes it was, "Bloody hell, what do I do *now?*"

The irony was that it was only a fraction of what was in the Beatles' business accounts. Although the Beatles gave the impression that they were worldly and wise, in business terms they knew very little. They were very like Elvis Presley with Colonel Parker in this respect. I believe that Elvis invented that magic phrase, "TCB," or "taking care of business," which is what the colonel did for him, and the Beatles were quick to understand that what it meant was that they didn't have to be responsible. I don't think they were capable of running their own lives, much less their careers, for some years. They presumed Brian and his secretary and people like me were there to TCB, and doubtless things would have continued to run on a fairly even keel, probably to this date, if Brian had not died.

Right from the start, it was almost as if there was a tacit understanding that Brian would handle everything, no matter what it was. If they had requested a sack of fresh manure, Brian would eventually shuffle the order down the line to some poor sod like me, who went out and found it. Then I would hand the sack to Brian, who would hand it to whichever Beatle had requested it. Then John, or Paul, or George, or Ringo would smile and say, "Thanks, Eppy!" as if Brian himself had done the job.

For a long time the four of them had no idea of what it took to get through a day. They had gone straight from regular school or art school or playing in a band at Butlin's holiday camp and had never done any real work. George had been the local butcher's Saturday delivery boy, and then, briefly, an apprentice electrician. As far as I know, the only job outside music that Paul and John had ever done was during the summer of 1960, when on holiday from college and school. They found work behind the bar of the Fox and Hounds, a pub at Caversham, near Reading, that was run by Paul's cousin, Elizabeth "Bett" and her husband, Mike Robbins. In return for pouring beer and wiping down the bar top, waiting on tables, sweeping up and being general dogsbodies, the boys were allowed to entertain the regulars on Saturday nights. Most of the money they legitimately earned was from gigging around Liverpool or Hamburg. When they went to Germany, not paid enough to eat properly, they had fallen into an almost deranged time of hunger and pills to keep them going.

In those days, it was very unusual for anyone to go off and do their own thing without ever having had some kind of day job first. Cliff Richard had been Harry Webb, a bus driver. Tommy Steele had been a merchant seaman, and Freddie Garrity of Freddie and the Dreamers had been a milkman. Everybody had a job, or was expected to get one. When you went to the Labour Exchange at that time, the bastards gave you a job, not a benefit check. If you didn't like that job, they gave you another one until you got the message.

The postwar generation bought stuff on the hire purchase, or saved up for it. There were no credit checks as there are today, and very few people had bank accounts. The banks treated ordinary people like scum. In order to get credit you needed to have rent books and a regular job that you'd had for several years. But for the Beatles when they first started out, doing anything as mundane as applying for an H.P. agreement would never have crossed their minds anyway— unless it was for a guitar, which was a different matter entirely. They didn't have rent books and gas bills, so if they wanted anything, they had to save up for it and pay cash. Even after they came down to London, they had no real concept of the outside world. Their world was Beatledom, which meant being silly and comic, as well as "creative." But that was about it. There was no track record before the Beatles, no blueprint to say, "This is how a pop star operates, this is how you run your life and your finances."

Their biggest decisions in life, even up to this point had been about sex and drugs, so it was not surprising that they were ill prepared to deal with a business that was generating millions. Everything connected with them turned to gold. Take T-shirts for instance. When I first asked Brian how much we should sell them for, he hadn't a clue. He looked in bookshops and libraries for some sort of manual, but all this was virgin territory, literally, a new frontier in business terms. There was no how-to book to follow. He even asked the old-time managers and had them flummoxed. In the end, all they could say was, "Charge whatever the market will stand." Brian should have gone to see Colonel Parker, and had a chat.

However, the money was flooding in and the Beatles were kept completely in the dark. Brian still made up their regular little pay packets, containing about fifty pounds after deductions, in five- and single-pound notes and the odd two-bob bit or half-a-crown. It was all a bit nonsensical because from the time they were in London, although they continued to get the pay packets, all aboveboard and correctly done, they stopped using cash. Houses were bought for cash through NEMS. Flats, cars, clothes, restaurants, groceries, were all on account, the bills paid by the office. They moved from being skint but having a few pound notes in their pockets, to being very rich and having none at all.

During their hippie period, they walked around barefooted, signing for everything. If they signed a check people would rarely cash it. They'd frame it. They were normal kids and grounded. They didn't overspend and run around making fools of themselves like a lot of the next generation of rock stars did. If one reads the press clippings from their early days, it's clear that they didn't embarrass themselves. There wasn't a breath of scandal, not a blemish until the little drug busts started. Journalists like Don Short, who got to know them well, said that looking back, it's incredible how well behaved they were even out on the road and under intense scrutiny and pressure. If you were in your midteens when you got into the Beatles, chances are your mum and dad liked them too. They were set up as role models and kept on their pedestals right up to the Summer of Love, when the Haight-Ashbury arrived in everyone's consciousness.

15

Songs were what John and Paul had always knocked out while bunking off from school, or on the way to gigs in the back of the van between a week's residency at Llandudno and nipping down to Birmingham to do *Thank Your Lucky Stars* on television before heading off to some theater at Great Yarmouth. Pop songs were a doddle.

Perhaps it was the world's press taking them too seriously and asking silly questions about the deeper meaning of their songs and about where the words came from that changed them from being simple songwriters. Songwriting became a "creative art" and was reinvented as being difficult. But even Franz Schubert—whom a serious critic compared their work to—used to "knock them out" at the rate of three, four, five a day. For John and Paul, songs were suddenly something that were "crafted" and then taken off to Abbey Road like a half-finished jigsaw puzzle for George Martin to work his alchemy on. It all became serious and expensive. Time was also taken seriously. Time was counted and valued by accountants and rationed.

Part of the problem was EMI itself. Whenever a new piece of studio equipment was invented or came on the market, EMI had an irritating habit of ensuring that after delivery, it was immediately taken away from Abbey Road to their laboratories "somewhere in the country" to be thoroughly inspected by white-coated boffins. They spent ages stripping it down, poking about in its in-nards, until with no more secrets left to reveal, it would be put back together with a few adjustments and new specifications. Only when an EMI stamp of ap-proval was finally awarded would it be returned to Abbey Road, by which time all the other studios were already using the latest equipment. For instance, Tri-dent Studios would get the new eight-track machines and use them. Abbey Road would get one too and it would be treated like the Enigma decoding ma-chine that they cracked at Bletchley and driven off in an olive-green camou-flaged truck with an armed guard to be returned—sometimes months later—like a new rocket installation, under conditions of great secrecy. Perhaps it was because of EMI's Thorn-Marconi connection. Marconi made missiles and guidance systems and most of their boffins were beavering away on hush-hush projects for top-secret government contracts. It seems far-fetched, but perhaps recording equipment from Germany or the United States was so cutting-edge that there were areas where Marconi could borrow or adapt for guided-missile or radar-listening systems.

Trident and Olympic studios were funky and groovy and easy to be creative at. But Abbey Road was run like the army, with signing in and out, 9:00 A.M. to 5:30 P.M. office hours and a sort of regime that wasn't far short of "Ten-hut! Stand by your guitar you 'orrible little musician, you." The result was that Abbey Road was always behind. The other studios had long gone sixteen-track when Abbey Road was still waiting for the return of the camouflaged truck.

Ultimately, when it was realized how much money they were earning for EMI, the Beatles got permission to record only when they really wanted to. Then they became a law unto themselves. It was now a matter of handing them the keys and telling them to get on with it.

It's true that when the Beatles first went into Abbey Road, they were nervous and shy, eager to please and stood almost at attention while performing. Ses-sions were quickly got out of the way and they escaped, as if from being lined up in the headmaster's study. Even long after they came to realize their own power, they still treated George Martin and his wife, Judy, with extreme reverence, as if they were royalty. They cowed to the record executives and were, in many re-spects, extremely polite, almost humble. This wasn't so much because they were provincials who had come down from Liverpool, but because in those days most people did tend to be in awe of authority figures, as Elvis was, even when he was the most successful pop star in the world.

We saw George Martin as Q in the James Bond films. You could imagine him saying, "Don't fiddle with those knobs, Double-0-Lennon, you'll blow us all to smithereens, there's a good chap." By that time, of course, John's head was so full of controlled substances that George would probably have been right. John was about to blow our minds, if not blow us up.

In the early days, I loved going into Abbey Road, no matter who was working there, whether it was Yehudi Menuhin, Cliff Richard, the Hollies or the English National Opera Company, because it was exciting. When I walked into a control room, something was always going on, tracks were being recorded, people were incredibly motivated and urgent. Then studios became a place of joints and takeaways and the energy and the fun went out of the windows with the fragrant smoke.

Just a few years earlier, Paul and John's degree of originality in Liverpool had consisted of wearing leathers and thrashing about with guitars. When they first got into concepts and ideas and video and films, they tiptoed a little, feeling their way cautiously. The Beatles did their first three albums more or less "live." This was not laying down track by track, say drums and bass first and then adding stuff. It was more like a count of 1-2-3-4 and they all started playing. That was how it used to be done, sometimes with a bit of ADT—automatic double tracking—on the vocals, to make it interesting.

Their first album took just twelve hours to record. "Hey Jude" was the first time the Beatles used eight tracks. It was done virtually simultaneously, "live" as before, but then the big buildup was overlaid and overlaid. It was like, "Let's use all eight tracks, eh?" Like wow! It was so fresh and exciting. They couldn't wait to get into the studio and put down their ideas. Even a concept as complex as *Sgt. Pepper* would be recorded on two four-track machines.

Their new power meant that they could pretty well do anything they wanted, but at a cost. Things changed. The passion went. Given the run of Abbey Road, they seemed to forget that a studio was there to *record,* not to write in. By November 1966, when they went in to record the first tracks on *Sgt. Pepper,* they were totally unprepared. Hardly anything was written, and far less rehearsed. But with the Beatles runaway success, they got—as George Martin often bemoaned—"Whatever the hell they want."

My time was still split between working at NEMS during the day, doing what was needed—which usually consisted of Brian asking me to take care of things for him, or sending me on special missions, such as organizing shows at the Saville or going around with Cilla. In the evenings, I would go to clubs. In between, I would hang out with the Beatles, so during this time, I came to see on a regular basis how the four of them would be slumped in a corner at Abbey Road, with cups of coffee and bits of paper and cigarettes and joints, not doing a thing. George Martin and the new engineer, Geoff Emerick (who had replaced Norman

Smith), would be sitting in the control room, or the canteen, bored out of their minds. Occasionally, John or Paul would say, "When is Mal going to get the bloody take-away?" George might ask, "Has John written anything today?" Or Paul might say to John, "Have you heard any new guitar sounds?"

This kind of minutiae would go on for days and days. Nothing of importance being said at all. Then, suddenly, "Fixing a Hole" would be transported from Paul's psychedelic den with the chrome fireplace at Cavendish Avenue and put together fast, recorded in a matter of hours. Then it would be more days of nothing. Into the boredom, Paul would say, "John's got this thing about some guy called Mr. Kite! Yeah, he's got a poster of, like, Mr. Kite's circus coming to town and he's gonna turn it into a song." A few more days would pass and then Paul would remember the idle images he'd had the night before as he dropped off to sleep, a nice little song for Ringo: "With a Little Help from My Friends."

Recording sessions jerked on for weeks on end of nothingness and boredom, all interspersed, of course, with flashes of brilliance. It was a far cry from the days when the Beatles went in with a well-rehearsed and polished song and their original engineer, Norman Smith, recorded it for them in a single take, and then they did one more just for kicks, just to be on the safe side.

🌟

Abbey Road was EMI's own studio and they could do as they pleased with it. The paperwork was done, studio time was charged and somehow the books were balanced. Although it was a bit regimented, it worked. The Beatles didn't record anywhere else at the time, so they had no idea what stupendous sums they were spending in this way. Anyone with real intent still could go into a studio and make a record for about thirty-five pounds in those days, but the Beatles' new recording method—and it was serendipitous—became the industry standard for doing that kind of big album. Musicians suddenly waited for the muse, the right vibes, man. *Sgt. Pepper's Lonely Hearts Club Band* moved the whole recording process into sitting in the creative area.

But despite this, *Sgt. Pepper,* the record album that started all the indulgences, was pure genius. It even changed the way people behaved and dressed. It changed the look of artwork, album covers and attitudes. Paul had thought it all up on a long flight back from Kenya, where he had been on holiday, staying at the Treetops Hotel during November 1966—the bush hotel where Princess Elizabeth was staying in 1952 when she heard that her father, the king, had died.

Paul thought that if the Beatles became Sergeant Pepper's Lonely Hearts Club Band instead of the Beatles, or even instead of John, Paul, George and Ringo, they would be free to do almost anything. They would be their alter egos, he said, different people. They would no longer have to do the cute little pop songs that they'd outgrown, along with the mohair suits, moptops and being good lads. Treetops had been a psychedelic experience. He said he "wanted to fly," creatively speaking.

Brian hadn't the faintest idea what Paul was talking about, what these alter egos were about, or what *Sgt. Pepper* was about. He only really understood making straightforward pop records and doing gigs, and he added these new worries to his already long list, the things that kept him awake and eventually drove him almost mad.

We were going to do a video for every one of the tracks on *Sgt. Pepper*. The idea was to get in a different director for each of them, so each one would have a different look, but with a linking theme. Quite a few were scripted, ready to be made, but Brian wasn't very happy about it. He said it would create an administrative nightmare for him.

"How will 'Lucy in the Sky with Diamonds' be achieved?" he asked, with a worried frown.

I knew what he was saying. They were taking acid like it was going out of fashion. John was eating tab after tab, week after week, before the album and after, though they never took acid while they were actually recording. But Brian was concerned with how legal the images would be because "Lucy" was scripted in an acid daze. He saw no point in making something that would end up banned. In addition, the musicians' union and the TV unions wouldn't leave anybody alone to do anything on an independent level. The cost of union camera crews and actors and overtime for little films made of every track on the album would have been huge. Overall it would end up bigger and more expensive than a movie. You needed a whole office bureaucracy in those days to deal with the paperwork involved, with the legalities and union aspects of a production. There were no faxes, no e-mails; only telephones and the Royal Mail, or a delivery boy. Everything had to be agreed, written back and forth in triplicate, the old-fashioned way with carbon paper, then signed, sealed and delivered. What had seemed a great idea in the Scotch last night became the Normandy landings the next day in the office.

Brian complained to me that this new venture created an enormous amount of work, and ultimately, the videos got shelved. Even the iconic *Sgt. Pepper* album sleeve, shot by Michael Cooper and with art direction by Peter Blake and Robert Fraser, was outrageously expensive. The final costs came to a staggering £2,867, a hundred times more than most album covers (you could have bought a couple of Jaguar cars for that sum). It burst EMI's "sleeves" budget—but John insisted that art was beyond price. He cracked, "If you can't stand the art, get out of the kitschen." Something that seemed a simple idea for Paul turned into a nightmare for Brian. I can't stress enough how ill it made him feel.

"All those people's faces on it," Brian said. "What's the point? Who are they all?" Also going on at that time was the renegotiation of the Beatles' EMI contract, which dragged on and was giving Brian additional sleepless nights.

Interestingly, *Sgt. Pepper* was put together almost accidentally in no particular sequence, but worked perfectly. It was brilliant. Yet, at a later stage, when the song order was rearranged to fit one of the new consumer-tape formats in the U.S., it didn't work. Strangely and inexplicably, it became a jumble. Make of that what you will.

Many people had talked about that kind of concept album but very few were capable of writing and performing such a feat. Perhaps Brian Wilson or Pete Townshend could. The songs were not so much linked by a continuing story, like a classical opera, or rock opera like *Tommy,* more by a *feel.* To bring it off they had the perfect partner in George Martin, a true genius of an arranger, and more importantly, an absolute anchor of organization and knowledge.

I saw firsthand that when your mind is flying at fifty ideas a minute, it is crucial to have someone around who not only *can* say, but *will* say, "Sure, we'll do this, then we'll do that, then we'll try so and so. Right! Let's get on with it."

By that time George Martin was on much more of a trust-like wavelength with them, and as they came to *Sgt. Pepper* he knew for sure that they were more than just singers and musicians. He'd come to respect their flair, and was happy to run with their musical indulgences rather than to merely indulge them. He was delighted to, in fact. He always enjoyed himself during some of the more creative sessions. At that time he was undoubtedly that fifth Beatle the press was always looking for, although Paul and John said he wasn't. Out of love and respect for his memory, the only "fifth Beatle" they would ever countenance was Stuart Sutcliffe.

🐾

Being there at a lot of the sessions is something I'll never forget, but my memories are tempered by the fact that naturally nobody had a clue how culturally important, how iconic, *Sgt. Pepper* would become. I clearly remember the filming of one of the final sessions for one of the tracks, "A Day in the Life," when Mr. McCartney had arranged with Mr. Martin for a full orchestra, or as Paul described it, "a set of penguins" to play nothing while he, Mr. McCartney, conducted.

When I say play nothing, I mean no scored music. Paul wanted each instrument to play its own ascending scale in meter, leading up to a grand crescendo. Obviously it worked because you can hear it on the album. Before we filmed we handed out loaded 16mm cameras to invited guests including, among others,

Mick and Marianne, and Mike Nesmith of the Monkees. They were shown what to press and told to film whatever they wanted. The BBC then banned the subsequent video. Not because of the content of the footage, but because the *song* itself had drug references.

Some time after banning the "A Day in the Life" video, the BBC telephoned me and said that they were planning an extravaganza of their own. It was to be the first worldwide satellite transmission linkup, and they were pompously calling it *Our World*. The 125-minute program would link live continents, bringing "man face-to-face with mankind." Would the Fabs consider writing and performing a new song to mark the event?

Still smarting from having their/our druggie video rejected, the lads said no initially, then reconsidered. They said that they would do it if they could do it like a party. Instantly suspicious, the BBC set up "a meet," and I was sent over to explain. I took with me the video for "A Day in the Life," which of course, as I suspected, they hadn't seen. And, as I knew they would, they loved it. We had a few drinks and played it continuously while we sang along. When we finally got down to business I produced a tape with two new songs on it and told them to choose which one they wanted for the forthcoming satellite transmission. The two songs were "Your Mother Should Know," and "All You Need Is Love."

In the fullness of time an official letter arrived from Broadcasting House. It informed us that they had chosen "All You Need Is Love," and furthermore, would agree to "a party atmosphere."

The lads went off to work on a backing track because they were going to sing along live on the night in the studio. It was probably the world's first live karaoke session. George Harrison was the one who finally cynically asked, "Hey? Who's gonna come to this party atmosphere, then? We've got less than two days!"

We all looked at each other. The solution was obvious. I got up and found Keith Moon quite easily at the Speakeasy. I didn't report back so fast though. After all, why ruin a good trawl around the clubs with an early goal? Keith was absolutely stonkers, throwing peanuts everywhere, and for once not dressed up as Queen Victoria or Hitler.

Tongue in cheek, I suggested he go home and get some rest. I told him about the BBC satellite linkup thing and said to him, "You've got an official rave-up tomorrow. The whole world will be there and we need you to be in top form."

He wasn't having any of it. He came close to me and slurred as Robert Newton had once done, after he'd turned up on a film set the worse for wear, "Don't chide me, dear boy, don't chide me." But Keith was in a much more confident mood. "Dear boy, I shall be there, but if it's all the same to you, I'll just keep going."

"The session will be live," I reminded him.

"Satellites? I know all about satellites. Worldwide linkups? A mere bagatelle," he said, grandly.

I left. It was exhausting work, but I persevered. I trawled the Cromwellian, the Bag, the Scotch of St. James and found Eric Clapton, Mick Jagger and Marianne Faithful, and friends. Mick said he'd come, no hassle, but he was a bit put out that the BBC hadn't asked the Stones. At the time they were doing their new album, *His Satanic Majesty's Request,* and he said you couldn't buy that kind of publicity.

He'd conveniently forgotten that his drug trial was coming up in two days and the case had been headlines for ages. There had been rallies in support of them, and numerous articles written. I said, "You're a bit persona non grata with the Establishment right now, Mick."

He grinned and drawled, "Yeah, you're right. Fuck 'em, there goes the knighthood." He didn't appear at all worried. *Satanic Majesty's* even had Mick saying in it, "Where's that joint?"

Eventually a reasonably sized party atmosphere was rounded up. Moon was early. Mick arrived wearing a beautiful silk coat with psychedelic eyes painted on it. Eppy came, looking very happy. He wore a black velvet suit but for once hadn't put a tie on. It made him look fresh-faced and far younger. I took many photographs that day and those of Brian with the Beatles are the last ones ever taken of them together.

I was still standing around the control room with George Martin and Brian drinking whisky when we were told we were on the air, forty seconds early. We stuffed the bottle and glasses under the mixing desk and rushed into position. Mick sat on the floor near Paul and puffed on a massive reefer, in front of 200 million people—and he was due in court the next morning. Eric Clapton had his hair permed specially in an Afro, the latest thing, like a Hendrix. The more narcissistic ones wanted to sit at John's feet because as the song's vocalist the cameras would be on him the most. He was so wired and speeding that all the way through he chewed gum incessantly. But everyone took a few mood elevators, and I appeared dancing and ringing bells, wearing a sandwich board which at one time probably used to read, THE END OF THE WORLD IS NIGH. This night it had LOVE LOVE LOVE.

After that, I was on a roll. I put myself in the "Penny Lane" video as a waiter, and waited for the calls, but unlike Mr. Moon, they didn't come.

16

Shortly before Jimi Hendrix formed his band, the Experience, I often used to bump into him and his manager, Brian "Chas" Chandler, former bass player for the Animals. Jimi loved Chas, really loved him. They would play some rock and roll, and some blues. This was before all the "Hey Joe" stuff. Chas was a wonderful, happy man, a bundle of fun, right from the time the Animals made their first sortie down to London, from Newcastle, knocked out "House of the Rising Sun" in twenty minutes and went for a pint. He was just so big and funny, unlike Eric Burdon, who wished he could sing like Ray Charles. I remember I had a girlfriend at the time and Chas really fancied her. Every time I turned around, Chas was there. He would phone up at the oddest times, trying to catch me "not there."

He had discovered Jimi playing in some obscure Greenwich Village dive and took control of his life and career. They were together twenty-four hours a day. He brought Jimi back to England and introduced him to people, getting him gigs by taking him around to all the clubs, from the Bag O'Nails and the Cromwellian, to the Speak. Whenever he found an opportunity, Chas would have Jimi on stage to jam so he could impress people and spread the news by word of mouth. And Jimi *was* very impressive. He would do his guitar histrionics, playing guitar behind his back and with his teeth. When he would finally set fire to it, the crowd would be almost baying for blood. Later, as is always the case, the histrionics were demanded. It became style over content. It got so that if Jimi didn't wreck his guitar and otherwise create havoc, the fans booed him off stage. Trying to keep up with the madness, and always feeling the expectations of violence and anarchy from the fans, was to have a profound effect on Jimi. He lost the plot and, eventually, his life.

Like John Lennon, Jimi was another absolute original. He never talked about anything but music and sometimes the army, where he had been a paratrooper. He had been in the famous 101st Airborne Division, the Screamin' Eagles, based at Fort Campbell on the Tennessee/Kentucky border. It was a wild, frontier-town atmosphere of blues, beer, bourbon and barroom brawls. That's where Jimi cut his teeth on the blues making forays down into Nashville and Memphis, picking and playing backup on all kinds of rock and roll revues, blues and soul shows.

I went out of my way to see him whenever he was on. He was so fantastic that I took Brian to the Bag to see him, sure that Brian would agree with me. He did. He was blown away and at once said, "I think I'll put him on at the Saville. He deserves his own show."

Brian kept his word, as he always did. He was proud of the Saville. We had proper lighting and everything. Not many acts then were used to playing in actual theaters where the sound was already acoustically good. They were more apt to be playing bars and pubs and basements and such, cranking up the amps and letting it rip. Jimi always tried to play as loud as he could to get the best sound that he had on his brain. In those days, the PA systems were adequate—except in stadiums, where they were hopeless—but they still couldn't cope with Jimi Hendrix. The whole industry, from recording to playing to marketing, was finding its feet, still so basic that it is almost unrecognizable by today's standards.

In the midsixties, the light show became as important as the music. Psychedelic lighting was paramount and matched the whole psychedelic craze, from magic mushrooms to lurid and bizarre fashions. Bands like Pink Floyd evolved more out of their light show than their "music," not the other way around. In a way, Jimi Hendrix seemed inspired by lighting. He suffered a great deal of pain from a back injury acquired after a bad parachute drop, and took handfuls of painkillers. We joked that he was getting high on Valderma, the antiseptic cream he used to rub into his face all the time to take care of his bad complexion. He also loved magic mushrooms, and on that combination, painkillers and mushrooms and a few lines of Charlie, snorted before the bright mirrors in his dressing room, Jimi seemed to fly to the stars and beyond when he was on stage.

I always thought he could see colors far beyond the spectrum. His eyes would get an "I'm seeing forever, and what I can see is what I'm gonna play" expression in them as he stood on stage during rehearsals, encircled within the lighting effects I devised, swirling orbs of magenta and lilac, acid green and gold.

Jimi was easy to work with, and very trusting. Anything went as long it enhanced his performance. Since I was relatively new to the lighting game, I was willing to experiment, to try anything from strobes to electric wheels. Jimi would try anything I suggested, from a swirling multicolored circular effect, to zigzags and vertical flashes. I remember him being pleased with that effect. "Hey man! It's like purple rain!" And that was all he had to say. He also loved the blue electric strobes that flashed on and off like lightning. They seemed to power him, as if he were actually plugged into the mains. His performances were incendiary.

The Saville was packed. The Lord Chancellor had ordained that people were not allowed to stand up in theaters, so everyone cheered wildly and stamped the ground while still seated. It was only in the Beatles' shows, where there was a more juvenile crowd, that kids ran wild. The Saville was more adult, more interested in listening to the music.

There were two forty-five-minute shows a night. Jimi sang "Purple Haze," "The Wind Cries Mary" and "All Along the Watchtower." He sang some blues, some Cream, some tracks off his album *Are You Experienced*. Most of the time he wore a silk shirt, velvet pants and Beatle boots, and on stage, an army jacket from a shop oddly named: I was Lord Kitchener's Valet. Another favorite way of dressing was in a powder-blue antique Hussars jacket with lashing of gold braid that he picked up at Granny Takes a Trip, a junk shop in the King's Road. Underneath, he wore army pants. It was an interesting look that became his trademark.

We put Jimi on three or four times at the Saville, and after that his career was off and running. He was always out there on his own and could already blow most guitar players off the planet. However, there was something about the Saville that seemed to move him into another league. Jimi Hendrix might have stayed just another guitar player had he remained in America. I think he had to come to Europe for his star to shine. It was just the right time and his progress was meteoric, from crowded, smoky, noisy little venues like the Speakeasy and the Bag O'Nails, to those bigger public performances and historic stage settings.

17

During the first few months of 1967 I often bumped into Paul on his own around town. At the time Jane was in the U.S. with the Old Vic Rep on a three-month tour of Shakespeare's plays and Paul had started going to experimental concerts, lectures and exhibitions, absorbing new ideas. He was rapidly becoming the most inventive and creative Beatle. In April, while John emerged from a haze long enough to commission The Fool, a Dutch design collective, to come up with designs for his Rolls to be decorated all over with bright psychedelic swirls and cartouches of flowers on a yellow background, Paul was jetting from L.A. to Denver in a Lear jet the Beatles' New York lawyer, Nat Weiss, had borrowed from Frank Sinatra. He had made up his mind to pay Jane a surprise visit for her twenty-first birthday. They spent only one day together, enjoying the scenery of the Rockies, before Jane had to return to work, and Paul went to Las Vegas to see some friends.

A few days later, somewhere in midair on his return journey home, his active mind dreamed up another wildly innovative concept: "A Magical Mystery Tour," complete with John-type sketches. Their pace of life was so hectic, so immediate, that within days, the Beatles would be at Abbey Road, starting the first recording sessions of the new album, with a film to follow.

The Beatles didn't take acid when they were in the studio, but earlier that year John had managed to take some accidentally. Perhaps influenced by Pink Floyd, who were making their first intergalactic pop album, *Piper at the Gates of Dawn,* in the next studio (with Norman Smith producing them), John spent the night perched on the roof of Abbey Road tripping, staring at the frosty stars and waiting for the dawn. Eventually, Paul and George went up to get him down before he fell off. Paul took him home and, to help John out, he also dropped some acid to get on the same plane and stayed up all night, keeping him company.

London was now buzzing with psychedelic sounds and dopes. "Strawberry Fields Forever" was being played to death, along with Jimi Hendrix's "Purple Haze" and "Paper Sun" by Traffic. To show the schizophrenic rift in taste and opinion between the generations, England's old guard bought "Roses of Picardy" by Vince Hill and wrote to the papers, complaining about the youth of today. But on the front line where it was all happening, studio work began to imitate *Sgt. Pepper,* including Pink Floyd's hit, "See Emily Play." Norman had to fight Floyd to be more melodic as well as psychedelic and he was right: it worked. Eventually, their main man, Syd Barret, became an acid casualty, a great pity because, as Norman told me when we heard the news, "Syd could write like John Lennon."

At the end of April I went to the first major psychedelic event in Europe, which took place in the massive space of Alexandra Palace—known to Londoners as Ally Pally—perched atop Muswell Hill in North London. Incongruously televised on BBC2, who normally only showed very highbrow programs, it was the precursor and model for all pop festivals that followed. It was billed as a benefit for the *International Times'* legal defense fund. The advertisements in the *Melody Maker* said it was "giant benefit against fuzz"—the fuzz being the cops who were attempting to close them down. In hippiedom it became known as the Fourteen-Hour Technicolor Dream. I knew most of the bands because I'd booked them all at the Saville.

Two large stages were set up and a smaller central stage for happenings, jugglers, fire-eaters and the like. Nobody expected ten thousand happy hippies to trek there, but they did. In one corner, from a plastic igloo, Suzy Creamcheese doled out yellow banana-skin joints, which were supposed to give you a blast, but since they were just banana skins, probably didn't—although Donovan sang that electrical bananas were apparently going to be one of the next big things. Pink Floyd headlined, and in addition there were seventy bands of every persuasion; light shows illuminating the massive walls and dancing.

I saw John come in with Dunbar and a couple of others, wearing an Afghan-embroidered skin coat and looking very stoned. I drifted across to speak to him. He said they had been watching TV down in Weybridge when they saw the concert on air. They jumped into the Rolls and came on up to London. As we were chatting—though not much could be heard above the music—John's attention was caught by Yoko, who was giving a Fluxus performance with stepladders and scissors center stage, beneath the acrobats and jugglers swinging from the soaring cast-iron gothic pillars. He watched, seemingly mesmerized.

In all that radiating joy and love, suddenly something strangely unpleasant happened around her. The dangerous amplified sound of the cutting scissors sawing through her clothing turned a few spectators nasty and they started to tear and drag at her, ripping off her pants, like dogs attacking a hare. She lay there, her features impassive and let them do it, as if it were some kind of experiment. When she was entirely naked, her little art groupies led her away to the side and surrounded her while she dressed in fresh clothes. Yoko might have lost her pants to a baying mob, but that night she found John, or at least, she gained his attention. Was it the kinky S & M–type happening he observed that fascinated him? Whatever it was, he became turned on. It was obvious in his face. And as I watched him, knowing John as I did, I sensed this would lead to trouble. Bizarrely, Yoko's husband, Tony Cox, had filmed the entire thing and at times, seemed to be urging on the mob. When he caught John's fixed expression, I saw a very knowing look flicker through Tony's eyes.

The most magical moment came at dawn. As the sky turned pink and sunlight flooded in, Pink Floyd took to the stage, for the first time wearing velvet flares and tight satin shirts. John was so overwhelmed that in a stoned way he had a vision of his future idyllic life. He came over and said, "I'm taking Cyn away. We're gonna live in Paradise." He was referring to the island he had bought by auction in remote Clew Bay the previous month, but hadn't yet seen.

The next day, John, Dunbar and Magic Alex flew to Dublin and got into a large black limousine that was waiting for them at the airport, and drove to the lonely West Coast. A local boatman took them from the mainland to John's island. He strode out the few hundred yards of damp heather and spiky sea grass he owned, before huddling out of the wind in the lee of a rock, to make a handful of nonsensical sketches of his future home, with an eye that saw only fantastic psychedelic visions. He wanted a place where he, Cynthia and Julian would find themselves, be happy and where there would be no deeply intense woman like Yoko to possess his mind. A place from which he would emerge occasionally to make a record or attend other psychedelic happenings. It was a dream that the exposed outlook and the cold winds from the sea blew away. The three intrepid adventurers returned to the madness of London and the island went back to sleep.

In a year that went down in folklore as the Summer of Love, Paul met Linda Eastman—the woman who was to be the love of his life—on May 15, 1967.

At the time, Linda was making a name for herself in New York. She had quickly gone from being a sixty-five-dollar-a-week receptionist at *Town and Country Magazine,* to a photographer, earning one thousand dollars per page on *Life.* She had achieved this by using an exclusive invitation sent to the magazine to attend one of the Rolling Stones' functions on the *SS Sea Panther,* moored on the Hudson. (The Stones were using this yacht as temporary headquarters, having been banned by every good hotel in New York.) Through fate and a little enterprise, Linda ended up being the only photographer invited on board. Subsequently, her pictures were the only ones available to the media, which quickly established her as a leading rock 'n' roll photographer. It was on the yacht that she first met the Stones' manager, Allen Klein, and also Peter Brown who was in New York on business.

Linda came to London to take photographs for a book to be entitled, *Rock and Other Four-Letter Words,* commissioned by Bantam Books. Her modest thousand-dollar advance had largely been used up on travel expenses and film, so Linda was staying with friends she had met in New York, such as the Animals, to save money on hotels. Georgie Fame was doing a gig at the Bag O'Nails when I dropped in with Paul and a small party. Linda was seated at a table some yards away near the front. I could see that someone had taken Paul's attention. I glanced in the direction he was looking. The girl he was looking at, Linda, wasn't cast in the usual mold of rock chicks with their generic pert features. She was striking, like a Veronica Lake, with angular features and strawberry-blonde hair, cut to swing over one cheek. When she walked back to go to the ladies' room, she moved like a forties star, with that kind of graceful stride. Paul "accidentally" stood up as she passed our table, blocking her path.

"Hi, I'm Paul McCartney. How're you doing?" he said.

Linda didn't gush, as many girls would have done when confronted by a Beatle. She introduced herself and they stood chatting. She told Paul what she was doing in London. Soon they were flirting and laughing, so it was no surprise when Paul said we were all going on to the Speakeasy to see Procol Harum, a new band—and would Linda like to tag along?

"Sure, love to," she said. "Let me ask the others."

Quick off the mark, Paul suggested that Linda travel with us, leaving the Animals to follow in their car. When we got to the Speakeasy we discovered that the obscurely named Procol Harum were in fact the Paramounts from Southend. Under a new name, cool new outfits and new music, they were tripping the light fandango and doing a sensational job, too. When they hit their stride with "A Whiter Shade of Pale," I immediately booked them for the Saville. That night we stayed on at the Speakeasy, but Linda left with the Animals when they went.

This was another unusual thing about her. Most girls would have hung on to the bitter end, hoping that Paul would invite them back to his place.

The launch party for *Sgt. Pepper* was four days later at Brian's house, an exclusive affair for just a dozen journalists and photographers. Linda dropped by the NEMS office with her portfolio. Paul wasn't there, and the girl at reception buzzed me. Linda pointed to her portfolio.

"I met Peter Brown in New York and told him I'd drop by with my portfolio."

We chatted some more, then I took her up to Peter's office and left her with him. Linda asked Peter to show her work to Brian, to see if she could shoot some snaps of the Beatles for her book. Brian loved Linda's portfolio and asked if he could buy some pictures—Linda declined politely—but she did get an invitation to the *Sgt. Pepper* launch. Brian himself almost didn't make the party. He had just spent a couple of days in a coma at the Priory.

Chapel Street was very elegant, with Louis Cinque rococo furniture covered with silk Regency stripes. The wallpaper was pale yellow. It was all tasteful and comfortable. Even the bedroom—where one would perhaps expect at least a little sybaritic décor—was restrained. There was a huge Napoleon bed, covered with a satin quilt. It was comfortable. I'd sat on it many times, talking to Brian when he was feeling "unwell."

When Paul met Linda for the second time, the attraction he had felt for her was reinforced. Her blond hair was clean and shiny, her clothes simple and American "preppy." More, her gaze was direct, her smile sincere. She seemed to have a way that made everyone feel special, quite different from most of the Fleet Street stiffos there, who never looked at you when they spoke. Their eyes always raked the room beyond, as if convinced they were about to miss a scoop.

Standing to one side with my drink and quietly observing, I noticed that Linda would lean forward and really listen. I saw how Paul liked her unpretentiousness. He seemed to me to be relaxed when talking to Linda in a way that he often wasn't with new people. He asked her for a date, but she said, "No, I have to return to New York."

"Oh," Paul said. "Well, another time, then."

"Sure, I'd like that," she said. I thought that only a girl who was well brought up and assured would turn down a Beatle. Most girls would have torn up their tickets and declared they could stay indefinitely.

She managed to get one of the most widely used shots of the evening, a relaxed pose of the Beatles just being themselves, laughing. Paul and John were shaking hands and John had his thumbs up as if saying, "Hey, ignore the rumors, we really are best mates."

Sgt. Pepper went to the top of the U.K. charts and went gold in the U.S. on the first day of release. Two weeks later, Jane flew back from the Old Vic's American tour. She wasn't too pleased by the state of the house, but she and Paul drifted back into their old habits, of Jane working hard and both of them going out on the town to clubs and opening nights, a fabled young couple.

Just after *Sgt. Pepper* came out, Jimi and Chas had dropped into the offices to discuss the Saville booking. I handed them a copy of the album. Jimi gazed at the cover silently, absorbing the multihued detail. I thought he'd gone into a trance. He put the record under his arm and left with it. Three days later, when he opened at the Saville again, Paul and I were there, hovering about backstage. Paul had considered Jimi the greatest guitarist in the world ever since hearing him perform at the Bag O'Nails and made a point of coming to see the show. We watched as Jimi walked on stage. Strobe lights flashed and liquid wheels bathed the whole place acid pinks and purples. And then, Jimi launched into a virtuoso medley from *Sgt. Pepper,* starting with the little track riff. I couldn't believe it. He must have done nothing else for three days but listen to the album.

Before Jimi got to the lyrics, Paul exclaimed, beaming, "Hey man, he's playing *Sgt. Pepper!*" He just stood there and absorbed Jimi's performance while the audience went wild. After it was over, Paul looked at me. "Tony, that was great. The album was released Thursday, it's now Sunday, and Jimi's already got it down." All I could do was nod in agreement, also amazed. Jimi Hendrix was that quick, and that good.

After the gigs at the Saville, he returned to the States to play the Monterey festival. Paul had made it a point to tell Derek Taylor, who was working over there putting the festival together, about Jimi's brilliance. At Monterey, the Who and Jimi were sort of the British contingent. Of course, this kind of cycle of events does not, and cannot, happen now. The circuit and system is gone. A performer like Jimi Hendrix being discovered and taken up by a manager-promoter type like Chas Chandler doesn't happen anymore. Now, all we've really got is the Shepherd's Bush Empire, and to play there you're already big, already able to sell out the place. But back in those days, musicians played small venues around London, Liverpool or Manchester. Bands would get the obligatory Bedford van, or later a Transit, and literally schlep from gig to gig until they got to the Marquee in Wardour Street. But then, those musicians were good. Or they'd better be if they wanted to last. It always sounds old-fartish to say "It's all gone, it's all changed," but the standard is so poor now that most artists and bands today couldn't come up through pure talent and a gig circuit.

18

So much was going on that spring and summer of 1967 that events blurred. At this point there was so little space at NEMS, all three floors being overcrowded with people like Stiggie and the burgeoning staff who ran the huge worldwide talent booking and promotions empire, that Brian got me and Vyvienne Moynihan our own little video and film offices at 3 Cork Street. Vyvienne had been a producer at ATV until Brian hired her. We had an efficient secretary, Angela Gatti, whose family owned the Vaudeville Theater and we were quite cozy away from the fishbowl, thankfully left alone to get on with our work.

I saw a great deal of Queenie and Harry, who used to come down from Liverpool to attend Brian's galas, like proud parents might go to their kid's sports day at school. Brian had retrenched more and more until he very rarely went in to NEMS—or even the "secret" offices he set up in Hille House, Stafford Street, with custom-built desks for himself and Peter Brown. The furniture was all black leather and gleaming cherry wood and enormously expensive. There was a fitted black carpet, Anglepoise lamps and modern artwork. From Eames, a leading contemporary designer, Brian ordered a black leather and cherrywood chair for himself, with a matching curved footrest, where he would sometimes sit when he wanted to think. Mostly, he was so filled with speed that he couldn't sit still for long.

He commuted almost daily between the Priory, which he hated, but which made him feel secure, and his house, where his secretary, Joanne, and his PA, Wendy Hanson, had a small office, and I whizzed between everyone, from Chapel Street, NEMS and the Beatles. There was so much showbiz going on at the time, I was constantly on the move, taking care of things, reporting back to Brian when he was available, doing what needed to be done when I couldn't reach him, or when he threw up his hands and couldn't take in what I was telling him.

And there was a lot happening that needed taking care of, with or without Brian. Cilla was still doing a three-month residency at the Savoy Hotel. Brian had ensured that it was a huge affair, very cabaret, very glam. I was at Abbey Road during the day and toddled off to the Savoy at night. Gerry Marsden was doing a musical at a theater in the Strand. NEMS had expanded into Nemperor, to take in General Artists Corporation, and through them we booked the Who and the Bee Gees and Donovan. Jimi Hendrix and Andy Williams were over from America.

Fuelled by drugs, a sense of love and peace was sweeping the world. A "Legalize Pot Rally and Smoke-In" was held at Speakers' Corner, Hyde Park; Ravi Shankar set up a sitar school in San Francisco; and the mood against the Vietnam War rumbled in intensity, with droves of conscripts fleeing from America, mostly to Europe. In our immediate circle, the most unlikely people were taking acid, including one or two of the desk jockeys at NEMS, who the Beatles disparagingly referred to as "the Suits," as well as the odd banker, accountant and record company executive, as well as, remarkably, David Jacobs—our very Establishment London solicitor.

By his own admission, Brian's assistant, Peter Brown, had given Brian his first tablet. Peter was a chubby man with thinning dark hair, close to Brian in interests as well as in age, though he looked older. He was always formally dressed, even at the height of flower power. He had managed one of the NEMS record shops in Liverpool before Brian brought him down to London within the last couple of years to help with the mountain of paperwork. His main role became fixer to the Beatles, to do whatever they wanted, particularly on the management side.

Brian's house at Kingsley Hill was very Lutyens, with a lovely Edwardian garden. He loved to show it off in spring and summer when it was looking its best. In May, he threw quite a lavish party garden to celebrate the launch of three new companies, two of which belonged to the Beatles and were incorporated for tax purposes: Apple Music and The Beatles & Company, which made them a legal partnership for ten years. The third company was Nemperor Inc.

set up in the U.S. in partnership with Nat Weiss. Brian invited Nat and his wife to the party and flew them over. He also provided Derek Taylor, ghostwriter of Brian's memoirs, with first-class tickets from Los Angeles. Derek had left his employment some time ago and set himself up as a successful Hollywood music publicist, with clients like the Byrds and the Monterey Rock Festival. Brian had bumped into him in Beverly Hills when he was on the Beatles' last American tour. They talked a little, then Brian whipped out his checkbook and wrote a check for one thousand pounds which he handed to Derek. "Here," he said. "You weren't paid enough to do my book."

On their arrival at Heathrow, Derek and his wife, Joan, were amazed to see John, Cynthia, George and Pattie waiting for them, waving gaily colored balloons. They looked incredible, dressed in rainbow silks and velvets, silver bells and bows, made and designed by The Fool, who were also in the carnival party. Apart from Paul, who didn't go, carloads of people drove down to Sussex, most of them tripping and dazed. Heightening the party mood were more brightly colored balloons that Brian had gotten his staff to tie at every crossroads along the quiet country lanes leading to Brian's house from the main London road.

John and friends floated in on his gaudy yellow Rolls, through bucolic country lanes adrift with clouds of May blossoms, as if in a magic pumpkin on the way to the ball. This gypsy car had so outraged a tweedy old lady when she saw it on its first outing that she had stepped into the traffic as it cruised down Piccadilly and whacked it with her umbrella, shouting, "You swine! How dare you do this to a Rolls Royce!" Naturally, John was delighted and repeated the story everywhere he went.

Since the time that Cyn had had a really bad trip shortly after coming to London, she'd refused to take drugs, but on that drive to Brian's party, she took a tab in an effort to get closer to John and not be seen as so square, something he regularly accused her of being. Her instincts told her that if she didn't do something to rekindle the embers of John's love for her, she would lose him. For a she-wolf garbed in black had descended on her quiet fold, ready to gobble them up and Cynthia admitted that she was scared.

Yoko had finally infiltrated their private family stronghold at Kenwood, though Cynthia told very few people because she wasn't entirely sure what was happening. She only knew that something about the intense, silent Japanese woman made her feel very uncomfortable. Cynthia's mum, Mrs. Powell, was under no doubt that Yoko was a force to reckon with and was quite vocal.

The first time Yoko came, she arrived uninvited, saying she had an appointment with John, a ploy many fans used. Cynthia didn't know her. John, whom Yoko claimed to know, wasn't around, so she wasn't asked in. When Cynthia glanced out of a window, she saw Yoko standing at the end of the drive on the side of the private road that wound past to other properties on the exclusive estate. She gazed steadfastly at the house, as if willing the gates to swing open and admit her. Hours later, Cynthia looked again, and Yoko was still there—Cynthia said, waiting for John to return. Eventually, as darkness fell, she disappeared. That was the thing about Yoko: she would appear from nowhere and then disappear.

When John did come home, Cynthia mentioned it, and John shrugged. "She's nuts," he said. Mrs. Powell, who always retired to her nearby bungalow before John got in, doubtless would have agreed. As the months passed John would say to me he wished Yoko would leave him alone.

The strange visitations to Kenwood continued in all weathers. Occasionally, when John was there, he might see Yoko's distant figure standing like a dark pillar of salt, and he would make sarcastic comments. He told Cynthia to ignore her. One cold day rain fell for hours. Taking pity on this forlorn creature who had become almost a fixture, Mrs. Powell let Yoko in to use the telephone to call a taxi to take her to the station. Yoko looked long and avidly about her, used the downstairs cloakroom, and left to wait for the taxi by the gate. Later, Mrs. Powell noticed that Yoko had left her ring in the cloakroom. "I think she'll be back," she said cryptically.

Then the letters and cards addressed to John started arriving through the mail on a daily basis, mysterious little notes with minuscule black drawings or incomprehensible one-liners. John would either say they were stupid, or look at them silently, then throw them away. Cynthia was too nervous to throw them away herself, but her mother had no such scruples. "Mark my words, that woman is dangerously stubborn," she said. If the word "stalker" had been in common usage then, no doubt she would have used it. When a box arrived addressed to John in Yoko's unmistakable handwriting, Mrs. Powell ripped it open. She and Cynthia were alarmed to find a broken white cup smeared with red paint inside a box of Kotex. The imagery and message seemed clear to Mrs. Powell, but according to Cynthia, she was too panic-stricken at the implications to accept it. It was like black magic.

John of course mentioned all this whenever he complained about Yoko's more outrageous activities, but I often wondered if he secretly relished her bizarre behavior. There is no doubt that John had a tendency for trouble.

I always thought that Cynthia was delightful. She was pretty, shy and well behaved, but if someone had told me that her mother had been a white rabbit and her father an ostrich, I would have believed it because she carried both those traits. Unfortunately, they were traits that infuriated John. He wanted some snap, crackle and pop.

Perhaps all these things were in Cynthia's mind when she took that tablet of LSD on the way to Brian's country party, but it made her feel ill. She stumbled into one of the guest bedrooms, opened the window for fresh air and looked down at everyone laughing on the lawn. She told Joanne Newfield that she wanted to fly out, fly above them, fly away to happiness. Instead, she got onto the bed and lay down for several hours until she felt better. Joanne, who had also taken some acid, later stumbled into the same room and threw up in a pair of Nat Weiss's shoes.

The Stones and the scene's new drugs guru, Robert Fraser, a heroin addict, had also been at Brian's party. Within a month, they were in court after a drug bust, when the police were tipped off by the *News of the World*, a sleazy newspaper that was planning a big series of exposés on the London scene. The Drug Squad raided Redlands, Keith Richards' home in West Wittering, which was very close to Kingsley Hill. They hit the jackpot. Marianne Faithful was found stoned and blissfully naked lying beneath a fur rug (she said she'd just had a bath) and while Mick and the rest of the party sat by, Robert Fraser—a former King's African Rifles Officer and son of a wealthy banker—fled through the garden. He was nabbed in a classic rugby tackle and found to have lots of heroin on him. The police ignored a large silver briefcase stuffed with drugs, owned by David "Acid King" Schneiderman, reinforcing a generally held opinion that he was the informer. Instead, the police took away suntan lotion and freebie bars of soap from hotels—collected during the Stones' tours—for forensic testing, but they also ignored a large cache of cocaine, simply because they hadn't seen cocaine before and didn't know what it was.

Mick had four amphetamine tablets, obtained perfectly legally in Italy, but they arrested him anyway, along with Robert Fraser and Keith Richards. Keith was charged for allowing his premises to be used. While the three of them were appearing in court (they were bailed to stand trial) the police raided Brian Jones' flat in London, where they found some pot. In a newspaper interview, the Drug Squad commented that they had three of the Rolling Stones "in the bag" and said that more raids would be conducted in their war against drugs.

※

During a glorious June in England the Beatles had agreed that the *Yellow Submarine* would be their third and last film for United Artists, and in California, the historic music festival was put together at Monterey, changing the shape of the way music was presented forever. Among an iconic cast of performers, it was notable for launching the careers of Janis Joplin, with Big Brother & the Holding Company, and of course, the Jimi Hendrix Experience, fresh from the

Saville. Ravi Shankar, who was to so influence George, also gave his first major concert in the West. The Byrds and Gram Parsons gave momentous performances.

At the end of the month, the Stones' drug trial came up. Robert Fraser pleaded guilty and got six months. We didn't believe it when we heard that Mick and Keith, who had pleaded not guilty, were respectively sentenced to three months and one year of hard labor. Outraged, the *Sunday Times* published its famously impassioned article by the editor, William Rees-Mogg, entitled, "Who Breaks a Butterfly on a Wheel?" In solidarity, the liberal and creative community rallied in support and paid for a full-page advertisement published in the *Times*. This was signed by a long list of sixty-five prominent names, including scientists, literary novelists, broadcasters, critics, Brian Epstein and the Beatles. Thinking he was helping, Paul admitted during a BBC interview that he had been on four acid trips. This admission created an international furor and the media went to town. Paul was splashed across the front pages of the papers, including London's *Evening Standard*. Many people in our circle had used acid, but Paul had forgotten how puritanical mainstream Britain could be. Brian made a futile attempt to calm things down, but made matters worse by holding a press conference, where he blew it by saying that he had taken acid and saw nothing wrong with it.

Oh dear! We discussed the faux pas around the office. Brian was at a loss which way to jump now. Whether to vigorously defend Paul and risk the total wrath of a staid citizenship or try and maintain what was called a LP (low profile, man) and hope it would go away soon.

"What do you think, Tony?" Brian asked, "Should we campaign?"

I said, "I think we should keep our heads down and let it blow over."

Mick and Keith got off on appeal, but Robert spent the Summer of Love in Wormwood Scrubs, where a succession of celebrity visitors arrived in their Rolls, Bentleys and Aston Martins to console him. Come back soon, they said, we miss your parties, we miss your gallery openings, we miss the fun you bring to our lives. In retrospect Marianne said he was "the nervous system of the sixties," and Yoko would say that he was "the driving force of the European avant-garde scene in the art world." Ho hum, we all sighed, knowing Robert's opinion of her.

In July, through NEMS, Brian broke the Monkees as an act in Europe, presenting them at the Empire Pool at Wembley. But he didn't go to the party thrown for them by Vic Lewis at the Speakeasy because once again, he was unwell.

The problems over his contract with the boys had never really gone away. He thought they were ignoring the subject and didn't know how to broach it himself. He stammered and stuttered when he mentioned it, was abnormally distressed, convincing himself that they weren't going to sign up again because they loathed him. Going through months of paranoia, he looked for reasons and forlornly asked the question, "Don't they like me anymore?"

It was so silly because it wasn't like that at all. At different times, all of them commented to me that they would never have signed another contract as "Beatles" but they would have signed individually with Brian. John expressed it best when he said, "We don't need a manager anymore, we don't do that kind of stuff anymore."

But their business affairs were so extensive, their lives so complex, their requirements so bizarre, that they really didn't know how to manage on their own and as individuals were perfectly happy with the idea of retaining Brian in some capacity. They never veered from their conviction that they needed someone to handle their affairs, as history was shortly to prove.

Poor Brian was constantly overacting and reacting, as when he made a fool of himself one night by turning up at Abbey Road with a boyfriend, trying to show off a bit to demonstrate to the boy how he exerted influence over the Beatles and knew his way around the studio. He flipped the intercom switch and told John that the vocals he'd just done weren't "quite right." Whether he was trying to make a joke, or being flippant, I'll never know. Everybody, including me, winced and cringed and waited for the inevitable, which came swiftly.

John just looked up at him without smiling and said, "You take care of the money, Brian, and we'll take care of the music." It was an awful, embarrassing put-down.

Brian fled. I can't remember now what song John was doing, but afterward, Brian anguished over it. "I've made such a fool of myself," he said. Such things affected him deeply. He looked pale and concerned.

"Don't worry about it, John didn't mean it," I said.

When Brian was down, he got depressed; then all his insecurities came to the surface and he was on a roll of self-flagellation. He said, "No, I think John hates me now. I don't know what I'll do if they don't sign. What will people think? I can see the headlines now: EPSTEIN DUMPED BY BEATLES."

"It will be okay," I said, but he wasn't listening. To cushion what he saw as the inevitable, Brian was running around doing deals. Six months earlier he had brought in Stigwood as a partner—though told everyone that it was a combining of forces on the agenting side and assured the Beatles at least that Stigwood had no share whatsoever in his management contract with them, their music, or anything else. He had also done that underhand deal with EMI whereby he retained 25 percent of the Beatles' records regardless of whether he managed them or not. More crucially, he had made two attempts at suicide. A few weeks earlier, in New York, Nat Weiss had roused him from a bad Seconal-induced coma, when Brain had been late for a radio interview, and had been surprised by the speed of his recovery. One moment Brian had been out of it, half dead; the next he was in the studio, offering lucid and interesting opinions.

Brian's manic moods continued as he made and canceled several appointments with Dr. Flood, his psychiatrist. He was now seriously unhappy, not just troubled. His personality had radically changed. Joanne would sometimes discuss it with me, telling me how concerned she was. Brian acted like Howard Hughes. He'd push notes with instructions and money under his bedroom door for when she arrived in the morning. When he emerged, round about five o'clock in the evening; he took lots of uppers to come fully awake. But lately, she said, he needed more. This made him so edgy that the smallest thing would cause him to rant and rave and throw stuff around. A wrong number could make him go berserk. Laden tea trays were flung, once at Joanne directly. In between the uppers and downers he drank heavily, didn't bother to eat and sometimes didn't bother to get dressed. Joanne promised herself she would quit every day, but never did. Brian had resident nurses, doctors who stayed, psychiatrists who lived in, all crowded into that little doll's house, getting on each other's nerves. At times he'd make an effort. He would sweet-talk everyone and then escape when they weren't looking.

He ran around looking for boys in ridiculously obvious places like the alleyways at Piccadilly underground station, or Times Square when he was in New York. He was out of control and, given that his orientation was unfortunately still illegal, was probably happiest when there were artificial parameters on his behavior. He felt he needed his sexual demons restricted by visits to clinics, or curtailed by visits by his mum, or simply by pressures of work. Left on his own, like many men with similar inclinations, he couldn't help but run away and do his own thing.

In July 1967, the law was changed to allow consensual homosexual acts in private between adults but it was years too late for Brian. He'd been ridden by guilt for too long. He told me he was badly in need of a holiday where he could fully rest and switch off. The Beatles were making leaving-noises, too. George and Pattie, who had been to San Francisco on holiday, had been hassled by a mob in the street who wanted George to play guitar for them. On George's return to England, the Beatles sat around discussing how they could never be free to be themselves, there were always cameras and fans. Three years before, all of the Beatles and their women had had a wonderful holiday cruising the Greek Islands in Peter Seller's yacht, a happy time they still remembered affectionately.

With that in mind, they started looking about for a retreat from the world, and Magic Alex was delighted to show them that he wasn't just a weird hippie who hung around them, that he was actually a person of some importance in his homeland. He used his Greek connections and found them a cluster of twenty-four idyllic islands for £95,000. Alistair Taylor even worked out that the sale of olives and olive oil would repay the purchase price in seven years. Brian, who was making his own plans to escape to Spain, took the Beatles seriously enough to write to Nat Weiss for advice.

At the time, the British government was in a financial crunch. British citizens were only allowed to take fifty pounds a year spending money out of the country. Capital foreign investments were levied a dollar premium. That is, for every pound spent abroad, an additional 25 percent had to be lodged with the Bank of England; but on top of that, a limit was still imposed on currency allowed out of the country. There was a minor flurry of concern when the accountants informed the Beatles that they only had about £137,000 in the bank. John thought they were alarmists. "I don't give a toss," he said. "We're going to live in Greece and that's it. Find the money."

The Chancellor of the Exchequer, James Callahan, got involved. He even wrote a personal letter to the Beatles, saying he would make an exception in their case over the limit allowed out, but would only allow them enough to buy the islands. His cryptic P.S. read: ". . . but not a penny more . . . how will you buy the furniture?"

John, with his son, Julian, and Alex went off to Greece to inspect the islands. Because of Alex's connections, they were met by a colonel or two and treated like royalty. Despite that, John hated the way in which they were exploited by the Greek press and a right-wing junta that disgusted him. Ultimately, the idea fizzled out.

19

The death of his father, Harry, of a heart attack while on holiday in Bournemouth on July 17, 1967, threw Brian into an even deeper slough of despondence and grief.

"I so wanted him to see me settled and happily married," Eppy said to me dolefully. "Now he never will, will he, Tony?" He stared at me, telling me something, willing me to understand.

I looked back at him in disbelief. I think that was when I realized what his pursuit of Alma, and then Marianne, had been all about. After his father died, a wife no longer mattered and Eppy dropped the charade.

There was little time for us to convey condolences since it was all so rushed. Jewish funerals were held within twenty-four hours. Brian disappeared to Bournemouth and escorted his father's body home to Liverpool for the funeral, which was attended only by his family and members of the Jewish community. After it was all over, he invited Queenie down to London so they could discuss the future. Brian wanted her to live in London near him and her sisters, but she had lived in Liverpool for thirty-four years and all her friends were there. At any rate, she came down to London on August 14 and stayed at her usual hotel. It was close enough for her to walk around to Chapel Street in the morning before Brian was up. She would tiptoe into his room and draw back his bedroom curtains so they could share breakfast and discuss what they would do that day. The constraints kicked in and we were all surprised to see how normal Brian could be. He even seemed calm and happy, though it was an empty sort of happiness, as if he were drained. At times, it seemed as if he were acting in a play.

They spent their days together, pottering about, doing a bit of shopping, seeing friends and the family in London. One day Brian took his mother to meet Cilla and Bobby at Euston Station on their return from Liverpool. They went on to lunch, a friendly informal meal, where they all talked of old times. However, Brian made a small error of judgment when he told Cilla he had arranged for her to represent England on the Eurovision song contest. She was instantly alarmed and defensive. It was far too risky—suppose she lost? It wouldn't look good. Her career was booming, she'd had hit after hit and recently had starting presenting her own TV show that looked as if it would run and run (it did, becoming an institution). She didn't need to enter a song contest; she wasn't a racehorse.

Brian's temper started to flare. He told Cilla that he knew what was best for her. She politely disagreed. The meal ended on an uneasy atmosphere, although Queenie affected not to notice.

On the twenty-third of August Brian took his mother to the Saville and seemed to gain a moment of his old sense of pride as he solicitously seated her in the royal box with its zebra-skin sofas. You could almost sense her looking about at the red damask walls, the gilded columns and thinking, "My boy has achieved all this, despite everything. Look how well he has done."

The next day, Brian took her to the station and put her on the train back home to Liverpool. He had done his duty as a good son and now it was time to frolic at Kingsley Hill. As if to save himself from rent boys, he asked Joanne and Lulu to go down with him over the approaching long bank-holiday weekend, but they had already made other plans.

While Brian was planning his weekend, Pattie and Alex had convinced the others to attend a lecture given at a West London hotel by a strange little fellow from India. His name was almost unpronounceable: the Maharishi Mahesh Yogi. Alex didn't approve of drugs and pressed hard for the meeting. He said that the yogi was wonderful, that his brand of magic, Transcendental Meditation, was far more powerful than drugs. On a whim, John, Paul and George, their entourage of women and Paul's brother, Mike, said they would go. At the lecture the Maharishi went into a deep trance and the Beatles were captivated. It looked so easy and to be able to go into a trance to order *without drugs* was a something they needed to know more about. Afterward, the Maharishi asked them for a private audience in his suite, during which he asked them to attend his induction course that bank-holiday weekend—starting the next day in fact—at Bangor, North Wales.

As they left the hotel, John and Cynthia went to get into their car when, out of nowhere, Yoko appeared and hopped into the car, to sit between them. Someone had tipped her off about John's attendance at the lecture and she had arrived, to wait quietly in the lobby for this moment. Cynthia froze. All the months of strange mail, the cut-off phone calls, the waiting silently at the gate were encapsulated in this tiny, terrifying woman. She glanced questioningly at John. He shrugged, as if to say, "I haven't a clue."

"I'd like a lift home," Yoko said. It wasn't a polite request; it was the order of an assured woman. Cynthia was seriously concerned when the car drove to Yoko's flat off Regent's Park, seeming to know the way without being told. The next day, Paul, George and Ringo and their women, together with Mick and Marianne, arrived at Euston Station to catch the train to Bangor. Cynthia and John arrived at the station in his painted Rolls. The station was packed with holidaymakers and the press. As John and Cynthia fought their way through the melee, a flashbulb went off in Cyn's face, blinding her. By the time she could see, everyone had vanished and she didn't know which was the correct platform. She raced along, but the police didn't recognize her and thought she was another hysterical fan. Suddenly, all the Beatles stuck their heads out of the windows of the train, urging her to run faster. "Run, Cyn, run!" John yelled. Those were the words Paul had used when chased by fans in their early touring days. As his car sped away, he'd put his head out of the window and called out, "Run, girls, run!" and the girls would redouble their efforts.

Cynthia stopped. It was no good; the train was going too fast. John hadn't come back for her, no one else bothered; it was as if she didn't exist. At that moment, she said, as she watched the train pull out, she saw how utterly irrelevant she was.

Meanwhile, on the other side of town, Brian was preparing to leave for Sussex. Geoffrey Ellis, the accountant from the NEMS office, and Peter Brown were also going down to Kingsley Hill, but Peter had to make a last-minute change in plans because he had to arrange to have Cynthia driven to Bangor. He arrived late in Sussex. Brian announced that he had expected to travel down with a particular young man, who hadn't shown up. After a quiet dinner served by the Australian butler, Brian spent time on the phone, trying to find some amusing people to join them. He even had a kind of key card to a call-boy agency—a rent now, pay later, kind of thing—and used that to try to drum up some fun, but was told it was too late, too far, and all the best boys were booked.

According to Peter and Geoffrey, when they described the events later, Brian said, "I'm going to town, I'll find some boys and bring them back."

"Leave it," Peter said. "It's late and you've had too much to drink."

But Brian was single-minded and left in his silver Bentley Continental convertible. He had been on his best behavior for days with his mother around and was ready for some action. Geoffrey Ellis called Brian's town house just after midnight, and Antonio, the Spanish "Town Butler" confirmed that Brian had arrived safely but gone straight to bed. Meanwhile, in response to Brian's previous frantic telephoning after dinner, three boys had arrived at Kingsley Hill in a taxi from London probably passing Brian on the road.

On the following day, Saturday, Brian called at about five in the afternoon and spoke to Peter Brown. He said he had been asleep most of the day but would drive on down that evening. Pete urged him to take the train instead. Brian agreed. He said he would call from Lewes Station when he arrived and Peter could pick him up. He never called. On the Sunday morning he still hadn't called and as usual, Peter and Geoffrey went to the village pub for a drink before lunch. The Australian butler was in the house to answer the phone if necessary.

In London, concerned that Brian had not emerged from his room since Friday night, and that everything was too quiet, Antonio telephoned down to Kingsley Hill to be advised what to do. But Peter and Geoffrey were still in the pub, so Antonio immediately telephoned Joanne at home in Edgware. He told her that Brian's car was still parked at the front; he'd tried the internal intercom and couldn't rouse Brian. Later, Joanne told me that she had instantly felt something was wrong. She telephoned Alistair Taylor to meet her at Chapel Street. On their arrival, they stood outside Brian's double bedroom doors with his chauffeur, Brian Barrett, and decided they should call a doctor. Brian's doctor was Norman Cowan, who lived too far away. The nearest one was Peter Brown's physician, Dr. John Gallway, who lived just two streets away. But it didn't matter anyway. Brian was already dead. Peter Brown and Geoffrey Ellis were back from the pub by then and were actually on the phone to Chapel Street, listening in while the bedroom doors were forced. They left immediately for town.

I had stayed in London that weekend to look after the Saville. Jimi Hendrix was on for two shows that Sunday, with Eric Burdon supporting. Brian had told me that he was having a party down at his house in Sussex, but would be returning on the Sunday and would be at the theater as usual.

"So you're not spending Monday at Kingsley Hill?" I had said. It was a three-day weekend so I expected Brian to take the extra day.

"No, I have too much to attend to," Brian said. He sounded normal for once, and I put this down to the influence of his mother during the past ten days.

I kept glancing up at the box, wondering if Brian would turn up. Whatever else he was doing, however out of it he was toward the end, it was a point of honor with him to make an effort to attend the Sunday shows, either alone or with a small party. He often brought Stigwood and Kit Lambert, the Who's manager, who was also gay, to a Sunday show. "All good queens together in the royal box," Lambert would say, and laugh. But the box remained empty. Toward the end of the first performance, we were just getting ready to open the doors to clear the theater for the second performance, when the phone call came from Brian Barrett.

"Brian's dead," he said. "We have just broken down the door of his bedroom and found him. He won't be at the show."

It was such a bizarre way of putting it, that I repeated it to the staff. We looked at each other, unable to take it in. I got Eric Burdon to go on stage and announce that the next show would be canceled. When the theater was cleared, we closed the doors on the second show, giving people their money back as they arrived. Eric and Jimi went out into the street to talk to the crowds, to explain why the show was canceled. Little groups of people stood about, talking. We sat in the dark theater in shock, going over memories of Brian, talking about the past as you do.

As I walked home that night from the Saville I couldn't help thinking about the day Brian took me on as the office boy at NEMS in Liverpool. My mum listened patiently to Brian, hoping I wasn't making a big mistake, that there was some sort of a career there for me, instead of going back to Ford. But she was worried all the same. Similarly, Brian's family had been worried. Patiently biding their time, his mum used to tell people in confidence that they were "letting Brian get this beat group thing out of his system." She seemed to think that it was just a fad, as so many of his fads were, and he would soon revert to running the proper business of selling records for the family stores.

I lived near Brian at the time. My way home led past his house, which was surrounded by lights, cameras, police. The square was cordoned off and police held back the gay mob that had turned up. It was horrible. I remembered Brian's pleasure when he first bought the Chapel Street house. He had been so proud of it, so delighted to have a smart, pretty place in the heart of town. He loved to throw small supper parties in the evening for a few intimate friends, after which there'd be a film show. Brian liked grim black-and-white films of the kitchen sink genre, films like *The Butterfly Collector,* or *Budgie,* or *The War Games,* a kind of documentary by Peter Whitehead. When I asked him what he wanted, he'd say, "Oh, you choose, Tony."

He adored Terry Stamp, one of the most beautiful young men of our generation. Cracking a little joke, he'd say, "You know I always enjoy Ugly Young Man films, get one of those."

I used to borrow these from the extensive library at the BFI (the British Film Institute) and take them round to Brian's, where invariably he'd be entertaining the kind of dreadful men I couldn't stand: parasites and hangers-on and people you felt would rob you blind. I'd set up the projector in the drawing room, get the film running, then go and sit in the kitchen in the basement and drink wine with Joanne. Sometimes I'd go to the pub. Later, I'd go back and rewind the film and put the projector away.

Brian was so different when around his beloved protégés. He became one of them. He was a friend, a chum, charming, trustworthy and kind. He set out to do what he promised and they all said it would never have happened without him. It was unbelievable that the man who had got all this going—the vast money-making machine and the culture shock that had changed the world, was gone.

If only he could have stopped and smelled the roses, not been such a perfectionist. The last few years had been a learning curve for us. We had all made many mistakes, but Brian took everything with such deadly earnest, anguished too much and bottled up most of it.

I sighed. Staring at the brightly lit house, filled with strangers and activity of a depressing nature, I wondered where Brian was now. I wondered if the Beatles had been told—would anyone have thought to do that? I think it was at that moment I realized that there was no one "in charge," Brian had no real second in command. Many people, like Peter Brown on the business side and Neil Aspinall, who was still only the road manager, or agents and managers like Stiggie and Vic Lewis, had specific jobs, but none controlled all the strings like the puppet master himself.

🌿

Joanne was in shock. She had seen him first. The doors had been broken down and there he was, curled up on his side in bed with Saturday's mail lying next to him. "We all knew at once that he was dead, but I heard myself say, 'It's all right, he's just asleep. He's fine,'" she said.

As soon as Peter Brown arrived from Kingsley Hill he called the Beatles in

Bangor. There is the famous story about the phone ringing and ringing off the hook in another room and Paul eventually saying, "Shouldn't somebody answer the phone?" Jane Asher then did so.

Fueling rumors that Brian's death hadn't been an accident, the *Daily Express* had apparently called out of the blue before anyone else knew that he was dead, to say they had heard that Brian Epstein was seriously ill. "Any truth in it?" the *Express* wanted to know. Nobody ever owned up to tipping them off. I watched the evening news which showed the scenes outside Brian's house in the late afternoon and TV cameras showing the Beatles leaving the Maharishi's conference a couple of hours before, heading back to London and a future without Brian. It was all very surreal. The coroner's verdict on September 8 was that Brian's death was accidental, due to an accumulation of bromide contained in Carbitral, the sleeping pills he had been prescribed.

His funeral, a Beatle-less family affair—to keep the press away—took place in Liverpool. He was buried at Long Lane Jewish Cemetery, not next to his father as his mother wanted but in a separate avenue. Nat Weiss was there and wept as he tossed a sunflower given to him by George into the open grave. The rabbi infuriated all Brian's friends by declaring pompously, "Brian Epstein was a symbol of the malaise of our generation." It was a very harsh epitaph for a man who had shown great kindness to so many and meant well.

◆

Everyone asked: who would manage the Beatles? The quibbling started at NEMS between the Suits and Stigwood by midafternoon on the Tuesday following the August bank holiday, only two days after his death. David Shaw joined Stigwood, who had been enjoying the break with the Bee Gees on a luxury yacht at Monte Carlo, for a pow-wow to plan their takeover of NEMS that had already been initiated by Brian. They made statements to the press, staking their claim. So too did other minor directors of NEMS. It was awful. But worse was that none of the pretenders and heirs apparent had grasped the fact that Brian hadn't really managed the Beatles for a long time, or at least, not in the same way as he did at the start, when they had nothing. They no longer gigged or toured. They turned up at Abbey Road and made records. They had just made *Sgt. Pepper,* their best ever. They might have appeared eccentric and woolly-minded, they might have surrounded themselves with many useless hangers-on who encouraged them to do vast quantities of drugs, but essentially, they were very tight and focused when it came to their work. I thought that they could manage quite well on their own, with a good staff to run things under their direction and initially, so did they.

It never occurred to me that in the wake of Brian's death my job might be at risk. Right from the start when I'd gone to work for Brian as a kid straight from school, he had always shown me special consideration. Some people resented this and did their best to whisper in Brian's ear, but office gossip and tittle-tattle annoyed him and such attempts to gain his favor usually rebounded. Generally in our world there was always a big turnover of staff. People who worked in the music business came and went, or they got fired. There were always office politics, or you screwed up and it was good-bye.

I know I was called teacher's pet, but I was easygoing and it didn't trouble me. I saw it as petty jealousy, as Brian did. Many wondered why I didn't get fired, or more to the point, why firing me was never an option. I was aware of the intense jealousy because I was close to Brian and the Beatles. Anybody new who came in to work at any level, whether as general manager or a director or as chief accountant, expressed bafflement at what my job description was. To them, I appeared to be doing nothing. All they saw was that I would be down at the Speakeasy or some club, or hanging out at the studios, or at a gig, or perhaps filming something around town, and to them it looked as if I was doing everything and nothing, just having fun. They had specific roles and titles and were very territorial, but I sort of weaved in and across other people's job descriptions. They simply didn't understand that Brian didn't want me to be "one thing." He wanted me to be very adaptable, always there to troubleshoot at a moment's notice, to scout, to produce, to promote, to manage, to TCB—"take care of business" like Elvis's boys did. In other words, to do whatever was required at that moment. I was good at what I did, I got on with people and was willing to learn. Lord knows, some of the jobsworths tried to get me fired—but Brian had promised my mum that I would have a career and he had meant it.

When he died, that sense of being suited up for all seasons continued. The Beatles respected Brian's wishes that I remain there as a multifaceted employee until I eventually left of my own accord. Not knowing what else to do, I continued as normal. My first task was to organize Traffic's first British show at the Saville. I was alarmed when I learned that some of the Suits intended to close down the Saville Theater. I pointed out that we had booked several acts, and had contracts to honor, the Bee Gees and the Bonzo Dog Doo Dah Band among many.

"Brian has never canceled a show yet," I said, quashing the panic. I continued until the contracted shows were done and the lease of the theater expired.

While the pretenders to Eppy's throne met and fought and schemed, rallied their troops, rattled their little sabers and called each other spiteful names, the Beatles met in Paul's house on the first of September to discuss the future. The fallout from Eppy's sudden death, and the realization that now they were on their own in the complex financial and business world, brought them together to seriously consider their future. What were they going to do, what did they want to do? On one subject they were united: it would not be what a bunch of greedy Suits wanted them to do. The Summer of Love was over and autumn coming.

PART IV

1967–1970

20

Because **Stigwood and Shaw** hadn't come up with the half-million pounds before Brian's death, the offer was considered withdrawn by NEMS's lawyers. The two Australians lost the boardroom battle to take over NEMS and were paid off with twenty-five thousand pounds plus clients like the Bee Gees that Stiggie had brought in. His severance from the Beatles complete, he went off to set up the highly successful Robert Stigwood Organization, and eventually produced *Saturday Night Fever* and *Grease.*

One by one, the Beatles drifted into the offices after Brian's death to make plans. I think only Neil Aspinall and Mal Evans were in evidence as we gathered in the usual office the Beatles always used. I think they felt the strangeness of being there for the first time without Brian around. Despite their firm intentions to be sensible and grown up and talk it through properly, the Beatles were confused, especially John, who voiced the opinion that without Brian, "They'd had it!"

They all knew that Stigwood had been a director of NEMS, but none of them had any idea of how involved he had been. When they learned for the first time about the proposed deal between Brian and Stigwood to sell NEMS, they were stunned, unable to believe that Brian had even contemplated it.

John was the most outraged and upset. "He was going to sell us down the river for a crap half million?" he said. "Was he out of his mind?"

The answer of course was that yes, Brian was deranged—but no one wanted to say it. Besides, Stiggie was out of the picture and they had to move on.

George said, "Without Brian, we're dead."

Paul said, "No, we're not. We just have to get on with it. We'll have to delegate."

They were under the microscope now, with the world looking to see what would happen next. George said, "Maybe we need some space. Let's go to India."

Before Brian's death, following their induction by the Maharishi at the level-one boot camp in Wales, it had been their intention to fly almost immediately to the ashram in the foothills of the Himalayas, to immerse themselves for at least six months in meditation at level two while the lessons the Maharishi had taught them were still fresh in their minds. But Paul questioned whether this activity would now appear a little flaky to the rest of the world. They would be gone for months at an exceptionally crucial time, just when they needed to get a grip on reality.

George thought it would do them good to get away and meditate. He said there was nothing flaky about it. He was convinced that the Maharishi was misunderstood. George and Pattie had already been to India, where George had done some recording of Indian music, and had gotten to know the people and the country. "Their culture is different from ours," he said. "They're deeper and know things on a different philosophical level." Enthusiastically, he exaggerated. The yogis were practically *magic!* They could *fly!* They could read your mind! Learning all this would surely help them enormously in business.

"Yeah, that's what we need. Learning how to read people's minds, so's we can tell if we're being ripped off," John said.

They argued it back and forth for a while, but ultimately they all agreed that the trip to the ashram had to be put on hold.

"Next topic," said Paul, who, as he often did, acted as chairman. The next topic was the *Magical Mystery Tour* film, which on paper sounded original and creative and all those artistic things, but which looked as if it might turn out to be a nightmare. Alistair Taylor was sent off to hire a sixty-seater coach for the *Mystery Tour*. Personally, I thought that filling it with an ill-assorted crowd in fancy dress and driving it here there and anywhere at all without an itinerary was bound to be seen by the media as being a bit airy-fairy and ripe for a well-placed custard pie unless the lads looked and sounded confident that it was the logical sequel to *Sgt. Pepper*.

"It's going to be great," Paul said and they all nodded in agreement. The title track to *Magical Mystery Tour* was already in the can and sessions for the rest of the soundtrack were booked at Abbey Road. They needed a script. They needed more songs. They needed organization. They needed Brian.

However, Brian was gone. Paul picked up the phone and called Denis O'Dell at Twickenham Studios, to ask him if he would produce *Mystery Tour* for them. During the conversation, in which John and Paul grabbed the phone from each other, they went even further and asked Denis if he would become head of Apple Films.

Paul turned to me. "You can be his assistant, Tone," he decided.

I was looking after the Saville, was head of promotions for NEMS and would do the same for Apple; but taking on another role didn't seem too much. *Nothing* seemed too much or impossible to achieve because none of this seemed real. It was almost an "are we playing at businessmen, or is this really happening?" feeling. But, now that it did look as if we were hurtling ahead into a complex film, George, who had been brooding, suddenly said he wanted to postpone the Magical Mystery Tour. He desperately wanted to go to India to study Hinduism and couldn't wait. John said, "Yeah, let's go." Ringo said he'd go along for the ride.

"Listen, we're gonna to stay here and do the Mystery Tour," Paul said firmly. "Then we can go to India."

"What about NEMS? And the staff?" Ringo wanted to know. "Any changes there?"

None of the Beatles really knew what the full situation was with regard to the running of NEMS, their role in it, or what influence the company had on their lives. As far as they were concerned, it was "Brian's company," set up to manage bands and tours, and they'd never questioned any of it.

Paul thought things should continue to run as they had before. He said, "Well, Eppy appointed everybody and they all know what they're doing. If it worked for him it will work for us, at least for now. There's no need to rock the boat when we've got so much to do. Let's stick to one thing at a time."

"But what about a manager?" John said. "Who's going to do that now?"

They looked at each other doubtfully. Paul said, "I don't think we need a manager. We don't tour anymore; we've always made our own decisions about records and films. Agreed?"

Everyone nodded. Satisfied they'd covered everything on the agenda, the meeting broke up.

I knew that Paul was really only doing the *Mystery Tour* as a project to keep the Beatles doing something. He said it was a kind of therapy that he thought would stop them from panicking and make them feel they were continuing as normal— and normal was working. Over the years, their work rate was astonishing.

They hardly ever had time off, hardly ever had a holiday—none of us did. Looking back, I think it was enthusiasm and passion for the amazing things that were happening on a daily basis that fired the entire structure of NEMS and the Beatles. We didn't want to stay away, we all wanted to be on the spot because it never ceased to be exciting. More and more we came to realize that Brian had driven it all. The big question in everyone's minds, including the Beatles themselves, was: could they pick up and carry the flame? Paul, who had a very quick and businesslike mind, was convinced that they could.

John started working on "I Am the Walrus" on September 5, only nine days after Brian's death. To most people it became a strange song for a strange time. I didn't think it was strange. I was used to John's gobbledygook, Lear-type poetry, which was just a bit further on from *Sgt. Pepper*. It didn't take long to do, nor much doing. John did it all himself in about two days, time which included recording other songs and simultaneously working on the film.

Most of "Walrus" was done on a Mellotron, a big, cumbersome machine that John was nuts about and swore was the future of music. In a way, he was right. It was used by musicians who liked to experiment a lot, and was a kind of tape recorder with a wide range of instrument sounds to choose from, all on tape loops. It also had a bank of backing tracks and percussion tracks. The machine was based on the principal invented by Harry Chamberlin, where each key set a length of tape in motion, and played back whatever was recorded.

When we listened to the playback, there was a sense of excitement that this was different, this was new. There was none of the feeling that it was too weird for words. To some extent, I could understand what it was that John had said he heard in his head from childhood—the sound of the sea. (When John underwent Janov's scream therapy a couple of years later, he remembered falling into a hole in the sand on the shore at Blackpool when he was five years old, and it all closing in on him. I wonder if his terror and the frightening sounds he heard from that event came out in "Walrus"?)

John had no idea when he wrote "Walrus" that it was based on a metaphor for capitalism. In Lewis Carroll's rhyme, the walrus gobbled up the shy little oysters. In his mind, he confused the walrus with a friendly seal. It was symbolic. I watched as John did his weird song and Paul followed with a beautiful one called "The Fool on the Hill." I felt that at the time that those two wildly different songs summed up the feelings of both writers, confusion on John's part, and strength and beauty in Paul's. Looking back, I love both songs equally.

The Beatles and a huge crowd of actors, technicians, journalists and camp followers disappeared around the country in the Mystery bus, like an army on the move. The bus was nothing special, just a yellow and blue one from a bus company, and definitely not luxurious. Nothing special was done to it, other than having bright fliers printed to be stuck on the sides. These were almost immediately ripped off by fans, and Mal spent most of his time pasting on new ones. When it was realized how visible the bus was, drawing hundreds of fans and streams of people following in its wake in dozens of cars—a situation that worried the police—the fliers were removed and not replaced. Not that it made any difference. By then the bus was so famous people recognized it wherever it went.

Paul visualized the film as being the kind of day out we all remembered from our childhood in Liverpool, when our mums would see an ad in the window of the local news agent for "a mystery coach trip." They were cheap days out to stop us kids from getting bored during the long summer holidays. We nearly always ended up at Blackpool, the traditional northern seaside resort with its piers, its brightly lit fairgrounds and miles of sandy beaches.

"It's a whole bunch of people, fat ones, thin ones, little ones, mad ones, like you get in real life. It's what they do, what they talk about, the fun they have, their eccentricities. You can't script it, it happens," Paul explained, frustrated when the actors asked, "Where's the script?"

When someone else complained we were behind schedule, I said, "No we're not. We don't have a schedule. The entire film is one big ad lib."

For me, the most bizarre moments were the two days I spent auditioning a room full of strippers from Raymond's Review Bar in Soho while John and George ogled them, strictly in the cause of art. Paul Raymond, the emperor of strip clubs, joined in enthusiastically, lining up his best girls and being as helpful as possible. He grew so wealthy he bought the Windmill Theater, famous for never closing during the war. It had always seemed the height of sophistication and sinfulness, the kind of place where sleek men with pencil mustaches and dinner jackets went for fun. This matched the camp style of the Bonzo Dog Doo Dah Band that Paul hired to play to the filmed striptease session. The band—founded by Vivian Stanshall and Rodney Slater, two Royal College of Art students—was originally named the Bonzo Dog Dada band, after a cute 1920s postcard puppy and Dadaism, the antiart movement.

Paul first saw the Bonzos at the Isle of Wight Pop Festival and was very taken with their mocking, louche take on bands like the Temperance Seven—though

Neil Innes, one of the original members who went on to be part of the whole Monty Python team, said, "We're not doing a Temperance Seven, we're murdering them." However, John wasn't as keen on them and openly argued with Paul over hiring them. Revenge was exacted when Rodney wore a T-shirt that stated LUMP IT JOHN in the publicity stills for the film.

During the auditions, we couldn't decide among a final handful of long-legged lovelies and asked several to come back. We narrowed it down to one: Jan Carson. I got her to repeatedly strip while the Bonzos played "Death Cab for Cutie" over and over again, in camp impersonations of Elvis dressed in silver sequined suits. The shoot itself, with all the male members of the Mystery Tour and John and George sitting slumped center stage gawping, was very funny in a macabre way, given that "Cutie" described the final moments of a pretty young thing and the driver of a cab that jumped the red lights and crashed. This was the final scene in the film; one that played it out to fade and final credits. Paul knew that the BBC would object to the nudity, so in the edit he slapped on a big placard that read CENSORED over Jan's bare breasts.

The best moment of all in the making of the film was after a day's filming on a sandy beach near Newquay in Cornwall. During a private little interlude of normality, Paul, Ringo, Neil Aspinall and Mal Evans dropped in to the Tywarhale pub in Perranporth one evening and were delighted to see an old friend, Spencer Davis (the Spencer Davis Group included Steve Winwood), propping up the bar. It seemed that the pub was owned by the parents-in-law of the Spencer Davis roadie. This instantly made them feel at home instead of among strangers.

The regulars couldn't believe it when Paul sat at the piano and shouted out, "Evening all! I'm the pub pianist and I'm taking requests." They spent the night in a good old singsong, with all the golden oldies, Paul thumping away on the Joanna and Ringo sometimes joining in on a mandolin with one string. When Ringo stopped strumming he said, "I think I've worn away me thumb." He held it out. They should have filmed that night—but in real life it never happens. The best moments remain the fond memories of a handful of lucky people.

🐜

The Beatles would record, then zoom off and film, then record another song, film that, and so on. We'd spend a day at Raymond's Revue Bar, filming, then it would be down to Maidstone, then back to the studio to finish off "Walrus"— and at the same time, they'd record "Hello Good-Bye," then it would be the next song, the next scene. It was very piecemeal and higgledy-piggledy, but it didn't matter. It was action, which was far better for everyone than inactivity.

The Magical Mystery Tour almost completely overwhelmed Denis. He didn't come into the office but once a week. He was like a lot of NEMS and then Apple men who were upper-echelon management but never invited to party, or to go to pubs and clubs with the Beatles: likable, but not one of the gang. At first, Denis and I got together scripts and books and ideas galore, which we would sift through for Apple Films in order to come up with a potential list of our first projects. One of the first was a film called *Walkabout*, which Nic Roeg wanted to do in Australia. Jenny Agutter was signed, but I think she only agreed because it was a Beatles' film. People were sent to Australia to scout locations. For all I know they're still in the outback because we heard no more from them—though Nic eventually made it with another producer and instead of the Beatles, John Barry and Rod Stewart did the music.

Another project was *Traffic Jam*, a film about a gridlock throughout Britain, a weird but very powerful early Mad Max type of idea. There were also a couple of Terry Southern projects, *Magic Christian* and *Candy*, which Ringo worked on. I was very eager to make the *Flashman* books into films. I thought if they were done properly they could be bigger than the Bond films. But so much nonsense was talked about who was going to play Flashman. Someone wanted John Alderton to play the lead, which was totally wrong. He was a kind of gentle bumbling comic, with no edge. Someone else suggested Dave Clark, which even Dave found hilarious. There were long discussions about the feel of the books, whether they should be changed in any way. I suppose they were a bit jingoistic, but that was part of what made them so different. Dinners were held with people like Dick Lester, who had made the Beatles films, John Davis, head of Rank, and Malcolm McDowell, who they had finally settled on as Flashman. I thought he was terribly miscast. I said if the right Flashman could be found, another Sean Connery, we would have a major hit. In the end someone else made *Flashman*, but it didn't achieve much.

It had long been John and Paul's ambition to make a surreal *Alice in Wonderland*. As writers, they felt that when they finished with pop music they would sit down together and be Rogers and Hammerstein. They bandied ideas about, but nothing much emerged. Mentally, they were ignoring the fact that United Artists were still due one film from the Beatles, the third film in the trio that Brian had signed them up to make. Although Brian was dead, the contract still had to be fulfilled—a situation that depressed all the Beatles except Ringo. Apart from him they had little interest in "Hollywood movies."

UA could have used up their option by picking up the Mystery Tour, but declined to do so because it was considered too risky and too far-out. Instead, they opted for *Yellow Submarine*, a cartoon made by King Features, which would show the Beatles as cartoon figures with their speaking voices. It was a bizarre movie, even though ultimately we had almost nothing to do with it. It was made during a period when things were even more confused than usual. George was still desperately trying to rope and hobble Pattie, who refused to act like the other wives and girlfriends. John was being stalked by Yoko, and Paul and Jane were trying to make a commitment to each other by getting engaged, when it seemed apparent to their friends that both of them had doubts. Little wonder, then, with so much going on in their private lives, that the Beatles had no time or inclination to focus on *Yellow Submarine* when it went into production.

By now, UA had made it clear that they wouldn't back any more Apple Films projects. "They think the Beatles are a bit too off the wall," was one comment I recall. This was all too much for Denis. He was a lovely man, very easy to get along with, but he was a different generation. Mostly he stayed at home and worked on film ideas. He smoked his cigars and drank his brandy. Before coming onto the Apple payroll, he'd been involved with *A Hard Day's Night* and *Help!* and the Michael Crawford film, *How I Won the War,* in which John had a small role as Private Gripweed. So, while the Mystery Tour rattled its way around the countryside, Denis had stayed at home. He continued to keep away from the office thereafter, and I found myself running the London office of Apple Films single-handed, taking orders from whichever Beatle came along with an instruction.

21

The accountants at **Bryce Hanmer** in Albemarle Street were still battling with the vast confusion of NEMS and Brian's accounts and the Beatles' tax affairs. What they found sobered them. Brian had been using NEMS as a personal piggy bank, advancing himself large sums of money, on which taxes would have to be paid. His personal wealth consisted mainly of his two homes, cars and art. His biggest asset of all, the Beatles management contract, was shortly due for renewal, although, cannily, he still had his percentages of their recording contracts and their publishing, all of which went to his estate. At that moment, EMI alone was holding a million pounds in royalties, due to be paid out immediately. Of that sum, thanks to the draconian 96 percent in the pound tax rate, the Beatles and Brian's estate would get forty thousand pounds between them.

Bryce Hanmer arranged a meeting with the Beatles and called in a tax expert to be on hand to offer his advice. Where the Beatles were concerned, I can't remember many meetings held behind closed doors, so we all trooped in to listen. The Beatles, it seemed, would owe a huge tax bill if they didn't offset most of the money flooding in from their worldwide operations.

Paul, the practical one, asked, "What does offset mean?"

The tax expert said, "In simple terms, it means if you don't spend the money, the government gets it. You can spend it on anything you want, provided it's a genuine business expense. You can't use it on your personal expenses."

"Anything?" the Beatles chorused.

"Buildings, businesses, investments—"

"Films?"

"Anything relating to what you already do," the expert confirmed. "Look on it as a tax shelter."

"How much can we spend?" Paul asked curiously.

"Two million pounds." The Beatles were speechless as the amount sunk in— about £25 million today.

Brian's brother, Clive, who had inherited NEMS along with Queenie, suggested that the Beatles should open a chain of retail stores, something he was familiar with. He was very taken with the idea of greeting-card shops. Nothing like them existed at the time and, to give him his due, it was a money-spinning concept.

The idea didn't appeal at all. The Beatles turned it down out of hand. John, who thought Clive was a second-rater who mentally had never left Queen's Drive in Liverpool, was very peeved that their business interests were now inextricably bound to this man, who in his opinion had never done a single thing for them. When Brian had been struggling to forge their career, Clive had constantly undermined him by telling Harry and Queenie that the Beatles were a waste of time. It was understandable that John stated flatly, "We don't want to be in that. We're not Woolworths."

Seeing an argument brewing, the accountants soothed, "I'm sure with your creative minds you'll come up with something. Ultimately, our plan for you is to build up, then consolidate all your companies and go public in about five years time."

Five years hence was not comprehensible to the Beatles. All they heard and gained from the discussion was the football-pool winner's credo: "Spend, spend, spend!" They delighted in the notion of thwarting the taxman. They would become the Medicis of the Western world and spread this sudden windfall of spending money around. As John put it, it would be like "playing Monopoly with real money." After the accountants and the Suits had packed up their papers into their briefcases, there were many group discussions, some at Cavendish Avenue, about how the Beatles would use their vast wealth and patronage to invest in talent and anything else that pleased them. It was like the game we all play as children: "If I were very very rich and could buy whatever I wanted, I would . . ." Now suddenly, they were very very rich—but not a single sensible idea emerged. They hadn't a clue what they would do.

The idea that they could do anything they wanted was very new to them. They had no education or experience in how to deal with it. Until Brian died the Beatles had never had any freedom. But with no restraints and no one to tell them what to do, George came out of himself and started playing with other musicians. Ringo got more into his own projects, including movies. His first non-Beatles film role was in *Candy,* which was filmed in Rome in December 1967. A month later, in February 1968, he was even a guest on his own, the first of many appearances, with Cilla on her series for the BBC. Paul grew even more experimental but in an interesting way, while John was now free not to spend all day in Weybridge waiting to go to the studio, which was basically what his life was all about after they decided to give up touring.

Apple was a fresh start. They had always said they would never be record producers, but now it seemed like a good idea. Ron Kass, an American, was recruited from his job as head of Liberty Records in the U.K. to be president of Apple Records. It was one of the Beatles' more sane decisions. Paul won't mind me saying that a less sane decision was when he and John went on the Johnny Carson show in New York and said to the world, "Send in yer tapes." They also placed full-page advertisements in newspapers for ideas. Tapes and manuscripts arrived by the sackful and that's where they had to stay, because there was nobody whose job it was to listen, or read, and recommend. The Beatles were busy, and no one really knows why Paul made that open invitation because Paul really wanted to sign the Stones, Donovan, the Byrds and all the groups he liked. There were certainly talks between the Stones and Beatles about getting together and forming a company. I don't think it happened because there would have been too many cooks.

　

They had always considered NEMS Brian's offices, but now that they had their own company—Apple—all four of them were doing office hours editing *Mystery Tour* and going to the pub for lunch like regular workers. They were meeting people without being protected by Mal, or Neil, or even me, or the chauffeur. People were going up to them and collaring them and telling them about their life and their ideas and plans and aspirations. This was not only new, it was a revelation. Suddenly they were living the life of Reilly. It was a bit like the kind of weird freedom some people experience in the aftermath of their parents dying, knowing that they are on their own to sink or swim, captains of their fate.

Paul said to me once, "We don't have to answer to anybody if we fuck up. Don't have to think, 'Ooh, what would Brian say?'" Even before, Paul had been the only one who went out on his own. Sometimes he would come out of his house in St. John's Wood, chat to the Apple Scruffs, escape them, get on a bus and go into the West End and walk around. He'd walk his sheepdog, Martha, on the Heath; he'd post a letter or pop into the corner shop to buy a newspaper. The others were chauffeur driven just about anywhere they ever went. In fact, as I write, Paul still acts like a regular guy. He gets on the train down to Brighton and waits in line outside the station for a taxi home. That's part of his great charm. He's more or less normal.

But then what's normal? Brian Epstein absolutely amazed me one time by getting out a very expensive cigarette case containing a row of perfectly rolled joints. He offered them around, saying, "I get one of my boys to do them for me." Normal is as normal does, and I suppose Brian saw how happy the Beatles were smoking dope and decided he'd have some. He always had huge amounts of LSD in his house—and I do mean loads.

When Apple announced that it was accepting proposals for funding ideas, Yoko struck immediately with a request for five thousand pounds—the equivalent today of about fifty-five thousand pounds—for an exhibition at the Lisson gallery. Considering that what she wanted to exhibit were things painted white and chopped in half, like half a chair or half a table, she could have gotten the lot from a junk shop and got change from a fiver. Rudely, Paul said, "Why don't you put half a person in?" He wasn't keen on giving her any money, but said John could if he wanted to. Paul's sarcastic comment had stuck with Yoko and she turned it to her advantage. She came into Apple and waylaid John to ask him, in a kind of shrugging, sycophantic, dimpling way, for the money. She got to him by saying that he was her inspiration. "I feel like only half," she intoned. "You are my other half, and I am yours. We have been lost in space searching, and now we have found each other. . . ."

John was taken aback and almost fled. However, as the idea sunk in, there was something about it that struck some kind of a chord with him. Ever since his childhood he had felt like half a person; he'd been looking for the missing pieces of the jigsaw. In fact, he'd always been in search of his parents. That dreadful moment when as a five-year-old child he had run from one to the other before choosing his mother had left an indelible impression. Then she had fooled him by dumping him at Mimi's and disappearing. While he pondered all this, Yoko apparently thought he was hesitating, so she turned up the heat. She said that if he didn't give her the money she must destroy herself. John must have had visions of Yoko committing hari-kari on the spot. Worse, he could probably visualize the headlines.

Abruptly he told her he'd fund her exhibition, on the condition she kept it secret. After she left, clutching a check from accounts, he still simmered with rage at her manipulation.

"Why did you agree?" I asked curiously.

"To get rid of her," he snapped. "With women like that you have to pay them off, or they never stop pestering you." Personally, I thought the opposite applied, but didn't comment. There seemed to be some contradiction between John's words and his behavior. Even when he was being dismissive of her, he was seeing her secretly. Perhaps his words were just a smoke screen.

Getting John to underwrite her show was a huge coup and there was no way on earth that Yoko was going to keep it to herself. Triumphantly, she instantly sent out a press release announcing that she and John were holding an art exhibition. The white catalogue stated, "Half a Wind: by Yoko Ono and John Lennon."

John was very annoyed. Had Robert Fraser not been in jail he would have said, "I told you so." All John could do to retaliate was to solicitously escort Cynthia to Brian's memorial service on October 17 and then very publicly hold her hand at the Earls' Court Motor Show a few days later.

▼

Although John was scornful about being a shopkeeper, he had set up his old school chum and fellow Quarryman, Pete Shotton, with his own grocery store in Hampshire and Pete had done well. The store was flourishing. However, the germ of an idea took root. They could open a store that was different. It would be the kind of place where people would flock in and have fun, buying stuff that they loved and wanted to own. Paul liked the idea of an all-white emporium where you could buy white china and so on, the kind of simple and stylish objects you had always wanted but couldn't find anywhere. He saw it as an inexpensive upmarket Marks and Spencer's where anyone could walk through the door without feeling threatened by it being too posh.

John extended their simple idea of free choice for everyone. He said "If they want the counter, sell them the fucking counter, if they want the carpet, sell 'em that as well."

I'm not sure who came up with the idea of giving The Fool £100,000— equivalent to over a million pounds in today's terms—to design the storefront and outfit the new boutique with anything from clothing to Moorish furniture, but it happened. They were given complete freedom to come up with their own designs and buy whatever they wanted. Magic Alex, who was sitting in on the meeting in his habitual position on the arm of John's chair, whispered in his ear and John said, "And we'll invest in a workshop for Alex. He can make us electronic gadgets we can sell to Sony and EMI and go into mass production and make lots of money."

The Beatles were under a lot of pressure at that time to prove themselves in the aftermath of Brian's death. Consequently, the people who worked for them, or for Apple, were under a lot of pressure not to take the piss out of even the smallest of the Beatles' bright ideas, including their involvement with the Maharishi, Alexis Mardas, or the Fool. They're looking at you saying: "Go on. Say it. Say what you're thinking! I can take it." And you're going, "No fucking way. One: you can't take it. Secondly: I like it here!"

To disagree would prove you were not tuned in and turned on, and drop out would mean something else completely—the door! Ergo, something's got to give, and usually it's common sense.

So, Magic Alex bought substantial premises in Boston Place, adjacent to Marylebone Railway Station. Apple Electronics was set up and he was told he could buy whatever a wizard needed. Ultimately, his brand of magic cost the Beatles some £300,000—over £3 million today. For someone who had said that like Prospero he could dangle the sun in the sky, he could make a spaceship by using the engines from John and George's brand-new Ferraris, he could construct a twenty-four-track studio, when eight-track was still the norm on both sides of the Atlantic, nothing was too much. But the only thing I can remember seeing that Alex made that actually worked was a miniature pocket radio, constructed from a few scraps of plastic and wire.

As a vehicle for all these ventures, and many more yet to be ill conceived, they would use Apple, the company Brian had set up for them, because whoever had signed all the checks at NEMS, still signed them for Apple. It was all tightly controlled financially, but a whim is a whim is a whim and £100,000 was a huge sum to draw for three young Dutch clowns whose only previous enterprise, a small clothing shop in Holland, had gone bust.

But, summing it up, George, who had embraced the karmic philosophies of the East, said, "There's more than enough laughter and fun to go round." Perhaps, but having too much money, or even a larger slice of the money they had actually generated, couldn't hurt. It had deeply shocked them when they had discovered that Brian had given away an estimated £100 million on the very foolish merchandising deal alone. After his death more of his foolish decisions would emerge. While none of the Beatles were greedy or cared that much for personal wealth, this windfall, although just a drop in the ocean, was a degree of compensation they could have had fun with.

They discovered that the accountants had bought a substantial corner building at 74 Baker Street some time ago as an investment, large enough for retail premises with offices above. John persuaded Pete Shotton to get his wife to manage his grocery store while he came to London as manager of the Apple Boutique. Pete wasn't keen, but John sweet-talked him into it. Peter said he wished he had not agreed because he found he was working for four bosses. In the morning Paul would have a partition erected. In the afternoon John would have it torn out. Pattie's sister, Jenny Boyd, agreed to be a salesgirl. It was very rushed, because we planned on opening fast, to show the world that Brian's death hadn't stopped the ideas or dissolved the Beatles partnership, as was being suggested by the press.

To demonstrate that their business was going to be very different, they even hired a full-time mystic. His name was Caleb and his chief role for over a year was to influence all company decisions by reading the Tarot and throwing I-Ching coins, an early version of Luke Reinhardt's Diceman ethos. Things got so nutty that Derek Taylor asked Paul if he—Derek—could be designated the office eccentric with a proper nameplate on his door. Paul thought it was a great idea, but having got a yes, Derek was too stoned to order the nameplate and it came to nothing. Derek's favorite position was seated in a majestic rattan chair in the long press room like some Eastern potentate, surrounded by tables on which stood telephones, bottles of booze and bowls of hash for people to help themselves. While the world flooded in and out, he drifted in a sea of happy oblivion.

The Fool would come into Apple and announce they were off on a buying spree. "Where are you going?" someone would ask. "We don't know—maybe India, or Morocco. . . . Wherever we can find what we want, man."

"How much do you need?"

"About ten grand because we've just had a couple of spliffs, listened to the new Santana album and we're going off with a camel train down the Old Silk Road." And without batting an eyelid, someone would sign the check, hand it over and say, "There you are. Send us a postcard, and try and bring back some receipts. We've got to have some receipts."

Sometime later, they'd come rolling back down Baker Street, smelling of exotic spices like Ali Baba and the Forty Thieves, singing, "Lovely Rita meter maid, where do we park our camel?"

Even the labels for Apple clothes were embroidered silk in five fantastic colors, but they cost a fortune. They cost as much as an entire piece of similar clothing in a department store or down the market. Miles of these special labels came tumbling off the assembly lines. It was like: "I'm a nouveau millionaire." "Oh really? What do you do?" "I make labels for Apple." Until then, it had been the pi-

rate T-shirt makers who made themselves a fortune doing souvenir business outside Beatles gigs; but now it was, "By appointment, label makers to Apple."

The buttons were specially imported too; it was all Milo Minderbinder stuff,
straight out of *Catch-22*. They'd buy buttons and hash in the cloth market in
Madagascar or Marrakech, get stoned, swap the buttons for figs in Tripoli. Wake
up, eat the figs, then remember they needed buttons. Go back, buy opium by the
pound and buttons at a penny a hundred, keep the opium, sell the buttons to
Apple for five shillings each, like Milo: everyone gets a share but no one was
any the wiser. It was as if they had worked out that there was an easy way to steal
a big pile of *bhat* with no effort.

They produced mountains of exotic, radiant pantaloons and caftans and bolts
of useless rainbow silks, velvets and batiks, but as we very quickly realized, no
matter what weekend hippie fantasies people entertained about getting it together in the country with a stoned earth mama from San Berdoo with flower de-
cals all over her beautiful body, most of them couldn't wear caftans or a djellaba
to work on Monday morning.

Even at the Apple office we were still quite conservative, with reasonably
conservative clothes. I always wore a tailored suit and tie because it would get
me into most places without any hassle. John turned up at Abbey Road once in
a silk turban and curl-toed slippers, full of Eastern promise, and the others
laughed so much they fell over. There were endless discussions about the
prices. The Beatles didn't want to look as if they ripped people off and insisted
that it didn't much matter what they charged anyway; it was all free money that
would otherwise go to taxes. It made perfect logic, put like that. To make it even
more logical, we should have put up a big placard that read: HELP YOURSELF, because people did. Tons of items were stolen from the racks. The Beatles were the
best customers. They'd choose tons of things I never saw them wear and ask the
sales staff to charge it to their account. The Fool looked like a band of medieval
jesters, so when they strolled in, jangling their bells and asked accounts for a
big wedge of money to get a few things for the shop, it was no good saying,
"You're joking," because they were. They were The Fool.

The boutique would eventually get it together like the competition down in
Carnaby Street. They got a guy named John Lyndon in as head of Apple Retail
and he got it organized. He banned The Fool from the clothing workrooms unless
they stopped taking garments without payment, he got the prices right, started
looking at items that would sell, but by that time the Beatles were "fed up with
being shopkeepers." Besides, John Lennon's life was getting very complicated.
He had a great deal on his mind—and her name was Yoko.

Meanwhile, Christmas was approaching and with it, the broadcast of *Magical*

Mystery Tour on BBC television. Paul had worked for weeks on the edit, delighting in the bright carnival colors. If he knew that it was all going to be broadcast in black-and-white, he didn't say. That Christmas of 1967, their first without Brian, Paul decided to organize a big fancy dress party to celebrate the broadcast of his film. It was to be held at the Royal Lancaster Hotel on December 21, with a sit-down Christmas dinner and a dance. The invitations were sent out secretly, and for once there was no leak. The press and the public didn't turn out in droves and the whole thing went very smoothly.

Fancy-dress balls and events were all the rage. Everyone seemed to dress up at the drop of a hat, whether for a wedding, a birthday or a dance. There was a fancy-dress party nearly every week at various London hotels and clubs or the posh houses in Hampstead, where you'd see the same people, dressed in the same outfits each time. We hired our costumes from Bermans, the theatrical costumiers. The Beatles nearly always wore the same outfits to these parties. I wonder if the fans ever found out that for a few pounds they could have walked around in John's rocker gear, which came with a black plastic jacket, or Paul's pearly king outfit. George Martin and Judy were always the queen and Prince Philip—and I was always the court jester with gold bells on my hat and the toes of my shoes.

At the dinner, *Mystery Tour* was toasted many times over, and everyone looked forward to watching it. It was ahead of its time. Without knowing it, Paul had created the blueprint for the first reality TV show. He should have won an Emmy. Instead, when it was broadcast in black-and-white on Boxing Day (December 26), watched by an audience of fifteen million, the critics panned it. In part it was because this was a revolutionary new format they didn't recognize, and in part it was because the charm of the film with its colorful costumes and makeup and special effects was lost in black-and-white. How could you show clowns dancing, or a magical sky where the clouds changed color, *without* color? It was enormously frustrating for Paul, having dreamed up something in Technicolor, and shooting it in color, being constrained by the shortcomings of the medium it was broadcast on. A year later, when color TV was launched, the film was shown again and redeemed itself, but by then, it was too late; the critics had done their worst. However, the album made something in the region of £11 million as soon as it was released, which satisfied the accountants.

22

Early in January 1968, shortly after we had moved from the overcrowded offices above the boutique to more spacious ones at 95 Wigmore Street, John suddenly made up his mind to accept the Maharishi's pressing invitations and persuaded the others to follow suit. That winter, all of the Beatles had been regular visitors to the Maharishi's luxurious flat in South Kensington; John had even taken Yoko. The Maharishi constantly stressed that the only way they could grow spiritually was to go far away to India and meditate with no outside influences and give him a large slice of their money.

But it wasn't an urgent desire to learn transcendental meditation or practice yogic flying that prompted John's decision to go to India. It was fear of his marriage being destroyed. Yoko had stepped up the pressure. Her stalking of him—which is what it amounted to—became more visible on a daily basis. At first, John, an inveterate tormentor, had slyly encouraged Yoko in the same way that one might prod a leopard in a cage with a very long stick. But the cage door had sprung open.

Yoko told John that their karmas called and their destinies were united, but for a long time John didn't hear. At heart, he was still a conservative. The normal middle-class side of his upbringing, the Aunt Mimi factor, made him fret about rocking his domestic boat. Back in the sixties, people valued their marriages. You couldn't just go in for a quickie divorce; it was very unpleasant and drawn out, the full Dixie knife finals.

For weeks, Yoko had been haunting Apple, something she could do very easily from the enormous flat she and her husband had laid their hands on at 25 Hanover Gate Mansions at the south end of Regent's Park. Her daily routine seemed to be to telephone our reception as soon as she had done her deep-breathing exercises, eaten her grapefruit, or shot up some smack, to find out if John were there, or when he was expected. All the Beatles were remarkably accessible now and the staff had instructions to be open and frank with callers, so tracking John down was not hard. It wasn't like calling MI5. It was perestroika. If more fans had realized this, the circus we already lived in would have been unbearable. Fortunately, most of the fans imagined that they would get the brush-off, so they didn't bother to telephone.

Only half of Yoko was inscrutably Japanese; the other half was pushy. She had so irritated Robert Fraser by constantly demanding space in his gallery that he told Paul she was the pushiest woman he had ever met. Omnisciently, he added, "She persists until she gets what she wants."

It seemed only moments after her preliminary telephone call before Yoko herself would turn up at Apple in person. We would spot her and say, "Oh God! She's here again!" This tiny figure dressed in black, usually wearing some kind of a hat or headdress, would slip in through the front door with a shy, downcast face behind the curtain of slightly frizzy long dark hair that hid a steely glint in her eyes. Then she would lisp in her high, Japanese-American little girl's voice, "John's expecting me."

If he was already in, someone would buzz him and he would appear. If he didn't feel like showing his face, Yoko would sit in the hall with an inscrutable expression and wait, sometimes for hours, like a living piece of installation art, until he gave in. At other times, if she felt that John were deliberately avoiding her, she would wait on the pavement, or hide behind a car or in a shop doorway. As soon as she saw John arriving or leaving, she would hurry up to him, often holding out some small token, such as her latest poem, an invitation to an art gallery or some happening event.

But almost perversely, sometimes John would sit in reception with her and they would talk. About what, none of us could even guess. At times, he seemed animated and amused, but I would guess that he was probably stoned. Other times, he would look anxious and hunted. Yet, as Robert Fraser had predicted, Yoko kept up the pressure, and John gradually began to cave in. I saw it happen and couldn't believe my eyes. Usually, when he'd been brusque, he would feel guilty and he'd take her to lunch or to dinner to compensate, almost as if he owed her something. The less charitable said she was hypnotizing him.

"Uh, Tone, just going out for a bite," John would mumble sheepishly, avoiding my eyes if I happened to bump into him. I would stand on the steps, shaking my head in disbelief as he strode off to some discrete local trattoria or the Japanese restaurant just across the road in Christopher Place, Yoko trotting to keep up with him. There was some problem over the Christmas period, which John spent at home with his family. Rumor has it that Yoko arrived at his electric gates at St. George's Hill in rural Surrey and peered through. Lord and master of the house he might have been, but with Mrs. Powell and Aunt Mimi there for the holidays, not even John had the nerve to open the gates and let Yoko in.

I don't know when this seesaw, one-sided relationship hatched—I can't bring myself to say *blossomed*—into an affair. It was a lot sooner than John ever admitted, a lot earlier than the date engraved in the Lennon iconography, the famed Night of the Two Virgins. I believe it was after the fourteen-hour Rainbow event at Alexandra Palace. According to John's chauffeur, Les Anthony, from that night John and Yoko regularly trysted—or bonked, as Les inelegantly put it—in the back of John's Rolls Royce. Even though, conveniently, John commissioned a folding double bed in place of the backseat, I couldn't see why they would need to put themselves to that degree of discomfort when Yoko had a perfectly good flat close to the action. Her husband, a con man she acted as if she despised, was no impediment to Yoko's bedding arrangements; the opinion of her husbands had apparently never concerned her. Although it seemed that they no longer shared a bed, Tony ran around after Yoko at her every whim. Their friends said he treated her like a princess. After several self-confessed abortions, Yoko didn't act like a natural mother with normal maternal instincts. It was Cox who looked after Kyoko. As a baby in New York, Kyoko had been left alone in their empty apartment while Cox and Yoko did their art thing.

Tony Cox had a criminal history in America, going back to before he met Yoko. He had mixed in John Cage's circles long before Yoko. In fact, he was said to have stolen Cage's car and changed the registration, though no charges were laid. A drug deal involving the Mafia went wrong. On the run, with both the Mob and the FBI on his tail, Tony Cox got cash from the publishing account of La Monte Young, who published *An Anthology*, and headed for an aunt's home in California. He had first heard about Yoko from La Monte Young, who explained that Toshi Ichiyanagi, Yoko's Japanese husband, was a celebrated, award-winning composer and pianist whom she had met in New York and married, much against her autocratic family's wishes. Toshi and Yoko were currently in

Japan. Yoko came from an ancient and noble family, one of the wealthiest in Japan before the war, and had gone to school as a child with the emperor's children. Cox surely homed in on one piece of information like an Exocet missile: Yoko's father was the president of a Japanese-American bank in New York. With the words "bank president" ringing in his ears and believing that Yoko would be a useful contact, Cox used some of the money he'd taken from La Monte Young and set sail for Japan.

The story continues that, to his dismay when he reached Tokyo, Cox found Yoko was in a secure psychiatric clinic after suffering deep depression and a severe mental breakdown. He still managed to get in to see her. She greeted him like a long-lost cousin and convinced him that she was a prisoner, fed heavy psychotropic drugs and unable to leave—which given the situation, was probably true. She saw in this American a tunnel out to the life she had grown accustomed to in New York. Between them, they hatched a plan to gain her freedom. Cox convinced the hospital director that he was a famous art critic and that he would inform the public of the way in which Yoko was being kept against her will. She was returned to her husband but was still mentally unstable. She and Cox met frequently at a cake shop in Tokyo where they wept over sweet rice cakes and tea as they talked nostalgically of the arty circle they had left behind in New York.

It seemed like fate when some members of that very circle, including John Cage and David Tudor, arrived for a cultural tour of Japan. Toshi was signed up to play piano for them, while Yoko was to be their interpreter. On that tour, she became rather more than an interpreter. She inveigled herself into the performances and was photographed lying fully stretched on the piano in high heels and cocktail dress, her long hair dangling, while Cage played. By the end of the tour, Yoko was pregnant by Cox. As Peggy Guggenheim, who was also there, wrote in her memoirs: "I allowed Tony to come and sleep in the room I shared with Yoko. The result was a beautiful half-Japanese, half-American baby."

Cox moved into the apartment Yoko shared with Toshi and became the one allowed into Yoko's bed, while Toshi slept on the floor. On November 28, 1962, Yoko bigamously married Cox at the American Embassy in Tokyo. Her family was appalled. They hired a lawyer and the mess was only fixed by Yoko "divorcing" Cox, divorcing Toshi, and then remarrying Cox. It seemed that whatever Yoko wanted, she achieved by any means. As Nixon once said, "There's no substitute for perseverance." In New York, just before sailing for London, the relationship between Cox and Yoko was sour because Tony didn't want to go to London and Yoko did. They had several marriage-counseling sessions with the Reverend Al Carmines. Rev. Carmines was a well-known Greenwich Village celebrity who was as famous for his parties as for the arts events he put on in his church, in which Yoko and Tony were involved. According to him, the counseling sessions were fruitless because Yoko refused to back down. In joint sessions with her husband, at first she gave the impression of being the subservient wife, but when Carmines asked her to come on her own, she revealed her true nature. He said, "Yoko Ono has a relentlessness about her own urges that is almost religious. . . . She is a woman of steel . . . one of the strongest-willed individuals I have ever met . . . I was a little frightened of that . . . and in awe."

Now she wanted John Lennon. Sleeping with him in the flat she shared with Tony Cox and their child was nothing new. She was a Bohemian artist, after all. Cox had kited checks on several London banks by telling them that he was a filmmaker expecting funds. The film, proposed as a eulogy to naked bottoms, existed; but the funds did not. However, with a father-in-law who was president of a bank, it was easy to pull off the con but it was risky. Yoko's visa had expired, and that winter of 1966–1967, a cold wind was whistling at their heels.

Dan Richter, a brilliant American mime artist who choreographed the start of Kubrick's *2001: A Space Odyssey* and played the part of Moonwatcher, was very tight with Yoko and Tony Cox. He was privy to their furious arguments as well as their financial problems. He had first met the Coxes in Tokyo, where he was studying mime. I met him when he came to London and hung out at Indica. He took an apartment at 26 Hanover Gate Mansions, and told the homeless Coxes when the adjoining number 25 on the same floor became available. He was a close confidant of both of them. He said he heard all their hopes and schemes to hook John, at first as a financial "angel," then, with dawning excitement, as a lover. What made the three of them even tighter was that they shared a common balcony overlooking the street and freely moved between both of their apartments. Often, Dan said, he would look down and see John's black Mini parked in the street below. He said to me, "After a while, it was always there." Eventually he moved to Ascot with John and Yoko and spent four years working with them on their film and music projects, including *Imagine*.

According to Dan, Tony Cox actively encouraged the affair between John and Yoko as a means of survival. He said that Cox would tell Yoko to "go get Lennon." When John proved elusive, as he was at first, Cox told Yoko she wasn't trying hard enough. For her part, when she saw how close she was to capturing their prey, Yoko told Dan that they'd soon be rich beyond their wildest dreams. Often, when Yoko made love to John in their apartment, Cox would bring Kyoko along the balcony and they'd wait in number 26 with Dan. At some stage, Cox began to feel fragile, thinking he might get cut out. In all seriousness, he drew up an agreement that he insisted Yoko sign. This single-page document—which was drawn up and signed at Dan's kitchen table—stated that when Yoko hooked John, they would split any cash she got from the endeavor.

🐾

One afternoon, John sidled furtively into my office and said, "Uh, Tone, are you doing anything?"

"Right now, do you mean?" I asked.

"When you've got a moment. I need you to do something . . . uh . . . confidential. I mean, secret, like."

"All right," I said, wondering what mess he wanted me to get him out of. This wasn't unusual. Like many young men of his age in the free and easy sixties, John was a demon for sex and had a contorted love life.

"I left some . . . uh . . . things at that woman's flat. I want you to go up there and get them back." He thrust a brown paper carrier bag at me, the kind with string handles. "And return all this stuff that she's given me."

I peered inside the bag. It appeared to be full of strange items made of cut-up cloth, wire coat hangers, folded paper and toilet rolls. On the top were some handmade cards with poems written in black ink, like black spiders crawling across the cards, and a few small books. It reminded me of a larger version of the kids' jamboree bags that sweet shops sold, except there was no fizzy sherbet dip or blackjacks, just the booby prize. The penny was beginning to drop, as John said, "Take a taxi. She's expecting me, so she'll let you in. You know Hanover Gate Mansions, don't you?"

"Of course. Will she have your things ready?" I asked.

"Well, probably not," John replied, looking off.

"I see. So what 'stuff' do you want back, John?" I said, sighing and getting to my feet. I wondered what I was getting myself into.

"Personal stuff," John said mysteriously.

"What, like pajamas and things?" I asked. John smiled, relaxing a little.

"Books," he said. "And some shirts . . . uh . . . maybe some socks and a sweater. She can keep the toothbrush and razor." He hesitated. If he'd been a small boy, he would have hopped from one foot to the other. *Here comes the whammy,* I thought. "And . . . uh . . . letters and written stuff, *you know,* Tone. That's the most important. *Stuff I've written.*"

I said, "Incriminating stuff, you mean? And she's just gonna give it to me, is she?"

Against my better judgment, I went to Hanover Mansions, and, like the Grand Old Duke who marched his men up the bloody hill and then down again because he was crazy, I didn't get anywhere. I didn't even get through the door.

When I explained what I wanted, Yoko looked coolly at me and said, "It's all mine. Tell him to come and get it himself."

It didn't much matter because I was to have this kind of conversation with John several times where Yoko Ono was concerned, as he slipped faster and faster down the slippery slope that led to the divorce courts in the Strand.

The production of *Yellow Submarine* had continued in the background to the confusion in the Beatles' lives. They still hadn't been anywhere near the film. They felt it was from a different era in their lives, on a contract with United Artists they'd outgrown and resented. They made their boredom quite obvious. In the end, even their voices were dubbed by various TV soap stars and film actors. However, when it was decided that a couple of minutes of film footage were needed to finish it off, their presence was insisted upon, and reluctantly, they drifted into the studios. They had no interest and even less enthusiasm, apart from when they needed two extra songs. Now, songs were another matter. Songs they could always come up with. (It was a different story at the premiere, which was the first time any of them had seen it. Then, it was "Wow, it's really good, that! Why weren't we more involved?")

By the beginning of February, the Beatles were hard at work in Abbey Road recording these additional songs. On February 11, they recorded "Hey Bulldog" at Abbey Road, while I filmed the entire process. We didn't need any promo material for "Bulldog," but Paul had also recorded "Lady Madonna," the song he had written in memory of his mother, which did need some promotional film. I cut the "Bulldog" shoot, using the bits of the lads playing and sitting about in the studio, and we used that. Then it vanished, completely disappeared. We thought it had been stolen, as things often were if not nailed down. (Over thirty years later, in August 1999, my original film was rediscovered and used with a reissue of "Bulldog" to go with the revamped digital version of *Yellow Submarine*.)

Despite the forays into the studio, John was still in turmoil over Yoko. She was impossible to ignore and seemed to pop up everywhere he turned. Once, she came to the studio. Somehow she conned her way in past the security guard, but at the last door was ejected. Instead of treading on hallowed turf, she suffered the ignominy of joining the Apple Scruffs huddled by the railings outside, among whom she remained silently for hours hoping that John would emerge. When it became obvious that he was in for an all-night session, she departed in a fury.

"I will never be thrown out again," she promised John the next time she waylaid him. I have visions of her going home and cooking up eye of newt and toe of frog, or perhaps making a juju doll and sticking in a few long pins, but none of the Beatles could have had an inkling of exactly what that promise meant to their future peace of mind.

John panicked at the accumulating threats from the Princess of Darkness. That was when he decided to go to India with Cynthia to put some distance between himself and Yoko. If he stayed away long enough, he could hope Yoko would just go away. Maybe she'd go back to America, or vanish in a puff of smoke. Her scissors act might go horribly wrong, or while she was bagged up one day the Royal Mail might frank the bag and deliver it to anywhere but India. Yes, a long trip to the ashram, where he could meditate and learn how to be calm and in control, give up drugs and spend romantic moments with Cynthia and glue his crumbling marriage back together, seemed opportune.

George, naturally, was very keen to go and had already packed his spice bag and a copy of *Chanting without Tears*. Paul, who embraced most new ideas, was also keen, although Jane was still as skeptical as she had been at Bangor. Ringo was deeply suspicious, particularly of the food he could expect at the ashram. I knew that he hated tomatoes and onions—the basis of many curries, which he also loathed—as he did yogurt and any fish that didn't come wrapped in news-paper with chips. As insurance, so he told me, he was going to take a large suit-case filled with Heinz baked beans.

"It'll weigh a ton," I said.

"They have elephants to carry the stuff, don't they?" Ringo asked. "If I can't take my beans, I won't go." I smiled. Ringo was going to India for an "English" experience.

A few days later, promising me a vast supply of 16mm film on their return, which I could edit into the entire Indian experience, the caravan of Beatles and Beatles' wives and girlfriends flew out of Heathrow. A day or two after that, I got a telephone call from Paul, who was always the most organized one.

"There's some kind of embargo here on undeveloped film," he said. "We're only allowed a certain amount." He wanted me to fly out to deal with it.

I flew to Delhi where I set up an unofficial consulate in the luxurious Taj Ho-tel as Apple attaché. I wallowed in absolute luxury, pampered at every turn and dined like a king, while they were starving in the retreat at Rishikesh in the re-mote and beautiful foothills of the Himalayas. Except for Ringo, of course, who was living on baked beans. My most onerous task was channeling hundreds of reels of movie film and rolls of Kodachrome up the mountain so that the Beatles

could film everything and take photographs of everything. I would send the film
back to London in a nonstop shuttle that would not offend the curious regulations put in place by the Indian government to protect their film industry. I was
to find out that India, rather like Russia, made wonderful film stock, top-class
stuff, but they used loads of silver nitrate and cyanide in the process. The waste
was dumped in the Ganges and had a remarkable knock-on effect on the environment. It killed all the crocodiles that traditionally took care of all the bodies
that were floated off to heaven down the sacred stream. The result was that vast
blockages of dead crocs and people built up into dams downstream, not a pleasant concept.

Thankfully, I was many miles away in Delhi, enjoying the cooling fountains
and the scented air of the Taj Hotel, taking care of business, which also included sending a steady supply of magazines, music papers and the latest
American records to the ashram via a courier. Even while meditating halfway up
a mountain with their heads in the clouds, the Beatles wanted to keep in touch.
I also forwarded their mail, including dozens of postcards from Yoko, who, even
at that distance, still peppered John with her poems on a daily basis. To save
any problems, I put these open cards in a plain manila envelope so Cynthia
wouldn't be upset.

After a week, Denis O'Dell, accompanied by Magic Alex, turned up at my
hotel in Delhi. Alex, whose luggage consisted of a small haversack containing
screwdrivers and a few electronic bits and pieces, had been sent for by John to
help the Maharishi build a miniature radio station that would beam the yogi's
message around the world. With any spare energy generated, they would light
up the ashram and neighboring villages. I casually asked how he would achieve
that with the few items what he had brought with him. It was like Yogi Bear and
BooBoo.

"Oh, India is very advanced electronically," he assured me. "I can get everything I need here. I've studied physics, you know." He might just as well have
said, "Because I'm smarter than the average bear!" His big thing was that since
the Maharishi was also a physics graduate, they would have a lot in common.

Denis, whose hefty suitcase also contained more tinned treasures to be carried by Ringo's obliging but nonexistent elephants, complained that the Beatles
had left behind in London a stack of scripts under consideration. "But I've
brought them all with me," he said, indicating a suitcase that was bursting at the
seams. "Stuck up there on top of that mountain, they can't have much else to do
but read."

The Beatles were eager to make the first book of Tolkein's *Rings* trilogy into
a film and they were negotiating an option. They had already talked to the

director, David Lean, but he was busy with *Ryan's Daughter*. They approached Stanley Kubrick, but he didn't think the books could be scripted. "I'm talking to Antonioni now," said Denis, filling me in.

"I think you'll find that the lads' hands are full, Denis," I said, but he wasn't having any discouraging comments.

What we didn't know—and would discover later on our return from India— was that UA had bought the option of *Lord of the Rings* behind our backs. Previously, they hadn't even considered it, but as soon as they heard that the Beatles were negotiating the rights, they slid in and picked it up themselves. They gave it to Saul Zaentz, who would make a nasty dark little cartoon film out of Tolkein's fabulous fantasy.

🐛

Unaware of this skulduggery, Denis left for the ashram, where he discovered that the Beatles were too high up in the clouds, literally, to care about films. George so desperately wanted to believe in this new religion that he called Denis into his hut and made him watch while he sat down cross-legged and levitated. When I asked Denis if he actually saw any space between George's bottom and the concrete floor, he said evasively, "I'm not sure. George was wearing a robe, and it was very dark in his hut." Denis was always very diplomatic.

He had planned on shooting a simple documentary at the ashram, but he and the Beatles quickly discovered that the Maharishi's PR machine had gone into overdrive. The Maharishi had his own film division ready to cash in on his famous visitors and had sold the rights to ABC Television in America—which infuriated the Beatles. Before they had even gone to India, the Maharishi had been beating the drum about his new disciples. Denis had even flown to Sweden, where the Maharishi then was on a lecture tour, to lay down the ground rules: no films, no publicity, no endorsements.

Blithely, the Maharishi acted as if he hadn't understood and continued to scarf up all the publicity he could, by selling the rights to deals which involved the Beatles, for lots of money. Denis returned to Sweden, this time with George and Paul, to again stress how seriously they felt about the ground rules; but to no avail. Knowing the kind of publicity freak he obviously was, it seemed contradictory of the Beatles to have continued their relationship with him. It seemed to me—and from what they said—that they were very earnest about meditation and Indian music, but found the Maharishi a faintly repulsive figure. They argued about it, but in the end they decided to give him the benefit of the doubt just in case he was some kind of magician and possessed some mystical secrets.

Denis had only been at the ashram for a day before other filmmakers arrived in droves and set up camp. Soon he was under siege, unable to film without fifty other opportunistic lenses zooming in. Probably he should have just had an anxiety attack and stayed home. The Beatles were also under siege and miserable, until they turned it into a game: "How to avoid the cameras." Drugs also arrived with the newcomers and John at least forgot his intention to give them up. He soon discovered that meditation was a lot easier when stoned.

Then Roger Corman and his brother arrived. Roger had made films with a young Jack Nicholson, and was a bit of a star himself. Joe Massot was there. He made *Wonderwall* with Jane Birkin, with George contributing to the soundtrack, and would make a film with Led Zeppelin. The Maharishi was the biggest film contender of all because he had so much at stake. His yogi money-gathering people were top-notch, many of them trained at Harvard. He was asserting a lot of pressure on the Beatles as well as being guru. And of course the incredibly "inventive" Magic Alex was there. A disaster on two legs was Alexis Mardas, in that he was convincing, clever with words and apparently a good technician— but he conjured up inventions that weren't possible at the time (if ever). He also wanted to make films. Naturally. Nothing was beyond Magic Alex's new film division. As I recall, at the time he had been busy in London building burglarproof force fields with either colored air or compressed air for going around Beatle homes and lots of other "Heath Robinson-Mardas" things that turned out to be useless. He, like Yoko, was very aggressive about his wants and needs. Ringo saw through the whole thing. He knew far-fetched when he heard it and the others would have done well to listen to him from time to time. (Though he believed in Magic Alex at the time, George would eventually acknowledge, "there wasn't anything he ever did, except he had a toilet with a radio in it, or something.")

Alex constantly wandered around in the background stirring up things. With his gift for gab and his unlikely inventions, many of us—though certainly not John—thought that he was, to use George Martin's term for him, preposterous. But then most of the people gathered out there were out to lunch, anyway. As for the film the Beatles shot, most of the footage was useless. There was no plan. It was all, "Hey, look what we did on our holidays, Mum." When we came to view it, some people uncharitably said that just because it was *filmed,* didn't make it sacred.

Ringo and Maureen fled the circus after ten days. It's not that Ringo ran out of beans, more that he just hated everything, while Maureen had a phobia about insects. As they visibly relaxed in the luxurious surroundings of the hotel, Ringo remarked that John called the ashram "the Butlin's of Bliss," but, Ringo said, he was wrong. It was worse than Butlin's. Maureen rolled her eyes expressively and hinted at worse horrors to come. I saw them to the airport and then returned to the hotel to await these horrors with interest. I didn't have to wait long.

One evening I was peeling a mango when Paul and Jane turned up in a battered taxi with Mia Farrow and her younger sister, Prudence. The girls, whose glamorous mother, Maureen O'Sullivan, had started out playing Jane to Johnny Weissmuller's Tarzan, were angry and tearful and wanted to leave.

George and John, who as usual were spaced out on drugs, stayed on until John, caught unstoned for an hour or two, was filled in by his constant acolyte, Magic Alex, who said he had seen some salacious happenings involving candlelit suppers with the Maharishi and disarranged clothing. Alex asked almost ingenuously, "Why would the Maharishi want a double four-poster bed?"

However, a few people thought that Alex had latched onto the sexual rumors as a means of escape because the Maharishi—the physics graduate—had taken a keen interest in the proposed radio station. He asked many searching questions that Alex was unable to answer and the young Greek panicked. It was then that he insisted that they all had to leave immediately over the sexual shenanigans. For some reason, John was always easily influenced by Alex. He turned on the Maharishi and persuaded the others to walk out with him. The Maharishi had toured the world, recruiting the rich and the famous to come to Rishikesh. It wasn't just the Beatles and their women sitting up there. It was a whole colony of would-be transcendentals, including some of the Beach Boys and Donovan.

In Delhi, discussing how they would present their trip to the world, they decided to simply keep their mouths shut. So on their return to England, the Beatles kept quiet and maintained a closed front about why they left the ashram. Paul told the press that he had gained a great deal of inner peace from the experience, and that he had been given a mantra—a kind of very personal inner voice—that he would always use. George remained a lifelong devotee, as did Pattie, and John, being John, said, "Whatever you do, you can always keep the good bits and throw out the crap," which he did.

John's words were ironic, because it seemed to me and to many of his friends that he was about to do just the opposite where the two women in his life were concerned. On the flight back from India, he had gotten very drunk and, for some reason, decided to confess all his affairs to Cynthia. Brutally, he ticked off a very long list, which included groupies, models, prostitutes, the wives and girlfriends of his and Cynthia's friends and, possibly cruelest of all, Cynthia's own girlfriends. Cynthia felt totally betrayed. As soon as they reached home, she packed and left with Julian, Magic Alex, Jenny Boyd, Donovan and his sidekick, Gypsy Dave, to go to Greece, a place where she had been happy cruising the islands the previous summer. Although I could understand why Cynthia wanted to distance herself from John, it was to prove a very unfortunate decision for everyone concerned.

*

Nothing was lost or wasted of their Indian experience and revenge of a kind was gained when the Beatles started work on the *White Album*. (It was actually titled *The Beatles* but got the unofficial name because of its white-on-white sleeve.) "Sexy Sadie," which was about the Maharishi, was a veiled reference to the goings-on at the ashram. However, the Beatles were keen to stress that they still supported the Maharishi. George never believed the stories anyway and poured millions into the Maharishi's work in England. He even bought the Rothschilds' huge mansion for them. He talked to John long and earnestly about the lessons they had learned, and eventually, John's attitude softened. He agreed that the Maharishi was some kind of a prophet, and he even started using his mantra again. Paul also came round, though it took a lot longer. As recently as the spring of 2004 he went to see the Maharishi in Holland, for guidance.

23

Paul was also about to experience a big change in his private life, one none of us saw coming. We all thought he and Jane would get married and settle down. He liked the idea of domesticity, a big happy family and a wife at home, someone who would replace the gap his mother had left by her death when he was so young. Perhaps the recent release of "Lady Madonna," with its haunting air, had brought his pain back to him. I do think Paul was coming to realize, despite being so recently engaged after a five-year courtship, that Jane's career was more important to her than he was.

On May 11, 1968, almost a year to the day since Paul had last seen Linda in London at the *Sgt. Pepper* launch party, he and John flew mob-handed to New York with Neil Aspinall, Ron Kass, Derek Taylor and Mal for four days to launch Apple Records and its associated companies in the U.S. Paul stayed with their New York lawyer, Nat Weiss, in his apartment on East Seventy-third Street. The others stayed in the St. Regis Hotel, where press interviews were held. On the fourteenth, the day they were flying out, they held a press conference at the Americana Hotel, and Linda was there, taking pictures. Paul was more than pleased to see her and made the first approach. "We met in London," he said.

"Yes, I remember," she acknowledged.

I was amused when Paul recounted this story. I mean, you would remember meeting a Beatle and hanging out with him, wouldn't you? But Paul enjoyed her response since he was so tired of American women gushing all over him. Linda was refreshing.

Paul said that they were leaving, and asked her for her telephone number. She scribbled it on the back of one of her checks and, tearing it out, gave it to Paul, under no illusions that he'd keep it. Much to Linda's surprise, the phone was ringing when she walked into her apartment.

"I'd like to see you tonight, but we're tied up. Do you want to come along for the ride out to the airport tomorrow?" he asked.

Of course, Linda jumped at the chance. She sat with her camera bag in the middle of the car, between John and Paul, and snapped pictures. When she returned to the city in the limo with Neil Aspinall and Nat Weiss, she wasn't sure what was happening. "Something was, but who knows what it was?" she said, still reluctant to believe that Paul McCartney was actually singling her out. Besides, with a living to earn and a young daughter, Heather, to take care of, she was far too busy for dreams. Linda was a down-to-earth lady, but she was also quite philosophical, believing in fate. What was intended would be. This was unlike Yoko, who philosophically believed that fate needed a kick in the ass.

While everyone was away, I was going through a very confused time in my private life, so welcomed some space. I was living with Diana Birchmore in a tiny mews house in Kinnerton Yard, the former stables of St. George's Hospital in Belgravia and now the swish Lansdowne Hotel. Dee was Vic Lewis and Don Black's secretary at NEMS. We had been together for a while, and were happy most of the time. When we had an argument, she would hop on the bus back to her mum's in Muswell Hill, hoping I would miss her. I didn't have the heart to tell Dee that I was also having an affair with a girl named Christine, whom I had met at the Speakeasy. Christine was beautiful in a fascinating way, great fun and very worldly, with a fabulous figure. Her flat was also conveniently close on the other side of Belgrave Square, behind St. George's Hospital. She lived there during the week, and went home to her parents in Staines on the weekends. When Dee was working, or at her mum's, Christine and I would have a great time at one of the regular haunts, the Speak, the Revolution or the Cromwellian, and then we'd go back to her place.

Everyone knew me around town. I was "the Beatles' Tony," so I had gotten used to the fact that some well-known people who were considered legends would introduce themselves to me in the hopes that I would be with a Beatle the next time we met. Despite this, I was still wet behind the ears because I think I was the last person in London to know that the girl I had been dating for several weeks was quite a celebrity, albeit one of a dubious variety. She had toppled the Minister of War from his post and almost brought down the government.

When we first met, she was just another girl at the clubs we went to. We'd have a chat and a drink and then we drifted into going out together in one of those casual on-off relationships that one had in those days. It was incredible because I just didn't put her together with the big scandal until one day at the office Jack Oliver (who was an assistant in Apple Publishing), said, "I see you're going out with Christine Keeler, then?"

I stared at him. "What did you say?"

Jack said, "You know, Christine Keeler."

I said: "Keeler? Is that who she is?" As the penny dropped with a huge clunk, I said, "Oh, God! No wonder I've been getting all those funny looks. I thought my flies were open."

Jack smiled.

People didn't talk about many personal things. It was all very genteel back then. They just said to each other, "Oh, I see Tony's going out with Christine Keeler, then?" Of course I was but nobody talked to me about it. When the writer and columnist Virginia Ironside had her biography out I sent her a note: "Do you remember me?" and she wrote back and said, "Of course I do. You used to pop round and have casual sex." In her book she says she once made love to about fifty men in as many days. She says her diary went something like, "Tony B, Arthur, Tony B, someone else, can't remember and Tony B . . ." And I'd thought I was the only one, such arrogance!

Christine suddenly felt too hot for me to handle. I eased out of our relationship and got back together with a girl called Rosemary Frankland, whom I had first met when she had a bit part in *A Hard Day's Night*. Now she was Miss World. One morning, once again Jack Oliver—someone with whom I was on the same wavelength—said to me, "Got to hand it to you, Tone. You know how to pick 'em. Call girls, Miss World—wow!"

I said, "What's up now? Are you jealous?" Jack shook his head sadly as if I were pretty slow on the uptake. He told me that Rose was Bob Hope's secret mistress in London—except that she was not really a secret, except to Bob's wife. (It turned out when Bob died that she wasn't a secret to Bob's wife, either.) She was on a tour entertaining the troops in Vietnam when Bob met her. He set her up with a nice flat and an allowance in London and when he came over, which was quite often, it was golf all day and Rose all night. It couldn't have been much of a secret if Jack Oliver knew, but once again I was completely in the dark. The last time I bumped into her it was in California. I was with Bruce

Springsteen and Phil Spector and she was with her new husband, Warren Ent-
ner, who was in the psychedelic group, the Grass Roots. They had six top-twenty
hits in the U.S. between 1967 and 1971. The first was "Let's Live for Today." A
couple of years ago Rosemary apparently committed suicide with a drink-and-
drug overdose. I was sorry: she was a lovely girl.

Paul and John had announced in New York that Apple was signing up new acts
and producing records for their own label. They repeated this mantra on their
return to London—and even took out ludicrous advertisements that showed
lads with huge cars and saying something like: "If you want to be rich, Apple is
looking for your talent." Not surprisingly, the offices became like a glorified
international rock and social club, with people constantly dropping by. Not all
of the talent that came our way was good, but sometimes it was outstanding. Bob
Dylan and Janis Joplin and many others came in and almost diffidently said
that they would love to be on this fresh and original label, but I especially remember the day when James Taylor happened to turn up. I believe "happened"
is the right word. He was one of those funny little people who arrived at just the
right moment.

At the time, Peter Asher and I had tiny offices next door to each other right
at the top of the building, well out of the way of the general melee and madness
that was going on all around. Peter was head of A & R and I was Promo/Apple
Films. People couldn't get to us without going to a lot of other places first, in true
music-biz tradition, which was the way we liked it. At one stage, I think Peter
and I were the only people who actually sat at a desk and got things done and on
time. Other people achieved things too; it just took them six days or six weeks.

That day, Peter must have been in a good mood, or bored, because when they
rang up from downstairs to say they had this peculiar American who wanted to
audition for somebody, Peter said, "Oh, okay, send him up." Shortly after, I
heard Peter say, "And what do you do?"

James Taylor just sat down cross-legged on the floor and sang a lovely song.
"The way she moves . . . forever . . ." It was so good that I sat up very straight,
stopped working and listened hard. By the time he had segued straight into
"Carolina in My Mind," I was in Peter's office. James Taylor was dressed in
Levis, a black shirt and Greek car-tire-sole versions of the usual Jesus boots.
But he had a beautiful guitar, a Martin or a Gibson, which he could most defi-
nitely play, and which showed he was serious.

I looked at Peter, my expression saying, "He's a bit good, isn't he?" Peter got
up and strolled to the top of the stairs.

"Is there a Beatle in the house?" he shouted down the stairwell.

Paul happened to be around and he came zooming up. James did a couple more songs and he was signed immediately to do an LP entitled *James Taylor*. Peter was given carte blanche and an unlimited budget to take James into Trident Studio, and Richard Hewson was brought in as musical director for the strings. We also brought in Richard Imrie to take pictures of James in a tweed suit, lying full-length on the floor for the album sleeve. The layout was perfect, the sleeve notes nicely designed. The ideal package was produced in a very short time. We took it to Bill Cotton Jr., head of BBC TV, and he instantly agreed to a television special, which was unheard of for an unknown performer.

I organized a couple of promotional gigs, putting James on at the Marquee with the Strawbs, when Dave Cousins was in the band and Rick Wakeman was the keyboard player. We also did a few radio shows, like *Country Meets Folk* with Wally Whyton and Gordon Giltrap. We took him to Cecil Sharpe House and the Troubadour to sit in so people could see that he didn't need props. Soon he was getting a bit of respect as word went round that he was for real, not just an overrated, overorchestrated folk singer on this obviously very expensive and ultimately overproduced album.

We soon discovered that he had a history of psychiatric illness due to his heavy use of drugs, particularly heroin, although at that time, as far as I know, he was clean. Ironically, he had fled New York for England to get away from drugs, believing we were drug-free—and he ended up in the hippie paradise of Apple.

Everything was going well until James had another nervous breakdown. He went home to recuperate in the bosom of the intellectual, wealthy psychosis that was Martha's Vineyard—probably not the best choice of environment for him at that time. It was to be some years before he "happened" into my life again.

24

Pete Shotton had resigned from the boutique before he sank with it and became John's personal assistant, in reality his companion. He went to stay with John after Cynthia went to Greece. They sat around, played some music, had had a few joints and some LSD when John suddenly made a spectacular announcement. "I think I'm Jesus Christ. . . . No, wait, I *am* Jesus Christ!"

Pete wasn't all that surprised. John had often made such bizarre pronouncements as a boy while we were all growing up in Liverpool. It was part of his eccentric character. "Oh yeah?" Pete said casually. "Fancy going out? Where shall we go? The Rock Garden, Gethsemane, or do you fancy a stroll across the Serpentine?"

But John wasn't joking. He was serious. He talked about the age Jesus was when he died. "They're gonna kill me, you know," he said, "But I've got at least four years to go, so I've got to do stuff." He insisted that Pete immediately call everyone and set up an urgent board meeting at Apple first thing the next morning.

It appeared so urgent that the other three Beatles came in, and together with Neil Aspinall and Derek Taylor, a few of us gathered in the boardroom. "I've got something very important to tell you," John said. "I am Jesus Christ. I have come back again. This is my thing."

The Beatles were annoyed that they'd been dragged in so early for such nonsense. It was John being John. They'd heard this kind of thing for years. Derek Taylor, who hadn't been around John from his youth, was the only one who was really surprised and worried. He thought John had flipped. "Right," said Ringo. "Meeting adjourned, let's go and have some lunch."

John mildly accepted that his messianic announcement had fallen on deaf years. We drifted across the road to a restaurant and ordered. While we were eating, a man came up to John and enthused over the Beatles, the usual kind of thing. John said, "Actually, I'm Jesus Christ." Without a blink, the man said, "Well, I still liked your last record."

That night at Kenwood, John and Pete hung out, took the usual drugs, gazed into space and did very little. Suddenly, John said he "fancied a woman." He picked up the phone and called Yoko, telling her to hop in a taxi, he'd pay. Yoko immediately hightailed it out to Weybridge.

At first, she appeared shy and modest. She sat with downcast eyes and mumbled scraps of her poetry. Pete made his excuses and went to bed. What happened that night can only be left to the imagination, but since it patently wasn't the coming together of two virgins for the very first time, did Yoko do her hypnotism thing, as some of John's friends thought she had, or did she have a powerful new drug in her arsenal? Nobody really believed that John fell in love overnight, because why hadn't he done so before? He'd been kicking Yoko in and out of his life for over a year. Mostly, he had given the impression that he resented and despised her. So it must have been something pretty potent that made John fall headlong out of his casual affair with her into a mad obsession. Perhaps it was that he really was mentally ill and like many schizoid personalities, got religious mania. If he really did believe that he was Jesus, Yoko would probably have convinced him she was the Virgin Mary. A virgin at any rate. John was shortly to tell the world that they spent the night at the top of the house in his bloodred music room, recording the *Two Virgins* tape. They say that a moose in heat can waken the dead and achieve the impossible with his bellows. John and Yoko spent the night screaming.

Pete Shotton also found John's remarkable change of heart hard to stomach the next morning when he got up. John was in the kitchen in a purple kimono, hungrily eating a boiled egg. "I'm starving and had to have something to eat," he said, "but I'm going back upstairs to Yoko. I can't bear to be away from her for even a minute." Pete was further stunned when John said, "I want you to find me a house to live in with Yoko."

"Just like that?" Pete said.

"Yeah, just like that. I'm going to be with her now."

The next day, John sent Pete up to town with Yoko to go shopping to get her some new outfits, whatever she wanted, and Yoko moved into Kenwood. By the time Cynthia arrived home that fateful morning from the airport, having made up her mind to forgive John for the sake of their son, Yoko had been installed for four days. As she walked in, Cynthia had some premonition of something being not quite right. The house was too quiet and appeared to be empty. She ran in ahead of Magic Alex and Jenny Boyd and found John and Yoko in the kitchen. Yoko was sitting with her back to Cynthia, in Cynthia's kimono, a pointed insult, because she must have known that Cynthia was due back.

"Oh, hi," John said casually.

Cynthia was so confused, she startled gabbling brightly about breakfast in Greece and lunch in Rome, and how they would all go out and have dinner in London. John destroyed her with a very disinterested, "No thanks."

It was then that Yoko turned and looked at her. It was a look that blasted Cynthia straight out of the water. Horrified, she turned and ran around the house in tears, stuffing a few possessions into bags before getting into the car and driving off. Pete did his best to get on with Yoko—he even said she seemed good for John—but according to him, the minute she had achieved her goal, Yoko turned. She started asserting herself and John meekly obeyed. Overnight, he no longer had a will of his own.

Yoko had turned thirty-five three months earlier on February 18, 1968, and perhaps she thought she had to do something fast to achieve her ends. Whatever it was that drove her so persistently after John, she finally won. But John did more than open the gates to his estate. He opened the floodgates on the Beatles partnership. Ever since Brian's death, they had been unsure of their future direction, but they were still together, still best mates. Yoko became a wedge. She went from being "that dreadful woman" to becoming the love of his life, his soul mate. To paraphrase the punch line from a wonderful Tim Hardin song: "The lady came from Tokyo. Got away with love."

At GHQ Apple, we only heard bits and pieces of all this as it went down. Most women whose husbands have betrayed them, get on the phone and call everyone who will listen and then start at the top of the list again. Cynthia was very shy and very private. As far as I know, the only person she fully confided in was Paul, who made her smile and feel better when he said, "Hey, Cyn, how's about you and I get married?" Paul really lit into John before he sat down and wrote "Hey Jude," one of his most beautiful and successful songs, to express his love and sympathy for Julian, who was caught up in the middle.

Paul, who believed strongly in the family and in family values, told me that he felt as if it was the Beatles themselves who were heading for divorce, not just

John and Cynthia. I think that perhaps Paul's anger and everyone's disapproval drove John further into Yoko's arms out of his usual sense of defiance. Far from taking Paul's message to heart, John even said that the words, "You have found her, now go and get her," in "Hey Jude," was Paul giving him permission to go get Yoko.

It was hardly surprising that everyone was confused by the way in which John did a complete somersault and fell madly in love with her almost to the point of obsession. She certainly got through his bullshit detector. "Hey! Here's a virtual hammer, John. Now why don't you go up this virtual ladder and bang in a virtual nail?" In the old days he would have just said, "Fuck off you stupid cow and take your ladder with you! I went to Liverpool Art School, I'll have you know. It may be up north but we're not that daft up there and if I find out you're taking the piss I'll fetch you a meaningful bunch of fucking fives! And what's more, my mate Paul's got just the song for you, it goes: "Bang bang Maxwell's silver hammer came down upon her head. Bang Bang Maxwell's silver hammer made sure that she was dead!"

▀

Shortly after this John started using heroin, to which Yoko had introduced him. They were getting very thick, not just as lovers but as heroin joyriders. According to John, Yoko snorted it, but I had no doubt that if she had used a needle, she would probably have said it was acupuncture. It was through heroin that John got closer to Robert Fraser. Robert had just been released from prison and very soon got back into his stride, opening a smart new gallery and throwing celebratory parties. His gallery was in Duke Street, an expensive address between Wigmore Street and Oxford Street, very convenient to our new offices. John was an experimenter, a daredevil by nature, so this new departure didn't surprise me although Paul was disgusted and we all said it was very risky.

"It's okay," John told me once when he'd had a few drinks, as if it made it better. "I hate needles. I'm too much of a coward. Sniffing's okay, it's not addictive."

"John," I wanted to say, "you're so wrong," but he wouldn't have listened. Generally speaking, he was very discreet, though we could all tell when John was using heroin. Paul would say, "Oh John's being John, he'll get over it." I didn't do drugs, beyond smoking a little pot or doing a few hits of speed as everyone did, and neither—as a rule—did I drink very much in the early days. Generally, a few beers would do me all evening. I rarely got to bed before three in the morning and was always up by eight. But to me, John seemed to be heading down a very dark and dangerous alley.

The first time John and Yoko were seen in public, before the press discovered that there was a scandal going on, was at the opening of Apple Tailoring in the King's Road on May 22. The Apple Boutique might have been an ill-conceived shambles, but Apple Tailoring was better. The idea was to make and sell bespoke suits and shirts by John Crittle, an Australian designer, who was the ballet dancer Darcy Bussell's father. It was lovely gear, but who needed a three-piece suit in a nice shade of yellow? Probably only the Beatles and half a dozen of their friends who could afford it. As John left the opening party, he walked along the Kings Road for photographers, and trotting in his wake, was Yoko. All the reporters and snappers missed a scoop, which John found very amusing. I don't think Yoko did. She wanted the attention. She wanted to become an official Beatles' woman. She made such a fuss that John obeyed next time she thought up another happening, which she very soon did, three weeks later at Coventry Cathedral, when they went public as a couple.

There were reports at the time that Yoko usurped an exhibition of modern art organized by the cathedral, by taking it over and calling it "Acorn Event" after she had a screaming match with the senior staff at the cathedral who didn't think acorns were art. The cathedral backed down and John and Yoko planted two acorns for peace on the greensward outside the cathedral, before smiling enigmatically for the cameras. Back at the office, they had us packing up dozens of little boxes of acorns—which, unbelievably, we actually dug up like squirrels in Regents Park—and a handwritten message from John and Yoko to be posted to all the world's leaders. One of the Apple Scruffs, now upgraded to a secretary, with her own desk, had to stagger along to the post office with a big sack to dispatch them posthaste. I'm not sure who did all the research to find out the names and addresses of all the leaders. It certainly wasn't John or Yoko. From the day Yoko went official as John's lover, she had another desk and chair moved into his office and started taking over, laying down the law, issuing orders. I have never seen anyone so assured, so completely in control, so much a pain in the ass.

By now, she was Yoko of Kenwood, much to Mrs. Powell's despair. She told Cynthia to put up a fight; but Cynthia was too upset and frightened of what she had seen in Yoko's eyes, and fled to Italy with Julian. With the press camped all around the house, Kenwood was impossible to live in, so John and Yoko escaped the back way and holed up in Ringo and Maureen's old home when they first came to London. This was a modest ground-floor and basement flat in Montagu Square. Ringo then lent it to Paul as a secret bolthole and studio. At one time,

Jimi Hendrix had even lived there, but he had painted the lurid purple shot-silk walls white, wrecked most of the furniture, and made so much noise fighting with his girlfriend the neighbors complained.

John and Yoko occupied the basement. It still hadn't been redecorated since Jimi's occupation, and I doubt the cupboards had even been emptied out. It wasn't long before the press discovered where the two lovebirds were. With windows opening right onto the street side and no other way in and out, they had no privacy. Within days, they made a run for it to Cavendish Avenue and sought sanctuary behind Paul's high brick walls. I went to bring in supplies for them as if for a siege, and found Paul fed up and John and Yoko stoned out of their minds. John showed me the avalanche of hate mail directed at Yoko and said, "Why do people treat her like this? Can't they see we're just two people in love?"

Paul was understandably annoyed for another reason. It seemed only a matter of a week or so since John had been complaining to anyone who would listen about Yoko making his life a misery, and now, here she was, actually installed in Paul's home, where she remained for a month, making Paul's life a misery. Only now, John declared that he loved her almost above life itself. It was a volte-face that bewildered all of us. What was more, she was always there and she had strong opinions which irritated everyone. Paul decided to seek sanity in work.

"Let's get this sorted, Tone," he said, coming into my office early and flinging open the windows. "What we need is a fresh start."

The words "fresh start" became the new Apple mantra around the offices. For some weeks the Beatles had been working on the *White Album*, or more properly, *The Beatles*. Oddly enough, like most Beatles' albums, it had started life with a working title, in this case, *A Doll's House*. Later, with a nod to the ashram and India, it was decided it would be renamed *Everest*. (The working title of *Rubber Soul* was *Abracadabra*; but after John's "Jesus" controversy, it was decided to steer clear of anything too magical. Songs also had working titles: for example, "Yesterday" started life as "Scrambled Eggs.")

Notably, Yoko was starting to influence John's writing and without being invited, was heard screaming on a bizarre unreleased song (one of the batch of demos recorded at George's home), "What's New Mary Jane." (It was said that Magic Alex wrote this, although it ended up credited to John and Paul.) Even though they were in the middle of recording a new album—a process that would take several months—George and Ringo escaped to California June 10. Ringo said it was a holiday to clear his head. George went to Big Sur where he and Ravi Shankar made a small film and did some recording. This dislocation set the pattern for the way things were to be. The Beatles still worked together, but they had started to drift. Ringo was unhappy and showed it, mostly by staying away and not being his usual funny self. By the end of July, Ringo was back at Abbey Road, recording two songs for the album: "Don't Pass Me By," written by him (was this a shot at recognition? I wondered), and one written by John, "Good Night."

The *White Album* was intended for release by EMI, but part of Paul's fresh-start approach was aimed at their long-held dissatisfaction with this company. The plan was to renegotiate their old, draconian five-into-a-penny contract, and to use the relatively new company of Capitol/EMI as distributors for Apple Records, which was their personal company, outside the EMI deal. It was decided I would produce a twenty-minute promotional film for the Apple launch in Los Angeles. Paul was very involved in this creative process which, it was intended, would show the people at Capitol/EMI the atmosphere at Apple and what it was all about.

The film we came up with was a little bit arty and airy-fairy. There was a sequence of James Taylor and Mary Hopkin and Paul doing "Blackbird," which I had filmed in early June; unshown footage that the BBC had banned of the Beatles doing "A Day in the Life" from *Sgt. Pepper;* a bit about the new Apple shop; some footage on the wildly experimental Indica Art Gallery and finally, the Beatles having a business meeting with "Uncle" Dick James in the new Apple offices in Wigmore Street. John insisted on including footage of Magic Alex in his habitual white coat, fiddling with a pile of junk. Overall, it was a pretty little film when it was finished and everyone said how well they thought it would go down. Ron Kass said it would be a very useful tool to show the record executives at the Capitol convention in L.A. what Apple was all about.

"Why don't you come too?" Ron said to Paul.

Paul said, "Okay," and, turning to me, he added, "and you come as well, Tone. And we'll take Ivan." This was Ivan Vaughan, Paul's oldest school friend, who had been in the Quarrymen. I think Paul agreed to go because he wanted to see Linda again. We literally rushed to the airport to get flights and, since we couldn't get a direct flight to L.A., had to make a stopover in New York. The first thing Paul did on arrival at Kennedy on June 20, 1968, was to dig out that check with Linda's number on it that, tellingly, he had carefully kept in his wallet, and telephoned her. She was out, so he got her answering service.

"Hey, I'm in America!" he said. "Come and hang out for a couple of days. I'm staying at the Beverly Hills Hotel." He seemed disappointed that she hadn't been in to answer the telephone herself.

"Do you think she'll come?" I asked.

Paul shrugged. "She's a very independent lady," he said. Like most men of his age, Paul's ideas about women had really been shaped in the fifties, when most mothers stayed home and looked after the kids. However, his own mother had managed to combine both a career as a midwife—earning more than his dad—with being a wonderful mother to Paul and his younger brother, Michael. Paul did have a fairly broad view about how women should be and Linda was fitting in with his images. The busy, independent woman. Someone who showed a genuine interest in him as a man and not as a Beatle. She was also like Jane Asher, in that she was smart and classy.

At the luxurious Beverly Hills Hotel we were given a bungalow beside the pool. It seemed like heaven! The first thing we did was change and go for a swim. Cliché it might be, but, *this is the life*, I thought, as Paul and I floated side by side on lilos, drinks in hand and gazing at the blue sky as the heavy scent of jasmine and orange blossom wafted on the air.

That afternoon, we decided to shop on Sunset Strip. To me, everything was wildly expensive, but Paul didn't care.

"Sign for anything you want," he told me. It was a bizarre situation. Here was a young man worth many millions who didn't have a penny on him. A bit like royalty, I suppose. At any rate, everyone was more than happy to have our signatures.

"Make the bill out to Apple," Ivan and I said grandly, collapsing into giggles around the corner on Rodeo Drive. It seemed unreal. Even Paul said that after several years he still couldn't get used to this way of life. Many years later, he loved to tell the story about how, when his young daughter, Mary, came home from their local school she was to say to him when they were out riding horses at their home in Sussex, "Dad, are you Paul McCartney?"

"It made me sit up and think about it," Paul said. "You know, sometimes, I would suddenly stop dead wherever I was and say, "Hey, you're Paul McCartney!" It's an eerie feeling, sort of like stepping outside yourself and asking, "Who the hell are you really?" Like you're someone playing the role of a Beatle, and some day you'll wake up, find it was just a dream and you're Pete Best!"

▰

Those few days in Beverly Hills were like that, very Hotel California, with the sun, the fun and the girls. On our shopping trip, Paul and I bought Nehru jackets. Paul's was red velvet and mine was white silk. We also bought several pairs of exotic sunglasses with pink lenses at a psychedelic optique, which we clowned around in. One pair would have done, but we couldn't make up our minds which we liked and in the end Paul said, "To hell with it. Let's have 'em all." Once again, as we signed the outrageous bill, we found it wildly funny and ran into the street, laughing like people who had done a runner from the Chinese restaurant without paying.

That night, after another dip in the warm silky water of the swimming pool, we dressed in our new gear, put the psychedelic glasses on, and swanned off in a limo with tinted windows, ten miles long. This was the sixties and in the accepted parameters of cool, we were the coolest of the cool.

"Man, we could play snooker in here," said Ivan. The Beatles had always had big cars when they went on tour, but this one was huge. We lolled back in the seats watching beautiful Californian girls roller-skate by with their fabulous tans and even more fabulous legs, their long blond hair blowing in the breeze behind them. All the girls seemed blond, and with tans. Sometimes a sports car would cruise up level with us and there would be some fabulous girl driving it. It was like they were all born to be in Hollywood.

"Must be something in the water," Paul said, and for some reason we found that hilarious. After all, it was all sun, sea and swimming pools.

As the news that Paul was in town spread like wildfire, the girls began to appear in their droves again. Our first stop was Romanoff's, Frank Sinatra's favorite restaurant, run by a sort of Russian prince. Then, we were off clubbing. The Factory was next on the agenda. Located in the middle of a large industrial warehouse, the members were mostly Hollywood elite, people like Paul Newman and Steve McQueen. Paul Wasserman, "Wasso," the top Hollywood press agent, sat with us, greeting and introducing, pointing names out. (He's still in the business, at the top of the tree as the Stones' press officer.) Sammy Davis Jr. was there and came over to our table for a chat.

"Hi, Paul, how're you doing, man? Glad to see ya." I was fascinated by the amount of gold jewelry this very short man could drape on his wiry little body and still dance. Ringo would have been impressed. Ringo loved gold, loved to dance, and he was good at it, too. Meanwhile, models and starlets were throwing themselves at us. If they couldn't grab Paul's attention, then Ron, Ivan or myself would do. The Scotch and Cokes didn't stop flowing until the early hours, all of us on such a natural high that we didn't feel any ill effects. We tipped out of the club, still accompanied by Wasso and several girls. I think I ended up with an air-hostess, but it was hard to tell. Dozens of girls were mobbing around and came back to the hotel with us. Traveling back down Sunset Strip to the hotel with a carload of girls, Wasso took great delight into bumping our car from behind with his equally gigantic Cadillac before he overtook us, waved, and roared off home.

The following morning Paul got up and swept out everyone like sweeping away the ashes with a broom because there was work to be done. On checking the equipment and promo film at the Beverly Hills Hilton, where the convention was due to be held that afternoon, I discovered that the film's soundtrack was on the wrong system for the American projector. For the next few hours we ran around in a panic trying to find somewhere open on a Saturday to transfer the sound. Al Corey, promotion man at Capitol, eventually took me to Hanna-Barbara Studios where this was done very fast and efficiently, and the day was saved.

Paul delivered a short speech to announce that EMI/Capitol would distribute Apple Records and, from now on, the Beatles were on the Apple label. That was a cue for me to show the film. Paul spent time doing the old meet-and-greet and being photographed with top Capitol executives, Alan Livingstone, Stanley Gortikov and Ken Fritz. It was a PR masterpiece. Relieved at how well it had gone we were ready to return to the hotel and leap into the swimming pool again. When we went into the bungalow to change, followed by the trail of girls, we were rather surprised to find Linda sitting there radiantly, totally spaced out, waiting for Paul. She had a joint in one hand and a beatific smile on her face. Paul immediately detached himself from the circus surrounding him and took Linda aside. As I looked across the room, I suddenly saw something happen. Right before my eyes, they fell in love. It was like the thunderbolt that Sicilians speak of, the *coup-de-foudre* that the French speak of in hushed tones, that once-in-a-lifetime feeling. Paul was struck almost dumb as he and Linda gazed at each other. Then he realized how crowded it was.

Like a poacher caught with a string of salmon, he pretended that the leggy beauties who were hanging around were not his catch. "They're with Ivan and Tony," he said. It was very difficult to carry this off because not only were the groupies arriving in droves, but models and starlets were trying to get access, calling incessantly, begging to be allowed around. We had to get hotel security to ask them to leave, but still, luscious little nymphets were breaking in, climbing over walls and crawling through the groves of orange blossom and jasmine. All they wanted was to see Paul, and all he wanted now was some privacy with Linda.

That night we all went clubbing again, to the Whiskey-A-Go-Go, where B. B. King and the Chicago Transit Authority (who later shortened their name to Chicago) were playing. The club was hot, dark and crowded. Paul and Linda sat in a corner booth while we acted as a kind of hedge. By a strange coincidence, both Eric Burden and Georgie Fame were in the booth next to us, a fact not missed by Linda or Paul in their state of heightened awareness. Eric and Georgie had been at the Bag O'Nails on the night they had met some thirteen months ago. Now here they were on the night they had fallen in love. It was a sign.

Paul and Linda left to be on their own back at the bungalow, while the rest of us partied into the early hours. The next day, even more fans turned up and mobbed the hotel. Crowds of fans were milling in and around the main entrance, lobby and grounds, while Paul and Linda were still in bed making love. Finally, to thank them all for coming, Paul got up and sat on the steps of the bungalow, playing his guitar and singing to them—I think it was "Blackbird"—while Linda kept quietly in the background, not wanting to be seen.

I wandered off into the main part of the hotel, where I bumped into Colonel Tom Parker, Elvis Presley's manager. He invited me to Elvis's comeback affair, an NBC concert in Hawaii the following week, handing me some tickets. I showed them to Paul later, and he said, "What a drag, we can't go! We'll be back in London."

"The colonel says it's Elvis's comeback concert," I said. "At the age of twenty-eight!"

I gave the tickets to Ray Connolly, the writer, and a major Elvis fan. Toward midday, Ivan was assigned to take care of Linda, while Paul, Ron and I visited Alan Livingstone, the president of Capitol Records, at his glamorous home in Beverly Hills. After a buffet lunch, we dropped in on Ken Fritz, where we spent the rest of the afternoon lazing around his pool.

On returning to the bungalow, Linda passed around a Victorian cloth drawstring bag stuffed full of grass. In London this bag became her trademark, the legendary "spice-bag" that Plonk Lane of the Faces wrote about in a song. All kinds of music people started to drop by, like Roger McGuinn from the Byrds. Boyce and Hart, the songwriters for the Monkees, telephoned to invite us to one of their notorious toga parties, a Hollywood version of a Roman orgy. Paul asked me to turn down all invitations so he could spend time alone with Linda. I did, but a leggy young starlet named Peggy Lipton, who had met Paul during their last American tour and still had designs on him, kept calling all through the night.

The next day, Ron Kass was invited to go sailing on the boat belonging to movie director Mike Nichols of *The Graduate*. Mike and Dustin Hoffman, the film's star, had always been two of Paul's biggest fans, and Mike extended the invitation to include us all, but Paul knew that if Linda went with him on the boat, the news would get out very quickly. He was torn between going, or keeping her a secret for a little longer by hiding her back in the bungalow. In the end he decided they would both go, and Linda could always say she was just taking pictures.

As we left the hotel to get into the limo, Peggy Lipton suddenly appeared, bikini and towel packed in her beach bag, ready to spend the day with us.

Somebody must have told her we were going sailing. "Oh my God," said Paul when he spotted her. "She can't come."

I had to tell her in the nicest possible way that it was a private party, while Linda stood quietly to one side pretending she wasn't with us. Peggy was very upset and got very argumentative. I realized that she needed the publicity for her career and had been told to make sure she got it, but Paul was tired of girls who used him. We drove off fast, leaving Peggy standing on the hotel steps in tears.

It was one of those perfect days, though not for Peggy, of course. We sailed to Catalina, feeling like Bogart and Bacall for whom the island was a favorite destination, along with the Flynns and the Fairbanks. We dived off the sides of the sailboat into the clear blue sea where dolphins swam, sunbathed on the decks, ate bacon sandwiches and drank champagne. It was a wonderful day, an antidote to the months of madness in London.

Late that afternoon, we checked out of the hotel to return to London. Paul and Linda were like Siamese twins, holding hands and gazing into each other's eyes all the way to the airport. In the VIP lounge, they sat apart from us on a small group of seats in a central aisle, the kind of seats that are back to back with another row. Suddenly, the doors burst open, like the sheriff and his men at the big bad saloon.

"FBI!" one of them barked, flashing a badge. "There's a bomb warning on your flight. Do you know of any Caucasian male with a grudge against you?"

Paul looked surprised. This was years before stars were assassinated and needed bodyguards. He said, "No, nobody."

"Do you mind if we search your baggage?" they asked.

Out of the corner of my eye, I noticed Linda very swiftly aiming a neat little backward kick with her heel. Her square vanity case, which she had placed on the floor beneath her seat, skidded to the row of empty seats and, fortunately, came to rest exactly underneath one of them. Casually, she stood up. "Well, guys, I guess this is good-bye," Linda said. "I'd better check on my flight."

"What flight are you on?" one of the agents asked.

"New York," Linda said. "I'm not traveling in Mr. McCartney's party." She smiled at us all and sauntered off through the door of the VIP lounge as if she had all the time in the world, and as if there wasn't enough marijuana packed into her vanity case to get a herd of elephants stoned.

We all wondered if Linda had managed to sneak back for her vanity case, or if it remained there. Who knows? I never asked.

25

Almost immediately upon our return from California, on June 29, 1968, a Saturday, Paul and I, with Peter Asher and Derek Taylor, together with dear old Martha, Paul's sheepdog, drove up to Saltair near Leeds to record the Black Dyke Mills Band do one of Paul's TV themes, "Thingumybob" and a brass band version of "Yellow Submarine."

They were an old-fashioned brass band from Yorkshire that had recently won the all-England brass bands competition at the Albert Hall—very much like the later film, *Brassed Off*. Ringo had discovered them through a builder working on his house, whose brother happened to be in the band. Paul loved their sound because it was so Northern, very working class and authentic. This recording was all part of Paul's ambitious plan to launch the Beatles' Apple record label with four new but totally diverse singles all on the same day. All in a promotional gift box, one of which would be delivered to the queen at Buckingham Palace.

Saltair was a traditional little Yorkshire town, full of masterpieces of the industrial age built by a millionaire mill owner. We did the first session in the village hall, which went fine. But between sessions, Paul roamed about with Martha and fell in love with the town itself. It was a beautiful day and he suggested a bit of authentic marching in the street, before finishing off in the village square. Everyone came to listen and watch and it went very well, with a carnival atmosphere.

We stayed over in an ancient hotel and I didn't know where to look when Paul handed Martha to the hall porter in a deadpan way with some cryptic instructions. "Er, remove her clinkers, would you?" Well, Martha was a shaggy sheepdog and sometimes things clung that shouldn't have clung. Without blinking, the porter said, "Why gladly, Mr. McCartney, and will Madam be requiring a dish of water and her supper?"

"Thanks," Paul said, and we all went off to sink a few pints of good Yorkshire ale.

We finished the recording on Sunday and then it was back to London. I noticed that Derek Taylor had washed down some LSD with his breakfast coffee and was out of his brain, but I didn't comment. You don't, do you? We were cruising along in the back of the big limo when the Stones' new single, "Jumping Jack Flash," came on the car radio. We couldn't believe it, and I leaned forward to turn the radio up loud.

Ever since radios were installed in cars we'd dreamed of bopping about, snapping our fingers, cruising our hometown's moonlight mile or hanging out and looking cool with the motor parked by the "monkey walk" with the windows down, a place where the girls paraded up and back. Wiggling. Giggling. Giving you the eye. Tossing the ponytail. Shaking that tail feather. "Here she comes again," sang Tom Petty, Bruce Springsteen and Willie de Ville—who all understood something of these matters.

And what a sales tool the car radio was! As a record promoter radio is my medium. My channel. Something sexy coming over the airwaves always does the trick but songs always sound so good in the car that musos with a bit of clout will often talk deejays into playing a newly recorded track over the radio just to hear how it will sound. To hell with the audiophiles and their two thousand bucks' worth of Bose; a car radio is where it's at. And in their own way, musos are as bad as the audiophiles. They will talk about the five to one sound compression that radio stations use to give it oomph and power. Turning a knob, squeezing the sound out to give it juice.

In fact they will all talk about what turns 'em on, but what it all comes down to—because everybody's somebody's punter, everybody's somebody's fan, is this: does Keef Richards' rhythm guitar getcha goin'? Does it bend your back? Does Charlie's snare drum make your neck move sideways to the offbeat? Do you wanna get up and dance in the back of a car?

In a discussion we had about the Stones once, I think it was Ringo who said, "You listen to the likes of 'Honky Tonk Women' and 'Brown Sugar' and tell me it doesn't make you wanna dance, and I'll tell you, you need help."

The Beatles were all fans of great music. Cruising along in the limo listening to "Jumping Jack Flash" blasting out of a little speaker, even Martha started to move. Derek Taylor tried to get up, gave up, and settled for grooving along in the corner, but Paul went nuts. That was the first time we'd heard it and it was a revelation. Mick and Keef may have been short of new songs when they borrowed "I Wanna be Your Man" from J & P, but my God, how they had caught up! The lyrics of "Jack Flash" said it all. "I may have started out as a no-hoper. Born in a storm but now it's okay! In fact, it's a bit better than that. It's bloody great! Let me tell you about it!"

We were just pulling into a gas station when it ended and Paul turned to me. Reverting to type he said, "Bloody 'ell! That's a bit tasty. 'Ere, Tone, do you think you could go and call up Alan Freeman and get him to play that again?"

"You want me to promote the Stones?"

"Yeah, why not?" There was a very funny look on Paul's face as I went off to find the phone. As if, not only was the whole world on his shoulders, but now the Stones were about to hit their stride. It wasn't jealousy as much as admiration. As far as the angels were concerned, the Stones had all the yearnings, and the Beatles had all the sighs.

I called "Fluff" Freeman as directed, and almost immediately, to our surprise, he announced on air, "Tony Bramwell of Apple Records has just called in from some gas station in the middle of nowhere. He's with Paul McCartney and they've made a request to play 'Jumping Jack Flash' again." And he turned to his producer, Dennis Jones and asked, "Can we do that?" Dennis said, "Why not?" So they did. We just sat there in the Daimler in this gas station listening. It was still fantastic. A year later, I was to take Billy Preston's record, "That's the Way God Planned It," to Kenny Everitt to play. Kenny and I were great friends. He was totally zany and a Beatles fanatic. I said to him half-jokingly, "Why don't you just play Billy's record a few seconds at a time between all the other records? Then when you feel like it you can play the whole thing?" And Kenny said to his producer, Derek Chinnery, "What about it?" Derek agreed, and so that's what they did all day. They played a few seconds here and there and then at the end of Kenny's program they played it all. It went straight into the top ten the next week. It was gratifying. You could suggest those kinds of things in those days but not now.

By the time we reached Bedfordshire, we had been driving for a long time on the A6 and were a bit bored. Paul wanted to let Martha stretch her legs and, to tell the truth, it was such a glorious day I don't think we were in any particular rush to return to London. Paul got out the road map and opened the page. He stuck a finger on it and we all looked. "Harrold" said Paul. "That sounds nice. Let's go and visit Harrold."

We struck lucky. Harrold was a most beautiful little medieval English village along the Great Ouse River. We drove through but all the pubs were closed. On the way out, we spotted a man cutting a hedge around a charming house. Paul said, "Stop!"

We all tumbled out of the car and Paul asked if there was anywhere we could have a snack. "And Martha needs some water," he said.

The man, a dentist, said, "There's nowhere open. But it's nearly teatime. Would you care to join us?"

We all trooped indoors, where the wife was preparing sandwiches and putting a cake or two on plates. She glanced up and smiled. If she recognized Paul she didn't say. They were far too polite. The children were called in from playing in the back garden. The oldest one, a very pretty little girl of about seven, recognized Paul like a shot, but again, had been nicely brought up and she didn't comment. However, she did have a guitar that was leaning up in a corner of the room, and after tea, Paul picked it up and, playing left-handed, sang "Blackbird" and "Rocky Raccoon" and a few other songs for the children, who clustered around him as if he were the pied piper.

After a while the dentist suggested that since the pubs would now be open we could have a drink. We strolled out into the dusk and down the High Street, passing a fourteenth-century church with a fine spire. The dentist, who was well informed on local history, told us the village was first founded in the time of King Stephen. The priory dated from about 1150 and there was a thirteenth-century stone bridge over the Ouse. While Martha splashed happily about in the rushes, he pointed over the bridge. "Chellington lies over there, or what's left of it," he said. He went to tell us the strange story of a disappearing village. At the time of the Black Death, the houses were pulled down—or burnt down—and the surviving villagers huddled together in the church praying for protection from the plague. When they emerged they said the village was haunted and most of them moved over the river to Harrold.

By the time we got to the pub, the word had spread and it was fairly packed. We drank beer while Paul sat at the piano and played a repertoire of Beatles songs, McCartney songs and a lot of rock and roll until closing time. I think in the back of his mind Paul would have liked to put tomorrow off indefinitely. At least here in the countryside was peace. In London there was none to be had. London was business and all its attendant problems. Lately most of them seemed to be sitting on his shoulders alone.

On the following Monday, John asked me if I would film yet another of Yoko's expensive events.

"What's this one called, John?" I asked.

"'Yoko Loves John,'" he admitted, a bit embarrassed. "But she might change it to 'You Are Here.'"

I filmed the "You Are Here" event on July 1, at Robert Fraser's gallery, the same Robert Fraser who said he wouldn't have one of Yoko's exhibitions in his gallery over his dead body. In fact, the exhibition was billed as John's but he didn't contribute a thing; it was all Yoko's. I thought probably the only reason she selected Robert's gallery was to teach him a lesson, and put him in his place—very cleverly, too. She filled the floor space up with loads of plaster-of-Paris charity collection-boxes that you used to see outside shops, life-size cute little begging dogs and crippled Dr. Barnardo's kids on crutches, embarrassing and tasteless when seen en masse. On the wall, center back, was a six-foot round circle of canvas, with the tiny words YOU ARE HERE handwritten with a black felt-tipped pen dead center like a miniature bull's-eye. I hid cameras behind two-way glass, like *Candid Camera*. The idea was to capture people's expressions when they came in, to see if they put money in the charity boxes, and film them in tight close-up as they read the tiny words on the canvas. John opened the event by launching thousands of white balloons for peace, one or two bearing prize-winning labels: IF YOU FIND THIS, SEND IT BACK TO JOHN AND YOKO, AND CLAIM YOUR FIVER. Very surrealistic, I thought, but I shot it all, and handed over the film without comment.

"What do you think?" John asked.

"Great, John, just great," I said, also handing him a prize-winning balloon I'd kept back, and claiming my prize, trying to keep a straight face.

"Sorry, Tone," he said, "I've given all my money to Yoko." I was entertained that John hadn't seen that I was pulling his leg. But then, when he was around Yoko, he seemed to lose his famous Liverpool sense of humor. Yoko took the films, with one of her little mysterious smiles, and I never saw them again. Somehow, I couldn't imagine her and John sitting up in bed watching them more than once.

Paul was someone who was also spending a great deal of time in bed. While John's love life was confusing in a dark way, rather like John's own personality, Paul was going through some important changes too. His engagement to Jane the previous Christmas seemed to herald the decline in their five-year relationship. No sooner were they back from India, than Jane returned to her work at the Bristol Old Vic, and Paul launched into what was probably the most relaxed time of his life. He opened wide the doors of Cavendish Avenue and the groupies, who had camped as faithfully outside as they had in Wimpole Street during the years that Paul had lived there with the Asher family, were astonished to find they were now invited in. Not only were they invited into the house, but also into Paul's bed. Whenever I went up to see Paul, the house was filled with giggling, half-naked girls, cooking meals, walking Martha, or glued to the phone for hours on end, calling the world.

"What's going on, mate?" I asked Paul. He knew what I meant.

"It's my bachelor phase," he told me with a leer.

Sometimes, it did get to him. I remember once arriving when he was trying to get rid of a more persistent American girl, who seemed to think she could move in on a permanent basis as Mrs. McCartney. Paul threw her suitcase over the surrounding garden wall, and locked the front door. But she retrieved the case, climbed back over the wall and in through a window. She was back inside even before he was.

"It's your own fault," I told him. "Once you let 'em in, you'll never get rid of 'em."

But Paul was rarely without a complex motive, that perhaps even he didn't understand. Essentially, he was always the very sweet Liverpool boy I had grown up with. Like me, he found it hard to hurt people's feelings, and he seemed to know that the only way to break his engagement was to make Jane do it herself. Intended or not, that's what happened. Has anyone analyzed the words *in flagrante delicto?* It's supposed to mean, "caught red-handed." Actually, it means "with the crime still blazing." In Paul's case, the bed was still blazing.

The engagement was over. Margaret Asher turned up to regretfully collect her daughter's belongings because she was very fond of Paul. It seemed Paul regretted falling out with Margaret more than with Jane. He adored that wonderful, motherly figure who had been so kind to him, but now the road was clear for him to go after a woman he could be true to.

The boutique was hemorrhaging money at a fantastic rate. It would have been easier if the Beatles had just walked up and down Baker Street once a week handing out cash. The catalyst to winding it up was an insulting newspaper article that wondered why the Beatles were scrabbling around as shopkeepers. They had become exactly what John had grandly told Clive Epstein they would never be. The boutique had been a mess from the start and had never lived up to their romantic idealism. They were so eager to dump it, they decided to give everything away rather than drag out the closure with an embarrassing sale. Two days before the great giveaway, John and Yoko arrived in John's unmissable Rolls Royce and they entered the shop. The staff were taken aback when Yoko spread yards of the beautiful silks and velvets on the floor and piled them high with whatever took her fancy, from clothing to bolts of silks and velvets. She knotted the corners and dragged the bundles out to the car like a bag lady. After she had helped herself—I imagine for official use in her theatrical events—everyone from Apple was told to go down and help themselves to the pick of anything that was left before the doors were opened to the public. I selected a weird assortment of a leather jacket, some hideous trousers and some flowery shirts, none of which I can remember ever wearing.

Apple had outgrown Baker Street and then Wigmore Street. For half a million pounds—cheap at the price—the Beatles purchased stylish new offices at 3 Savile Row in the heart of Mayfair, an historic building that had once been Lady Hamilton's town house while she was Nelson's mistress. Paul loved both the history and the building, which was very beautiful with spacious, graceful rooms and a sweeping circular staircase. Before we moved in, it was freshly decorated throughout with a scheme of white walls and woodwork and fitted sage green carpets throughout—all except for George's office. George wanted to chant his mantra in the right atmosphere, so he had it decorated in Day-Glo pink. Prints and fabric tapestries of jeweled elephants and six-armed Hindi goddesses hung from the walls. The finishing touch was to install fake ceiling beams painted gold, and to smother the floor with cushions and thick Indian rugs.

We spent days packing up our old offices and waited for Pickford's removal vans. It was only a journey of about half a mile, but loads of things just vanished on the way from one of the vans. It's a total mystery to me where all the stuff went. I lost my personal filing cabinet—and I'm talking about one of those tall metal cabinets with four deep drawers—which was full of films and photos and rare theater programs from years gone by and other irreplaceable items that I had collected. All gone. I was devastated. No explanation was ever given and none of it was ever recovered. The accounts department fared no better. They piled all their paperwork into a taxi, which they never saw again.

Paul was the one who, the previous year, had come up with the word "Apple" for their new corporation, basing it on the first letter of the alphabet: "A is for Apple, like kiddies' alphabet blocks. Simple and nice and starting at the beginning." He said it would be easy to remember, while John's take was that the image was both pagan and arcane with its connotations of forbidden fruit, as in Adam and Eve and the Garden of Eden. But they all loved the pun on Apple Corp. "Apple core, get it?" John said, laughing wildly.

Paul liked that so much he wanted to call the company Apple Core; but was told he couldn't; it had to be a properly designated corporation. Some hippie designers were brought in and they came up with artwork depicting an old-fashioned variety of Cox's orange pippin, all rosy red, green and yellow, which everyone loved because it was so friendly and nice, the kind of apple you'd find stuffed into your Christmas stocking. Initially, this logo was used on things for the Apple shop and for the notepaper. It was all very relaxed and harmonious but apparently not very businesslike. Ron Kass and the lawyers explained that the Beatles had to copyright the name and trademark in order to make it the consistent Apple symbol anywhere in the world, or they ran the risk of being copied without legal redress.

Alan Aldridge and Gene Mahon, from the Beatles' new advertising agency, declared that they would come up with the ultimate apple, an apple with meaning, an apple that said APPLE, just as Coca-Cola said "Coke" anywhere on the planet. For months, they came in with pictures of apples, paintings of apples, photos of apples of every hue, and apples placed on a variety of colored backgrounds. But none of them had that WOW! factor.

When the English Apple Growers Association launched National Apple Week, Paul immediately saw that as a rare marketing opportunity.

"Yeah, we're Apple, so let's promote ourselves as well," he said enthusiastically.

About this time, an almost unknown Welsh singer named Mary Hopkin had also been recommended to him by the famous model, Twiggy, who had first seen her performing some months earlier on *Opportunity Knocks* on television. When he telephoned her at home in Wales and said, "This is Paul McCartney," she was so overwhelmed that she dropped the receiver and shouted to her mother to come and talk. Mary's shyness was one of her lovely features, like her long blond hair, straight from a fairy story, and her pure voice. Paul called her down to London, auditioned her singing six of her whimsical, pretty folk songs in Dick James's studios in New Oxford Street, and like everyone who heard it, fell in love with her incredible voice. That was when I filmed her and Paul singing "Blackbird" to an acoustic guitar, which we used in the PR film we showed in Los Angeles.

Paul found "Those Were the Days" for Mary and brought her back to London to record it at Abbey Road. It was decided that we would make a film to promote the record. One hot summer's day in early August when I was filming Mary down by the folly in the green wilderness at the end of Paul's garden, Robert Fraser, who was commissioned by Paul to buy paintings for him, dropped by with a special painting, a Magritte entitled *Le Jeu de Mourre*, in which a green apple filled the canvas. On being told that Paul was down in the wilderness with us, as a surprise, Robert left the picture propped up against a vase on a table in the dining room and slipped away. When Paul came indoors from the brightness of the garden, he saw this cool green apple, almost glowing in the shade of the room. It was a magic moment. They had found their apple.

♈

All the literature on the Beatles states that EMI refused to release the catalogue number Apple 1. History has it that "Hey Jude" was the first Apple release, with no catalogue number, and "Those Were the Days" was Apple 2. This isn't so. The truth is far more interesting.

Harrisons was the company who did the EMI labels. They had endless problems with fixing the exact color of the Apple logo. One of the printers, a good, solid English craftsman who took a pride in his work, came up with a solution. He showed us a superior new printing press, which was really a forerunner of a laser ink-jet machine, and was used for luxury, hand-operated work. After fiddling around a while, he came up with some near-perfect blanks, with no label information on them.

"That looks lovely, great, it's perfect," Paul said, and passed the labels around.

"Right, then," said the printer. "Where's your first record?"

Beatles looked at each other and muttered among themselves for a bit because they didn't have one ready for this momentous occasion. However, it so happened that it was Maureen's twenty-second birthday on August 4, and Ron Kass got absurdly excited over the idea of doing something really special for her. He telephoned his friend Sammy Cahn in Hollywood and got him to rewrite the lyrics to "The Lady Is a Tramp" so it related to Ringo and Maureen. Nobody thought Sammy would do it, but he did. Then he amazed us by calling Sinatra and asking him to record it. Off they went to Capitol Studios, in the Capitol Tower in Hollywood. The finished tape was air-couriered to Ron to be mastered. (Frank, a fan of Beatles songs, was to include versions of "Blackbird" and "Yesterday" and "Something" in his stage act.)

Meanwhile, our printer chum at Harrisons had run off a single label that read: "The Lady is a Tramp," by Frank Sinatra. I'm not sure if it said "Happy Birthday, Maureen" or not. We took the master to EMI's factory for a test and Apple 1 was pressed, both sides the same. There was a big party and with due ceremony the record was played. It was quite something. Then Ron ordered the master stampers crushed. The tape was cut up and destroyed.

Ringo gave the one and only copy in the world to Maureen, and she's dead now. I don't know where Apple 1 is these days, but it is an incredibly rare object, a record collector's Holy Grail.

On August 30 we launched Apple Records. True to the spirit of the whole Apple ethos, I gave myself a "field" promotion to head of promotion. There was nobody else with my experience, probably nobody else in the entire industry. I had done it from the start, when we first came down to London when no such job existed. On "The First Day Of Apple" all the media got a box full of cheer labeled, OUR FIRST FOUR. This was a presentation pack of four records, two of which became chart-toppers: "Hey Jude"; "Those Were The Days"; "Sour Milk Sea", which George wrote and produced for Jackie Lomax; and "Thingummybob" by the Black Dyke Mills Band, backed by "Yellow Submarine." And, a friendly touch, typical of the Beatles, as in a Christmas stocking, there were apples and oranges, some nuts and some gold chocolate money.

For some reason, Sandie Shaw, who was an established singer, rushed out her version of "Those Were the Days"—how this happened I don't know—but many thought she could have cast a damper on Mary's party. Instead of saying, "Ours is best," Paul put out ads that said, "Listen to Sandie's, listen to Mary's, then buy the one you like best." Fortunately, everyone preferred Mary's version. Her single shot rapidly up the charts to number one. Within four months, it sold four million copies worldwide. All four records were simultaneously released in more than thirty countries worldwide. It was all a great deal of work, with few of us to do it, but it got done. The gold chocolate coins were very soon replaced with the crash of gold, real gold, pouring into Apple's coffers. Apple Records was a very successful company and made a great deal of money.

The one that gave me the most pleasure to promote was "Hey Jude." Definitely! The reaction was unbelievable. It was the first Beatles single on Apple and just to go along with the very first advance package for the bright new company was wonderful. The BBC had recently started Radio One, a station that played nonstop pop for at least eight hours a day. It was the first time that we'd had that kind of radio access to the public and I'd found myself walking around with boxes of "Hey Jude," giving away about one hundred advance copies instead of the more usual ten. More importantly, it was also the first long single that had ever been out. It was about seven minutes and everybody thought that the deejays would just fade it, after about three minutes, never mind getting to the repetitive "La la la la" bit at the end. But right from the launch date, everyone played the whole thing.

Mary Hopkin's first album, *Postcard*, was a fun promo example. Billy Butlin, owner of the Butlin's holiday camps our little gang had gone to with our families as kids and where Ringo played with Rory Storm, ran the restaurant at the top of the Post Office Tower. It revolved, and as you ate you could watch London unfold in a magnificent panorama. The first time Paul had gone, shortly after the restaurant first opened, he was still living at the Asher's house in Wimpole Street. Dr. Asher decided he wanted the full guided tour and arranged for the entire family to go, including Paul.

Sometime later I was sitting in the restaurant, having dinner with a girlfriend, when Bobby Butlin, Sir Billy's son, came over to my table and told me all about Paul's earlier visit. He said, "If there's anything I can ever do for you, or Paul, or Apple, let me know." When we launched "Postcard" the question of a location for the launch party arose. Paul said, "Hey Tone? Do you think by any chance they would let us have the Post Office Tower restaurant?"

I acted nonchalant and said, "Oh, I dunno. Hang on and I'll have a word with them." I picked up the phone, quickly made the arrangements. Paul looked at his watch and said, "Great. Tell you what. Why don't we do some location scouting?" So we all went off to lunch at the Tower. We had a smashing time, and suitably oiled, Paul and I decided to have a race down the stairs to the door. It was a very stupid idea, especially after a big lunch. There are some photos somewhere of us lying at the bottom gasping for breath and probably trying to light a cigarette.

The launch party for "Postcard" was marvelous, with a really good turnout of rock stars. Jimi Hendrix came and Brian Jones and Donovan, as well as Mary's future husband, Tony Visconti. I was going out with Mary at the time but he fancied her too, and eventually they got married. He would later produce Mary, David Bowie, T Rex, Lou Reed and loads of other stars.

There was no doubt Apple Music Publishing was seriously successful but, much to the confusion of many hard-working people in the industry, Terry Doran was appointed managing director. Terry was Brian's old partner in his car company—a car dealer with no experience whatsoever in the music industry and even less in publishing. But he was into music, as were most of Brian's crowd from Liverpool and, given the timing, he couldn't go wrong. Though he did make some silly decisions—such as selling George Harrison's song catalogue off to Doris Day's son, Terry Melcher, who produced the Byrds for CBS. The Beatles had been introduced to Melcher through Derek Taylor, among whose clients were the Beach Boys and the Byrds. To counteract his lack of industry knowledge, Terry hired Mike Berry, a former assistant at Sparta Music Publishing to do the copyrights and offer advice.

The writers we signed were fantastic. Many were big behind-the-scenes talent who did not become household names but nevertheless wrote commercially and well. Gallagher and Lyle were both great writers but Graham Lyle was probably the luckier. He became one of the biggest songwriters in the world because he wrote hits for Tina Turner in her heyday. The Family was signed as a band. Jim Cregan, Rod Stewart's guitar player and co-writer for many years was signed, as were Steve Miller; Dr. John; Tony Ashton of Ashton, Gardner and Dyke and numerous others.

Apple Records, under the brilliant and experienced Ron Kass, flew from its inception to survive in a tough field for some eight years. One of Ron's first tasks when he was hired was to buy back George's catalogue from Terry Melcher. On the downside there was resistance to poor old Jackie Lomax. We tried and tried. The material was great but we just couldn't get it to fly. The big image at the time was Jim Morrison, so, in modern-day business parlance, that's where we "positioned" him: the moody genius with the great voice. We even brought in Justin de Villeneauve, who was Twiggy's manager and beau, to manage him. We had super production by George Harrison. It looked good, sounded good—and didn't work. Apple's product was licensed through EMI and maybe some wires got crossed occasionally. They worked on what appealed to them, but went slow on most other records. Ultimately, all they were really interested in was the Beatles because their records jumped off the shelves. It was very much a case of "We like this, we don't like that, when's the new Beatles LP coming out?"

Paul went through his late adolescence after he broke up with Jane. Previously, he and Jane had small dinner parties or went to the theater, or occasionally he might have gone to a club. But immediately after Jane and he split up, he was in one every night. His catch-up period lasted about six months—but what a six months. Then, suddenly he sickened of it. He flew to New York to stay with Linda, not in an expensive hotel, but in her small, two-room walk-up off Lexington Avenue. Yorktown was a safe and cosmopolitan district three blocks from Central Park and the Metropolitan Museum of Art. It was easy to hop on and off the subway to Harlem, or to wander into Irish bars and listen to music. Linda showed Paul where she shopped for clothes, in Goodwill, or thrift stores. He bought an ex-Vietnam combat jacket and a herringbone tweed overcoat that he wore for years. Paul loved the sense of freedom, and for ten days they ate in little German and Italian restaurants and hung out. Paul admired the way that Linda looked after her child. He would lie on the couch and watch while she fed Heather with real food and not take-out. "She had a wonderful maternal instinct," he said. "I suppose in a way I was remembering how my own mum used to look after us."

Paul returned home after the ten days, but couldn't settle. Casual flings no longer held any charm for him. As the nostalgic smells of autumn filled the air and the leaves started to turn to gold, Paul quietly told me that he had asked Linda to fly over and join him. He missed her and had spent long hours every day talking to her on the phone in New York. He wanted to see if they could make a go of it. Paul wasn't really a womanizer at heart and was burnt out by the almost deranged chaos of the groupie-scruffs period. He felt ready to settle down, to get some normality into his life.

Linda arrived while Paul was going through a particularly intensive period in the studio with the others, working on the *White Album.* Mal collected her from the airport and dropped her off at Cavendish Avenue, telling her to give Paul a call at the studio if she needed anything. Linda walked into the house, tired from the trans-Atlantic flight, to find Martha running wild, dog hair and dog crap everywhere because Paul had gotten rid of the scruffs who walked Martha, and he had no time himself. There was no food, just a carton of stale milk. Linda was amazed that this man, who could have bought up the entire food hall in Harrods, had nothing at all to eat and lived in such squalor, with a minuscule refrigerator instead of the big American ones she had been used to, and a television set that barely worked. She telephoned the studio and got me on the line. I said, "Hey, shall I get Paul?" She told me not to disturb Paul if he was working, but she was going to clean up the pigsty.

"I'd love to see you, Tony," Linda added. "And if you come, would you pick up some dog food, milk and some coffee?" It wasn't the first time I'd been asked to transport groceries around town, or the last. And Linda was nice. She didn't treat people like they were there to work for her because of her relationship with Paul, as Yoko did with John. The comparison is unfair anyway because Linda was warm, funny, and talented. She also organized Paul's life which even he said needed organizing badly. His house was a tip from the minute Jane left, to when Linda turned up. Previously, Paul had invited people like Nico the blond druggy singer from the Velvet Underground to stay. People like her never helped out. Being a star and OD'ing was all they ever did. Like a lot of stars, they used to spout crap about equality, but someone else always had to pick up the pieces, the clothes, the mess. People like that who mistake success for talent, or are just arrogant and selfish and lazy by nature, will never change, something Paul came to appreciate when he saw how grounded Linda was. He stopped inviting hangers-on to stay. Linda sent for her daughter and the two of them were never to live permanently in America again. Paul and Linda closed ranks and the front door on their private lives.

26

John and Yoko's *Two Virgins* album evolved from their conviction that everything they did, from their first lovemaking, to the first argument, to their first boiling of an egg, was important art. In the cause of important art everything they did had to be chronicled, documented, filmed, taped, the dots joined up and colored in carefully—with their tongues sticking out to show concentration and focus.

My contribution to the cause started on a quiet Saturday afternoon in late September or early October when I was gently dozing in bed. The phone rang. It was John.

"Hey, Tone, can you do us a favor? We're up at Montagu Square. It's not far from you, is it?" I agreed that it was close. "Well, can you bring us a couple of bottles of milk?"

In those days I had one of those miniature Honda monkey motorbikes. Lots of people, including Twiggy, had one, finding them ideal for whizzing around town. I got dressed and was soon zipping up Park Lane, looking to buy milk. A deli was open; I bought the milk and was soon chaining the little bike to the railings in Montagu Square. John opened the door to the flat, took the milk, and shuffled about a bit. I waited.

"Uh, Tone," he said. "While you're here, could you set up the camera for us? I want to . . . uh . . . you know about cameras, don't you? 'Cos we want to . . . uh . . . could you set it up in that room there and get the light right and everything to . . . uh . . . and all that stuff . . . uh . . . how do you use the timer?"

"You want to use a timer?"

"Yes . . . uh . . . like to take pictures and stuff later." He smiled. "You know, later on," he said meaningfully. I took hold of the camera and talked him through it.

"Well, you push that back to there, do this there, push this button and then this makes this noise and then you do it again." John watched intently.

"All right, Tone, thanks very much, I think I've got it," he said. "Thanks for the milk." And off I went on my little monkey bike.

Next day, Sunday afternoon, gently dozing, the phone rang again.

"John here. Could you pop round for a chat? And could you bring some more milk? And while you're at it, could you bring some coffee?"

It wasn't as easy finding milk and coffee back then in the West End on a Sunday afternoon, but eventually I succeeded. When I arrived, I handed John the milk and a jar of Nescafé.

"By the way," John said, "could you take the film out of the camera?"

I did, while he watched me intently, so he would know how to do it next time.

"Uh, Tone, you know when you've got some dodgy pictures . . . uh . . . you know the sort of thing, like . . . uh . . . page-three nudies . . . well, how do you get them developed? Where do they get them done?"

These were obviously the "later on" pictures.

"Well, you don't want to take them to Boots the Chemist," I said. "You take them to Sky labs in Soho."

"Do you know them there?" John asked tentatively.

"Yeah, of course. We get everything done there, like album covers."

John's face brightened. "Album covers? Right, then, Tone, so can you get these ones done? I mean, they're a bit risqué, you know. Don't let anyone see them, know what I mean?"

"Well, *someone* will have to see them, John," I said.

"Yeah, I know, but they're sort of our people there, aren't they? Like on the team. We can trust 'em, eh?"

I took the reel of film into Sky the next morning and asked if they could do a rush job on them. Back at the office, the phone rang. It was the developer at Sky.

"Ah, Tone, do you know what's on these pix?" I said I had no idea. "Oh," he said and seemed surprised. Then he started laughing. "I'll send 'em round in a brown envelope."

When the brown envelope came, I opened it and shuffled through the ten-by-eights, then shot them straight back into the envelope. John's idea of page-three

stuff was a wild understatement. These pictures were hairy. That's an unin-
tended pun, but in America they would call them muff shots.

John came into the office later that afternoon. Casually he asked, "Did you
sort out the pictures?"

"I did John, I certainly did," I said, handing the envelope over. That was the
last I heard of it until Jack Oliver came in a couple of days later, holding up two
large prints that he had just collected from Sky.

"This is going to be the cover of John and Yoko's new album," he said, handing one around for us to look at. We all fell about laughing. As I have said before,
Yoko was not a pretty sight, but she and John in the buff together were plain embarrassing. None of us thought they would go through with it, but we hadn't figured on "Art" having the last word, as it often does. A couple of days later, there
was a big pow-wow with me, John, Ron Kass, Jack and Derek Taylor to discuss
the new album. Unfortunately, before we got down to the discussion, John made
us sit and listen to the *Two Virgins* gibberish all the way through. Since most us
were stone-cold sober, it was probably against the Geneva Convention and when
Yoko's last scream died away, John got out the by now familiar album-sized prints
that we had already seen and had hysterics over, and cleared his throat.

"This pic is gonna be on the cover," he announced, "and this one here is
gonna be the back."

Ron Kass, who was Mr. Straight, Mr. Clean-Cut-American-from-Connecticut,
was so appalled he seemed to have gone into shock. Recovering some of his
composure, he said, "John, you can't do this!"

But John started giggling his head off, whether out of nerves, marijuana or
delight, I don't know, and said, "I don't care, Ron. I'm doing it anyway." The
meeting broke up soon after, because it was obvious that Yoko had made up
John's mind and nothing Ron or anyone could say would change it.

Sir Joseph Lockwood, the chairman of EMI, always took an interest in these
matters, and as soon as the pictures hit his desk, he almost had a heart attack.
He sent for Ron Kass immediately, for some kind of an explanation.

"Yes, John says it's art," Ron said weakly.

"He's determined, is he?" Sir Joe said.

"You could say that," Ron agreed.

"Well, I'll have to show it to the people at the pressing plant at Hayes," Sir
Joe said. "As you are no doubt aware, we have to deal with the shop stewards
and the unions, you know. Some of them can be very Bolshie. It's not as straightforward as John seems to think to print up this kind of obscenity."

But the unions and their view were nothing compared with Brother McCartney's reaction. Paul got to hear of it and then saw the photos. He had seven

thousand kinds of fits. He thought it was disgusting and was absolutely appalled that John was seriously intending to go through with it. Paul, of course, blamed Yoko's influence. He was bang on target. John had been very prudish before he met Yoko. Now he said she had released his inhibitions.

"Doesn't John realize that we're all in this together?" Paul said. "It might be him and Yoko, but people will say it's the Beatles who are out of their tree and getting into straight porn now."

Paul demanded an immediate meeting with Sir Joe, John and Yoko. It was a very uneasy gathering and I was surprised that John and Yoko, given their stubborn frame of mind at the time, attended. Sir Joe said he didn't think the pictures were obscene, he had seen much worse, an opinion which confused John and Yoko. They wanted to be seen as avant-garde and enfants terribles. Worse was to come. In his opinion, said Sir Joe, not mincing words, John and Yoko looked revolting. He agreed with Paul that the public's perception still was that the Beatles were nice kids who had made it to the big time. These pictures would blow that perception right out of the water. John grinned. Yoko squeezed his hand and closed her eyes.

In the end, as Sir Joseph knew, EMI was able to pull out when the brothers and sisters in the union at Hayes said they wouldn't touch the *Two Virgins* album cover with a barge pole, refusing to work on it point blank. Sir Joe called Ron with the good news.

"They said take it away, we're not doing it here. I'm afraid this means that while EMI will press the album, we are not able to handle the distribution of this record," he said, with deep satisfaction.

For Ron, it was not a case of "Say it ain't so, Joe." There wasn't a person at Apple who didn't think the album and cover were rubbish. But John, with Yoko goading him from the rear, wouldn't let it rest there. He nagged Ron ceaselessly until, in the end, Ron roped in Roy Silver, a friend of his who was the unusual combination of being a restaurateur and Bill Cosby's manager. Roy had a company called the Campbell Silver Cosby Corp. and a record company called Tetragrammaton, run by Arty Mogul and Greg Smith, with such groups as Deep Purple signed to them in the States. However, it was much more complicated than anyone realized; it always is. By innocently asking Roy Silver's help, Ron opened a hornet's nest because Tetra's own pressing and distribution was with the English record company, Track. Track in turn had a similar P & D deal with Polydor, which was part of Polygram—which was owned by EMI. In the end everybody, involved by weirdness of contractual obligation got involved in *Two Virgins;* and the problem was, since EMI had expressed the opinion that it was pornographic, the others didn't want to know.

Soon after, John arrived at the offices with a new idea that I suspect originated either from the large brown envelope that Sky had delivered his prints in, or quite possibly from the plain paper bag that dirty magazines left Soho porn shops in. Whatever it was, the plain brown wrapper from Soho was about to become art.

"Tone? I want to put the album out in a brown paper bag," was John's next less-than-earth-shattering pronouncement. "Oh, and one other thing—"

"What's that?"

Then as my heart sunk, John elaborated on his "best idea of all." He wanted to make a blue movie to package with the album. The two together would fit nicely in said paper bag, a grab bag of goodies that he was sure would have the record-buying public lining up in droves to purchase. Lining up exactly *where*, he didn't say, given that the distribution arrangement was dissolving.

Nevertheless, urged on by John's greater vision, we rented a great deal of expensive, very technical camera equipment from Cambridge Scientific, the people who shoot mosquitoes mating magnified four million times, or time-lapse flowers opening once a year on the floor of the Amazon basin, and now, John and Yoko. The high-speed cameras that shot ten thousand feet per second or whatever, were the size of refrigerators, all so John could catch his own erection, or the ideas he had in mind while his mind was elsewhere. Cambridge Scientific was so busy that I could only get the equipment on weekends, when they weren't using it themselves. When they said that, I wanted to laugh. It was like "something for the weekend, sir?" Why John needed such technical stuff, I'll never know. I asked him if it was really necessary.

"Yeah, I've read about it, see," he said vaguely.

I was given the job of editing the soundtrack from the album to John's high-speed film even though I told him I wasn't a high-speed expert. In the end, I got in Ray Millichope of *Monty Python* fame from the BBC, who understood something of these matters; at any rate, he nodded wisely when I told him what had to be done. We did it, but almost predictably, like Yoko's "You Are Here" event, the film was not aired. And what was on this expensive high-speed film? John Lennon's *face*. I have heard recently that Yoko had released it somewhere or another. I often wonder what the credits on it are.

I used to dread taking John and Yoko's arty stuff into radio stations and asking them to play it. For me, it was a bad experience because it was unplayable and unlistenable. Who can you recommend it to? John was on at me to get in there and plug it. So I thought I'd better give it my best shot. The reaction was a bored, "Why are you bringing this crap to us?" At first I argued with radio producers about it, though not on a very artistic level. I even heard myself saying, "Because he pays my wages. That's why!" It was so embarrassing.

27

Probably a sense of being alienated from the world got John interested in
heroin originally. As far as Yoko was concerned, if you spout all this magical,
healing, antiwar, be kind to everybody, all-seeing, all-caring, all-macrobiotic
stuff, being pregnant on heroin would seem to be the last thing she would need.
And how does all that stuff equate with shooting up smack? How does all that
spiritual pontificating gel with the teaspoon and the needle, unless you're a
fraud? Hunter Thompson once said that if you live with someone who is using
the spike, you come to terms with it yourself or split up. So, psychologically it
looked more and more like it might have been a power thing on Yoko's part to
draw John in closer to her and farther away from other people. An "It's you and
me against the world now, baby" feeling.

For us at Apple when we did wonder what was going on with John, it was
hard to see it any other way because John used to like life. He used to like to get
on a roll. Laugh, eat and drink. Steak sandwiches were his favorite. Any time of
the day it was steak sandwiches. But he'd eat anything tasty: proper breakfasts,
an old-fashioned fry-up, pie and chips, fish and chips, fried chicken, a roast
dinner on a Sunday, Chinese food, curry, spaghetti Bolognese. Everything. Then
he met Yoko, grew his beard, and it was every variety of peace possible: hair
peace, bed peace, bag peace. From Irish navvy's food, he went to heroin and

macrobiotics. I think if Yoko had said it was spiritual to snort bean curd instead of eat it John would have done it.

We all thought that Yoko's way of showing her power was her ability to spend as much of John's or Apple's money as she wished, whenever she wished. This was demonstrated by her wasteful caviar phase. It was totally out of whack with what they were spouting about the world, and starvation and peace. John had his beard and said he was Jesus so technically he should have made do with loaves and fishes; but Yoko was too crass. She'd step out of John's office on the ground floor and autocratically send the office boy—an American student named Richard DiLello—down to Fortnum and Mason's every day for some of their finest Beluga in that big white enamel pot with the special lid, and the chefs would start making toast in the kitchen. John wasn't keen on caviar, but they'd ignore the hot toast and feed each other a couple of spoonfuls, get stoned and leave the rest of the pot sitting on the desk with the two spoons sticking out, Or they'd go to a bag-in and forget to put it in the special fridge. Five hundred pounds' worth, left to rot. Thousands of pounds' worth of lovely caviar went to waste because Princess Yoko could get a fresh pot the next day. It infuriated the Apple staff. We used to mutter, "So much for those sit-ins, and bed-ins and feeding the starving millions." We failed to see how you could stop the war in Vietnam by sending a lad down the road to Piccadilly for caviar from posh Fortnum's. *Hair! Peace! Caviar!* It didn't play. But it didn't bother Yoko, now that she had landed the big fish. She probably thought: "Let them eat toast." It was Yoko's way of saying, "You minions get paid thirty pounds a week—and I am richer than any of you now." She would never have seen the irony in James Bond's comment in *Casino Royale*: "The problem with ordering caviar is not that you can't get enough caviar, but that you can't get enough toast."

When George came in, he'd survey John 'n' Yoko feeding each other like a couple of cooing love birds, and say cynically, "Yeah! Right on! But don't leave the lid off yer caviar."

We didn't see much of George because he was mostly holed up in Kinfauns, his home in Esher. I think he had seen the writing on the wall and was looking to the future where his own compositions would be every bit as important as John and Paul's. This was the period when he wrote and produced a classic, "While My Guitar Gently Weeps," on which Eric Clapton played. The song was selected for the *White Album.* They had started the process of selecting the songs in Kinfaun's by making twenty-three demos on George's four-track Ampex mobile machine.

Many of the songs were wonderfully fresh and original in concept, like John's "Revolution" and Paul's "Blackbird"; two others, written by John, "Sexy

Sadie" and "Dear Prudence," were satires based on their experiences in India. Yoko's constant presence in Esher was unexpected and an irritant, but after the notorious night of May 19 when she'd first spent the night at Kenwood, she and John were like Siamese twins.

The Beatles started working at Abbey Road—some of which was filmed by me, for the first time, capturing shades of things to come with Yoko still in constant attendance.

With all this chaos in our lives, it was asking for trouble when Derek Taylor, the press officer, continued to encourage his open-house policy, with half the world dropping into Apple. Cases upon cases of spirits and crates of beer flowed into the press office making it like his old Fleet Street local, an arty El Vinos. Not everyone drank; many smoked dope and hung out. Peter Asher and I tried our best to impose some kind of order, asking the girls in reception and the doorman to filter out the less-welcome callers. Among the less welcome was a young student named Richard Branson.

As I've said, it was another Richard by the name of Nixon who said, "There's no substitute for perseverance." Richard Branson, of course, would have been against everything Nixon stood for, but as far as perseverance was concerned, Branson put Nixon to shame.

I'm sure that Richard has mellowed with time, but in those early days he was a student geek whom no one could bear. He'd try to get in all the time, hoping to grab some contact with the Beatles and chatting with anyone who wasn't being too physical with him by helping him back out into Savile Row. Most annoying, but top marks for trying.

Richard hoped to interest the Fab Four in his student magazine. Well, sometimes, help comes from strange areas and it so happened that around this time, Yoko demanded her own office at Apple; that is, she asked that a desk and a chair be moved into John's office so she could sit side by side with him. She wanted to learn the ropes. There weren't any ropes to learn, but Yoko wasn't to know that. You could see by the determined set of her jaw that by next Thursday— Friday at the latest—she would make a supreme bid for Apple power in the name of either the people, art, or Yoko Inc.

Branson happened to make it past reception one day and caught John and Yoko. John, being quite sociable, would have a word with anyone. Despite inner groans and sinking hearts from the staff who would have to get rid of these people, he would say, "Come on in, have a chat," and in the cranks, the unwashed, the loonies, and the others, would come. John, bless him, even held the door open for Richard and the young student shot in and, showing John a copy of his rag, asked if John would answer a few questions.

"Sure," John agreed affably.

Almost unable to believe that he was getting this interview, which in fact was quite a scoop, Richard followed John around for some hours, asking earnest questions until he had enough material. Bolstered by this, he got a bit brave and asked John for a song. They stopped moving.

"A *song?*" John said, confused, thinking that Richard meant him to sing something live for his entertainment.

Richard explained that he wanted a tape that he would press up and give away as a freebie record with the magazine. John loved the word "free"—he even used to stop off at reception and ask hopefully if any free gifts had come in that morning—but with Richard being so eager and persistent, John began to panic a bit and said, "Oh all right. We'll sort something out for you." By then, Yoko had had enough of John's attention being taken up by someone else for so long and she got the heavies to propel the fledgling boy wonder outside.

From then on, a serious game of persistence set in. We were plagued by this student who wanted a song from the Beatles to give away with his mag. Finally, when it was obvious that John was avoiding him, Richard insisted on having a meeting with Ron Kass, who, in turn, insisted on me handling it. I explained that we did give away similar flimsy records to magazines like *FAB* and such, but they were organized on a commercial level.

"You can't expect to have a Beatles record for nothing," Ron had said. "They're under contract to . . . it's over to you, Tone."

"EMI and Apple," I told Richard. He was very upset and played the children's ace.

"But John promised," he said, bottom lip trembling, pushing his square frames back up his nose. "John's a Beatle isn't he? All he has to do is give me a tape and I'll return it. It's not like I'm selling it or anything. I told John this was a freebie."

"There's no such thing as a give-away Beatles record," I said. "We would have to pay EMI royalties on it."

But Richard Branson wouldn't take no for an answer. A reign of "that student's here again" terror began. The whole building was put on a "Branson watch." We were all vigilant, except for Derek Taylor, whose office was stacked so high with cases of booze he couldn't see the door. Branson was in, but Ron Kass threw him out again, saying, "We can't have this invasion on a daily basis." John himself was now in such terror that he threatened to sack anyone who let strangers near him.

On October 18, 1968, Sergeant Norman Pilcher, together with his trusty hound and several uniformed policemen, knocked on John's basement door at

Montagu Square. Eventually, John staggered to the door, looking dazed and un-kempt. He'd deliberately kept the police waiting while he telephoned his lawyer. He was late for a press conference at Apple and suddenly genuinely alarmed as he realized the seriousness of his situation. He gazed blindly at the seven burly policemen and the one policewoman—brought along for Yoko—who were standing on the doorstep. Pilcher handed John a warrant.

"Right lads," he said officiously. His boys in blue burst in on the double; one of Pilcher's notorious drug raids was on.

Neither John nor Yoko should have been surprised, but they were. Heroin is like that—it can make time stand still. Only a couple of days earlier they had been warned about a raid by our old chum, Don Short, who was the chief show-biz correspondent on the *Daily Mirror*. In a frenzy, John had rounded up Pete Shotton to clean up the flat. Pete went reluctantly because his feelings had been deeply wounded by the arrogant way John and Yoko treated him, calling upon him to clean up the pigsty of an apartment when the mess got to be too much for them. The final straw was when he was expected to do Yoko's laundry. He had said to John: "John, it's me, Pete—remember?" before storming off.

Nevertheless, he was there when John needed him. They'd gone through the flat like a whirlwind, getting rid of the traces of every drug. Pete was carrying out piles of trash when Yoko turned up. "Get rid of him!" she screamed at John. Pete left. If he had remained, perhaps he would have found the various small caches of marijuana around the place that he and John had missed, particularly the larger amount hidden in an old film can under the sink which Sergeant Pilcher and "Sniffer" Willy discovered in the raid, or so it was asserted.

John said it wasn't his, he didn't even know it was there. Possibly it had be-longed to Jimi Hendrix, who had also once lived there; but the favorite theory was that it had been planted. This wasn't too far-fetched. In his zeal to reduce the country's drug problem, Pilcher was later caught planting evidence and served some time in prison. John and Yoko were formally charged with possession and of willful obstruction due to the few moments John had spent flushing some drugs down the loo before answering the door. John was allowed to telephone Neil at Apple HQ and the news went round the offices like wildfire. By the time they were marched out to the waiting police cars, looking wan and scared, the press had arrived and flashbulbs popped. At the police station, to save Yoko, who was pregnant, more grief, John took the rap. A few hours later Yoko was rushed to the hospital with an imminent miscarriage.

We were amazed when Richard Branson turned up at Apple one day toward the end of November with two suits. One was Charlie Levison, a top man at Har-bottle and Lewis, and the other suit was Branson's father, who just happened to be a judge. Harbottle and Lewis—made famous by Goons fans, who would call them Bluebottle and Lewis—also happened to be Apple's lawyers. While some of us hovered in the background with Goon voices, saying, "You'll never get out of here alive with a free song! Here comes that student with Bluebottle and Lewis, quick run before we all get deaded," in the reception area, without a glimmer of a smile Levinson explained to Ron Kass and me that young Richard had gone ahead and planned the new edition of his student magazine based on John Lennon's promise of a free record. He had ordered extra copies and, despite being still at boarding school, had worked very hard—after finishing his Latin prep no doubt—at raking in more advertising because this was going to be his huge, multimillion sale edition.

We all thought that this seventeen-year-old public schoolboy was threatening to take John Lennon, the Apple Corporation and the Beatles to court for substantial damages with our own lawyers. There was utter disbelief. We *were* deaded.

John walked in through the front door in the middle of this row. Yoko had just had a very public miscarriage in her fifth month and obviously John was still anxious and upset. He glared at Charlie Levison.

"Whose solicitor are you anyway?" he demanded. Levison's reply went unheard because John suddenly lost it. I don't know where he got it from—maybe he had come fresh from the hospital from seeing Yoko and had it in his pocket—but with a manic expression on his face, he stuffed a tape into Richard's hand. "There's your fucking tape, a John Lennon Productions production. Get out and don't ever come back again," he snarled.

Levison said, "But what's it a tape of?"

"Our baby's heartbeat and eventual miscarriage," John said, stalking off, leaving us stunned. There wasn't a lot anyone could add to that. Throats were cleared, feet were shuffled, watches were checked and the legal conference fizzled out. It was a strange day. A week later, John's trial came up. He pleaded guilty and was fined £150. A small amount, perhaps, but taking no responsibility for their own actions, he and Yoko said Sergeant Pilcher had cost them their baby. John's drug's bust was also to have endless repercussions when he decided to go and live in America.

I have no idea what happened to that tape or whether it was used in any way. Given Richard's admitted penchant for dressing up as a woman, maybe Ron Kass should have commissioned another version of "The Lady is a Tramp" for the young Branson. Now, that also would have been a rarity. Those were strange times indeed.

Stranger times were to come. When George had been in San Francisco some months previously, wandering around in the Haight-Ashbury district in a daze, he'd met up with Ken Kesey and invited him to London. Ken and the Merry Pranksters had traveled America in Ken's psychedelic bus, driven by Neil Cassady, while doing the notorious Electric Kool-Aid Acid Tests. Unfortunately, the entire tribe took poor George up on his offer. They arrived with two Hells Angels, Frisco Pete and Billy Tumbleweed, and sixteen hangers-on. Ken did have the grace to contact George first, and he in his wisdom left us a note which, to paraphrase, read something like: *Hell's Angels arriving to stay at Apple. Let them hang out, be cool, don't give them a hard time, but don't let them take over the gaff—Love and Peace, George.*

We scarcely had time to absorb the contents of the note, which was passed from hand to hand, with rising derision, when the bikers did indeed roar in at the end of November on two gleaming Harley Davidsons they had air-freighted in at Apple's expense. Ten more arrived in taxis and swarmed into the offices like locusts. They scattered throughout the premises to check us out, and the accommodation. Deciding on the entire top floor, they started to carry their goods and chattels up the stairs, and there wasn't a thing we could do about it. Many people might think it cool to have Ken Kesey there, but at the end of the day, Apple was still a work environment.

We'd barely gotten used to them stomping all over the place, when a family of American hippies arrived with their four children, who ran riot and added to the noise and confusion. It was like a scouting party of old, where the men went on ahead to stake claim to the land and the tribe followed behind. They spent all day smoking dope, making hash cakes and drinking their weird 150-proof whiskey-egg nog concoction which was mixed by the lethal gallon jug using the amply supplied Apple liquor store. Shortly, Derek Taylor could see over the top of his diminishing stack of spirits, but wisely, he kept his head down.

From the start, the new arrivals were just a big interruption in the building and they scared the horses—not to mention the secretaries, who were terrified by them. They called them the Unwashed Pirates of Savile Row. Apple had their own Cordon Bleu chefs—two bright girls called Sally and Diana, who served three-course lunches at Apple every day, if you were there to enjoy it. The Pranksters took over the kitchens, raided the pantries, cooked huge hashcakes and trays of all-American hash brownies which the children guzzled, and eventually they drank Derek Taylor dry. Their washing was hung all over the fire escapes, until our grand offices in refined Mayfair resembled a tenement house in a Rio slum. The neighbors were horrified and started drumming up a petition. We'd only just gotten over the petition from the Baker Street residents which had led to the removal of the Fool's giant mural on the boutique wall, and now it looked as if a similar situation were about to arise.

Around this time, John and Yoko came up with the idea of a new label on Apple to be called Zapple. The original intention was to make this just for spoken-word albums. In fact, the first thing to be produced was to be John and Yoko's unfinished music; and then George's new electronic music. They also had a stoned wish list of other people they wanted to contribute material including Richard Brautigan and Allen Ginsberg—an eccentric American intellectual who lived in a flat above Indica, and who used to turn up and walk around Apple all the time. I think it was Ginsberg who had suggested we do his fellow beat poets, William Burroughs, and Jack Kerouac. Expanding the idea further, Zapple would put out some Charles Bukowski, Lawrence Ferlinghetti, and some old Lenny Bruce tapings.

Some of this got turned into songs. "Tomorrow Never Knows," the last track on *Revolver,* was written by John after he bought Timothy Leary's *Tibetan Book of the Dead* at Indica. He took it home to read, and the next day, in Abbey Road, I watched him write one of his masterpieces. As songwriters, both John and Paul could be remarkably fast. "Hey Jude" was written on Paul's drive down to see Cynthia and Julian when John walked out. It was recorded in one day. I've been with them when they sat around with nothing, then at the studio the very next morning, Paul would walk in with some perfect, polished songs tailored for the tone of the album they were working on. This would happen sometimes day after day. They were amazingly prolific.

When Kesey arrived on our doorstep, it was about the time that he had finished *One Flew Over the Cuckoo's Nest,* or maybe it was when it was just being published; but it was decided that he would also do a "Spoken Word" of *Cuckoo's Nest* and maybe write and record some new stuff for Zapple. He was given an expensive tape machine to work and an IBM Golfball typewriter, which at the time were brand new to the market. They were like gold dust, even hard to get for a Beatle, and which Derek Taylor had fought tooth and nail to acquire. Both tape recorder and the Golfball disappeared immediately, never to be seen again.

Meanwhile, Ken was practically in rags, and unwashed rags at that. He had come with no luggage whatsoever and looked as if he had gotten off the plane with what he stood up in. In my capacity as head of promotions, I was given the job of taking him off to Carnaby Street and getting him kitted out so he could be put on show and be interviewed, photographed by the media and so on. With money no object, he soon got the knack of shopping. I can't say I blame him. It was all free, and Carnaby Street had some wonderful things to offer.

Christmas was a big event in the life of the Beatles. Each year until they had stopped touring they had put on a wonderful Beatles Christmas show at the Hammersmith Odeon that was always sold out a year ahead. They also released absolutely unique Christmas records every year strictly through their fan club. In addition, they always threw a marvelous Apple party. In the past, Brian had organized this, with caterers and special gifts, which he himself went to a great deal of trouble to choose. Come the day, shortly after the arrival of Kesey and friends, we were astonished to see John and Yoko walk in, dressed up as Mr. and Mrs. Christmas. They wandered around, going Ho Ho Ho and Yo-ko-ko, patting people on the head, doling out presents to staff, family of staff and loved ones and significant others. We all got lovely presents. I think I got a set of goblets that year. But, as it turned out, no dinner.

When it was time to sit down to lunch in the boardroom, and we all trooped in, we found the Merry Pranksters had already been there. They had smelled all the appetizing aromas drifting up from the kitchen and swooped down from their lair up on the top floor like vultures. The table had been stripped bare while all the present-giving was happening in another room. Our turkeys, stuffing, and plum duff were all gone, with only a few bones chucked under the table and a few crumbs of mince pies on plates to show what had been there. The Fab Four were mortified. They were still more or less normal and loved Christmas, but like the Grinch, the Merry Pranksters had stolen Christmas. They'd shredded the turkeys, drunk the champagne and port, scoffed everything.

This wasn't simply a case of a few laid-back hippies smoking a few doobies, sniffing the air and getting the munchies. It looked like a scene after a Viking raid on a village hall with some small barefoot urchins still crawling around on the huge table after the big guys had been hacking and tearing at the sumptuous food with hands, knives and axes. Most of the cutlery and glasses was unused so probably they'd just stuffed fists full of grub in their mouths and the rest in their pockets as they went. They swigged all the wine from the bottles. There was nothing left. This was before George and John and then Paul and some of the others at Apple went veggie, so there should have been enough turkeys and hams for an army. Sally and Diana were upset that their lavish, long-planned, carefully arranged gourmet Christmas banquet with crackers and candles and all the trimmings had been demolished. It looked like a battlefield.

The Merry Pranksters had ruined the whole event and now they were seriously drunk and mean. They threw up on carpets and insulted their hosts. Enough was enough and a few days later they were turfed out of the building by George who was very embarrassed and by Derek Taylor who also shouldered some of the blame. There was a bit of a skirmish and the "guard"—me and some other big lads—was called to help them out into Savile Row. A couple of pretty girls who had come over with them stayed on as personal assistants or secretaries. Pretty girls are pretty girls.

28

In many ways, the Beatles were a metaphor for the 1960s. London seemed to be doing amazingly well throughout that decade, a magnet for the youth and talent of the world. Music, fashion and fun all originated in the capital. Jobs were easy to come by, there were no dossers in the streets, there was a good feeling in the air; everything was fine, all of it underwritten by our manufacturing industries. It all seemed to implode with the turn of the decade. As the sixties gave way to the seventies, the fun left. It was like a carousel on a merry-go-round slowly grinding to a halt, with the music dying and the lights going dim.

In the wider scheme of things, I blamed the British prime minister, Harold Wilson, head of the Labour Party, and told him so. I couldn't understand why he had suddenly devalued the pound in 1967 when everything at home was booming. Things staggered along for a while, but a recession loomed. At the same time, his thought police took over. There were enough new regulations and red tape to tie up free enterprise for years. Licenses were brought in to regulate live music in pubs and public places. One minute Swinging London was like a giant theme park, the envy of the world, then they—Wilson and his gang—closed it down. It was as if they went out and stamped on it. Live music, cinemas, theaters, pirate radio stations, Carnaby Street, the Kings Road—everything that was fun about Britain got stamped on.

The Beatles had strong socialist convictions, as had most Liverpudlians, but we became convinced that this 'orrible little man with his smelly pipe was a Communist mole. We were depressed that in 1964, on the eve of the general election, Brian had even sent him a telegram, wishing him success. To make matters worse, he was also our local member of Parliament for Huyton in Liverpool. We felt cheated. I saw my chance to vent my feelings when I was invited on *Start the Week*, a morning radio magazine show presented by Melvin Bragg, and heard that my fellow guest would be Comrade Wilson, who was there to promote some kind of expo, which would put the oomph back into Swinging London. On air, I turned on him angrily.

"It's all gone. You've killed it off. You blew it. You can't just resurrect it when it's convenient."

He stopped sucking on his pipe and stared at me. He blustered a bit, but I said, "It's no good. You've done us in; you've wrecked the country. You're a pathetic, tawdry, horrible little man. Liverpool doesn't deserve you, let alone Britain." Shortly afterward, his party lost the next election; but the rot had already set in.

If Harold Wilson was the evil emperor who had brought down England and pushed it toward a gloomy era of strikes, the three-day working week, rising crime and sacks of uncollected garbage littering the streets, then Yoko Ono was thought of as the snake-haired Wicked Witch of the East who destroyed the Beatles.

When Yoko turned up she pushed the other three Beatles and their relationships with each other and with John to the limit. Northern working men simply didn't take their wives and girlfriends to work. Not only would it make them look stupid, it was also against the unwritten "pal's code." John, it seemed, suddenly didn't mind appearing stupid; he didn't appear to notice—or even care—that Yoko's constant presence was annoying, irritating and otherwise pissing off his friends. The Beatles came to one conclusion: he was either mad, or had been hypnotized. Yoko herself later insisted it was because John was so paranoid, he didn't want her out of his sight.

Whatever the truth, she was such a core of negativity that she sucked the air out of the room whenever she entered. She wanted to possess John and she was the one who was exceptionally jealous. She could not cope with the fact that John could love three other guys. The gradual erosion of the fun and trust that had been between the Beatles from the early days was like going through a divorce. You had to be there to see it happen, to understand how powerful the anger, hate and jealousy were, the emotions that surged around them. It was like being inside the pages of Tolkein. I was around them a great deal at this time, filming their daily activities, and saw the tensions building.

When John got the drift about how the others felt, instead of keeping Yoko away out of sensitivity for their feelings and out of concern for the group dynamics, he said, "I don't want to play with youse lot anymore." Paul desperately wanted things to work out. He was enormously patient. It was only his great love for John and for the whole Beatles thing that stopped it from blowing up sooner than it did. I remember the exasperation on his face away from the studio. At the time he *was* Abbey Road far more than John, who mostly kept away. John's input was minimal, except on his tracks, or the ones he featured on. George's input was pretty strong, but Paul was the most visible one, perhaps to the point of being overwhelming. Not in a nasty way, but just being creatively in the lead. I think this was because his personal life was very happy. John, newly obsessed with Yoko, should have been happy, but was exhausted and in torment. Looking for some release, he and George had even taking up chanting together.

I think after John and Yoko got busted together they got worse. Maybe as far as John was concerned, the reality of the Beatles splitting up, a plethora of crooks and silly deals, together with the public's absolute dislike of Yoko overwhelmed him. He was prone to wake up in a deep funk and ask: "Why am I doing this? This crap means nothing. What's it all about?"

From the moment Yoko was inflicted upon the Beatles, the atmosphere became grim. The previous autumn, Ringo had been the first to break. Yoko's constant, grating presence was behind it, but it was impossible to tell John anything. When Ringo returned from a break in the studio to find Paul—who could play many instruments well—experimenting on his drum kit, all his resentment and bottled-up insecurities surfaced, and he walked out. John and Paul were in a dilemma.

They asked my opinion. "If you want him back," I said, "then maybe you'll have to crawl a bit, you know, like, apologize." So John and Paul, cap in hand, went round to Ringo's house to plead with him to come back, but he refused. He disappeared on a holiday to Sardinia with Maureen. He always struck me as the "grown-up" Beatle, perfectly happy with his more sophisticated movie friends, like Peter Sellers whose substantial house he had bought, and on planning a movie career. If anyone could do without the other Beatles, it was Ringo.

Eventually, he did return to the fold. The boys were so delighted they got Mal to decorate his drum kit with garlands of flowers. Nothing was said. Ringo came into the studio and simply started drumming again. For a while at least, everything was harmonious.

Paul suggested that they needed to start over again, to try to recapture whatever it was that had drawn them so closely together as more than friends—as brothers—for so many years. They had been through so many shared experiences; they clicked, their music clicked. "Back to basics," Paul said. "I think we should play live again. It grounded us."

John agreed with Paul, and for a moment, there was a brief period of nostalgia as they talked of some of the fantastic moments they had shared. Nodding away at John's shoulder like a marionette, Yoko kept butting in, describing some of *her* live performances. Gritting their teeth in the cause of harmony, the others ignored her. Unfortunately, the new way was to be anything but back to basics.

Alexis Mardas probably contributed to a lot of John's problems and insecurity by coming up with expensive, artistic, and futuristic ideas that didn't, couldn't work. Because his ideas were challenging in an unproven way, Yoko and John became his champions, but John ended up by being lumped in with Alex's failed inventions. The now-legendary crunch came when Alex said he could design a futuristic state-of-the-art twenty-four-track studio in the basement of Apple HQ in Savile Row, when the most that existed then was eight-track. John believed him and Alex was authorized to order whatever he required to achieve this miracle of technology on which to record their back-to-basics album, *Get Back*.

When John got enough personal clout, he always vested his money and his beliefs in people like Alex instead of talking to people who knew what they were talking about, like George Martin. Alex should have just read his copy of *Future Electronics and Toys Monthly* and kept schtumm. Instead he spewed other people's inventions as if they were his own, but worse, he said he could do it "*even more* better!*"

George wandered in the day before they were due to start recording and was stunned into silence when he saw Alex wiring up twenty-four tiny individual speakers and hanging them all over the basement walls. The equipment Alex said he had designed and built himself was still in boxes all over the basement floor, and was clearly labeled with the manufacturer's name from Germany. Ringo and Paul had always been skeptical of Alex; now George saw him for what he was. The more John protested that his little Greek necromancer was a genius, the more they saw John as deluded or mad. Eight-track mixing desks had to be hired in a hurry, but the basement studio was a mess, and not soundproofed, with the heating system thumping away in the corner. They couldn't work there and ended up back at Abbey Road.

As usual, the sessions were filmed as a promotional tool, with Denis O'Dell and me in charge of filming. During the studio period, while they recorded the tracks over several weeks, things were very tense. Yoko was even more of a permanent fixture at John's shoulder, kissing him, nibbling at his ear, whispering to him. She even went to the bathroom with him, and everyone would look at each other and wonder. They seem glued together. Things came to a head when Yoko started making musical suggestions.

It's quite conceivable that Yoko wasn't aware that she was interfering or in the way. For the most part, her behavior was unforgivable, but she might have just been ignorant. She just plonked herself down, either on John's amp or on a chair at his side and joined in without being invited. It infuriated the others, and the more it did, the more aggressive she became.

Almost every photograph taken at the time shows Yoko as John's shadow. The Beatles would lean out of a window to be photographed, and Yoko would be there, with the hint of a triumphant smile, pushing her way to the front, in a large hat that filled the frame. John would be seated on a chair playing guitar, Yoko beside him, and you'd suddenly see that the entire time her arm was outstretched, her hand resting against his back, ready to prod, to command. I don't know how she snowed him so totally.

She and John used to whisper away in their corner, with a completely different, us-against-the-world perspective to everyone. I know they did, because filming quietly on the sidelines, I heard. Having discussed life and its ins and outs and meanings, and worked out that *it all means nothing,* John and Yoko didn't want to, couldn't possibly, give the edifice of the Beatles any credit, or indeed any respect. She wanted it to be a cooperative, with her included. John wanted it to be both a co-op to assuage Yoko, and a rock band to assuage his inner child, his inner Elvis. Around a Beatle meeting table, or around a Beatle rehearsal and recording or writing situation, that kind of dichotomy wasn't going to work.

It was probably in retaliation for Yoko's constant presence that Paul started to bring Linda into the studio sometimes. Or perhaps, in a nonconflictive way, he wanted John to understand the problems he caused by having Yoko around. But if that was Paul's plan, it backfired. Linda was so low-key no one could object to her presence. She took pictures, but she didn't get in the way and she certainly didn't venture an opinion about their work. She was relaxed and intelligent, with a sense of humor. She has been accused of being pushy. I never observed this in her. She was always pleasant, never in the way. Yoko demanded service as if we were her personal servants. If she were our employer, the one who paid our wages, there might—just—have been an excuse. But she abused her position as John's new girlfriend. She wouldn't accept that she wasn't a Beatle. She was actively encouraged in this by John. He expected everyone to treat her in the same

way as the entire Apple staff treated him. Everyone, whoever it was, had to do
her bidding. But John was always courteous and could be endearing and funny.
We came to hate Yoko all the more because she didn't have a very nice way of
asking for things. She would point at someone and demand quite imperiously,
"Get me a jar of caviar," or "Put my chair next to John's." Linda on the other
hand would smile nicely and ask politely for what she needed.

George always felt that he was seriously underappreciated. Although, as a unit,
the Beatles were the biggest band in the world and generated the most influence, as individuals they were perceived in different ways. George felt that he
was the Beatle people took the least notice of and it always bugged him. Paul
was, of course, Paul. He was great looking, the singer and frontman with John.
John was also John. That's all they had to be. It was like the king being the king.
Together, they were Lennon-McCartney, a powerful force.

Ringo was a character, always very popular, especially in America where he
ended up living after he moved more into films. But George had been insecure for
years. He had never seemed to know who he was and he bottled it all up. I always
sensed this dark moodiness and tension about him, and while I thought it was
mostly to do with his almost insane jealousy over Pattie, it was obvious that for a
long time he felt inferior creatively to Paul and John. Eventually, he gave up being
a Beatle round about the time Apple was formed. He started playing with other
musicians and came to appreciate that he was a better musician than he thought
he was. He was playing with his old love-rival, Eric Clapton, and Delaney and
Bonnie, backing other people and recording with Billie Preston. He produced the
album with Jackie Lomax, who used to have a Liverpool group called the Under-
takers. They wore undertaker suits, top hats and black ribbons. George loved it.

All this gave him a new degree of confidence, but even as he began to find his
own creative niche in the group, here was an interloper who in a few months had
changed the fragile balance of power. At the start of John's affair George had remarked that Yoko was "nothing but a Bohemian tart from New York who had
been such a troublemaker there she was given the cold shoulder," but he didn't
lose his cool until the so-called *Get Back* recording sessions, which I filmed in
Twickenham Studios early in January 1969. The original idea was to make a film
of the making of the album, but not only did it spiral into a disorganized mess,
with the Beatles loosely jamming their way through more than a hundred songs,
but the air almost sparked with tension and animosity toward Yoko. George was
affected the most. When Yoko made yet another musical suggestion directed at
him, he turned on Paul instead of her. He just put his guitar down and said to

Paul, "I'm through. You want to play all the guitar bits, then you fucking play 'em, 'cos I'm going." Then, like Ringo, he walked out.

John said, "Fuck it. If he's not back by Monday we'll get Eric in." (He meant Eric Clapton.) Without missing a beat, Yoko immediately went and sat in George's still-warm blue cloth chair and began wailing. She called it "playing air." Trust me, it was *wailing*. Our cameras moved in for a close-up and, for the first time ever, Yoko Ono was recorded smiling. Much to their own bewilderment, the remaining Beatles picked up their instruments and found themselves jamming with Yoko. It was unbelievable. But it wasn't a sharing. It was a room full of angry people beating the hell out of their instruments in a fury. George did return after a bit of meditating, but the atmosphere was uneasy.

Later, John expressed how upset he was. "Yoko only wants to be accepted," he said. "She wants to be one of us. It's hateful that someone can be treated with so much hostility just because they love someone." Ringo snapped, "Well, she's not a Beatle, John, and she never will be." They hoped that he would soon tire of her, as he had tired of most of his other momentary crazes. But he got tight-faced. "Yoko is part of me now. We're John-and-Yoko, we're together," he insisted. That was what they all feared almost more than anything.

━━

When it had come to choosing a venue for the promo film for the ultimately aborted *Get Back* double album, the Beatles had grand ideas way beyond their then financial position. One moment it was going to be at the Roundhouse in London with Yoko's Middle Earth hippies and freaks who were into the heavy rock band UFO; but the Middle Earth people started raving and shouting like crazed capitalists about bread—in other words, their split. They squabbled like some alternative bazaar about money and seating and selling their tie-dyed T-shirts. Then it was going to be a George-type charity thing, something to feed the starving masses. Jeffrey Archer, then a conservative MP and publicity hound, turned up at the offices, sensing a great scoop for himself. In 1964 he had invited the Beatles and Brian to a dinner at Brasenose, his old college at Oxford to mark the twenty-first anniversary of Oxfam. Of course, there just happened to be reporters and cameramen handy. Before they knew it, the headlines the next day had said, BEATLES TO BACK JUNIOR CONSERVATIVE MINISTER'S CHARITY CAMPAIGN which—as socialists—didn't please them. Since then, Archer was always popping up with a proprietal air, and sure enough, there he was again, ready to sign them up. It was explained that while they did support charity, they couldn't be seen to be political.

Instead, they told Archer that they had decided to film in a Roman amphitheater in somewhere like Tripoli, with thousands of Bedouins streaming in from every direction, followed by people of every race and color. It was to be like an earlier version of what eventually became the Coca-Cola ad: "I'd Like to Teach the World to Sing." Warming to the multihued psychedelic visions they still shared, they imagined that as the sun set over the vast panorama with the Mediterranean as a backdrop, they would come on stage and sing. It was all incredibly expensive, like a Cecil B. De Mille movie, and remembering the food he'd been forced to eat in India (when he wasn't eating beans) Ringo killed the idea stone dead. No way would he go to Tripoli, he said flatly. In truth, Ringo didn't even know where Tripoli was, but he said it sounded "too foreign."

They decided that the same thing might work in the middle of some desert in America. Mal was to be dispatched to scout a good empty location miles from anywhere. Neil Aspinall looked worried. "Can you imagine the insurance claims if thousands of fans turn up and get lost in the middle of nowhere?" he said. "And how will we truck enough lavatories in?"

George started to laugh. "A great idea, scuppered by portable toilets!" he said.

Paul's creative idea was to book a club in Germany under the name he liked, Ricky and the Red Streaks. "Hey, can you imagine the expression on their faces when we walk in?" he said. "That would be great to film."

Promoted to "Head of the Foreign Department," Jack Oliver was told to set it up. "You can't keep a thing like that a secret," he said. "The place would be mobbed. It would be bedlam."

The Beatles talked idea after mad idea through, until they simply ran out of time. In the end, two days before the last date scheduled for filming, Denis O'Dell and I suggested we should film the rehearsals for the filming of the concert, which now looked as if it would never happen, just to have something in the can. One of them, Paul, I think, said, "Oh, let's just do it the day after tomorrow on the roof."

Tired and fed up, the Beatles looked at each other. At first, they were surprised, then the idea grew on them. John said, "Bugger it, the roof's a good idea. We can always film something for real later." We didn't bother to tell him that this was it—there would be no later. We needed a film to be released soon, in conjunction with the *Get Back* album, not at some time in the distant future. George was the only one who was a bit reluctant, but in the end he agreed. They decided to do six songs and worked out the running order.

I hastily made all the arrangements. Neil Aspinall, who had nothing particular to do at the time, became the producer. Michael Lindsay-Hogg, who had gone on to direct "Jumping Jack Flash" and "Rock and Roll Circus" for the Rolling Stones after "Paperback Writer," was hired to direct in 35mm. A bit of scaffolding was erected on the roof of Apple Headquarters. The sound went downstairs via a snake directly into the mixing board in the studio. I set up the lights and called the press; they turned up.

What had seemed a bit of an anticlimax turned out to be an iconic moment. On January 30, 1969, warmly wrapped up against the cold, rarefied air, people were on the rooftops as far as the eye could see, hanging onto freezing chimney pots and half of London came to a standstill as thousands stopped to listen and watch. Office workers hung from windows and passers-by lined the streets.

My job was finished and I retreated to my office to listen to the circus from a distance. Now and then, I would amble down to the street to chat with the junior shopkeepers at Gieves and Hawkes, who clustered in their doorway, or just to watch the reactions of people passing by. Carried on the chilly and damp January air, for forty minutes, the music swept over the rooftops of London. It was only one two-hundred-watt sound system, but apparently you could hear it as far away as Park Lane and Soho, a mile distant. As I watched the office workers excitedly hanging out of their windows, laughing with pleasure, I suddenly saw that this was a wonderful and unique event.

Of all the six songs they performed—some of them twice and not counting an impromptu "God Save the Queen"—the one that struck me most was "Don't Let Me Down." I knew that this concert was really the end. Poignantly I felt that although John had written that particular song as a tribute to Yoko, it seemed to be directed at the Beatles themselves in their relationship with each other, and was also a plea to the world to understand them and all that they had tried to achieve. The song that achieved the most reaction from the crowd because it was a bit of a belter and they could hop about to it, was "Get Back." This also said a lot about the way things were. It was a heartfelt plea from John and Paul, mostly to each other, saying, "Let's get back to where we were in the beginning."

The phones kept ringing, but everyone was outside, having a good time. Eventually, when someone answered, it was the BBC, asking questions for the six o'clock news. Then the senior tailors from Gieves and Hawkes complained about the noise and sent for the police, who were on their way round anyway. The police arrived and we got the doorman to stall them, by asking if they had backstage passes. They were stalled further inside with the office boy using the same ploy. The boys in blue fought their way bravely through secretaries and Apple Scruffs and whoever else put out a foot to trip them up, until they reached the very top. It was all very good humored. We negotiated with them for more time, and to give them their due, they watched out of sight for twenty minutes or so while the boys went on playing. Finally, they said, "Look lads, it's too loud, you're going to have to stop." The open-air concert had started at about noon and ended at about a quarter to one when the police pulled the plug.

Afterward, everybody went downstairs and had a cup of tea and sandwiches. It was very civilized. Then they all went their merry way—as if it had been just another day in the life of the Beatles. In fact, it was the last time they ever played together as a unit. Sadly, this strange little rooftop concert was to prove a farewell to the most incredible years in the history of pop music. The Beatles were at the top of the building; now there was nowhere left to go, but down.

We sat in Alex's miserably inefficient basement studio and listened to the tape. It was grim. External sounds intruded, like traffic, car horns, and, worst of all, the roar of the central heating plant and even the drains gurgling. In their capacity as "quality control," the Beatles shook their heads. Paul said, "It's awful. We can't use it." They listened several times, and decided that only the "Get Back" track was good enough for a single, the rest was too poor to allow out. The album was initially redone at Abbey Road with George Martin under more controlled conditions and, with a lot of new material later added by Phil Spector, it was eventually released as *Let It Be*. To give George his due, he just got on with the task and didn't say, "I told you so."

They spent three weeks during December 1968 and January 1969 filming at Twickenham for material to make a proper movie. Much if it, like the rooftop tapes, was a mess. What was intended as a short promo film ended up being an awful pseudodocumentary with no story line. It was so bad that few people wanted their names in the credits. In the end, as a typical Beatle joke, Mal Evans—their roadie—ended up being listed as producer.

In the larger picture, the Beatles started to implode at a time when the accountants prepared yet another report saying they would soon be broke if costs weren't controlled. John claimed to be the only person who read the report, but instead of discussing it properly, he announced to the press, "We're going broke, we need to stop this Apple business."

Paul heard someone say, "You'll need a Beeching to get you out of this mess." At once he contacted Lord Beeching, the government minister who had wielded his famous "axe" to drastically prune the railway system by closing down hundreds of stations and lines in order to make it profitable. However, Beeching was probably the only person in the country who didn't know who the Beatles were, and pompously, he declined Paul's invitation. Other important names were tossed in the air. Even Caleb, the Apple soothsayer, was consulted. His magic runes advised against any of the contenders. It was perhaps fortunate for the Beatles that shortly after, Caleb's runes instructed him to move on from Apple.

29

The Beatles always knew, and never begrudged the fact, that Brian got 25 percent of the gross on everything. What they hadn't quite taken on board was what this represented. He gave them their money after taxes, and they never questioned how he had arrived at that sum. All expenses, including his own (and he had very expensive tastes) were deducted from the remaining 75 percent, after which it was split four ways among the Beatles. So Brian earned more than any of them.

There was more than enough to go around, even taking that into account, but right from the start, Brian didn't realize the enormity of the Beatles' earning capacity and negotiated some very foolish deals, particularly with John and Paul's song publishing and the merchandising, which turned into a nightmare when it was calculated that he had probably given away the equivalent of about £100 million (£1 billion in today's currency). It was only after Brian's death that the Beatles came to realize how badly their affairs had been handled. Maybe it wasn't their fault. Irving Azoff—manager of the Eagles—once said that when you cross the creative business with the accounting business, you'll get chaos. The Beatles made the music and they felt it was up to Brian to make the money.

There were trips to America with Ron Kass to discuss business. The Beatles still weren't mature enough or experienced enough to treat Apple seriously. This was hardly surprising considering that they were still only in their twenties. Apple was like a leaky bucket, a personal plaything that was on the verge of collapse. The company was expanding wildly out of control, with no one in charge of it overall. The accountants—the same ones who had told them that they had to spend money or it would be taken away, now told the Beatles that for every £10,000 spent, they had to bring in £120,000 because of their huge tax exposure.

To add to their woes, when the Beatles had moved out of the old building in Wigmore Street to Savile Row, all their financial paperwork and tax returns were put into that London taxi, never to be seen again, and now the taxmen were breathing heavily down their necks. One of the biggest problems that emerged was that the Epsteins had substantial estate duties to pay on Brian's estate. Despite saying he would never "sell them down the river," Clive quickly tired of the confusion, the muddle and the bickering and wanted a simpler life. He started looking for a buyer for Nemperor, the company that had absorbed NEMS and the part of Northern Songs that he and Queenie had inherited. Thanks to Brian's underhand personal insurance deal with EMI, Nemperor didn't have to do anything but they'd still collect 25 percent of the Beatles' earnings for a further nine years. When the Beatles heard that a city investment company, Triumph Investment Trust, had offered a million pounds for Nemperor, they were enraged at the idea that some big anonymous corporation could take them over through the back door. Almost any sacrifice would be worth it to get out from under such an insult.

Paul immediately got on the telephone to Linda's father, Lee Eastman, to ask if he could come over as a matter of urgency to help sort things out, but Lee was so busy he made the tactical error of sending his son. John Eastman had studied law at Harvard. He was sharp, but young and the other three Beatles wanted someone with gravitas. They discussed it among themselves and came to the conclusion that while Eastman Jr. might lack his father's status when put up against the big-city guns, he was all they had. John Eastman set up a meeting with Sir Joseph Lockwood and Lazards, the merchant bankers, to work something out. All four Beatles, plus Yoko—who had a high and lonely opinion of her business acumen, and perhaps she was eager to find out about the money—met at EMI to discuss Nemperor and Apple matters over tea and biscuits.

Eastman had a solution. He suggested that the Beatles buy Nemperor themselves. "How much of an advance do you need?" Sir Jo asked. When told the amount was £1.25 million, he looked at Lord Poole, who nodded. He said they would look at the figures, but it appeared a sound investment. He further said he would help sort out their affairs at no charge. It was a generous offer and the Beatles should have accepted; but they dithered and a monster moved in.

I took this photo of Paul in a poolside bungalow at the Beverly Hills Hotel, June 1968, when he and Linda first got together. Paul has just had a swim and he is sitting in his swimsuit, playing and singing "Blackbird." CREDIT: Tony Bramwell. Used by permission of London Features International Ltd.

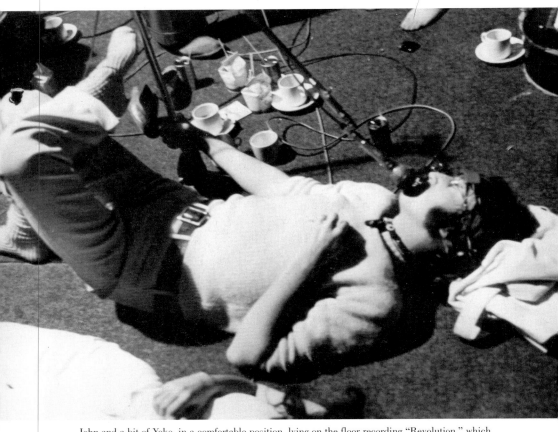

John and a bit of Yoko, in a comfortable position, lying on the floor recording "Revolution," which was all about peace. There were never any drugs or alcohol at Beatles sessions—note the vast quantity of teacups all over the floor! CREDIT: Tony Bramwell. Used by permission of London Features International Ltd.

Twiggy, absorbed, watching Paul and
George recording at Abbey Road.
In this photograph taken by me, she
looks very small and waiflike. She was
always around, one of the very few
people allowed in to watch the Beatles
at work. CREDIT: Tony Bramwell
Archive. Used by permission of
London Features International Ltd.

Paul, looking very dandy in a striped blazer, talks to Al Brodax, head of King Features and producer of
the *Yellow Submarine* cartoon film. I snapped this at Abbey Road while they discussed the music for the
film. CREDIT: Tony Bramwell. Used by permission of London Features International Ltd.

ABOVE: John and a scowling Yoko at Abbey Road. CREDIT: Tony Bramwell. Used by permission of London Features International Ltd.

LEFT: Paul, smiling up at the control booth, listens happily to a playback at Abbey Road. CREDIT: Tony Bramwell Archive. Used by permission of London Features International Ltd.

Thumbs up for Lesley Cavendish as he cuts George's hair at Apple Hairdressing in the Kings Road. It was a nice little salon run by Lesley, but after it was discovered by fans he would pop into our offices and we'd all line up for a trim. I wish I'd photographed *that!* CREDIT: Tony Bramwell. Used by permission of London Features International Ltd.

I took this study in concentration of George Martin, "lord of all he surveys" at Abbey Road, during the making of the *White Album* as he works out a piece at the piano while surrounded by Beatles. CREDIT: Tony Bramwell. Used by permission of London Features International Ltd.

I always loved this photo of George in a flowered shirt and striped pants. I took it in August 1968, at the time of "While My Guitar Gently Weeps," because I thought he looked a bit serene.

I snapped this unusual high-powered board meeting in the Apple boardroom at 3 Savile Row before any furniture was moved in. Amongst the various bodies are John, Yoko, Paul, Francie Schwartz, Neil Aspinall, Derek Taylor, Mal Evans, Peter Brown and Magic Alex Mardas. I think we were planning how to spend about £2 million in as short a time as possible! CREDIT: Tony Bramwell. Used by permission of London Features International Ltd.

I took this during our Catalina trip, summer of 1968. Paul is on the right and Linda is second from left. At top left is Ron Kass. The director Mike Nichols is below Ron, facing the camera. And that's the film producer Billy Graham holding the videocam. CREDIT: Tony Bramwell. Used by permission of London Features International Ltd.

Linda, Paul and Ivan Vaughan enjoying the sun and the sea on the Catalina trip. Ivan, who was Paul's old schoolfriend from Liverpool, had brought Paul and John together. CREDIT: Tony Bramwell. Used by permission of London Features International Ltd.

Falling in Love during the Summer of Love, 1968. I took this on Mike Nichols's yacht while we were sailing to Catalina. Paul and Linda have a quiet moment in the cabin. CREDIT: Tony Bramwell. Used by permission of London Features International Ltd.

Mary Hopkin and Paul sit on a bench seat in front of the mixing desk and listen to a playback of "Those Were the Days"—which launched Mary's career. Twiggy discovered Mary on *Opportunity Knocks* and recommended her to Paul. CREDIT: Tony Bramwell. Used by permission of London Features International Ltd.

LEFT: Paul with the manager of the GPO Tower restaurant—then the highest building in London—which was run by Butlins. I'm behind them. We went along to have lunch to check it out as a venue for the launch party for Mary Hopkin. This was in the days before terrorists, when the restaurant still revolved. CREDIT: Andrew Mulligan, Tower Photographer. Used by permission of Butlins.

BELOW: In the revolving restaurant at the top of the Post Office Tower in London, with Jack Oliver, Paul, the manager of the restaurant, Mal Evans and me. CREDIT: Andrew Mulligan, Tower Photographer. Used by permission of Butlins.

Shooting the video for "Hey Jude" at Twickenham Studios, Wednesday, September 4, 1968. We went out into the streets to round up an audience of about three hundred. It was shown the following Sunday on *David Frost*, in the U.K., and the next month on the *Smothers Brothers Show*, in the U.S.

I also took this atmospheric photograph of Ringo, John, Paul and George at Twickenham Studios while making the video for "Hey Jude," the song Paul wrote for Julian Lennon after John and Cynthia split up.
CREDIT: Tony Bramwell. Used by permission of London Features International Ltd.

I snapped Paul and George just doodling on two pianos as Peter Asher leans against the bar in the penthouse suite of the Lancaster Gate Hotel. We had flown EMI executives in from around the world to launch the *White Album* in 1969, and the pianos just happened to be there. CREDIT: Tony Bramwell. Used by permission of London Features International Ltd.

I took this study of Ringo at Abbey Road, quietly composing at the piano. CREDIT: Tony Bramwell. Used by permission of London Features International Ltd.

LEFT: I caught Paul unawares in an introspective mood at Abbey Road, 1969. He's wearing a Shetland wool sweater and is miles away. CREDIT: Tony Bramwell. Used by permission of London Features International Ltd.

BELOW: A candid shot I took of Paul and Linda, stoned and happy at a party to launch a Wings tour at the Hammersmith Odeon, 1974. That's Neil Aspinall to the right, who still runs Apple. I promoted all of Wings' records. CREDIT: Tony Bramwell. Used by permission of London Features International Ltd.

This is a typical business discussion at Apple, with everyone smoking their heads off around a table in the main office. From left is George Harrison, Peter Asher, me, John Frewin (a director of EMI), Jack Oliver (squatting on the floor), Yoko, John, Ron Kass (on a bad profile day), and the back of Neil Aspinall's head (on a bad hair day). We were discussing a John-Yoko record, probably *Unfinished Music No. 2*. I'm not sure what George was doing there, because the other three Beatles usually showed little interest in John and Yoko's flights of fancy! CREDIT: Tom Hanley/Camera Press/Retna Ltd.

At the film premier of *The Optimist of Nine Elms,* a lovely little film starring Peter Sellers and produced by Ron Kass. That's Ron on the left; his wife, the lovely Joan Collins, looking glamorous in black velvet; and me, happy because my company did the music (by Lionel Bart and Don Crown) and it was great. Peter Sellers played an old busker and sang the theme song, "Mr Bass Drum Man," which George Martin produced. CREDIT: Michael Putland. Used by permission of London Features International Ltd.

I took this snap of me and Bruce Springsteen around the pool of the Sunset Marquis motel when I was in Hollywood working with Phil Spector. It was a manic time—and then Springsteen breezed into town with his entourage. A few days later we flew to London, where Bruce opened to great acclaim at the Hammersmith Odeon. CREDIT: Tony Bramwell, from Badlands Collection. www.badlands.co.uk.

Me (center) with Vangelis and Demis Roussos (some cigar!) to celebrate the Oscar for Best Music for *Chariots of Fire*, 1981. We're at Seacy, a restaurant in Knightsbridge, just behind Harrods. CREDIT: Tony Bramwell Archive

Allen Klein was fat and grubby. He was a multimillionaire but used to wear filthy white polo-neck sweaters under food-stained jackets. From the moment he had heard the news of Brian's death, he had tried to get his foot in the door, but he had only one telephone number, that of our office manager, Peter Brown, whom he had first met on the Stones' boat in New York. He called repeatedly, begging to be allowed to talk to John. Why John, I don't know. Perhaps he had already figured out that Paul would be a hard nut to crack where fraudsters like himself were concerned. But Peter, who had no intention of letting this brash New Yorker in, continued to stonewall him. Klein tried another route. He got Tony Calder, a former comanager of the Stones, to approach Derek Taylor, with whom he was friends. Tony came by the offices, and over a glass or two of vodka, broached the subject. Derek passed on the message to John that Allen Klein was staying at the Inn on the Park and urgently wanted to meet with him.

"What for?" said John. "What for?" said the echo.

In all innocence, Derek said, "Look, he got an amazing deal for the Stones with Decca. They gave them a huge advance and a heavy percentage on their record sales, unlike Brian, who got you no advance and a joke royalty. He wants to help you."

"He's American," said Yoko. "I like Americans."

John and Yoko turned up at the brand-new glass and marble hotel that evening for dinner with Klein. Instead of being put off by Klein's squalid appearance, they decided they liked his down-to-earth attitude. I had met him around the Stones before his assault on Apple and there is no doubt that he was amusing and good company. He had cleverly prepared his brief by heavily researching his target. First, he had asked Mick Jagger who was who and what was what in the Beatles' social structure. Mick was the one who, early on, when he was pro-Klein and their business affairs were a mess, unwittingly told him to focus on John, something he regretted.

As they chitchatted over dinner, Klein artlessly told John and Yoko about his struggle in life, how he was an orphan who had clawed his way up out of the gutter to become a highly successful accountant with top clients in the music field. John admired that. Then Klein discussed every one of the Beatles' records, cleverly picking out the lyrics that John had written. Klein couldn't have known that John was sensitive about being slightly dyslexic, but he had guessed correctly that John resented being seen as the junior partner. John and Yoko were very pleased with Klein's obvious interest in music. None of the other possible managers had a clue what they were about. Most of all, they were taken in by his magnificent promises. He trotted out the old chestnut he used on all potential clients of how he had approached Bobby Darin at a wedding where they were both guests. "I can get you one hundred thousand dollars," he told Bobby.

"How?" Bobby asked suspiciously.

"No catch—no cost to you. Let me just go through your books." The story of how he had then conjured the money out of thin air unrolled like a magician's Persian carpet. He concluded by telling them he could get them Nemperor Holdings for nothing; he could get a deal from EMI similar to the Stones' deal with Decca and—the clincher—he could get Yoko a huge distribution advance for her films. He hadn't seen one, but called them great.

John and Yoko were beguiled. John immediately wrote on the piece of hotel notepaper that Klein proffered, *From now on Allen Klein handles all my stuff.* He signed it and gave it to Klein. When a copy of this note was handed around our offices the next day, it really put the cat among the pigeons.

"We haven't agreed to this," Paul said. "We've got John and Lee Eastman to help sort us out."

"No," John said. *"You've* got John and Lee. I've got Allen Klein."

John and Yoko somehow convinced George and Ringo to appoint Klein in charge of their affairs as well. He said that Klein knew a great deal about music, managed their buddies, the Stones, and, crucially, he was independent, while the Eastman clique of Paul-Linda-John-Lee was all one sided. When news got out of the ill-advised appointment, Mick Jagger came straight round and told the Beatles under no circumstances should they go with the shady accountant. The Stones had been with Klein for some time and wanted out.

Mick and Keith both had exotic houses in Cheyne Walk in Chelsea down by the river, each of them decorated in rich fabrics and dark, sludgy colors. When John and I dropped in to one of Mick's parties, the conversation soon got around to Klein. Mick immediately said, "Keep away. He's messed us right up, man."

Keith agreed. "We had to escape to the Matto fuckin' Grosso to get away. It's how 'Honky Tonk Women' came about."

John was instantly interested, because he loved everything about it. Keef smiled and said, "We're in the Matto fuckin' Grosso on this ranch, and there's more cowboys around than in Texas. And me and Mick are like, hanging out on the front porch and doin' all this country stuff which I love. We're doin' our Hank Williams thing drinking loads of Jack Black and beer and wearing all the gear. Three sheets to the wind, I play him a thing I've got called 'Country Honk.' We did it really slow and we work it up and we're thinking, Jesus! Can't give this to the Stones. They'll take the piss. What? Charlie? Bill? No way! They'll down tools and fuck off to the pub.

"But, we did. We took a chance and it might have been the words or whatever, I don't know, but they just locked into that offbeat and it got louder and it changed and it got more raucous but it was still country."

At this point Keith picked up an acoustic and played it as it started out, Hank Williams' style, like "Your Cheating Heart." Then he played it how it ended up.

"But only the Americans really cottoned on," said Mick. "They sussed us out and they didn't care. They worked it out and took it to their bosom but in those days in England if you said you're doing a country song they laughed their bollocks off. Still do."

John said, "Yeah. You're right. Good song that, but if me and Paul wrote it we would have had to give it to Ringo to sing. Then, next thing you know, because he fancies himself as a fookin' dancer he'd wanna be out front like Mick giving it all the moves and all the pouting and—I mean, we can't be having that in the Beatles can we?"

And the night went on, singing, pantomiming, dancing and dissecting the song and apportioning lines and parts to various friends. Funnily enough I still love the song. Written by two very talented hillbilly shouters from Dartford Kent while they drank and played at being cowboys out on the Matto "fuckin" Grosso. That's the music business for you.

That night was a welcome relief from what was still a big issue yet to be resolved. Despite Mick and Keith's warning, John had this sort of New York/New Jersey "street-fighting" idea of Klein being his champion now against the London accountants, upper-class crooks, and against Paul's choice of the gentlemanly Eastman as their new white knight. Yoko always professed to being a businesswoman. It's possible she may have picked up a few financial buzzwords along the way; after all, she was a banker's daughter. She also had John's money to play with; but it was obvious she knew nothing. She hadn't proven herself yet. At the time, even the arts community didn't take her seriously. In my opinion, Yoko thrived on conflict. Voting for Klein was another way of stirring things up. It was a matter of: "You want to get through to John? Then talk to me. I have his ear."

We mocked her around the office: "I have his caviar. I have his toast. I was on the barricades. I played Middle Earth, you know. Call me number one. Bring me my ladder. Bring me my hammer of burning gold. Bring me, bring me . . ."

Meanwhile, Yoko and Tony Cox had been hard at work negotiating their divorce. John had rather unwisely told Yoko that he would settle with Cox for whatever it took, so perhaps not surprisingly, what it took was a very large amount of money. During their time in London Mr. and Mrs. Cox had earned next to nothing. Mr. Cox had charmed money out of banks and film labs. In a similar way, long before they had a real relationship, Yoko had used John's name as collateral for her art exhibitions and numerous other expenses. They owed money for back rent, and loans. It all came to a massive £100,000. In addition, John agreed to give Cox a substantial sum that would enable him to resettle himself and Kyoko in comfort in the Virgin Isles. John's lawyers and business advisers at NEMS winced, but John Winston Lennon didn't care what it cost. He wanted Cox gone and he was convinced that he wanted Yoko. Later, it may have been love, but I have no doubt that, from the start, at least where the Coxes were concerned, it had all been about money.

♈

The Beatles had changed dramatically in appearance and attitude from the lovable "moptops." Since its inception, they had been at the forefront of the hippie movement. But since the offices were in Savile Row, it was an upmarket kind of peace, love and brown rice. In fact, it was a bank waiting for Butch and Sundance to turn up and rob it. As it turned out, the robbers were not nearly as charming and well mannered as Butch and Sundance. Helplessly, our hands tied, we stood there and watched it happen.

Klein moved to London early in 1969 for a solid block of time. In the U.S. he used to manage Sam Cooke and the Cameo Parkway label. Many of the big British acts he owned a part or all of ended up under his banner because initially he had negotiated contracts for what was called the British Invasion. He had signed the Stones to Atlantic, Herman's Hermits to MGM, and Dave Clark to Epic in the U.S.—and then he signed them to himself.

He took a flat nearby at Hyde Park Gate—paid for by Apple—so he could be in early and out late. He basically moved into Apple from that moment. He didn't go to lunch, had sandwiches at his desk, while he pored over the vast amount of paperwork that had accumulated over the years. What he saw must have filled his heart with joy. Page after page of bank statements with rows of zeroes at the bottom showed him the hundreds of millions that had poured in, and were still pouring in. But, where was it going? Who had it all? Klein told the Beatles he would get to the bottom of everything and make them richer than they believed possible. In the process, he would enrich himself as well, since three of the four Beatles had blindly agreed to give him 20 percent of everything extra he brought in over and above what they had already been earning. In effect, he had become an equal shareholder with them, all on his unproven assurance that he was equal to the job and without having to expend any of Brian's early efforts.

Paul was the only thorn in his side. Paul refused to sign the contract and walked out of the offices. This left things in limbo, since according to the terms of the Beatles' partnership agreement, all their business decisions had to be agreed by quorum. It might seem remarkable that Klein so quickly acquired this degree of power over the Beatles' affairs. But bizarre at it might seem, the matter of the quorum was totally ignored. It might even have been that none of the Beatles were really aware that this clause had been written into their partnership contract by Brian. I doubt if at that stage any of them even had a copy. Three Beatles backed Klein, blindly following John's lead, and he had walked in, given himself an office and corralled all the paperwork. Some of the old-timers, like Neil Aspinall and Peter Brown, had objected, but Klein was a like a Panzer tank—solid, aggressive and ruthless—and besides, three Beatles supported him. For Paul, it was wildly frustrating, but he simply didn't know how to get rid of him without physically ejecting him and changing the locks, and obviously he couldn't do that on his own without support. Paul even shouted at Klein and told him to go away but Klein baldly ignored him and continued to take charge.

Paul didn't want what was happening at Apple to overshadow a more important event in his life. He and Linda were married at Marylebone Registry Office on March 12, 1969. I knew his plans, as did Mal and Peter Brown, who were Paul and Linda's witnesses, but apart from that, very few people were informed. The press heard and arrived in force at an affair so low key that Linda dressed in an old tweed overcoat, tailored plain wool frock and sensible shoes. George and Pattie rushed in late for the wedding breakfast because the drug squad had raided them that morning. Once again, the raid was led by Sergeant Norman Pilcher, the same policeman who had raided John and Mick Jagger and Keith Richard, accompanied by his notorious drug-sniffing dog, Willie.

George was at the office with us when Pattie telephoned about the bust. He was very angry, but calm. He asked to speak to Sergeant Pilcher and said, "Birds have nests, animals have holes, but man hath nowhere to lay his head." He told Pattie to give them the grass kept in a box on the mantelpiece, "or they'll wreck the joint."

By way of a honeymoon, Paul and Linda flew to New York to introduce Paul to the family. They spent two weeks at the handsome Eastman house in the wealthy suburb of Scarsdale where Linda's father, John, and her stepmother lived. They also went to see Linda's mother. On their return to the U.K., they disappeared to Scotland, a country Linda had fallen in love with. The run-down farmhouse with its primitive furniture—much of it made by Paul from orange boxes and mattresses—was a big contrast to the luxurious houses the Eastmans lived in, but Paul and Linda felt far more relaxed there. They remained out of sight for months. Paul wanted to get away from everything while he secretly wrote and recorded an album entirely on his own, to be called *McCartney*. He completed it himself in Cavendish Avenue, assisted by Linda, using hired recording and mixing equipment.

Two days after Paul and Linda were married, as if scoring points, John and Yoko attempted to do the same, on a ferry sailing out of Southampton. They drove to Hampshire to pick up Mimi for the event (later Mimi was to say about Yoko, "I should have told John what I really thought") but their plans were thwarted because the captain didn't "do" weddings at sea; and more importantly, Yoko's U.K. visa had long expired. Instead, they flew to Paris in a private plane, neatly evading passport control, but they couldn't marry in Paris either and ended up on "the Rock." Gibraltar was British territory, and finally they married on March 20.

Cynthia had divorced John in the High Court of London on the grounds of his adultery with Yoko on October 28 the previous year. This first stage is known as a decree nisi. The decree absolute comes through six months later, which allows time for a reconciliation or for any legal issues to surface. When Yoko announced that she was pregnant—although she shortly miscarried—it seems that the judge made the decree absolute with immediate effect. Had this not happened, since Gibraltar was British territory, they would have married while John was still technically married to Cynthia. John and Yoko had already tried a marriage of sorts in an artistic event they described as "An Alchemical Wedding" on December 18, 1968, at the Royal Albert Hall. Dressed entirely in white, they writhed around a bit within a large white bag while their *Two Virgins* tapes played away in the background.

The other Beatles told the press that they didn't know John and Yoko had married until they bought the record, "The Ballad of John and Yoko." They were making a point because Paul, who had worked on it, was credited, not in his name but as "A Beatle."

"It's all nihilism, man," John said about the bag-in, the bed-in, and the record credit. To my mind smoking a cigarette at the ceremony in Gib while Yoko fidgeted was not enough nihilism. Living in sin with Yoko instead of running around Europe looking for some preacher/ship's captain/justice of the peace to get a wedding certificate was more nihilistic. John sidestepped the issue neatly by saying, "Yoko gave me the inner strength to break up my other marriage—my real marriage—to the Beatles."

It was during his long, hermitlike exile in Scotland that the rumors about Paul being dead started to surface, then to circulate widely. They had started when an anonymous caller named "Tom" had telephoned a Michigan disc jockey, John Small on WKNR, sounding very knowledgeable about "Paul's death" and offering many clues. He didn't say that he had found these clues in *Northern Star,* a campus newspaper. His real name turned out to be Tom Zarski, a student at Eastern Michigan University. John Small thought it was all nonsense, but as a hoax, he and a couple of other deejays decided to perpetuate it for fun and to get a lively on-air debate going. They never really expected it to take off in such a dramatic way.

Our phones started to ring off the hook. Journalists wanted to interview Paul. The office refused to say where he was—and in fact, most of the time, we simply didn't know. He had dropped off the radar. He and Linda would be walking the hills, giving birth, growing vegetables, writing, sailing on fishing boats to the lonely offshore islands, contentedly learning how to be a family. However, the rumors grew. People started to look for "signs" in the strangest places. Paul was photographed wearing a black carnation when the others had red (the florist had run out of red). On the shoulder of his uniform on the *Sgt. Pepper* album sleeve was patch that said OPD. The fans said it meant "Officially Pronounced Dead"— in fact, it was a uniform badge that Paul picked up in Ontario that stood for "Ontario Police Department." He walked across the famous zebra crossing on Abbey Road in bare feet while the others wore shoes (it was a hot day and Paul liked to walk around bare-footed).

The death-theorists dug deeper and examined everything for "clues." There was a coffin on the sleeve of *Sgt. Pepper* and a guitar made of flowers; song lyrics were dredged through, like the Bonzo's song "Death Cab for Cutie" which, so it was said, described the fatal accident in which Paul had died. He died on November 9, 1966. He was buried on September 27, 1968. A double had been brought in to be Paul.

The rumors flourished and grew more ridiculous. It didn't help that Allan Klein, who was in New York, encouraged them when he saw how sales of old Beatles records suddenly took off in America. It has long been said by faded rock stars: "You're worth more dead"—and this certainly proved it. Derek Taylor telephoned Klein and told him that he would appreciate it if Klein could deny the rumors, but Klein seemed to find it amusing. He laughed and said that it didn't hurt sales.

When Paul checked in one day, I said, "We have to do something to scotch this. Can you come down so we can hold a press conference, and so people can see you?"

Paul sighed. "I can't be bothered. It's all so silly. Why won't they leave me alone?"

I said, "Well, we have to do something."

Paul said, "Look, Tone, do whatever you think is best."

Well, I took that as carte blanche to be creative, but first I discussed it with Derek Taylor and a couple of others while we sat around late one afternoon, relaxing over a couple of drinks. Pretending to be Paul, something I was able to do given that we were born within a mile or two of each other, I telephoned Richie Yorke, an English deejay we knew on CING-FM, at Burlington Ontario, and said, "This is Paul McCartney. As you can hear, I'm alive and kicking."

It certainly caused a reaction, but one I didn't expect. The short interview shot around the radio stations like bush fire, and two of the stations, WKNR—the station that had originated and perpetuated the hoax—and one in Miami, submitted the tape to scientific voice recognition analysis. Professor Oscar Tossey of Michigan State University concluded that the voice on the tape was not Paul's, as did Dr. Henry M. Truby, director of the Miami University's language and linguistics research laboratory. "I hear three different McCartneys," said Dr. Truby.

The furor that started was astonishing. This was irrefutable proof that Paul was dead! Finally, Derek Taylor issued a somewhat ambiguous statement purporting to come from Paul: "I am alive and well and concerned about the rumors of my death, but if I were dead, I would be the last to know." But still the rumors grew and Derek issued a statement of his own: "Paul refuses to say anything more than that. Even if he appeared in public, it wouldn't do any good. If people want to believe he's dead, then they'll believe it. The truth is not at all persuasive."

The rumors were finally laid to rest—as much as any conspiracy theory is ever laid to rest—when *Life* magazine sent an intrepid reporter and photographer to Scotland in search of Paul. They trekked across a couple of bogs and finally found their quarry tending vegetables. Paul was very annoyed and threw a bucket of water over the reporter. He retreated indoors, but emerged shortly with Linda, Heather and baby Mary. Aware of the damage his display of temper might cause, sheepishly he apologized and offered a short interview and a couple of photographs in return for the film in the camera that showed him throwing the water. The subsequent photograph, showing the family group with Paul holding their bonny new baby—the first time she had been photographed—and Heather defensively clutching a shepherd's crook, made the front cover of *Life*.

There were a couple more nice photographs inside, with Paul, who undeniably looked like himself, explaining how he really did want to be left alone. But even with that evidence many people still thought that Paul had a double and the rumors still persisted. That tape of me impersonating Paul is used all the time as ultimate "proof" by the rumormongers, which just goes to show that silly people are silly people.

30

On their return from their bizarre honeymoon, the first of their very public bed-ins for peace, held in the Amsterdam Hilton, John and Yoko got me to help do the soundtrack to the *Two Virgins* film, such as it was, and their "Smile" film thing. I call it that because it wasn't really recognizable as a film. It was nothing but that slow motion of John's face.

There was however, a connection in the title with the Beach Boys' legendary, lost *Smile* sessions. The work was done in their "Good Vibrations" period, which all the Beatles were almost obsessed about. They played their Beach Boys albums and listened repeatedly to the harmonies, discussing how they could achieve a similar sound. I went on tour with the Beach Boys, and ironically learned that they all, particularly Brian Wilson, idolized Paul. He was always asking me about him. At the time, surfing music was terminally uncool. I thought it ironic that these two groups had so much admiration for each other and each didn't really know it. I also found out that Brian Wilson had tracked down Norman Smith, the Beatles' first sound engineer at Abbey Road to work for him. Norman said, "Surely you want their producer, George Martin?" Brian replied, "No, Norman, I can produce. What I need is their sound!"

Shortly, Paul went to Los Angeles to work with Brian on their new concept album, *Smile*. Everyone who heard it said it was highly original and stunning, but it disappeared and became the thing of legends. They said they lost the tapes on the way to the pressing plant. However, it is more likely that Brian lost the plot and didn't finish it. It remained in the sandbox until 2004, when he and Van Dyke Parks completed it and Brian performed it in concert. And at last it has been released as a studio album.

♔

George didn't come in to town very much during this period. He had gotten into the habit of being reclusive. Unlike the other Beatles, Ringo was very organized, with a nanny and a secretary. His social life was very full and busy but we didn't see much of him. He and Maureen moved in glitzy circles with a coterie of exotic and beautiful people. We called their crowd "the Dorchester Mob"— the Dorchester being a grand hotel in Park Lane, where women in couture gowns arrived in Bentleys and Rolls Royces and danced to an orchestra in the grand ballroom. He also went to different clubs than we did, very toffee-nosed places and private Mayfair gambling joints where you had to dress in evening clothes to get through the door, like Les Ambassadeurs and the Saddle Room. Occasionally, I went to Les Ambassadeurs because I sometimes enjoyed putting on a dinner suit, and they served an excellent steak au poivre. On the whole though, we stuck to the Scotch and the Bag.

There was a nervous mood at Apple now, with everyone looking over their shoulders in case the axe descended on them. Before, the atmosphere had been easy-going. With Klein there, it became like George's song, "Sour Milk Sea," a place no one wanted to be. Previously, we had always wandered into meetings, been a part of everything. Photographs from pre-Klein showed a typical Apple board meeting, with everyone lying about the floor of the large boardroom, which wasn't furnished with anything other than beanbags. After Klein, we couldn't just wander round like before. It became a closed-door environment. Conspiracy, rumors and secrets flourished. We furtively looked over our shoulders, waiting for the chop, which Klein unpleasantly promised would come. A gloomy and highly suspicious atmosphere took over. No one turned on and tuned in anymore. The only people dropping in were accountants and lawyers.

Klein wanted everything to go through him. He didn't want anyone having close personal contact with the Beatles in case they whispered treacherous advice in their ears. Brian had been exactly the same, possessive, not so much with the money, but with his boys. Brian fancied himself as an artistic peer of the Fabs and there were dollops of sexual longing and angst thrown in for good measure. One of Klein's first actions was to fix a time-and-motion study to see what we all did—except for the Fabulous Four, of course.

First of all, there was an official employee head count—who does what? who gets what?—which was pretty stupid because after NEMS and Brian I couldn't ever remember getting a pay slip, let alone paying National Insurance. It was like going into an American restaurant but getting, "Hi, my name's Kevin and I'll be your time-and-motion person today. I'll be following you around all your working day. Okay. Now tell me, what are you doing right now?"

"Right now? Well I was thinking about going down the pub."

"Oh."

"Or, possibly, John might turn up in a minute and sit on the edge of my—"

"This John? What does he do? What's his job?"

"He sings a bit. Anyway, as I was saying. He might be a bit bored and he'll perch on my desk and say, 'Hi Tone. What yer doin'?' and we'll go off to Kilburn to see Mick and Keef and watch them do their dru—"

"Mick? Keef? I see. And which bit of the Apple do they work in?"

The chap who was assigned to me gave up after about four days of falling out of the Scotch of St. James at three or four in the morning. He couldn't handle it. Nor could I really, but I was determined to give him a run for his money—or Apple money, as it was paying his fee. Before he disappeared from my life he typed out a quick memo, which he left in the typewriter. It read: *I don't know what Tony Bramwell does but I'm very tired and I'm going home now. In all probability, I will not be back.* I added, *Get back Jo-Jo* at the bottom of his note and left it there for weeks. He never did.

I think the guy they put on Jack Oliver lasted for an even shorter time. What none of these statisticians appreciated was that when you're talking to deejays and music people, or meeting flying rock stars who sleep a good part of the day, the only time you can do this is after midnight in a club or restaurant. How do you separate rock 'n' roll time from normal time? To the T & M people, I was having fun. But it was my job to do that. If the bottom line shows that you're selling a lot of records by doing what you do, then don't tinker with it. It's already fine-tuned.

❦

I was close to Ron Kass. At the time we were both "bachelors," recently out of long-term relationships. We'd team up to go to industry functions and lunches during the day. More frequently, we'd meet up in the evening at Tramp, and go on to dinner and then we'd go club hopping. Through Ron I got to know Joan Collins, who became his wife, and Joan's sister, Jackie. I worked on promoting the music for two of the films made from Jackie's books, in which Joan starred:

The Stud and *The Bitch*. Both of them were filmed in England and notable for poor scripts but a vast quantity of beautiful girls and nudes. Pan's People danced in one and Joan, who was fabulously glamorous, appeared in many scenes wearing black corsets and stockings.

The real fun we had was an antidote to the vile atmosphere at the office. Because of my friendship with Ron, Klein didn't want me around; he hated Ron, who was honest. Klein wanted to get rid of everybody so he could cook the books and milk the company dry. He spent his days conspiring about how to get rid of us, whispering about everybody behind their backs to John and George, who thought he was some kind of New York financial genius. Ringo was rarely around and so cannily managed not to get embroiled, which was his style. He always took what he needed without hurting anyone's feelings. He sidestepped trouble. But for the rest of us, it was a strange and unsettling time.

Klein's tentacles were long. He tore everything apart. Within a few months of him taking over, I was the only member of the old staff left in the company. Derek Taylor went to California again. Alistair Taylor and Peter Brown resigned. Ron Kass was fired and replaced by Jack Oliver, which was a strange appointment, considering how junior Jack's position was. It was probably intended as a slap in the face for Kass, to show how unimportant his position was. Until his promotion, Jack had been hired as Terry Doran's assistant in Apple Publishing, with responsibility for "Foreign." To his bewilderment, he was suddenly appointed head of Apple Records but at a far lower remuneration than Ron had received. But Jack wasn't allowed to do anything because Klein rushed around, trying to do it all. He had set up a system of cutouts, hiring a cardboard army with a single agenda: to report directly to him. It was only after Klein had fired everyone that his T & M people discovered what we did. It was everything that the people he fired used to do, and what Klein was unable to do.

Many things slipped through the net in Klein's reign, including a big stage musical that ran and ran for years. The first big musical in London after *Hair* was *Jesus Christ Superstar*, the first of a dynastic series of musicals from Andrew Lloyd Webber and Tim Rice. *Jesus Christ Superstar* was brought to Apple as a new project because Ian Gillan from Deep Purple sang on the demo and another friend, Johnny Gustafson, the bass player from Liverpool's the Big Three, played on it. I can remember hearing it around the building at the time, with everyone singing snatches of the very catchy big theme song. But it was Robert Stigwood who ended up producing it. (Not everything Stigwood touched turned out golden. In 1979 he produced the infamous film version of *Sgt. Pepper's Lonely Hearts Club Band,* which starred people like Peter Frampton, Steve Martin,

Alice Cooper and the Bee Gees—but, believing that Americans couldn't understand English accents, he used George Burns to do the narration. The fans loathed
it and the movie bombed so badly that the video wasn't released until 1997.)

I've always thought that when Klein threw Peter Brown out, Peter must have
popped the tapes in his briefcase when he cleared his desk and took them with
him to Stiggie's place on the basis that there wasn't a lot of interest in them at
number 3 Savile Row. If he did, he was right. In fact Peter Brown is still Andrew
Lloyd Webber's PR man in the States. If Klein had kept his eye on the ball and
hadn't been too concerned with feathering his nest, Apple could have signed
Lloyd Webber and Tim Rice up and produced all their other big musicals after
Superstar, like *Evita, Cats* and *Les Miserables.* I was at Polydor after Apple and
ironically, I promoted *Cats, Starlight Express, Tell Me on a Sunday* and *Song
and Dance.* I did a lot of work for Andrew, which in the way of promotion mostly
involved taking people to lunch. I was out every day at London's top restaurants
with journalists and radio and TV people. I don't know how I managed it. Sometimes we'd start off at Andrew's wine cellar—one of the best in London, given
his hobby of attending the top wine auctions—and then we'd go out. Yes, it was
fun, but sometimes fun can be hard work if there's little respite.

I have been asked many times why it was that the Beatles didn't just hire an
office manager to handle their business affairs and pay him or her a salary. It
would have made sense. But it never occurred to them. They just went blindly
on, trying to find someone to replace Brian, like it was some kind of law. They
seemed to think that they had to have a manager, to whom they had to give
25 percent of their gross income, or they'd be arrested or drummed out of the
Brownies.

Even without the Beatles, Apple was a very successful record and music
publishing company. All it needed was a good office manager to run things and
do some pruning. Everything needed to be trimmed, including such lunatic ex-
penditures as Yoko's caviar and the lavish gourmet lunches with the finest wines
that Peter Brown and Neil Aspinall had served up to them each day, cooked by
Sally and Diana. Many people believed—because of the myths about the
breakup of Apple, widely reported in the press, by way of the pastiche band The
Rutles (a send-up of the Beatles by some of the Monty Pythons), and inaccurate
little documentary films—that Apple was broke, or that all the money was given
away. This simply wasn't true. It was, and is enormously successful despite the
astronomical 95 percent tax they paid. The visible problem was that there was
no control at all over expenses.

We used to go to clubs like the Revolution or the Speakeasy and I, or whoever was there, would sign the bills. I suppose they would be sent to Apple to be

paid, and I suppose they might have been paid. There were no credit cards then and nobody in their right mind was going to take a check, so you signed for things and an account was sent in to GHQ. This of course led to an enormous amount of abuse. Half the "in scene" in London signed for everything, from clubs, restaurants, taxis, and stores, and said they were Apple. The bills just kept coming in and someone paid some of them—then they probably went to lunch and signed for it. So it goes and so it went.

In theory, each individual Beatle would have an Apple account for purchases and for stuff they wanted, and their individual assistants would ask for things like air tickets, and they would be sorted out and supplied. Ringo and George were low-key and pretty self-sufficient, while Paul and John, who actively did far more, used the staff to get things for them. They all had personal assistants, but I have to say that for musicians and rock stars, George and John's assistants weren't much assistance. They kept asking us what to do. For a while, influenced by Yoko's obsession for all things arty, John employed an art gallery type named Anthony Fawcett, who helped them produce some of their exhibitions and outlandish experimental films—referred to around the office as their "home movies." He didn't last long.

Individual requests yielded petty jealousies. For instance, John and Yoko's "home movies," which were in no way Apple projects yet charged to Apple, aggravated the other Beatles because they were enormously expensive and earned nothing. I think that John and Yoko must have believed they were doing solid projects. In the great scheme of Beatle-life, most of their personal indulgences were small beer, hobby stuff to while away the time, or to experiment. With all the money that was around it seemed nitpicking to criticize and mostly people didn't. Those were weird times, after all. Everybody was experimenting with something and moving on to the latest idea. It was mostly the acid casualties who still dressed like *Sgt. Pepper* and got stuck in the groove. It was a fun thing at the time, but not even the Beatles wanted to go around looking like they just stepped out of their *Yellow Submarine*.

Alex's electronics department was a big waste of time and money, but it had nothing to do with Apple. It was a fantasy created by John and Alex. The boutique was also a waste of time and money, but it was money that they could afford to waste, money that was earmarked to go to taxes anyway. They could as well have had a public bonfire on the roof of Apple with the money they wasted—but it would probably have rained. There was considerable waste—including the lead from the Apple roof that some enterprising office boy was stealing by the sackload and strolling out of the front door with like Santa, until the upstairs started to leak—but nobody cared. George even wrote it in a song:

it was all written off to the taxman. As Mario Puzo once said, "If you wanna get rich, you gotta get rich in the dark."

Apple probably put more kids through Eton than any merchant bank. Looking back, one can see how it straightened out a lot of misconceptions about how to run a worldwide entertainment business. Its logo should have been a slyly smiling python with the apple. We should have attached a big blue plaque on the wall at number 3 Savile Row, saying in Latin, GET IT RIGHT OR THEY'LL STEAL THE LEAD OFF YER FUCKIN' ROOF, or perhaps nailed up one of the big signs erected around London by Syd Bishop, a leading demolitions company: WATCH IT COME DOWN.

But, despite all, Apple was amazing. It sold hundreds of millions of records, in real figures, not hyped up to move sales along. We used to get sales figures showing a quarter of a million album sales a day, *every day!* The place was so knee-deep in platinum and gold and silver discs, there was nowhere to put them. Klein got 20 percent of it all, but John, who brought him in, was crackers at the time and shouldn't have been taken seriously. They didn't need Klein or anybody like him. Ron Kass was doing a great job. We all adored Ron, but there was no way that Ron and Yoko would ever see eye to eye. He was a smashing bloke. He dressed well, he was polite and he was educated. He knew and understood the music industry. In fact, he was one of the best things that happened to Apple. But Klein hated him and Yoko hated him and those two were forces to reckon with.

31

Despite Klein's presence among us, somehow business proceeded as usual, with some high spots. Janis Joplin was one of those high spots. I met her quite a few times. Albert Grossman, Bob Dylan's manager, managed her. He was a legend, a cuddly, great bear of a man with a gray ponytail. Because he wore nothing else but blue denim shirts and jeans, it always appeared that he only had one set. We often bumped into each other at MIDEM (the annual music industry convention in Cannes) where he was always a very generous host.

The first time Janis came to England, it was in early in 1969 to play the Royal Albert Hall in London. It was a fantastic show and far exceeded her wildest expectations. She had always heard that we British were a stuffy lot, but when everyone starting dancing in the aisles, she reacted with a mind-blowing performance. Afterward, while still out of breath, she said, "God, is that exciting, man!" On a roll, she continued, "Nobody, nobody even . . . thought it would be that good! I didn't . . . That was more good than any other good. . . . Yeah, London was the best. Nobody's ever got up and danced and dug it . . . and they did, man! They fuckin' got up and grooved, and then they listened. That was dynamite." Fine words indeed.

Like many other musicians when in London, Janis took to hanging out at the Apple offices. I can still see her in my mind today, wearing a great big sort of

Cossack hat. The corner of my desk seemed to attract them all like magnets. She would perch on the corner with a joint and a glass of bourbon or Southern Comfort from Derek's huge stash and gossip a mile a minute. She wasn't attractive, but she was a really nice, funny woman. She swung both ways, but gave little indication of it, at least, not to me. I didn't see any sign that she was mainlining at the time—in fact, I don't think she used many drugs at that stage. She got into them when she got more successful.

Janis, Albert and I would hang out at the Speakeasy listening to White Trash, a Scottish band signed to Apple. Ian Mclean was their lead singer and Ronnie Leahy was on keyboards. Ronnie's wife Joan famously became Mrs. Richard Branson. Ronnie always complained that Richard, who did incredibly well while still at school by importing records from Europe, stole her away by flashing his money. White Trash's music was bluesy and cool but we never sold any records. The closest they came to having a hit was their version of the Beatles' "Golden Slumbers," which Paul wrote while staying with his father in Liverpool. The story of the song is interesting, in that it shows the various sources Paul used to draw on for his material. Jim McCartney had remarried and had a daughter, Ruth (Paul's stepsister). Paul was sitting doodling at the piano when he noticed some of Ruth's sheet music on the piano, "Golden Slumbers" among it. He didn't read music, but liked the words. It was out of copyright, written by Thomas Dekker in 1603, and Paul decided to write his own tune. As usual, John and he are credited, but Paul actually wrote it.

The basic problem with White Trash was the BBC banned them from their play list because they thought their name was racist. Somebody then compounded the fact that the BBC had missed the point by 180 degrees and they changed it to Trash, which was even worse. Janis adored their bluesy sound. She would get up with them at the Speak and sing. She'd get silly and drunk and have great fun. The office boy and general junior dogsbody at Apple at the time, the keen young American, Richard DiLello, was assigned the job of hauling Janis and White Trash/Trash around. They became a sort of project with him and he started taking lots of pictures. One snap was of Janis in the hat outside the Albert Hall, not long before she died. At the time, Richard wasn't a very good photographer, but that one became famous. He observed enough of what a manic place Apple was in those days to write a book about it, *The Longest Cocktail Party*.

Despite the arguments and the wrangling, at heart the Beatles remained close friends who really cared about each other. Without outside influences, they could still get together as a unit in the studio and work amicably. This was the case in July 1969, when they settled their differences long enough to start the long process of recording *Abbey Road,* a process which would continue during July and August. It was to be the last big opus, a swan song to the Beatles. It became one of their most evocative and beautiful albums. At first, they resurrected "Everest," the previous working title for the *White Album,* and decided to use it. They wanted the album to reflect the eternal, soaring images of the mountain itself and they even discussed going to India to film and take that classic photograph. The idea of the Beatles trekking through Nepal at that stage in their lives was ludicrous. I think it was George who suddenly had a Zen moment when he said, "Well, we're here—in Abbey Road. It's our spiritual home. Let's call it that."

Paul was keen. He lived just across the road and to him this was home anyway. For once there was no disagreement. They set up a photo shoot and the famous "zebra crossing" shot was taken of them striding across the black-and-white stripes of the pedestrian crossing that led to Cavendish Avenue.

If this was going to be their last album—which they suspected it would be— they wanted to go out with a bang. They had almost too much material to choose from, some going back years and years from when John and Paul had first started writing songs. Even George, who had come to songwriting late, had enough for what would become his triple album. I remember being with them when they sat around the studio for days listening to tapes and drawing up lists. They rejected "Jealous Guy" and "Mother Nature's Son"; and they even rejected John's classic "Imagine" because it wasn't finished—the song that was to be called the greatest song of all time, equal only to Paul's "Yesterday."

They wanted all four of them to have something on the album. Many people thought that George stole the show with his wonderfully uplifting "Here Comes the Sun" and "Something"—which has been called one of the loveliest of ballads. Ringo did the cute "Octopus's Garden," and John did three songs, his magnificent "Sun King," "Mean Mr. Mustard" and "Polythene Pam" (this last one harked back to his student days at art school). Paul, who was the driving force behind the project, did all the rest, including "Golden Slumbers."

The title of one of John's songs included the word "heavy," as in, "I Want You (She's So Heavy)." The hip contemporary use of the word has been attributed to me, at least by Paul in his biography, *Many Years from Now.* It came about one day at Apple when the atmosphere was more poisonous than usual and everyone was feeling glum and despondent, as if the weight of the world was on their shoulders.

I said, "Man, the atmosphere sucks. It's so heavy."

Paul, who was in love with words, looked up and said, "Wow!" Soon, they were all using the word, as in "it's so heavy, man" and it went from there. Around the world? I have no idea, but it did at least go all the way to John's song.

One clever idea on the other side of *Abbey Road* was the medley. This used up a large swathe of the Beatles' unfinished songs, ones that possibly might never get finished. I think George Martin and Paul were responsible for that innovative notion, and it worked.

✒

Paul, George and Ringo immediately started work on the *Abbey Road* sessions on July 1, but John and Yoko decided to go on a family holiday with Julian and Kyoko to Scotland to stay with one of Mimi's sisters, where John had spent almost all of his childhood vacations. It was a standing joke in the office how bad at driving John was. He rarely got behind the wheel himself because his sight was so poor. But, this time, he was determined to be a family man—a very stoned family man—but still, they all set off on a meandering journey. Within a couple of days news came that John had wrecked the car, an Austin Maxi, on a lonely stretch of road, and he, Yoko and Kyoko had been injured and were in the hospital. All three were badly gashed and needed extensive stitches, while Yoko had a badly wrenched back and couldn't move. After the accident, Cynthia removed Julian and Tony Cox swooped on Kyoko and took her to Denmark. John tenderly arranged for Yoko to be transferred by helicopter from the hospital lawn to Glasgow Airport, where she was put into a private plane and taken to Heathrow. From there, a helicopter flew her to the spacious lawns of their new home, Tittenhurst Park.

John had bought this huge mansion the previous year, and had it completely renovated. The renovations included a state-of-the-art studio and an enormous white music room that contained nothing else but a white grand piano and drifting white voile curtains. It was in this room that "Imagine" was finally finished the following year, inspired by Yoko's ability to play classical piano, her *Grapefruit* book, and their joint quest for peace. It would have been nice if things had remained simple, but to everyone's astonishment, after the accident John ordered a big bed from Harrods and had it installed at the studio for Yoko. A microphone was dangled in the right position above the bed, to enable Yoko to pass comment. I don't think such a thing had ever happened before in the history of recorded music. People didn't know where to look, or what to say. The other three Beatles should have said no. One depressing repercussion of Yoko's back pain was that heroin came into John's and Yoko's lives in a major way and they disappeared from sight. Holed up in the huge bedroom of their new home, they dreamed the summer away, like Coleridge and a geisha. In the end, they went cold turkey on their own—even wrote a song about it, the first recording they ever did on their own at Abbey Road—saying that they pulled through with pure willpower and inner strength. Maybe so, but it's documented that they were definitely checked in at the London Clinic and numerous friends visited them there.

With *Abbey Road* in the bag, ready to be launched, Klein announced that we would be going to the Capitol Records/Apple Convention, to be held in Hawaii. Capitol, a part of EMI, distributed Apple in the U.S. and he stressed that it was important to meet all the heads of the divisions and for them to get to know us better. This made some of us laugh. We had originally attended the first convention in Las Vegas two summers earlier, long before Klein's arrival in our midst. Our team was mainly a very happy Allen Klein, who was finally in charge of the Beatles, and me and Jack Oliver who were in charge of drinking since I didn't think Klein would allow us to say much and we had no intention of hanging out with him anyway.

But I must admit it was wonderful to fly to Hawaii in a Boeing 707 in 1969 before it became so touristy. It was like being in the start of a Bond movie, the one where Ursula Andress came up out of the sea in that white swimsuit. The whole island smelled as if it had been sprayed all over with the most wonderful subtle perfume. It was quite heady. As well as the small British contingent, Klein brought a load of his own people from New York, including executives from Invictus Records, who launched the group, Chairmen of the Board, at the convention. Klein was very buoyant, practically bouncing around like a beach ball, slapping backs and beaming. "Look at me! Top of the world, Ma!" He spent the afternoons playing tennis with the Italian crowd from New York, running all over the court showing off, while Jack and I did the PR thing from our lounge chairs on the terrace, with lots of tropical booze served in hollowed-out pineapples. Every now and then, Jack would glance across at Klein and say, "Look at that fat bastard. I'd like to stuff this pineapple right up his jaxsey."

I said, "Nice thought. Great waste."

Our hotel, which was right on Waikiki Beach, was the hotel where the TV series, *Hawaii Five*-O was filmed. About a thousand drunks, in what is now known as "the full Jimmy Buffett" of lurid shirts and baggy shorts, staggered around with their pineapples slopping, laughing and mimicking Jack Lord's big closing line: "Book him Dann-O. Murder One." The cabaret was Freda Payne, doing "Band of Gold," and Glen Campbell and Joe South—big mates of Elvis—also performed. Elvis himself happened to be making a film there at the time and Glen and Joe introduced us to him. We didn't say a great deal; one never does in those situations. It was just a handshake and, "How do you do?"

I was totally in awe. His voice sounded as if he was speaking the words to "American Trilogy," as if he'd said, "Look away, Dixieland!" He looked fantastic and I remembered how that earlier summer in Los Angeles, the colonel had given me some tickets for his "comeback"—which also happened to be in Hawaii. Sadly, he wasn't in concert this time, so I never did get to hear him sing live.

32

In many respects, Ringo had drifted sideways from the mess at Apple some time ago. He drifted for a while and even said, "I wondered what I should do with my life now that it's all over." He decided to go back to his roots by producing an album of big band and show tunes from his childhood. He asked his mother to remind him of a few and friends came up with others. From September 1969 to early 1970 he got on with making his own album on Apple, *Sentimental Journey*. It was produced by George Martin, and friends, such as Paul, contributed with the arrangements. Ringo said in an interview: "The great thing was that it got me moving. It got me going. Okay, let's go, not very fast, but just moving in some way. It was like the first shovel of coal in the furnace that makes the train inch forward."

While Ringo got on quietly with making things happen, George was the first to express his annoyance over his own position. He felt that the records he was making with Jackie Lomax, Doris Troy and Billy Preston were not getting the same push as an individual Beatle album. The only real hits were Billy Preston's single, "That's the Way God Planned It," and the two Hare Krishna records, which were seen as novelties. He couldn't get Apple to sign Delaney and Bonnie and Friends, whom George was passionate about. To get some space, he went out on tour with them. It wasn't structured, like the tours Brian had worked hard on with the Beatles. It was much looser and it was fun. I think that was when he realized there was a whole different world out there.

By the autumn of 1969 the Hare Krishnas became George's big passion; unfortunately it was one that nobody else wanted anything to do with. But, somehow, George charmed and suckered everyone in. I guess he had his Indian stuff like John had his *Two Virgins* stuff. After their experience in India, for a couple of years all the Beatles took to dressing in an Eastern way, which was also quite hippie-ish, with brightly colored satin or velvet tunics, collarless shirts, beads, floppy hats and so on. George, however, took it to extremes, draping himself in layers and layers of beads. He grew his hair and beard very long. He gave up wearing shoes, preferring sandals instead—what are called *chaplis* in India. At times, he even came into the offices dressed in some togalike white robes, his own cheesecloth interpretation of the Krishnas' orange gear. To this, he added a garland of their sacred marigolds draped around his neck. He would give us all the V peace sign, which John also took up.

We hid our smiles and condescendingly called it "George's Hare Krishna thing," but the seriousness that we had to treat it with was a right royal pain in the arse. Every time the subject came up, we all made loud snoring noises, looked at our watches and said, "Put the telly on and we'll catch the *Magic Roundabout.*" In fact, the *Magic Roundabout* made more sense. (This was a cult TV show for toddlers in which some of the names were drug related, something the staid BBC producers didn't realize—just as they didn't realize about Bill and Ben, the Flowerpot Men and their friend Weed in another popular kiddies' show—while *Captain Pugwash* had two characters named Master Bates and Seaman Staines.)

We might have joked about George's new interest, but it wasn't very funny. Not only was it hard work drumming up sufficient Krishnas to placate George when he wanted them around, but we were all bored to death at having to go along with the bunch of dropouts who marched up and down, chanting, clanging bells and begging for money.

The London Radha-Krishna temple, fully funded by George, was in Oxford Street and too close to our office on Savile Row for comfort. Passing by the temple, one would always catch a whiff of joss sticks and pot floating on the air. I often saw the members begging on the street, bent and shuffling along, sometimes wearing only sandals in the snow, no coats, their noses runny with cold, their pigtails ratty and their eyes red-rimmed. It was a nightmare that these same people were now turning up at our office, and in the TV studios, ringing their incessant bloody bells and looking for George. I was the one who had to deal with them most of the time, and I have little patience for people whose kids are taken away by social workers because they're suffering from malnutrition. I happen to believe in feeding kids, not making them pray all night and live on bean shoots and curds.

When George went into the studio with his pals we all thought nothing would come of it—how could it? But, somehow, Joe Public came to believe that this stuff was deep, like: "If you're not into it then you must be an insensitive moron who will be punished in the next incarnation." I saw it as emotional blackmail, a kind of weird religious peer pressure that says if you don't give until it hurts, you're gonna pay for it later. As John said, "The karma will get you."

I said, "I'll take my chances. I'll tell God he gave us Yoko and Klein and I was busy with them on his behalf." At the time, John lacked his usual sense of humor, so he stared at me suspiciously.

The Krishnas' conviction might have been believable except for the fact that many were reformed junkies. I personally never saw a bona fide Indian among them. Most of these guys were not only British, many of them were from Liverpool! I said to Paul, "How are you going to send out for a chicken tikka masala if all the guys who work in the tandoori are down on Oxford Street with George, marching, clanging and begging?"

Paul grinned and said, "George doesn't clang, he's too busy."

He was. When the Hare Krishnas got on *Top of the Pops* that September they had to be taken seriously because *TOTP* was the most popular TV show in England. The unlikely Krishna impetus had started during the summer of 1969, when George had released his single, "Hare Krishna Mantra," with the temple members chanting away in the background. It had quickly gone to number one in Europe and Asia. We cynics were all greatly surprised by this commercial success. There was some jocular eating of hats and stepping over "my dead bodies." Then the producer of *TOTP* rang me up.

"Tony? How many Hare Krishnas can you lay on at the studio for this week's show?" he inquired. Amazed, I asked George this metaphysical question.

"How many Hare Krishnas can we get, George?" He did a slow mental head count. "Uh . . . thirty-seven," he said, then frowned. "Hang on, maybe it's . . . uh . . . thirty-eight."

Leaving George to count the pigtails, I got back on the phone to the *TOTP* producer. "We could let you have thirty-seven, give or take a clang," I said.

The man at the Beeb said, "Oh dear. We've only got room for five. Send us your five best chanters."

I had to go down to the Krishna GHQ and, feeling more than faintly ridiculous, said, "Hey, Hare, can five of you get yourselves down to *Top of the Pops* tomorrow?"

"No!" they said, helping themselves to another macrobiotic onion bhajee.

"We all have to do it, or not at all. Have a bhajee. Leave a peace offering."

I thought I was in deep water when I called the guy at the Beeb to tell him that he couldn't break up the set. "It's a whole temple or nothing," I said. He groaned.

"Well, since it's George Harrison," he said, reluctantly, "I don't suppose I've much choice."

An extra corridor of dressing rooms had to be opened and a couple dozen vases brought in to hold all the marigolds. Taping the show itself wasn't easy, considering it's difficult to step around, and over, that many Hare Krishnas. There they all were in those orange robes, meditating, counting beads and getting in the way of the cameras, not to mention all those electrical cables that were snaking about. But the show was taped and aired, and this was how America got wind that George Harrison had a new mantra to match his raised consciousness.

All those Krishna bells must have sounded like cash registers. As often happens when any religion rears its head, opportunists saw the political, not to mention commercial, possibilities. George and his little orange friends with the red, runny noses were suddenly big business. Capitol Records immediately sent a Magi to find that star shining in the East: the president, Stan Gortikov. Instead of frankincense or myrrh, Stan arrived bearing a big smile. He was eager to check things out, or so he told me.

"It's been an ambition of mine to see the Beatles in action at Abbey Road," he confided, "with George Martin producing." In short, he wanted to see the whole legendary shebang and it fell to my unfortunate lot to set it up for him. Unfortunately, because Stan was still stuck in the land of "She Loves You" and "I Wanna Hold Your Hand," what he got instead was one of those wild nights when George was doing his "Hare Krishna thing." Most of the Oxford Street Temple was there to chant along, swaying like orange reeds. Everywhere Stan looked he saw sitars, incense, tambourines and beads. It was "Clang! Clang! Clang!" instead of "Yeah! Yeah! Yeah!" Yogis in loincloths sat cross-legged upon mattresses around the room, making occasional leaps into the air, using their arse muscles to propel them. Even life in Los Angeles hadn't prepared Stan Gortikov for yogic flying. His face was a picture and I gently led him away to the pub.

A loony September wasn't done with me yet. John was feeling lots better after his treatment for heroin addiction in the London Clinic and several months of an attempt to use Primal Scream Therapy under Arthur Janov by telephone, to free him from his heroin addiction. He and Yoko had started dropping into the offices regularly.

The Beatles had been invited to play the Toronto Rock Festival but hadn't accepted, though John had muttered something about going for the Live Peace part of it. Two days before the event, I was chatting to Mal in the office when John drifted in. Something was obviously on his mind.

"Oh, hi. I was thinking—" he started. Mal and I interrupted our conversation and waited for what John had to say. "Uh," John continued, quietly summing up the situation in a detached way, "I'm going to need a drummer and a bass player, and me and Yoko, and you, Mal."

I suddenly realized that John was talking about a pick-up band for the concert in Toronto. It was like a Monty Python sketch: "You doctor, me patient, she nurse, you Tone, you Mal, find people, get tickets for big silver bird for heap big gig, man."

"Yeah, leave it to us, John," I said. But this was Thursday and the concert was Saturday. Why had John, as always, left it until the last minute? Then again, Mal and I were interchangeable, "Appleman and Robin—superfixers!" We could have a quick nervous breakdown, get on the phone and still be in the pub by six, just like doing business in any other Batcave in London. But John was talking again.

"I asked Allen and he said it, yeah, go ahead—do it." I wondered why he needed permission, especially from Klein, but didn't comment. However, I could see Mal was wondering the same thing. Then, just before John drifted off, he turned and said, "Oh, Tone, can you get us some music? And . . . uh . . . we'll meet you at the airport."

"Music, John? What music?"

"Yeah, you know, all those songs from way back when . . . uh . . . you know, those songs we used to do. All that Chuck Berry stuff and Little Richard stuff and Fats Domino stuff . . . get all the top lines for all that stuff . . . know what I mean?"

"What about musicians?" Mal asked.

"I'll sort that out," John said, which of course he didn't do.

Getting the lineup wasn't easy. By then, it was Saturday, after all, and most people, like Eric Clapton, were still in a coma and not answering their phones. In the end, the lineup consisted of Eric—who was finally roused; bass player Klaus Voorman, who John knew way back from their first trip to Hamburg; drummer Alan White, whom George's assistant, Terry Doran (demoted from being head of publishing), rounded up. At the time, Alan played for a band called Skip Bifferty, one of Don Arden's fledgling groups. Later, he joined Yes.

Having organized the tickets and the hotels, I was wandering around Tin Pan Alley and the top end of Charing Cross Road with my flight bag, going into publishers and buying all the rock classics on sheet music I could lay my hands on. I schlepped out to Heathrow, to the VIP lounge, where Eric, John, Yoko, Mal and the rest of the lineup were drinking green tea and mango juice, waiting to board.

"Thanks, Tone," John said as I arrived. He took the large package of sheet music from me. "Great stuff. We'll rehearse on the plane, know what I mean?" I looked at the group crowding around with instrument cases and said, "By the way, the flight was full. So I'm not coming."

To tell the truth, I wasn't disappointed even though I learned later that John and the rest of them had rehearsed on the plane with acoustic guitars, a rare treat for the other passengers, and one I'm sure few of them will ever forget. Back at the office when I walked in and was asked what had happened, the joke started to circulate that Yoko was given an acoustic stepladder to rehearse on the plane so that her chops would be "up" for the gig.

They got to Toronto just in time. It was John and Yoko's first public outing as the Plastic Ono Band. We heard that it went over extremely well, all except for Yoko, who rolled around in a white sack on stage while John was singing. Then he stepped back and said, "Well, folks, this is the bit you've all been waiting for!"

Yoko wailed a lost and lonely banshee scream for twenty minutes or so. The audience wholeheartedly booed her, despite their respect for John and the others. Nonetheless, the *Live Peace in Toronto* album was great, with some of the best straight-ahead rock and roll you'll ever hear.

Many people have asked me if Yoko thought she was artistic or avant-garde. To tell the truth, I don't really know. At parties people were saying, "Oh, yes, Yoko . . . uh . . . she's with John, who is enormously talented, and *he* admires her stuff but, personally, I think, well . . . I don't know." Then doubt set in because some critics and reviewers gave her favorable reviews in the press and on TV. You'd find yourself wondering if you were an intellectual failure, unable to spot the hidden value in Yoko's art and music. I can remember those discussions and the debates among John's friends, particularly when it was obvious that John was obsessively smitten. He had a reputation as something of an intellect, so somehow it became important to judge Yoko as impartially as possible, mostly out of regard for John. The problem was we couldn't accept that he could be so blinded.

I wonder now if we'd all said, "John, she's bloody awful—you know it, we know it, and the whole world knows it," he would have *realized,* and maybe Yoko Ono would never have happened. But we all covered it up. We all told him she was good when he asked our opinion—as he often did at first. In retrospect, we are all to blame for Yoko's artistic rise. It was a case of collective guilt and also the emperor's new clothes. As a result, Yoko ended up practically fireproof where John was concerned. After a time, he was too far lost in Yoko for the truth to have mattered.

▀

Over the years, working closely with so many stars, getting closer to them than most people do, has led to a certain cynicism. I developed the somewhat old-fashioned attitude that a pop star's job, if that word is correct, is to sing songs and make records, not to comment on politics, be it John Lennon or whoever. I think what led John into believing that he had the right to talk about world peace was that people took his opinion seriously on any subject, whether it was jelly babies or the bomb. Hunter Thompson once said that when people like Lennon started ranting on about politics, all they did was get in the way. People deferred to John because he looked the peacenik part. He was shortsighted and wore glasses, which made him look political and academic. He looked concerned. He probably was concerned. He looked deep, but he was not Socrates. There was a famous Rigby cartoon in the *Sun* at the time when John and Yoko were cutting off their long hair for peace and wrapping themselves up in bags. It was all bag-peace-love-hair. The cartoon depicted grinning dustmen picking up the wrong bag—the one with John and Yoko's shaven heads sticking out, not the one with the hair—to throw them in the grinder at the rear of the dustcart.

The shorn hair event was not a political issue at all. It was a stoned issue. Yoko had permission from Tony to go and see her daughter in Denmark for Christmas. During that visit, she and John were persuaded by Cox to shave their heads. It was a strange moment, and one apparently more to do with Cox convincing them that it was a good idea, but playing a spiteful prank that they simply didn't see. On their return to England they got in thick with Michael X, otherwise known as Michael Abdul-Malik, the leader of the Black Muslims and president of the Racial Adjustment Action Society. Linked with the Black Eagles and the Black Panthers, their base was the Black House, the complex of adjoining terrace houses, shops and empty factories in Holloway Road. Described as a social commune it was financially helped by pop singers, actors, churchmen and such. John and Yoko enthusiastically endorsed all that the movement stood for and donated their shorn hair to raise money for the Black House. (In return they were given the gift of a pair of Muhammad Ali's sweaty shorts.) Abdul Malik's eventual fate was to be hanged in Jamaica, for murder. I often wonder who bought that hair, and if they still have it. Sometimes I have bizarre fantasies about it, like could you actually *clone* John from his hair?

John rarely insulted people or was rude to anyone. Occasionally, he'd say witty little things in a Lewis Carroll or an Edward Lear way, or maybe in a *Goon Show* type of way, but he didn't ever say anything racist or nasty. He would make the odd V sign behind someone's back, but he was never frightening. On the other hand, Yoko Ono *was* frightening. Trying to promote her records was downright scary.

I can remember taking her product into radio stations. The nearest it got to a play list was the producer's bin. Or they would smile and say, "Thanks, Tone," and then sail the record across the studio like a Frisbee. This was light-years removed from the avid reception I got when I went in with a new Beatles record. Deejays would interrupt their shows to put it on the turntable at once. I can remember the various studios filling up with producers, and secretaries lining the walls, just to watch the Beatles' latest release actually spinning around on the turntable while they listened.

The idea of Zapple, Apple's Poetry and Spoken Word project, which had started well, and then faded with the disappearance of Ken Kesey and the Merry Pranksters, hadn't really gone away. Paul was very open to ideas and John and Yoko were also still keen on it and they mentioned it to Klein. Naturally, he took a good look at it. I wasn't particularly into beat poetry and all the Kerouac *On The Road*, Tangerine-Flake Streamline Baby type of writings, and looking back, neither were most of the staff at Apple. We just liked rock music I suppose and didn't see any market, or more to the point, didn't really see any reason for Apple to be doing this spoken-word experimentation. But while the walls had been resonating at Savile Row with endless bickering and in-fighting, Barry Miles, one of the founders of Indica, had been out of sight and almost out of touch for months, roaming around the United States with a mobile recording unit, compiling interviews and recording sessions with the new breed of avant-garde writers.

What killed it all stone dead was one of Miles's big ideas to make an album in New York with the granddaddy of beat poets, Allen Ginsberg, whom he had first met in London, at Indica. Ginsberg agreed, but perturbingly businesslike for a hippie, he said he wanted some sort of special contract with Zapple, a real piece of paper with words and percentages and amounts on it. He didn't know what a mistake this was because Klein was now involved in the financial Apple/Zapple setup. Klein said he and Ginsberg would have to have a meeting to discuss this piece of paper. Miles brought Ginsberg along. To say that the pair of them didn't hit it off was something of an understatement. Here comes the shuffling unkempt Jewish beat poet with peanut butter in his beard talking about his projected royalties, and across the desk there's a glaring Klein the archcapitalist Jewish lawyer/accountant, who abhorred the idea of giving anybody any royalties, especially to what he called a "fake fagellah poet."

No, they did not get on. Ginsberg apparently adopted the asana position and was doing a quick "Ommmmmm." He invited Klein to join in to get the right vibes going. Klein would have none of it. He shouted, "Get offa my carpet and outa my office, you goddamn queer hippie!"

Soon, strange as it may seem, Klein withdrew all Zapple funding and scrapped the whole idea forthwith. Miles was mortified. He was stuck with all these tapes and living in the Chelsea Hotel in New York, absolutely out of money, out of everything, and going out of his mind. Eventually he got his tapes compiled and they were released by various other specialist labels.

Paul had put money into the Indica bookshop, which Miles ran, above which Ginsberg came and lived for a while. Ginsberg had been heavily involved in the great Pro Pot rally at Hyde Park, at Speakers' Corner. Gonzo Ginzo, as we called him, had gotten up on a soapbox, played his little squeezebox and declaimed his poetry, but most of the thousands of people who went along that sunny afternoon did so because Eric Clapton was playing. As for Bukowski, I met him in Los Angeles, but it was impossible to hold a conversation because he was always falling over drunk. Mickey Rourke played Bukowski in a movie, but William Burroughs was a different kettle of fish. A beat novelist as against a beat poet, he was around London all the time and came into Apple a lot. For a while, like Ginsberg he lived virtually next door to the Indica bookshop in Masons Yard. Eventually, Zapple joined Apple Electronics and the Apple Boutique in losing money and being closed down.

33

I **had met Phil Spector** for the first time when Brian was still alive. He'd come to England for a tour with Billy J. Kramer, who was signed to NEMS, although I don't recall what Phil was actually going to do. However, Andrew Loog Oldham gave him the complete living legend treatment and I was delegated to promote the tour. Cilla had also recorded a cover version of "You've Lost That Loving Feeling," Phil's big hit with the Righteous Brothers. Before they even knew him, the Beatles were in awe of Phil Spector's music. They did his big hit, "To Know Him Is to Love Him" at their failed audition for Decca. Despite the failure of the audition, the Beatles were still in awe of Phil Spector's work when they met him.

Paul's rejection of Spector originated from when Klein secretly called Spector in to "rescue" the *Get Back* tapes, which had never been issued. After the rooftop sessions and the filming at Twickenham, the masses of film and all the tapes were put into storage. Some of it was accidentally thrown away and was stolen. (Down the years, it got released out of Holland by bootleg pirates.) From going through the Abbey Road accounts and discovering that studio time had been charged for work that hadn't been used, Klein did some detective work and learned about the *Get Back* sessions. Well, to him, this was potential gold dust. It was lost Beatles material that could be issued and earn him tons of money.

John and George were keen on Phil Spector and when Allen Klein, who was busy trying to please them, asked them who could rescue these tapes, they suggested Phil. In the spring of 1970 Phil smothered the lot with strings, horns and female choruses, and it was released as *Let It Be*.

When Paul heard it, particularly what he referred to as Spector's sickly sweet version of "The Long and Winding Road," he was furious. He rushed straight into Apple and berated Klein so loudly you could hear him throughout the building. "It's not us anymore!" he shouted.

Klein's rude comment was, "Your original material sucked. It was unusable. John thinks Phil is a genius and I agree with him."

Ironically, the movie *Let It Be* won an Oscar in 1971 for best original score. The only ones who bothered to attend the ceremony were Paul and Linda, who picked up the statue on behalf of the Beatles. (Thirty years on, Paul and Ringo got together and had the album de-Spectorized for re-release.)

Phil took a shine to me, perhaps because I was a good listener and he was a world-class talker. Every time he flew over, he would come into Apple and perch himself on the end of my desk like a little fishing garden gnome. He talked about Life, about anything and everything. Mostly, he talked about himself, so I got to know him and his phobias quite well. He was still married to Veronica, "Ronnie" of the Ronettes, for whom he produced his Wall of Sound–style hits, like "Da Doo Ron Ron," "Be My Baby" and "Baby I Love You," records that took the pop world by both storm and surprise. The American music industry's surprise that he could do so much so well soon turned to hate. He was the first pop multimillionaire with about $38 million in the bank, but he was also a renegade who refused to follow the rulebook. It infuriated and baffled them. His black groups had pushed many white stars off the stage. The music industry couldn't stand uncontrollable geniuses and Phil was convinced that they were conspiring to get rid of him because he was just too powerful. His reaction was to fan the flames of his natural New York poor boy paranoia by hiring a huge bodyguard by the name of George, and equipping him with the biggest handguns imaginable.

I don't think I'd seen a gun carried by anyone until I met Spector. George had been a cop in L.A. and was licensed to carry arms around the world. "He's licensed to kill," Phil told me, telling George to show me his two shoulder holsters. Phil didn't have a gun license in the U.K., but he always told me that he was never without his big U.S. police .38s—which he kept stuffed into his belt and in a shoulder holster concealed beneath his cloak. John was fascinated by the weapons and discussed them at length with Phil or mostly George, who would show him how to load and unload and do the cowboy twirl.

Phil was a self-confessed ex-control freak, self-confessed ex-schizoid para-
noiac, who carried around more baggage than Pan Am. He was so terrified of flying that when he arrived in London after a flight, for a few hours he would be at
the speechless stage beyond rant. When the Beatles and Phil flew to New York
once, Phil wouldn't sit down, but walked up and down the aisles. Ringo said,
"He's as mad as a hatter. He walked the Atlantic, you know?" Another time that
we flew, Phil got some kind of psychic warning. He freaked out and refused to
get on the plane, so we all had to wait for the next flight.

When his father killed himself in the garage in New York with exhaust
fumes, his mom put on his gravestone the epitaph: TO KNOW HIM IS TO LOVE HIM.
Phil went one step further and turned that epitaph into a song. Always a manic-
compulsive-obsessive, no doubt part of his peculiar attraction, charm and success, he decided to overemphasize by doubling up the words of the catchy little
mantra—"To know-know-know him is to love-love-love him . . ."—and it shot
to the top of the charts with the Teddy Bears, who consisted of seventeen-year-
old Phil and two friends.

Sometimes, he talked about England. As an example of his schizoid personality, he would rant on about how much he hated England because his best
friend, Lenny Bruce, had been deported from London. "Bastards!" he shrieked.
"This country sucks."

John was a bit of a renegade; he'd nod in agreement and make his rude V
sign, but Paul was very patriotic. "If you don't like it, go home," Paul would say.

Phil would glare and squawk, "Hell, no! This is a great place! I love it here."
He could be quite bizarre because his mind didn't work like most people's. He
might have been a record-producing genius but he was also out of his tree. He
would get worked up over almost anything and yell like a little Demosthenes.
Unlike Paul, I let him rant. I nodded and now and then said tentatively, "Y-e-s,"
like a Norman Rockwell professor who was Professor Emeritus of Rant at Columbia encouraging someone to elaborate—although Phil needed little encouragement.

It didn't help that he looked weird, with his little velvet outfits, his strange
wigs and his cloak. There was the time he went to Berkeley Square to buy a Rolls
Royce wearing the cloak and looking like his friend, Bela Lugosi. The sales staff
thought he was a deranged tramp and gave him a hard time. When they refused
him permission to take the car on a test-drive, he jumped in behind the wheel of
the latest model and drove it out through the showroom window, singing

"A Nightingale Sang in Berkeley Square" at the top of his voice. He told me all about it from his usual perch on my desk and asked me to get him the whole lyric. Laughed like a maniac. Said he'd produce it. Take it round the showroom and put it through the mailbox. Lennon thought this was hilarious and the two of them cackled like witches. Yoko had no sense of humor at all and she loathed Phil as much as Phil hated her. Each of them was implacable and paranoid.

But if someone else from the outside was going to produce them, she didn't see why it couldn't be her. When Yoko and Phil confronted each other, sparks would fly and I fully expected Phil to grab a gun or karate chop Yoko into slices. Phil was very good at martial arts. I don't know who had taught him, but they included experts like Bruce Lee and Elvis's bodyguard, Mike Stone, who was to run off with Priscilla. I was surprised, then, when Phil told me that he'd had a punch-up with David Geffen, Spielberg's partner in DreamWorks. Weedy though Phil was, he could have killed the record mogul, but restrained himself. So obviously, he did know how far he could go.

When Phil came over to rescue the "Let It Be" recordings, which had gone horribly wrong and which the Beatles had lost all interest in, we had to sort through the hundreds of tapes stacked up all over the place, offcuts of music and hours of conversation from shooting the film. There were so many that many were dumped and surfaced as part of the stash that was "discovered" in 2003 by the police and said to be worth millions.

Phil carted them all off to Abbey Road and holed up for months while he worked. He seemed to live on tandoori chicken takeaways during this time and ordered it in by the crate. It was his passion for this dish that introduced us to it big time and it became an Apple staple. When the Beatles finally heard the finished tape, John and George loved it. "It's not the Beatles," Paul said stubbornly, refusing to be convinced. "It's not our sound." It got so bad that Paul couldn't stand to be in the same room as Phil. When Phil walked in, Paul walked out—as he did very publicly many years later, during an awards ceremony. However, when the album won a Grammy, it was Paul who collected it—like he had also collected the Oscar for the film score.

With Christmas approaching, Klein decided we would put out Phil's famous Christmas album again. Phil's genius had been to take straightforward Christmas songs like "Rudolph" and "Frosty" and turn them into Wall of Sound works of art. The album had been released a few years earlier, on the day that John Kennedy died, but those in the music industry said it was the day the music died because record sales plunged. Nobody wanted bright Christmassy stuff so Phil's record was withdrawn. Since then, it had become rare and very collectable.

Klein's idea for the reissue was sound, but Phil didn't help. I arranged some interviews with him with the press, who hated him, and which he did with very bad grace. He was scathing about everything in his horrible, squeaky, high-pitched little voice that came out of the kind of neck most people would want to throttle within a minute or two. He just seemed to go out of his way to aggravate everybody with his attitude. As I have said, great producer—pity about the man. However, everyone likes a nice Christmas album and there was no doubt his production was brilliant. Apple's coffers—and Klein—garnered several million more pounds.

Phil's guns and his bodyguards were always much in evidence and eventually he retreated and got fortressed up in his own asylum with his own rules. It was to prove impossible to deal with him, although I admired his talent so much I tried over many years. I put my heart and soul into trying. I worked with him, managed him at one time, promoted him, visited him—and almost ended up as crazy as he was.

34

While the Beatles had split up—at least emotionally and creatively, though not legally—and were doing their own thing, I continued to do whatever was required of me at Apple, and indeed at NEMS, which was still in existence. Mostly, I promoted records or brought in new talent. However, I did have bags more spare time than I had before, and my social life expanded accordingly. In many ways, I saw far more of the daily "in" life of London, because I was always around, dropping in on places and meeting people the Beatles couldn't because of their fame.

I was always running into *enfant terrible* Keith Moon around town. He was known for greater excesses than any of the other rock stars. Even the Stones were tame in comparison. I liked him because he was so amusing. One evening, Moon gave me his flat, "just like that," as comedian Tommy Cooper would say. The lease on my flat in Chelsea was about to expire and having been too busy to pay attention to such domestic details as renewal letters from the agent, I suddenly found myself homeless. This coincided with Jack Oliver having difficulties with his wife. She asked him to leave their Chiswick flat, or he wanted to. At any rate, we decided to drop into the Speakeasy and have a few drinks. The solution to our problems arrived unexpectedly. Keith Moon was there and soon was a party to our tale of woe.

"Dear boy, dear boy, fret no more," Keith said to me. "I have a flat in High-gate, above a car showroom as it happens, very handy when you run out of cars. You can have it, Tone. It's at Thirty-two Highgate High Street. Here you are." And he handed me a set of keys.

"Have it, Keith?" I asked, picking up the keys. "What do you mean by *have it?*"

"It's yours, dear boy, lock stock and barrel. I own it. It's furnished, every-thing's kosher, you won't need a thing." I looked at him suspiciously.

Rather like that story where the Austrian prince is told that the Russian am-bassador has died, and says, "Really? I wonder what his game is?" I said, "What are you up to, Keith?" I had visions of him having sawed a large circle in the living room floor above the car showroom. Jack and I would walk in, descend rather rapidly in a sea of plaster, get taken to the hospital, where Moon would turn up with flowers, laughter, brandy and dynamite, asking "How are you, dear boy? Have you got a match?"

"I'm bored with it," Keith said. "I don't want it anymore." That made sense and I pocketed the keys.

Some time after midnight, Jack and I hopped into a taxi and I gave the ad-dress. In that world, in those days, life really was a magical mystery tour and anything was possible. The flat was just as Keith had assured us, fully and very comfortably furnished, which was more than you could say for most hotel rooms after Moon had occupied them. A nice decorative touch was the bottom half of a bottle of champagne sticking out of the living room wall. Apparently, in a famil-iar fit of pique, Moon had flung a full magnum at the wall and instead of smash-ing, as champagne bottles tend to when hurled at walls or prows of ships, it had embedded itself deep in the plaster. Later, I put a nice frame around it, making an instant *objet d'art*. I lived in Keith Moon's flat until I fell for Julie Ege. In March 1970 I moved to Belgravia with her, leaving the flat to Jack, where he continued to live, rent-free.

Julie Ege, a Norwegian film star and model, was my girlfriend for five or six years. Rosemary Frankland, my previous girlfriend, had been Miss World and Julie represented Norway in the Miss Universe competition. Both of them were incredibly beautiful. When I met Julie, she had just made a film with Marty Feldman called *Every Home Should Have One*. After that she took off like dyna-mite as the "sex symbol of the 70s." You couldn't open a newspaper or a maga-zine without seeing her photograph. Literally every day, there she was, naked and gorgeous, in the papers, on the front mat. We must have gone to a million showbiz parties simply because I was with the Beatles and she was in the nude. That is to say, in the papers she was often photographed in the nude. For a while we lived in a flat in Chesham Place, just off Pont Street, Belgravia, a very smart central district of London between Buckingham Place and Victoria Station. However, I yearned to live in Barnes again. One of the first places I rented when Brian moved NEMS down to London was a two-up two-down by the river in Barnes. I liked it because while it felt like a real country village, the kind of place you'd escape to for the weekend, it was just twenty minutes on the train from the West End. I convinced Julie that it was the perfect place to live, and when we found a lovely four-bedroomed house with a big garden in Suffolk Road just around the corner from where I had lived before, we took it. We finished moving in the late afternoon, early evening. The place was still piled high with unpacked tea chests and suitcases, but we were starving so after the removal van left so did we. We just locked the door and went to the nearest Indian restaurant, where we met some people we knew. Afterward, we went to the pub and had a jolly time. When we strolled back home at about twelve thirty to one o'clock, we found the place had been stripped. We'd moved in; burglars had moved us out.

It was very depressing. Julie was just about the top photographic model in the country and had lots of really good jewelry. I think she was probably targeted—maybe someone was even watching. They probably followed us as far as the Indian restaurant and knew that they had at least a couple of hours. The police came and looked at the open window that we pointed at and said, "Yes, they came in through there." Then they licked the stubs of their pencils, made a few notes and left. That was that. We lay down on the bed and went to sleep. But the next day it got much worse. I called the insurance company to tell them we'd been burgled and they denied liability on the grounds that we hadn't told them that we were moving from Chesham Place to Barnes. "Read the small print," they lectured smugly. "You should have called us," they said. "Every area is different, but even so, we can't transfer the insurance unless you call us." To be honest I had to admit that they did have a point. When we started to list what was missing, I suddenly realized that all my Beatles memorabilia had gone, all the presents the boys and Brian had given me over the years. The list is too long to give here, but it included a very nice inscribed gold Rolex watch engraved FROM THE FAB FOUR; a lighter that said FROM J & Y; gold discs. All gone. They'd even taken my heirloom Faberge cuff links with the family crest.

The only thing that I ever heard about was over thirty years later when someone sent me an e-mail saying that they'd bought a gold disc at a boot sale of a smash hit number-one record which was presented to me for getting it to the top. (I won't name and shame the artist.) They didn't want to get into trouble but could they possibly keep it? I e-mailed them straight back and said, "Please!

Be my guest! Keep it." My largesse lasted until they e-mailed again, to ask if I had any others I didn't want.

A lot of interesting, showbiz types of people lived in Barnes. It was one of those leafy, traditional places where very little has changed over the years, yet trendy, with Olympic Studios where the Stones did their early stuff, the Eagles recorded their first album, and all sorts of rock stars used it regularly. They liked it because the pace was slower. You could take a break and stroll around the village or go to the Sun Inn, a nice old-fashioned pub right by the Village Green. The Sun was always full of actors and rock stars, sitting inside and out, and drinking beer.

There was also a bowling club that went back to Tudor times and a cricket team. It was all very sedate and quaint. A lot of people joined so they could carry on drinking when the pub was supposed to be closed. I was elected captain of the bowling team because I lived close by and seemed to have plenty of time on my hands. The members were people like comedian Billy Connolly, Roger Chapman from the band Family and Captain Sensible from the Damned. It was a real mixture. We had a team but very little competition, and there was a good reason for this. The rules we played by and the layout of our bowling green were almost unique. Only one other club had similar rules and green. This was the ancient bowling club at the Tower of London, and once a year the Beefeater Bowlers from the Tower would invite us to play a grand match against them. We always thought it was a great honor to play these eccentric-looking men with their mutton-chop whiskers and their historic red-and-gold uniforms. The first match was actually played at the Tower on their marvelous green, which was like velvet. Imagine playing on grass that Anne Boleyn, Elizabeth I and Henry VIII used to play on, not to mention Drake and Raleigh! The return match at the Sun Inn was an event, but still, it didn't have exactly the same cachet. We always used to win, too.

Brian May, of Queen, wasn't a member of the bowling club, but I got to know him very well because he was another neighbor of mine. Brian would come along to drink beer and cheer us on. He and I had met when the Beatles first tried out Trident Studios in Soho. Trident always kept way ahead of anybody else technically. The Beatles cut "Hey Jude" there and Apple did "Those Were the Days," with Mary Hopkin. Trident was owned by two brothers, Barry and Norman Sheffield, ex-musos from the early sixties. They also had an American guy called Jack Nelson working for them. I would drop by at Trident to do some business for Apple or maybe just to hang out. That's when Jack and a mate of mine named Ronnie Beck would play me these Queen tracks, probably hoping that I would take it to Paul or John, and Queen would get signed to Apple.

I liked what I heard, but never took it further. Sometime late in 1973 or early 1974, Jack and Ronnie talked me into going to a Queen gig at a technical college. Maybe it was an off night, but I wasn't knocked out. Before I left, Ronnie gave me a tape, or acetate, and I played it for John Lennon, who hated it.

"It's dreadful," John said. "Rubbish." At that time, John thought most things were rubbish, except the genuine article that Yoko was creating. However, I liked the sound of the group's music and persisted a little.

"It's different, John," I said. I think "Seven Seas of Rhye" was on the tape, and "Killer Queen." It was almost the finished album, all ready to be taken up by someone. Looking back, there was really no excuse not to do anything with it, but we didn't. Despite that, all the members of Queen, including Freddie Mercury, who was very disappointed, stayed friends with me. I used to chat to Brian while he was mowing his back lawn, and we would often go to the pub for a beer. About a year after this, "Killer Queen" went massive.

"You should have signed us, Tone," was all Brian said.

"I wish we had," I said, ruefully.

After that, it all happened for Queen. If John had been more positive, I would have given the other Beatles a listen, but once you got a negative from one Beatle, you didn't pursue it. That's how it worked at Apple—except for Ringo. Ringo didn't really participate in the A & R thing at Apple. He had his own ideas about things. In fact, he didn't spend all that much time at Apple if he could help it. For a long time after Brian's death, John and Paul would come in virtually daily, and George about once a week after Yoko moved in. After Klein's installation, it was a matter of tracking them down at home.

Often I would drop in on Jack Oliver, who continued living in Moon's flat, dusting the framed champagne. At GHQ Apple, things were tense. Jack and Alan Klein, who hated each other, continued to fight, but plotting and intrigue takes on a much more positive feel if you have the power to hire and fire as Klein had. Eventually, Jack got the chop, something that was always in the cards. He went to work with Peter Asher in L.A., but first he "bequeathed" the Moon flat to his brother, Jeff. On the grapevine, I heard that Jack had left Peter's employ to set up on his own in a decorating business, importing English fireplaces and Anglicizing wealthy people's homes around Malibu. Many years on, living in Devon with my wife, Lesley, and our two boys, I called a cab to take me to the train station to get to London on business. The driver had a London accent.

"I've seen you in the papers, haven't I?" he asked. "You're in the music business." I agreed that I was. "My best mate, Jeff, is in the music biz. He lives in Highgate," the driver continued. "Maybe you know him? His name's Jeff Oliver."

And that was how I learned that Jack's brother Jeff had lived in "my" Moon flat for twenty years, gotten married, had three children and had never been asked for a penny in rent. Nobody had ever asked, since the night Moon gave me the keys in the Speakeasy, and of course, ironically poor old Keith Moon—who'd gobble down and drink anything he was given or got his mitts on—died in 1979 from taking some proper medication he was prescribed. There is another a strange little footnote to this story. In 1997, I was in Chicago while managing the Falling Wallendas, when I got a telephone call from Butch Vig, who produced among other big acts the likes of the Smashing Pumpkins and Garbage. Butch was doing the music for the Nicolas Cage movie, *Wild Card*. He had put the Smashing Pumpkins on the soundtrack and also wanted to use the Falling Wallendas.

"Nick Cage is very hands-on with his movies and would want to discuss the situation, Tony," Butch said. "Why don't you give him a bell?" Then he gave me Nicolas Cage's home number in Los Angeles. A very English voice answered the phone. I got as far as saying, "This is Tony Bramwell," when I was interrupted.

"Fuckin' 'ell, is that you, Tone? Jack Oliver 'ere. Yeah, I'm Nick Cage's fucking manager, ain't I?" That's how I learned that Jack now lived in Hollywood and also managed Roseanne Arquette, Cage's sister-in-law. Two weeks later he and Cage came to England for a vintage Lamborghini sale and we caught up on gossip, mostly about Keith Moon.

Dear old Moon was larger in life than most, so it wouldn't be stretching the imagination to wonder if he's not in charge of some weird accommodation in Paradise. Handing out keys in the heavenly speakeasy to the wifeless and flatless, hurling magnums of pop at the clouds, dressing up as Queen Victoria, driving the odd Cadillac into God's swimming pool and blowing up the gates of Eden. I miss him.

35

March 18, 1970, was a momentous day. Paul was convinced that Klein was crooked and issued a writ to try to dissolve the Beatles partnership. It would take a year for the case to come to trial, but meanwhile, he and Linda, who they also blamed, became pariahs in the eyes of the other three Beatles. They couldn't believe that Paul would take such a step. He tried to explain that he had nothing against them personally, that this was the legal way, but they wouldn't listen. He insisted that the lawyers had advised him that the only way they could sort the mess out, get rid of Klein and start again with a clean slate, was to start over.

Previously, the Beatles had tried to get along; now there were factions. It was like walking on a knife-edge of conspiracies and backbiting. I watched the madness and the slow disintegration of Apple as barriers went up and years of lawsuits and wrangling began. Work became boring since there was nothing to do in the world of the Beatles, where nothing was going on. Klein tried even harder to get rid of me, as he had gotten rid of all the old guard, but strange as it sounds, he didn't seem capable of coming up to me with the words, "You're fired." In the absence of that, if I saw a job that needed being done, I did it; but mostly I did my own thing and continued to draw my salary.

People who worked for the Beatles and Apple were supposed to be totally faithful, but it was impossible to be loyal to everybody. Paul stayed away, but he still expected me to be faithful to him, and I was. He called me regularly and said things like, "Don't tell anybody but . . ." Sometimes he varied it by asking me what was happening, who was doing what.

George expected the same. No sooner had I put the phone down on Paul, then it would be George. "Hey what's happening?" I knew what he was asking, "Have you heard from Paul? What's he up to?" Then John would call and beat about the bush a bit trying to gauge if I knew something he didn't. I'd try to walk the line. We had been friends for a long time, and I felt equally loyal to all of them. Ringo was the only one who was out there, quite happy doing his thing, making records and being a pop star. As Klein thrashed about angrily, making waves, determined not to give up his position, and as the lawyers prepared for trial, the scene got ever more bitter. Everyone tried to get their "team" behind them; but the problem was the team was the same small handful of people, getting smaller.

Nasty comments started to fly. There had been a time when most people and the Beatles in particular had been pleasant to each other. They squabbled, yes, but real affection and regard underpinned their relationship. Now it seemed they didn't care what they said. Yoko and John were the worst. They seemed to go out of their way to give long interviews in which they came up with some very nasty comments about Linda's arrival in their midst. They got personal, describing her looks. But the worst that John could say about Paul was that he was a "Beatleholic."

During the long run-up to Paul's High Court writ to dissolve their partnership, the Beatles were shocked to discover that Dick James had secretly sold Northern Songs to ATV for a very large sum. He had been able to do this because not only was his company the major shareholder, but Brian had persuaded the Beatles to go public on the Stock Exchange with Northern Songs. It was true that they made about £365,000 in the deal—which was a lot of tax-free money back when John's house, Kenwood, was bought for £20,000—but they lost control of the best of their early work.

In addition, Paul found that any new songs now had to be signed to ATV Publishing. He was busy writing songs for his own albums and he had no intention of "giving them away" to ATV. Instead, he said that Linda worked on them. Lew Grade—boss of ATV—didn't believe that Linda was doing any songwriting— even though she was, and continued to do so—and he bought a case against Paul for breach of contract, which Paul settled out of court. Part of the deal was Paul agreed to make *James Paul McCartney*, a TV special made for ATV, Lew's television company.

Research showed that in the past judges had always ruled for the publisher against writers no matter what the circumstances. Paul made a big effort to get to grips with the music publishing side of the business. With Lee Eastman's help he made headway, although it was too late to save his early work. John also signed a separate deal with ATV and things appeared to be on a better and more equitable footing.

🐛

I was relieved when I was asked to take Mary Hopkin to the U.S. and Canada for her opening at the Maple Leaf Gardens in Toronto. All this was a long way from Wales, and she was very excited. She looked very beautiful, seated alone on stage with just her guitar, her golden hair falling over her shoulders. When she started singing everyone was quiet and entranced throughout. After the booking, we headed to Greenwich Village, where James Taylor was at the Bottom Line. This was the best folk club and the place to play. I had installed myself comfortably at the Drake Hotel, where The Who also happened to be staying, and when I returned to the hotel in the early hours, the telephone rang. It was Peter Asher in London, saying he was joining me. "Is anything happening?" he asked.

"Yes, tons of talent to check out," I said. I think Klein was glad to see the back of Peter for a while. To Klein, we were all annoying little reminders of Brian and the old guard. He wanted a clean sweep, but so far Paul at least had resisted my dismissal. He was a bit more ambivalent about Peter though, because of his breakup with Peter's sister, Jane. Paul was far too decent to have fired him out of hand, but there was always that slight awkwardness.

Peter was fixed to stay with Gloria Stavers, the editor on *16* magazine. He adored Gloria. She was the most powerful woman in the record world, since *16* was *the* mag! Gloria was fast, funny and very attractive. She had run off at fifteen to marry some guy. By sixteen she was in New York trying to become a model, which didn't work. When she was offered the job of subscription clerk for the teen-idol magazine, it was take it or starve. A year later in 1958, at the age of seventeen, she was editor in chief. Single-handedly, she pushed the circulation up from a couple of hundred thousand to one and a quarter million. Her method was simple: she thought like the teenager she was. She worked hand in glove with *American Bandstand* promoter and fledgling TV producer, Dick Clark: she wrote about the acts he promoted; he promoted the acts she wrote about. Together, they helped shape the teen scene in the U.S., but it was Gloria's passionate love affair with Jim Morrison, the beautiful and doomed singer of the

Doors, and the black-and-white pictures she took with an old-fashioned press camera that made her into a legend.

By the time I knew her, unbelievably she was Frank Barselona's wife. Frank was a big-time promoter. He had a great deal of clout and had promoted a couple of the Beatles' U.S. stadium concerts, as well some for The Who. He would soon get to work with Bruce Springsteen among many other legendary bands, in the U.S. In those days, there were always union problems but Frank was always able to sort them out. He and Linda had been close when she was a photographer in New York. Often she would photograph the acts Frank promoted at the Fillmore East in the Village. She was there when Keith Moon went deranged in Franks' house. He'd gone back to the Gorham Hotel and blew up his toilet with a cherry bomb. Then he climbed out onto the ledge and started hurling cherry bombs into the street at the police. Barselona managed to keep Keith out of jail, but The Who were thrown out of the Gorham. They spent the night sleeping at Grant's tomb, draped with a Union Jack—which made for great photos—and the next day checked into the Waldorf. It was Keith all over—he always came up smelling of roses.

That night, the Scene was booked solid, but we got in because the doorman was Paul Simon's little brother. He looked exactly like him too. When we went inside, Jimi Hendrix was jamming onstage with Stephen Stills. It was absolutely amazing. At that time Jimi was probably the biggest thing in America and Stills was of Crosby Stills and Nash and Young, possibly the best West Coast soft-rock group around. David Crosby had been with the Byrds, Graham Nash with the Hollies. Stephen and Neil Young joined from Buffalo Springfield. They had played Woodstock, along with all the greats and many of their songs, like "Marrakesh Express" and "Woodstock," were anthems of a generation. At the Bottom Line the next night James Taylor was out of this world. It was just him and an acoustic guitar, but what made his performance particularly poignant was this was the first time he had played for almost a year. After finally kicking his heroin habit, he had made a successful comeback at the Troubadour in Los Angeles, but shortly afterward, had broken both hands in a motorcycle accident, and been unable to play for many months.

He was just great. I sat there and listened, thinking back to how different things had been when he first walked into Apple. We had been excited, fresh and looking to the future. Now, all we were doing was scattering. James was tremendous, but Klein had already decided to drop him from Apple—a real smart move. Apart from the little bit of money the first album cost, artistically speaking what it had to do with Klein I really don't know. He was making decisions way beyond his brief and there was nobody to stop him.

However, watching the reaction of the audience, Peter Asher sat there like the cat that had gotten the cream. He had decided to manage James and very wisely was saving the news for when Klein dumped him. Peter had worked with James on his eponymous album, *James Taylor*, for Apple, mostly at Trident Studios. James used to sleep at his flat and sometimes at my place on the couch. When the album didn't set the world alight, Klein acted aghast, shocked that James hadn't made a fortune immediately and that was when he decided to get rid of him. I don't think he had any idea what James was about.

As I sat there brooding about the past, the present and the future, I suddenly felt that I'd had enough. It was already crazy at Apple and I sensed that it would be getting crazier, especially now that Paul had set the cat among the pigeons by instigating the lawsuit against Klein. Instead of returning to London right away, I flew to Los Angeles. I checked into the Capitol Tower for a week or two to get away from it all. Shortly, Peter arrived in L.A. and finally told me he had made up his mind to quit Apple and stay in the U.S.

"I've got James Taylor away from that bastard and signed him to Warner," he told me with a gleam in his eye. I had to hand it to him. James quickly released *Sweet Baby James*, which did set the world alight. We should have set Klein's pants alight and watched him run down Savile Row.

One of the tracks on *Sweet Baby James* was "You've Got a Friend," written by Carole King. It was a massive hit and became the single. This revived her career and she went on to make *Tapestry*, which turned her into a superstar. Carole's career began in a comic way. Neil Sedaka wrote "Oh! Carol," dedicated it to her. It was a big hit. In return, she wrote "Oh! Neil," dedicated to him. It was a big flop, but it did get her noticed. Linda Ronstadt also signed with Peter, and went on to be a star, with her backing band, who went on to be the Eagles. For Peter, being booted out of the once-cozy environment of Apple gave him just the impetus he needed to reach his potential.

▼

The combative and competitive mood increased between the Beatles, particularly between John and Paul as they vied to release separate work at exactly the same time. In April 1970, Phil Spector finished work on the Beatles' *Let It Be* album, and on a roll, he went on to produce the *Instant Karma* album for John and Yoko's Plastic Ono Band. Excitedly, John telephoned George to come play *that instant!* on the song, "Instant Karma," saying it had to be done that night, then released the next day. Oddly, George accepted this and turned up at the studio. John played piano, George played acoustic guitar, Klaus Voormann was on bass (because John wasn't talking to Paul) and Alan White was on drums because

Ringo was in Hollywood. The album itself was mixed in record time by Phil and brought out on EMI that same week. It was quite an achievement.

Paul's own album, *McCartney,* was slated for an EMI release in April, in the same week that *Let It Be* was to be released. Without discussing it with Paul, Klein personally oversaw some work on the mix, and then told EMI to delay Paul's album until June 4, at the big Apple convention in Hawaii. Paul wrote Klein a stinking letter, telling him to never do that again. "And don't ever fiddle with the mix either," he added. He also said he was through with being a Beatle.

George telephoned Paul, said, "You'll stay on this fucking label! Hare Krishna!" and hung up quickly.

Paul's reaction was to issue a news story, on April 10, 1970, stating that the Beatles had officially split. Angry at being gazumped, John announced at a press conference, "I left first, before Paul, I just didn't say it first!" The beautiful dream was officially over, except of course in the eyes of the public, who clamored for more. As soon as it was released, *Let It Be* became another smash.

☙

Klein was still determined to get rid of me, but the Fab Four united in that at least and wouldn't allow me to be gotten rid off. In retaliation, he made petty exclusionary rules that subtly sent me to Coventry. He ignored me, doors were shut in my face and people didn't want to be seen with me. Suddenly it was all "Secret Squirrel stuff." It was pathetic and very off-putting, but it worked. I began to give serious thought to doing something else with my day. I knew that like Peter I had been around long enough to have numerous options. I could take an industry job. After all, I was always getting asked. I could find myself a rock 'n' roll band to manage and promote. I knew how to do it. I knew how to sign, produce, promote, video and plug.

I could go into virtually any company, any music business office, or any club, frontstage or backstage, or whatever-stage and they knew who I was. They would let me in, be glad to see me. The music people knew what I did, and what I could probably do for them if let loose. I was liked—I was even envied. Up until Klein, even though I wasn't earning a fortune, I had been enjoying myself a lot. I used to be invited back to the deejay's offices. I'd hang out with Tommy Vance, John Peel and Kenny Everett. We would drink alcohol, smoke cigarettes, talk openly about women—as in being silly, leering and lecherous—and I would play records to them that I thought were good and fine and worthy of attention. The complete record pluggers' shtick!

Before I could make up my mind which way to turn, I wangled it so that I was sent to the U.S. to run Apple Films and Apple Records between New York and

L.A. In Los Angeles, I lived in the rarefied atmosphere of a suite in the Chateau Marmont during the entire period, being entertained by the likes of Jerry Moss (head of A&M) and the legendary manager and film producer, Jerry Weintraub, while the famous and the destructive, who all seem to live for the excitement of the moment, filtered in and out of my life. It seemed as if some of the old life was unraveling when, in September, Hendrix died alone in a London flat and, two weeks later, Janis Joplin died in America.

I returned to London for Christmas 1970 and was at a cocktail party on New Year's Eve when I bumped into Ron Kass again with Joan, who was in sparkling form. After Ron was fired by Allen Klein he had gone to work for Warner Bros. Records in America, where I often saw him and we would have lunch, or a drink. He told me that he had left Warner, married Joan, and was back in England to work with Harry Saltzman, who had set up a new company with Cubby Broccoli to produce the James Bond movies. Ron introduced me to Harry Saltzman, who was chatting to Michael Caine and Michael's wife, Shakira.

"This is Tony Bramwell," said Ron. "He works for the Beatles and Apple."

Harry promptly said, "Why don't you come and work with us, Tony?"

"Love to, Harry," I said. "Doing what?"

"I'll think of something," he said. "We just need someone like you."

It was Ron who said, "What about a company that does film music? I'd be interested in getting involved."

I had always wanted to be involved in films and grew excited. "We could do regular records too," I said. "I hear new singers and groups every day."

"Great! Great!" Harry said very enthusiastically. "Let's have a meet, set it up."

Despite the enthusiasm, it sounded to me like the usual cocktail party talk and I said something like, "Sure. Give me a bell." I wasn't about to say no, obviously, but I certainly didn't take it seriously. However, a gossip columnist overheard the conversation and the next thing I knew, a piece appeared in one of the movie magazines, probably *Screen International*, saying, "At the party, Tony Bramwell, Harry Saltzman and Ron Kass were discussing forming a new record company."

Inevitably, it was brought to Klein's attention and he went through the roof. He came rushing up to me as soon as I walked into the office after the holidays.

"What are you up to?" He was ranting and yelling. "What does this mean? Is it true? Are you doing this?"

"Yes, you creep," I said. I was just so annoyed by his attitude, and I hated him so utterly that it was a relief. "I'm resigning."

"You're not! You're fired!" he screamed.

It all seemed rather academic because I had been in departure for months, if not years. So I strolled across to Harry's offices in South Audley Street in Mayfair.

"Now, about our new company . . . ," I said.

"Yes, yes," said Harry, enthusiastically. "I'll form the company and you can run it." That sounded to me like a wonderful arrangement.

PART V

1971–Present

36

Everything fell effortlessly into place. Harry Saltzman, Ron Kass and I duly formed Hilary Music, named after Harry's daughter. The idea was to have a little record company and a music publishing company and make good soundtracks for movies. My premise was that most contemporary film music wasn't very good and didn't work. We could do it better. In those days you got a theme tune and then a lot of incidental stuff which didn't sell records. Harry had seen Shirley Bassey sell a million copies of the song "Goldfinger" and wondered where the money went since he hadn't done a decent deal. I had seen the Beatles do *Yellow Submarine* with songs on one side of the record and George Martin's "Yellow Submarine Symphony" concept on the other side. It turned the whole album into "a work," which was nice. But these were an exception. On the whole, soundtracks up until then were an unfocused mish mash.

We went down to MIDEM, the annual music industry convention in Cannes, threw a launch party for our new company and licensed various other companies and subpublishers around the world to take our product and set it all up to flow smoothly. It was agreed that I should get a salary of, as I remember, one hundred pounds a week, plus running around expenses. We would split the royalties. These would be sent to the company's account in Switzerland where they would be held, apportioned, and distributed, each to his share. I was very happy. I felt that I had fallen on my feet into a situation doing what I knew and loved best, at several times my previous income.

I started work at once. The first film for which I commissioned a soundtrack was the new Bond film, *Live and Let Die,* which was almost finished. By this time, Albert "Cubby" Broccoli and Harry, who were joint producers and owned the Bond franchise, were barely speaking. They had started a loose system where they took it in turns to produce the next Bond. Before the bust-up, Harry told me that he and Cubby had intended to go the usual route and get John Barry to do the score.

"Why not try something different?" I suggested.

"John Barry is good," Harry said.

"I know he is. But what about Paul McCartney? He's always wanted to do the music to mainstream films."

Harry was very enthusiastic. "Great idea," he said. "Do you think Paul will do it?"

"Well, it's James Bond and that's pretty irresistible," I said. "I'll go and ask him." I went round to Paul's house and described the film to him. Then I asked if he'd like to score it.

"It depends," said Paul. He was supposed to bite my arm off.

"On what?" I asked, somewhat chastened. I thought he would be really pleased with the idea.

"I've never written to order," he said. "My music sort of evolves. The upfront music for the Bond films is very specific, isn't it?"

We sat and discussed it at length. Paul wanted to know where the track would go and, if it was at the front, how it would look. I went and saw Maurice Binder, who did all those fantastic James Bond opening titles graphics at the start of every Bond movie. He was a smashing guy. I always joked with him that he must have spent half his time filming nudes who were swimming underwater, or nudes who were sitting astride guns, and all the nudes that's fit to read. They were semipornographic little movies that introduced all the Bond films.

I arranged for Maurice to do a complete mock-up show reel of how the opening credits would look, with the gun firing and the naked woman. I hired a viewing theater, and Paul and I watched this reel a few times. He seemed relieved. Possibly ideas came into his head while he was watching because he said, "I'll do it. Thanks for asking me." Always very polite, was Paul.

Binder and Paul had great fun working out frame by frame what went where, and what bit of film would be shown with what bit of song. It sounded easy, but it wasn't. It was like doing a tight little movie. About a week later I went to George Martin's Air Studios in Oxford Street where Paul and his band, Wings, did the basic track for the theme song. The next day, George Martin did the rest, adding the special effects and explosions. When we played it, everybody was floored. It was a very powerful, huge piece of music, especially when you heard it for the first time. It turned out to be one of the biggest movie themes of all time, a big, big seller. In a way, although Paul was already one of the brightest songwriters of our generation, I think that writing something to order like that showed him how good he was. It also revealed different ways in which he could use his potential, moving into areas he had not explored before.

In the background, I was still aware of what was going on with Apple. Not only was the High Court action splashed all over the newspapers and on the news daily during the actual hearing, which started on January 19, 1971 and lasted for nine days, but it was discussed daily among everyone I knew. Paul was the only Beatle who attended. The judge, Mr. Justice Stamp, ruled that the Beatles' financial situation was "confused, uncertain and inconclusive" and that the condition of those accounts was "quite intolerable." He appointed a Mr. J. D. Spooner to act as both receiver and manager. Worried that Klein might nevertheless be able to dip into the funds they were holding for the Beatles, EMI froze all royalties until matters were resolved at a full hearing. John, George and Ringo immediately appealed, but dropped their appeal a month later on April 27, which landed them with an estimated £100,000 in legal costs. Ultimately, the case against Klein would drag on for many years, during which time Klein would be imprisoned for IRS offenses in America, unrelated to Apple. It was eventually decided in Paul's favor January 9, 1975. Klein was taken out of the picture, the Beatles' partnership was formally dissolved and the bulk of their assets—held in escrow for long years—was released.

I still sometimes bumped into John, or Paul filled me in with what was happening on the Apple front, or I'd have a beer with friends such as Dan Richter— who was working for John and Yoko at Tittenhurst Park. I heard that they were still struggling with heroin. Finally, they had spent most of April 1970 in California at Janov's Institute doing Primal Scream Therapy, before flying off to Majorca with Dan, where they had learned Tony Cox was with Kyoko. At the time there was a custody battle over the child and from all accounts John and Yoko decided to take matters into their own hands and snatch her back. The attempt ended in their arrest and deportation from the island. Tony Cox and Kyoko disappeared and it was to be over thirty years before Yoko saw her daughter again.

The beautiful song, "Imagine"—on which George played guitar—was born from the confusion in their lives. The album of the same title was recorded at the studio at Tittenhurst Park during June and July of 1971. But it wasn't all peace and light. One of the tracks on it, "How Do You Sleep," was a direct attack on Paul. According to Allen Klein, who happened to be there, Yoko wrote most of the vitriolic words on it. She would race into the studio, waving a piece of paper when she came up with a nasty new line, joyfully shouting, "Look, John, look!" Lapping up being part of the circle for once, Allen even contributed a few lines himself. Many of the session musicians—members of the band, Badfinger—felt uncomfortable, but the only person who felt really embarrassed was Ringo, who had gone along to drum. He kept telling John they'd gone far enough, but he was ignored.

Grateful that I was no longer embroiled in the bitter rock and roll circus at Apple, my work with Hilary Music continued. After *Live and Let Die* came *The Man with the Golden Gun*. I racked my brains to come up with something original again, something to blow people away. I wanted Elton John or Cat Stevens; but this was Cubby's turn for Bond and he had his own ideas. Behind the scenes he got John Barry and Don Black to do a pretty mundane song which Lulu recorded. I didn't think it was being very creative and wouldn't have anything to do with it.

However, and it's one of the biggest howevers, someone I had the bad misfortune to encounter was a guy named Kenneth Richards. He was the company accountant, based in Switzerland—which was where all Harry Saltzman's companies were based. Harry had Stephen Films SA (named after his son), Jacky Films SA (named after his wife) and of course our company, Hilary Music SA (named after his daughter). All were named after members of his family. Harry Saltzman also owned Technicolor Laboratories (which was losing money at the time), and a large slice of the company that made Éclair movie cameras. He also had, of all things, something to do with the Open University. He had companies and properties like some people collect paintings. He also acquired scripts and plays and was always running out of cash. It didn't trouble him too much. His films earned tons of money and his royalties were accruing very cozily in the Alps.

Sean Connery was also involved with Harry in the Bond movies and other ventures, which were fed through one of Sean's Swiss companies, handled by Richards. For those of us who had businesses that were handled by Richards, it was a bit under the table at the time because in the U.K. we were in the depths of a big recession and draconian money laws. We still had a V Form that restricted us to fifty pounds a year spending limit when we went abroad and that sort of thing.

After Bond, we moved on to a David Puttnam project, *Melody SWALK (Sealed with a Loving Kiss)*. The film starred Jack Wild and Mark Lester, who had starred in *Oliver*. I put together the soundtrack for that with the Bee Gees and Crosby Stills and Nash. For the era it was novel to have music that was not specially recorded for a film, but something that made it work, that the audience related to. The record came out on Polydor, with whom I had done a nice little deal for Hilary Music. The film didn't do well in the U.K. but was huge in Japan. There were crowds around the block and the soundtrack album flew out the door. When the sales figures started to come in, there was much rubbing of the hands in anticipation of the loadsa royalties which Kenneth J. Richards would collect and distribute.

Next I helped put the music together for *That'll Be the Day,* another Puttnam project starring David Essex and Ringo. Still coining it in, we did all of the music for Michael Caine's film of *Kidnapped,* for which I got Mary Hopkin to sing the title song. I signed up Tony Joe White as a songwriter. (In the eighties Tina Turner used a lot of Tony Joe's music. By then, he had hits without giving anyone his publishing, so he had it all, 100 percent.) Martin Scorsese also asked me to get Spector—who I managed—to do the soundtrack for *Mean Streets*, the film that established Scorsese's reputation.

One day in about 1972, I called the office in Switzerland for some money to be sent over to pay for something or other. The phone rang and rang. There was no reply. The ringing had a hollow, very lonely sound. *Brrrrr . . . Brrrrr . . .* Nobody answered. I put the phone down and I knew, did I ever know. Right then and there it dawned. I called Ron. He called the others. Someone flew out. Kenneth J. Richards had done a bunk. It turned out to be a very successful bunk. All Harry's money. All Sean Connery's money. My accrued royalties in Hilary Music. Ron Kass's royalties in Hilary Music. All flown away. Gone.

I don't know exactly how much I lost because the accountant had all the figures. I believe it was in the region of £50,000 to £100,000. In today's buying power you would have to multiply it by ten, so it hurt. It wasn't particularly to start some exotic lifestyle with, it was to invest and build a company with. But when it vanished that all went out of the window. What he stole was the work that had gone in, plus the future. The others lost millions. We had done very well from all the music and publishing—even Elvis had recorded one of our songs: "I've Got a Thing About You, Baby." Harry had to sell his entire rights to his share of Bond, to MGM, I think. Afterward, he went to work for H. M. Tennant's, the theater people. He even had to sell his flat on the corner of Grosvenor Square and South Audley Street. Frank Sinatra stayed there so many times people thought it was his. Frank loved it because it overlooked the American

Embassy, and he liked that. He felt safe because he could park his car behind the embassy, where the U.S. marines kept an eye on it. It wasn't a great flat by any means. In fact it was very ordinary but it saw some great parties. Saltzman sold it to Martin "Marty" Machat, an influential New York music industry lawyer who became a close friend of mine, the parties continued and Sinatra continued to stay there when he was in town.

Sean had lost all his Bond money, his retirement nest egg, as well as numerous other investments. He had to start over, accepting many roles just for the money, I'm sure. Sean was more vocal than any of us, threatening serious Bond-type death and destruction if he ever got ahold of Richards. Years later someone working for Sean got "a sighting," so to speak, and Sean started lawsuits to recover, but Richards slipped through the net again and nothing ever came of it.

37

A couple of years after the famous Christmas album that Apple had put out while I still worked there, Marty Machat—who was Phil Spector's longtime lawyer—telephoned me. Marty, who was well connected in New York, represented among others, Freddy Bienstock of Carlin Music, a publisher who had a lot of songs that Elvis cut. In fact, Marty was also Elvis' lawyer. He managed Leonard Cohen and—God help us—he was Allen Klein's lawyer too. But Marty and I got on very well. I went out of my way to be as much help as I could be in London on various projects. We became good friends. He was like my godfather.

"Phil sends his love and wants you personally to set up a new record company for him, based in London, and re-release every record he's ever made," Marty said genially, talking fast in case I smelled a rat. "Phil speaks very highly of you. He thinks you're great, remembers all those great talks you had."

"What exactly do you mean?" I asked.

"His entire catalogue. A lifetime's work," Marty explained, as if it were an everyday event.

I should have smelled a rat. I probably did, but didn't admit it, which sums the record business up pretty neatly. Off I went to see Warner—a phrase that also summed up the music business in those days. They were more than keen on the proposal, and hoping that Phil wouldn't take affront at the credit sequence, we set up a unique situation, called Warner/Spector. Then I flew to Los Angeles to have a word with Phil. I checked into the hotel and I took a cab up to his home.

In the front hall were two complete suits of armor that Phil was especially proud of. The next thing that struck me were the placards and posters lining the walls in the hallways and up the sweeping staircases, many with strange mottoes, including a strangely prescient one: IT'S BETTER TO HAVE A GUN AND NOT NEED IT, THAN TO NEED A GUN AND NOT HAVE ONE. There was also a huge wanted poster of Nixon depicted as a crook and another of Phil, armed to the teeth. He had an obsession with Nixon, whom he believed to be the devil. Once he had famously called the ex-president up and told him he wanted to make an album of the Watergate Tapes.

Getting down to business, I said, "What's the concept, Phil?" All very innocent.

"Concept! You moron!" he screamed. "I hate him! That's the concept!" I didn't realize that he was still on about Nixon.

Then he calmed down and said, "It'll be a great album. You've heard of my Wall of Sound, this will be the Sound of the same Walls. Closing in on the bastard! Ha ha!"

Phil's paranoia, I believe, was there all his life. He was still, simply, the little Jewish orphan geek on the tough block in New York, getting constantly ridiculed and slapped around. Sammy Davis once said that his own whole success had been due to a "must make it, can't fail" syndrome. He was thrust onward because, as far as he knew, he was the only black, redheaded, one-eyed singer turned Jew who could dance and act. Equally, what Phil went through early may have been character building, but the character it built was a little genius monster with deep fears and life-long psychoses.

It didn't help that even when Phil was hugely successful, big record companies still screwed him. He made great records, original, innovative, multimillion selling, with all his black girl groups, way ahead of his time, records that inspired generations of musicians, guys like John Lennon. He created other record companies and whole industries employing thousands, but he had no personal peace. He was the *enfant* Mozart of his time. Virtually single-handedly, he invented the role of record producer, as we now understand it. Before Phil Spector there were non-music-loving, arrogant, ex-army boffins in white coats, tut-tutting at the behavior of the " 'orrible little musicians" or "punk kids" they were forced to deal with in the studio. All they usually did was turn on the recording machine or change a dusty valve here and there. Quite simply, there were no totally original record producers before Phil—apart from Sam Phillips at Sun Studios in Memphis, who produced Elvis—and Sam was pretty basic.

There would have been no Tamla Motown without Spector, no black record industry. He did it all because he *could* do it all. He could take a three-girl black singing group like the Crystals and record a kids' song like "Frosty the Snowman," or "Santa Claus is Coming to Town," and put them on his Christmas album, and sell it over and over again.

When I arrived Phil was sans the usual cape I fully expected to see him wearing. He led me to his pantry, where, incredibly, he kept his life's work. All the master tapes were stacked there, everything he'd ever recorded from the days at his Goldstar Studios onward. *Gold dust* in fact. I wondered where he kept his food. I should have remembered that Americans keep everything in the fridge, including cigarettes.

"Better get it all crated up, huh?" he said.

Bear in mind that this was a guy who in his own words did not trust nobody with nothing. Despite the deeply paranoid wobblers on a par with a King George when he had just lost America; or a Hunter Thompson who had just misplaced his entire stash, his Wild Turkey, his Ballentine Ale *and* his grapefruits, Phil let me crate up his life's work while he lurked in the shadows, watching every move I made. He would twirl loaded pistols and have panic attacks that would deposit most people in the funeral parlor. But, much to my amazement—and it was a mammoth task, insuring, logging and crating them all up—he let them go.

In London, we ran oxidization checks and numerous other diagnostic tests on the tapes in order to work out how to preserve them and keep them in perfect condition. Then we started putting it all out on the market. Naturally, that's when Phil suggested that we put out his *Christmas Album* first, but we pointed out that it was only March. Instead, we kicked off with the *Phil Spector Real Masters Series* volumes 1 and 2 and 3. *The Best of the Ronettes; the Best of the Crystals;* unreleased *Masters* volumes 1–50. . . . It was a lavish cornucopia of brilliant, legendary sound seemingly without end. This was a show that was going to run and run and I started to think about tempting the fates. Studied those magazines that offer islands in the sun for sale and private yachts and planes.

At first, things proceeded well. Periodically, Phil wanted me to go on over to L.A. where I would report to Camp Dracula to give him an update. There was the album with Leonard Cohen. We survived. Phil and Len; ego versus ego; lunacy to the power of two—one in his fortress, the other in his monastery. But then the real madness set in once again. John Lennon was experiencing what is called in La La Land: "big problems, baby" with Phil on his seminal *Rock 'N' Roll* album.

John once famously sang a song about "mind games." I don't know who John was really referring to in this acid lyric but Phil Spector, who went to New York in 1972 to produce the *Rock 'N' Roll* album, was a master at them. Marty told me that Phil and Yoko almost shorted out when they confronted each other again, because they were both control freaks, used to having their own way at whatever the cost. What's more, they both knew it.

I was having big problems, too, a really bad time. Wobblers and tantrums at Camp Dracula of mega proportions where Phil would wave his arms like a deranged Kermit, screaming, "It's all mine!" and "Who are you? Who brought you in? You're a fucking Nazi spy!" All that and more. Eventually, it went from great art back to a kindergarten, and Phil took the tapes away.

It was an absolute nightmare. It was straitjacket time. Except, when you're rich, it's everybody else who is crackers, not you. Marty Machat tried again and again to sort unsortable things out and succeeded to some extent, but it must have been a big strain on him. I continued working, but in my heart I knew it was hopeless. Eventually, I went home.

38

Everyone hopped in and out of bed like rabbits in the seventies. It didn't seem a big deal and most people had fun. One woman who I will never forget—and with whom I had a very pleasant four-day affair—was the vivacious Welsh actress, Rachel Roberts. I met her at one of Nancy Holmes's famous soirees. Nancy was a very beautiful Texan in her mid-fifties who cultivated me because she thought I was a sort of "West End swinger," and knew a lot of people. I did. She had a flat just around the corner from San Lorenzo (a very in restaurant later beloved by Princess Diana), where she would entertain the strangest group of people, and Rachel was one of them. Nancy's friends went right across the social spectrum and she asked only two things of them: that they were interesting and amusing. They were people like Lady Warwick and old Lord Warwick who owned Warwick Films and also of course, a wonderful Gothic pile, Warwick Castle. The diarist, Hawk Allan, was another. And to complete the gossip-column set were the young Nigel Dempster, then Hawk's apprentice on the *Daily Mail,* before Nigel married the Duke of Leeds' daughter; also star columnist, Jack Tinker, from the *Daily Express;* and Jack Martin, who was with the *Hollywood Reporter* and *National Enquirer*. It was an assorted group, big on gossip and big on G & Ts.

At the time I first met Rachel, she was having an off-on relationship with her boyfriend, Darren Ramirez, a Mexican-American window dresser who worked for one of the stores on Rodeo Drive. She wasn't very happy because he irritated the hell out of her; besides which, she didn't really want him. She wanted her former husband, the love of her life, Rex Harrison—the trouble was, Rex didn't want her. Rex had had enough.

One night when I walked into Nancy's flat, Rachel spotted me and sashayed over. She was full of fun and madness, red hair, green eyes. I couldn't say that she was beautiful, but she was vital and vibrant. I knew she must have had something special about her or Rex Harrison—professor Higgins in *My Fair Lady* personified—wouldn't have married her. He was known as the most dicriminatory man in town. Rachel was exciting, no doubt about that. I found her irresistible. It wasn't long before she said, her green eyes glinting with a sense of mischief, "I think I've fallen in love with you, Tony darling." It would have been nice to have believed her, but since I wasn't Rex, I knew it was all very ephemeral, which it proved to be.

I wasn't aware that Rachel carried the reputation around as a world-class nymphomaniac. To me, she was a lot of fun, a woman I'd seen around the film parties I was now going to more frequently, thanks to Harry Saltzman. The first three days of our affair consisted of complete and utter lunacy, sex and drink. I was twenty-seven at the time, and Rachel was forty-five. She had recently split from Rex. "My darling sexy Rexy," she used to call him. I found out later that she would call Rex several times a night, for nine years, driving him and his new wives crazy.

When they were still married, fueled by booze and prescription drugs, she used to walk out of a dinner with Rex to seduce the chauffeur in Rex's Rolls Royce. And then she'd return to the table, lipstick smudged, stockings torn, and announce to everyone, "I've just fucked the chauffeur." Rex—straight out of *My Fair Lady*—would continue to coolly eat, not batting an eyelid, which drove Rachel wild. She only wanted his attention and some reaction. I have seen Rachel crawl across tables full of glasses in pubs, no underwear on, to grab total strangers, begging them for sex, offering blowjobs. At parties, she would disappear outside with almost anyone, and come back grinning like a cat, only to repeat her knee trembler in the cloakroom five minutes later with someone else. Yes, she had quite a reputation, but I liked her. She was entertaining, very amusing, a brilliant actress, a very giving and generous friend and great fun to be with. I soon realized that she was also very lonely, deeply insecure and quite impossible.

I was living two lives: on the one hand was the young music crowd, all the rock and pop stars I had always been close to—and on the other was the faster-living, very wealthy, old-money set. As time progressed, of course, the two sets merged and rock stars became the new aristocracy. Sometimes I dropped in at Paul Getty's place in Cheyne Walk. That is, Jean Paul Getty II, later to be made Sir Paul because he was such an amazing philanthropist, giving away something like £200 million to good causes, much of it anonymously. It was his son, John Paul Getty III who was kidnapped in Rome and had his ear cut off before his crabby old miser of a grandfather paid the million-dollar ransom. Jean Paul III lost his inheritance because he married too young. He ended up paralyzed and blind due to an overdose of heroin. But then, members from every generation, and many of their wives, were addicts. It was a terrible burden and curse.

At the time, Paul II loved to party and was always completely bombed, or out of it on heroin. Pale and hollow-eyed, stumbling about like something from an old Hammer horror flick. This creepy effect was added to because it was always dark and gloomy at his place in Cheyne Walk. To me it was like being inside that Rolling Stone song, about going down to the Chelsea drugstore and getting your scrip filled, which is in effect, Mick and Keef doing their version of St. James's Infirmary. "I went down to St. James's Infirmary, to see my baby there. She was lying on a long white table, so young, so cold, so fair." Speaking of which, Paul II's Polynesian Dutch wife, Talitha Pol, was very beautiful. A model, she got a few small roles in films such as *Barbarella*. Unfortunately, like Rachel, she was known not so much for her beauty as for being a "slag," as we say in Liverpool: a sex maniac. But, unlike Rachel, she had no sense of humour, no spark, probably because of her heroin addiction. I have to confess that I went to bed with Talitha, but then, so did half of London. I had her, or she had me. It wasn't an affair as much as a happening that had the timing of inevitability about it. I mean, it was not a case of who has been to bed with Talitha, but who *hasn't?* She was an awfully pathetic human being.

For people like Mick Jagger, Talitha was yet another scalp. At Cheyne Walk I was always bumping into people like Mick and Keith (Richards), David Geffen and Lord Lambton, who was involved in the Norma Levy scandal that involved police bribery, prostitutes and Lord Jellicoe, leader of the House of Lords. I met Tony Lambton down at Paul Getty Senior's great gothic pile in Surrey, Sutton Place. I got to know Getty Senior well, and never revised my opinion: that he was really bizarre—even more bizarre than Bette Davis, who was a fellow guest at dinner parties in that circle. She was enjoying a modest revival of her career in her twilight years, and had some incredible stories to tell. She took a shine to me and would hold out her hand, heavily laden with huge jewelled rings, and say, "Young man, come and sit by me." Her face was always deathly white, her lips a vermilion square, her hooded eyes set deep into her skull. Evening after evening, she appeared always wearing the same black frock.

Paul II also had massive estates in the country and in Italy. His villa in Rome was like a Roman palace, where they held orgies which would have impressed Caligula. When Talitha died of an overdose in their beautiful pool, surrounded by orange trees, cypresses and palm trees and with a view of the Roman Hills, the whisper that went around London was that Paul II had given her the overdose because she was such a slut, such an addict, and he yearned to break free of drugs and clean himself up—which of course you can't do when your partner is a junkie, heading for that long table. So young, so cold, so fair.

So there I was the following year, in 1973, walking down Broadway in New York and on my way to see Allen Klein on Apple business when I bumped into Engelbert Humperdinck.

"Hello, Tone, what are you doing?" he asked.

When I said nothing much, Engelbert told me he was staying at the Mayfair, and asked me to give him a call. I did that same night.

"Do you have your tux?" he asked. I did. I always took a tux because I never knew when I would need it. In those days, a dinner jacket was *de rigeur* for many events. "Okay," Engelbert said. "Put your tux on and we'll have a night out."

Later that evening I left the Drake, where I was staying, and caught a cab over to the Mayfair, to meet up with Engelbert, Mickey Green (who was a guitar hero of mine way back when he was one of Johnny Kidd's Pirates on those old Liverpool riverboat shuffles) and Tony Cartwright, Engelbert's roadie. We went to all the cabaret rooms in town including the Wonderbar and the Coconut Grove, where we saw the Supremes, Fifth Dimension, and Bobby Darin. I'd seen Bobby when he'd come to Liverpool when I was a kid and thought he was a god.

However, I was stunned when I saw him come on stage. He had just gone through some sort of breakdown and now he was wearing tuxedo trousers, shiny cowboy boots, a frilly shirt and a denim jacket. He carried a guitar and did Tim Hardin songs, like "If I Were a Carpenter." The audience hated it. They wanted "Mack the Knife," "Dream Baby," "Splish Splash" and "Nature Boy," all the Darin songs they had come to hear. They shouted for them, and Bobby hissed back at them.

"Fuck off!" he snarled, very diplomatic. Then he took his Vegas wig off, picked up a banjo and went crazy on it. It was wonderful, absolutely unbelievable. He looked great and he sounded great. The guys and I whooped and cheered, trying to drown out the hecklers. It was a very eventful and exhilarating evening.

A couple days later, I went to L.A. and Bobby Darin was there as well, doing the Troubadour this time, with Roger McGuinn from the Byrds backing him with banjo and twelve-string. I went to see him on the last night and was again blown away. The Troubadour was the perfect venue for the metamorphosed Bobby Darin. The buzz went around, "You've got to see Darin, he's totally flipped." Every night more and more people were going to see the show for themselves. By the end of the week, everyone from Crosby, Stills and Nash, Joni Mitchell, and the Byrds were all on stage with Bobby, a huge, star-studded folk-rock band, all picking away or singing. Acts like the Mamas and the Papas and Lovin' Spoonful were packing the venues out in New York, and the Troubadour had picked up on this very quickly. They had taken a leap of faith by booking Bobby Darin and they were vindicated, too. It was wonderful to see this rebirth of a man whose career had hit the bottom.

39

I **was sitting around** one slow day in London with David Mindal, a friend and neighbor of mine in Barnes. Dave, a songwriter and a jingle writer, married Cherry of Pan's People—the dancers on *Top of the Pops*—thereby breaking a million hearts. We were debating what to do, when he said, "Come on, Tone, let's go to L.A."

It was early in March 1974, my birthday was looming, so I thought, why not? Packing nothing, not even a toothbrush, we hopped on a plane. On our arrival, we checked into a lavish suite at the Sunset Marquis and after a rest and a swim, called a few friends. It so happened that Jane Seymour, another of our neighbors in Barnes, was in L.A. at the time. I knew Jane well, because, apart from being a neighbor, she was in *Live and Let Die*. I had also just been to her wedding.

When I telephoned her, she said, "Let's go out to dinner. Susan's here, and Olivia and her sister." She was referring to Susan George and Olivia Newton-John.

That night, we met up and ate in a Mexican restaurant in Santa Monica. Included in the party, which seemed to grow larger as we progressed through the evening, were some people from Chrysalis Records. We got totally jugged out of our heads on margaritas and were served mind-blowingly hot chili. In those days even guacamole dip seemed hot to anybody who grew up on roast lamb and mint sauce and fish and chips. I can remember how our eyes watered. We all grabbed the margarita jugs and drank from them.

The following day, having barely recovered from the night before, I was wandering down the street—that nice bit along Santa Monica and la Cienega with palm trees and a view of the sea—when I bumped into Ron Kass and his wife, Joan Collins, whom I hadn't seen for a long time—not since Kenneth Richards had run off with all our money. Joan had gotten Ron into the English habit of taking a stroll before lunch to sharpen the appetite. They asked if I would join them. We went to the Brown Derby and while ordering, I casually mentioned that it was my birthday.

"Are you having a party, Tony?" Joan immediately asked.

I said, "No, I thought I would just go out for a few beers with the lads."

"Oh, you must have a party," Joan said, her eyes sparkling. She was really lovely, with her huge eyes, cute nose and fantastic skin and profile. She was a very beautiful woman—and still is.

I shook my head, "It's okay, I'll just hang out."

"No, you will have a party, I insist," said Joan. "Talk to him, Ron."

Ron grinned and shrugged. "You heard the lady," he said. "She's unstoppable when she gets an idea. You'd better just lie back and enjoy it, Tony, because it's gonna happen."

Joan winkled out of me that I was staying at the Sunset and she said, "Right, I shall send a car for you at eight." It was job done, so to speak, so we settled down to lunch and a good gossip.

That night, the huge limo swished me up to Joan and Ron's amazing home in Beverly Hills. I thought I'd seen it all, but this was very swish, very Hollywood. I don't know how or where she had conjured them up at such short notice—obviously Joan had some kind of a magic wand—but when Dave and I walked in we found big smiles and gifts for the birthday boy, Tina Sinatra, Roger Moore and his wife, Luisa, Cybill Shepherd—and of course, Jane Seymour and friends.

My gift from Roger was an obscene pair of Y-fronts with a rude message printed across the front and a ruder picture on the rear. He suggested I put them on immediately. I didn't, of course. I wish I still had them. I like to think they might still be floating in the pool where they ended up. I fancied Tina, but wasn't sure about the potential father-in-law. However, it started to dawn on me during the course of the evening that Joan had decided to do a little matchmaking of her own. She decided that Cybill and I were just made for each other. Sadly, despite some neat footwork on Joan's part, it never happened.

I was back in L.A. a few weeks later and this time the Don was involved—Don Arden, that is. I was head of promotions for Polydor with whom Don had a big distribution deal. One of his stars was Lynsey de Paul, who was Ringo's current girlfriend. Ringo and Maureen were still married, and wouldn't get divorced until July 1, 1975, but Ringo suddenly decided he didn't want to be married and was playing the field. I promoted Lynsey's single "Sugar Me" for Don, and did a good job.

After leaving Apple, Ron Kass went to Warner Bros., home to Don's Jet Records. Under Ron, Jet soon became a real contender in the industry. One day in 1974 Ron asked my help with promoting Lynsey's new release, the title song from the TV sitcom, *No, Honestly,* which starred John Alderton and his wife, Pauline Collins—who eventually played "Shirley Valentine." I dropped into Ron's top-floor office in Greek Street and we chewed the fat a bit, catching up on news and gossip while we waited for Don to arrive.

Don came in and he's all business, no how are you, no polite chitchat. He said, "So! When yer gonna start then, Tone?"

I did some quick mental calculations. Pressing plant. Advance copies. PR handouts. I said, "Probably tomorrow, Don. That okay?"

He said, "Thursday, huh? Yeah I suppose that'll be all right. Just make sure you're on the case. I got a lot riding on this record." He hadn't. He was doing a number on me, a power trip, flapping his wings, playing the heavy.

I hid a grin and said, "No problem. Come tomorrow, I'll be round the radio stations, on the phone. Doing the business."

"Make sure you are," he said, wanting to get in the last word. I thought to myself, "Prat!"

That night, while I was having dinner at home in Barnes, Marty Machat called from New York. "Can you come over tomorrow, Tony? Phil Spector's doing an album with Leonard Cohen and wants to discuss the promotion with you. I'll meet you in L.A. In fact, I'll buy you lunch at the Polo Lounge."

I jumped on an early plane, flew over the pole and arrived in L.A. When I walked into the Polo Lounge of the Beverly Hills Hotel, there was Marty, sitting with Phil, Leonard Cohen, Steve Marriot—and Don Arden. Don's mouth dropped open when he saw me. Everyone got up and greeted me warmly except of course Don, who was scowling. The others looked at him and thought, "Oh-oh! Heads down. Incoming."

Don glowered at me and said in his best menacing hood voice, "You shit! It's Thursday! You're s'posed to be promoting my record in London."

I looked at him as if I didn't quite understand, looked at my watch and said, "I'm here on regional promotion, Don. I just popped over for this meeting, okay?

I don't know why you're giving me a hard time. After all, it's only a time-zone thing. It may be lunchtime here on the West Coast but we're so far ahead of London that in fact it's still yesterday there and when I get back it'll still be today." Don went to say something. Stopped. Shut his mouth. Frowned.

Marty cracked up and waved me to sit down with them. Besides handling Phil Spector's affairs, Marty was also heavily involved with ELO, who were signed to Warner Bros. Records—who also distributed Jet for Ron and Don. Mo Ostin, who was running Warner in the States, had just put out a worldwide memo to the staff that they should not allow themselves, or Warner, to be intimidated by faux gangsters or hooligans, and that Jet Records must be dropped.

Don had managed to get hold of a copy of this confidential memo and waved it about while he ate. "They've called me a *persona non grata!*" he said. "What the fuck's going on?"

Several decades earlier, Warner had the reputation of being connected to the mob through Bugsy Siegel, so it became a hilarious joke within the music industry for Warner to say they wanted no truck with the mob. Unbelievably, the memo started quite a panic and, as well as Jet Records, a lot of vowels got dropped. Overnight, according to the rumor mills, top executives at Warner went from being "Mr. Rossi" to being "Mr. Ross"—that kind of thing.

Don and Marty had met up in L.A. to discuss some kind of united policy. It was agreed that with Jet doing so well they could look for another deal. After the meeting, Marty, as Don's lawyer and representative, went straight to Walter Yetnikoff at CBS to negotiate a deal. Yetnikoff was delighted, always happy to pull a stroke on Warner. In fact, Walter, whose intake of recreational products rivaled Keith Richards's, was always happy to pull a stroke on anyone. "Wildman" Walt took care of Michael Jackson, the Stones, Bob Dylan, Barbra Streisand and Bruce Springsteen. He "never kissed anybody's ass"—except for "the Japs at Sony," who Walt was secretly talking into buying CBS for $2 billion. This would make Walt very powerful. He was so arrogant and rude that if someone like Keith Richards interrupted his flow, he'd tell him to fuck off to Switzerland and get a brain change to go with the blood change. Anything would rile him. After a heated argument over a joint with one rock star on his roster, the star moved to a new label.

The fact that Jet was falling into Walt's lap because of an antigangster memo at Warner didn't alarm him at all. Walter appreciated the joke and was delighted to pay off the opposition to the tune of $15 million for ELO. This might seem a lot of money, but not many people appreciated that the record divisions of the huge conglomerates and industrials like CBS and Phillips were considered "toys" and "sidelines." Another consideration was that companies like CBS had radio and television stations and if they didn't have music, they had nothing popular to broadcast. It was a case of "feed the beast."

Similarly, Polygram (which was part of Phillips) and Thorn/EMI made hardware such as record players and tape machines. So it made perfect business sense to make records so that consumers would have something to listen to, *and* a reason to buy their equipment. Sony said that they bought CBS purely for the sake of getting software for their hardware, not for the records themselves. At first, these toy-town divisions made a few pennies here and there until suddenly the whole record industry caught fire in the wake of the Beatles and billions were pouring into their coffers. Music was very, very lucrative, but, as usual, no one was ready for it. Accountants were put in charge to run these enterprises. Alarmingly, accountants were even made head of A & R. After dithering for years, one day the American stock market crashed and Akio Morita—the man from Sony—stepped in, and picked up CBS Records for a song.

At the close of the meal at the Polo Lounge, I could see that something else was still bugging Don. "So it'll still be today when you get back to London, will it?" he suddenly said.

"That's right," I replied. "Like I said, it's all a matter of timing."

Don got his pen out and, frowning, while giving me the occasional evil eye, started to work it out on a napkin. Marty and I got up. Phil followed suit. As I made my escape, I looked back over my shoulder and saw Don still drawing diagrams and Steve Marriot, rocking back and forth, trying to drink some beer but laughing so much his hand was shaking.

On the way out, we bumped into Jerry Weintraub, who owned a country club in Beverly Hills. He also managed Bob Dylan, John Denver and the Moody Blues and was married to Jane Morgan, who had a big hit many years ago with "The Day that the Rains Came Down." I'd had dinner with him just the week before in London to discuss the promotion of the Blue Jays, the offshoot from the Moodies. He looked delighted to see me and pumped my hand enthusiastically. He shook hands with Phil, who looked completely mystified, and with Marty.

"Hi Tony! What are you doing in L.A.?" I jerked my thumb over my shoulder, and said, "Right now I'm escaping from Don Arden."

Jerry nodded knowingly and quick as a flash, insisted that we accompany him to his club. Marty was all for it, so we leaped into a taxi to the club, where we spent the afternoon drinking and hiding. I got to work on Lynsey's record a few days late, but since it did well, Don was none the wiser. At least, he seemed a happy man as it steadily climbed the charts. It even won an Ivor Novello award. Big kudos for me, and I still had a full complement of legs.

In September 1974, Warner asked me to promote Ronnie Wood's first solo album with the strange title of *I've Got My Own Album to Do*. The reception to launch it was held at Ronnie Scott's club in Soho. It was the usual lavish Warner Bros. Records bash with a continuous buffet lunch and drinks all afternoon so it was almost inevitable that everyone got well oiled, especially, I have to admit, me and Ronnie.

At some stage we got into a huddle with the American contingent who had flown over: Jerry Moss, head of A&M, and Mo Ostin, Warner's famed L.A. boss, he of the notorious antimob memo. As afternoon gave way to the evening and we were still partying, I suddenly remembered in a bit of an alcoholic haze that Ravi Shankar was performing that night at the Albert Hall. George had asked me to come, but I told him that I had the record company bash to attend.

"Well, bring all the lads," George had said, enthusiastically.

"Right," I'd said. Well, I didn't want to let George down, so I announced, "C'mon boys, we've got to go to the Albert Hall for one of George's things." I hustled Ronnie, Jerry, Mo, Eric Clapton and a couple of others out of the club and into a taxi. We arrived at the Albert Hall a bit late and a lot noisy. Very rowdy and boisterous. Thoughtfully, George had laid on the royal box and drinks for us. On the stage, seated cross-legged on a cushion, Ravi was doing his thing.

Somewhat baffled, Mo leaned across and asked, rather loudly, as only someone quite drunk can do, "What kind of music is that, Tony?"

"Ravi is doing a raga, Mo," I said. At least, it was what I presumed was a raga, because that's the only word I knew for describing a jolly Indian tune for the sitar and tabla and the various other Eastern instruments littering the stage.

"Is he? A raga, huh?" Mo repeated, doubtfully. Then, he nodded solemnly as he sipped his Scotch. "Raga," he muttered. "How 'bout that? A fuckin' raga!"

Some twenty minutes later, when Ravi finally finished the long and tedious number, mainly for George's sake—because it had bored the pants off us—we started applauding. In fact, being in a very generous mood, we gave Ravi a standing ovation, holding up our cigarette lighters, whistling and shouting, "More! More! Author! Author!" It must have been obvious to everyone that we were well plastered.

George went potty. He came running into the box, waving his arms and yelling. He had a walkie-talkie clamped to his head. I suppose this was in order to be in touch with the engineers on the desk and to help his mate Ravi get a really good sound balance. But now George was in a really bad temper.

"You're being disrespectful to a great artist!" George shouted.

"But, George, we're cheering," I protested.

"He's only been tuning up!" George ranted. I was about to say something smart, but George wasn't done. I think he was embarrassed because people mistook Ravi's "tuning" for the real thing so frequently that he had come to use his tuning-up thing as a bit of a gimmick. George went on to accuse us of being "leeches" and "living off the music industry." From the stage, Ravi squinted up at our box, wondering what his mate and best benefactor, George Harrison, was up to. During all this time, the audience gazed up at the right royal rumpus in the royal box. George finally calmed down, we settled down, and Ravi started his performance in earnest. I have to say it was grim from that moment onward.

Afterward, there was a party for Ravi in what I always called "the house of green tiles" up Holland Park way. This was a house with white stucco walls and an emerald green roof, famous for its "strangeness," for its for bizarre happenings and the peculiar people who drifted in and out of its doors. Plenty of Indian vegetarian and macrobiotic food was laid out. Eric Clapton and Ronnie Wood evidently didn't approve of the offerings because they started a food fight, with beanshoot bhajis and handfuls of brown rice hitting the assembled guests and spattering the walls. That did it. George hit the roof.

"There are people starving out in India, you know!" he shouted at them. We knew that, we really did. We'd just had too many drinks at the record company bash, and now it was too late for any decorum. The "house of green tiles" ended up a mess and with George almost in tears. We left to party on through the night, I'm not sure where—but it was somewhere without sitars, green tiles, brown rice and George.

40

Toward the end of 1975, I got another phone call from Marty Machat in New York. This time it was to say that after a long period of derangement, Phil had calmed down. I immediately looked at the calendar. Yes, Christmas was coming round again and—guess what?—Phil wanted to put out the famous *Christmas Album, again.* Foolishly, I agreed to help. I went back to Warner and set up another nice deal. I told them that we should call the album, *Phil Spector— Out of His Christmas Tree,* but in the end we just pressed it up in blue vinyl, packaged it in a seasonal Christmas-balls effect, used the proper title, made it nice, and once more it did really well.

Naturally, about three minutes later (metaphorically speaking) Phil fell out with Warner. I picked up the phone and learned that he had gone bonkers big time in Warner's Los Angeles offices with the company heads like Mo Ostin, men you can have a laugh with, but who you just don't abuse. Predictably, Warner had decided to drop Warner/Spector. I took it to Polydor and we started again with Phil Spector International. But things had gone crazy so fast it was still Christmas, so we put out the famous album *again,* in another nice wrapping and sold another two hundred thousand in quick time. It sold so fast that sometimes it became out of stock and was changing hands for thirty-five quid—a weekly wage to many people. Inevitably, Phil fell out with Polydor and we released it yet again, on another label. Every time we released it, it would sell another quarter of a million copies. It was crazy, but we all made pots of money. Well, I thought in a quietly reflective moment, we've gone from Warner/Spector to Phil Spector International and done well. It couldn't last, and it didn't. The vampire awoke, reached out of his coffin for the phone, woke me up, wanted me to form "Phil Spector's World Records!" It had to happen.

Phil was screaming down the phone at me in his terrifying, high-pitched voice. "Come on over! I want to release everything now! I want to take over the world! Get out of bed!"

I did. I went to the airport, checked in and went back to sleep. In L.A. again, I woke and drove up to Castle Spector, Phil's fortress high on Mulholland Drive. My previous experiences had taught me that the temperature at Phil's fortress was kept about the same as Christmas in England. The A/C was cranked to maximum all the year round, and I soon got used to people laughing at me when I went over to his place in an army greatcoat and mittens. "Hey Buddy," cab drivers would say when I hailed them outside the Sunset Marquis, at noon. "Where ya going? The fuckin' North Pole?" Of course when they hear your English accent they know you're some kind of eccentric anyway.

Since I'd last been there, Phil had found time to turn his Bela Lugosi home into a real fortress. It had even more machine-gun turrets at the corners and razor wire to keep out the nasty, thieving world. To stop her running away, he locked Veronica "Ronnie" Ronette up like she was some black Transylvanian princess in a tower and not the beautiful girl who sang "Baby I Love You," and won the hearts of millions. But, while making her the Prisoner of Mullholland Drive, Phil forgot to lock up his secret liquor cabinet, which Ronnie, bored to death, accidentally discovered. Soon she was out of it, on whiskey and broken dreams. It was all Raymond Chandler in black-and-white, like *The Big Sleep*.

Sometimes, when I arrived, Phil would be firing guns down the long drive. I never knew what he'd look like because he changed his hair, his makeup and his complete outfit every hour. I wondered if he would end up like Howard Hughes, who also changed his clothes constantly, before he stopped wearing any at all. After the second of two very bad car smashes, when Phil was pulled out of the wreck clinically dead, but revived, the experience left him convinced that he was still dead. Maybe that was his fascination with Bela Lugosi. His other best friend was Stan Laurel. Before they died, he'd often had all three of his pals—Lugosi, Laurel and Lenny Bruce—around for dinner. The conversation must have been like something out of a surreal movie. When Lenny died, heartbroken, Phil organized the most spectacular New Orleans–style funeral, complete with plumed black horses and marching bands, in the middle of L.A. I often thought he still had his friends around for dinner after they died, in spirit.

His fascination for the macabre also extended to his décor, which was like the set of Gloria Swanson's movie, *Sunset Boulevard.* Most of the rooms were pitch dark. A fish tank illuminated the living room. This could have been to hide the mess the car crash had made of his face. He had needed a thousand stitches and covered the livid scars with thick pancake makeup. I will always remember during our marathon drinking sessions how he would stroll around like a wandering minstrel singing "Baby I Love You" and playing a guitar with a .38, hitting it like an Irish drum, using the barrel as a sort of industrial pick. I would gingerly edge away and find a corner to hide around, convinced that I would be hit by a flying bullet. Happiness was definitely a warm gun—though how he didn't shoot himself I never knew.

It wasn't all bad. His three adopted children, aged about eight, six and five when I first met them, lived with him. Who looked after them, I have no idea. I have a sneaky feeling it could have been Phil's bodyguard, George, who fed them and made sure they went to school and to bed. There never seemed to be any sign of a woman after Ronnie tunneled out. But they appeared to be delightful, charming, well-adjusted kids and it was obvious that Phil adored them. He would hold their hands, stroke their hair and smile indulgently at them.

However, when Phil once showed them a photograph of himself in the studio with Ike and Tina Turner, the kids said, "Which one's you, Daddy?"

Sometimes when I arrived, Phil would say, "I'll be back in a minute—" Then he'd disappear like the malevolent genie he was and leave me alone.

After I'd gotten used to his little games, I'd think, "Oh-oh. Here we go again. It's mind-game time." Often he wouldn't be back for hours. Or he would go shopping! When I ran out of patience and got up to leave, somehow he always seemed to know, and he'd come running in, a strange smile flickering about his face like swamp lightning, to challenge me to some crazy drinking contest. These contests were a bit one sided. I would have to drink a bottle of vodka— though Phil could only have a bottle of diabetic Cab Sauv. Ten minutes later I'd be out of my brain singing along to "Frosty the Snowman" at top volume, and he'd be doing a war dance and shouting, "I won! I beat the fuckin' Limey!" Surreal! It was hardly surprising, considering that above the bar was another of the placards that read: HANGOVERS INSTALLED AND RESERVICED.

Once, Phil really didn't come back for hours. I was half convinced he was either watching me on a CCTV camera, or hiding behind the paneling watching me through a peephole, so I stuck it out. In the end I decided that not even Spector would hide that long staring at a bored Tony Bramwell, so I poured myself a large drink, then another and wandered off around the house making V signs wherever I thought I'd come across a CCTV camera.

Eventually I got tired of that and, stumbling across a room that contained a beautiful pool table, I decided to play myself. Why not? Unlike the drinking contest, I might even win. The balls were all over the table, so I collected them, racked 'em up, tossed a coin to see who would go first. I won and broke the pack like I was in the final of the Budweiser World Championships in Las Vegas. I went back and forth, had a few drinks. Got into it. Smoked a cigar from the stash in the humidor on the bar. Took off my army greatcoat. Loosened my tie. I was about to go for a difficult three-cushion shot, needing plenty of Body English, when I thought I could hear the crowd cheering me on, shouting, "Go for it, Bramwell! Go, baby, go!"

But it was George, Phil's huge minder, going apeshit, shouting, "Oh no! Bramwell!" George had come looking for me.

Great, I'll play George. "Rack 'em up," I shouted back.

George was waving his arms and shouting, "No no no! Oh my God! Phil's gonna kill me!" He was white. I thought it was the cold and offered him my coat. Eventually, when he could speak coherently, he said, "Look, Brammers, this is a hell of a mess. Both our jobs are on the line."

"But I didn't leave the house, George," I said, "and I only poured a few drinks. Oh, and I smoked a cigar or two."

He completely ignored me. "Do you remember where the balls were before you racked 'em?" he demanded in a trembling voice.

I said, "Not really, George. They were everywhere. All over the table."

George said, "That's right. But you better start remembering quick, because that's how Minnesota Fats left those balls when he was playing Phil. And as Fats is dead, he ain't coming back to finish the game. In fact, he packed his cue and ran out on the game, first time in his career, Fats said, and a ton of money riding on it. But he told me he ain't never seen nothing like Phil—and never wanted to again. So this table, Tony, it's a shrine. Fats is Phil's all-time hero. It was gonna stay the way it was when Fats left it, forever."

I looked at him and said, "George, don't worry. I have a photographic memory, and I've just remembered where every ball was."

It was freezing in that mausoleum of a poolroom, but George mopped his brow. He smiled. "Know what?" he said, "I think I believe you."

I replaced the balls and we removed all traces of my presence before returning to the living room to wait for Phil. Obviously he hadn't been watching me on CCTV, because when he came in, nothing at all was said, and we got on with taking over the world. Again.

In the middle of all this Phil decided to go into the studio and produce an album with Dion DiMucci, as in Dion and the Belmonts. Mostly I left him to it, and took time to do some sunbathing around the famous pool at the Sunset Marquis. I was amazed to see a constant stream of people I knew well staying at my hotel. Elton John was doing his famous Benny and the Jets concerts at the Dodger Stadium, dressed in his glittery baseball outfit. He had flown all the showbiz press and media over from the U.K. including Bob Harris and the Old Grey Whistle Test people. During a respite from the fortress, I was sitting by the pool, reading *Rolling Stone*, when I heard Bruce Springsteen's familiar New Jersey voice behind me.

"Hi Bramwell—what's happening?"

When Bruce heard I was working with Spector, his eyes lit up. "My hero! Introduce me," he begged.

The E Street Band used Spector's Wall of Sound a hell of a lot—indeed, *Born to Run* sounded as if it could have been a Spector production, it was so close. Bruce was doing a week's residency at the Roxy in L.A. and when the press found out where he was staying, they turned up in force. However, he already had a reputation with the press, so they were terrified to approach him. Even the hardened music journos and drunks circled at a distance like jackals, waving and trying to attract my attention. In the end, when I went to the men's room, I was besieged. "'Ere, Tone, 'ow about introducing us to Bruce, eh?" I quickly became Bruce's unofficial PR rep. "Bruce, this is Ray Coleman. Tony Parsons, this is Bruce Springsteen."

The shows at the Roxy were little short of phenomenal. Everything Bruce had been working toward came together. He was on the top of his form. Combat trousers and knitted hat. A complete showbiz band fronted by a magic tramp, the sort of show that usually only happens in the movies. This was before Bruce got into the bodybuilding. He was still skinny, fey looking, really. Stealing all the girls' hearts. At the first show I sat with Annette Funicello, the beach-movie icon and head Mouseketeer for Disney. Also with us was Carol Connors, who was one of Phil Spector's Teddy Bears, when Phil had written, "To Know Him Is to Love Him." After the show, I introduced Bruce to the girls. He decided that he wanted to go to Disneyland. We all went the next day, getting VIP passes through Carol, who now wrote for Disney. We spent a wonderfully silly day there, and had the best pirate-hatted, all-the-ride-taking time ever. It felt unreal. Me at Disney with the head mouse and the E Street Band. Only in America.

Before we left town, I knew Bruce would ask me again to introduce him to Phil. Funny as it seemed to me for a Brit from Liverpool to introduce one

American icon to another, I did it gladly. I reasoned that if Phil grabbed Bruce round the neck, throttled him, shouting, "You stole my sound, ya bum, I'm gonna rip ya fuckin' neck off!" there would be little I could do, except perhaps offer to put out Phil's Christmas album again. Happily, they got on. It blew Bruce's mind (his words) especially when he found that Phil was doing an album with Dion, who was another of Bruce's all-time heroes. It was like, here are your fantasies, Bruce—fill your boots up. It made me go all fuzzy, too.

While I had seen the press go weak at the knees for Springsteen, Bruce himself was now "in awe." He was shy, both with Spector and Dion. Cool, however, was recovered, and he and Phil joined in and helped with a couple of the tracks. Bruce, Phil and Roy Carr, a journalist on the *New Music Express,* became the Belmonts for Dion for the day, clapping and cooing, doowopping and oohing and aahing away in the background. What the Eagles once called "oohs for dollars"—except this was free and fun. I watched as bliss set in for once around Phil Spector for a few hours. Born to Run? Time to go.

Phil moved out of the fortress eventually—too many bad memories, he said— and into his new Alhambra home, where a dead body was discovered in 2003, leading to his arrest. I was sorry to hear about it. In all the years I knew him, although women seemed to find him fascinating, and he often had affairs with female singers he produced, I had never known him pick women up or have a casual one-night stand, as appears to be the case with the woman found shot in his home. But I know one thing: whoever is still left from the old days will not be surprised.

It was almost predictable. The miracle is, it took so long. As John Lennon, who fatefully cowrote with Paul "Happiness is a Warm Gun," once said to me, "Phil's a genius but he's nuts." John would have recognized Phil's flawed personality because it described John himself perfectly.

George and Ringo and especially Paul were pretty normal lads, but there is no doubt that John was different. He used to see other faces in mirrors when he looked into them and heard voices. Much like Phil—or Philip, as he preferred to be called when I managed him—though frankly, he was unmanageable. There's no escaping the fact he was, as John said, nuts. Wobblers in the studio, shooting out the lights when the musos weren't doing what he wanted, shooting the Coke machine, blowing the end of the gun like Billy the Kid. He was always in court, always in turmoil. Fortressed up. Pulling his cloak around him up there on the west turret, staring through the Nitesight on his Armalite for intruders, but maybe seeing only three black girls hanging out by the gate who wanted to make a record. "Come down and let us in, Phil."

♏

At the end of October, I escaped the madness of Spector's castle. I flew back to London, along with Bruce, and all the Old Grey Whistle Testers and the music press. The whole contingent was now as thick as thieves. They wrote their articles on the plane and in London the next morning, the newspapers said: "Is London Ready for Bruce Springsteen?"

The long flight left me plenty of time to reflect on both Phil and Bruce, each of them brilliant in different ways, both prone to depression. One could cope and one didn't try. In the midseventies, long before producer Jon Landau over in the U.S. had coined the immortal dictum, "I have seen the future of rock and roll and it's Bruce Springsteen," and *Time* and *Newsweek* sat up and paid some attention, Bruce was already known as a sort of "Noo Joysey Bob Dylan" anyway.

I had promoted Bruce's first album, *Greetings from Asbury Park,* in the U.K. Right off, it started to get some good airplay, and I managed to make it Noel Edmunds' Album of the Week, and Kid Jensen's Radio Luxembourg Album of the Week. It wasn't long before I realized that, incredibly, nobody this side of the Atlantic was interested in Springsteen's music publishing. I asked his manager, Mike Appel, if I could help find him a publishing deal. Mike jumped on the idea so Adrian Rudge and I took the material to Intersong, Polygram's publishing arm, and Bruce was signed up. Then Adrian persuaded Manfred Mann to cut his "Blinded by the Light." It was a hit. I persuaded the Hollies and their singer, Allan Clarke, to cut songs, like the "Fourth of July," "Asbury Park," and "The Priest." Bruce was a happy man and we struck up quite a friendship.

However, Bruce ground to a halt. He'd reached a plateau and was still doing gigs at the Bottom Line in New York, or the Stone Pony in Asbury Park, and although these were nice gigs to do, his backing band, soon to be feted as possibly *the* backing band of all time, was constantly falling apart because Bruce couldn't pay them properly or regularly. Bruce also had his own personal problems and was often depressed. Looking back on these situations it seems like a dream. Bruce Springsteen depressed and having nobody to talk to? But, it happens all the time. Memories like mine are filled with talented people who didn't make it out the other end to success. There is no guarantee that just because you have what it takes, that you'll be lucky and win.

Bruce would call me at all hours, for some light relief and to cheer himself up. Later, he called more often because more was happening for him in Europe. We became "phone pals," our conversations ranging far and wide until *Born to Run* broke in the States. He was like Spector on adrenaline. "Chrome wheeled, fuel injected and stepping out over the line . . ." Nice.

He made the front covers of *Time, Newsweek* and *Rolling Stone* and his career was up and running. How good it is to see someone who is talented take flight.

When we arrived in London, Bruce checked into the Churchill on Portman Square and we went down to do a sound check at the Hammersmith Odeon, where he was to do a gig. By now, it was like a traveling road show with Bruce as a sort of Pied Piper. The Whistle Test people were filming, journos scribbling. The place was hopping. It was as if everybody sensed that something explosive in the music world was happening before their very eyes. History tells us it was.

However, I was watching Bruce very carefully, and something else was also happening. As Bob Dylan once said about a hapless journo, "You know that something's happening, but you don't know what it is, do you, Mr. Jones?" I don't know if Bruce was jet-lagged, or just plain tired, or if events were moving so fast that they were doing him in. He certainly wasn't drunk or speeding. But I could see that something was building up inside him. He was getting very impatient, especially with the people who had been sent along from CBS, his record company.

The record business is, has always been, staffed with more than its fair share of prats, and CBS had sent along a prime example of an over-the-top smarmy "artist relations" guy who quite simply was the wrong man for the job. Perhaps they were expecting some kind of spoiled American superstar who wanted a lot of oil, but Bruce wasn't that kind of guy. Walter Yetnikoff has called him boring, but he wasn't. He was just very down to earth and remarkably normal.

Suddenly, he disappeared. He was found out front of the Odeon, seriously pissed off and ripping and trashing the bunting, pictures and displays. In the process he tore his fingers up. Despite that, the show was good, but not as good as the show in L.A., nowhere near as good. It was good enough, however, to show the people in London what he was about. But he was still very angry and stormed off the stage.

The entire hierarchy at CBS, Mo Oberstein and Paul Russell among them, came backstage to glad-hand, backstab, and to cart Bruce off like a triumphant hero to the postconcert bash. Stretch limos were lined up, but our man was in a rage.

"Get those people away from me, now!" he shouted. He locked his dressing room door, refusing even to talk to them. The hierarchy drifted off, hoping that the star would soon calm down and turn up at the party later. As soon as their dust had disappeared, Bruce unlocked the door. "Can you get me out of here?" he asked. "Let's go somewhere."

I found a taxi and we went back to my place in Barnes, where we sat up all night talking. His spirits should have been up, but instead he was very down. Everybody wants a piece of a hero, I suppose, but sometimes the hero says, "What took you so long? Where have you been hiding? Do you remember when you treated me like Mr. Nobody?" And that's what this night had been all about, as far as Bruce was concerned. All the niggling little things came to a head. He moaned bitterly about CBS Records, saying he just wasn't prepared to play their "star" game. At least, not just switching it on for their benefit.

Well, there's nothing new about a rock star trashing his or her record company. When the steam had gone from his rant, I suggested that we watch a video. Home video had just started and I was proud of my huge, clunky Phillips machine. I stuck the tape in and we sprawled on the carpet watching a film about James Dean's life. Bruce loved it, so we watched it again.

At dawn, Bruce went off to the Churchill and a couple of hours later, I went into my office at Polydor. Word had gotten around about what happened at the starless bash and even there, my name was mud. There they were, waiting to pour the champagne and no conquering hero to fete. "He can't treat us like this!" Mo had apparently said. "We've sunk a lot of money into him. Has he flipped or what? Is he on something?"

Bruce went off to do some European dates, then returned to another concert at Hammersmith. This time, it was amazing. He blew them all away. Later, it all came apart at the seams again: his manager, the music publishing, his band, his career. The "future of rock and roll" ground to a dead halt. To be reborn yet again—and again.

41

I met Jack Nicholson when the Stones played Knebworth in 1976. We were up at the main house, all very convivial, getting on like two houses on fire, really hitting it off. After a while, I had to leave to go backstage to sort something out with the Stones. Jack asked me for a lift on my Harley Davidson, around the crowd, and into the main area.

I said, "Hop on."

So there was Jack on the back of my Harley, waving away and giving that big stoned grin. It was just like that scene in *Easy Rider* where they played the song, "Wasn't Born to Follow." But this wasn't a movie set or a road. I'd had a couple of drinks and the grass was very wet. We skidded sideways and crashed. The bike, Jack and I tumbled over and around, all arms and legs and spinning wheels.

Jack got up cussing at me and staggering about. So I just threw him into the Moet tent and ran off. I heard later that they helped him up and made him very welcome.

Somewhere else where the champagne flowed like water in those days was the big music industry market, known as MIDEM (le Marche International de la Musique). It was always held in Cannes, first at the old Casino, and then at the new purpose-built Palais. Right back from my Apple days, I had gone every year, as regular as clockwork. You soon got to know all the same old faces, who also turned up year after year. When we launched Apple Records, we papered the walls of our stand with the Apple logo, and had cases of apples to give away that, ridiculously, we shipped from London. I have a photograph of myself on the stand, with long hair and wearing a trendy wild silk gray suit. It sums the era up: a big carton of apples, stamped APPLE—LONDON, two open bottles of French beer and a Gauloise.

One year I was down there, it was perfect South of France weather for January: sensational food, blue skies, sparkling sea. I went to the Piano Bar, which was around the corner from the Martinez, where, naturally enough, someone was sitting playing the piano. Usually, they're just tinklers, but this player was sensational. I sat and listened for a while, sipping a cold beer or two. In a break, I asked if he had a tape, not expecting one. He had one available. Back in London, at the Polydor post-MIDEM meeting, I was asked if I had found anything worthwhile. I said, "Yes, there was this pianist at the Piano Bar and he was rather good."

We put the tape on and they went, ho-hum. "What does he look like?" I said, "He's cute, a bit like Bobby Crush." There were collective sighs around the table and someone said, "What the hell do we need another Bobby Crush for?" I subsided because I thought, quite right, they must know what they're talking about. The pianist I didn't discover was Richard Clayderman, who was discovered by someone else and went on to sell about 93 million albums.

Some MIDEMs are more memorable than others. In 1977 I attended as usual, with Marty Machat—Don Arden's lawyer—because Don, who managed the careers of many stars such as Black Sabbath and Ozzy Osbourne, had just done a huge deal for ELO. As a birthday present, he had given the job of managing Lynsey De Paul to his "little girl," his sassy dark-eyed daughter, Sharon, who was about eighteen and stunning. I was with Marty, Don, Sharon and Lynsey de Paul—a real beauty with a waterfall of wavy blond hair and a sexy mole above her pouting mouth. We were in the Grand Casino, about to order dinner, but something seemed to be troubling them. Marty smiled and chatted, but I could sense a pervading undercurrent of tension.

I was aware that there was a "handbags at dawn" running battle between Patrick Meehan, who at the time ran NEMS, and Don—and then I saw Meehan sitting at the bar, tossing them back and glaring at our table. Before long, he was shouting, "Hey! Arden! You can't do nothing right. You're a fuckin' wanker." He gave a demonstration with his free hand.

I was just thinking, *This should be interesting*, when Sharon and Lynsey joined forces in giving him some verbal back. Next thing I knew, Patrick jumped up from the bar, came across and smacked Don in the middle of his face so hard his nose all but disappeared. It was one hell of a punch. There was bone showing, blood gushing like a geyser, claret everywhere. Marty immediately jumped up and ran out fast. I should have joined him, but I was too slow. Then a big guy, like a gorilla, appeared out of nowhere. Lynsey jumped on his back, grabbed him round the neck and started scratching and clawing the hell out of him. Sharon jumped up, shouted at Patrick, "You leave my dad alone!" She kicked his shins and pummeled his face as she yelled.

I was still watching, but it now had all the makings of a saloon bar brawl. The gorilla disengaged from Lynsey with a bellow and looked like he was about to give her a good smack so I got up and drew one off. Hammered him. He went right across the dinner table. That did it. Noise. Chaos. Screaming. Suddenly there was a French siren straight out of a Clousseau film. Gendarmes came rushing in, batons waving, the whole bit. We all got arrested—except the guy I'd hit. He smirked evilly in my direction and rattled off a volley of French.

It transpired that he was head of security for the whole casino, so it was not looking terribly good as far as getting any dinner was concerned. Certainly no one came to take our order. Don was very upset, of course, shouting loud threats which, apart from the string of expletives, were unintelligible, because what was left of his nose was blocked with blood. I couldn't move my hand, which felt broken. The gendarmes had painfully twisted my arm up behind my back. The girls were still screaming abuse and the waiters were gathered around in a circle, clapping. An ambulance was summoned for Don, and he was stretchered off to the hospital, with a towel around his head. We were carted off to the nick.

It took time to locate Marty the running lawyer, whose tennis habit seemed to have finally paid off. He had it on his toes at the first punch, but somehow, in a town of drunken music-biz lawyers (and without mobile phones) we found him. He turned up sheepishly but soon got into his shtick. Smoked his cigar furiously. Acted like George Burns who has been dragged out of bed. Leaned over the desk. Issued a couple of ultimatums. Said he'd call his buddy, the mayor of Cannes. The gendarmes decided to take no chances and we were sprung.

The next day it was all plaster of paris and bandages around the pool. Stiff drinks. Strong painkillers. We nursed the damage and talked of revenge and lawsuits. Lynsey was out-of-control angry, Don was vowing all kinds of murder and mayhem like an angry Schnozzle Durante which sounded like, "Arb godda hab ids guds fer fuffin' garders. I phwhere I'll fuffin' rib is tids ock!" He'd probably already been on the phone to Horst Fascher in Hamburg with Sharon in her black mood egging him on.

I still have the photographs I took of our black eyes. In them, Sharon has the biggest shiner of all. The irony was that at the time Lynsey was locked in a vicious lawsuit with Don, whom she was suing for all manner of things. It seemed remarkable that not only was she about to break bread with him, but she had fought his corner in the casino, and that they could sit around the pool comparing notes and plotting revenge like comrades in arms.

The entire family was well known for being dysfunctional and over the top. Sharon's brother, David, was jailed for locking the family accountant in a cupboard in the man's own office. It was straight out of a gangster comedy, "Get in the cupboard Mister Number Cruncher! I'm not letting you out until you tell me what you done wid our money and then I'm gonna kill you." Someone called the police. They were not amused. When he got out of the cupboard, the accountant was delighted, convinced that he was off the hook. In the fullness of time, David was jailed and the accountant sued the Arden family for kidnapping, brutality, false imprisonment and millions. Once again Don was not a happy man.

The kidnap events were pre-Ozzy and pre-Don as Ozzy's father-in-law. Sharon's then-boyfriend was Adrian the driver, who went on to become head of promotion for Sony. Don was managing Ozzy's band, Black Sabbath, at the time. There are two versions of how Sharon got together with Ozzy, and there is truth in both. When her parents split up, Sharon took her mum's side. To put the boot in, she took Ozzy away from him and didn't speak to Daddy for years. On the other side, it's said that Don gave her Ozzy's management contract as a wedding present, but it's generally accepted that it was a matter of push and shove and expediency. Sharon had Ozzy, she wasn't going to let her father manage him, so Don did the decent thing. But Sharon was very hard-nosed in those days. She was Lynsey de Paul's road manager for a while and according to Lynsey, who had hysterics (and to Sharon herself, who bragged about it), when they fell out Sharon took a dump in Lynsey's suitcase and then closed the lid. It's also said Don put many of his business affairs, as well as his L.A. mansion, in Sharon's name when he ran into some little tax difficulties. When it was all sorted, and he asked for everything back, Sharon smiled sweetly and told him to take a hike.

I first met Ozzy when Black Sabbath was living on a boat on the Thames. For four guys who were making big money, it was unbelievable. I have never seen such squalor in all my days. It was like a floating Dumpster, with a door instead of a lid. It stank of dead winos, vomit and blocked bilges. There were empty glassine baggies, overflowing ashtrays, rotten socks, dirty underwear, a blocked-up lavatory. It was a nightmare.

In complete contrast were the Osmonds, who Polydor asked me to promote. They were like babes in a sea of sharks. The Scotti Brothers, Tony and Ben, looked after them in the U.S. The Osmonds were signed to MGM Records. The promotion for most of MGM product was handled by the Scottis, probably because Ben and Tony had an excellent reputation for getting stuff played on the radio. Their track record was unparalleled in the industry. I had a similar reputation but the difference was simple. I went round *asking* people to play a record. They went round *telling* people to play a record.

Meanwhile, practically every party I went to in L.A. in some two or three decades had bowls of coke on every table, as casually placed as bowls of peanuts. The deals that went down were celebrated not with a glass of champagne, but with a dish of cocaine. It was like, "Help yourself." I always stayed cool. I'd laugh and say, "No thanks, I'd rather have a drink"—which happened to be true. I'm a drinker, not a drugger; but it would have been so easy to slip into that way of life and obviously many people did. I saw scenes, which would seem wildly beyond belief, with some big names, big executives. It was all happening, continued to happen, still happens.

42

I **first met a girl** named Lesley Woodcock when I was head of International Press and Promotions at Polydor and I needed a new secretary. I got the personnel office to seek out some girls and interviewed about a dozen. But they'd all worked in the music industry before and I had my own way of doing things. I didn't want anybody who had come from another record company, because they always seemed to say, "That's not the way it was done at Chrysalis/EMI/Sony."

Lesley was working for the *Times Literary Supplement* when the entire staff of the *Times* group went on strike for over a year from November 1978 to November 1979 because the union objected to new technology being brought in which they said would lose jobs. Everyone was getting union scale but weren't doing anything and Lesley was a doer. After a couple of months she was bored to death with just sitting around and being paid for nothing. She put job applications in to various places and had two appointments: me and the drama department at Thames TV. She had more or less made up her mind to take the TV job but I talked her into coming to work for me. She was lovely. Very shy, didn't argue and seemed to know just how to do things. Right from the start, she had a feel for it all and just got on with the job. She was so good at it that I didn't take much notice of her for a long time. I was very busy and was living with someone else, a delightful and fiery Irish girl named Bernadette Sheridan.

It was round about the time that The Who got together again shortly after Keith Moon died, with ex-Faces drummer, Kenney Jones, and I set up a small promotion tour to launch their 1979 movie, *The Kids Are Alright*. They were doing Glasgow on a Friday night and I was sitting in the office wondering what I should do and suddenly I said to Lesley, who was working late, "Book a couple of flights up to Glasgow and a hotel and we'll go up and see the lads." I thought it might be fun and that we ought to show the group some support from Polydor. I didn't really need a reason, but think I said to her something like, "It's about time that you saw what it's like for a band on the road. You've never been to any of the gigs. This will be a good start." I was joking. The Who were pretty wild. I should have said, "Come on, jump in at the deep end."

Lesley was very excited. She phoned her mum, said she was off to Glasgow for the night. I think her mum was a bit stunned. She was a woman to reckon with. She had been the editor in chief's assistant at the Mirror Group of newspapers, then she worked for Robert Maxwell, who bought the Mirror Group, until he ran off with all the money and was eventually found dead, having either been pushed or jumped from his yacht off the Canary Islands. As he was a former secret agent, many rumors circulated about his demise.

Glasgow was fantastic, a wonderful baptism for Lesley into that world. The Who were incredible. As always, the volume was just unbelievable. They just tore the roof off. When they'd finished, we went backstage, but true to their reputation, by the time we got there "backstage" didn't really exist as such anymore. It was like a building site in Berlin at the end of the war. To say that The Who had trashed it completely wouldn't do the havoc, or them, justice. The ceiling had been smashed. What must have once been delivered to the dressing room as, "the catering," was now everywhere: all over the walls, all over the floor, all over The Who. It was like a "work in progress."

Keith Moon must have been smiling down. Without getting in the way, I smiled at the lads and waved. Lesley's mouth dropped open. Without missing a beat, Pete would pass by holding a guitar by the neck like an axe, manic grin, huge spliff between his teeth—obviously on a mission of mayhem and mass destruction—and mumble, "All right, Tone?" HACK! BANG! CRUNCH! SMASH!

"Fine Pete. And yourself?"

John Wolf, their tour manager, was standing to one side gnawing at a complete haunch of venison en croute. It was a fit and proper "Return of The Who"—and I was delighted. We went back to the hotel and were up the rest of the night just laughing and drinking as we swapped old Keith stories. He really did seem to be there that night. Pete Townshend and Roger Daltrey are extremely funny and entertaining men, and that night they were happy and on form. Lesley was just speechless. It was the stuff that she had only read about, and she loved it. The theater of rock 'n' roll. The Electric Circus.

In the morning we went to a preview of *The Kids Are Alright*. Afterward, I said to her, "Would you like to stay over and go on to the gig at Edinburgh tomorrow?" She said, "Oh can we?" So we did.

When we got back to the office I started to look at her in a new light. As the weeks went by I occasionally took her for lunch or drinks after work, but nothing came of it because of Bernadette. Then I went freelance and Lesley and I lost touch for two or three years. She went to work for Elton John at Rocket Records. Apparently, she enjoyed the reputation of being the butchest person in the building. She said it was fun, but that there was "lots of daily emotion." From the office boy upward, the tantrums and backstabbing atmosphere got to her in the end and she went to work for Richard Branson at Virgin Records as a promotions assistant.

I continued to keep in touch with Paul, promoting Wings. On January 16, 1980 when they arrived for a tour of Japan, Paul was arrested at Tokyo International Airport after narcotics agents found two plastic bags in his suitcases containing almost eight ounces of marijuana. Japan was famous for its hard stand on drugs and Paul knew that. I suppose he thought the agents would never think he'd try getting pot past them. But they did. They searched his suitcases and Paul was soon handcuffed. To his shock, a rope was tied around him and he was carted off to jail where he spent nine days.

On the face of it, it looked his fault. But I wasn't the only one who believed that Paul was set up by Yoko Ono. Not only was Yoko Japanese, she was from an influential and very wealthy banking family. Paul and Linda and everyone in the inner circle believed that Yoko had informed the Japanese police that Paul was more than likely to have marijuana in his luggage. Even though Paul had been quite outspoken about his use of cannabis, and even though he may have been naive about getting caught, I think there had to be some "Japanese politics" involved. For one thing, Yoko was jealous that Paul was doing a concert in Japan before her own Plastic Ono Band had the opportunity. Japan was *her* territory, and for a long time she'd had every intention of flying there in a blaze of glory, the conquering heroine returns, only she hadn't gotten around to it—and now here was Wings, with Linda, intruding on her turf.

To make matters worse, Linda was also performing with Paul. A great deal was said when Paul was let out of jail and he, Linda and the band eventually returned home. None of it was pleasant. It was believed that Linda had been the one to pack the pot in their cases, and Paul graciously took the blame because of their children, who were young. "I was fully convinced that I would be imprisoned for nine or ten years," he said when he was released. "I was scared out of my wits."

I was at MIDEM shortly afterward, when Denny Laine, who was in Wings, and his wife Jo Jo, disgraced themselves. At least Jo Jo did. She had a bit too much Pol Roger and started slagging everybody off, left, right and center, and calling Paul and Linda all sorts of names over the pot fiasco. Jo Jo complained that the whole tour had been cancelled and no one made any money. Not only did Wings lose the money they would have made from the concerts, but they had to pay back all the Japanese promoters what they would have made too. Denny depended on work coming in and he said he ended up so broke he had to sell all his copyrights. As for Jo Jo, she went off to be one of Lord Weymouth's numerous wifelets at Longleat, his vast stately pile in Wiltshire. I think Denny—who started out with the Moody Blues and sang lead on their first big hit, "Go Now"—and Jo Jo got back together again after she tired of being part of a harem. He was an original with a great voice and had studied Spanish guitar, especially Flamenco. He had a string section with his band, long before ELO thought of it. I often mused on the fact that ELO also came from Birmingham, and wondered if there had been any synergy. The public dusting of Denny's feelings spelled out the end of his relationship with Paul and Linda and was the reason why he left Wings. Later, Denny organized a band, a sort of tribute band, to do "Denny Laine sings the songs of Wings." Very kindly, Paul gave his blessing, but according to the band, Denny failed to show up for rehearsals and it fizzled out.

♏

In February 1982 I started doing some freelance work for Virgin, promoting Mike Oldfield's *Five Miles Out* and an album named *Rhythm of Youth* for a Canadian band with the ridiculous name of "Men Without Hats." It seemed strange that Richard Branson—the odd little student pest who'd haunted us at Apple all those years ago—was now an enormously successful businessman. He'd grown into his clothes and full potential and gained a great deal of influence along the way, with a £2.6 billion fortune that encompassed a record label, publishing, wine, holidays, airlines, banks, railways and islands. Despite his lifelong passion for the music industry, I'm not sure that Richard ever really understood the record business, but he had some good people working for him, like Simon Draper. Virgin Records' attitude wasn't industry standard. It seemed to be more like "throw a lot of shit against a wall and see if any stays up there." The amount of records they put out and acts they signed was phenomenal. Unfortunately, there were too many one-off single deals that went nowhere and died. It baffled me how they survived. Shrewder men like Mickie Most would put out only a few records and promote them intensely. Magnet were the same. The word to describe Virgin's modus operandi was serendipity: see what comes along, sign it, tell them they're wonderful, do a record and then like George III with America in 1776, say, "America? I don't recall. Who are they?" Despite Mike Oldfield's *Tubular Bells,* Virgin Records struggled until Culture Club and Human League came along.

At Virgin, Lesley's first job was promoting Culture Club with Boy George. They had made two records for Virgin when she arrived and the label was about to drop them, so their third record was the make it or break it one. It was a matter of "you'd better sell some records, boys and girls, or you get dumped." Virgin put out their single, "Love Is Cold," and booked them on the BBC's *Pebble Mill* lunchtime show, which had a big audience for daytime telly. Lesley went to Birmingham to look after them. They sang the song which was the A-side and then later in the show they sang the B-side which was, "Do You Really Wanna Hurt Me?" Lesley fell in love with it, as did the audience. She went back to Virgin and told them about the audience reaction. Bravely, she said, "Flip the record. The hit is on the B-side." Naturally they begged to differ. They didn't really want to know, but she was so sure, so adamant, she believed in it so much that she battered them until they said, "All right, all right! Go for it—but on your head be it."

It was a massive hit, as she knew it would be. Lesley gained a great deal of respect and was taken seriously after that. Their next single was "Karma Chameleon" which put them firmly on the map. In fact, blowing my own trumpet, there's a family history of "flipping" records. When I was still at Polydor, Gloria Gaynor was signed to us and had a couple of hits, including "Never Can Say Goodbye." Then she had a minor hit in the U.S. with "Substitute," a song that was also covered by a South African girl group called Clout, who made it to number two in the U.K. I decided that there was little point in trying to compete against that, and almost idly, I listened to the B-side and was electrified. It was "I Will Survive." We put that out as the A-side and it shot straight to the top of the charts. All these years later, it is still a world-class sing-along anthem.

So Lesley was at Virgin, doing well when we met again. I asked her out. This time round, we fell in love. Of course there was Bernadette, my long-term girlfriend, in the background. She came from a very strong Catholic family, who lived out at Epsom, near the racecourse where the Derby was run. Her dad was a builder and when he met me he'd asked me what I did in the war, and I thought, *war? What fucking war?* Immediately I went and looked in the mirror to see if I looked old, or if I looked like I was suffering from battle fatigue.

Then it was, "What religion are you, then?" I blurted out, "I'm Church of England," which was stretching things a bit, but that's what you wrote on any official forms in those days. He looked at me and it was like, "You've got no chance here, mate!"

When I told Bernadette about Lesley, she lived up to being Irish and fiery. In fast order, she met and married Peter Reichert, the head of EMI Music Publishing in London. Peter was Jewish. Not only that, but he was a serial divorcer at that time so quite what Bernie's old man made of all that I don't know, but I can hazard a wild guess. However, Bernadette and Peter are still together, still happy.

Lesley and I rented a wonderful old Jacobean house on Barnes High Street, with a garden that went down to the Thames, virtually at the end of the Boat Race course. It was next door to the White Hart pub, opposite a little village-type green. It was perfect.

🦇

One of the most interesting double acts signed to Polydor when I was there were Demis Roussos and Vangelis Papathanassiou, known simply as "Vangelis." But I didn't sign them as a duo by any means. They were very individualistic as musicians; the duet really came to life in the kitchen. At the time I met him, Demis was enjoying massive middle-of-the-road musical success but real fame still eluded Vangelis. This was mostly because Vangelis insisted on just doing his own thing. He was extraordinarily talented but very difficult to deal with. I became very fond of him. Notwithstanding the fact that he was a lavish host, sometimes he was quite perverse, a real character in many ways. He made a beautiful album called *China*. It was stunning, very Left Wing and esoteric, based on Mao's famous long march and the Chinese Revolution. I thought it would be very hard to market, but quality always shines through. It did well and everybody copied it.

Lesley and I used to go and visit him frequently at his luxurious flat near the Albert Hall, and we all became great friends. Demis was often around, too, and if he was, we were always in for a treat. They were great together, a double act, with Demis cooking away. They had been in the Greek band, Aphrodite's Child, a very successful band in Europe, one filled with large men with big appetites for food and life. Sometimes, in idle moments, I imagined having to supply the buffet for that band.

Sometime later, when David Puttnam wanted something different for a little film that he was putting together, called *Chariots of Fire*, I immediately thought of Vangelis because of the magical way he used electronic instruments. I talked him into it because I knew nobody else could do it. It had to be him. Even before we started, I had a sense of how it should sound, but first, we had to do a lot of talking, and cooking and eating and uncorking of wine.

The film was a very slow burn, one of those things that live in your memory, something you can watch again and again. The music had to match that and be spacey and ethereal and haunting, yet triumphal. We used to go to Nemo, Vangelis's studio in Edgware Road, where each day the rushes would be delivered so he could put sound to picture. It took ages and he got very frustrated because they kept changing stuff and there was no dialogue on the rushes. We used to spend days and evenings at Nemo with him.

At the first preview, the producers showed the film without music and it was embarrassing beyond belief. People just didn't know what to say, or which way to look. They didn't think it worked, and didn't think it could even be rescued. I heard someone say quite loudly into the silence, "Well, it's a turkey in the oven." It was a quirky little Hugh Hudson–period British film and they can be buggers to sell. Then later they showed it again, with the music added and those famous six notes just fitted it so well. It was instantly so uplifting that people were standing up and cheering the runner on. I knew as soon as I heard the finished soundtrack that it had lifted the film into Oscar territory. Of course it did—and it coined the Colin Welland premature soundbite: "The British are coming" at the awards ceremony.

I didn't supervise Vangelis as such for Polydor. In fact, he was probably unsupervisable. When *China* had come out, Polydor International was so keen they wanted to launch Vangelis as a major new star. We put him on at the Royal Festival Hall. Poly people came from all over the world; journalists and broadcasting people as well were all flown in at great expense and put up in expensive London hotels. But instead of playing what everybody came to hear, those wonderful, trademark soaring compositions that could make you weep, Vangelis played some avant-garde, straight-off-the-wall, electronic noodling with a percussionist. My heart sank. I couldn't escape but many people walked out, saying it was a load of rubbish.

At the after-gig party it was quite embarrassing because nobody knew what to say. No one went up to Vangelis to congratulate him, so he stood there looking quite glum. But not as glum as we all were. A generous point of view would be to say that he was not at all commercially minded. He really didn't see why he should play what people came to hear. Personally, I could have throttled him. It was a good thing he wasn't on CBS or Jet. He could have ended up at the bottom of the Aegean.

As an indication of how good Vangelis was, Hans Zimmer was his assistant.

Zimmer is now the wunderkind, a leading composer of movie music and much more commercially viable on a film-to-film basis than his former mentor. I have no doubt that he probably watched what happened when he was working for Vangelis and listened to the critics more, knew all the pitfalls and learned how to do it right. After *Chariots*, I asked Vangelis to do *Blade Runner,* which started life as another quirky little film. As usual, the production was blighted by many financial problems, with different backers coming and going, and kept changing shape. The executives changed. It was all change, all the time except for the director, Ridley Scott.

Ridley was another genius, one who kept his head. Vangelis was doing this storming music but the film wasn't shot in sequence and came in to him in obscure chunks. He was going up the wall, unable to see it clearly as a whole, and felt that he would never be able to complete a comprehensive soundtrack. In the end, the soundtrack album wasn't released for about fifteen years, and the rights to the music had changed hands several times by then. Eventually, Warner put it out on the off-chance, on one of their el cheapo labels. It's stunning music, and although it has made a great deal of money, it's not anywhere near the kind of money it should have earned had it been released with the film. The funny thing is that Vangelis will go on stage and perform unstructured stuff when he feels he's being constrained, but when he works to film he wants it absolutely structured.

🐾

Vincenzo La Bella also came into my life during this period. He was head of the Vatican Film and TV Service, which, yes, dear reader, does exist—and so too does the Office of the Inquisition. He had a very bizarre job of running a huge budget, which was invested in films around the world on behalf of the Vatican. They also produced TV programs and records. It was an incredibly well-paid job, as were many Vatican gigs. Vincenzo toured the world, staying in the very best hotels and eating in the best restaurants. Dining with him was an experience on its own. I saw the lavishness of how the really rich live.

The Beatles, for all their wealth, actually lived very modestly, even if an awful lot of vintage wine and caviar flowed into the Apple kitchens and dining rooms for the hangers-on. With Vincenzo, we often met and discussed film investment, though nothing much came of it. To me, it was a way of life not enjoyed since Nero fiddled in Rome. I think I preferred being with Vangelis and Demis, watching them cooking up a storm, laughing and eating and drinking. It all seemed far more real.

43

For a long time, the only Beatle I saw with any frequency was Paul, but I kept up with the news via conversations with Paul and mutual friends. John went to America on October 16, 1971, and would remain there for the rest of his life, for a long time under a deportation order, embroiled with visa and residency problems and unable to leave. But for eighteen months, during 1974 and 1975, he split with Yoko and had an affair with their assistant, May Pang. Initially—and somewhat contrarily, given his ambivalent feelings for Yoko—Paul played a part in helping to bring them back together. I heard that Yoko had telephoned Paul and asked his help. Paul said, "She sounded so sad that I found myself agreeing to act as negotiator by telling John that she wanted him back. And Linda said that we were so happy, I should bury my differences." Paul was going to Nashville to record, and he made a detour to Los Angeles, where John was leading a highly publicized life of debauchery. Ultimately, John did return to Yoko, but reluctantly. She was supposed to have invited him to the Dakota for a mysterious "smoke cure." May Pang is convinced that once again, Yoko had bewitched John because he called May sobbing to say he wanted to return to her, but was a virtual prisoner. From all accounts, for years he continued to write in his diaries how much he missed and wanted to be with May.

I was sad when Ringo and Maureen—my old teenage buddy, Mitch—were divorced in 1975. Six years later Ringo married the American film star, Barbara Bach, while Maureen would marry Isaac Tigret, a founder of the Hard Rock Cafes, in 1989. Poignantly when Maureen died of leukemia five years later, her four children, her husband, and Ringo were by her side. George and Pattie, who had also been apart for some time, were divorced in 1977. Pattie married her longtime love, Eric Clapton, and the following year, George married Olivia Arias, a secretary at his record label's L.A. headquarters. A big shock within our once close-knit ranks was hearing about the death of Mal Evans under very strange circumstances in an L.A. motel. He was in the middle of a drug psychosis when his girlfriend called the police. They burst in and shot Mal dead. Such a violent end for a man who always enjoyed life upset everyone who knew him, and reinforced my own aversion to drugs.

Happier times were ahead for me. Lesley and I were married on August 6, 1982, which was a Friday. It was also the day that Roxy Music started rehearsing for a new tour—which I happened to be promoting. They were rehearsing in Cork in Ireland, so Lesley and I joined them for our honeymoon. It was an unusual one, to say the least, shared with Brian Ferry and the road crew. After a few days in Cork we went to Limerick to a little theater to tighten up the show, then did a week in Dublin before hitting the U.K. We've always had fun saying that they came on our honeymoon with us, though strictly speaking it was the other way around!

When Lesley got pregnant the first time, she gave up working and the world of record promotion lost a rising star. She convinced me that it was time we had some bricks and mortar of our own, so we bought a house in Mortlake where we lived until we had the two boys, and we decided to move down to Devon.

I had been going to Devon quite frequently over the years, right back from when I stayed with Brian Epstein when he was working on his memoirs. When Simon was about two months old, Lesley and I went down to a little village we'd discovered near Exeter for some fly-fishing. We stayed for three weeks in a fishing lodge, a lovely place with fresh air and clean water burbling away to the sea, which was close. We bought a place to use for weekends, then the weekend turned into four days, then entire weeks until we just weren't going back to London anymore. When the boys started school, we had to make some decisions about where we wanted to be permanently. Devon won, hands down. To some extent, economy was important because shortly after I married Lesley, I lost all my money again.

This time, it wasn't as spectacular as the huge loss through Hilary Music, because when you're building a company with the likes of Harry Saltzman, the producer of the Bond films, and Ron Kass, the sky's the limit. The second time round happened like this: I got involved with IDS (Independent Distribution Services), a company put together by ex-members of various record labels and financed by a merchant bank. I agreed to do promotion for them for royalty points of 3 percent plus a reasonable lump sum of five hundred pounds for each record I promoted. At the time, being given points for exploiting a record through your promotion work was quite innovative.

The first record was a break-dance single, put together by the team who brought us the Village People. It was the first break-dance hit record in the States, where it made the top five. In the U.K. it sold about half a million units. The follow-up sold about the same and the album sold about a quarter of a million. I was very happy with 3 percent of that. Next up was Evelyn Thomas with "High Energy," which went to number one. We had a smaller hit with "So Many Men, So Little Time," with Miquel Brown (who happened to be the mother of the American dance music queen, Sinitta). Then a couple of reggae versions of Lionel Richie songs which made the top five. So money was building up. I felt it had been a year or so of quite remarkable success from a standing start.

I promoted "Gloria," a big hit with Laura Brannigan, on Warner the summer my son, Simon, was born in 1984. It was followed by a letter with my usual five-hundred-pound check and a summary of what had accrued to date. The statement ended with the words, "Royalties are being computed de da de da de da . . ." Within days, another letter came with the information that IDS had gone into receivership. "If you have any claim against it, send it to Henry Ansbacher Bank at—" I lost about one hundred thousand pounds, which twenty or so years ago was a lot of money.

They say once bitten, twice shy. There's also the phrase, "Once is happenstance, twice is a coincidence, three times is enemy action." So maybe the gods decided to play a long running joke on me, because I lost all my money three times.

The first time was when Kenneth J. Richards, may he rot in hell, ran off with untold millions—some of it mine. The second time was when IDS went down; and the third time was in 1988, when my dear friend, Marty Machat died. He was Allen Klein's lawyer in the U.S. That's how initially I got to know him. He was also Leonard Cohen's lawyer. Leonard was someone else who was very difficult to deal with, though not as hard as Klein. Nobody was as hard as Klein, except maybe Phil Spector, and I've already been there. However, whether by accident or design, Marty got the last laugh on Leonard.

There has always been a running joke in the industry about Leonard Cohen. It is said that his records are *music to commit suicide by.* But, as Elton John pointed out, sad songs say so much. And it's true. Leonard can write sad songs with the best, and if there was ever a sad song to write it's the one about all of Leonard's money going missing somewhere in numbered accounts in the Caymans. In fact, Marty looked after clients' money, including mine, and Leonard's, like it was his own. But, when you hide money, you create mysteries, like pirates with buried treasure. X might mark the spot, but only if you have the map and can find the X.

Marty often called me, sometimes for business, often just to chat about this and that. I always felt he was a kindly and benign father figure, so I had given him some of my American money to keep in an offshore account, as a sort of pension for the future. Marty took a shine to me and we became good friends. He was an Anglophile, who loved going to English pubs and doing English things while all the time being like my American godfather. There's no denying that while he was alive, he did look after me. He'd line up projects, tell people to call me, and make sure my name and ability were put about. If I needed a thousand pounds to pay for something, the next day it would be there.

Once I'd gone entirely freelance, my payment usually came partly in a fee, plus expenses and on top of that, royalties. Through Marty, I promoted the music for *Dirty Dancing* which I had some points in, which was nice, because the album was massive, something nobody expected. The story of how this came about is a little contorted. Originally, Jennifer Warnes had done an album of Leonard Cohen songs for a little label called Cypress Records who were distributed by RCA. It was called *The Famous Blue Raincoat,* and it was a lovely album, dedicated to Leonard, who dueted on one track. Stevie Ray Vaughn played some guitar. It really turned Cohen's music into something special and I fell in love with it.

I'd already worked with Laura Brannigan; she and Jennifer had been Leonard's backup singers. One day, Marty called to say, "If you promote *Blue Raincoat,* Tony, I'll see that you get five pence per record."

"Fair enough," I said. "Is that for the world?"

Yes, he said, because like a lot of things, he believed that if it broke first in the U.K. then America would follow. I got immediate airplay from everywhere. People who'd never ever thought about playing a Leonard Cohen record—probably because a large percentage of their listeners would do themselves harm or commit hari kiri, and they'd get sued—played Jennifer's Cohen album. As it took off, she was sent over to London. I found her difficult. She suffered from a lot of anxieties, but we threw her into television so that she didn't have time to think, and suddenly I got the feeling that it was all about to happen. You know it! You can feel it when the audience is just about to catch onto what it's all about and rush out to the shops. It was a combination of many things: Jennifer's great voice, a perfect choice of songs and promotion, all coming together and working.

Then Marty called up and out of the blue said, "Can you stop it?"

I didn't get it. "Stop what?"

He said, "Stop promoting *Blue Raincoat*."

I was stunned. Marty explained. It seemed that RCA in the States were about to release a strange little soundtrack to a movie called *Dirty Dancing*. It featured Jennifer and the Righteous Brothers, as well as all kinds of every star you can imagine. "They want to give it first shot, before *Raincoat* takes off. And would you promote it?"

"But Marty," I said, "I've been working my socks off. *Blue Raincoat* is just about to fly."

"Yes, but not in America," he said. I was speechless. Marty said he'd organize some percentages for me. Feebly, since RCA was picking up the tab, I agreed. I can't take all the credit for *Dirty Dancing* going so massive because it was also being promoted in-house by RCA as well, but it took off like a jet fighter. Then came *Dirty Dancing 2* and so on. By the time all the hoo-hah had died down, I couldn't get Jennifer's old *Blue Raincoat* album going again for love or money. It was dead as a dodo, gone. Good-bye. Farewell.

I called Marty to tell him and he called me back from somewhere in the Caymans where he was playing tennis. Marty played a lot of tennis despite the fact that he was in his late sixties. We discussed it and Marty said he'd have a think, talk to some people and get back to me. I didn't think he sounded all that bright, and said, "How are you, Marty?"

"To be honest, Tony, I don't feel all that good," he said. He sounded worried. "I have an appointment with a doctor in New York in a couple of days. I'm here in the Caymans, sorting things out. I've been making notes on my affairs, listing all the numbered accounts and the various holdings I have for my clients."

"Oh, I'm sure it will be all right, Marty," I reassured him.

"Well, a man in my position has to put things in order, Tony," he said. "Everyone will get their numbers if anything happens to me." I thought it was all a bit doom-laden and laughed it off. We finished our chat and I wished him good luck.

The next day I was having dinner and I got a phone call. Marty was dead. I called his family. He'd collapsed. They'd flown him back to New York where the doctors opened him up for a look and he was riddled with cancer. There was nothing to be done, and he died in the hospital.

I thought to myself, Oh well! Somebody will sort out the money in the end. Then I shook myself and said, *Don't be silly, Tony. Nobody will sort it out in the end. Move on*. But nevertheless after a few days I spoke to one of his sons. He said there were problems. Someone had intimated that Marty had possibly been poisoned. Should he be interred? Should he be put on ice? It quickly became like an episode of *Law and Order*.

The big question was "Where's the money?" It was a difficult subject to broach, so close to Marty's death, but the son, who was also in the music business like Marty's other children, knew that Marty was looking after a great deal of money for many people. I called him and repeated the last conversation I had with Marty, and asked if his father had indeed left any instructions for me, or for anyone. I asked, "Did he leave a list of numbers?"

He sounded quite concerned. "We've been through Dad's papers with a fine-tooth comb, Tony," he said, "and we can't find anything. Leonard's having a fit because he stands to lose the most. For the most, read everything."

"What do you mean, everything?" I asked cautiously, hoping it didn't sound like it did.

I can only assume that the money is probably still out there, out of reach, and earning interest to eternity. I went into the pub. Phil Spector went into a rage. Leonard Cohen went into a monastery, and the New York lawyers went into a huddle until one of them said, "Did you eat yet?" and then that was the end of that. As Leonard said when he heard the bad news: "What else is there to do?"

Over the years, the Beatles continued to keep in touch with me. I considered Paul a friend and saw the most of him. I promoted all Wings' records and tours, and did the same for the NEMS roster and for Apple. The other three would call me from time to time if they were around, if they wanted me to promote a record for them, or to ask me to some event. I had also kept in touch with our little inner circle at Apple. Sometimes months or even years would pass and I'd bump into one of them somewhere.

The last time I talked to John was when I was with Polydor and he was recording again after a long hiatus while he played househusband. I went to New York and I kept just missing him. This was hardly surprising. He had stopped seeing his oldest friends, like Pete Shotton and even Paul. Pete had called him once and he and Yoko met him for a Japanese meal of raw fish and macrobiotic rice. "Call me tomorrow," John said. But Yoko glowered. The next day, when Pete called, he heard Yoko screech down the phone, "Tell him to get lost!" John told him it wasn't a good time and they never met again.

It was the same when Paul spontaneously dropped by the Dakota with his guitar, hoping that he and John could jam a little. He called John from the reception downstairs. Distantly, John had said, "Look Paul, it's not like it used to be when we were kids, going round each other's houses. We've grown up since then." Well, Aunt Mimi didn't like him playing and jamming, either. There was always a reason back then, too. The wrong haircut, the wrong clothes, leading John astray. I don't know what Yoko's reasons were.

Little wonder, then, that I couldn't get through to him. I knew he was looking for a new deal, a new label for the album he was working on. I wrote to him from London and asked him if he wanted to sign with Polydor, who were as big as anybody. I heard nothing and forgot it. I was working late at the office—it was seven or eight in the evening, when the worst janitor in the world—I'll call him Bloggs—came looking for me. Remember this was before the days of proper phone systems. I had given John my direct number but he had probably lost it.

When Bloggs found me he said, "There's a guy called John Lennon on the phone for you." Now Bloggs was a man who just lately had refused entry to a "fat unshaven foreign geezer who calls hisself Frank Ellis." This was Vangelis, whom I was expecting. But Bloggs was Bloggs and he continued to be a pain. He once insisted on keeping "some poncey-looking guy" outside in the rain while he found out who he was. It was Brian Ferry of Roxy Music. So when Bloggs put John Lennon on hold, I shouldn't have been surprised or even annoyed.

Back in his lair, Bloggs put John through and we just had time to say hello to each other before there was a "blip" and Bloggs said, "Sorry, I think I just cut you off."

I tried to call John back but I couldn't reach him. The switchboard security at Stalag Dakota wouldn't let me through. Two weeks later, on December 8, 1980, my phone rang. It was five A.M. I answered it, still half-asleep. It was a deejay calling from a radio station in New York. "John Lennon is dead," he told me. "How do you feel about it? We're on the air right now, live."

I simply couldn't believe what I was hearing. "Are you sure?" I asked.

On-air, very excited, he told me what had happened, how some nut had shot John as he was going into the Dakota apartment building with Yoko. I choked up, trying my best to say the right things.

"He was a great singer and a great person," I said. "He'll be badly missed." It was all so trite. How can anyone explain? None of the Beatles could; none of them had the right words either. And then I hung up and sat there, in the early dawn, thinking back on my years with John, the boy who set fire to our village hall. It was the end of an era, no doubt about it. And then my phone began to ring, and continued to ring for days, hundreds of calls. So it was true, then. John really was dead.

But that morning, I had to pull myself together, get dressed, get on the train

to the Water Mill Theater at Newbury in Berkshire where Marti Webb was taping a big special on Andrew Lloyd Webber's *Tell Me on a Sunday*. I was committed to the show but I didn't want to do anything except stay at home and be
private. It was a case of "the show must go on." While I was there, I was grabbed
to talk about John on the midday news on the radio. TV and radio shows kept up
their demands for comment on John. Like a lot of people all over the world, I
was in shock, and I have no idea what I said.

Apart from the long wealth of memories, I dwelt on how our conversation on
the telephone had been cut short. I wondered what John had wanted. Was he re-
sponding to my letter, to say he wanted to sign up to Polydor—or was it deeper
than that? I had heard on the grapevine that John wanted to leave Yoko and
come back home. He had even telephoned Mimi just three days before his death
and his half sisters and cousins in Liverpool to say just that. "I'm homesick, I'm
coming home," he had said.

It was hard to explain to myself how I felt that our conversation was cut short.
It seemed to develop some mystical significance. Maybe John just wanted to say
hello. The sad part is, I'll never know—but "hello" would have been just fine.

🐾

At some time in his tenure, probably when he first started working there, someone had said to Bloggs: "Now, a word to the wise. Be very careful who you let
in," and he'd taken it too much heart. It was either that, or he really was stupid.
Case in point: Ringo, who actually was signed to Polydor, came to see me once.
Downstairs in the lobby, Bloggs said to him, "What do you want?"

"I'm here to see Tony Bramwell."

"Are you now? And who are you?"

"Ringo Starr."

My phone went *Ring-ring. Ring-ring*. I picked up the receiver. "Hello?"

"Someone to see you called . . . what was your name again?"

"Ringo Starr."

"Says he's Ringo Starr."

"Send him up."

As Ringo got in the lift, Bloggs shouted after him: "I thought it was you!"
Ringo got out of the lift, still laughing. He said to me, "Where did you find
him?" We both remembered at Apple when the girl on the front desk, who was
surrounded daily by all kinds of nutters, buzzed Derek Taylor one morning and
said, "Derek? There's a Mr. Hitler in reception for you."

"Send him up!" Ringo and I both had chorused.

Derek had even said to me, "Tony, I'm serious. Even if it had been Hitler I was so out of it, I would have given him a job. But just imagine the hissy fit with him being there the next time Keith Moon comes in dressed up as the Fuhrer. Oh! Clash! Clash!"

Ringo's eponymous record label was signed to Polydor and I was promoting *Rotogravure,* his first album for us. To give it its initial push, I organized a big international press conference and dinner in Paris and flew everyone in from all around the world. We stayed at the George V, scene of that euphoric night so many years ago when Brian and the Beatles had heard they had gone to number one in the U.S. So much water had flowed under the bridge since then. When Ringo walked into the hotel, I did a double-take. He had shaved his head! Ringo caught my expression and smiled. He rubbed his head, a little ruefully. "I wanted to see what I looked like bald," he said.

"What do you think?"

"I think I look bald," he said.

Down the years, working from my home in Devon, I continued to promote records, often for Ringo, Paul or George. One of my biggest successes was launching Eva Cassidy's career on an international level with *Songbird.* The tragedy was Eva wasn't around anymore to receive the awards and plaudits. Her album went straight to the top of the charts in the U.K. as well as Europe, Japan and Australia. Eva had already recorded some albums before her untimely death from cancer at her Washington home, but they largely passed unnoticed. How it came about was I heard a track one day and I loved it. Her voice just captivated me but I wasn't sure how I could be involved.

I was thinking about it in the next day in the car while I was listening for the first time in ages to the new revamped Radio 2. It had been so awful the year before, I had stopped listening to it. Now it was completely new and improved and I sat up. I made a few calls, talked to some people to get some background and it transpired that a producer called Jim Moir had performed wonders. The old audience was flocking back in droves. It occurred to me very quickly that this new Radio 2 would be the perfect medium to promote Eva. She just sounded right for what the station was doing. I thought, well, although she's not with us anymore, her magical voice could live on. She could be as big as a James Taylor or a Carole King. The quality of her voice with the songs she had liked to do was a perfect match.

I went up to London and dropped in half a dozen copies to producers Paul Walters for the legendary deejay Terry Wogan, Roger Bowman for Sarah Kennedy, and a few others. I followed it up the next day with a fax saying simply that I'd dropped some records off yesterday that I thought they might like to hear. The following day, Paul Walters faxed me and said it was wonderful. "We're playing it tomorrow." The next day Terry Wogan played it and while he was playing it, for the first time he read to himself the little release sheet and realized Eva was dead. He was both stunned and shocked and I think, quite emotional. His on-air emotional reaction was so sincere that people took notice.

From there Eva started to take off. I had known that given one break the audience would be with her, simply because her voice touches you and her story says so much about personal tragedy. The things that are important in life that can just disappear in a moment and that we should cherish. The message is: stop for a moment and listen to a thing of beauty. Listen to her singing Sting's "Fields of Gold." It says it all. It makes you tingle. It not only makes the hairs on your arms or on the back of your neck stand up, but it puts you right there in those fields and tells you about a time and a place and a love. To be able to do that with a voice and a song is no small thing. To me, this is what it's all about, like listening to Paul do Buddy Holly's "True Love Ways."

Eva didn't take off when she did the songs initially because she didn't come in a package, didn't come wrapped in a big bow like Celine Dion or a singer like that. Promoting records is a business where you see the potential or the angle and know how to place it, but many people don't want to work at it, or think about it too hard, whatever you do. They just take what the big companies give them. Pop music can be great fun, but sometimes it can also throw up a great artist, sometimes by accident. Sometimes it comes with a combination of things that move you, make you feel alive or perhaps gives you emotions that you thought you didn't have anymore.

Eva's "fault" was that she didn't want to be pigeonholed as a folk singer, or rhythm and blues or a diva or whatever. She just wanted to sing some of the songs that she liked. Mick Fleetwood loved her voice. He said that when she covered a song it was like hearing it again for the first time. She played at his club, Fleetwood's, in Washington, D.C. Atlantic Records came down and she did a showcase for them, but Mick said they just didn't get it. She did a couple of others there too but she didn't get taken up and Eva told Mick philosophically, "If they don't want me as I am, then I don't want to be with them."

He said that if he did have a soul, and he hoped he did, Eva touched it with her voice. I didn't push her as this fantastic voice from the other side, or exploit the fact that she was ignored while she was alive. But, human nature being what it is I'm sure some people found that compulsive. It is very poignant, after all. Within months, *Songbird* had achieved triple platinum status. With four more

Eva Cassidy albums waiting in the wings for Hot Records to release in Europe, I attended MIDEM and sold it worldwide.

Recently I read that "Yesterday" is now the most recorded song ever, with over three thousand versions. Eva recorded one of them. It was a beautiful performance, one Paul fell in love with. We were both sad when we considered this wonderful voice would never again make music. Paul and I discussed making a duet—"Eva and McCartney sing 'Yesterday'." It was a seductive idea. We'd have to go into the studio and he would have to add his vocals to Eva's, but it wouldn't have been difficult.

I got very excited about it—we both did—but sadly it didn't happen. It wasn't anything to do with Eva or Paul, but with legal issues. Sometimes, dreams and great ideas fade away and you just have to accept it. Just like I accept that, all things being equal, and that all things must pass, there are probably more yesterdays in me now than tomorrows. Still, doing this book has put it in some perspective.

At least I do have tomorrows. I'm still here, John and George and Linda, Maureen, and Eppy are gone, as are many others. I miss them, but along with a lot of fond, funny, and Fab Four memories, I have a wife and family and that makes me a very lucky man. Looking back, it still seems pretty amazing that so much happened. At the time, it didn't seem that it was an era that influenced so many things and so many people. We had no idea at all that the Beatles and those roller-coaster years were at the heart of a "Cultural Revolution." They were just four lads from Liverpool and yet, they changed the world. I feel honored and very grateful that I was a part of it.

So, here's to yesterday, and tomorrow. Cheers!

epilogue

The last time I saw George was in the winter of 1998. I was walking down from South Kensington tube on my way to the Genesis–Phil Collins office to discuss some promotion with their manager, Tony Smith. George was coming toward me in his overcoat, long scarf thrown around his neck, frowning slightly. He saw me almost as if he'd suddenly woken from a dream, or deep thoughts.

"Hel-lo!" A two-note hello. A high one, a lower one with a tail to it. And there's a big smile. He grabs me, gives me a big hug and says, "Where you going?"

It was the same question I'd asked him that night long ago on the bus when we were kids.

"Into Genesis, to see Phil," I said.

He told me he was on his way to the Apple offices, which were just around the corner. He said, "After you've finished here, come round and have a drink."

"Lovely," I said. Well, my meeting went on much longer than I expected, as they do sometimes, and when I finally got to Apple, George had left a message saying he had to go. I had a drink with Neil Aspinall, but it was all a bit sad because Derek Taylor had just died of lung cancer, and George had just been diagnosed with it. We sipped our drinks and sat in silence, memories chasing through our minds. It seemed that one minute I was young, the next, we were confronting our mortality.

Some days are like that. You remember being in the back of an old van bombing down the road late for a gig. There's Neil and Mal up front and four Beatles in the back practicing the weird harmony at the end of "She Loves You," where George has to hit a sixth on the last "yeah". And John says, "Fookin' George Martin says he doesn't reckon it. Can you believe it? He says it sounds old fashioned. Well, bollocks to him is what I say. If it sounds good, we'll fookin' do it."

George laughed so much in the back of the van that when they came to record it everybody was sure he'd remember what John said and screw it up. But he hit the note spot on. The memory of that day, and so many others like it, brought tears to my eyes.

The first time I saw George, he was just a kid, running into our house in Liverpool to play. Fifty years on, the last time I saw him, he was walking away, down a road. John, Paul, George and Ringo. How I loved them. It was, as George said about John, "All those years ago."

Tony Bramwell
Devon, January 11, 2004

acknowledgments

With many, many thanks to all those people who pulled hard together to make this book happen. They include the excellent team at Thomas Dunne Books and St. Martin's Press: the publisher, Tom Dunne; the editor, John Parsley; and the production editor, Mark Steven Long. Warmest thanks to Barbara Gratch Cohen for her wisdom. And the greatest appreciation to my literary agent, Jeff Kleinman, for efforts far beyond the call of duty. Without Don Short, who introduced me to my coauthor, Rosemary Kingsland, this book never would have happened. Finally, but not least, very many thanks to Neal Jefferies.

index